LIBRARY OF THE HISTORY OF IDEAS

VOLUME XI

The American Enlightenment

LIBRARY OF THE HISTORY OF IDEAS

ISSN 1050–1053

Series Editor: JOHN W. YOLTON

THE

AMERICAN ENLIGHTENMENT

Edited by

FRANK SHUFFELTON

UNIVERSITY OF ROCHESTER PRESS

This collection first published 1993

University of Rochester Press
200 Administration Building, University of Rochester
Rochester, New York 14627, USA
and at PO Box 9, Woodbridge, Suffolk IP12 3DF, UK

ISBN 1 878822 24 1

Library of Congress Cataloging-in-Publication Data
The American enlightenment / edited by Frank Shuffelton.
    p.   cm. – (Library of the history of ideas, ISSN 1050–1053 ;
v. 11)
    Includes bibliographical references.
    ISBN 1–878822–24–1 (alk. paper)
    1. United States – Intellectual life – 18th century.   2. United
States – Intellectual life – 1783–1865.   3. Enlightenment – United
States.   4. Theology, Doctrinal – United States – History – 18th
century.   5. Philosophy, American – 18th century.   6. Political
science – United States – Philosophy – History – 18th century.
I. Shuffelton, Frank, 1940– .   II. Series.
E162.A5137   1993
001.1'0973–dc20   93–15719

    British Library Cataloguing-in-Publication Data
    American Enlightenment. – (Library of the
    History of Ideas, ISSN 1050–1053;Vol.11)
        I. Shuffelton, Frank   II. Series
        191
        ISBN 1–878822–24–1

This publication is printed on acid-free paper

Printed in the United States of America

TABLE OF CONTENTS

PART TWO: DISCOURSES OF POLITICS AND NATION

ACKNOWLEDGEMENTS

The articles in this volume first appeared in the *Journal of the History of Ideas* as indicated below, by volume, year and pages, in order.

Anderson, Wallace E., "Immaterialism in Jonathan Edwards' Early Philosophical Notes," 25 (1964) 181–200.

Bidney, David, "The Idea of the Savage in North American Ethnohistory," 15 (1954) 322–27.

Blau, Joseph L., "Joel Barlow, Enlightened Religionist," 10 (1949) 430–44.

Branson, Roy, "James Madison and the Scottish Enlightenment," 40 (1979) 235–50.

Bynack, V. P., "Noah Webster's Linguistic Thought and the Idea of an American National Culture," 45 (1984) 99–114.

Chinard, Gilbert, "Polybius and the American Constitution," 1 (1940) 38–58.

Cohen, Lester H., "The American Revolution and Natural Law Theory," 39 (1978) 491–502.

Cooke, J. W., "Jefferson on Liberty," 34 (1973) 568–76.

D'Elia, Donald J., "Dr. Benjamin Rush and the Negro," 30 (1969) 413–22.

Fiering, Norman S., "Irresistible Compassion: An Aspect of Eighteenth-Century Sympathy and Humanitarianism," 37 (1976) 195–218.

Greene, John C., "The American Debate on the Negro's Place in Nature, 1780–1815," 15 (1954) 384–96.

Hofstadter, Richard, "Parrington and the Jeffersonian Tradition," 2 (1941) 391–400.

Jeske, Jeffrey, "Cotton Mather, Physico-Theologian," 47 (1986) 583–94.

Kammen, Michael J., "The Meaning of Colonization in American Revolutionary Thought," 31 (1970) 337–58.

Kates, Gary, "From Liberalism to Radicalism: Tom Paine's *Rights of Man*," 50 (1989) 569–87.

Kennedy, Rick, "The Alliance Between Puritanism and Cartesian Logic at Harvard, 1687–1735," 51 (1990) 549–72.

Ketcham, Ralph L., "James Madison and the Nature of Man," 19 (1958) 62–76.

Maestro, Marcello, "Benjamin Franklin and the Penal Laws," 36 (1975) 551–62.

Miles, Edwin A., "The Young American Nation and the Classical World," 35 (1974) 259–74.

Pocock, J. G. A., "Between Gog and Magog: The Republican Thesis and the *Ideologia Americana*," 48 (1987) 325–46.

Post, David M., "Jeffersonian Revisions of Locke: Education, Property-Rights, and Liberty," 47 (1986) 147–57.

Riker, William H., "Dutch and American Federalism," 18 (1957) 495–521.

Sandler, S. Gerald, "Lockean Ideas in Thomas Jefferson's *Bill for Establishing Religious Freedom*," 21 (1960) 110–16.

Schulz, Constance B., "John Adams on 'The Best of All Possible Worlds,' " 44 (1983) 561–77.

Yarbrough, Stephen R., "Jonathan Edwards on Rhetorical Authority," 47 (1986) 395–408.

INTRODUCTION

By Frank Shuffelton

Peter Gay opened his two-volume interpretation of the Enlightenment with the observation that "There were many philosophes in the eighteenth century, but there was only one Enlightenment."[1] Entitling a collection of essays *The American Enlightenment* might thus seem to be one more brash act of exceptionalist American historiography, claiming special features for the American mind that separate it from the paradigmatic ideas of eighteenth-century Atlantic civilization. The thinkers who variously participated in what Kant called man's emergence from his self-imposed tutelage lived in a world extending from Uppsala and St. Petersburg to Philadelphia and Charlottesville, Virginia, and it would clearly be a mistake to overlook the power of their shared concerns to draw them together in communities of debate and mutual support. Thomas Jefferson's *Notes on the State of Virginia*, for example, a defining study of his native state (and of the whole United States by a sort of synecdoche), began as an answer to queries by François Marbois, secretary of the French legation in Philadelphia, and ultimately emerged as a rebuttal of the environmental theories of Buffon, Reynal, and de Pauw. Jefferson's awareness of the range of contended questions in Enlightenment discourse helped him to lift his text above its potentially parochial limitations and give it a cosmopolitan significance. To refer to an American Enlightenment, then, is to insist that the American experiment of the eighteenth century is, for better or worse, inextricably part of the ongoing experience of the western world with itself and with the rest of humanity.

Nevertheless, it seems equally clear that the numerous voices of the Enlightenment were modulated differently across the different nations of the Atlantic world and within its different languages. The Enlightenment, the *siècle des lumières*, and the *Aufklärung* are not perfectly synonymous; Benjamin Franklin would surely not have been Benjamin Franklin had he been born in Königsberg nor Kant Kant in Philadelphia. The political and intellectual ambitions of the *petit bourgeois* printer would probably have been stifled in East Prussia, and the philosopher of transcendental reason would have found scant support in the brand new College of Philadelphia. The neighborhoods within the Enlightenment

---

[1] Peter Gay, *The Enlightenment: An Interpretation: The Rise of Modern Paganism* (New York: Knopf, 1966), 3.

community were marked by different conditions of discourse and culture, and in this sense we can argue for the American Enlightenment as
in effect a local culture defined by its selective attention to some particular themes chosen from the range of questions and concerns taken up by
the larger Enlightened world.

Ironically, the differences that mark this American Enlightenment
have sometimes tended to interfere with its recognition. Henry F. May in
1976 observed as "a surprising paradox of American historiography"
that while "most American historians of recent times [were] partisans of
the Enlightenment: of liberalism, progress, and rationality, . . . yet there
[was] no good book on the Enlightenment in America." He observed
that there was, however, a "splendid and rapidly growing literature on
the ideas of American Protestantism," and implicitly suggested that the
attention to Protestantism, which he described as a "cluster of ideas"
distinct from that of the Enlightenment, obscured or overlooked the
phenomenon of the Enlightenment.[2] We thus might note that in one of
his most well-known and important essays Perry Miller argued for an
intellectual tradition in New England that went from Edwards to
Emerson, leap-frogging over several generations of secular politicians
and revolutionaries who demonstrated a distinctly different variety of
consciousness.[3] Miller's contention elsewhere that Edwards was deci-
sively influenced by his reading of Locke was perhaps a strategic move
to include the subject of the Enlightenment within that of American
Protestantism. Miller's argument has been seriously questioned by more
recent scholarship on Edwards, much of it energized by his example, but
his work and that of numerous other scholars of American Protestantism
nevertheless force us to recognize a Calvinist concern for the relationships among grace, human consciousness, and history as one of the local
characteristics of the American Enlightenment.[4]

In addition to May's recognition of the apparent appeal of Protestantism over Enlightenment as a category of scholarly inquiry, one might
also think about how the subject of the American Revolution has

[2] Henry F. May, *The Enlightenment in America* (New York: Oxford University
Press, 1976), xii. Obviously one reason to title this collection of essays *The American Enlightenment* is to avoid confusion with May's important study, but I would
like to suggest as well the need to think about Americans' participation in the
Enlightenment on their own terms and not merely about their reception of its ideas.

[3] Perry Miller, "From Edwards to Emerson" in *Errand into the Wilderness*
(Cambridge: Harvard University Press, 1956), 184–203.

[4] cf. Perry Miller, *Jonathan Edwards* (New York: William Sloane Associates,
1949); Norman Fiering, "The Rationalist Foundations of Edwards's Metaphysics"
in *Jonathan Edwards and the American Experience*, ed. Nathan O. Hatch and
Harry S. Stout (New York: Oxford University Press, 1988), 76–77.

curiously diverted attention away from the subject of the Enlightenment. In earlier years the Revolution was a motive for some of the wildest excesses of American exceptionalism as it on the one hand sought to celebrate a myth of independence as a sort of national parthenogenesis, and on the other anxiously tried to dissociate the American Revolution from its radical successor in France. Conservative efforts that went so far as to deny that the American Revolution was a revolution at all tended to distance it from discussions of the Enlightenment, since they sought to depict the French Revolution and the Terror as the ultimate fulfillment of a delusive Enlightenment. More recently the brilliant work of the interpreters of the traditions of republicanism and civic humanism – J. G. A. Pocock, Bernard Bailyn, Gordon S. Wood, et al. – has offered a context for the American Revolution that originates not in the Enlightenment, although it becomes a powerful stream of discourse within it, but in the Renaissance of Machiavelli and Harrington. Dissenting historians such as Isaac Kramnick and Joyce Appleby have pointed to the importance of a seemingly contradictory tradition of Lockean liberalism that originated in the Enlightenment and might be regarded as one of its defining ideas. However, taken as a whole, the work of historians as different as Pocock and Appleby situates the Revolution, the major political and social phenomenon of the late eighteenth century in America, as a function of the international Enlightenment. Furthermore, the historians of republicanism and civic humanism by paying careful attention to the language of political debate in revolutionary America have identified for us a second key voice modulating the local culture of the American Enlightenment.

The subjects of the Great Awakening and the American Revolution, which on one level have tended to displace a fuller consideration of the Enlightenment in America, are in fact the major paradigms within which we must understand most Americans' participation in the international Enlightenment. The instrumentality of much of American thought is perhaps a commonplace, but in the eighteenth-century it certainly seems true that the most powerful intellectual currents in America swirled around questions about the soul confronted by nature and nature's God and about man in political society, about salvation and government. Even the not inconsiderable discourses of science and belles lettres frequently, perhaps typically, oriented themselves to these two paradigmatic concerns. In bringing together the best of the essays on the American Enlightenment that have appeared in the *Journal of the History of Ideas*, I have discovered that they tended to locate themselves most conveniently within one or the other of these paradigms. More specific groupings have suggested themselves, some of which I will discuss below, but I have resisted additional subheads and divisions because I have been struck by the sometimes surprising ways many of these essays both inform each other and point beyond conventional understandings. While May rightly lamented the absence in 1976 of a systematic treatment of the Enlightenment in America, periodicals such as the *Journal* had offered and have continued to offer an array of rich and suggestive studies of Enlightenment subjects that are perhaps more useful for being unsystematic and specific. Drawn from more than fifty years of the *Journal*, the essays in this volume can suggest a working definition of the Enlightenment that reflects the sense of many scholars – systematic sometimes means idiosyncratic – as well as changes in scholarly focus and method over the last half century. Taken together, they testify to the unity of the American Enlightenment, but they also recognize the variety of the philosophes, to use Peter Gay's term, who spoke to it in voices that were by no means unanimous.

II

The first essays in this collection establish some boundaries to the chronological limits and to the ruling conceptions of an American Enlightenment. Rick Kennedy's "The Alliance between Puritanism and Cartesian Logic at Harvard, 1687–1735" focuses on the impact of William Brattle's two text books that were based upon the Cartesian *Port-Royal Logic* (1662) of Antoine Arnauld. Because Brattle and his brother Thomas were connected with the founding of the Brattle Street Church in Boston, Brattle's Cartesianism has been linked to the same liberalizing impulses that asserted the church's covenant to be based not on Scripture or the traditions of New England but on "the Law of Nature."[5] At the same time, however, Cartesian logic has been seen as of only minor significance in the curriculum, contributing to the end of Puritanism's intellectual dominance before giving way fairly quickly to Lockean empiricism, but Kennedy demonstrates that "an alliance between Puritanism and Cartesian logic existed at Harvard after 1687 and served to strengthen Puritanism's intellectual hegemony." He argues that Brattle's Cartesianism, emphasizing the assurance of clear and distinct ideas revealed by God and method based "on a universally applicable model of geometrical demonstration from clear and distinct axioms," was neither liberal in intention nor a mere philosophical interlude. Brattle's texts remained a part of the curriculum until 1767, often used along with Ramist texts in the earlier years and apparently in conjunction with Locke in the second quarter of the eighteenth century.

5   Perry Miller, *The New England Mind: From Colony to Province* (Cambridge: Harvard University Press, 1953), 242. Note, however, that Miller says,"liberal historians have exaggerated the importance of Brattle Street." 254.

The compatibility of Brattle's Cartesian logics with both Ramus and Locke suggests, however, that they may not be entirely the conservative presence Kennedy suggests. If they supported the older Puritan theism by drawing a connection between divine revelation and first principles, their connection of logic with "an epistemology that put logic into a similar intellectual category with theology" opened unsettling questions about the human will. In his concluding sentence Kennedy situates the Cartesian logics "during the crucial beginnings of the Enlightenment in New England," but we might go beyond that and think of them *as* the beginning. When Brattle told the students and teachers of Harvard that "knowledge must reach our affects and change our hearts, it must transform us," he spoke a language closer to that of Jonathan Edwards than to John Cotton.[6] Kennedy cautions that no one at Harvard seems to have made an explicit connection between knowledge and election, but by implicitly bringing together grace and knowledge and by praising science, "that certain and evident knowledge which we have of anything," the Cartesian logics set into play questions that prepared some young men, Edwards among them, to read Locke and Newton.[7]

Leon Howard was one of the first to note the influence of Cartesian ideas and the *Port-Royal Logic* on Edwards, but Wallace E. Anderson has more recently described the problems of Cartesian dualism and mechanism as a challenge to Edwards's evolving philosophical understanding.[8] In his important early essay in this journal Anderson examines Edwards's generation of his own philosophical position in response to his readings of Newton, Henry More and distinguishes it from those of Locke and Berkeley. When Anderson's essay was published here in 1964, scholarship on Edwards was taking a corrective course to Perry Miller's challenging but overstated claims about Locke's influence on Edwards.[9] Although Anderson does not take up here the issue of the possible Port-Royal influence, his portrayal of a rationalistic Edwards

6 Quoted by Kennedy, 570.
7 Quoted by Kennedy, 566. Although less active in scientific matters than his brother, William Brattle was also a member of the Royal Society.
8 Howard, *"The Mind" of Jonathan Edwards: A Reconstructed Text* (Berkeley: University of California Press, 1963), 7–9; Anderson, "Editor's Introduction," *The Works of Jonathan Edwards: Scientific and Philosophic Writings*, v.6 (New Haven: Yale University Press, 1980), 59–63.
9 One year earlier the *Journal* published Edward Davidson's "From Locke to Edwards" 24(1963), 355–72, which reasserted the importance of Lockean influence but also pointed to significant differences with Locke. Because he focused on the Lockean questions, Davidson concluded that "Edwards was an anomaly" (372). He was hardly an anomaly if one considers his impact on subsequent religious thought in America, and Anderson's essay suggests that in the context of a

responding to Newton locates him not merely as a figure in the history of American Protestantism but as a participant in the Enlightenment's organized habit of criticism. Or in a different context, as Stephen R. Yarbrough claims in his essay, "Edwards describes the effects of grace much as Kant will describe the effects of assuming the aesthetic standpoint" (397). Yarbrough re-states a connection between Edwards and Locke but now on the level of rhetoric rather than of metaphysics or even epistemology. For him Edwards expresses his key insight as a moral thinker lies in his recognition that moral government is a product of rhetorical forces, immediately experienced as our conversation with other intelligent beings, ultimately felt as "God's communicating his mind to us by word or conversation" (401). If Anderson's immaterialist Edwards defines a limiting example of rationalism in the American Enlightenment, one about as distant from Thomas Jefferson as it is possible to go, Yarbrough's theorist of moral rhetoric is fully compatible with the man who founded a university to improve the republican conversation of young Virginians.[10]

Jeffrey Jeske's "Cotton Mather, Physico-Theologian" describes a very different example of the transition from Puritan theism to the Enlightenment rationalism. Mather's *Christian Philosopher*, which Jeske points out was in some ways an exception among Mather's writings, demonstrated his "Enlightenment-like" regard for reason (588), an enthusiasm for a mechanistic interpretation of the universe, and an "essential secularity" (592). Mather and his father opposed Thomas and William Brattle and the Brattle Street Church, but Mather's demand in 1700, "Instead of saying Shew your selves Regenerate Christians, we will only say, Shew your selves Rational Creatures" (588), reveals shared language, even if John Ray and the *Port-Royal Logic* value reason differently. The "empirical bent" (589) of Mather's physico-theological persona, claims Jeske, was one of the "intellectual forces inexorably drawing Puritanism toward deism."

Norman Fiering, our best historian of moral philosophy in early America, supplies a broadly contextualizing essay that points to the eighteenth-century connections between compassion, imaginative sympathy, and humanitarianism. His essay begins by quoting Thomas Jefferson on the moral instinct in 1814, closes with a discussion of Edward Wigglesworth, Hollis Professor of Divinity at Harvard in the

---

larger Enlightenment he was certainly not anomalous in grappling with issues raised by Locke.

[10] Kennedy's essay on the Cartesian rhetorics also allows us to situate Yarbrough's analysis more clearly than he is able to do with his claim for the continuing influence of the Ramist logics.

early eighteenth century, and in between surveys the development of the modern emphasis on the significance of compassion. Enclosed by American references, his essay focuses on the work of British thinkers from Henry More through Richard Cumberland, Shaftesbury, Berkeley, Hutcheson, Hume, and Adam Smith. Fiering's rhetorical strategy reminds us, if we had needed reminding, that Enlightenment is a cosmopolitan term and the notion of enlightened America should always resist any notions of exceptionalism. Similarly, his counter-chronological strategy of beginning with Jefferson and closing with Wigglesworth's difficulties in reconciling the new ideas about compassion with the old Puritan theism is an implicit reminder that if the men of the Enlightenment liked to think of themselves as progressive, progress may have been one of their profoundest illusions. His sympathy for the predicament of Wigglesworth is the response of a modern thinker who has learned to be suspicious when, as he puts it, "a human feeling is elevated to a moral absolute" (218).

Fiering links the development of ideas about irresistible compassion with the rise of humanitarianism in the course of the eighteenth century and in extension with the emergence of the antislavery movement, although he makes several important qualifications about this latter connection.[11] If compassion involved "an imaginary change of situations with the person principally concerned," as Smith put it (211), then it was frequently put to the test when the men of the Enlightenment encountered racial others. Nowhere was this more true than in the Americas where relations with Native Americans and the practice of chattel slavery were sometimes threatening everyday realities and not merely the stuff of abstracted theory or theatrical sentiment. The next three essays each deal with this problem differently: David Bidney's 1954 review essay of important studies by J. H. Kennedy and Roy Harvey Pearce notes a two-way exchange of ideas and ethnographic facts between the Old World and the New. For French intellectuals such as Rousseau and Voltaire, the savage became a means to champion freedom and equality against the Church. On the other hand, Bidney

---

[11] The relationship between humanitarianism and antislavery has recently become the subject of some debate. Thomas L. Haskell's two-part essay "Capitalism and the Origins of the Humanitarian Sensibility," *American Historical Review* 90(1985), 339–61, 547–66, has argued that the rise of capitalism enabled the emergence a humanitarian spirit that motivated the antislavery movement. David Brion Davis, whom Haskell had criticized, has written a strong rejoinder, as has John Ashworth. The documents in this controversy have been conveniently brought together in *The Antislavery Debate: Capitalism and Abolitionism as a Problem in Historical Interpretation*, ed. Thomas Bender (Berkeley: University of California Press, 1992).

rejects Pearce's thesis that the idea of savagism derived from Scottish Enlightenment thinkers necessarily prepared the way for negative evaluations of the Indian. Not Enlightenment ideas, which as logically could support positive evaluations of Native Americans, but "the hunger for land, a growing population, and the economic development of the country" (326) determined attitudes toward the natives. John C. Greene's survey of "The American Debate on the Negro's Place in Nature, 1780–1815" finds that the discussion of the Negro's origin and characteristics had more to do with the credibility of revealed religion than with the search for a "scientific" defense of slavery which would come later. Nevertheless, if Greene discovers a wide range of notions about the character of black Africans, it is readily apparent that this essay, published in the year of Brown vs. the Board of Education, encounters racism everywhere. Donald J. D'Elia's "Dr. Benjamin Rush and the Negro" examines the Enlightened good intentions and the ideological and practical failure of one of the most important scientific thinkers in late eighteenth-century America. D'Elia's concluding, somewhat edgy, recognition that the promise of freedom and equality is not yet fulfilled for African Americans is a reminder of the continuing importance in our century of the Enlightenment's ambiguous bequest.

Humanitarianism was able to flower, says Fiering, because of "the discrediting of rational justifications for inhumanity by opposing to them the *divine authority* of natural and instinctive compassionate feeling" (208). If divine authority functioned on the level of individual feeling, then for many enlightened Americans this necessitated championing of religious freedom on the one hand and on the other a suspicion that religion came down in the end not to the practices of sects but to the private motions of the moral sense. Gerald Sandler documents the close affinities between Locke's *A Letter Concerning Toleration* and Jefferson's *Bill for Establishing Religious Freedom*, and the next essays explore the ways in which three major participants in the American Enlightenment worked out their particular understandings of human moral freedom. It was James Madison who actually saw Jefferson's *Bill* through the Virginia Legislature, and his belief in toleration was, if anything, stronger than Jefferson's because it grew out of more complex and nuanced view of human possibility. As Ralph Ketcham claims, it was grounded in a "constant strain of skepticism and even pessimism about human nature that runs like a stream . . . through his writings" (64). In order to resolve the ambivalence between his faith in men's ability to govern themselves and his recognition of the frailty of human character, Madison emphasized the diversity of human talents and the multiplicity of human desires and interests. Ketcham locates one source of Madison's "realistic, sagacious, moderation" (75) in classical literature, particularly Thucydides, but Constance B. Schulz shows John Adams critically reading a pair of classical writers and displaying a surprising optimism. Often described as a prickly conservative, suspicious of human nature, Adams's response to the Marquis d'Argens' translation of and comments on Ocellus and Timaeus Locrus "repeatedly reaffirms the essential happiness of human experience," says Schulz. Furthermore, the combination of classical Greek texts, commented on by D'Argens, the anticlerical Frenchman, and read by the American Adams demonstrates a fundamentally Enlightened intertextuality in which the American reader has the last word. Joseph Blau's Joel Barlow is perhaps the clearest example of the American philosophe, if that means a commitment to liberty, anticlericalism, progress, and the brotherhood of man. If we are to understand the divine authority of natural compassion as supporting religious toleration, then the example of Barlow suggests that one consequence of toleration might be rejection of all clerical hierarchies and church forms in the interests of "the great realities of liberty" (441). Educated for the ministry at Yale, Barlow ultimately embraced an "enlightened religion" that sought to eliminate the church and its hierarchy and symbols, a republican civil religion for post-revolutionary America.

III

Joel Barlow, thought that Americans were

> Predestined here to methodize and mold
> New codes of empire to reform the old.
> A work so vast a second world required,
> By oceans bourn'd, from elder states retired;
> Where, uncontaminated, unconfined,
> Free contemplation might expand the mind,
> To form, fix, prove the well adjusted plan
> And base and build the commonwealth of man.

He celebrated the possibilities of the coming commonwealth of man in his epic poem *The Columbiad*, written to satisfy the new country's need for a national epic as described by Herder. As this introduction is being written in 1992, Columbus is being castigated as the snake who poisoned the American Eden, but Barlow celebrated him as the European discoverer – the Enlightenment liked to think of itself as the age of discoveries – who brought mind to America even as he sought to Americanize him and distance him from the European contamination. The two essays leading off this second part of our collection, which looks at aspects of building the commonwealth of man, each consider different but analogous strategies by which Americans reconceived their history in order to justify their revolutionary present.

Michael Kammen looks at the reconception of the historical meaning of British colonization of North America that finds its ultimate expression in Thomas Jefferson's and John Adams's defences of legislative independence. The argument that American settlers built the colonies with little assistance from the mother country typically relied upon a narrow focus on seventeenth-century colonial origins because that period had already been staked out as constitutionally determinative by writers who portrayed settlement as a consequence of British failure to provide economic opportunity or civil and religious liberty. This notion of colonial origins underwrote views of sovereignty very different from those of imperial administrators who focused on the Crown's expense in defending colonists from troubles caused by their own greed for land and mistreatment of the natives. Furthermore, Kammen points out, as colonists looked to the histories of other colonies' origins to bolster their own arguments, the meaning of colonization in revolutionary thought came to transcend the provincial bounds of experience. Lester H. Cohen discusses Revolution-era historians who justified separation from England as a similar case of Americans' re-historicization of themselves by the "blending of empirical historical analysis and the metaphysics of Natural Law" (491). He points out how writers like Mercy Warren, James Wilson, and David Ramsay historicized Natural Law, substituting an understanding of it as a process "by which fundamental principles were made concrete in the course of history itself" for an older conception of it as a static body of immutable principles (497). Warren's belief that Natural Rights were "improved in society" so that they had become "a part of the religious creed of a nation" (500) almost echoes Jonathan Edwards's affirmation of moral government grounded in conversation, as described in Yarbrough's essay above, but where Edwards sought to argue from first principles, Warren's appeal to the implicitly pragmatic verdict of history in effect repudiated a faith in the transcendent as a knowable, certain standard.

Conversations about the relevance of historical example for the new nation were a basic fact of American intellectual and political life in the second half of the eighteenth century, because the light of history was a key value, sometimes a controversial one, for republican discourse. One of the strongest historiographical forces in the last twenty-five years has been the uncovering and explanation of this discourse in its most wide-reaching implications. The work of Bernard Bailyn, Gordon S. Wood, J. G. A. Pocock and numerous other scholars has called our attention to the rich array of arguments and texts that seized the imaginations of the people struggling to shape American institutions. The essays by Gilbert Chinard and William H. Riker preceded the accomplishments of the historians of republican discourse, but in significant ways they suggested the possibilities of the work of later scholars and also offer grounds to reflect on it.

Gilbert Chinard's "Polybius and the American Constitution," originally appearing in the first issue of the *Journal*, is an important forerunner of contemporary scholars' attempts to uncover the American Enlightenment's critical involvement with the texts of the past. Chinard, two generations before the present-day intellectual historians of republicanism, was one of the most effective and responsible delineators of the cosmopolitan dimensions of revolutionary thought, particularly in the case of Thomas Jefferson. His editions of the correspondence between Jefferson and Du Pont, Volney, and others clarified the nature of French and American intellectual relationships in the years after the Revolution, and his editions of Jefferson's literary and political commonplace books made explicit the force of the classical presence for the generation of founding fathers. His essay here goes so far as to make the Constitutional Convention of 1787 sound as if it were a debate about the Amphictyonic League, but in demonstrating the passionate commitment to the historical enactments of political ideas, he reinforces Ernst Cassirer's reminder that Enlightenment philosophy was "no longer the isolated substance of the intellect" but an effort to transform "the fixed and finished forms" of the past "into imperatives."[12]

Riker's essay gives a complementary view of how the founders used the example of a more recent republic in their deliberations over the Constitution. The United Netherlands, as Riker demonstrates, might almost be called "the republic that wasn't there" for the members of the Convention in spite of their referring to it more often than to any other modern European government except that of Great Britain. The framers' knowledge of Dutch affairs was based on only a few sketchy and dated texts, and Riker consequently argues that we ought to regard their discussion of Dutch institutions "as an elaborate figure of speech, an extended but not wholly conscious metaphor" (516). Before any talk about the "linguistic turn" taken by contemporary historiography, Riker noticed that "In the eighteenth century, when political propositions attained intellectual respectability only under the guise of universals, the service of the metaphor was of some emotional value" (517). The classical presence described by Chinard was equally a metaphor, but at the same time we might do well to consider the differences between metaphors supported by extensive knowledge and those that are almost empty names. Riker, a political scientist and distinguished scholar of federalism, suggests that the absence of a real Dutch historical example

---

[12] Ernst Cassirer, *The Philosophy of the Enlightenment* (Princeton: Princeton University Press, 1951), vii.

for the framers, despite their seeming claims, may show the Constitution to be more indigenous than often thought. If we take seriously the problem of the "emotional value" of metaphor, however, we might also reflect on the framers' desire, expressed differently here and in their discussions of the Amphictyonic League, to insert their debates in 1787 into a cosmopolitan, enlightened discourse.

Roy Branson's discussion of the relevance of the social and political theory of the Scottish Enlightenment for Madison and his contemporaries recognizes another dimension of Americans' philosophical conversation with the world. Branson claims that Madison's affinities with the social and political thought of John Millar, Adam Smith, David Hume and Adam Ferguson distinguish him from his somewhat older colleague and friend, Thomas Jefferson. Madison backed away from Jefferson's belief in the necessity of "a little rebellion now and then" in part because of his recognition that all nations were in a constant process of development. Madison was immune to the more primitivistic implications of Jefferson's pastoral agrarianism, worrying more about the threat of regression to savagery than of the perils of the manufactory. Branson's consideration of the social dimensions of Madison's ideas can be usefully linked to Ketcham's discussion above that shows how they are grounded in his conception of human nature.

Reading the essays on Jefferson included here in the light of Branson's distinction between the two Virginians suggests differences between what we might regard as early and late phases of the "high enlightenment" in America. J. W. Cooke begins his essay by quoting Schelling, "The beginning and end of all philosophy is – Freedom," a totalizing statement of principle with which Jefferson could easily agree but to which Madison would almost surely wish to give qualifications and nuances. Cooke's systematic description of the conceptions of liberty and reason entertained by Jefferson delineates the thinking that lay behind his vision for an "Empire for liberty," but to encounter this description after Branson's presentation of Madison's debt to the Scottish Enlightenment makes us recognize an essentially utopian dimension of Jefferson's thought. Jefferson's seemingly ahistorical vision of society, as sketched by Cooke, was perhaps more typical of a pre-revolutionary mentality untested by power and practice, but the Jeffersonian position was not simply a passive formation of received concepts about liberty. David M. Post's Jefferson is thus the eponymous leader of a group of thinkers who transformed Lockean ideas about property and education in order to articulate an emerging developmental concept of liberty. Following the cue of C. B. Macpherson, Post sees Jefferson and the Jeffersonians as initiating "a divergent view of individual liberty" that in its divergence marked a reformulation of classic

Enlightenment ideals of freedom. The more purely philosophical notions about liberty expressed in the Declaration of Independence were followed by the rationalizing practice of Madison's Constitution and Jefferson's University, institutions that signalled both a culmination of Enlightenment ambitions and the beginning of a new era.

Post's label of the Jeffersonians as "early U. S. thinkers" suggests an historical and national boundary to the American Enlightenment, but the essays by Marcello Maestro on "Benjamin Franklin and the Penal Laws" and by Gary Kates on "Tom Paine's *Rights of Man*" reinforce the cosmopolitan nature of the Enlightenment even as they point to late eighteenth-century American contributions to the European Enlightenment. Maestro describes a transatlantic exchange of ideas between Franklin and Gaetano Filangieri that illustrates the transmission westward of Cesare Beccaria's ideas about criminal legislation as well as the passage in the other direction of Franklinian theorizing and news of Pennsylvanian reforms. Kates examines what amounts to an American export to France, Thomas Paine, and skillfully analyzes the transformation of his ideological position while participating in the French Revolution. Arguing that the two, separately published parts of *Rights of Man* demonstrate an ideological shift from liberalism to radicalism, Kates points out how the example of the United States becomes central to Paine's arguments in Part Two, ironically after dropping Part One's focus on Lafayette, the standard-bearer of American-style revolutionary moderation.

If Maestro's and Kates's essays suggest emerging national differences in the Enlightened world, the essays by Edwin A. Miles and V. P. Bynack contribute toward a definition of its historical boundaries. Miles argues that "different attitudes toward the relevance of the classical world . . . demonstrates the political and intellectual chasm that existed between the Revolutionary generation and their descendants who lived during the quarter century prior to the Civil War." Describing the gradual disappearance of the classical tradition from public discourse and the college curricula, he reveals both a triumph of Enlightened ideas, democracy, materialism, science, and progress (but also anti-intellectualism), and the loss of an important element of Enlightened discourse. Southerners' attraction to "a cult of Greece" only strengthens the sense of an end of a period, since the Greek example was used not ultimately to support freedom but slavery. Bynack demonstrates how Noah Webster's Herderian project to create an American national culture by defining a national language collapsed in the face of his conversion experience during the Second Great Awakening. Rejecting the conception of language as "a human construct, an artificial system of conventions fabricated to express truths that are external to language," he understood it as in effect a means of grace, "the immediate gift of God" to Adam and Eve in Paradise. If the beginnings of the American Enlightenment are marked by Jonathan Edwards's rationalized theism, its conclusion is thus signalled by Webster's retreat from secularized rationality to a theocentric linguistics. The Enlightened attempt in America to disenchant the world ended, as Bynack suggests, in the reenchantments of romanticism and a resurgent evangelical Christianity.

The final two essays in this collection, each of which reviews earlier attempts to define American intellect, are in part intended to point up the changes in historical method and conceptual focus from the early volumes of this journal to its most recent. Richard Hofstadter's review essay on V. L. Parrington's *Main Currents in American Thought* appeared in 1941 the second volume of *Journal of the History of Ideas*. It looked back on a great achievement of a yet earlier generation of scholarship, and at the same time it expressed the values of an emerging school of consensus historians. Hofstadter takes aim at Parrington's emphasis on the influence of French economic thought on the Jeffersonians and argues that not Physiocracy but empirical and pragmatic liberalism shaped the American spirit, along with a healthy dose of Adam Smith. Hofstadter contends that the ideas of Jeffersonian democracy survived in the Jacksonian era and that by accepting "fundamental economic premises which elsewhere served magnificently to rationalize the capitalist order," Jeffersonian democracy made room for Hamiltonian principles. In volume 48 of the *Journal* (1987) J. G. A. Pocock takes up the question of the "American spirit" in a new guise, here the "*ideologia americana*" that Renzo Pecchioli has described as engaging in an offensive against Marxist historiography. Pocock, responding to Pecchioli and to John P. Diggins, re-states his understanding of the relationship between the republican tradition, which he had famously articulated in *The Machiavellian Moment* (1975), and the Lockean, liberal discourse, which Diggins, Isaac Kramnick and Joyce Appleby have variously urged as of greater significance. Pocock's vigorous defense and clarification of his position demonstrates the terminology and issues in which the most recent debates about the meaning of the political and social meaning of the American Enlightenment have worked themselves out. The shift from Hofstadter's concern with democratic ideas to Pocock's with the "intensively contested dialogue" between discourses of republicanism and liberalism illustrates the sea change that has come over the historiography of ideas in the last half century.

Pocock claims that his dominant concern as an historian has been the "plurality of languages interacting in a given society, not the majestic *translatio imperii* from one 'paradigm' to another." The essays in the present volume similarly pursue the syntax of the significant languages in our society as they were spoken in the eighteenth-century, and in the course of doing so have contributed toward a map of the local enlightened culture. They suggest that the most important languages had to do with politics and religion, and certainly the scientific, aesthetic and historical theorizing that marked many of the other Enlightenments never in this country matched the concern for political and religious questions. Considerations of human nature, character or possibility stayed close to religious concerns, and while Americans like Franklin, Adams and Barlow expressed a rational religion comprehensible to philosophes anywhere, the distinctively local and American accents in which they spoke may have been shaped by the efforts of enlightened Puritans to analyze the rhetoric of God's conversations with us.[13] Similarly, the founding fathers' discourse of freedom drew upon and was received by the philosophical conversation of the West that was the Enlightenment, but their peculiar opportunity to put their own thinking into practice inflected their discourse with a local accent and tone. The essays in this collection seek to recognize both the plurality of voices that enlightened Americans heard and the distinctiveness of their responses, to plumb not just the Enlightenment in America but America's Enlightenment. These essays, then, are implicitly attentive to Pocock's warning that any search for an "American spirit" or "*ideologia americana*" has more to do with the mythopoietic needs of its portrayers than with the actual situation of American thought should bear on any attempt to define an American Enlightenment. If we are to understand the peculiarities of the American neighborhood, we must listen to his enlightened suggestion that "Americans might be happier if they shared their history with other people." These essays are therefore presented in the spirit of a shared history.

[13] May, *Enlightenment*, xiii–xiv; also *The Divided Heart: Essays on Protestantism and the Enlightenment in America*, ed. Henry F. May, New York: Oxford University Press, 1991. May sees Protestantism in conflict with the Enlightenment, and while I agree that the Enlightenment in America closes with the Second Great Awakening and its symptomatic rejection of rationalism, the thinking of people like William Brattle, Cotton Mather and Jonathan Edwards, as examined in the first essays of this volume, represents a movement toward Enlightenment rather than away from it, as in the case of Noah Webster.

PART ONE

DISCOURSES OF RELIGION,
SCIENCE, AND
THE NATURE OF MAN

The Alliance between Puritanism and Cartesian Logic at Harvard, 1687-1735

Rick Kennedy

William Brattle (1662-1717), a much-loved tutor at Harvard and later minister to the college, formally introduced Cartesian logic into the Harvard curriculum in 1687; and the Cartesian compendium that he wrote, along with a later Cartesian catechism, were the basis of a Harvard student's logic education for at least fifty years.[1] These two logic textbooks were passed around in manuscript and transcribed into student notebooks until 1735, when the catechism was published with extensive footnotes by an anonymous editor.[2] From 1687 through 1730s and 1740s there existed an alliance between Puritanism and Cartesian logic at Harvard. That this alliance existed runs counter to historical interpretation up to now.

Nineteenth-century historians of Puritanism began to interpret the introduction of Cartesian logic as an ominous event which introduced self-reliant intellectuality into a society based on the authority of the Bible. Later Perry Miller expanded upon this interpretation and wrote that Cartesian logic in the curriculum indicated a crumbling of Puritan intellectual assurance. For him and the many who have followed his work, Cartesianism only foreshadowed the fall of Puritanism.[3] This interpreta-

---

[1] The author appreciates the help of Norman Fiering, William Rumsey, Thomas Siegel, Barbara Shapiro, Steven Nadler, and Tim Vivian, along with the financial assistance of the National Endowment for the Humanities and Indiana University Southeast.

[2] For the textbooks and reforms at Harvard, see Thomas J. Siegel, *Harvard College in the Eighteenth Century* (Ph.D. diss., Harvard University, 1990).

[3] Perry Miller, *The New England Mind: From Colony to Province* (Cambridge, Mass., 1953), 253, 428, and Samuel E. Morison's *Harvard College In the Seventeenth Century* (2 vols.; Cambridge, Mass., 1936), I, 185-93. Morison errs by taking Brattle's two texts for one, by asserting that New England had access to Descartes's *Rules for the Direction of the Mind* in the 1656 edition of the *Opera Philosophica*, by stating that Brattle's text[s] were "based on the works of Descartes and Pascal," by failing to distinguish the changes from the manuscript to the published versions of Brattle's logic, and by delineating too rigidly between Aristotelian, Ramist, and Cartesian texts.

tion has been taken for granted by most historians who, after noting the place of this insidious new logic in the curriculum at Harvard, quickly move to discussions of the influence of Locke's *Essay Concerning Human Understanding* (1690). The standard interpretation, therefore, of New England's intellectual development is that Cartesian logic briefly helped end Puritanism's intellectual dominance before Lockean empiricism quickly filled the resulting void.[4]

This article proposes, instead, that an alliance between Puritanism and Cartesian logic existed at Harvard after 1687 and served to strengthen Puritanism's intellectual hegemony. This article will first explain how Cartesian logic, having already been formed into a system compatible with Augustinian epistemological principles and useful for dogmatically-minded Christians, came to be taught at the provincial Puritan college. More importantly, this article will then explain how Brattle used it to strengthen rather than diminish Harvard's commitment to Christian orthodoxy and biblical authority.

Brattle's first logic text was *A Compendium of Logick, According to the Modern Philosophy extracted from Le Grand & Others, their systems* (1687). His second text was written within the following five years and was a much shorter Latin catechetical version of the first, more useful for recitation in the classroom. This second text was less precisely titled *Compendium Logicae secundum Principia D. Renati Cartesii* (1693?).[5] As these titles illustrate, Brattle was not exactly an author; in fact he was third in a line of textbook authors who at each step removed the logic from its source in René Descartes and adapted the logic to a specific Christian use. In the manner of the time Brattle was an epitomizer who extracted the principles and systems of others, adapting them to a specific educational situation. Although his textbooks have a cut-and-paste quality that mix Aristotelian-scholastic, Ramist, and Cartesian logic, the text-

---

[4] For example, Lawrence A. Cremin in *American Education: The Colonial Experience 1607-1783* (New York, 1970), 256; Henry May in *The American Enlightenment* (New York, 1976), 38; and Elizabeth Flower and Murray G. Murphey in *A History of Philosophy in America* (2 vols.; New York, 1977) I, 365-73. Important exceptions to the dominant interpretation are Norman Fiering's *Moral Philosophy at Seventeenth-Century Harvard* (Chapel Hill, N.C., 1981), *Jonathan Edwards's Moral Thought and Its British Context* (Chapel Hill, N.C., 1981), and "The First American Enlightenment: Tillotson, Leverett, and Philosophical Anglicanism,"*New England Quarterly*, 54 (1981), 307-44.

[5] There are manuscript copies of both of these texts in several New England archives; for a partial list see Arthur O. Norton, "Harvard Text-Books and Reference Books of the Seventeenth Century," *Publications of the Colonial Society of Massachusetts* (Henceforth *CSM*), 28 (1933), 393-94. Page numbers for *A Compendium of Logick* are from the easily accessible transcription by David Jefferies (1704?) in the Houghton Library at Harvard University. The earliest extant transcription of the 1687 text is by William Partridge in the Beineke Library at Yale University; that of the second text is in the 1693 notebook of Thomas Phips that is described in Norton, 393. For the dating of the text, see footnote 32.

books are essentially Cartesian with a direct intellectual lineage to Descartes through Antoine Arnauld. In order to understand Brattle's provincial role as an epitomizer and the central Cartesianism of the logic, we must first begin by describing the intellectual lineage of his textbooks.

Descartes first published his method of inquiry in his *Discourse on Method* (1637), written in French rather than Latin in the hope of a large audience. He believed he had a divine commission to disseminate his strategy for attaining sure knowledge against the increasing influence of various forms of skepticism.[6] Descartes believed "that all whom God has given the use of . . . reason are obligated to use it principally to try to know him and to know themselves" and that skeptics were just seeking reputations by "boldly attacking whatever is most sound."[7] Descartes was a conscientious Roman Catholic who believed Christianity was threatened by encroaching uncertainty. "My whole aim," he announced in his *Discourse*, "was to reach certainty—to cast aside the loose earth and sand, so as to come upon rock or clay."[8] To accomplish this aim Descartes wrote what he hoped would become a popular textbook for "Christian teaching," the *Principles of Philosophy* (1644); however, it was another textbook that spread Cartesian logic throughout the schools of Europe and America in the service of Christianity.[9] "The hard fact is that no school adopted . . . Descartes' *Method*," wrote a logic textbook author in 1724; instead, *The Port-Royal Logic* "came upon the scene, and its repeated editions in our own century will justly arouse admiration."[10]

The Port-Royal Logic (1662, revised 1674) was written principally by Antoine Arnauld, a brilliant theologian who has long been studied as an intellectual foil to Descartes, Leibniz, and Malebranche, whose Jansenism has been considered both a literary stimulant and bad influence on Pascal. Recently, Arnauld has begun to receive the attention he deserves for his work in philosophy, grammar, and the emergence of thinking in terms of

---

[6] See Bernard Williams, *Descartes: The Project of Pure Enquiry*, (Atlantic Highlands, N.J., 1978), 16, henceforth "Williams."

[7] Quoted in E. M. Curley, *Descartes Against the Skeptics* (Cambridge, Mass., 1978), 13n. René Descartes, *The Philosophical Writings of Descartes*, tr. John Cottingham, Robert Stoothoff, Dugald Murdoch (2 vols.; Cambridge, 1985), II, 5, henceforth "Descartes."

[8] Descartes, I, 125.

[9] Descartes, I, 177-78.

[10] Quoted in Wilbur Samuel Howell, *Eighteenth-Century British Logic and Rhetoric* (Princeton, N.J., 1971), 326. What I refer to as *The Port-Royal Logic*, was first published in French as *L'Art de Penser* and usually cited in seventeenth-century New England as the *Ars Cogitandi*. For a facsimile of the 1662 edition and publication history, see *L'Art de Penser: La Logique de Port-Royal*, eds. Bruno Baron von Freytag Löringhoff and Hervert E. Brekle (2 vols.; Stuttgart, 1965). Citations here are from Antoine Arnauld, *The Art of Thinking*, tr. James Dickoff and Patricia James (Indianapolis, Ind., 1964), which includes the 1674 revisions; henceforth "Arnauld."

mathematical probability.[11] As a young theologian, Antoine Arnauld was asked to write what became the "Fourth Set of Objections" to Descartes's *Meditations*. In his "objections" Arnauld is credited with first noting the problem of Descartes's "reasoning in a circle," which Leibniz later criticized as "Take what you need, and do what you should, and you will get what you want."[12] Although circular reasoning would later be part of the downfall of Cartesian epistemology, Arnauld was satisfied by Descartes's response to his objections.[13]

That Arnauld was so easily convinced by Descartes is attributable more to his own intense religiosity than to Descartes's persuasiveness. Arnauld was the intellectual leader of seventeenth-century Jansenism, which was a repressed minority movement within the French Roman Catholic Church. The Jansenists believed they held to the true Roman Catholicism of St. Augustine while the hierarchy of the church was being led astray by Jesuits and skeptics advocating a lazy-thinking, human-centered Christianity. Cartesianism's attack on skepticism, its epistemology based on a God who did not deceive, and its promise of intellectual certainty reassured Arnauld of the intellectual stability of his religious beliefs. Even in his "Fourth Set of Objections" Arnauld compared Cartesianism favorably to Augustinianism; and throughout the rest of his life he mingled his Augustinianism and Cartesianism in statements such as, "St. Augustine realized, long before M. Descartes, that in order to arrive at the truth we cannot begin with anything more certain than this proposition: I think, therefore, I am."[14] Augustinian subjectivity led Arnauld to embrace Descartes's circular reasoning; and this same subjectivity connected Arnauld to John Calvin, who also attempted "to objectify subjective certitude by attaching it to God."[15]

[11] See Steven Nadler, *Arnauld and the Cartesian Philosophy of Ideas* (Princeton, N.J., 1989), henceforth "Nadler," and Ian Hacking, *The Emergence of Probability* (Cambridge, 1975), 73-85. For the wide use and influence of *The Port-Royal Logic*, see L. W. B. Brockliss, *French Higher Education in the Seventeenth and Eighteenth Centuries: A Cultural History* (Oxford, 1987), 197-205. There are also important discussions of *The Port-Royal Logic* in Wilbur Samuel Howell's *Logic and Rhetoric in England 1500-1700* (Princeton, N. J., 1956), 342-63, and his *Eighteenth-Century British Logic and Rhetoric*.

[12] Descartes, II, 150; Leibniz is quoted in Williams, 32.

[13] Arnauld expressed his satisfaction with Descartes's responses in two letters, see Nadler, 23-25.

[14] For Jansenism and Arnauld's role in it, see Alexander Sedgwick, *Jansenism in Seventeenth-Century France* (Charlottesville, 1977); the quote is translated in Nadler, 40. There is a scholarly debate, most recently between Jan Miel in "Pascal, Port-Royal and Cartesian Linguistics," *JHI*, 30 (1969), 262, and Steven M. Nadler, 14-15, as to whether Arnauld was principally a Cartesian or Augustinian. In the specific discipline of logic, William and Martha Kneale in *The Development of Logic* (Oxford, 1962), 316, assert that Arnauld was a Cartesian "chiefly because [he] saw it as a revival of Augustinian thought and therefore an ally of [his] own kind of theology." This article assumes that this was true of Brattle.

[15] Richard Popkin, *The History of Skepticism From Erasmus to Descartes* (Assen, 1964), 195. See also, Edward Downey, *The Knowledge of God in Calvin's Theology* (New York: 1952).

Convinced of Cartesianism's support for Augustinian Christianity, Arnauld, probably with the help of Pierre Nicole and other Jansenist teachers, wrote *The Port-Royal Logic* principally for the use of Jansenism's Little Schools of Port-Royal. Even though the Little Schools were at the time being politically repressed and officially disbanded, Arnauld succeeded in creating not a turgid logic textbook but rather a lucid and powerful essay on "the art of thinking" that was quickly published and adopted in schools throughout Europe.[16] In it the Cartesian method of inquiry and system of logic were fully explained, and Arnauld even used Descartes's unpublished *Rules for the Direction of the Mind* (1628, published in Dutch in 1684 and Latin in 1701) when dealing with the geometrical method of proof. Most importantly, *The Port-Royal Logic* popularized the Cartesian unity of logic and epistemology, linking it to Augustinianism and pointedly using it to attack skepticism.

The Port-Royal Logic bore directly on Brattle's logics; but, as his title indicates, Brattle's first text was based on a textbook by a Franciscan Recollect missionary to England named Anthony (or Antoine) LeGrand (1629-99).[17] LeGrand was born and educated in Douai, where he joined the Recollects, a strict branch of the Franciscan Order inspired by the seventeenth-century spiritual revival in France. In accord with the missionary zeal of that revival, LeGrand accepted a post in the heart of enemy territory, Oxfordshire, England. From 1656 until his death forty-three years later, LeGrand worked among the Roman Catholics of Oxfordshire and London, where he probably served as a tutor to many young Roman Catholics. Christian missionary activity often emphasizes education, but LeGrand could not establish a formal school because Roman Catholicism was officially repressed in England. He could, however, publish a textbook "In usum juventatis Academicae" for the use of his own students and those in the Protestant schools of England.

In 1672 Legrand reduced the whole of Cartesian philosophy and science into the *Institutio Philosophiae secundum Principia D. Renati Des-Cartes, Nova Methodo adornata et explicata, In usum juventatis Academicae*, published two years before the first English edition of *The Port-Royal Logic*. Soon the two would be the principal textbooks during a Cartesian

---

[16] *The Port-Royal Logic* was first used as a manuscript textbook before it was published anonymously. Several people might have helped with its authorship, and certainly, Pierre Nicole, one of the Jansenist tutors in the Little Schools, had something to do with writing the book; however, Arnauld was its principal author, and I follow Dickoff and James in citing him without reference to Nicole or others.

[17] See John K. Ryan, "Anthony Legrand 1629-99: Franciscan and Cartesian," *New Scholasticism*, 9 (1935), 226-50; 10 (1936), 39-55, and the *Dictionary of National Biography*. Richard Watson in *The Breakdown of Cartesian Metaphysics* (Atlantic Highlands, N.J., 1987), 93-96, analyzes LeGrand's Cartesianism and writes that the *Institutio* (using the 1694 date of its English translation) was the "last major exposition of Cartesianism" and heralded "the close of the Cartesian era"; but as this article shows, the use of Cartesian logic did not end with LeGrand.

trend in the 1670s and 1680s.[18] Seven editions of *The Port-Royal Logic*
were published in England before 1700, three in English and four in Latin.
LeGrand revised and expanded his textbook in 1680 with this larger work
going through four editions in England between 1680 and 1694, the latter
being an English translation entitled *An Entire Body of Philosophy*.[19] Only
the first part of LeGrand's text dealt with logic, and in this section the
Franciscan followed the format of *The Port-Royal Logic* and even lifted
whole paragraphs from Arnauld's text.

Unlike *The Port-Royal Logic*, which is pugnaciously filled with anti-
Protestant examples and insistence on Roman Catholic orthodoxy, the
Institutio possesses a missionary quality which makes it more insinuating
than pugnacious. Without copying any of Arnauld's anti-Protestant examples or specific proofs for such doctrines as eucharistic transubstantiation,
LeGrand demanded that those seeking knowledge should follow the example of the Roman Catholic "Renatus Descartes . . . , who by a method,
before his time but imperfectly known, restored philosophy from the very
foundations, opening a sure and solid way to mankind into the inmost
recesses of nature."[20] Sending this out among English youth was apparently meant to accomplish two goals: first, to diminish the influence of
skepticism in England and, second, to build a Roman Catholic foundation
for English students. The latter goal seems to have rested on a premise
similar to Arnauld's: set people on the course of right thinking, and it
will lead them eventually to the "universal Church," which was Roman
Catholic, not Protestant.[21]

It must have disheartened LeGrand to realize that wide use of his text
did not lead to large numbers of converts to Roman Catholicism. In fact,
during the two decades before publication of Locke's *Essay*, the most
dogmatic sort of Protestants appropriated his and Arnauld's textbooks
into their Dissenting Academies. It became apparent that Cartesian logic
could equally support various types of Christian dogmatism, whether
Roman Catholic or Puritan. Even though Joseph Glanvill advocated
Cartesian doubt because it would lead to intellectual humility and show
"the vanity of dogmatizing," two logic textbook authors, Henry Aldrich

---

[18] See Sterling P. Lamprecht, "The Role of Descartes in Seventeenth-Century England," *Studies in the History of Ideas*, 3 (1935), 180-240; and Marjorie Nicholson, "The
Early Stages of Cartesianism in England," *Studies in Philology*, 26 (1929), 356-74.

[19] Anthony LeGrand, *An Entire Body of Philosophy*, tr. R. Blome (London, 1694):
English quotations of the *Institutio* are Blome's, but citations are from the 1680 Latin
edition.

[20] LeGrand, "The Preface" to Blome translation, n.p.

[21] Arnauld wrote of the "universal Church" as a never-changing Roman Catholic
tradition that "cannot err" (p. 287) and "is completely decisive" (p. 286). For Bishop
Bossuet's approval of Arnauld's view of a universal church, see Owen Chadwick, *From
Bossuet to Newman*, (2nd ed, Cambridge, 1987), 12-13.

and John Sergeant, showed that they understood Cartesianism's appeal to the dogmatically-inclined of any theistic persuasion.[22]

Aldrich ended his *Artis Logicae Compendium* (1691) with an oration against *The Port-Royal Logic* as the work of a dogmatic mind. "Everything which [Arnauld] puts forth on his own behalf," Aldrich wrote, "he pronounces haughtily, as if ex cathedra"; and "he perspires in explaining them as if he were giving assistance to a collapsing world."[23] Sergeant particularly criticized both *The Port-Royal Logic* and the *Institutio* in his *The Method of Science* (1696) and generally criticized Cartesian logic as the "method of fanatics." Sergeant characterized Cartesian logic as "spiritual alchemy" based on "whimsical fancies" ultimately bringing "a kind of enthusiasm to philosophy." And for the most cutting critique: "Was ever such Quakerism heard among philosophers?" Judging from the people who seemed most inclined to Cartesianism, Sergeant concluded that people with a "melancholy temper"—defined partially in the seventeenth century as a susceptibility to dogmatic religion—were those most easily seduced by the French philosophy.[24] He was right in the case of many Puritans who supported the Dissenting Academies in England and the Puritans who supported Harvard.

The Dissenting Academies of England were a bit like the Little Schools of Port-Royal: they were not corporately organized, there were no professorships, they depended upon the interaction of a small number of students with often only one tutor, they existed at the displeasure of the state, and they shared among themselves a progressive view of education which entailed an openness to new ideas and textbooks. Most importantly, the Little Schools and the Dissenting Academies were bastions of theological out-groups opposing what they perceived as a tendency to laxity and skepticism in their respective cultural contexts. In the 1680s and 1690s Harvard College can be viewed as the most far-flung and actually most impressive example of a Dissenting Academy.[25]

With their intellectual support of dogmatism and antagonism to skepticism, *The Port-Royal Logic* and the *Institutio* were useful textbooks in the English Dissenting Academies; and it was an academy master, Charles

---

[22] See Joseph Glanvill, *The Vanity of Dogmatizing* (London, 1661), 69-74.

[23] The paragraph of Aldrich's text is translated by Howell in *Eighteenth-Century Logic and Rhetoric*, 55.

[24] John Sergeant, *The Method of Science* (London, 1696), "Preface Dedicatory," n.p. and *Solid Philosophy Asserted* (London, 1697), "Preface," n.p. For the dominant definition of religious melancholy, see Richard Burton, *The Anatomy of Melancholy*, ed. Floyd Dell and Paul Jordon-Smith (New York, 1927), 866, 873, 901.

[25] See Herbert McLachlan, *English Education under the Test Acts: Being a History of the Nonconformist Academies, 1662-1820* (Manchester, 1931), and J. W. Ashley Smith, *The Birth of Modern Education: The Contribution of the Dissenting Academies* (London, 1954). Ashley Smith's appendix gives available textbook lists, most too late for information on the 1680s and 90s, but they do show the continued influence of *The Port-Royal Logic*; he errs in attributing the *Ars Cogitandi* (sometimes written *Ars Cogitando*) to Jean LeClerc.

Morton (1627-98), who carried those two textbooks and a logic text of his own across the Atlantic to Harvard College, where William Brattle used them and other books probably brought by Morton to create his own textbooks.[26] In England Morton had been a progressive master. Like Arnauld, he advocated education in the vernacular, writing two manuscript textbooks in English: the *Compendium Physicae* (no date) and *A System of Logick* (no date). The preface to his logic, which justifies writing in the vernacular, directly influenced Brattle, who also wrote his first textbook in English—although he went back to Latin in his other textbooks. That Morton supplied the books that Brattle used to produce his logic text is suggested by the fact not only that Brattle wrote his *Compendium of Logick* soon after Morton's arrival in Massachusetts but also that in his own works Morton cites two of the Roman Catholic and Cartesian authors that Brattle would explicitly quote, LeGrand and Kenhelm Digby.[27]

Upon arrival in New England, Morton joined immediately with the new president, Increase Mather, and the new tutors Mather had picked, William Brattle and John Leverett, in a coalition for invigorating the college which for some time had been in a "low, sinking state."[28] Over the next decade the four of them increased enrollments, started a building program, reformed the content of the curriculum, and in general restored and reinvigorated the provincial college. Morton's own physics text was introduced into the curriculum, but his logic text seems not to have been used much, even though it was epitomized in the 1690s by Tutor Jabez Fitch.[29] Aside from logic, Brattle and Leverett both introduced material copied directly from the Cambridge Platonist, Henry More. Brattle introduced the *Enchiridion Metaphysicae* in 1688 and Leverett the *Enchiridion Ethicum* in 1694.[30] Of all these textbook reforms of the curriculum, the

[26] For biographical information about Morton see *The Dictionary of American Biography*; Samuel Eliot Morison's introduction to Morton's *Compendium Physicae, CSM*, 33 (1940); Ashley Smith, 56-61; and Norman Fiering, *Moral Philosophy at Seventeenth-Century Harvard*, 207-38.

[27] Morton cites LeGrand in the appendix to his *The Spirit of Man*, published in Boston in 1693, five years after arriving in America, and Digby in the preface to his *A System of Logick*, transcribed in the manuscript notebook of William Partridge (1687). On Digby's relationship to Descartes, see Lamprecht, 189-92.

[28] "Diary of Increase Mather," *Proceedings of the Massachusetts Historical Society 1855-58*), 317.

[29] Fitch's 12-page epitome, *A Treatise of Logic extracted from Mr. Morton*, is included in the 1697 ms. notebook of Daniel Greenleaf at the Massachusetts Historical Society, including both logic texts by Brattle and John Leverett's Cartesian catechism.

[30] There is no warrant for Samuel Eliot Morison's statement that "it is difficult to find any positive achievement of Mr. Mather's on behalf of his alma mater" (*Harvard College in the Seventeenth Century*, II, 504). Mather was in charge, he was a patron for both Morton and Brattle, and his own speeches indicate that he was at the forefront of an invigorated humanist atmosphere at Harvard. See Michael Hall's *The Last Puritan: The Life of Increase Mather* (Middletown, Conn., 1988), 198-201. For the building program

longest lasting and most progressive addition was Brattle's logic texts. Other textbooks from this period of reform came and went, such as Morton's *A System of Logick* and Leverett's own condensation of Brattle and LeGrand.

Having traced the geographical and intellectual lineage of Cartesian logic from France to New England, from Descartes through Arnauld and LeGrand to Brattle, we can now understand Brattle's provincial role. In establishing an alliance between Puritanism and Cartesian logic at Harvard, Brattle did not create a new intellectual synthesis; rather, he adapted a synthesis already created by Arnauld between Jansenism and the Cartesian logic which had been used in England by LeGrand. Brattle, although not the architect of the alliance nor an original thinker, was a crucial figure in the history of Harvard and Massachusetts Congregationalism.[31] While Mather, Morton, and Leverett encouraged and contributed to the curriculum reform, it was Brattle who took Morton's ideas and books and led the way in the most significant reform of the intellectual content of the curriculum. In an age when logic was of crucial importance, when every member of the faculty and administration of the college—Mather, Morton, Leverett, and Brattle—wrote their own manuscript logic textbooks, it was Brattle's logics that prevailed.[32]

Cartesianism in general was not new at Harvard, but Brattle gave it its first distinctive role in the curriculum. The year before Brattle wrote his version of LeGrand's *Institutio*, Nathaniel Mather, reviewing the masters'

which accompanied the curriculum reform and manifests some of the mathematical ideals of Descartes, see Rick Kennedy, "Thomas Brattle, Mathematician-Architect in the Transition of the New England Mind, 1690-1700," *Winterthur Portfolio*, 24 (1989), 231-45. The importance of More's ideas at Harvard are discussed by Fiering, *Moral Philosophy at Seventeenth-Century Harvard*, 239-94. Fiering deals with Leverett's Cambridge Platonists textbooks in "The First American Enlightenment: Tillotson, Leverett, and Philosophical Anglicanism," 322-23, and places his emphasis on an English-Latitudinarian-Leverett connection, whereas I place more emphasis on the French-Cartesian-Brattle connection.

[31] For his role in Congregationalism, see Rick Kennedy, *Thy Patriarchs' Desire: Thomas and William Brattle in Puritan Massachusetts* (Ph.D. diss., University of California, Santa Barbara, 1987).

[32] Mather's *Catechismus Logicus ex Petri Rami, Alexandri Richardsoni, et Guiliemi Amesii* (1683) is included in the 1692-93 notebook of Walter Prince at the American Antiquarian Society; Leverett's *Compendium Logicae Vera, Renati Descartes Collectae in usum Pupillorum* (1692) was transcribed in 1720 by Stephen Greenleaf into the notebook of Daniel Greenleaf. President Mather returned from England in 1692, and the 1692 date of Leverett's catechism indicates that Mather did not wish to continue Morton's emphasis on vernacular textbooks but instead asked that Brattle's logic textbook be reformed into a catechism. A few years later, Morton's text was also made into a Latin catechism. I date Brattle's catechism, therefore, to the period after Mather's return and possibly after Leverett's catechism which it mostly replaced. The 1693 date of the earliest extant transcription is the likely date of its composition.

theses of the last few years, wrote from Dublin to his brother Increase: "I perceive the Cartesian philosophy begins to obteyn in New England."[33] Cartesianism had entered the Harvard curriculum in bits and pieces through English mechanical philosophy and mathematics. It also entered through books and textbooks coming from Holland, a country with a close theological relationship to New England and where Descartes lived and published from 1628 to 1649.[34]

With a general Cartesianism beginning "to obteyn" by 1686, Brattle himself was crucial in the adoption of Cartesian logic in New England. The speed and ease with which the alliance between Puritanism and Cartesian logic was accomplished is attributable to Brattle's own reputation and influence at the college and in Massachusetts. By examining his educational ideals, the sources he used in creating his cut-and-paste *Compendium of Logick*, and the way he used Cartesian logic in his sermons to students, we can understand the core of the alliance between Puritanism and Cartesian logic at Harvard and the source of its influence over the many students who graduated into influential posts as ministers and tutors over others in New England.

One parent whose son was greatly influenced by Brattle, remarked in his diary that William Brattle was regarded as a "father to the students of the College."[35] Unlike Morton, Leverett, or Mather, Brattle remained at the college throughout his life. Increase Mather was his patron for most of his career, first bringing him in as a tutor in 1686. Mather also recommended him in 1697 to the church in Cambridge as minister, a position which Brattle held until his death in 1717. This important pulpit carried with it the duties of unofficial chaplain to the college and *de facto* "professor" of divinity.[36] For three decades, a long stream of students and tutors were taught by him and sought his counsel with many of them leaving tributes to his intelligence, compassion, and godly example. In 1702 Increase Mather recommended Brattle to be the on-site vice president of Harvard—at forty he was too young to be president, Mather wrote, but "I take him to be sincerely pious, and fully as orthodox as [the Rev. Samuel Willard, then vice president]." Mather noted that, with Brattle in control of day-to-day affairs, the president could be a distin-

---

[33] *Massachusetts Historical Society Collections*, ser. 4, vol. 8, 63.

[34] Thomas McGahagan in his *Cartesianism in the Netherlands, 1639-1676: The New Science and the Calvinist Counter-Reformation* (Ph.D. diss, University of Pennsylvania, 1976) discusses the Cartesian influence on authors popular at Harvard such as Franco Bergersdijck and Adrien Heereboord. For another comparable situation, see Michael Heyd, *Between Orthodoxy and The Enlightenment: Jean-Robert Chouet and the Introduction of Cartesian Science in the Academy of Geneva* (The Hague, 1982).

[35] *The Diary of Samuel Sewall*, ed. M. Halsey Thomas (2 vols.; New York, 1973), II, 846. Though this phrase was common in an era when tutors worked *in loco parentis*, the title was used inordinantly often when people wrote of Brattle.

[36] Josiah Cotton even refers to Brattle as "professor" of divinity in his diary, printed in *CSM*, 26, 280.

guished absentee figurehead.[37] Brattle did not desire the politically contentious post but was in fact the on-site administrator of the college for much
of his career, beginning with Mather's four-year absence, when he and
Leverett ruled the college, through Leverett's absence after 1697 and the
absentee presidencies of Mather and Samuel Willard, finally sharing the
administration when John Leverett was elected to presidency in 1707.
When Brattle died in 1717, tutor Henry Flynt—himself to become a
Harvard institution—mourned that "God has taken away a minister
watchman father."[38]

Brattle was concerned with education even before he became a tutor.
His first publication was an almanac, *An Ephemeris of Cælestial Motions*
(1682), that gave the standard information but added a postcript essay
stating that he wanted his readers to know not simply *when* an eclipse
would occur but *why*. In this essay Brattle also explained why the Protestant English should accept the Roman Catholic Gregorian calendar. This
was the first published American statement on the subject. His fundamental commitment to education was his belief that unthinking acceptance of
authority, especially one so obviously defective as the Julian calendar,
should be characteristic of only irrational creatures. "Reading without
understanding is one way to introduce the tongue of a parrot into the
head of a rational creature," he wrote, and laid his youthful disdain on
men who "parrot-like . . . talk of things by rote."[39]

Five years later and a year after being named a tutor, Brattle's *Compendium of Logick* carefully organized, strengthened, and expanded the individual intellectual responsibility that he had recommended in his almanac.
Brattle had signed his almanac as "Philomath," lover of learning, and he
dedicated the rest of his life to the pursuit and dissemination of the
type of rigorous analysis that disdained "parrot-like" thinking. Brattle's
Compendium of Logick was principally dedicated against the evil of skepticism in any form. "Right thinking" based on initial doubt and argument
from clear and distinct ideas would yield certain knowledge. The Ramist

[37] *CSM*, 49, 195-96. Brattle's Congregational orthodoxy has long been impugned by
historians, principally on the basis of remarks from a former student, Henry Newman,
who converted to the Church of England and in London became secretary to the Society
for the Promotion of Christian Knowledge (SPCK). Newman's characterizations of Leverett and Brattle in 1713-14 were greatly exaggerated, as in his statement that Brattle would
gladly take orders in the Church of England if he was not afraid of crossing the Atlantic.
This statement and others were written in an attempt to save his job when the influential
Francis Nicholson was attacking Newman's loyalty for corresponding with Brattle, "a
rigid Independent [Congregationalist]." See Newman letters in *SPCK*, Society Letters, to
Dr. Smallridge (March 9, 1713-14) 18, and to Mr. Taylor (March 29, 1714), 31-32. For
further discussion, see Rick Kennedy, *Thy Patriarchs' Desire*, 268-78.

[38] *Diary of Henry Flynt, 1675-1760*, 2-volume transcription by Edward Dunn, Harvard
University Archives, I, 197.

[39] William Brattle, "Postcript," *An Ephemeris of Cælestial Motions* (Cambridge, 1682),
n.p.

doubt (derived from Aristotelian and Humanist traditions) that Brattle had been trained in and was the basis of his attack on "parrot-like" thinking had served only to better establish already known truths. Cartesian doubt, recently learned from Arnauld and LeGrand, entailed even more rigor and promised to yield even greater results. This was the appeal of Cartesianism to young Brattle.

Brattle's *Compendium* followed *The Port-Royal Logic* and the *Institutio* in condemning skepticism, but there is no evidence that there was an actual trend toward a formal philosophical skepticism among Harvard students or in Massachusetts. Brattle apparently learned of the insidious ideas of Montaigne from Arnauld and wrote his logic as a pre-emptive strike against any future skepticism that might insinuate itself into Massachusetts. Skepticism was portrayed by all three textbook authors as something easily fallen into, a form of sin that one must be constantly vigilant to avoid. The most diabolical aspect of skepticism was its seductive humility. Montaigne had not argued against Christianity, only that it was embraced by faith and was not a matter of knowledge. He explained that it was the mentality of theological certainty that made it so easy for Christians to "excel at hating enemies." He asked his readers to question their dogmatisms and to consider "man in isolation—man with no outside help."[40] This was completely wrong-headed to dogmatists because they asserted that humanity was not alone, that divine revelation and human knowledge were intertwined, and that the Holy Spirit had worked and still worked with human reason to guide Christians to true doctrines. Brattle found in Arnauld not only an argument for the sinfulness of skepticism but also dogmatism's most rigorous defense in Cartesian epistemology.

In the vigorous Cartesianism of Arnauld, Brattle wrote that logic "makes the way clear for knowledge in general" and delivers "such precepts as may direct and assist the mind when enquiring into the nature of anything whatsoever."[41] "If we would philosophize in earnest," Brattle insisted using the standard Cartesian phrase, "we must lay aside all the prejudices of infancy and youth."[42] Doubt, however, must be understood only as a means to truth, not an end. "A skeptick," Brattle wrote, was full of "folly and unreasonableness," whereas, "to doubt of things and to suppose them to be all false only for the obtaining of more full and direct knowledge is a laudable method."[43] Doubt was only a beginning to a

---

[40] Michel de Montaigne, *An Apology for Raymond Sebond*, tr. M. A. Screech (London, 1987), 7, 13.

[41] Brattle, *A Compendium of Logick*, "Prolegomenon," chap. i, 5; For equivalent, see LeGrand, "Prolegomenon," chap. ii, sec. iv, 1.

[42] Brattle, *Compendium of Logick*, "Prolegomenon," chap. iii, 16; for equivalent, LeGrand, pt. 1, chap. ii, sec. iii.

[43] Brattle, *Compendium of Logick*, "Prolegomenon," chap. iii, 18; adapted from LeGrand, pt. I, chap. ii, sect. iii-iv.

system that culminated when "we infallibly prove a truth and demonstrate the same to others."[44]

It should be noted here, however, that this method and its goals were not completely new and aspects of it could be found in other forms of logic. Cartesian logic, itself, strengthened aspects in Aristotelian-scholastic and Ramist logic rather than completely overthrew them. The goal of the Cartesian logic texts dealt with here was wide use, not anti-Aristotelian or anti-Ramist polemic. *The Port-Royal Logic* made this perfectly clear: "Our policy concerning what was to be included from the common logic books was this: . . . to incorporate . . . all that was really useful from other logics."[45] Brattle assured his readers that beginning with doubt was "not peculiar to Descartes but was approved by Aristotle."[46] Following Arnauld, Brattle criticized Aristotle only for "faulty" and "unprofitable" categorizing, as in the case of dividing the *ens* into substance and accidence.[47] Aristotle was partially vindicated, however, in a section drawn neither from LeGrand nor Arnauld. In a long quote from Kenhelm Digby, Brattle separated Aristotle from "pretenders of Aristotle" who "alledge texts" just as "hereticks do out of scripture to prove their assertions."[48] As for Ramist logic, Brattle only criticized it once in a section derived directly from Arnauld which condemned Ramus's Topics and over-dichotomizing. Following Arnauld, Brattle advocated "common sense" and the more "accurate" classifications of Topics by a German textbook writer, Johann Clauberg (1622-55).[49]

Therefore, Perry Miller was partially correct to downplay the reforms of Brattle's *Compendium of Logick* in New England when he wrote that it "represents no radical break with Ramist methodology; for in the *Compendium* Brattle did not utterly discard Ramus but rather rewrote the system, following the same scheme of organization, dropping outmoded concepts and inserting instead those of Descartes or else merely translating Ramist terms into Cartesian nomenclature."[50] The problem with Miller's

[44] Brattle, *Compendium of Logick*, "Prolegomenon," chap. i, 8; for equivalent, LeGrand, "Prolegomenon," chap. i, sect. xiii.

[45] Arnauld, 13.

[46] Brattle, *Compendium of Logick*, "Prolegomenon," chap. iii, 17; adapted from LeGrand, pt. I, chap. ii, sect. v, 9, and Arnauld, 24-28.

[47] Brattle, *Compendium of Logick*, pt. I, chap. ii, 42; adapted from Arnauld, 42-45. Arnauld and LeGrand both insist that essence and accidents are not separated in their proofs for the immortality of the soul: LeGrand, pt. IV, chap. xxi, sect. x, 96, and Arnauld, 306.

[48] Brattle, *Compendium of Logick*, pt. I, chap. ii, 49-51.

[49] Brattle, *Compendium of Logick*, pt. III, chap. iv, 178-80; for equivalent, Arnauld, 236-40.

[50] Perry Miller, *The New England Mind: The Seventeenth Century* (Cambridge, 1939), 121. Two disciples of Perry Miller, Elizabeth Flower and Murray G. Murphey, have continued this perspective of the *Compendium Logicae* in their *A History of Philosophy in America* (New York, 1977), I, 367-71.

criticism is that it looked for a systematically radical break between Cartesianism and its precursors that neither Descartes, Arnauld, Le-Grand, nor Brattle wanted to make. LeGrand explained that Descartes only strengthened what was "before his time but imperfectly known."[51] Descartes's followers sought only increased rigor and stronger conclusions, not the creation of a completely new system. Their principal enemy was skepticism, not Aristotle or Ramus. For the Cartesians discussed here, they built upon and reordered former systems of logic in order to counteract what Arnauld called lazy and inattentive thinking which led to "voluntary uncertainty concerning matters of religion."[52]

Following Arnauld and LeGrand, Brattle separated his logic into four parts: perception, judgment, discourse, and method. Aristotelian-scholastic logics and Ramist logics of the seventeenth century covered similar material but with different frameworks, different levels of emphasis, and different meanings for perception and method. The important Ramist development in the sixteenth century had been its emphasis on method.[53] The most influential aspects of Arnauld's development of this four-part structure was, first, to make the section on perception a treatise on Cartesian epistemology, emphasizing the assurance of clear and distinct ideas revealed by a God who did not deceive, and second, to go beyond Ramus and follow Descartes's method, basing it on a universally applicable model of geometrical demonstration from clear and distinct axioms. These are the two crucial Cartesianisms that Brattle imported into Harvard—though not without some moderation and changes.

In his "Prolegomenon" Brattle most clearly lays out the epistemological basis of perception in ten "Rules of Truth." The predecessor of this set of methodological rules, derived from Arnauld and LeGrand, was Descartes's *Rules for the Direction of the Mind*.[54] The first rule explained the importance of doubting in order to attain knowledge. The second, that internal and external senses are deceitful, set up the importance of the third: "whatever we perceive we perceive only by the mind." The fourth rule declared that "the only rule which we can go by in discovering truth is a clear and distinct perception or a perception that excludes all doubt."[55] As an example of the fourth rule, Brattle cited Descartes's proof of the existence of a deity.

[51] LeGrand, *An Entire Body of Philosophy*, "The Preface," n.p.

[52] Arnauld, 11.

[53] See Walter J. Ong, *Ramus, Method, and the Decay of Dialogue* (Cambridge, Mass., 1958).

[54] Ramists avoided lists of rules, but there was a tradition of rules for easy memorizing in Aristotelian-scholastic logics; see John Milton's preface to his *Artis Logicae Plenior Institutio* (1672), a good example of a Ramist logic. A copy owned by William Brattle is in the Prince Collection of the Boston Public Library.

[55] Brattle, *Compendium of Logick*, "Prolegomenon," chap. iii, 22-23; see LeGrand's "Rules of Truth," Pt. I, chap. ii, 8-15.

Earlier logics used at Harvard took innate knowledge for granted, but unlike Brattle's *Compendium of Logick* they avoided or quickly passed over rules for distinguishing true knowledge. Alexander Richardson's *Logicians School-Master* (1629) succinctly begins with "Ens est quod est" and Franco Bergersdijck's *Institutionum Logicarum* (1647) begins simply with "themes" which are anything whatsoever that may be proposed to the understanding to be known.[56] Morton's mostly Aristotelian *A Logick System* began with "terms" or "notions" which are "not so much outward words as the inward conceptions."[57] Brattle's logic went further than these other logics by introducing a full-fledged epistemology into the Harvard logic curriculum; and with Cartesian epistemology as interpreted through Arnauld, the students were taught a more precisely delineated version of the anti-skeptical epistemology of Augustine. It was not a new epistemology; rather readers of Puritanism's leading theologians—the apostle Paul, Augustine, Calvin, and William Ames—could find in it a direct support of their own vaguely developed epistemology. Harvard had never taught a specific epistemology in its curriculum; but in the late seventeenth century, hearing of the rise of skepticism and feeling its threat, Harvard's leaders answered the need of an epistemology with Cartesian logic.

Even though the introduction of an epistemology in Cartesian logic did not lead to a shift in their theology, it does indicate a subtle shift within the Puritan world-view at Harvard. Formerly, Ramist texts had emphasized logic as the basis of dialectic; and drawing on Ciceronian rhetoric, Ramists demanded that the "end of logic . . . is simply discoursing well."[58] The premise of dialectic was the process which ended in winning or losing arguments. As Walter Ong points out, "You knew you were right because no one could prove you wrong."[59] Obviously this was appealing in the post-Reformation world of confrontation and debate between Roman Catholics and Protestants who accepted fundamental ground-rules such as the authority of the Bible, the wisdom of the Church Fathers, and the correct ecclesiology of the Early Church. Yet it could not work against slippery skeptics like Montaigne who could refuse to acknowledge that either side had a sure foundation for the debate. Ramist logic, like Aristotelian logic, had no epistemology capable of answering the increasingly prevalent skepticism of the seventeenth century and could not "win" debates against the skeptics. *The Port-Royal Logic* and its

---

[56] Alexander Richardson, *The Logicians School-Master: or A Comment upon Ramus Logicke* (London, 1629), 1; Franco Bergersdijck, *Institutionum Logicarum Libri Duo* (Cambridge, 1647), 6.

[57] Morton, *A Logick System*, notebook of William Partridge, 27.

[58] John Milton, *A Fuller Course in the Art of Logic Conformed to the Method of Peter Ramus, 1672*, introduced by Walter J. Ong, ed. and tr. Walter J. Ong and Charles J. Ermatinger in *Complete Prose Works of John Milton* (8 vols.; New Haven, Conn., 1982) 8, 214.

[59] Milton, 161.

followers abandoned discourse as the end of logic; and instead made convincing others secondary to personal assurance. One can lose debates and still be right. Overriding all of the particular differences between Ramist and Cartesian logic at Harvard is the basic truth that Cartesian logic is the perfect logic for an out-group, for dissenters, for a minority who insist on truths different than the majority. The shift from Ramist to Cartesian logic at Harvard, therefore, was a conscious or subconscious recognition that Puritanism could no longer logically win a religious debate with the dominant intellectuals of Europe in the late seventeenth century and must settle for strengthening the personal assurance of its members.

That a reorientation of Puritanism's role in the world was necessary in 1687 is evident in the political and social history of Massachusetts. In the three years before 1687 the Massachusetts charter was revoked, a royal governor took control, religious toleration was imposed, an Anglican priest began conducting services in a Congregational meeting house, and the Puritan control of Harvard College tenuously hung in the balance as its administration waited to see if the Church of England and the Crown would assert their legal right of control over higher education. It is no wonder that Brattle was influenced by Arnauld's logic, a logic written at a time when Jansenism was suffering a wave of political repression and authored by a man perspiring "as if he were giving assistance to a collapsing world."

As for method, the second important innovation in Arnauld's logic, Brattle followed LeGrand in avoiding some of Arnauld's extremes but still used Arnauld's version of Cartesianism. Descartes's *Rules for the Direction of the Mind* and *Discourse on Method* advocated a radical extension beyond Ramist method. Ramus had led the way to Descartes by advocating a method of organizing knowledge from the general to the specific in a manner that lended itself to schematic drawings that appeared in many textbooks. For Ramus there was only the analytical method which involved manipulating knowledge already possessed. Ramist method had no need of a divinely guaranteed knowledge and was systematically limited to putting each bit of knowledge in its particular place, based on its discipline and object. Descartes took the method of general to specific but opened the system up in a way that no longer supported schematic drawings. Descartes rejected the tradition of "distinguishing the sciences by the differences of their objects" and insisted that every discipline "is to be valued not so much for its own sake as for its contribution to universal wisdom."[60] The Ramists did not deny universal wisdom; rather, they insisted on distinctions between disciplines and objects "not in regard to God, but in respect of the frame of the thing where we see

---

[60] Descartes, I, 9.

it."[61] Descartes, on the other hand, reversed the viewpoint, emphasizing divine knowledge over the human perspective.

For Descartes arithmetic and geometry showed the way toward universal wisdom, and so he advocated the synthetic method over the analytical: "in seeking the right path of truth we ought to concern ourselves only with objects which admit of as much certainty as the demonstrations of arithmetic and geometry."[62] Arnauld embraced this liberating ideal and began his section on method with the model of Euclidean geometrical demonstration.

The key to geometrical demonstration for Arnauld was the gathering of a treasury of axioms which could be mixed in various ways "to prove and discover what is obscure and abstruse."[63] For Arnauld and his followers, axioms were those clear and distinct bits of knowledge that no honest person could doubt. Following Descartes, Arnauld insisted on the certainty of axioms and the certainty of proofs geometrically derived from those axioms.[64] For Descartes and Arnauld, there was also another means of knowledge that was the equivalent of an axiom: divine testimony. A God who did not deceive already guaranteed the certainty of axioms such as "the whole is greater than its part"; yet God also revealed information to humanity in other ways. For Descartes and Arnauld, God's authority backed the authority of the Roman Catholic Church and the Bible. Brattle gave no such authority to any church; but since for him the Bible was divine testimony, any clear and distinct statement found in it was the equivalent of an axiom from which "convincing and incontestable" proofs could be created.

In the *Institutio* the use of the Bible as axiomatic divine testimony is very clear. Advocating the collection of "a good store of axioms," LeGrand offered a long list of sources for axioms which included "From Divine Authority." "The testimony of a being sovereignly intelligent, wise, and true," LeGrand began in his explanation, "is of greater efficacy to persuade, than any other the most strong and evident reasons that may be." Then as an example LeGrand used a biblical quote: "Thus since God tells us that they are blessed who are persecuted for righteousness sake, we are to hold it for an undoubted truth."[65] At this crucial juncture in Cartesian logic, Jansenists, Puritans, and Roman Catholics in England— each a group persecuted for righteousness sake—found intellectual assurance capable of supporting them through their dark trials.

The particular certainty of Christian doctrines known from divine testimony was also clearly asserted in the section on demonstration, where

[61] Richardson, 16.
[62] Descartes, I, 12.
[63] LeGrand, pt. IV, chap. xxii, sect. v, 100.
[64] See Arnauld, 328.
[65] LeGrand, pt. 4, chap. xxii, sect. v, 107; derived from Arnauld, 337-40.

LeGrand and Brattle distinguished between science, opinion, error, and faith. Arnauld, in his confident assertion of the possibilities of geometrical demonstration, removed it from its traditional position among forms of syllogisms and placed it at the head of the Method section.[66] LeGrand and Brattle followed Arnauld in emphasizing geometrical demonstration but conservatively put it back among the syllogisms of part three: Discourse. Even though changing its position in the text, LeGrand and Brattle followed Arnauld's use of the four terms—terms derived from Augustine's *De Utilitate Credindi*.[67] "Science," Brattle wrote, "is that certain and evident knowledge which we have of anything." Opinion "is not plainly certain knowledge but is attended with a certain fear or wavering of the understanding." Faith "is a proposition grounded on the testimony of another, which may be true or doubtful according to the difference of the authority on which it relies. Thus the faith which we have in God is most firm because we know that he is true and cannot lie. But human faith has always something of uncertainty in it."[68]

Note the two levels of Faith, one human and one divine. One bases its authority on humanity and the other on God. This was crucial because the latter type of Faith is absolutely certain and the equivalent of Science. In the logics of Arnauld, LeGrand, and Brattle, divine testimony could serve as an axiom from which to create geometrical demonstrations that yielded absolute certainty. Brattle made the connection between divine revelation and first principles when he wrote "there is a power innate with us whereby we do assent to first principles," and that these first principles are "true and immediate" and *"cause faith"* (my emphasis).[69]

This is a crucial section of the text for the alliance between Puritanism and Cartesian logic, and so it should be put into context with the logics that it replaced. No logic textbook at Harvard overtly argued that logic should have direct influence on theology or that logic could prove the certainty of a theological doctrine. In the schematic presentations popular before Brattle's text, logic was one part of what Keith Sprunger has called "a six-sided view of life," in which logic (or discourse), grammar, rhetoric, mathematics, physics, and theology were separate pursuits with theology being the only one divinely imputed into humans.[70] "The principles of other arts," wrote William Ames, the most influential thinker in the early Harvard curriculum, "can be developed through sense perception,

---

[66] Arnauld added this section to *The Port-Royal Logic* in 1674.

[67] Arnauld cites Augustine on "understanding, belief, and opinion" in his "Fourth Set of Objections" (Descartes, II, 152); in *The Port-Royal Logic* these distinctions are developed on p. 293.

[68] Brattle, *Compendium of Logick*, pt. III, chap. iii, 166-68; for equivalent, LeGrand, pt. III, chap. xix, sects. i-iv, 85-86.

[69] Brattle, *Compendium of Logick*, pt. III, chap. iii, 168.

[70] Keith L. Sprunger, *The Learned Doctor William Ames: Dutch Backgrounds of English and American Puritanism* (Urbana, Ill., 1972), 117.

observation, experience, and induction"; however, true theology was revealed only to those predestined by God.[71] Formally, the Harvard curriculum had separated logic and theology, and it continued to do so during
Brattle's life. Logic was a human endeavor, and theology was of divine
origin with little human influence. Logic dealt primarily with the intellect,
while theology dealt with the will.

Informally, of course, keeping such boundaries was impossible in the
Massachusetts Bay Company, one of history's most vigorous social experiments uniting right living and right thinking. *The Logicians School-Master*
expressed the spirit of inquiry that permeated Puritan education: "Now
there must be reason in every thing, because I am to see every thing by
my logicke, which is the rule of reason, ergo all things must be lyable to
it."[72] When dealing with Faith and Science, Brattle's logic mixed the
formal and informal, the old and the new logic. As we have seen, the
geometrical method could yield certainty in the area of Faith when built
upon axioms revealed by a God who did not deceive but earlier in his
textbook Brattle followed the Puritan tradition of insisting that "Logic is
not medicinal to the mind in relation to sin, nor cures defects in theology
and ethics."[73] Though Brattle defined the synthetic method of geometry
as "the method of handling a doctrine," he did not follow LeGrand or
Arnauld in giving examples of provable Christian doctrines.[74] In this way
Brattle continued the Puritan tradition of having an intellectual safety-
valve when their human intellectual arts began to press against their
theology. The mysteries of the faith could still be held aloof from the
human mind. However, Cartesian logic's great assistance to Puritanism
was combining logic with an epistemology that put logic into a similar
intellectual category with theology in that both depended upon a God
who revealed knowledge to humanity. In both logic and theology there
were things known clearly and distinctly on an axiomatic level which were
absolutely certain and upon which other doctrines could be demonstrated
by geometrical method.

For an example of how Brattle used Cartesian logic with theology, we
must turn to his sermons (since he did not give examples in his text).
Brattle's manuscript sermons are still extant, and in them we can see the
glosses that Brattle might have given to his text while he was a tutor. One
sermon in particular offers an example of how a tutor could "puritanize" a
discipline. John Morgan in *Godly Knowledge* has shown that "the puritan

---

[71] William Ames, *The Marrow of Theology*, tr. and ed. John Dykstra Eusden (Durham, N.C., 1968), 77.

[72] Richardson, 9.

[73] Brattle, *Compendium of Logick*, "Prolegomenon," chap. ii, 11. This is one of the places where Brattle breaks from LeGrand's language: in an equivalent passage, LeGrand wrote that logic "is necessary to cure the diseases of the Soul, and to direct and guide its operations," ("Prolegomenon," chap. ii, sect. ix).

[74] Brattle, *Compendium of Logick*, pt. IV, chap, ii, 191.

approach was to accept the basic curriculum, though to modify texts and subjects; to work within existing structures, though to introduce activities which would *in practice* demonstrate the aphorism that learning was but a handmaid to divinity."[75] Brattle's logic texts already showed a certain amount of "puritanization" of a new philosophy, and his sermon to the students and tutors at Harvard in 1711 shows it even more.

"The trinity," Brattle often preached, was a mystery beyond the reach of certainty, and yet "belief of this mystery is the duty" of a Christian.[76] In 1711 he preached on what was "certain" in the scriptures. He began with the trinity which was "a mystery; but the declarations of God's holy word do plainly teach us this mystery."[77] In this Brattle echoed *The Port-Royal Logic* which made a similar distinction between mystery and certainty: "There are some things which are certain in their existence, yet incomprehensible in the manner of their existence: Though unable to conceive *how* they can be, we are certain that they are. What is more incomprehensible than eternity? And yet what is more certain?"[78] For Brattle the nature of the trinity was a mystery of faith, but since its existence could be demonstrated clearly from biblical references, its existence was certain. For Brattle there was a clear and distinct divine testimony of the trinity in 1 John 5:7-8, which mentions three witnesses: the Father, the Son, and the Holy Spirit.[79]

It should be noted that the validity of this verse was hotly debated in the sixteenth and seventeenth centuries ever since Erasmus had shown that it was an addition to the text in the Middle Ages. However, many dogmatists on both the Catholic and the Protestant side argued for its biblical veracity; and although almost all Bibles no longer include this statement, the King James version that Brattle used did not remove it. Brattle was not unaware of the debate but believed that Erasmus had not given enough evidence to warrant the deletion of that crucial proof-text for the doctrine of the trinity.[80] The important point is that concerning the trinity, Brattle, in complete consistency with the epistemology and logic taught at Harvard, could show the certainty of its existence while still maintaining the mystery of its workings.

The trinity, however, was only beginning to be a debatable subject

---

[75] John Morgan, *Godly Learning: Puritan Attitudes towards Reason, Learning, and Education, 1550-1640* (Cambridge, 1986), 232.

[76] Brattle sermon on baptism, date obscured but probably December 1696, 1. Unless otherwise noted, all Brattle sermons are from the Houghton Library at Harvard University.

[77] Brattle Sermon, August 26, 1711 PM, 3.

[78] Arnauld, 298.

[79] The doctrine of the trinity was also taken for granted as divine testimony by Le-Grand, pt. IV, chap. xxii, sect. xiv, 110. Arnauld discusses the trinity on p. 339.

[80] Brattle never offered arguments for the validity of 1 John 5: 7-8; however, he probably agreed with Cotton Mather's arguments in *A Christian Conversation . . . The Mystery of Trinity* (Boston, 1709), 4-6.

among New Englanders in the first two decades of the eighteenth century. More pressing was the certainty of the doctrine of predestination, and Brattle gave more time to proving its certainty. He recognized that the doctrine was the "occasion of many disputes . . . but it is very clear that the holy scriptures do assert the doctrine."[81] Using the same distinction he had used when discussing the trinity, Brattle explained that God's will in predestining the elect was a mystery but that the doctrine of predestination was a certainty. Again consistent with Arnauld's epistemology and logic, he demonstrated the doctrine's certainty from the standard proof-texts from Paul's Epistle to the Romans.

Throughout this sermon Brattle consistently returned to such phrases as "the scriptures do plainly teach" and "it is very clear" in the "Word of God." Of course these were the phrases of Christian polemics since at least the Reformation; but given the context that these words were spoken to students by the author of their principal logic textbook, we can see that they could also be understood as catch-phrases of Cartesian logic, hardly different from their old polemic usage but just more precisely understood as part of the logical language necessary to establish the certainty of doctrine. Throughout that sermon and others, Brattle used the language of Cartesian certainty in order to insist that Christian orthodoxy was built upon an intellectual rock, not on the shifting sand of skeptical insecurity.

Cartesian epistemology, the certainty of geometrical demonstration from axioms, and the equivalence of divine testimony in the Bible with axioms were the most significant developments in the logic curriculum at Harvard after the introduction of Brattle's texts. There was also an important development of the role of human will in logic. The standard practice was to distinguish between logic and theology, the former dealing with the intellect and the latter with the will; but Descartes, Arnauld, LeGrand, and Brattle posited the lack of certainty in a sinful disposition of a skeptic's will.

In the over seven hundred pages of manuscript sermons that still exist, Brattle often preached on "contending for the faith," and the vigorous logic of Cartesian certainty supported the arguments throughout. Brattle emphasized at the end of his *Compendium of Logick* that, as logicians, the teacher and the student were duty bound to apply human reason "as far as we can."[82] The goal was to "leave nothing obscure, ambiguous, or equivocal." Only the "limits of man's mind," he advised, should hold a person back.[83] In his textbook and sermons he trained his students to avoid lazy skepticism and advocated vigorous application of Cartesian logic in order to expand the boundaries of certain knowledge. The bound-

---

[81] Brattle Sermon, August 26, 1711PM, 5.
[82] Brattle, *Compendium of Logick*, pt. IV, chap. iv, 205.
[83] Brattle, *Compendium of Logick*, pt. IV, chap. iv, 203-5.

ary of certainty could not include the intricacies of the trinity or God's will in predestination, but the doctrines of trinity and predestination themselves were included.

Brattle ended his sermon to the students and teachers with an appeal that his listeners heed the certainties of scriptures and apply them to their hearts and not just their minds. In this he followed the same argument that appears at the end of *The Port-Royal Logic*. Brattle preached that "this knowledge must reach our affects and change our hearts, it must transform us." Brattle knew the questions and weaknesses in the orthodoxy of tutors like Henry Flynt in his congregation. He spoke directly to them when he concluded that they should make their students wise by "teaching their heads and hearts the things of God."[84]

For the Cartesians we have been discussing, right thinking depended on having the right heart. Throughout his logic, Arnauld criticized the lack of proper will in skeptics: they were lazy, inattentive, and egocentric. He warned that minds not continuously pursuing knowledge would "shrink imperceptibly" and become "incapable of understanding."[85] Arnauld, quoting Aristotle, recognized that "nothing is so well demonstrated that it may not be denied by an obstinate man" and therefore taught that "the wranglings of men are no basis for a judgment concerning the certitude or clarity of a proposition, for everything can be disputed."[86] A version of Bergersdijck's logic taught the same Aristotelian principle: "A person may deny an axiom rather than confess himself to be overcome."[87] As in other things, the Cartesians took this older principle further as in the last sentence of *The Port-Royal Logic* where Arnauld warned that those who do not have salvation as their ultimate concern "are labeled by the Scriptures as fools and imbeciles and make ill use of logic and of reason and of life."[88]

Puritan theology as developed by William Ames demanded that logic was not a matter of the human will. However, because Cartesian logic entailed a fully developed epistemology as the basis of Perception, the will came into logic with the epistemology. Although Brattle did not copy it into his textbook, one section of the *Institutio* clearly showed the role of the will in epistemology: "Since therefore falsehood consists in the hasty consent of the will, it can by no means be imputed to the intellect, because error is not to be found in perceptions, neither is it in any way intelligi-

---

[84] Brattle Sermon, August 26, 1711PM, 10. See also Edward Dunn's *Tutor Henry Flynt of Harvard College, 1675-1760* (Ph.D. diss., University of Rochester, 1968).

[85] Arnauld, 14.

[86] Arnauld, 319, 318.

[87] Quote is an additional comment to Bergersdijck's bk. II, chap. xxii, by "A Gentleman" in *Monitio Logica or, An Abstract and Translation of Bergersdicius his Logick* (London, 1697), 112.

[88] Arnauld, 357.

ble."[89] When Brattle pleaded with the tutors to teach the "things of God" both to the heads and to the hearts of their students, he was speaking, at least in part, from a Cartesian epistemological imperative.

Here again the usefulness of Cartesian logic for religious dissenters is apparent—especially dissenters who believed in the Augustinian theology of election. If knowledge was fundamentally tied to opening one's mind to God's testimony, then knowledge was intimately entwined with grace— and grace was offered only to a minority of people. In a sermon given to the students while still a tutor, Brattle confirmed the Puritan worldview that "Christendom is but a small part of the world, and yet even in Christendom itself, there are but few that are the true disciples." "Many are called," he quoted, "but few are chosen."[90]

Although Arnauld and Brattle never explicitly wrote that right think- ing was tied to grace and election, it was an obvious conclusion to be drawn from their Cartesian/Augustinian epistemology and belief that wrong thinking was a matter of the human will. The closest anyone at Harvard came to explicitly connecting knowledge and election was Charles Morton, who, though influenced by *The Port-Royal Logic*, wrote a mostly Aristotelian text. In a section on Assent Morton began with knowledge "infused by God immediately, as Grace"; and in the accompa- nying schematic drawing, he wrote that "Assent without fear to a true proposition" is either acquired or "infused divine faith gotten by the testimony of God's Word or Spirit."[91] Although Morton's logic was not used often, Morton was an influential mentor to William Brattle, and Brattle's Cartesian logic was consistent with such statements.

By the 1690s Brattle's *Compendium of Logick* had reformed the logic curriculum. Even though Ramist logic continued to be taught along with Brattle's logics, the latter was referred to as the "new" as opposed to the "old" logic. There is no list of textbooks from that period of Brattle's life, but Tutor Flynt submitted a list to the Overseers in 1723 that included Bergersdijck's logic and "a manuscript called the new logic extracted from LeGrand and Ars Cogitandi."[92] Earlier in 1718 a 1709 graduate of Harvard wrote that his father was "well acquainted with the Philosophy & Logick in reputation in his day"—taking it for granted that a new logic ruled his own time.[93] Ramist logic did not disappear from Harvard in the first half of the eighteenth century, yet its role is indicated by a doggerel verse added in 1753 to a copy of the *Logicians School-Master*:

[89] LeGrand, pt. I, chap. iii, sect. xiii, 26.

[90] William Brattle ms sermon, Oct. 6?, 1695, John Carter Brown Library.

[91] Morton, *A Logick System*, 40.

[92] Henry Flynt, "A Particular Account of the Present Stated Exercises Enjoyned the Students," is printed in Morison's *Harvard College in the Seventeenth Century*, I, 146-47.

[93] John Barnard, "An Autobiographical Fragment of John Barnard," *Congregational Quarterly*, 4, 381.

The Author's knowledge sure was great,
But it is grown now out of date.[94]

The question of Locke's role in the "new logic" of the second quarter of the eighteenth century still remains to be studied carefully. From 1687 to 1735 the "new logic" was based in Brattle's *Compendium of Logick* and his cathechetical reduction in the *Compendium Logicae secundum Principia D. Renati Des-Cartes propositum in usum Pupillorum*.[95] Until a published version of the catechism was available in 1735, both of Brattle's logic texts were often transcribed into student notebooks. Although Benjamin Rand, in his history of philosophical instruction at Harvard, considered it "doubtless" that the tutors "moulded their instruction" on Locke's *Essay* soon after 1690, he offers no evidence of its regular use in the curriculum until 1743, when the *Essay* joined Brattle's logic.[96] Not until 1767 when the tutorial system of instruction was reformed and Simeon Howard was specifically named Harvard's Instructor in Logic, did Brattle's logics disappear from Harvard's curriculum. Howard preferred to teach from Isaac Watts's logic—which, though mostly Lockean, paid homage to *The Port-Royal Logic*.

From 1687 until at least 1735, Brattle's Cartesian logic served to support Puritanism's intellectual hegemony based on biblical authority at Harvard. The new logic had much to offer Puritans, who perceived themselves surrounded by an encroaching skepticism that threatened their intellectual hegemony in New England. The history of the logic curriculum at Harvard seems to prove Norman Fiering's general rule that "the long term impetus in America was toward philosophical structures that would reinforce and protect the essential elements of the inherited religious tradition."[97] With an explicit epistemology based in a God who guaranteed the validity of knowledge, an understanding of axioms as that which was clearly and distinctly revealed by God, a view that the divine testimony in the Bible was the equivalent of an axiom, and the method of geometrical demonstration that yielded intellectual assurance, Cartesian logic served to reinforce and protect the essential elements of Puritanism's intellectual hegemony in New England during the crucial beginnings of the Enlightenment in New England.

Indiana University Southeast.

---

[94] Norton, 426.

[95] The size difference between Brattle's texts in the Greenleaf notebook is *Compendium of Logick*, 52 pages, and *Compendium Logicae*, 33 pages. Given the question and answer format of the catechism, the *Compendium Logicae* has about one third the content of the *Compendium of Logick*.

[96] Benjamin Rand, "Philosophical Instruction in Harvard University from 1636 to 1900," *Harvard Graduates Magazine*, 37 (1928-29), 36; see also Siegel for evidence of the use of Locke's *Essay* before 1743.

[97] Fiering, *Moral Philosophy at Seventeenth-Century Harvard*, 241.

II

IMMATERIALISM IN JONATHAN EDWARDS' EARLY PHILOSOPHICAL NOTES

By Wallace E. Anderson

Jonathan Edwards has become a singularly puzzling figure in the history of ideas. Those who refer to him as an idealist have principally in mind the several series of manuscript notes which he wrote mainly between the years 1716 and 1726, during his residence at Yale College. The oddity is that no one had suspected him of idealism until these notes appeared in 1830,[1] though Edwards was widely known from his own lifetime through his published works.

In commenting upon these notes their editor, Sereno Dwight, remarked the author had arrived independently at a position comparable to Berkeley's on the question of the independent existence of the physical world. At a later time, others regarded Edwards as another American disciple of Berkeley. It has since become clear that no such relationship existed between the two, and all evidence points to the view that Edwards' position was developed completely independently of Berkeleyan influence, as Dwight had supposed.[2]

There is, nevertheless, the mystery of Edwards' idealism. The materials from which it was developed, their sources, and the ways in which Edwards used them to arrive at his conclusions are all matters that deserve to be brought to light. They form the central issues of this paper. Other questions that are equally pertinent—why idealism was not developed as a key position in any of his published works, the extent to which it influenced his mature thought as presented in those works, and so on—must be set aside for the time.

As the title suggests, I shall speak of Edwards as an immaterialist rather than as an idealist. This preference is dictated, not so much by the fact that that term is in current vogue, as by its more apparent fitness for the position which I take to be central to our understanding of what is attempted in the notes. It has been disputed whether Edwards really was an idealist, particularly in the sense in which that term is applied to Berkeley. But it is much more clear that he rejected all metaphysical commitments to material substance, that he did so at a relatively early period, and on the ground of what he believed were good reasons. Furthermore, there is no passage in his later works which clearly shows that he had readmitted matter as an ultimate constituent of the world.

---

[1] In *The Works of President Edwards, With A Memoir of His Life*, Sereno E. Dwight, ed. (10 vols., New York, 1829–30). "The Mind" and "Notes on Natural Science," the two series with which this paper is primarily concerned, appear as Appendixes H and I respectively, in Vol. I.

[2] For a complete discussion of the question, see I. W. Riley, *American Philosophy: The Early Schools* (New York, 1907), 144–51. Cf. also Douglas Elwood, *The Philosophical Theology of Jonathan Edwards* (New York, 1960), 169 n.51, for a recent summary.

In order to locate and clarify the grounds of Edwards' immaterialism, we must deal at length with the theory of atomism, which was apparently his point of departure. The early essay which Dwight entitled "Of Atoms and of Perfectly Solid Bodies" is entirely concerned with it. In every other passage among the early notes where the status of matter is at issue, the discussion proceeds, in part, in terms of concepts which are explored in this essay. Furthermore, the essay contains a passage in which he explicitly denies the existence of a material substratum.

The evidence indicates that Edwards' attention was drawn to atomism through a study of Newton's *Opticks*. The pre-college papers "Of Insects," "The Rainbow," and "Of Colors" [3] show that he had read parts of this work before the age of thirteen. In "The Notes on Natural Science" there are a number of passages treating optical phenomena, in which the corpuscular theory of light is invoked. For example, differences in the reflexibility of light are to be explained by the different densities of the rays. The passage concludes with a "Corollary": "Because there is such a difference in the Density of the rays of light, it appears that the Atoms, of which the rays of light are composed, are immensely less than the rays themselves." [4]

This passage suggests that Edwards adopted Newton's corpuscular theory of light as part and parcel of the general theory of atomism, as set forth in the third book of the *Opticks*. There is no single scientific text which Edwards more thoroughly appropriated or persistently incorporated into his own image of nature that this of Newton's:

All those things being considered, it seems probable to me, that God in the beginning formed Matter in solid, massy, hard, impenetrable, moving Particles, of such Sizes and Figures, and in such proportion to Space, as most conduced to the End for which He form'd them; and that these Primitive Particles being Solids, are incomparably harder than any porous Bodies compounded of them, even so hard as never to wear or break in pieces; no ordinary Power being able to divide what God himself made one in the first Creation.[5]

Atomism is applied, somewhat naïvely, to optical phenomena, heat and cold, elasticity, the atmosphere, freezing. From it Edwards deduced the proposition that water is compressible, a performance that is sometimes cited as evidence of his scientific ingenuity.[6] Scattered

---

[3] The first of these in *Works*, I, 23–28; the other two in Egbert C. Smyth, "Some Early Writings of Jonathan Edwards," *Proceedings of The American Antiquarian Society*, X (1895), 218ff.

[4] "Things to be Considered or Written Fully About" (second series), No. 46. *Works*, I, 727. Also Cf. No. 80, *ibid.*, 756.

[5] *Opticks* (New York, 1952), Bk. III, pt. i, 400.

[6] For a more conservative appraisal of Edwards' scientific ability, cf. Clarence Faust, "Jonathan Edwards as a Scientist," *American Literature*, I (1930), 393–404.

among these purportedly scientific notes are a large number of passages in which the theory of atomism itself is examined.

From these different notes we may gather that Edwards' view countenanced most of the main points of the Newtonian hypothesis. Atoms are the real and indivisible parts of material bodies, have size and shape, are impenetrable, have simple location, and are movable in real space. In addition Edwards ascribes attractive forces to them. Contrary to Newton, he treats these forces as original and essential properties of atoms. "Solidity is gravity," he writes in one place, "so that, in some sense the Essence of bodies is Gravity." [7] Newton took great pains to deny this thesis in both the *Opticks* and the *Principia*, and again in his letters to Bentley. There are other difficulties in Edwards' conception of Newtonian mechanics. He often uses the term 'gravity' to refer to any attraction whatever. In proving that the essence of bodies is gravity, he not only erred in his application of the inverse square law, but his argument rests entirely on either a misinterpretation or ignorance of Newton's proposition concerning the composition of forces.[8] It is evident that he was much more an enthusiastic proponent of a general Newtonian world view than a serious student of Newtonian science.

In the passage quoted above from the third book of the *Opticks*, Newton offered his atomism as a plausible or probable hypothesis whose merit for science lay in its simplicity and explanatory fruitfulness. Perhaps Edwards' greatest departure from Newton, both in spirit and method, comes in his attempt to give an a priori demonstration of the theory. His demonstration, so far as it is given, is found in the essay "Of Atoms and of Perfectly Solid Bodies." [9]

This remarkable paper consists of two propositions, each defended in a quasi-geometrical argument, and each followed by a series of corollaries. The first proposition states, "all bodies whatsoever, except Atoms themselves, must, of absolute necessity, be composed of Atoms, or of bodies that are indiscerpible, that cannot be made less, or whose parts cannot, by any finite power, be separated one from another." [10] Edwards could hardly have failed to recognize how far this claim to absolute necessity goes beyond Newton's more modest statement. The second proposition of the essay reads, "Two or more atoms, or perfect solids, touching each other by surfaces, . . . thereby become one and the same atom, or perfect solid." [11] Let us begin with the first of these propositions.

The argument is articulated through a series of homely and somewhat obscure examples. We are to suppose a body which is perfectly solid, a plenum, and then consider whether this body can be broken or crushed by other bodies. If the body is broken at all, it must be broken in some parts but not others; "and indeed, breaking of a body

[7] *Works*, I, 723. Cf. *ibid.*, 744.   [8] *Principia*, Bk. I, Prop. LXXXVIII.
[9] *Works*, I, 708–715.   [10] *Ibid.*, I, 708–9.   [11] *Ibid.*, I, 712.

all over, or in every part, is the same as to annihilate it. . . . But a body perfectly solid and absolutely full, is everywhere equally solid, equally full, and equally strong, and indeed everywhere absolutely alike, so that there is nothing that should cause a fraction in one place sooner than in another." [12] Hence, if a solid body can be broken at all by the pressure of other bodies, it can be annihilated by them. To the objection that we can suppose a small part might be broken from a perfectly solid body without supposing the annihilation of the body, Edwards replies, in effect, that the smallest piece should then be the first broken off, but the smallest piece is infinitely small. "They had as good say, at first, that none at all would be broken, for, as I take it, an infinitely small body, and no body at all, are the same thing, or rather, the same nothing." [13] The requisite inference is drawn in the first corollary:

From what has been proved by the second figure, it plainly appears, that the breaking of a perfectly solid body, and the annihilating of it, are the same thing, so far that the breaking of it would be the annihilating of it.[14]

For Newton, the indivisibility of atoms ensures some sort of constancy in nature. Turning again to those pages in the *Opticks* with which Edwards was well acquainted, and which were of such moment for him:

While the Particles continue entire, they may compose Bodies of one and the same Nature and Texture in all ages; But should they wear away or break in pieces, the Nature of Things depending on them, would be changed. Water and Earth, composed of old worn Particles and Fragments of Particles, would not be of the same Nature and Texture now, with Water and Earth composed of entire Particles in the Beginning.[15]

Edwards, on the other hand, considered the indivisibility of atoms to be the very condition for the existence of matter.

It is unlikely that Edwards produced such an argument entirely on his own, and unnecessary to suppose that he did so. There are a number of indications that the works of Henry More furnished him with both the basic form and much of the materials of his reasoning. Though the works of the Cambridge Platonists have often been mentioned in a general way as having a bearing upon Edwards' early thought, the influence of a part of More's writings on these passages concerning atoms has, until now, gone unnoticed.

In More's *Immortality of the Soul* there is a substantial passage concerning the divisibility of matter, in which appears the statement, "I have taken the boldness to assert, that Matter consists of parts indiscerpible, understanding by indiscerpible parts, particles that have indeed real extension, but so little, that they cannot have less and be

---

[12] *Works*, I, 709, Cf. "Preliminary Propositions," post. 4–7, *ibid.*, 705.
[13] *Ibid.*, I, 710.   [14] *Ibid.*, I, 710.   [15] *Opticks*, 400.

anything at all, and therefore cannot be actually divided." [16] The appearance of the word 'indiscerpible' both here and in Edwards' statement of his first proposition as quoted above, together with the fact that it was a rarely used word apart from More's writings, suggests a connection between the two. An examination of More's argument in support of the above statement will serve to show both the plausibility and the significance of the connection.

More put his premises in the form of axioms, four of which bear directly upon the problem:

Axiome XII: The least that is conceivable is so little, that it cannot be conceived to be discerpible into less.

Axiome XIII: As little as this is, the repetition of it will amount to considerable magnitudes.

Axiome XIV: Magnitude cannot arise out of mere non-magnitude.

Axiome XV: The same thing, by reason of its extreme littleness may be utterly indiscerpible, though intellectually Divisible.[17]

By axiom XII, the least conceivable parts of extended substance are indiscerptible, but by axioms XII and XIV these parts are extended. Extension implies divisibility; hence, by axiom XV, the same thing is both indiscerptible and divisible. More sought to avoid an outright contradiction in axiom XV by distinguishing between discerptibility (the separation of a thing into lesser parts) and "intellectual" divisibility (the discerning of lesser parts in the thing).[18] The argument for the indiscerptibility of extended parts is as follows:

To take away all Extension, is to reduce a thing only to a Mathematical point, which is nothing else but pure Negation or Non-Entity; and there being no medium betwixt Entity and Non-Entity; it is plain that if a thing be at all, it must be extended.[19]

The similarity between Edwards and More is now quite apparent. For both, there must be some extended parts of matter such that, should these be divided, matter itself would cease to exist.

In the fact, the major, if not the only significant difference between the two at this point is that More emphasized the small size of indiscerptible atoms, that they are of the least conceivable magnitude, while Edwards explicitly rejected size as relevant.

[16] In *A Collection of Several Philosophical Writings of Dr. Henry More*, 2nd ed. (London, 1662), Bk. I, Ch. ii, sect. 1, C 2–3. This collection, in its fourth (1712) edition, was among the volumes received by Yale College at the beginning of its history, the gift of Jeremiah Dummer. Cf. Ann Stokely Pratt, "The Books sent from England by Jeremiah Dummer to Yale College," *Papers in Honor of Andrew Keogh* (New Haven, 1938), 7–44. There is no question that Edwards had access to this or another edition of More's work while he resided in the college as a student, and later, as tutor.

[17] *A Collection of Several Philosophical Writings*, C 26–27.

[18] Boyle's concept also reflects this distinction. Cf. *The Origine of Formes and Qualities* (Oxford, 1664), 71.

[19] *A Collection of Several Philosophical Writings*, C 3.

From what has been said, it appears that the nature of an Atom or a *Minimum Physicum* (that is, if we mean by these terms, *a body which cannot be made less*, which is the only sensible meaning of the words), does not at all consist in littleness, as generally used to be thought; for by our philosophy an Atom may be as big as the Universe; because any body, of whatsoever bigness, were an atom, if it were a perfect solid.[20]

This point must be returned to later, for it is also clear that a mathematical concept of three-dimensional extension is involved in the arguments of both. In fact, it is one of the principle meanings assignable to Edwards' term "solidity."

There is a further crucial difficulty to be found in More's demonstration, similar to that which led Leibniz to reject the atomistic doctrine that simple substances are extended.[21] Turning again to More's axioms, we find that axioms XII and XV together yield the inference, that the least that is conceivable is also intellectually divisible, that is, that in it we may discern lesser parts. The significant thing here is that Edwards was aware of the difficulty, and that his most fundamental, probably also his earliest denial that matter is substance, appears as a consequence of his formulation and treatment of it.

Edwards' treatment reflects the claims, explicit and implicit, in classical atomism. Any determinate magnitude is divisible into parts, and is an aggregate of all its parts. An individual thing of determinate magnitude, a body, is divisible accordingly. The parts of a body are bodies. Thus, in Edwards,

In every body, or part of a body, however small, there is a middle, between the two extremes of that body, or that part of a body. . . . There may be bodies of any infinite degree of smallness. That is, in any of these infinite divisions of matter, it is possible that matter, or body, may extend so far as the extremes of that part, and no farther; and then that part will be a distinct body.[22]

It is thus that gross material objects are conceived as composites of lesser bodies. Similarly, the division of a gross body into parts is understood simply as the dislocation of the lesser bodies which compose it. All this proceeds on the basis that the parts of a body have an independent status as bodies, even while they are its components. Since the least conceivable part of any magnitude, that is, a part which is itself not composed of parts, is non-extended, the least parts of a body must be without magnitude. More conceded that such parts are distinguishable, but held that they are not separable. His reason as well as Edwards', is that these least conceivable parts are not bodies. More important, they are not entities at all.

[20] *Works*, I, 711.   [22] *Works*, I, 705.
[21] Cf. "New System of Nature," No. 3, in *Leibniz, Selections*, P. P. Wiener, ed. (New York, 1951), 107. Also "The Monadology," Nos. 2–3, 533.

What Edwards deduced from all this is that atoms are not merely three-dimensional compositions of lesser parts, but that they offer an infinite resistance to division into parts. The concept of such resistance provides a second distinct meaning for Edwards' term "perfect solidity." This is the sense of the term which is employed in the corollaries to his two propositions. From the paradoxical result that the least conceivable parts of a body are non-entities, he attempts to show that bodies which are solid in the sense of being three-dimensional wholes, are of necessity solid in the sense of being infinitely resistant.

Corollary 1: From what was proved by the 2nd figure, it plainly appears, that the breaking of a perfectly solid, body, and the annihilating of it, are the same thing, so far that the breaking of it would be the annihilating of it.

Corollary 2: Hence it appears that Solidity, Impenetrability, and Indivisibility, are the same thing, if run up to their first principles. . . .

Corollary 3: It appears from the two Demonstrations, and from the two first Corollaries, that Solidity, Indivisibility, and resisting to be annihilated are the same thing; and that bodies resist division and penetration, only as they obstinately persevere *to be*.[23]

In the succeeding corollary, Edwards identified body as such with solidity.

Since Annihilation and Breaking are the same; their contraries, Being, and Indivisibility, must also be the same; and since Indivisibility and Solidity are the same, it follows, that the Solidity of bodies and the Being of bodies are the same; so that Body and Solidity are the same.[24]

The identification, as it were, of a thing with its basic properties constituted Edwards' point of departure in considering matter or body in other important passages in the essays "Of Being" and "The Mind." In this context, of course, it is another, almost hidden premiss in his move to abandon material substance.

In Newtonian mechanics the term "resistance" is used primarily as it appears in the definition of inertia, for "the '*vis insita*' or innate force of matter, . . . by which every body, as much as in it lies, continues in its present state." [25] The differences in Edwards' use of the term in these arguments is obvious. Solidity, as a characteristic of atoms, is not a resistance to change of state, but a resistance to annihilation. Moreover, Edwards regards it as an active, not a passive force. It is as though each atom, so far as it is merely extended, is constantly threatened with dissolution into nothing. Hence it is that, for Edwards, active resistance is not simply to be taken as another in the list of properties we ascribe to atoms; it is that upon which all the properties of body depend.

If here it shall be said, by way of objection, that body has other qualities besides solidity; I believe it will appear, to a nice eye, that it hath no more real ones. "What do you say," they say, "to Extension, Figure, and Mobil-

[23] *Works*, I, 710–11.   [24] *Ibid.*, 711.   [25] *Principia*, Bk. I, Def. III.

ity?"—As to extension, I say, I am satisfied, that it has none, any more than space without body, except what results from solidity. As for figure, it is nothing but a modification of solidity, or of the extension of the solidity. And as to mobility, it is but the communicability of this solidity, from one part of space to another.[26]

The argument for the second of Edwards' two propositions, to wit: "Two or more atoms, or perfect solids, touching each other by surfaces, . . . thereby become one and the same atom, or perfect solid," is not difficult to see through. Given solidity in the sense of a three-dimensional whole, the proposition is analytic. Two atoms so disposed do indeed become a single three-dimensional whole. It is of greater moment to show that atoms which are thus mathematically contiguous cannot be separated. The argument for this thesis we must fashion out of the materials at hand from the first proposition and its corollaries. If we suppose that any given finite force will divide a body, a three-dimensional whole, into lesser parts, we must suppose that an equal force will divide it in every part, or into infinitely small parts. If we ascribe nothing but three-dimensional magnitude to bodies, then whatever divides them will equally destroy them. But bodies are not destructible. Therefore we must ascribe to bodies an infinite resistance to division through their three-dimensional parts. The concept of such resistance and the evidence for its presence in bodies are both a priori.

The resistance cannot depend upon extension or the arrangement of parts; these depend upon resistance. Resistance itself, being constant and active, must depend upon God.

We have already as much as proved, that it is God himself, or the immediate exercise of his power, which keeps the parts of atoms, or two bodies tending by surfaces, together; for it is self evident that barely two atoms being together, and that alone, is no power at all, much less an infinite power; and if any say that the nature of atoms is an infinite, they say the same that I do; for all the nature of them, that is not absolutely themselves, must be God exerting his power upon them.[27]

[26] *Works*, I, 711.

[27] *Works*, I, 712. Leibniz at one time made a similar point, i.e. that the purely geometrical properties of bodies do not explain their active force. "In considering the matter closely, we perceive that we must add to them some *higher* or *metaphysical notion, namely, that of substance, action, and force;* and these notions imply that anything which *is acted on* must act reciprocally, *and anything which acts must receive some reaction.* . . . For *the extended signifies* but the repetition and continued multiplicity of what is spread out, a *plurality, continuity, and coexistence of parts,* and consequently it does not suffice to explain the very nature of the substance spread out or repeated, whose notion is prior to that of its repetition" ("Whether the Essence of a Body Consists in Extension," *Journal des Savans,* 1691; "Further Discussion of the Same Subject," *Journal des Savans,* 1693; in Wiener, ed., *Leibniz, Selections,* 101, 104). Despite the differences in Leibniz' and Edwards' concepts of force as such, both argue that it is ontologically prior to extension.

With the thesis that God's power is necessary to cause the infinite resistance of atoms, and with his identification of body with solidity, Edwards has prepared the ground for a general statement of immaterialism. First, since indivisibility and solidity are the same, solidity must result from the immediate exercise of God's power, ". . . causing there to be an indefinite resistance in that place where it is." [28] Finally:

It follows that that, which Philosophers used to think a certain unknown substance, that subsists by itself, (called the *Unknown Substratum*), which stood underneath and kept up solidity, is nothing at all distinct from solidity itself;—or that, if they must needs apply that word to something else, that does really and properly subsist by itself, and support all properties, they must apply it to the Divine Being or power itself. And here I believe all these philosophers would apply it, if they knew what they meant themselves. So that the substance of bodies at last becomes either nothing, or nothing but the Deity, acting in that particular manner, in those parts of space where he thinks fit; so that, speaking most strictly, there is no proper substance but God himself. We speak at present with respect to *Bodies* only; how truly is he said to be *Ens Entium*.[29]

The position expressed in this conclusion is far from complete or coherent. In later passages in the notes Edwards attempts to clear up some of its logical muddles. But there can be no doubt that, as a doctrine, it constitutes a persistent, if not always an apparent theme throughout the philosophical notes. At this juncture, Edwards should be regarded at least as having banished altogether from his metaphysics that concept of ultimate prime matter which was implicit in the writings of most XVIIth-century atomists, and explicitly assumed by some.[30] In its place he put God's action, causing resistance in certain parts of space. All the primary properties normally ascribed to bodies—shape, size, mobility, as well as their creation and duration—are now explicable in terms of resistance in parts of space, the result of divine power. Similarly, the laws of nature are

the stated methods of God's acting with respect to bodies, and the stated conditions of the alteration of the manner of his acting. . . . Hence we learn, that there is no such thing as *Mechanism;* if that word is intended to denote that, whereby bodies act, each upon the other, purely and properly by themselves.[31]

These thoughts are further developed through scattered passages in the two series of "Things to be Considered and Written Fully About," which constitute a large part of the "Notes on Natural Science." Following his attempt to demonstrate the solidity of bodies from the Newtonian law of gravitation, Edwards concludes, "Solidity is gravity; so that, in some sense, the Essence of bodies is Gravity,

[28] *Works*, I, 713.   [29] *Ibid.*
[30] For example, see Boyle, *The Origine of Formes and Qualities*, 3.
[31] *Works*, I, 714.

and to show the folly of seeking for a mechanical cause of Gravity." [32] In a slightly later passage, he reminded himself "To bring in an observation, somewhere in the proper place, that—instead of Hobbes' notion, that God is matter, and that all substance is matter—that nothing, that is matter, can possibly be God; and that no matter is, in the most proper sense, matter." [33] Later still, he observes that since bodies are not substance, they cannot literally have properties; "So that there is neither real substance, nor property, belonging to bodies; but all that is real is immediately in the First Being." [34]

Among the consequences of his denial of the existence of matter, the decisive overthrow of Hobbesian theology must have been one of the most significant for Edwards. In a similar way, Berkeley's earliest efforts to work out the hypothesis of immaterialism took into account its implications for the philosophy of religion. A note in Berkeley's *Philosophical Commentaries* reads, "Matter once allow'd. I defy any man to prove that God is not matter." [35] Being prepared with the arguments, or at least the concepts explored in "Of Atoms and of Perfectly Solid Bodies," Edwards was able to state summarily in the essay "Of Being": "This Infinite and Omnipresent being cannot be solid. Let us see how contradictory it is, to say that an infinite being is solid; for solidity surely is nothing, but resistance to other solidities." [36]

The arguments in "Of Atoms and of Perfectly Solid Bodies," together with those related passages from later parts of the "Notes on Natural Science" (the second series of "Things to be Considered") give us relatively little which can be directly compared with Berkeley's immaterialism. His conclusion denying the existence of an unknown material substratum is similar to Berkeley's inasmuch as it clears the way for identifying substance with spirit and for making body depend-

---

[32] *Works*, I, 723–4. In his "Subjects to be Handled in the Treatise on the Mind" (No. 36), he writes, " . . . it is Laws, that constitute all permanent being, in created things, both corporeal and spiritual" (*Works*, I, 667). Cf. James Tufts, "Edwards and Newton," *Philosophical Review*, XLIX (1940), 610–12.

[33] *Works*, 724. Hobbes is mentioned again in an early entry in the "Miscellaneous Observations" (Harvey Townsend, ed., *The Philosophy of Jonathan Edwards from his Private Notebooks* [Eugene, Oregon, 1955], 193), and frequently in the *Treatise on the Freedom Of the Will*. There, however, Edwards wrote, "I confess, it happens I never read Mr. Hobbes." Paul Ramsey, ed., *Jonathan Edwards' Freedom of the Will* (New Haven, 1957), 374. His understanding of Hobbes probably derived from reading the Cambridge Platonists, Bayle's *Dictionary*, or some other compendium.

[34] *Ibid.*, 725. This passage does indeed encourage the interpretation of Edwards as a pan-entheist. Cf. Elwood, *The Philosophical Theology of Jonathan Edwards*, 21ff. We might more cautiously suppose, however, that he speaks here with respect to bodies only, as in the former instance.

[35] *The Works of George Berkeley*, A. A. Luce and T. E. Jessop, ed., 9 vols. (London, 1948–57), I, 77.   [36] *Works*, I, 706.

ent upon spirit. But the dissimilarities are just as apparent. His arguments are totally unlike Berkeley's. Edwards did not raise the question of the "external" world, except so far as the existence of material substance is involved in it. His conclusion leaves bodies as much external to the *perceiving* mind as any materialist or dualist would have them, though the dependence of bodies upon their being perceived is a claim that Edwards can now support, and soon in fact does support. But for now, bodies depend upon the creative power of God's spirit, rather than upon their being the objects of perception for some spirit or other, as in Berkeley's principle arguments. Last, we have found no need whatever to appeal to the concepts or doctrines of Locke for either the sources or the interpretation of Edwards' arguments here, though Locke's *Essay* is supposed by many to have had a leading rôle in moving him to their formulation.[37] They are not based upon appeals to experience of any kind, and there is a notable absence of characteristically Lockean terminology, with the possible exception of the expression "unknown substratum." Even here, however, Edwards' argument is not that we cannot consistently affirm the existence of something we say is unknown. While it is probable that Edwards had some acquaintance with Locke's *Essay* at the time he wrote "Of Atoms and of Perfectly Solid Bodies," the connection between the two is at best very much more tenuous than that between Berkeley and Locke.

It is in "Of Being," in its concluding argument, that Edwards first introduced anything like an empirical consciousness into his position. This is also the earliest place, presumably, where he is found to affirm that bodies exist only in the mind.[38] The entire passage is very significant in the development of a coherent immaterialism, since in it Edwards responds to the demand that thought come to terms with experience. It seems to be implicitly understood that bodies exist only so far as they are, or can be, objects of empirical enquiry.

The passage begins with a statement of his thesis. Its similarity to Berkeley's can hardly escape notice:

And how doth it grate upon the mind, to think that Something should be from all eternity, and yet Nothing all the while be conscious of it. To illus-

---

[37] Cf. Tufts, 609. The source of the current belief that Edwards read Locke's work at a very early age seems to be his first biographer, Samuel Hopkins, who wrote, "In his second year at college, and the thirteenth year of his age, he read Locke on the human understanding, with great delight and profit. . . . Taking that book into his hand, upon some occasion, not long before his death, he said to some of his select friends, who were then with him, that he was beyond expression entertain'd and pleas'd with it, when he read it in his youth at college; that he was much engaged, and had more satisfaction and pleasure in studying it, than the most greedy miser in gathering up handfuls of silver and gold from some new discovered treasure." *Life and Character of the Late Reverend Mr. Jonathan Edwards* (Boston, 1765), 11–12.   [38] For the date of "Of Being," see Smyth, 218ff.

trate this: Let us suppose that the World had a being from all eternity, and had many great changes, and wonderful revolutions, and all the while Nothing knew it, there was no knowledge in the Universe of any such thing. How is it possible to bring the mind to imagine this? Yea, it is really impossible it should be, that anything should exist, and Nothing know it. Then you will say, If it be so, it is, because Nothing has any existence but in consciousness: No, certainly, no where else, but either in created or uncreated consciousness.[39]

As a preliminary to his argument, Edwards gives three more illustrations which he supposes serve both to explain the proposition and to make its truth more evident. For the first, we are to suppose another universe at a great distance from this, containing nothing but senseless bodies, " . . . created in excellent order, harmonious motions, and a beautiful variety, . . . and nothing but God knew anything of it." Such a universe could exist only in God's consciousness. "There would be figures, and magnitudes, and motions, and proportions; but where, where else, except in the Almighty's knowledge? How is it possible there should?"

The second illustration is perhaps more illuminating:

For the same reason, in a room closely shut up, which nobody sees, there is nothing, except in God's knowledge. . . . Created beings are conscious of the effects of what is in the room; for, perhaps there is not one leaf of a tree, nor a spire of grass, but what produces effects, all over the Universe and will produce them, to the end of eternity. But otherwise, there is nothing in a room so shut up, but only in God's consciousness.[40]

The consciousness of created beings which is referred to here is apparently that of immediate sense experience. At least, Edwards ignores the possibility of our remembering, or our inferring the existence of real contents of the room from their effects which, as he holds, we do experience.

For the last illustration, we are to suppose that all minds in the universe were deprived of consciousness for a time, and that God's consciousness too were interrupted during that time. "I say that the Universe, for that time, would cease to be, of itself; and this not merely as we speak, because the Almighty could not attend to uphold it; but because God could know nothing of it." We suppose otherwise only because we imagine that figures, magnitudes, relations and properties can exist without their being known. But here our imagination misleads us. Edwards takes it that the demonstration of his claim, that bodies exist only in consciousness, rests entirely upon the refutation of this supposition. We are first asked to suppose the universe is entirely deprived of light. In such a case

the universe would really be immediately deprived of all its colors. . . . There would be no visible distinction between the Universe and the rest of the incomprehensible void; . . . there would be no difference, in these respects, between the Universe and Nothing . . . All, in these respects is alike confounded with, and undistinguished from, infinite emptiness.[41]

As the visible world depends upon light, so does the tactual world depend upon motion. If we suppose the universe deprived of motion:

> Then, also, solidity would cease. All that we mean, or can be meant, by solidity, is resistance; resistance to touch, the resistance of some parts of space. This is all the knowledge we get of solidity, by our senses, and, I am sure, all that we can get, any other way. But solidity shall be shown to be nothing else, more fully, hereafter.[42]

The reference to another discussion of solidity as resistance is most probably to the arguments in "Of Atoms and of Perfectly Solid Bodies." [43] The first noticeable difference between this passage and those arguments is Edwards' treatment of resistance here as an object of sense experience, rather than as the exercise of an infinite power. It is an indication that the concept of body has been subjected to a re-examination under the influence of Locke.[44] Equally noticeable is the fact that a connection between resistance—the essence of body— and motion has been established. This connection is more fully analyzed later, in passages in "The Mind."

Without motion, the argument proceeds, there will not only be no perception of resistance, there will be no resistance whatever. "One body cannot resist another, when there is perfect rest among them." [45] To the objection that there would nevertheless be potential resistance, Edwards replies, "This is all that I would have, that there is no solidity now; not but that God could cause there to be, on occasion. And if there is no solidity, there is no extension, for extension is the extendness of the solidity. Then all figure, and magnitude, and proportion, immediately cease." [46] That all other real or primary properties of body depend upon resistance is a claim we have already found in Edwards' discussion of atoms. That resistance itself is found to be a dispositional property, conceived as actual only in the context of motion, constitutes an advance beyond that discussion. Conjoining the two suppositions, that the universe is deprived entirely of both

[41] *Ibid.*, 708. For the connection with Newton's theory of colors, cf. Tufts, 612–13.   [42] *Works*, I, 708.

[43] Townsend suggests that the reference is to "The Mind" No. 61 (*The Philosophy of Jonathan Edwards from his Private Notebooks*, 8, n.11). Though the two discussions are very similar, Dwight believed that "The Mind" No. 61 was written probably at a somewhat later period in Edwards' life (*Works*, I, 674n.). Edwards could hardly have referred to a demonstration of solidity as resistance which he had not already prepared.

[44] Cf. *An Essay Concerning Human Understanding*, Bk. II, Ch. iv.

[45] *Works*, I, 708. Cf. Leibniz' statement, "Primary matter is nothing if considered at rest," in the fragment "On Aristotle's and Descartes' Theories of Matter" (Wiener, 90).

light and motion, we find that we must conceive it to be divested of all properties, relations, events, even of all bodies and all spirits.

What, then, is to become of the Universe? Certainly, it exists no where, but in the Divine Mind. This will be abundantly clearer to one, after having read what I have further to say of solidity, etc.: so that we see that a Universe, without motion, can exist no where else, but in the mind—either infinite or finite.[47]

Under no interpretation could this argument be made to justify the conclusion stated. The claim that body itself ceases to exist when resistance ceases, as in a state where everything is at rest, apparently rests on the assumption that body is identical with resistance. This assumption is made, as we have found, in Edwards' treating the primary properties of bodies as properties of solidity. It would seem, in view of this, that much of the force of this argument is to be found in his demonstration from the solidity of atoms to the conclusion that there is no material substratum, In fact, the question of the existence of material substance is not directly posed in the argument "Of Being" presents, though the essay ends with a denial of it:

It follows from hence, that those beings, which have knowledge and consciousness, are the only proper, and real, and substantial beings; inasmuch as the being of other things is only by these. From hence, we may see the gross mistake of those, who think material things the most substantial beings, and spirits more like a shadow; whereas spirits only are properly substance.[48]

Just as the idealistic conclusion in "Of Being" seems to come out of, and refer back to, the concept of body as solidity and the denial of substratum in "Of Atoms and of Perfectly Solid Bodies," so a similar relation is found to obtain between many passages in "The Mind" and those two earlier papers. There are, for example, a number of entries in which the hypothesis that the universe exists only in the mind is worked out in some detail, in an effort to reconcile it with seemingly incompatible assumptions of science and common sense.[49] Since we are concerned primarily with the underlying critical arguments by which Edwards sought to establish his immaterialism, only two of the entries in "The Mind" are of immediate importance to the

---

[46] *Works*, I, 708.   [47] *Ibid*.   [48] *Works*, I, 708.

[49] E.g. "We would not therefore be understood to deny, that things are what they seem to be. For the principles we lay down, if they are narrowly looked into, do not infer that. Nor will it be found, that they at all make void Natural Philosophy, or the science of the Causes or Reasons of corporeal changes: for to find out the reasons of Things, in Natural Philosophy, is only to find out the portion of God's acting" (No. 34, *Works*, I, 699). The question of the status of sense organs and the brain, and the meaning of the preposition in the expression 'in the mind,' are examined in No. 51; that of the existence of things which are not actually perceived by created minds, in No. 36 and No. 40 (*Works*, I, 670–1). The reconstruction of the Newtonian distinction between real and apparent motion is in No. 65 (*ibid*., 678).

discussion here. They are numbers 27, entitled "Existence," and 61, entitled "Substance." [50]

Of these two, only the first is directed to the explicit conclusion that bodies exist only in the mind. In some respects, it resembles the argument in "Of Being," though it is worked out with far more care. As in the earlier essay, the existence of bodies is considered first from the point of view of our visual experience of them, and then from the point of view of their solidity. For the first, Locke's doctrine of secondary qualities is apparently Edwards' source:

> If we had only the sense of Seeing, we should not be as ready to conclude the visible world to have been an existence independent of perception as we do; because the ideas we have by the sense of Feeling, are as much mere ideas, as those we have by the sense of Seeing. But we know . . . all that the mind views by seeing, are merely mental Existences; because all these things, with all their modes, do exist in a looking-glass, where all will acknowledge, they exist only mentally.[51]

It was particularly appropriate for Edwards to incorporate the Lockean term 'idea,' as standing for a mind-dependent item, the immediate object of consciousness in all sense perception. He found it to be, not only a happy substitute for the Newtonian concept of color, as we find that used in "Of Being," but it also afforded him the means of logically clarifying the concept of resistance.

In order to do so, Edwards began again with the concepts found in "Of Atoms and of Perfectly Solid Bodies," taking resistance as the essence of body:

> I think that Colour may have an existence out of the mind, with equal reason as anything in Body has any existence out of the mind, beside the very substance of the body itself, which is nothing but the Divine power, or rather the Constant Exertion of it. For what idea is that, which we call by the name of Body? I find Colour has the chief share in it. 'Tis nothing but Colour, and Figure, which is the Termination of this Colour, together with some powers, such as the power of resisting, and motion, &c. that wholly makes up what we call Body. And if that, which we principally mean by the thing itself, cannot be said to be in the thing itself, I think nothing can be. If Colour exists not out of the mind, then nothing belonging to Body, exists out of the mind but Resistance, which is Solidity, and the termination of this Resistance, with its relations, which is Figure, and the communication of this Resistance from space to space, which is Motion; though the latter are nothing but modes of the former.[52]

In thus returning to the earlier arguments, the question of the existence of bodies external to the perceiving mind, when it is at last explicitly raised, is conceived in view of those conclusions denying the existence of material substance. The question is not whether *matter*

[50] *Works*, I, 668–9 and 674–6 respectively; No. 13 (673–4) includes a well-known general statement of Edwards' central position, but adds nothing new to the argument.   [51] *Works*, I, 688.   [52] *Ibid.*, I, 668–9.

exists externally, but whether the result of the exercise of God's power is independent of perceiving minds.

In accordance with the discussion in "Of Being," Edwards first distinguishes actual resistance from the power to resist. In neither case, it is shown, can we give a coherent account of the existence of resistance external to the mind. In the case of actual resistance, we must say that resistance both resists and is resisted. "There must be something resisted before there can be resistance; but to say Resistance is resisted, is ridiculously to suppose Resistance, before there is anything to be resisted." [53] The difficulty Edwards points to is one of his own making, for it brings out the absurdity of his own former view that body is not merely the subject of resistance, but is itself resistance.

Equally ridiculous is the supposition that the power to resist exists external to the mind. In the case of two globes existing external to the mind, we should suppose nothing but the law that all parts of two spherical spaces will resist under certain conditions. It apparently follows that, when the globes actually resist each other, we must suppose that one such power of resistance resists another. The crucial problem, that is, what it is that resists, has become a problem only because Edwards had disposed of the subject of the properties of bodies when he disposed of their substratum. If resistance is held to be external to the mind, it must assume the status that was formerly assigned to material bodies. But while it is proper to say that one body resists another, or has the power to do so, it is not proper to say that one power of resistance resists another.

Edwards resolved the problem by construing resistance as a feature of ideas, defined by the laws of behavior of ideas:

But now it is easy to conceive of Resistance, as a mode of an idea. It is easy to conceive of such a power, or constant manner of stopping or resisting a colour. The idea may be resisted, it may move, and stop and rebound; but how a mere power, which is nothing real, can move and stop, is inconceivable, and it is impossible to say a word about it without contradiction. The world is therefore an ideal one; and the Law of creating, and the succession, of these ideas is constant and regular.[54]

Given that resistance is the mode of an idea, it is dependent upon the mind just as the idea is. There is a superficial difficulty in Edwards' statement that one color resists another. What he apparently wished to assert is, first, ideas or shaped colors are the particulars to which the predicate term 'resists' applies, and second, that this predicate term must be analyzed, in terms of the moving, stopping, and rebounding of shaped colors. The power of resistance is then properly understood as the law or "constant manner" according to which these alterations occur.

[53] *Works*, I, 669.   [54] *Ibid.*

Despite the fact that Edwards was deeply indebted to Locke for many of his concepts and arguments, this passage shows a number of important points in which he clearly departed from the assertions found in Locke's *Essay*. Locke, for example, considered solidity as a simple idea received by touch,[55] while for Edwards it is a mode of an idea. Locke ranked motion among the simple ideas common to both sight and touch,[56] but Edwards considers motion, in this passage, only as a visual datum. In another passage, Edwards approaches Berkeley's thought in distinguishing the ideas received by several senses.

As to any idea of Space, Extension, Distance, or Motion, that a man born blind might form, it would be nothing like what we call by those names. All that he could have would be only certain sensations or feelings, that in themselves would be no more like what we intend by Space, Motion, etc., than the pain we have by the scratch of a pin, or than the ideas of taste and smell.[57]

Yet a further, and perhaps more important difference between Locke and Edwards appears in the latter's use of "idea." Ideas, for Edwards, are particulars, shaped colors, subject to motion and rest. They, like Hume's impressions, more nearly resemble the colored patches discussed by modern sense datum theorists than do ideas of sensation as understood by Locke. The point, though it is basically a logical one, is important for the inference Edwards draws. Locke found it necessary to posit a substratum in which qualities must inhere, and considered ideas only from the point of view of their being or presenting these qualities. For the most part, his statements do not suggest that the idea of motion, for example, is a moving idea. This is exactly what Edwards maintains, and it is what permits him to infer that resistance is in the mind.

The article on "Existence," as we have seen, is mainly concerned with raising and resolving the problem of the thing which is understood to resist, or to have the power of resisting. The article on "Substance," the last to be considered here, is concerned with a different problem, namely, what is the proper cause of resistance.

Edwards was compelled to raise the question again, after having answered it once in "Of Atoms and of Perfectly Solid Bodies," since his concept of resistance had been radically altered, as we found in "Of Being" and the earlier entry in "The Mind." 'Solidity' no longer stands for the inseparability of the parts of perfectly solid bodies, but rather for regular alterations in the motions of things, as understood through the laws of nature:

The whole of what we any way observe, whereby we get the idea of Solidity, or Solid Body, are certain parts of Space, from whence we receive the ideas

---

[55] *Essay*, Bk. II, Ch. iv, s. 1.   [56] *Ibid.*, Bk. II, Ch. v.
[57] "The Mind," No. 13; *Works*, I, 674. Cf. Berkeley, *Principles of Human Knowledge*, sect. 44 (*Works*, II, 58–9).

of light and colours; and certain sensations by the sense of feeling; and we observe that the places, whence we receive these sensations, are not constantly the same, but are successively different, and this light and colours are communicated from one part of space to another. And we observe that these parts of space, from whence we receive these sensations, resist and stop other bodies, which we observe communicated successively through the parts of Space adjacent; and those that were before at rest, or existing constantly in one and the same part of Space, after this exist successively in different parts of Space, and these observations are according to certain stated rules.[58]

In his care to present a purely phenomenalistic account of solidity, Edwards even replaced the term 'motion' with others which he held to properly define it.[59]

Not only solidity, but gravity also is a concept we form from the observable phenomena of motion and rest. "In either case, there is nothing observed, but the beginning, increasing, directing, diminishing and ceasing of motion." [60] Solidity is not identified with gravity, as Edwards had done in passages in his "Notes on Natural Science," but both are reduced to phenomena of the same type. Edwards was not disturbed by the problem of "action at a distance," which all gravitational phenomena seemed to involve. He had long since rejected the possibility of there being a mechanical cause for such phenomena, and applied instead to the immediate and harmonious exercise of God's power for their explanation.

Why is it not as reasonable to seek a reason or cause of these actions, as well in the one case as in the other case? We do not think it sufficient to say, It is the nature of the unknown substance, in the one case; and why should we think it a sufficient explication of the same actions or effects, in the other? . . . It was before agreed on all hands, that there is something there, that supports that resistance. It must be granted now, that that Something is a Being, that acts there, as much as that Being that causes bodies to descent towards the Centre. Here is something in these parts of space, that of itself produces effects, without previously being acted upon; for that Being that lays an arrest on bodies in motion, and immediately stops them when they come to such limits and bounds, certainly does as much, as that Being that sets a body in motion, that before was at rest. Now this Being, acting altogether of itself, producing new effects, that are perfectly arbitrary, and that are no way necessary of themselves; must be Intelligent and Voluntary.[61]

In other passages, Edwards defined cause simply as the antecedents to a given event in a uniform succession.[62] In some contexts, we should construe the uniform succession as the regular temporal sequence of changes, which we grasp inductively through the observation of phenomena. It is in this way that we come by the concept of solidity. In other contexts, the antecedents are those understood as

[58] *Works*, I, 676.
[59] Cf. the definition of motion in "The Mind" No. 48 (*ibid.*, 691).   [60] *Ibid.*, 675.

rationally necessary to the production of regular sequences of phenomena. In these contexts, no one phenomenon is understood to be rationally necessary to the occurrence of any other. It is the absence of necessary connections among phenomena, Edwards holds, that leads us to posit a hidden substance.

The reason, why it is so exceedingly natural to men, to suppose that there is some Latent *Substance,* or Something that is altogether his, that upholds the properties of bodies, is, because all see at first sight, that the properties of bodies are such as need some Cause, that shall every moment have influence to their continuance, as well as a Cause of their first existence.[63]

The case here is just as we have discovered it to be in every relevant passage after the arguments in "Of Atoms and of Perfectly Solid Bodies." The substance to be inferred cannot be body, since body is solidity and solidity is the very sequence of phenomena to be explained. Otherwise, material substance is not even mentioned in the passage. We cannot reasonably infer mere substance as the cause, since "By Substance, I suppose it is confessed, we mean only Something; because of Abstract Substance we have no idea, that is more particular than only existence in general." [64] Throughout this discussion, the phenomena are referred to as completely neutral, neither mental nor physical. In this respect, it appears to stand closer to Edwards' early discussions in the "Notes on Natural Science," than to many of the important entries in "The Mind," which presumably precede it. Much the same conclusion is drawn in an earlier entry in "The Mind," however, in which the dependence of phenomena upon the mind is explicitly supposed:

And indeed the secret lies here: That, which truly is the Substance of all Bodies, is *the infinitely exact, and precise, and perfectly stable Idea, in God's mind, together with his stable Will, that the same shall gradually be communicated to us, and to other minds, according to certain fixed and exact established Methods and Laws.*[65]

In view of the foregoing analyses, it is pertinent for purposes of comparison to distinguish the conclusions to which Edwards was drawn, from the arguments which yielded them. For while the conclusions are often strikingly similar to those of Berkeley, we find that the arguments of the two are almost completely unlike.

In one or another passage, Edwards drew inferences to the effect that there is no material substance or substratum, either in the sense of that in which the properties of bodies inhere, or in the sense of that which causes or supports those properties. Neither bodies nor their properties have an "absolute" existence independent of spirits. In every passage we have investigated, Edwards explicitly affirms that the proper cause of bodies and their properties is an active substance,

[61] *Works,* I, 675.   [62] "The Mind" Nos. 12, 29 (*ibid.,* 668, 681).   [63] *Ibid.,* 676.
[64] *Works,* I, 675.   [65] "The Mind" No. 13, *ibid.,* 674.

spirit or God. In some passages, Edwards also argues that bodies exist "in" the mind, or that their existence is simply as idea. Finally, in view of the phenomenalistic analysis of solidity which Edwards provides, he seems, like Berkeley, to hold that in the judgments of science and common sense, our concepts and language are fitted to deal with the complex structures and uniform successions which are arbitrarily established among phenomena by their creator, rather than with individual isolated phenomena as such.

These conclusions of Edwards are not only similar to Berkeley's themselves, the similarity continues through many passages in "The Mind," in which Edwards proceeds from them to give a more detailed account of the existence and order of the physical world. How genuine the similarity is must depend in large part upon the extent to which Edwards' view is conditioned by his acceptance of abstract ideas. In the one relevant passage cited above, Edwards admits the abstract idea of substance, as Berkeley would not, nevertheless, Edwards did not accept an appeal to this abstract idea as furnishing an adequate answer to the question what it is that causes and upholds bodies.

When we turn to the arguments by which Edwards established his various claims, we find them to be just as markedly dissimilar to Berkeley's arguments as their conclusions are similar. Edwards' attack on material substance as such is virtually confined to a few paragraphs in "Of Atoms and of Perfectly Solid Bodies." In every other discussion of the existence of bodies, as we have found, the identity of body with resistance which was produced in that argument comes to be assumed as a premiss. This assumption, by itself, ruled out the possibility of treating bodies as substances. Moreover, the development of his immaterialism from those early and thoroughly rationalistic beginnings is traceable to those revisions in his concept of solidity or resistance which he found to be necessary in the course of further study and reflection. The development of an empirical, and eventually a phenomenalistic account of the concept of resistance is of greatest importance in understanding the later passages. But the initial identification of body with resistance, once established, was never again put in question.

The importance of the concept of solidity for Edwards is shown in the originality with which he explicated it. At different places, he understood by this term a three-dimensional whole, an infinite resistance to separation into parts of such a whole, God's power exerted in a part of space, the mode of an idea, and a characteristic uniformity in the sequence of observed phenomena. Though in each case it is possible to mark out the predominant influences of Newton, More, and Locke, neither Edwards' concepts nor the immaterialism they allowed him to formulate were directly adopted from those sources.

Ohio State University.

III

JONATHAN EDWARDS ON RHETORICAL AUTHORITY

By Stephen R. Yarbrough

Throughout his life Jonathan Edwards worked on a treatise entitled a "Rational Account of the Main Doctrines of the Christian Religion Attempted." He managed to finish very little of it. To get an idea of what he had intended to say, we have to reconstruct it from bits and pieces of materials not published in his lifetime and fill in the gaps with published works and our own conjectures.

The "Account" apparently tries to prove the unity of history, nature, and theology by way of a new kind of rhetoric. The treatise was also to be somewhat polemical: according to Perry Miller, Edwards was "highly resolved not to let science itself, as a mere description of phenomena, take the place of a philosophy or theology of nature."[1]

We are, Edwards believed, persuaded to a right and proper understanding of the world by an encompassing rhetorical process of which science, though important, is only a single aspect. The problem with science, as with any discipline whose immediate aim is not obviously the illumination of the moral dimension of our lives, is that its ends tend to supplant the properly ultimate ends of God. In Edwards's view the origins and grounds of discourse determine its ends; thus the aim of rhetoric (had Edwards used this term) should be to reveal the possibility and explicate the means of God's communication with man. For the problem is not that communication among men is impossible without its being originated in God, but that it *is* possible. Coherent and rational visions of the world *can* be accomplished in a Godless society, yet they may damn the beings who live by them.

Edwards's basically Lockean position, which has been argued and re-argued, is that words refer to ideas rather than to things themselves, that complex ideas are built from simple ideas which are themselves sensible, that men have the same sense organs with approximately the same capacities, and therefore that language can serve as the basis for a coherently organized society—for through language we can have certainty of nature "not only *as great* as our frame can attain to, but *as our Condition needs.*"[2] To Edwards, however, man's needs go well beyond those enabling him to deal pragmatically with nature and to maintain a stable society precisely because "our condition," first and foremost, is that of fallen creatures. The world's languages are in a state of Babel: men born

---

[1] Perry Miller (ed.), *Images or Shadows of Divine Things,* by Jonathan Edwards (New Haven, Conn., 1948), 28.

[2] John Locke, *An Essay Concerning Human Understanding,* ed. Peter H. Nidditch (London, 1975), 634.

into societies whose languages are in such a state are destined to damnation because they cannot receive the Word.

Puritan theology asserted that God gave His Word to the children of Abraham (and the Puritans counted themselves among this small number), so that they might live within a social order that could prepare them to receive grace and eventual regeneration. The problem, of course, was that the Bible is as subject to multiple interpretation as any other text, as the dissension among the Protestants themselves forcefully demonstrated.

A paradox arose here. The Word was a necessary preparation for receiving grace, yet one's interpretation of the Word was suspect unless one had received grace. This paradox lies at the very center of Puritan theology, yet as far as I can determine, it was never stated explicitly. It was crucially important to the Puritan saint in two respects, however. If he had not properly received the Word, his own election was uncertain. Just as important, the Word stood as the proper paradigm for his own words; and since, accepting Abraham's covenant, he was responsible for the preparation of his seed, his faulty teaching could result in God's imputing the sins of his children to him.

Therefore, the Puritan could not help but sense, if he did not consciously recognize, that interpretive and rhetorical acts had to be capable of being grounded in the divine order. Mere speculation or secondary testimony would not suffice. The right understanding of language must rest upon the rock that no Puritan saint could afford to deny—the experience of a saving grace. Accordingly, the Puritan conception of grace had to be formulated in such a way that it could perform this function within a theory of language. The usual image for grace as a light was an epistemological metaphor and unsatisfactory in this context. Perhaps this is the reason the curious paradox was never stated. Toward the end of the Puritan era, however, Jonathan Edwards formulated the metaphor that could solve the problem and possibly provide the foundation for that unified view of history, nature, and theology that Edwards was unable to complete.

The question of what Edwards believed grace is and how it functions must be answered if we are to understand his view of language. Those who have asserted Edwards's Lockeanism, most notably Perry Miller[3] and Michael Colacurcio,[4] have argued that to Edwards grace functions as a "new simple idea." As Colacurcio put it, "If nature is nothing but so many of God's ideas regularly communicated to all men's minds, then

---

[3] Perry Miller, "Edwards, Locke, and the Rhetoric of Sensation," in William J. Scheick (ed.), *Critical Essays on Jonathan Edwards* (Boston, 1980), 120-35.

[4] Michael J. Colacurcio, "The Example of Edwards: Idealist Imagination and the Metaphysics of Sovereignty," in Emory Elliot (ed.), *Puritan Influences in American Literature* (Urbana, 1979), 55-106.

what could grace *conceivably* be but one very special idea communicated to the saints alone?" (71). Yet this claim is fairly simply refuted: to Locke *all* simple ideas are derived from sensory experience; there are *no* innate ideas or principles. For Edwards grace is not, of course, a sensory experience, although it is a state that will alter our sensory experience in a very special way. Furthermore, the alternative to be found in Locke's philosophy, that grace might be a type of the first degree of knowledge, intuitive knowledge, which "forces itself immediately to be perceived," is out of the question. To Locke intuition is always a perception of difference: "Thus the mind perceived at the first sight of Two *Ideas* together, by bare *Intuition,* without the intervention of any other *Idea.* . . . 'Tis only [on] this *Intuition,* that depends all the Certainty and Evidence of all our Knowledge. . ." (531). But as we shall see, to Edwards grace provides an intuition of sameness. And whereas to the Puritans the conference of grace is a partial restoration of an unlearned harmony with nature, to Locke identity is not an innate idea (*ibid.,* 85) but a product of experience. Moreover, to Locke there are no identical ideas— only ideas understood as identical through the category of relation (*ibid.,* 526).

In Edwards's theology grace is not understood as a "new simple idea." It adds no new element to experience; rather, it alters our experience by altering the perspective of our experience. Thus Edwards describes the effects of grace much as Kant will describe the effects of assuming the aesthetic standpoint. Like the aesthetic, the standpoint of grace provides a sort of universal position, a common ground on which all men can agree. Just as one can be assured of perceiving beauty when seeing it, so one can be assured of perceiving the effects of grace when in a state of grace. Thus, like the aesthetic standpoint, grace confers authority upon the individual within it. But of course the authority of the saint is not like what Kant conceived for the artist: God alone is the moral artist. The saint can merely appreciate His masterpieces—His Nature and His Word. Yet the saint's appreciation confers an authority upon him that goes well beyond that of the aesthete, for his perception of the right order of nature and his grasp of the right order of language establish his authority with regard to the word of God and therefore with regard to society.

Consider the following statement from a too little regarded thesis of Edwards entitled "On the Medium of Moral Government—Particularly Conversation": "By all that we see and experience, the *moral* world and the *conversible* world, are the same thing. . . ."[5] This passage exemplifies Edwards's view that rhetorical and moral authority issue from the same ground. Yet beyond this it contends that what can be said and what can

[5] Sereno E. Dwight (ed.), *The Works of President Edwards* (New York, 1829), VII, 281.

be judged are identical. To put it another way, the world one apprehends is determined by the words one speaks. This notion lies at the center of Edwards's concerns. The passage therefore should be carefully considered in its full context.

In both "On the Medium of Moral Government" and its companion piece "The Insufficiency of Reason as a Substitute for Revelation," Edwards attempts to defend the doctrines of revealed religion against attacks on all sides by deistic thinkers. Men like Anthony Collins, John Toland, Matthew Tindal, and Lord Bolingbroke had by the early decades of the eighteenth century argued that man could discover the essential principles of religion purely through the use of reason. Edwards's purpose in these two treatises is to demonstrate that reason has its limits.

Edwards's argument in "The Insufficiency of Reason" is, for all its length, a simple one. After defining reason as "that power or faculty an intelligent being has to judge the truth of propositions" (261), he argues that the truth of any proposition in a chain of argument will always depend upon the truth of the proposition which precedes it. Original propositions will always depend upon some sort of experience, so that rational statements are only as valid as the experience grounding the original propositions. Experience is then classified into various sorts of "testimonies," including the testimonies of the senses, the memory, and history or tradition.

Once Edwards has shown that reason can judge only against a pre-given background of one or more kinds of testimony, he observes

that when any general proposition is recommended to us as true, by any testimony . . . that seems sufficient, without contrary testimony . . . and the difficulties that attend that proposition . . . are no greater . . . than what might reasonably be expected to attend true propositions of that kind, then these difficulties are not only no valid or sufficient objection against that proposition, but they are no objection at all. (267)

Having said this, Edwards can easily conclude that revelation is a kind of testimony subsumed under the heading of history and tradition, and that the difficulties attending revelation are the very sort of difficulties one might expect to have concerning messages from God. In short man has no reason not to accept revelation.

Next, Edwards turns to argue that revelation is necessary. To summarize briefly his conclusions: Inasmuch as we are creatures, as creatures the light of nature alone can *possibly* give what must be known of the moral. But it is highly improbable, since the light of nature does not have "a *sufficiency of tendency* actually to reach the effect" (276) or else it would have reached that effect, whereas the facts show that it has not. Furthermore, inasmuch as we are sinners, as sinners we cannot be led to what we need to know of religion by the light of nature "in any sense whatsoever" (277). Why not? Edwards does not explain here.

The explanation, of course, lies in the Calvinist doctrine of original sin. In his "Doctrine of Original Sin Defended" Edwards defines original sin primarily in terms of the *"depravity of nature"* (Dwight, II, 309). The first man was governed by two kinds of principles, the natural and the divine: "When man sinned, and broke God's covenant . . . these superior principles left his heart . . . ," whereupon "Man did immediately set up *himself,* and the objects of his private affections and appetites, as supreme; and so they took the place of *God"* (537).

The important thing to note here is that original sin is defined as a shift in point of view from the infinite and divine to the finite and human. The proof of original sin is that men "come into the world mere *flesh"* (538). The horizon of man's perception is reduced because of his bodily existence, so that the result of original sin is "self-love"—man can constitute his world and its values only from their relations to himself. Edwards's doctrine of revealed religion, and consequently his entire moral philosophy and (our concern here) his theory of language, are guided by his conception of man as a sinner: man as a finite being.

But Edwards saw man as a finite being with an infinite purpose. The nature of man's end, indeed the end of all creation, Edwards consistently conceived in terms of communication: "The great and universal end of God's creating the world was to communicate himself. God is a communicating being."[6] God's own essence defines Him as a communicating being (Misc. #94, 253). The pure being of God is generated by the reflexive act of God's having a perfect image of himself, and "the Son of God is that image of God which he infinitely loves" (Misc. #94, 255). The Holy Spirit is that reflexive act holding between the two; thus the trinity. The union of the trinity, being perfect, cannot be added to, yet God grants the possibility of man's participation in his glory by "an inclination in God to cause His internal glory to flow out *ad extra* . . . not that he may receive but that he may go forth." "For it can't be that He can receive anything from the creature" (Misc. #448, 133-34). The highest end of finite man, therefore, is to become able to be a recipient of communication from God.

Precisely how man can receive communication from God is the subject of "On the Medium of Moral Government." Its point is that if conversation is to serve as such a medium, there must be a social authority in the form of speakers who have been partially restored to the original point of view that was removed by Adam's sin.

Edwards begins by distinguishing between "God's *moral* government of his creatures, that have an understanding and will, and his general government of providential disposal" (Dwight, VII, 278). The latter refers

---

[6] Harvey G. Townsend (ed.), *The Philosophy of Jonathan Edwards from His Private Notebooks* (Eugene, Oregon, 1955), 130. All the "Miscellanies" used here are from Townsend and will hereafter be referred to simply as "Misc."

to the operation of the material world. A satisfactory explanation of Edwards's understanding of the material world would take us far afield from our immediate concern, and the topic has been thoroughly discussed elsewhere.[7] It is sufficient to say here that since the relationships among God and man and the world as material are sustained by God, inasmuch as the testimony of the senses is reliable, man is capable of understanding the material world. Consequently, in "On the Medium of Moral Government" Edwards is justified in saying that "the nature, design, and ends of the material world, by no means require that it should be declared and made visible by a revelation of the methods, rules, particular views, designs, and ends of it . . ." (Dwight, VII, 278). Science and man's reason are adequate instruments for understanding the material world.

The moral world, however, is a different matter. Here, even when the objects of perception are the same as those of the material world, the relationships with which the perceiver is concerned are different. Moral perception is concerned with the objects' relationships to one another within a whole of value. Just as things are *beautiful* insofar as they maintain a proportionate or symmetrical bearing toward the other objects considered along with them (Dwight, I, 693-95), beings are *excellent* (the analog of beautiful) insofar as they reflect the totality of the spiritual realm within which men judge them. *Consent,* the relationship holding between spiritual beings, is one being's recognition of another's status as spiritual and as within a spiritual totality. Thus the greater the totality of the spiritual world within which a being is consented to, and the greater totality to which the being consented to consents, the greater the excellency; or, as Edwards says, "The more the Consent is, and the more extensive, the greater is the Excellency" (696). The highest of all possible excellencies is summed up in Edwards's famous phrase, "consent to Being in general."

As we have already seen, man has been reduced by original sin to judging all relationships in terms merely of his own being—his own ends and aims. Since the relationships that hold in the moral world are relations of proportion, of part to whole, perspective is everything; and since the whole exists in terms of God's communication with Himself, man is by necessity doomed, unless God extends His communication to him.

Edwards's conception of unregenerate man is indeed that of the poor spider dangling helplessly over the flames. Man is unable by his own fallen essence to perceive the excellency of being in general or even to perceive that his final end should be to receive communication from God. Yet God has determined that man shall live within a moral government,

---

[7] Cf. George Rupp, "The 'Idealism' of Jonathan Edwards," *Harvard Theological Review,* 62 (1969), 209-26; Leonard R. Riforgiato, "The Unified Thought of Jonathan Edwards," *Thought,* 47 (1972), 599-610; and Claude A. Smith, "Jonathan Edwards and 'The Way of Ideas,'" *Harvard Theological Review,* 59 (1966), 153-73.

and therefore it is necessary that he should receive communication from God: "The moral government of a society, in the very nature of it, implies, and consists in an application to their understandings, in directions to the intelligent will, and [in] enforcing the direction by the declaration made" (Dwight, VII, 278). He uses the analogy of a political government here, the relationship between a king and his subjects, to illustrate his conception of the relationship between man and God. The analogy is legitimate, for in either case the subjects cannot act in accordance with the ends of the state unless the subjects can partially foresee the ends the ruler has in mind. The answer is the same in both cases: only through the word can the subject receive an understanding of what he should do.

Edwards therefore begins "On the Medium of Moral Government" with a definition of the key term:

By *conversation*, I mean intelligent beings expressing their minds one to another, in words, or other signs intentionally directed to us for our notice, whose immediate and main design is to be significations of the mind of him who gives them. Those signs are evidences distinguished from works done by any, from which we may argue their minds. The first and most immediate design of the work is something else than a mere signification to us of the mind of the efficient. Thus, I distinguish God's communicating his mind to us by word or conversation, from his giving us opportunity to learn it by philosophical reasoning; or by God's works which we observe in the natural world. (Dwight, VII, 278)

Once again, for us to be able to grasp fully Edwards's meaning we must turn elsewhere—this time to his private notebooks, where he discusses the nature of the sign. There we find that a "great part of our thoughts and the discourse of our minds concerning things without the actual ideas of those things of which we discourse and reason; but the mind makes use of signs instead of ideas" (Misc. #782, 113). This statement seems Lockean enough, but it has a different import than Locke would have given it. Differentiating between *"mere cogitation"* and *"apprehension,"* Edwards sees that most of the time we recognize the relations among things by recognizing the relations among the signs that refer to them. But when we do so we are not necessarily affected by them—that is, we ourselves do not change because our attitude toward the things has not changed. When we apprehend, however, we change in our attitude toward the things, so that the very appearances of the things change as well. For this reason Edwards calls the same differentiation one between "merely speculative" and "sensible" knowledge (Misc. #782, 119). This differentiation extends "to all the knowledge we have of all objects whatsoever" (Misc. #782, 120).

Interpretation, then, can take place at two distinct levels. When Edwards applies this differentiation to the end for which man was created—to receive communication from God—it becomes clear that man can receive that communication in two ways. The first is a preparatory communication, by a sign, i.e., through revelation. The second is an apprehension of the meaning of that same sign through grace. Another possibility is God's direct inspiration, the inspiration that produced revelation in the first place. Thus, the "extraordinary influence of the Spirit of God in inspiration imparts speculative knowledge to the soul, but the ordinary influence of God's Spirit communicates only a sensible knowledge of those things that the mind had a speculative knowledge of before" (Misc. #782, 121). Since knowledge of revelation without apprehension has already been classified by Edwards as a kind of speculative knowledge earlier in the same essay, man *as an individual* clearly has no way of knowing before receiving grace what knowledge is or is not truly revelation or how to gauge the relevance of a true revelation.

Here Edwards's categorization of revelation as a kind of history or tradition takes on its full significance. He makes it clear in the fourteenth section of "On the Medium of Moral Government" that the kind of thoughts that people can think, indeed the kinds of phenomena that they can experience, are determined by the traditions they receive. "The heathens," for example, "received and believed many great truths, of vast importance, that were incomprehensible..." (Dwight, VII, 287) and "received many traditions, rules, and laws, as supposing they came from God, or the gods, by revelation" (288). Unquestionably, without the testimony of visible saints to confirm the validity of the tradition, based upon the authority of their own conversion experience, the unconverted may very well accept a tradition that will prepare for them a way straight to hell. Edwards's view is clear: without first accepting the true tradition—the revealed Word—and without a knowledge of his intended final end, people have little chance of preparing themselves for that end.

The pilgrims' preparatory journeys toward their destined communion with the Father, consequently, are less individual than social acts. The possibility of the sinner's salvation is founded on the fact that human nature is a social nature, since language, as conversation, is sustained by society through the speech and actions of the visible saints. Only through language, as the Word of God, can sinners perceive relationships as God would have them seen. Moral behavior is for Edwards, then, a product of rhetorical forces: "The *ground* of moral behavior, and all moral government and regulation, is society, or mutual intercourse and social regards. The special medium of union and communication of the members of the society, and the being of society as such, is conversation..." (282). Though finite human beings can judge the material world with some certainty insofar as the testimony of the senses and the framework of reason are trustworthy, they can judge the moral world with certainty only insofar as the testimony of tradition is sound. Here Edwards is obviously getting very close to a notion of cultural relativity. Perhaps he would have been forced into such a position if he had not already had the doctrine (and his experience) of grace ready at hand to authenticate revelation. Yet even the experience of grace does not *absolutely* confirm the Gospel to be the Word of God:

The truth that the soul is most immediately convinced of . . . is not that the Gospel is the word of God. But this is the truth that the mind firstly and more directly falls under a conviction of, viz. that the way of salvation that the Gospel reveals is a proper, suitable, and sufficient way, perfectly agreeable to reason and the nature of things, and that which tend to answer the ends proposed. (Misc. #752, 126)

According to Edwards, only by inference do we suppose the Gospel to be the true Word of God.

This inference, though obvious, is extremely important for our understanding of Edwards's thought: grace can ground neither statements of apodeictic truth, such as mathematical proofs, nor empirically valid assertions of scientific truth; rather, grace supports statements which induce persuasion and conviction. Grace is a seat of rhetorical authority in exactly the same way as, to the rationalists whom Edwards opposed, such as the Earl of Shaftesbury, taste would be a seat of rhetorical authority. In other words we might say, without stretching the facts too far, that the effect of a saint's receiving grace would be analogous to a barbarian's receiving taste. The one who had once seen the forms of the world in a material, grasping, self-serving way now begins to see the order and proportion of God's great art.

Even after grace, of course, one remains a finite being but with an essence no longer of *radical* finitude. We have already seen that for Edwards, as with Berkeley, anything is *as* it is perceived. Once one believes and is allowed by grace to apprehend God's communication through nature, one's perception of oneself changes; therefore the person changes, becoming a saint. In "The Nature of True Virtue" we find that the primary result of grace is a shift in the direction of one's perception from consent to beings in particular to consent to Being in General, which is at the same time a shift of motives from love of self to love of God.[8] In "A Divine and Supernatural Light" we find that grace is accompanied by an intensification of one's appreciation of speculative truths of divine things (Austin, VIII, 298). For our purpose now, however, what grace does not do is more interesting.

"This spiritual light," writes Edwards, "is not the suggesting of any new truths or propositions not contained in the word of God" (296). When unregenerate man becomes saint, the Word remains the same, though his relationship toward the Word changes:

Indeed a person cannot have spiritual light without the word. But that does not argue, that the word properly causes that light. The mind cannot see the ex-

---

[8] Samuel Austin (ed.), *The Works of President Edwards* (Worcester, 1808-09), II, 395-404; 424-37.

cellency of any doctrine, unless that doctrine be first in the mind, but the seeing of the excellency of the doctrine may be immediately from the Spirit of God; though the conveying of the doctrine or proposition itself may be by the word. (302)

As we have already seen, what Edwards usually means by "excellency" is a thing's fittingness within or its appropriateness for the world as perceived. If grace does not add to one's knowledge beyond the Word as the saint has already received it, grace does alter one's perception of the world, according to Edwards's testimony of his own experience:

The appearance of everything was altered; there seemed to be, as it were, a calm, sweet cast, or appearance of divine glory, in almost everything. God's excellency, his wisdom, his purity and love, seemed to appear in everything; in the sun, moon and stars; in the cloud, and blue sky; in the grass, flowers, trees; in the water and all nature; which used greatly to fix my mind. (Dwight, I, 61)

Norman Grabo has called attention to the contrast between the way Edwards describes grace as altering the appearance of nature and the more typical descriptions of those like Edward Taylor, who saw "God's grace" as an epistemological change which "like light, shines upon the rational soul and awakens it to the source of all wisdom, Christ."[9]

Yet Grabo has misinterpreted the implications of Edwards's experience, for he implies that "although Edwards sidesteps the error of pantheism, his expressions walk the very brink of that abyss," whereas Taylor's cosmology remains transcendental, so that "the world glorifies its maker, but it always remains apart from him" (45). However, in view of what Edwards has said about grace in various places, it seems best to infer from this description that neither the Word nor the world changes but that the perspective of the recipient of grace changes, so that although nothing new is perceived in the Word or the world, they seem to be of a piece, a unified, coherent, and beautiful work of the Master Artist.

God's two chief means of communication with man, nature and revelation, were coherent because they were unified. Edwards described this conjunction between natural structure and Biblical scripture by advancing his new typology, one which went beyond the traditional interpretation of Old Testament events in view of their New Testament fulfillment, to include also the interpretation of revelatory statements in view of natural facts. The saints could communicate this correspondence to listeners as yet unconverted, thus preparing them for grace, only if the Word and the world were the same for regenerate and unregenerate alike. Therefore, Edwards could not have understood grace as a new Lockean idea. Such ideas are derived from sensory experience, so that the world would have to change before the saint could receive such an

[9] Norman S. Grabo, *Edward Taylor* (New Haven, 1961), 46.

idea. The work of the ministry could not be effective if the spiritual truths the preacher spoke about were not visible in the world in which the congregation lived.

Finally we begin to understand the full significance of the short passage with which we began: "By all that we see and experience, the *moral* world, and the *conversible* world, are the same thing. . . ." Conversation—language—brings into being those relationships which are in fact the moral world. Language itself is sustained by society, which in turn received the Word from tradition—the Bible as interpreted by the exemplary speech and behavior of the saints.

Thus it seems odd that in his brilliant introduction to *Images or Shadows of Divine Things,* Perry Miller, who recognized that for Edwards only the saints could properly "see" a type (27) and who claimed that Edwards's theology was "an exaltation of nature to a level of authority co-equal with revelation—nature as seen by the regenerate eye . . ." (28), would nevertheless describe grace as a simple idea. As Miller says, "Any dullard with the help of a little logic can argue a priori; any scholar can repeat the argument from design, and all men can read or hear the Bible" (13). Yet just as obviously, any scientist can measure the Newtonian universe. The important, dramatic shift in Edwards's theology from the orthodoxy that justified his shift in rhetoric—from the spiritualization of the commonplace through metaphor to the integration of nature and scripture through typology—is not so much his assertion of the authority of Newtonian physics as his re-assertion of the stature and authority of the Puritan saint, an authority that had begun to degenerate from the time of his own grandfather's successful battle against the Half-way Covenant.

There is nothing in Edwards's works to suggest that nature, as such, is anything but corrupt. Lockean empiricism and Newtonian physics may have confirmed that God sustains the world regularly enough for its phenomena to serve as types for spiritual antitypes:

The system of created being may be divided into two parts, the typical world, and the antitypical world. The inferior and carnal, i.e. the more external and transitory part of the universe, that part of it which is inchoative, imperfect, and subservient, is typical of the superior, more spiritual, perfect, and durable part of it which is the end, and as it were, the substance and consummation of the other. (Dwight, IX, 110-11)

But neither Locke's psychology nor Newton's science can provide the link between the typical and antitypical. Science is important rhetorically only because it confirms the existence of structures and laws that all men can understand.

But if all men can understand the material world, the typical world, only the saints can apprehend the antitypical. Therefore when Edwards describes the structures of excellency, he draws his analogy not to a commonly accessible domain, but to an elitist one—the aesthetic. This is a move that cannot be anticipated by reading Locke, yet it is not a move without precedent or influence. Although Edwards's aesthetic analogy for the means of entry to this elitist realm, grace, is somewhat radical, its corollary, his aesthetic analogy for the moral world itself, certainly is not. In fact it finds its source in one of the most venerable of Puritan traditions.

That Puritan thought was heavily influenced by Peter Ramus's *Institutiones dialecticae libri duo* (1543) is a thesis fully accepted by contemporary scholarship. But the fact that Ramus's influence was most often exerted through his commentators is less commonly noted. Alexander Richardson's *The Logicians School-Master,* John Yates's *A Modell of Divinitie,* and Williams Ames's *Technometry* were all heavily influenced by Ramus and commonly read in Puritan America.[10] Unlike Ramus, any one of these could have sparked Edwards's analogy of the moral to the aesthetic.

However, of these three Richardson was the first to take Ramus's reform of the liberal arts and ground it "in an essentially Thomist metaphysics and epistemology" (John Charles Adams, 4). From the thesis that the world created by God was just that—a created work, a piece of art—Richardson developed his theory of encyclopedia. It held that all things begin and end in the same source, God, not as an extension of God's being, but as "God's Idea." For Richardson "God's Idea" and "art" (created being) were synonymous: "There is not Art but is an eternal rule in the Idea of God, as a precept of that thing whereof it is an Art, to guide it to its *eupraxie* [well doing] . . ." (Richardson, in Adams, p. 122). Thus Richardson's first epistemological premise sounds strangely similar to the notions of Edwards and of Locke: "Derived being is intelligible because God's creative power (i.e., His efficiency) causes it to be in accord with His Primordial Idea" (Adams, 21).

Here the resemblance to Locke ends. For Richardson the regularity of perceived ideas is a necessary though not a sufficient cause of intelligibility. As John Charles Adams has pointed out, "although the perceptible world is intelligible, to know it is not enough. The natural world is good as well as intelligible" (30). Richardson's teleology is based on his understanding of finitude. Since derivative being is finite, all things have limits and therefore quantity. Similarly, since no derivative being is pure act, it "has a form acting upon a matter" (*ibid.,* 130), which determines its quality. Richardson believed that all beings are derived from primary being—the prime mover, God—and since "the *highest, most blessed act* must do nothing in vain" (*ibid.,* 126), form cannot be

---

[10] John Charles Adams, "An Explication and Edition of 'The Preface or Entrance into Book,' 'Grammatical Notes,' and 'Rhetorical Notes,' from Alexander Richardson's *The Logicians School-Master*" (Diss., Univ. of Washington, 1983), 2-7.

imposed upon matter without purpose. *"Quality,"* therefore, *"is nature and goodness" (ibid.,* 130). The nature of things lies in their matter and form; their goodness lies in the ends for which they were made.

The unity between nature and goodness grounds Richardson's definition of his great project, encyclopedia: *"Encyclopedia is that by which all arts are comprehended for the ordering of their ends" (ibid.,* 131). In creating the world, God gave man the great paradigm of the proper relationship between art and artist. Creatures and plants subordinate their acts to God's will. Only man rebels. So Richardson's great theme was that "the arts must be held together, before there be encyclopedia . . ." *(ibid.,* 134). All the particular arts, by which Richardson meant all the activities of man, must be linked together *"for the subordination of their ends" (ibid.)* if the City of God is to be established on earth.

For Richardson the proper ends for man's activity were readily revealed by the scripture. His problem, then, was to explicate the proper relationships that should exist among the various arts. He found them to be thoroughly interdependent, so that each artist needed to be conversant with both the arts his art depended upon and the arts that depended upon his. The general art is the art of speaking, and accordingly Richardson set out to explain the principles of grammar, rhetoric, and logic.

For Edwards, however, the interpretation of Scripture had itself become problematic. Richardson's coordination of scholastic epistemology and metaphysics with the Puritan worldview could not help Edwards in post-Newtonian America, but Richardson's elaborate analogy of the world as art could.

Richardson quite possibly helped Edwards in another way as well. He may have influenced Edwards to posit grace as the source of rhetorical authority. In the "Ethical Notes" to *The Logicians School-Master* Richardson writes: "For he that will be a good Ethician must not only be an honest man, but such one as hath those things which do attend *bonum* both *corporis et animi:* now as I said before this *gratia* maketh good estimation among men; and from this ariseth *authoritas,* whereby he can do much with men."[11] Here Richardson means grace in the classical not the Christian sense, as acting in a proper manner. Grace is the product of ethics, and "Ethica est ars bene gerendise" (128).

At first Richardson appears merely to be repeating the classical "good man theory," which asserts that inner virtue will be reflected in outward actions, in the way a man carries himself. Yet he had previously drawn a distinction between the right actions of the sanctified man and those of the "civic man which wanteth Faith" (128). The civic man "keepeth the rule of Ethicks by the spirit of restraint," whereas the sanctified man

---

[11] Alexander Richardson, *The Logicians School-Master* (London, 1657), 132.

is inclined to do good by the spirit of faith. Such an inclination is, as we have already seen, one of the effects of grace as Edwards describes them.

Thus, although Richardson defines *gratia* as an effect of sanctification while to Edwards grace is its cause, and although Richardson describes *gratia* as a harmony between the spirit and the body whereas to Edwards grace produces a harmony between the spiritual truths of revelation and the material forms of nature, for both Richardson and Edwards grace is the seat of rhetorical authority. Such authority arises from a harmony of the corporal and spiritual that even the unsanctified could sense if not understand. This is the power the Puritan divine would need to persuade his flock. If God's grace had given the saint a new simple idea—as if He had given him the power to perceive a new color—how could the saint ever convey such an experience?

Although Edwards undoubtedly drew his conceptions of the material world from the science of his day, he very likely drew his views on spiritual matters from a deeper, more reliable wellspring of Puritan thought. Edwards must have recognized the fundamental differences of attitude one must assume in order to shift from viewing the scholastic world of spirit to viewing the empirical world of matter. It is no wonder, then, that in many ways Edwards's work foreshadows the categorical understanding of transcendental philosophy. Very shortly, Kant would describe the aesthetic standpoint in terms of a capacity to see form as purposiveness when there is no apparent purpose. Edwards defined the moral standpoint in terms of a capacity to see in form a very special purpose. Only God's grace could confer this capacity. It was as unlearned as it was undeserved. Yet once conferred, grace brought a man's vision back into focus, so that he saw as a unity both Scripture and Nature communicating God's harmonious, proportionate, beautiful work of art. This communication gave the Puritan saint his authority to interpret and to teach.

Texas A & M University.

IV

COTTON MATHER: PHYSICO-THEOLOGIAN

By Jeffrey Jeske

By the late seventeenth century the failure of New England Puritanism to synthesize its disparate intellectual traditions resulted in a variety of Puritan voices. Juxtapositions of Calvinism, Scholasticism, humanism, and seventeenth-century ideas produced strange hybrids, offering multiple personae to the orthodox thinker. Examination of the Puritan response to physical nature, for example, reveals irreconcilable philosophical modes issuing in equally irreconcilable rhetorical stances.

The founders of Puritanism, of course, had emphasized a Calvinist interpretation of nature as inherently flawed and of little ontological or epistemological value to man. Hence the pervasiveness of the literary image of nature as "wilderness" and the ascetic rhetoric of John Winthrop: "O Lord, crucifie the world unto me, that though I cannot avoyd to live among the baits and snares of it, yet it may be . . . truely dead unto me and I unto it."[1] This "otherworldly" attitude toward nature, an inheritance from Paul, Augustine, and Calvin, remained a staple of pietistic Puritanism and underlay sermonic use of garden-wilderness imagery well into the 1700s, as ministers continued to encourage a disinterestedness akin to that of the early Puritan models.

Within a generation of the founders, however, a contrary interpretation of nature, based on Scholastic and Ramist philosophical assumptions, became prevalent, producing a more positive assessment and emphasizing a second literary image: nature-as-book. Confidence that nature was a vast organized blueprint setting down God's wisdom in rational terms generated a minor renaissance of science at Harvard, and enthusiastic—if non-Calvinist—rhetoric in Harvard textbooks, such as Charles Morton's influential *Compendium Physicae*, and in theological treatises such as the *Kometographia*, in which Increase Mather enthusiastically cited contemporary scientists like Kepler and Hooke to conclude that even the secular mind can and should interpret the "great and glorious volume" of God's works.

Not recognizing the latent dangers to orthodoxy in objectifying the world picture, many New Englanders displayed great admiration for the new learning, while still professing the conventional pietism. After all, there were successful exemplars of science in England. When the Royal

---

[1] Cited in Edmund Morgan, *The Puritan Dilemma: The Story of John Winthrop* (Boston, 1958), 11. For typical use of garden-wilderness imagery, see John Cotton, *A Brief Exposition with Practical Observations on the Book of Canticles* (London, 1655), *God's Mercie Mixed With His Justice* (London, 1641), and *God's Promise to His Plantations* (Boston, 1686).

Society was founded in 1663, forty-two of the sixty-eight members were Puritans, and the stated goals of this highly-regarded organization were quite religious and consonant with Puritan orthodoxy, at least as the latter was expressed in Scholastic assumptions regarding God's operation in the universe through secondary causes.[2]

In the early eighteenth century these two main, diverging lines of thought regarding nature reveal a fundamental split in the Puritan mind, shown on the one hand in sermonic declarations that nature is awry and its epistemological potential destroyed by man's blasted faculties, and on the other hand by *thesae technologicae* with their confidence in nature's knowableness. In this context the protean Cotton Mather, attempting both to preserve the Calvinist core of Puritan belief and to accommodate the new science, adopts different personae with contradictory philosophical assumptions, depending on situation and audience. A Calvinist persona, steeped in mythic identifications and belief in the inscrutability and immediacy of Divine Providence, speaks in selected sermons, diaries, and meditative works. In sermons like *The Way to Prosperity*, for example, Mather follows his father and other second-generation ministers in employing the familiar garden-wilderness imagery to rekindle commitment to the Puritan mission and a sense of the supernatural character of the covenanted community.[3] Throughout is a sense of myth, as in the diaries, and a confidence, earlier documented in his *Memorable Providences Relating to Witchcrafts and Possessions* (Boston, 1689), that natural phenomena are but fleeting expressions of God's eternal will.

Mather abandons the Calvinist frame, however, when writing as a scientist. Instead of devaluing natural investigations, as had his famous grandfather,[4] he adopts the persona of the "physico-theologian," cele-

---

[2] In defending the Royal Society in his "Some considerations touching the usefulness of Experimental Natural Philosophy" against attacks by clerical opponents of natural science, Robert Boyle states two Scholastic principles succinctly in declaring that "two of God's principal ends were the manifestation of his own glory and the good of men" and thus argues that "those, who do labor to deter men from sedulous inquiries into nature, do take a course which tends to defeat God of both of these mentioned ends." Cited in Friedrich Klemm, *A History of Western Technology*, trans. Dorothea Waley Singer (Cambridge, 1964), 190.

[3] He declares: "If the Lord had been with us, would he have made our Wall so feeble, that (as they said of Jerusalem) the going up of a poor Fox upon it should break it down? If the Lord had been with us, had all the wild Creatures that passed by this vineyard, found such opportunities to be plucking at it? No, our God would have kept us, as a vineyard of red wine and lest any should have hurt us, He, [the Lord] would have kept it, night and day" (Boston, 1689), 12. Cf. also Samuel Danforth, *A Brief Recognition of New England's Errand into the Wilderness* (Cambridge, Mass., 1671), 68-69; Increase Mather, *The Day of Trouble is Near* (Cambridge, Mass., 1674), 6; Urian Oakes, *New England Pleaded With* (Cambridge, Mass., 1673), 17.

[4] Repeating the familiar Platonic view that our knowledge of external nature is unstable, John Cotton asks, "How should that which is restlesse . . . procure us setled rest and tranquillity, which accompanieth true happiness?" The saint seeking intellectual

brating the same physical world which in the Calvinist mode he condemns, and copying a specific English tradition of natural theology which was at its peak in the late seventeenth and early eighteenth centuries. Natural theology had always been implicit in the Judaeo-Christian heritage; but in Mather's period, the scientific revelations of law and design contributed by Sir Isaac Newton, Robert Boyle, and others prompted a number of English science-minded theologians as well as devout scientists to define the "new" order in nature in systematic treatises. The Puritan chemist Robert Boyle (1627-1691) inaugurated the heyday of the tradition with his *Usefulness of Experimental Natural Philosophy* (1663); important subsequent works included John Ray's *Wisdom of God manifested in the Works of the Creation* (1691), Richard Bentley's *A Confutation of Atheism* (1964), and William Wiston's *A New Theory of the Earth* (1696). Together these volumes enunciated a new Christian attitude, which, partially through Mather's reception, facilitated Puritan orthodoxy's evolution toward mechanism and Deism.

Mather read Boyle's *Usefulness of Experimental Natural Philosophy* in the 1680s, finding its enthusiasm similar to his own. An inheritor of Increase's scientific scholarship, Cotton displayed an interest in science throughout most of his life, being "an avid dilettante, with an encyclopaedic range of interests and a predisposition toward the experimental and the pragmatic."[5] What is more important, Mather found in Boyle a useful model to copy. As early as *The Wonderful Works of God Commemorated* (Boston, 1690), a Thanksgiving Day sermon, Mather incorporated a number of Boyle's remarks about the amazing number of new species which the naturalists had discovered and demonstrated a stance toward nature different from that providing the basis of *Memorable Providences*, published the preceding year, which praised the irregularity of phenomena in manifesting God's direct and inscrutable participation in nature.[6]

---

stability had better avoid nature, for "the mind of man . . . is somewhat assimilated into the nature of the object which it studieth" (*A Brief Exposition with Practicall Observations upon the Whole Book of Ecclesiastes* [London, 1654], 13, 21).

[5] Sacvan Bercovitch, *Major Writers of Early American Literature*, ed. Everett Emerson (Madison, 1972), 130. While a student at Harvard, Mather prepared for a possible career in medicine and maintained an active, empirical involvement in the field over the course of his long career, playing a direct—and controversial—pro-inoculation role in the Boston smallpox epidemic of 1721. Otho T. Beall, Jr., and Richard H. Shryock present a full discussion of the medical aspect of Mather's career in *Cotton Mather: First Significant Figure in American Medicine* (Baltimore, 1954).

[6] Even in *Memorable Providences*, with its full acceptance of the activity of witches and demons, Mather exhibits the developing methodology of empirical science. Describing himself as a "Critical Eye-Witness," he uses a primitive form of case study to discuss the affected Goodwin children and describes careful experiments both to determine whether neighborwoman Glover was a witch and to assess the precise nature of one of the Goodwin girl's demonic possession. To accomplish the latter, for example, Mather

Mather was also reading Bentley's *Confutation* and Whiston's *New Theory* in the 1680s and '90s, extracting a Newtonian concept of gravity and the inspiration for his *Biblia Americana*, a series of biblical commentaries garnishing the hexameron with Newtonian concepts.[7] At this time Mather combined an interest in synthesis with an empirical spirit. Thus, in a *Biblia* extract sent to the Royal Society in 1712, he glossed Genesis 6:4 ("There were giants on the earth in those days") with a reference to the remains of a giant found near Clavarack as well as to an Indian tradition regarding this giant but then added the uncharacteristic admonition, "there is very little in any Tradition of our Salvages [*sic*], to be rely'd upon."[8] Nevertheless, despite the *Biblia*'s affirmation of the method and ideas of contemporary experimental science—particularly pertaining to Newtonian dynamics and the anamicular [*sic*] hypothesis—the work remained largely medieval, locating heaven, for example, beyond the outermost Aristotelian sphere. Within a few years of the *Biblia* (completed in 1712), however, Mather dropped the arduous attempt to reconcile the new science with the traditional Puritan world view. And in *The Christian Philosopher: A Collection of the Best Discoveries in Nature, With Religious Improvements*,[9] he adopted the physico-theologian persona, drawing from many of the contemporary treatises and modeling his work directly on Ray's *Wisdom of God*.[10]

---

exposes her to a number of books—popish books, books dealing with witches, the Testaments—and studies her reactions, finding with some degree of pleasure that his grandfather John Cotton's works induce "hideous convulsions" (23).

[7] Never published, the *Biblia*'s seven large manuscript volumes remain in the Massachusetts Historical Society. Mather did send portions of the *Biblia* commentaries as part of his early correspondence with the Royal Society. Collectively titled the "Curiosa Americana" (1712-1724), Mather's approximately 82 letters to that body further demonstrate the wide range of his scientific interests. In the letters, he presents data on American curiosities in fields from medicine to zoology to meteorology. In 1713 Mather became one of the first Americans to be awarded membership in the Society.

George Lyman Kittredge has identified and annotated each of the "Curiosa" letters in "Cotton Mather's Scientific Communications to the Royal Society," *Proceedings of the American Antiquarian Society*, XXVI (1916), 18-57. See also Otho M. Beall, "Cotton Mather's Early 'Curiosa Americana' and the Boston Philosophical Society of 1683," *William and Mary Quarterly*, 3rd Ser., XVIII (1961), 360-72. Beall demonstrates that the early "Curiosa" are outgrowths of the data collections which Mather contributed to the Boston Philosophical Society, an enterprise founded by Increase in 1683. This connection further verifies the early genesis of Mather's scientific interests. And when comparing Mather's seventeenth and eighteenth century scientific writings, we see a definite decline in his preoccupation with religious implications.

[8] Cited in Kittredge, 23.

[9] (rpt., Gainesville, Florida, 1968). Subsequent citations are entered in the text.

[10] Mather acknowledges an equal debt to William Derham ("there are especially Two, unto whom I have been more indebted, than unto many others; the Industrious Mr. Ray and the Inquisitive Mr. Derham." [3]) but it is the far more distinguished Ray who actually provides the *Christian Philosopher*'s main source, as *Wisdom of God* is also *Physico-Theology*'s chief model. Derham follows Ray closely, though not as closely as

The *Christian Philosopher*, completed in 1715 and published in 1721, enunciates a voice distinctly different from that of either the jeremiads or the meditative spiritualizing tracts Mather was writing throughout this period. His choice of model had much to do with this. Rather than being a clergyman with scientific interests, Ray (1627–1705) was a scientist with a theological veneer. *Wisdom*, his masterpiece, clearly subordinates theology to concrete observation and the empirical method; modern-day naturalists consider Ray the founder of modern botany and zoology largely on the basis of this book, a direct ancestor of Darwin's *On the Origin of Species*.[11] Mather repeats the shift in emphasis from theology to science. Despite its subtitle—*"Religio Philosophica"*—the *Christian Philosopher*'s balance is noticeably different from that of the *Biblia*, where Mather focused on Scripture, using science as a subordinate principle of explanation. In the *Christian Philosopher* physical nature is the subject and theology a peripheral source of edifying improvement. Nature itself becomes more solid and prosaic and Mather's tone necessarily more objective.

The extent of Mather's indebtedness to Ray in the formation of the *Christian Philosopher*'s speaking persona is readily apparent. Mather organizes his work in an almost identical format. Both works present an ordered survey of the universe, beginning with chapters on the celestial bodies and then successively on atmospheric phenomena, minerals, plants, and animals, with large concluding sections on man. Each work laces objective description with observation on how well the parts of the whole connect and how wisely God displays His providence. And in many cases Mather lifts passages from Ray with little change. Ray, for example, considers "the manner of the Rain's descent, distilling [*sic*] down gradually and by drops, which is most convenient for the watering of the Earth, whereas if it should fall down in a continued Stream like a River, it would gall the Ground . . . and greatly incommode, if not suffocate Animals" (65). Similarly, Mather describes how "the gradual Falling of the Rain by Drops is an admirable Accommodation of [Providence] to the Intention of watering the Earth. 'Tis the best way imaginable. If it should fall in a continual Stream, like a River, everything would be vastly incommoded with it" (53).

The actual persona which Ray helped Mather fashion consists of three interrelated elements, each running counter to the founders' orthodoxy, though an implicit part of the Puritan intellectual heritage. The

---

Mather, and refers to him constantly; in his prefatory "To the Reader" Derham notes that in comparing his treatise with his sources, especially "my friend, the late great Mr. Ray," he finds that in many things he has been "anticipated," and hopes that his reader "will candidly think me no Plagiary."

[11] Charles E. Raven, *John Ray, Naturalist: His Life and Works* (Cambridge, 1950), 425ff.

first is an Enlightenment-like regard for reason. Mather declared a high valuation of man's rational faculty, equating regeneracy with reasonableness. In *Reasonable Religion* (Boston, 1700), for example, he comments that "Instead of saying, Shew your selves Regenerate Christians, we will only say, Shew your selves Rational Creatures"; and he depicts God addressing idolaters with the words, "Do but act Reasonably, and you will no more be such Transgressors of my Holy Laws." (6)[12] In *Reason Satisfied* he attempts to "prove" a miracle by appealing to reason, signalling an important change in attitudes toward Scriptural authority: even while confirming Christian mystery, he suggests its accessibility to reason. And six years later he revises John Cotton's nature epistemology; speaking of the Divine Pattern revealed in the natural order, he declares, "By the light of this precious and wondrous Candle [reason], we discern the Connection & Relation of Things to one another."[13] At this point and earlier, however, he speaks as a Ramist, assuming that the purposes of relations discovered in nature are chiefly the exploration of the Divine Mind through its reflection in nature and man's increased understanding of his own relatedness in the theophanic cosmic scene.

In the *Christian Philosopher* Mather organizes these motifs but with a shift of allegiance from Ramus and Ames to contemporary scientists whose primary interest was not necessarily the nexus of nature and Divine Wisdom. By adopting Ray, Mather's persona agrees with empirical science not only that reason is "right" but that its primary uses might not be secular and its authority exclusive in the natural realm. Ray, insisting that man make a just evaluation of his "Gifts and Endowments," unquestionably substitutes reason for Scripture and traditional authorities as interpreter of the book of nature. In *Wisdom*, assuming that man's unaided reason can ultimately explain all, Ray refuses to accept irrational or supernatural interpretations and applies the experimental method rigorously, with no recourse to a *deus ex machina*. He discounts "supernatural Demonstrations" of the existence of God which depend upon miracles, for these are "not common to all Persons or Times"; instead he prefers rational proofs from "Effects and Operations, exposed to every Man's view, [which are] not to be denied or questioned by any" (Pref.).

Mather, the author of *Memorable Providences*, does not dispute Ray. Instead he marshals the same high praise for the rational faculty: "Reason, what is it but a Faculty formed by God, in the Mind of Man, enabling him to discern certain Maxims of Truth, which God himself has established" (*CP*, 283). And whereas the "Maxims of Truth" appears in contemporary Matherian works as moral principles leading to theological truths, the *Christian Philosopher* stresses objective discoveries issuing in

---

[12] Similarly, in *Reason Satisfied: and Faith Established* (Boston, 1712) he further equates sinfulness and irrationality in calling his opponents "Unreasonable Infidels" (18).

[13] *Man of Reason* (Boston, 1718), 3.

pragmatic results. God has only recently unlocked human understanding; now one must marvel at the "Progress which the Invention of Man has made" (289). Medicine, astronomy, and the technological arts have all profited from the application of reason to the book of nature, and there is no end in sight.

A second primary feature of Mather's persona as enlightened eighteenth-century physico-theologian is his enthusiasm for a mechanistic interpretation of the universe, one whose biases are not only non-Calvinist but thoroughly more empirical and secular than the Ramistic counterparts. The foundations of the "modern" view are present in Mather's earlier works as an almost necessary consequence of his view of reason; as he declares in *Reasonable Religion*, "let Reason look upon the World, the Various Parts of it, the curious Ends of it, the incomparable order of it; it will see a World of Reason" (15). Viewing the world as reasonable did not, of course, inevitably lead to unorthodoxy. Ramism, with its book image, assumes rational order. And Mather does use Ramist rhetoric in the *Christian Philosopher*. Assuming that there is in Christ "the original Idea and Archetype of everything that offers the infinite Wisdom of God to our Admiration" (301), Mather suggests that creatures systematically reflect these archetypes, organized by man into arts forming a "Circle of Learning" analogous to Richardson's *Encyclopaidia*, whose beginning and endpoint are both God. Hence nature, though subordinate to Scripture, is a rich source of knowledge about God: Mather insists that there is "a Twofold Book of God: the Book of the Creatures, and the Book of Scripture: God having taught first of all . . . by his Works, did it afterwards . . . by his words" (8).

Because of the persona's empirical bent, however, Mather does not focus on nature's order in chiefly theological terms. One index is his abandonment of traditional Scholastic and Ramist authorities, who assumed a firm connection between natural and spiritual truth and who emphasized the latter. In this he departs from his own customary procedures and imitates Ray's pragmatic rejection of Scholastic learning. In place of the old authorities Mather substitutes contemporary scientists, continually invoking the names of Boyle, Hook, Halley, and Newton, and highly recommends study of the new learning.

There is a considerable difference between the philosophy of Thomas Aquinas and that of Boyle, whose atomist hypothesis, condemned by many Puritans as the basis of atheism, assumes God's absence from the universe He has set in motion and posits a system of inviolable law into which God does not intrude. In approving Boyle's experiments, Mather adopts the underpinnings of a secular, even irreligious, perspective of natural order. And in copying Ray's *Wisdom*, whose specific interests are problems of form and function, of adaptation to environment, the *Christian Philosopher* becomes less a true believer's handbook than a storehouse of data supporting the secular perspective, apparent especially when Mather chronicles the recent astronomical discoveries of Newton and Hooke (24ff.) or presents anatomical descriptions of the human skeletal system and musculature (230).

In the context of shifting attitudes toward natural order, a particularly graphic illustration of Mather's divergence from orthodoxy in the guise of physico-theologian is his treatment of comets, whose traditional role as direct messengers of God Increase Mather had attempted to reaffirm. In the *Kometographia* (Boston, 1683) Increase defends the numinosity and ultimate unpredictability of the universe by combining Calvinist rhetoric and Scholastic arguments. Comets, he suggests, are indeed portents revealing God's active providence, and as history demonstrates, they have both signal and causal importance: when such "Ensigns" appear "admist the Heavenly host," man observes the hand of God "writing its 'Mene, Mene, tekel upharsin' " (Pref.). Increase documents the work by using the customary Scholastic formula, the marshalling of past authorities, here comprising "all the wise Men who lived in all former Ages" (131), and gives an exhaustive account of all recorded comets from Creation through 1682. Despite reference to contemporary authorities like Kepler and Hooke and making potentially damaging concessions to avoid contradicting his scientific colleagues,[14] his primary purpose is theological and his interpretation of natural order traditional.

In the *Christian Philosopher*, on the other hand, rather than allowing the mystery of comets to remain, Cotton applies the extensive researches of Tycho Brahe, Kepler, and Newton to elaborate a "true system of Comets." Citing Seneca's prediction "That a time should come, when our Mysteries of Comets should be unfolded," he avers that such time "seems almost accomplished," especially given Halley's calculations for predicting a comet's return (43-44).

Nominally, Mather repudiates mechanism. With the *Christian Philosopher*'s schematization of a universal order with God at its head, he can optimistically declare that all "Mechanicall Accounts" are "at an end," for "we step into the Glorious God immediately" (8). Despite his denunciations, however, Mather himself characterizes nature mechanistically. Throughout the work he displays great admiration for the "harmonious Regularity in the Motion of Bodies" (36). He applies the term "machine" to nature as a whole (87) and to its constitutent parts. "Brutes" are "simple Machines" (209); man, a more complex organism, is "a Machine composed of so many Parts, to the right Form, Order, and

---

[14] In dealing with the current observation that the conjunction of planets seems to produce comets, for example, he states, "yet I will not deny, but that a probable conjecture, as to the year of a Comets appearance, may be made from the conjunction of the superiour Planets" (*CP*, 16). If successful conjectures regarding comets can be made by observing natural phenomena, even God's special providences may be bound by natural law.

Motion whereof there are such infinite number of Intentions required" (232). Such anatomical elements as the "motory muscles we find in the Wheels of our Clocks" (271). Mather may deny that a mechanical agency conducts natural phenomena,[15] yet he describes the actual working of those phenomena in mechanical terms. In so doing, and by suggesting that a clock-like stability and precision are the properties of all nature, he comes to conclusions regarding providence similar to those of his contemporary mechanists, especially regarding the traditional "special providences," which seem to interrupt order and to be substantially different from more orthodox Puritan usages of mechanistic imagery.[16]

A necessary consequence of *Christian Philosopher*'s extreme rationality and empirical ambience is the third prominent feature of Mather's physico-theologian persona: a lessening of the sacerdotal and affective preoccupations characterizing his other works, even those dealing with scientific topics.[17] In adopting an objectified world-picture, Mather in effect abandons the numinous universe of both Calvinist and Scholastic traditions. Essential features of the thought of the last several decades had been the Ramist contentions that nature is theophany and, more importantly, that man's epistemological contact with nature is quasi-mystical; had not the popular Alexander Richardson, highly praised by Increase, averred that "as flowers doe send out a sent" [sic], so does nature-as-encyclopedia irradiate the human mind with the Divine Wisdom, enabling indirect contact with God?[18] Mather elsewhere champions this position, as do other prominent Puritans of the early eighteenth century.[19]

Even in *Christian Philosopher* Mather appears to suggest that elucidation of theophany is his chief purpose. Ultimately, all creatures point toward the Maker in some way: each has, in addition to its observable identity in the "Scale of Nature," a sacred character that one can likewise recognize and employ. "There are no Creatures," Mather insists, "but

[15] For instance, he vigorously repudiates Ray regarding "plastick nature," a contemporary concept of an inferior, non-divine manager of creation.

[16] Numerous early theologians refer, for example, to the "wheels of providence," such that when Ebeneezer Pemberton, a contemporary of Mather's, describes how God "Has in all Ages so turned the Wheels of Providence as might suit the End of Government" or notes how according to God's direction "the Wheels and Living Creatures move below" (*The Divine Original and Dignity of Government* [Boston, 1710]), he is recapitulating a long tradition.

[17] Cf., for example, *The Angel of Bethesda*, ed. Gordon W. Jones (Barre, Mass., 1972).

[18] *The Logician's Schole-Master* (London, 1629), 18.

[19] Experience Mayhew, for example, declares how "it hath pleased Him to create the World to be a kind of Mirror wherein His own Glory may be seen and admired; and to make a Number of Creatures capable of viewing His Perfections shining forth therein" (*A Discourse shewing that God Dealeth with Men as Reasonable Creatures* [Boston, 1729], 18).

what are His Models, on every one of them the Name of Jesus is to be found inscribed" (298). Man's duty, according to Mather, is chiefly to assist in the manifestation of the Divine Glory in matter: nature is "the temple of God" (13), and man is to "do the part of a Priest for the rest of the Creation" (221). Because man alone has the ability to know God and the speech to express this knowledge, only he can, as it were, complete the theophanic order already present by naming it and recreating it in the consciousness of mankind.

This conventional rhetoric is, however, only a superficial layer in *Christian Philosopher*. By emulating Ray, Mather reverses the key Scholastic relationship of natural philosophy to theology, where the first is handmaiden to the second. In subordinating the priestly role to the scientific, he submerges theophany in empirical knowledge, disallowing a numinous response; the predominance of secular authorities and Mather's hesitance to make Scriptural analogies or citations testify to the changed relationship.

A second reason for the essential secularity of Mather's work proceeds from his taking a physico-theological step encouraged by the Ramist tradition itself: the shifting of attention from God to the creatures. In effect, Ramism reversed Thomistic teleology, making immediate ends—representing the actual working out in multiplicity of the unitary Divine Wisdom—more pressing than the final, more abstract end of the return of the creatures to God. In its preoccupation with creaturely activity conducted in harmony with the arts, Ramism theoretically lost sight of the divine in studying nature, especially given the great efficiency in this task of the inductive and experimental methods, for which influential Ramists like William Ames had high praise.[20] In other words, if pragmatic considerations were best served by a not-immediately-theological perspective, then Ramism encouraged such a perspective, assuming of course that one ultimately returned to a consciousness of the Divine Purpose.

In taking this step, characteristic of the physico-theology of the period, Mather begins to exchange the vision of nature as theophanic reflection for the interpretation, assumed by his scientific authorities, that nature is a well-designed artifact indirectly testifying to the grandeur of the Divine Mind. As a consequence, the priestly function of Mather's persona no longer involves presiding over the intimate contact between man and Deity which is at the core of Puritanism, but rather initiating an inductive process of "improvements" culminating in ephemeral affective responses. Natural phenomena become "Engines of Piety," which theoretically stimulate man to experience appropriate emotions not otherwise a product of the scientific method.

Hence Mather attempts to add awe-filled wonder, and then piety, to rational observation. "Consider," he declared repeatedly, "into what As-

[20] Cf. *Technometria Omnium & Singularum Artium* (London, 1633), 20.

tonishments must we find the Grandeur and Glory of the Creator to grow upon us" (16). In surveying the Newtonian heavens, for example, he notes that it would take 700,000 years for a cannonball to reach the nearest fixed star; exclaiming, "Great God, what is thy Immensity" (18), he evidently expects the reader to convert his own experienced awe, humility, and gratitude into a state of piety. But being tacked onto the work's scientific contents and inconsistent with their secular tone, the improvements actually betray the Puritan commitment to piety under-lying most of Mather's contemporary works by negating the numinous contact with God which the Puritan response to nature formerly offered.

Elements of Mather's physico-theological persona appear in subse-quent Matherian works, most notably the *Manuductio ad Ministerium* (Boston, 1726), admonishing the reader to "be sure, The Experimental Philosophy is that, in which alone your Mind can be at all established" (50). In this ministerial handbook Mather not only exalts the new learning but dispenses with the old Scholastic theories upon which a great deal of Puritan piety depended: the *Manuductio* contains no mention of *tech-nologia*, for example, and rejects traditional logic and metaphysics: "to weave any more Cobwebs in your Brains, to what Purpose is it?" (37). Claiming that natural philosophy is now a part of orthodoxy, Mather assumes that the new material, "if well-pursued, would Compel you to come in to a Strong Faith, wherewith you would give Glory to Him, on all Occasions" (51). But by substituting this new foundation for piety, Mather clearly gives away more than he obtains.

Elsewhere, however, Mather strikes a more traditional pose, reflecting reservations about reason and its applications. And in fact the *Christian Philosopher* marks Mather's last attempt at formal natural theology and final use of the physico-theological persona modeled on John Ray. Per-haps recognizing the secularizing implications in his writings, he contin-ues to praise science but does not employ it in the same way. His turns from and to natural theology anticipate the later repudiation of science by the American Pietistic movement.

Appropriately, his last major treatment of nature, *Agricola* (Boston, 1727), published the year before his death, is a spiritualizing tract. Here the model is *Husbandry Spiritualized* (London, 1669) by John Flavel, a Presbyterian minister noted for his evangelical sentiments, and the treat-ment is profoundly religious. No longer is the chief objective rational appreciation of the Divine Wisdom; rather it is that the practitioner of spiritualizing become "boiling hot in its use." When, upon occasion, Mather begins to speak in the physico-theological mode, he immediately shifts to a narrower perspective. Thus in discussing clouds, he begins "The Philosopher will tell you, That a Cloud is a Collection of little, but concave, Globules, which therefore ascend unto that Heighth, wherein they are of equal Weight with the Air; where they remain suspended, until by a motion in the Air, they are Broken, and so come down in drops"; but almost immediately he separates himself from the "Philosopher" and declares, "but it is the Religion of these Watry Meteors, with which we are now to be entertained" (121). If anything, his *Agricola*, with its profuse garden imagery and obvious scriptural orientation, represents an attempt to recapture earlier mythic conceptions of nature and man's relationship to it.

But the past was no longer accessible, chiefly because of developments to which Mather himself had contributed. The three chief elements of the Matherian physico-theological persona were pervading Puritan thought, severing traditional ties, and substituting rationality and empiricism. Nature remained an integral part of New England theology but as a tool of comfortable piety rather than as meeting-ground of man and God; for when Puritanism assimilated the mechanistic outlook of contemporary science, nature necessarily became a prosaic machine uninhabited by the supernatural, into which the spiritualizer attempted to breath theological life. Mather's persona in the *Christian Philosopher* thus reflects one facet of a complex mind; but also, in a larger sense, it performs a barometer-like function, measuring and revealing the intellectual forces inexorably drawing Puritanism toward deism.[21]

University of California, Los Angeles.

---

[21] For further discussion of Mather's role in the evolution of Puritanism in the eighteenth century, see Pershing Vartanian, "Cotton Mather and the Puritan Transition into the Enlightenment," *Early American Literature*, VII (1973), 213-24.

V

IRRESISTIBLE COMPASSION: AN ASPECT OF EIGHTEENTH-CENTURY SYMPATHY AND HUMANITARIANISM

By Norman S. Fiering

In a well-known letter written late in life, Thomas Jefferson reiterated some of the essential elements in his ethical philosophy. At one point he asserted, "Nature hath implanted in our breasts a love of others, a sense of duty to them, a moral instinct, in short, which prompts us irresistibly to feel and to succor their distresses. . . ."[1] At least four distinct "natural" ethico-psychological qualities are reflected in these few words, though Jefferson unwittingly conflated them all into a single innate "moral instinct" and worried little about the separate historical life of the parts. Of the variety of interesting and typical eighteenth-century assumptions in the passage, it is the last one that is the subject of this paper: the belief that men irresistibly have compassion for the sufferings of others and are equally irresistibly moved to alleviate that suffering. My purpose is to trace back to its modern origins the assumptions about compassion that not only Thomas Jefferson but numerous other figures in the eighteenth century treated as self-evident fact.

The belief in what we shall call "irresistible compassion" expresses great confidence in the human personality, a confidence that goes considerably beyond trust in the free exercise of reason as a moral guide or political safeguard. Here we are presented with an automatic mechanism for social good, not simply an intellectual option. To a twentieth-century mind, doubts about the reality and the reliability of this mechanism arise quickly; history and analysis both undercut it. We know more about the perversions of "nature." But in the eighteenth century, among some groups, as Jefferson is a witness, the trust in certain qualities of human emotion was unbounded, as impressive certainly as the more often noted trust in rational faculties.

Irresistible compassion has another name commonly used in the eighteenth-century, "sympathy"; it was also called "humanity." When the ideal was truly practiced, or when the alleged mechanism really worked, we have one of the essentials of humanitarianism. Modern humanitarianism may be defined as the widespread inclination to protest against obvious and pointless physical suffering.[2]

---

[1] Jefferson to Thomas Law, June 13, 1814, in Andrew Lipscomb and Albert Bergh, *The Writings of Thomas Jefferson* (Washington, D.C., 1903), XIV, 141.

[2] The suffering must be obvious because usually even humane souls would rather avoid than have to confront the physical pain of others. It must be pointless because most humane men and women do not object to self-incurred purposeful suffering—let

The doctrine of irresistible compassion as found in the eighteenth century was probably not more than a hundred years old.[3] It grew up with and was one of the motivating forces behind humanitarianism, and it contributed to the spread of humanitarianism by establishing an image or an idea of human nature that made humanitarian feelings insistently "natural." If human beings were by nature irresistibly moved to relieve suffering, then those who were coldly indifferent to suffering were, by definition, something less than human.[4]

The seventeenth century inherited from the ancient world many of the ingredients of the doctrine of irresistible compassion. The most famous expression of the idea from classical times appears in the fifteenth satire of Juvenal. I quote from the translation best known in the eighteenth century, viz., John Dryden's edition of the *Satires* (1693):

> Compassion proper to mankind appears;
> Which Nature witness'd, when she lent us tears:
> Of tender sentiments we only give
> These proofs: to weep is our prerogative;
> To show, by pitying looks and melting eyes,
> How with a suffering friend we sympathize!
> Nay, tears will e'en from a wrong'd orphan slide,
> When his false guardian at the bar is tried:
>
>   *   *   *
>
> By impulse of nature (though to us unknown
> The party be) we make the loss our own;
> And tears steal from our eyes, when in the street
> With some betrothed virgin's hearse we meet;
>
>   *   *   *

---

us say, for example, to the rigors of certain kinds of athletic training or to a moderate ascetic regimen—nor do they protest against suffering imposed from outside when the goal is humane, as, for example, in some medical treatments. Finally, most kinds of *mental* suffering, because of the subtlety and intangibility of the event, far less readily stir up humanitarian concern. Maria Ossowska, *Social Determinants of Moral Ideas* (Philadelphia, 1970), 8, points out that we ignore suffering that is the result of the personal search for excellence.

[3] I agree with Geoffroy Atkinson, *The Sentimental Revolution: French Writers 1690–1740* (Seattle, 1965), v, that "what is important in the history of ideas is always their expression and frequency of expression by different authors, for the date of onset of ideas is impossible to find."

[4] Of all the great themes of eighteenth-century social thought, humanitarianism has received the least study in intellectual history. The new international edition of the *Encyclopedia of the Social Sciences* (1968) has no entry under the subject, though the 1932 edition, vol. VII, had an interesting and promising short essay by Crane Brinton. A. R. Humphrey's, " 'The Friend of Mankind,' 1700–1760—An Aspect of Eighteenth-Century Sensibility," *Review of English Studies, 24* (July 1948), 203–18, expertly relates humanitarianism to sentimentalism. An archaic treatment but worth reading is Maurice Parmalee, "The Rise of Modern Humanitarianism," *American Journal of Sociology, 21* (Nov. 1915), 345–59. Many standard studies of the enlightenment take up the subject, but there is need for extended treatment.

> Who can all sense of others ills escape
> Is but a brute, at best, in human shape.[5]

In twentieth-century translations these words read somewhat differently, suggesting that Juvenal had been distorted in this version to conform to the already existing predispositions of Dryden's time.

Next to the influence of Juvenal's words, probably most deeply received into eighteenth-century consciousness were various passages in Cicero. In the *De Officiis,* for example, Cicero is arguing against the rule of expediency in international relations:

The appearance of profit [may be the occasion in public affairs] of making false steps. . . . Thus our fathers, for instance, did ill in destroying and rasing of Corinth; the Athenians yet worse in making an order, that the people of Aegina should all have their thumbs cut off, because they were powerful at sea. This, no question, was thought a profitable decree . . . ; but nothing can be truly profitable that is cruel; for the nature of man, which we ought to follow as the guide of our actions, of all things in the world is most opposite to cruelty.[6]

One other inheritance from the ancient world should be mentioned here since it is frequently found in eighteenth-century moral philosophy: the idea of *storgè,* a Greek word meaning "natural affections," which St. Paul uses in *Romans* 1:31, and which appears also in *Timothy* 3:3.[7] Thus, to cite one example of many possible, the Scottish moralist George Turnbull in 1740 called attention to the social passions given us by nature that counter-balance the powerful natural feelings directed toward the preservation and care of our own bodies:

Our moral desires and affections are strengthened . . . by uneasy strong sensations to maintain a just balance [against bodily appetites]; so is plainly the Στοργὴ or natural affection to children, so is compassion or pity to the dis-

[5] The translation of this satire was by Nahum Tate (1652–1715).

[6] Thomas Cockman's translation from 1699, reprinted in the Everyman Library edition (London, 1909), 132. Humane remarks occur, too, in Euripides, Seneca, Plutarch, and some others. But the prevailing tone in the ancient world, it seems, was along the lines of Plato's warning in the tenth book of the *Republic* against indulgence in pity and compassion. Cf. David Hume's opinion: "Epictetus has scarcely ever mentioned the sentiment of humanity and compassion but in order to put his disciples on their guard against it." *An Inquiry Concerning the Principles of Morals,* ed. Charles Hendel (Indianapolis, 1957), 136. Of course, this refers to the Stoic view. Grace H. Macurdy, *The Quality of Mercy: The Gentler Virtues in Greek Literature* (New Haven, 1940), makes a case for the widespread existence of humanitarian feeling in Greek literature from Homer to Socrates, but her point is often forced. John Ferguson, *Moral Values in the Ancient World* (New York, 1958), gives many examples of the expression of pity among the ancients, but he notes that it always existed in defiance of other greater values. The Greek "philanthropia" and the Latin "clementia" were tinged with the quality of condescension, according to Ferguson, if not for which they could have become words of "immense moral power." Ferguson is writing out of a definite Christian commitment.

[7] It is also used in works by Plutarch, Antoninus, and Athanasius.

tressed, and many other moral passions, that thus the public and social ones might not be too weak and feeble. . . .[8]

Storgè differed from irresistible compassion, as it will be studied here, in that it was primarily applied to the natural affections between parents and children rather than to compassionate relations between all humans.[9]

The humanitarian principles asserted in the eighteenth century had much in common with those in classical literature. But the modern period added (often implicitly) all of the weight of Christian providential design to the authority of Cicero's "nature." The mere phrase "the author of nature," so frequently adverted to in the eighteenth century, said enough. In addition to a kind of secular sanctification of compassion in the eighteenth century, there was also a vast increase in the number of express advocates of the principle. The idea of irresistible compassion became a psychological dogma, and more than ever a touchstone not only of true civility but of human status itself. Finally, the discussion of irresistible compassion was at the very center of the general discussion in the eighteenth century of the nature of sympathy and in that way contributed mightily to the ramifications of the idea of sympathy in both philosophy and literature.

In the seventeenth century from both religious and secular sources human nature was widely disparaged. Puritan examples of this tendency are easy to find, of course, and in secular thought there were many other figures besides Hobbes who took a similar line.[10] The dominant theory was pessimistic: men were almost always guided in their behavior by self-interest or self-love. In Hobbes's definition even pity was egoistic: the "imagination or fiction of future calamity to ourselves," albeit provoked by the calamity of another man. Pity, that is, is a species of personal fear. Few human virtues seemed to be immune from the shrewd analyses of the cynics in France or England.

Not surprisingly, it was among the Cambridge Platonists, who as a school objected to both the Calvinistic and the Hobbesian depreciation of human nature, that the modern emphasis on the significance of compassion has its beginnings. In Henry More's *Enchiridion Ethicum* (1666, Latin ed.; 1690, English ed.), the phenomenon of natural com-

[8]*The Principles of Moral Philosophy. An Enquiry into the Wise and Good Government of the Moral World* (London, 1740), 73.

[9]In Classical literature the negative concept of *"astorge"* was more commonly in use, with reference to the man who was little more than a brute insofar as he lacked sympathetic feeling.

[10]The fullest discussion is in F. B. Kaye's introduction to his edition of Bernard Mandeville, *The Fable of the Bees,* 2 vols. (Oxford, 1924), lxxvii–cxiii. Equally informative is A. O. Lovejoy, *Reflections on Human Nature* (Baltimore, 1961). For valuable discussion of optimistic, pessimistic, and neutral views: J. A. Passmore, "The Malleability of Man in Eighteenth-Century Thought," in Earl R. Wasserman, ed., *Aspects of the Eighteenth Century* (Baltimore, 1965).

passion was introduced with new force and meaning. More asserted, in opposition to the prevailing neo-Stoic opinion, that the passions in general were good in themselves, and "singularly needful to the perfecting of human life. . . ." "These Natural and Radical Affections" were peculiarly important, More argued, because it is obvious they do not come from our own effort; they are not "the result of freethinking or speculation," nor can they be acquired. They are "in us antecedent to all notion and cogitation whatever," and hence " 'tis manifest they are from Nature and from God." Therefore, More deduced, "whatever they dictate as Good and Just, is really Good and Just," and even further, "we are bound to embrace and prosecute the same."

Our passions and affections reveal to us the authentic version of the Law of Nature that "bears sway in the animal Region," and they are, therefore, "a sort of confused Muttering, or Whisper of . . . Divine Law," though the same message is, of course, "more clear and audible" to the intellect.[11] More's trust in the passions was an extension of the similar but narrower Augustinian trust in the nonrational influence of divine grace upon the soul. The sanctified will in the seventeenth-century Augustinian conception was synonymous with a heart imbued with love, and essentially a passively experienced effect upon the self rather than a matter of effort or deliberation. In short, will itself was a form of passion (psychologically "suffered" instead of "acted"), rather than a function of intellect. More seems to have transferred to natural passions the authority of the sanctified heart.[12]

However, the main driving force behind the avidity with which More and eighteenth-century moralists studied human nature was the belief that all of nature is a form of divine revelation, and human nature particularly. Thus, More said, in order to learn how the passions are "rightly to be moderated and used," it is necessary simply to observe "the end unto which Nature, or rather God, who is the Parent of Nature, has destined each of them. . .."[13] As we noted earlier, this device put the full weight of the Judaeo-Christian God behind the results of psychological investigation, an authority it is doubtful that Cicero could muster in his own time, even though he, too, believed, according to one eighteenth-century commentator, that "the natural end for which man is made, can only be inferred from the consideration of his

[11]Henry More, *Enchiridion Ethicum: The English Translation of 1690* (New York, 1930), 41, 78, 54, 78-79. On the neo-Stoic disparagement of the ethical value of the passions: Anthony Levi, *French Moralists: The Theory of the Passions, 1585-1649* (Oxford, 1964); Peter Gay, *The Enlightenment: An Interpretation, The Rise of Modern Paganism* (New York, 1966), 295-304, and the bibliography, 522-23; Rae Blanchard, "Introduction" to Richard Steele, *The Christian Hero* (Oxford, 1932), and Rudolph Kirk, "Introduction" to Joseph Hall, *Heaven Upon Earth and Characters of Vertues and Vices* (New Brunswick, N.J., 1948).

[12]For discussion of this point, see my "Will and Intellect in the New England Mind," *William and Mary Quarterly,* 3rd Ser., **24** (Oct. 1972), 515-58.

[13]More, *Enchiridion,* 54.

natural faculties and dispositions as they make one whole."[14] More
then proceeded to give a number of examples of how the passions
themselves declare their purposes and ends. Two of his examples are
directly related to our theme.

Even unpleasant passions have their special purposes, More noted.
Thus, we see, he said, in some of the manifestations of grief, those
"efficacious sorts of Eloquence she has bestowed on so many of the
Creatures when they are oppressed, for the drawing of Compassion
towards them," such as a "lamenting tone of the Voice, the dejection of
the Eyes and Countenance, Groaning, Howling, Sighs, and Tears, and
the like." These involuntary expressions have the "Power to incline the
Mind to Compassion, whether it be to quicken or Help, or to retard the
Mischiefs we intended." Similar to this example is another based on the
passion of "commiseration." "The use hereof," More said, "is in suc-
coring the distressed, and defending him that has right. For to take
away the Life of an innocent Man, is so monstrous a Crime, as tears the
very Bowels of Nature, and forces sighs from the Breasts of all Men."
In other words, the emotional effects of grief on the sufferer bring
about a psychologically determined compassionate response in the observer, and both the grief and the reciprocal compassion serve as
natural revelations of God's moral expectations of us. Likewise, the
emotion of commiseration reinforces justice and plainly exists in us for
that purpose.[15]

In the great *Treatise of the Laws of Nature* published by the
Latitudinarian bishop, Richard Cumberland, in Latin in 1672, one finds
some of the assumptions in More's work stated with greater explicit-
ness. Cumberland also sets forth clearly the basic methodological
axiom behind most eighteenth-century reasoning about ethical questions: human nature itself, he said, "suggests certain Rules of life . . . ,"
and from the study of it we can learn "for what kind of Action Man is
fitted by his Inward Frame."[16] Cumberland was nowhere near as favorably disposed towards the usefulness and verity of the passions as
More. He is often spoken of as the founder of utilitarian ethics because
of the preeminent place he gave to universal benevolence as the basic
moral commandment, but the source of the benevolence, according to
Cumberland, is intellectual, not passional or sentimental. Even so, included in the evidence that he ingeniously amassed to demonstrate the
natural, empirical, and necessary foundation of the law of benevolence,
was the observation that men have "both an expectation of Compassion" from other men, which presumably would not exist if they
were not entitled to it, "and a sympathy . . . by which they rejoice with
those that rejoice, and weep with those that weep."[17]

[14]Turnbull, *Principles*, 9, referring to Cicero's *De Finibus*.
[15]More, *Enchiridion*, 59, 70.
[16]Richard Cumberland, *A Treatise of the Laws of Nature*, trans. John Maxwell
(London, 1727), 99.
[17]*Ibid.*, 96; for similar material in Cudworth: Passmore, "Malleability," 24.

Other Latitudinarian Anglican preachers contemporary with Cumberland struck the same note. For example, Isaac Barrow, who was also a famous mathematician, delivered sermons that were a model for many other ministers in Britain and America. When Barrow turned to attack Hobbesian egoism he called attention to natural benevolence and compassion: "the constitution and frame of our nature disposeth to [natural affection]," he said; we cannot but feel this "when our bowels are touched with a sensible pain at the view of any calamitous object; when our fancies are disturbed at the report of any disaster befalling a man; when the sight of a tragedy wringeth compassion and tears from us. . . ."[18]

The most astute and original psychologist of the passions in the seventeenth century, the French Augustinian monk Nicolas Malebranche, whose main work, *The Search After Truth,* appeared in 1674 (and in English in 1694 in two separate translations), contributed his great authority to the argument and deepened it considerably. It is "chiefly by the Passions," Malebranche said, speaking directly against the neo-Stoics, "that the soul expands herself abroad, and finds she is actually related to all surrounding Beings. . . ." God has so "artfully united us with all things about us, and especially with those Beings of the same *Species* as our selves, that their Evils naturally afflict us, their Joy rejoyces us; their Rise, their Fall, or Diminution, seem to augment or diminish respectively our own Being. . . ." "The strongest *Natural Union* which God has established between us and his Works, is that which cements and binds us to our Fellow-Brethren, Men. God has commanded us to love them as our second-Selves," and He "supports and strengthens" this love

continually with a Natural Love which he impresses on us: and for that purpose has given us some invisible Bonds which bind and oblige us necessarily to love them. . . . All this secret Chain-work is a Miracle, which can never be sufficiently admir'd, nor can ever be understood. Upon the Sense of some sudden surprising Evil, which a Man finds, as it were, too strong for him to overcome by his own Strength, he raises, suppose, a Loud Cry. This cry forc'd out frequently without thinking on it, by the disposition of the *Machine,* strikes infallibly into the Ears of those who are near enough to afford the Assistance that is wanted: It pierces them, and makes them understand it, let them be of what nation or Quality soever; for 'tis a Cry of all Nations and all Conditions, as indeed it ought to be. It makes a Commotion in the Brain, and instantly changes the whole Disposition of Body in those that are struck with it; and makes them run to give succour, without so much as knowing it. . . .[19]

By the turn of the century, ideas like those of More, Cumberland,

[18]*Theological Works* (Oxford, 1830), II, 78–79.
[19]*Father Malebranche his Treatise concerning the Search After Truth . . .* , trans. T. Taylor, 2 vols. (2nd ed., London, 1700), I, 165–66. Malebranche's status in English-speaking countries was enhanced by the fervid admiration of his disciple, John Norris of Bemerton. Atkinson, *Sentimental Revolution,* fails to mention Malebranche.

and Malebranche found immensely influential expression in the famous *Characteristics* of the third Earl of Shaftesbury and in the journalism and other work of Addison and Steele and their associates. Shaftesbury is virtually identified with the view that "in the passions and affections of particular creatures there is a constant relation to the interest" of all. This is demonstrated, he said, in the many examples of men's "natural affection, parental kindness, zeal for posterity, concern for the propagation and nurture of the young, love of fellowship and company, compassion, mutual succour, and the rest of this kind." He developed a whole "economy of the passions," which had to do with their proper balancing in the general social interest. Selfish as well as social passions are included in, and even necessary to, this economy when they are properly integrated into the whole divine system. Indeed, all human emotions are important to virtue and well-being—except for one class: those passions that have *neither* the public nor private interest as their end. These so-called "unnatural passions" were rejected as perversions or abnormalities of nature. Examples of unnatural passions or feelings, Shaftesbury wrote, are those in which there is an

unnatural and inhuman delight in beholding torments, and in viewing distress, calamity, blood, massacre and destruction, with a peculiar joy and pleasure. . . . To delight in the torture and pain of other creatures indifferently, natives or foreigners, of our own or of another species, kindred or no kindred, known or unknown; to feed as it were on death, and be entertained with dying agonies; this has nothing in it accountable in the way of self-interest or private good . . . , but is wholly and absolutely unnatural, as it is horrid and miserable.[20]

Animal victims were included in Shaftesbury's condemnation of unnatural passions, whereas Cumberland's benevolence had extended only to "rational creatures."[21] The cluster of English words cognate to "human" that refer essentially to compassion as a trait, such as "humane," "humanitarian," "humanity," have their firmest philosophical origins in the work of Shaftesbury. No one before him had argued so eloquently for the identification of fellow-feeling with the essence of true human nature.[22]

The genteel moral journalism of the early eighteenth century, exemplified by the *Spectator,* contains a number of references to the ethical significance of compassion. Ten years before Francis Hutcheson

[20]Anthony, Earl of Shaftesbury, *Characteristics of Men, Manners, Opinions, Times,* ed. John M. Robertson, 2 vols. in one (Indianapolis, 1964), I, 280, 289, 331; II, 287.

[21]Shaftesbury explicitly rejected Descartes's theory of animal insensibility. But others in the seventeenth century, including Henry More, had done so before. For a brilliant survey of the development of "humanity" towards nonhumans: John Passmore, "The Treatment of Animals," *JHI,* 36 (1975), 195–218.

[22]This is not to deny predecessors: Ficino's letter to Thomas Minerbetti, in Paul O. Kristeller, *The Philosophy of Ficino* (New York, 1943), 113.

set out to refute Bernard Mandeville's renewal of cynicism and psychological pessimism,[23] irresistible compassion was already being cited as proof of the real existence of unadulterated altruism. Thus, in *Spectator,* no. 588 (1714), a dissenting minister, Henry Grove, who went on later to become a moderately distinguished lecturer on moral philosophy, presented an argument for the irreducibility of kind and benevolent propensities in humankind:

[The] Contriver of human nature hath wisely furnished it with two principles of action, self-love and benevolence; designed one of them to render men wakeful to his own personal interest, the other to dispose him for giving his utmost assistance to all engaged in the same pursuit.

Man is led to "pursue the general happiness" through his reason, according to Grove, for he sees that this is the way "to procure and establish" his own happiness. Yet

if besides this consideration, there were not a natural instinct, prompting men to desire the welfare and satisfaction of others, self-love, in defiance of the admonitions of reason, would quickly run all things into a state of war and confusion.

But we are happily saved from this Hobbesian nightmare by "inclinations which anticipate our reason, and like a bias draw the mind strongly towards" social ends. As part of the evidence for this thesis, Grove adduced the following observation: "The pity which arises on sight of persons in distress, and the satisfaction of mind which is the consequence of having removed them into a happier state, are instead of a thousand arguments to prove such a thing as disinterested benevolence."[24]

Bishop George Berkeley, the famous philosopher, was a dedicated opponent of Shaftesbury, but his contributions in early life to Steele's *Guardian* of 1713, paralleled the Shaftesburian disposition: "Nothing is made in vain," Berkeley wrote, "much less the instincts and appetites of animals." This is a maxim that holds "throughout the whole system of created beings. . . ." And using a gravity image with antecedents from long before the time of Newton, Berkeley wrote:

As the attractive power in bodies is the most universal principle which produceth innumerable effects, and is the key to explain the various

---

[23]Bernard Gert, "Hobbes and Psychological Egoism," *JHI,* **28** (Oct. 1967), 503–20, has argued convincingly that for most purposes the term psychological "pessimism" is preferable to the term psychological "egoism." True egoism, Gert observes, defined as the view that "men *never* act in order to benefit others, or because they believe a course of action to be morally right," is almost never explicitly defended by anybody. The term "pessimism" is appropriate for the view that "most actions of most men are motivated by self-interest. . . ."

[24]Donald F. Bond, ed., *The Spectator,* 4 vols. (Oxford, 1965); also numbers 213, 243, 302, 397, 488, 601. This is the earliest use of the term "disinterested benevolence" that I have seen. It has a long career thereafter in American religious thought.

phenomena of nature; so the corresponding social appetite in human souls is the great spring and source of moral actions. This it is that inclines each individual to an intercourse with his species, and models everyone to that behaviour which best suits with common well-being. Hence that sympathy in our nature whereby we feel the pains and joys of our fellow-creatures. . . . Hence arises that diffusive sense of humanity so unaccountable to the selfish man who is untouched with it, and is, indeed, a sort of monster or anomalous production. . . ."[25]

It is easy to find similar statements to Berkeley's from the pens of others at the time, not only in *The Spectator* and *The Guardian* but in Richard Steele's *The Christian Hero* (1701).

Writing in 1722 for his brother's newspaper, when he was still a youth in Boston, Benjamin Franklin casually referred to that "natural compassion to . . . Fellow-Creatures" that brings "Tears at the Sight of an Object of Charity, who by a bear [sic] Relation of his Circumstances" seems "to demand the Assistance of those about him."[26] Franklin may have gotten this idea from one of the English periodicals. But the doctrine of irresistible compassion, even before this time, was hardly unknown to the New England clergy. Solomon Stoddard, a clerical leader from the Connecticut River valley town of Northampton, in a discussion of the proposition, axiomatic for him, that "natural men are under the government of self-love," had to take cognizance of the fact that men are

sometimes over-ruled by a spirit of compassion. Men that are devoted to themselves, are so over-born sometimes with a Spirit of Compassion, that they forget their own Interest. . . . There is no man so void of compassion, but upon some occasions [it] will prevail upon him. The seeing or hearing of the miseries of others, will extort acts of compassion, and they will be under a necessity to deny themselves, and relieve them. Men have not the command of their own compassions, their compassion doth prevail sometimes whether they will or no, and they are forced to neglect their own interest to relieve others in their distress: and this compassion is not only to friends, but to strangers, persons that they have no acquaintance with; . . . yea, to brute Creatures also.[27]

It is notable, however, that Stoddard, the Puritan, does not use this phenomenon of irresistible compassion as the foundation for a new philosophical anthropology; nor does he give compassionate impulses an authority comparable to the acting of divine grace in the soul.

By mid-eighteenth century, the opinion that a person who is unmoved by the pains and joys of others is a kind of monster, an unnatural creation, and that God has given men and women inborn feel-

[25]*Guardian,* No. 49 (May 7, 1713), and No. 126 (Aug. 5, 1713), printed in A. A. Luce and T. E. Jessop, eds., *The Works of George Berkeley* (London, 1955), VII, 194, 227.

[26]*The Papers of Benjamin Franklin,* ed. L. W. Labaree and W. J. Bell, Jr. (New Haven, 1959), I, 37.

[27]Stoddard, *Three Sermons Lately Preach'd at Boston* (Boston, 1717), 37.

ings of compassion, sympathy, and benevolence as a way of directly guiding mankind to virtue, this opinion became a virtual philosophical and psychological dogma. Part of the reason for this popular success was the authoritative confirmation given to these ideas by the two moralists whose writings were probably more widely approved of in Britain and America in the second quarter of the century than those of any other philosophers: William Wollaston and Francis Hutcheson.

Wollaston's *The Religion of Nature Delineated* first appeared in 1722 and was printed in eight other editions before 1759. It quickly won an esteemed place in the genre of writing on "natural religion." Wollaston was distinctly not a sentimentalist, and humanitarian arguments usually are not associated with him.[28] But all of the dogmas that I have already recounted are as clear in Wollaston as in Hutcheson a few years later.

There is something in *human* nature resulting from our very make and constitution ... which renders us obnoxious to the pains of others, causes us to sympathize with them, and almost comprehends us in their case. It is grievous to see or hear (and almost to hear of) any man, or even any animal whatever, in *torment*. This *compassion* appears eminently in them, who upon other accounts are justly reckoned amongst the *best of men:* in some degree it appears in *almost* all ... It is therefore according to *nature* to be affected with the sufferings of other people: and the contrary is *inhuman* and *unnatural*.

The difference between Wollaston and Hutcheson for our purposes may be summed up by noting that in *The Religion of Nature Delineated* this reliance on natural compassion was carefully qualified, whereas for Hutcheson it becomes the very cornerstone of his system. "The reports of sense may be taken for true, when there is no reason against it," Wollaston wrote, and "the same may be said ... of every *affection, passion, inclination in general. ... Sympathy* ought not to be overruled, if there be not a *good* reason for it. On the contrary, it ought to be taken as a *suggestion* of nature, which should always be regarded, when it is not superseded by something superior; that is, by *reason*."[29] Wollaston's position on this matter, then, is something like Henry More's.

Wollaston also introduced into his book what was possibly the most interesting discussion of pleasure and pain in English thought between

---

[28]Atkinson, *Sentimental Revolution,* 157, e.g., is puzzled by the praise from the translator in the preface to a French edition of the *Religion of Nature:* "Wollaston proceeds from one logical step to the next in his treatment of virtues and vices among men," according to Atkinson, "without much evidence of passion or emotion. ... One can only conclude that his translator was reading emotions into its pages, or else that he may have been counting upon the emotional nature of prospective readers. As for the 'natural outpourings of a heart ... ,' those qualities are precisely what is most absent in this theoretical work."

[29]Wollaston, *The Religion of Nature Delineated* (London, 1726), 139–40, 165; French trans. *Ébauche de la Religion naturelle ...* (The Hague, 1726).

Hobbes and Bentham. This in itself is significant, for perhaps underlying even the widespread justification of natural compassion was some sort of profound change in the phenomenology of pain and pleasure. This possibility has recently been suggested by Professor Sheldon Wolin, who refers to the "exposed nerve ends of modern man," and his "heightened . . . sensitivity to pain." [30] Wollaston's extraordinary discussion in 1722 would support this opinion. On the basis of the necessary subjectivity of all experience of pleasure and pain, Wollaston called upon "princes, lawgivers, judges, juries, and even masters," to put aside what might be called rationalistic legal considerations and to mete out punishment *not* on the basis of what "a stout, resolute, obstinate, hardened criminal may bear," but on the basis of what "the weaker sort . . . can bear." [31] In effect, Wollaston advocated an expanded role for compassion in all penal matters.

The Scottish philosopher, Francis Hutcheson, as it is now well known, reduced reason to an ancillary role in ethics a half-generation before David Hume issued his famous dictum that reason "is and only ought to be the slave of the passions." [32] This fact, in addition to Hutcheson's remarkably pervasive role in British and American moral thought for fifty years or more, makes the publication of his first book, the *Inquiry into the Original of our Ideas of Beauty and Virtue,* a significant event in the history of humanitarianism. [33]

Hutcheson's *Inquiry* was in many ways the culmination of the trend in the preceding seventy-five years. He was greatly indebted to More,

[30]Wolin, *Politics and Vision* (Boston, 1960), 326. Nietzsche suggested that in earlier days "pain did not hurt as much as it does today. . . . For my part, I am convinced that, compared with one night's pain endured by a hysterical bluestocking, all the suffering of all the animals that have been used to date for scientific experiments is as nothing." *The Birth of Tragedy and the Genealogy of Morals,* trans. F. Golffing (New York, 1956), 200.

[31]Wollaston, *Religion,* 34. Wollaston was used as a text at Yale College under Thomas Clap's administration, which began in 1740 and ran for more than twenty years. But as early as 1726, James Logan, the learned Philadelphia Quaker, considered it "a piece for which one may justly . . . congratulate the age." Frederick B. Tolles, *James Logan and the Culture of Provincial America* (Boston, 1957), 198. And ca. 1727 or 1728, Jonathan Edwards entered in his "Catalogue" of reading: "Wollaston's Religion of Nature which I have been told Mr. Williams of Lebanon [Conn.] says is the best piece on the subject that he has ever read." I have deliberately excluded Edwards from treatment in this paper, since I am preparing a separate discussion of his relation to humanitarianism.

[32]*A Treatise of Human Nature* [1739–40] ed. L. A. Selby-Bigge (Oxford, 1928), 415.

[33]William Frankena, who has extensively studied eighteenth-century British ethics, has estimated that if the moral thinkers of that century were asked who was the most original and important among them Hutcheson would take the laurels; and this is probably true of America also, despite the fact that in the eyes of posterity figures like Bishop Joseph Butler and David Hume are far greater moralists; Frankena, "Hutcheson's Moral Sense Theory," *JHI,* 16 (June 1955), 356–75; also Adam Smith's famous tribute to Hutcheson, his teacher, in *The Theory of Moral Sentiments,* Part VII, Sec. ii. Hutcheson's *Inquiry* was well-known in America in the second quarter of

Cumberland, Malebranche, and Shaftesbury among the moderns. The class of passions that Shaftesbury and others had despised, abominated, and designated as unnatural was treated by Hutcheson as not only unnatural but as somewhat improbable. "Human nature," the Scottish philosopher wrote, "seems scarce capable of malicious disinterested hatred, or a sedate delight in the misery of others, when we imagine them no way pernicious to us, or opposite to our interests. . . ." Moreover, the psychological determinism that had been implicit in this benevolist trend from the beginning is overt in Hutcheson. God has determined "the very frame of our nature" to feelingful benevolence, and this fact is considered a great testimony to the divine element in human affairs. There is a "determination of our nature to study the good of others; or some instinct, antecedent to all reason from interest, which influences us to the love of others. . . ."

Hutcheson has also an economy and a teleology of the passions. Part of it is the close circle of emotions nature has established, whereby benefits to others evoke gratitude in the recipients, which is unfailingly pleasing to the benefactors, which in turn further stimulates benevolence. But beyond that, there is "a universal determination to benevolence in mankind, even toward the most distant parts of the species." Compassion is just one of a number of human traits that "strongly proves benevolence to be natural to us." And Hutcheson reiterated the by then commonplace example of how "Every mortal is made uneasy by any grievous misery he sees another involv'd in. . . ." Sounding much like Malebranche, whose work he knew well, Hutcheson wrote: "How wonderfully the constitution of human nature is adapted to move compassion. Our misery and distress immediately appears in our countenance . . . and propagates some pain to all spectators. . . . We mechanically send forth shrieks and groans . . . : Thus all who are present are rouz'd to our assistance." Hutcheson was not blind to the selfishness and depravity to be found everywhere. The point was that because of the intrinsic goodness of human nature, vice was a quite surmountable obstacle. The vicious passions do not necessarily disappear, but they are balanced out by divinely established benevolent affections.

Aristotle had persistently stressed the importance of "choice" in moral action. By choice he meant not just that an act was free or voluntary but that it was the result of conscious deliberation and right reason. The benevolists like Hutcheson turned this upside down and held, in effect, that deliberation was vicious if the suffering of another

---

the century; and the work of a thorough and unquestioning disciple, the *Elements of Moral Philosophy* by David Fordyce of Aberdeen, became the primary text in ethics at Harvard in the last half of the century. Fordyce's book first appeared in *The Preceptor,* ed. Robert Dodsley, 2 vols. (London, 1748), and in a separate edition in 1754. One or another of Hutcheson's works were used at the College of Philadelphia, Columbia (i.e., King's College), and Brown in the course of the century.

human being was before our senses. Rather than deliberation, the measure of the good person was to be found in the instantaneity of response, the unthinking, unreasoned animal (or spiritual) act of the virtuous soul. "Notwithstanding the mighty reason we boast of above other animals," Hutcheson wrote, "its processes are too slow, too full of doubt and hesitation to serve us in every exigency, either for our own preservation..., or to direct our actions for the good of the whole...."[34]

Wylie Sypher, Sr., has called Hutcheson "the first writer in any language fully to apply to the moral problem of slavery the 'romantic' ethics of pity instead of the 'classical' ethics of reason." According to Sypher, in Hutcheson the strong " 'sense of pity' swallows up all reasoning about 'just' and 'unjust' wars," or about natural inferiority.[35] In the lectures that Hutcheson was delivering at the University of Glasgow in the 1730s (but which were not published until 1755, nine years after his death), the essential principle that marks the "revolution in ethics" Sypher wished to emphasize, comes across clearly: "Must not all the sentiments of compassion and humanity, as well as reflection upon the general interest of mankind, dissuade from such usage of captives [i.e., enslavement], *even tho' it could be vindicated by some plea of external right?*"[36]

The main innovation in ethics and psychology that allowed unqualified humanitarianism to flower was the discrediting of rational justifications for inhumanity by opposing to them the *divine authority* of natural and instinctive compassionate feeling. A benevolent God gave man authoritative benevolent feelings, according to this reasoning. But it is important to note what is often overlooked in this matter, that in this case the discovery of the benevolent feelings seems to have preceded and forced the change in the understanding of God's will. Eventually, flogging, torture, chattel slavery, mistreatment of children, the sick, and the insane, and of animals, and "cruel and unusual punish-

[34]*An Inquiry into the Original of our Ideas of Beauty and Virtue...* (London, 1723), 132, 182, 137–40, 176–77, 143, 195, 215–17, 245.

[35]"Hutcheson and the 'Classical' Theory of Slavery," *Journal of Negro History,* 24 (July 1939), 263–80. David Brion Davis, *The Problem of Slavery in Western Culture* (Ithaca, 1966), 378, has pointed out that Sypher exaggerated Hutcheson's originality in antislavery arguments.

[36]Quoted by Sypher from Hutcheson, *A System of Moral Philosophy...* (Glasgow, 1755), II, 202–03; my italics. It should be kept in mind that antislavery sentiments and humanitarianism are not identical. But the success of the antislavery movement, when it used the presentation of the horrors of slavery to win converts, owed a great deal to humanitarianism. If humanitarianism is defined as active protest against obvious suffering, ostensibly benign slavery might not attract the opposition of the humanitarian. On the complex and paradoxical relationship of humanitarianism to the antislavery cause, see the excellent discussion in Winthrop Jordan, *White Over Black, American Attitudes Toward the Negro 1550–1812* (Chapel Hill, 1968), 365–72.

ments," would all come under powerful condemnation in the name of plain feeling.[37]

Both Hutcheson and his contemporary, Bishop Joseph Butler, were intent on proving that not all benevolent behavior was reducible to self-love, as Hobbes, Mandeville, and others had claimed. In this debate with the cynics (or the egoists or pessimists), the nature of spontaneous compassion was a prominent issue. Butler conceded implicitly that pity sprang from the imaginary substitution of the spectator in the place of the sufferer, but he denied that one could then correctly conclude that "it is *not another* you are at all concerned about, but *your self* only." (The imaginary substitution, we can see, is required for an accurate comprehension of the event, but it does not alter its nature.) Butler observed that in fact there were often "three distinct perceptions or inward feelings upon sight of persons in distress: [1] real sorrow and concern for the misery of our fellow-creatures; [2] some degree of satisfaction from a consciousness of our freedom from that misery; [3] and as the mind passes on from one thing to another, it is not unnatural from such an occasion to reflect upon our own liableness to the same or other calamities."

Hobbes, however, was "absurdly mistaken," according to Butler, in taking for the whole of pity what are concomitant elements only. Hobbes's interpretation, Butler noted, would make fear and compassion the "same idea, and a fearful and a compassionate man the same character, which every one immediately sees are totally different." Butler asserted categorically that "accidental obstacles removed, [men] naturally compassionate all in some degree whom they see in distress, so far as they have any real perception or sense of that distress."[38]

It would be hard to find anything in Thomas Jefferson's moral thought at the end of the eighteenth century that was not already present in some measure in Hutcheson and Butler fifty or more years earlier. The great Scottish moral psychologists of the second half of the century, David Hume and Adam Smith, contributed some finer discriminations, more extended analyses, and magisterial authority, but in the area of theory of the moral passions fewer new ideas than is sometimes supposed. Hume's tremendous powers of analysis came to a dead stop on the subject of compassion. After reviewing the familiar facts— "that the very aspect of happiness, joy, prosperity gives pleasure; that

[37]Amendment VIII to the American Constitution, which prohibits "cruel and unusual punishments," is one of the least studied of all the parts of the Constitution. Beccaria's *On Crimes and Punishments* (1764) readily comes to mind as an influence in this case. But it should be recognized that humane sentiments, if not all of the cogency of Beccaria's reasoning, were already present in America and Britain by 1750.

[38]*The Works of Joseph Butler,* ed. W. E. Gladstone, 2 vols. (Oxford, 1896), II, Sermon V.

of pain, suffering, sorrow communicates uneasiness. . . . Tears and cries and groans, never fail to infuse compassion and un- easiness . . ."—the great philosopher remarked in a footnote:

It is needless to push our researches so far as to ask, Why we have humanity or a fellow-feeling with others? It is sufficient that this is experienced to be a prin- ciple in human nature. We must stop somewhere in our examination of causes; and there are, in every science, some general principles beyond which we can- not hope to find any principle more general. No man is absolutely indifferent to the happiness and misery of others. The first has a natural tendency to give pleasure, the second pain. This everyone may find in himself. It is not probable that these principles can be resolved into principles more simple and universal. . . .[39]

Like Hutcheson, Hume believed that "absolute, unprovoked, disin- terested malice has never, perhaps, place in any human breast."[40]

The story of the idea of compassion in the eighteenth century is, of course, incomplete without some reference to Adam Smith, who gave the subject more extended treatment than any one else before and probably since. It is striking evidence of the central position the doc- trine of irresistible compassion held in this period that Smith's *Theory of Moral Sentiments* (1759) in its very opening words refers to it: "How selfish soever man may be supposed, there are evidently some principles in his nature, which interest him in the fortune of others. . . . Of this kind is pity or compassion, the emotion which we feel for the misery of others, when we either see it, or are made to conceive it in a very lively manner. That we often derive sorrow from the sorrow of others, is a matter of fact too obvious to require any instances to prove it."[41]

Smith paid much more attention than any of his predecessors to the nature of the imaginative projection that makes possible not only pity but all forms of sympathetic response. "As we have no immediate experience of what other men feel, we can form no idea of the manner in which they are affected, but by conceiving what we ourselves should feel in the like situation." Our physical senses alone can never inform us directly of the suffering of "our brother . . . upon the rack"; but

[39]*An Inquiry Concerning the Principles of Morals,* ed Charles W. Hendel (In- dianapolis, 1957), 47–48. Hume quotes another ancient source in this context, Horace's *Ars Poetica,* 101–02: "Ut ridentibus arrident, ita flentibus adflent/Humani vultus." "As the human face smiles at those who smile so does it weep at those who weep."

[40]Hume, *Inquiry,* 42. Glenn R. Morrow in "The Significance of the Doctrine of Sympathy in Hume and Adam Smith," *Philosophical Review,* 32 (1923), 60–78, dem- onstrates that Hume and certainly Adam Smith went further than their predecessors in grasping the social (i.e., the non-individualistic) nature of sympathy, defining sympathy as "the communication of feelings and sentiments from man to man" rather than as simply pity or compassion, and making sympathy in this broad sense the very basis of moral approbation.

[41]*The Theory of Moral Sentiments,* 2 vols. (10th ed., London, 1804), I, 1–2.

through the use of imagination we can form a conception of his sensations. Yet even imagination cannot "help us to this any other way, than by representing to us what would be our own, if we were in his case." Thus, our imagination discovers our own sensations, not the sufferer's.

By the imagination we place ourselves in his situation, we conceive ourselves enduring all the same torments, we enter as it were into his body, and become in some measure the same person with him, and thence form some idea of his sensations. . . . His agonies, when they are thus brought home to ourselves, when we have thus adopted and made them our own, begin at last to affect us, and we then tremble and shudder at the thought of what he feels.

But for all this, Smith remained quite convinced that sympathy "cannot, in any sense, be regarded as a selfish principle." Compassion or commiseration does "arise from an imaginary change of situations with the person principally concerned," but "this imaginary change is not supposed to happen to me in my own person and character, but in that of the person with whom I sympathize."

When I condole with you for the loss of your only son, in order to enter into your grief I do not consider what I, a person of such a character and profession, should suffer, if I had a son, and if that son was unfortunately to die: but I consider what I should suffer if I was really you, and I not only change circumstances with you, but I change persons and characters. My grief, therefore, is entirely upon your account, and not in the least upon my own.

As another example of the independence of compassion from self-interest, Smith cited the case of the man sympathizing with a woman in child-bed. "It is impossible that he should conceive himself as suffering her pains in his own proper person and character."[42]

Smith's book is full of subtle perceptions about the functioning of compassion, and of sympathy in general. He truly brought to fulfillment a hundred years of interest and investigation. One further instance of his extraordinary analysis of compassion deserves extended quotation:

The emotions of the spectator will . . . be very apt to fall short of the violence of what is felt by the sufferer. Mankind, though naturally sympathetic, never conceive, for what has befallen another, that degree of passion which naturally animates the person principally concerned. That imaginary change of situation, upon which their sympathy is founded, is but momentary. The thought of their own safety, the thought that they themselves are not really the sufferers, continually intrudes itself upon them; and though it does not hinder them from conceiving a passion somewhat analogous to what is felt by the sufferer, hinders them from conceiving anything that approaches to the same degree of violence.

[42]*Ibid.*, I, 2–3; II, 283–84.

Meanwhile, the miserable sufferer is aware of the spectators' detachment, and yet "passionately desires a more complete sympathy."

He longs for that relief which nothing can afford him but the entire concord of the affections of the spectators with his own. To see the emotions of their hearts, in every respect, beat time to his own, in the violent and disagreeable passions, constitutes his sole consolation.

Ironically, however, the sufferer can only hope to obtain this degree of commiseration "by lowering his passion to that pitch in which the spectators are capable of going along with him."

He must flatten . . . the sharpness of its natural tone, in order to reduce it to harmony and concord with the emotions of those who are about him. What they feel will indeed always be, in some respects, different from what he feels. . . . Though they will never be unisons, they may be concords, and this is all that is wanted or required.[43]

The doctrine of irresistible compassion has played a large part in the establishment of Western humanitarianism insofar as it was presented in the eighteenth century as both a normative and a descriptive concept. Men *are* natively humane; if not they *ought to be,* and those who are not so are something less than human. Humanitarianism in this sense is a historical stage in the education of the emotions. The "man of feeling" was a new social type as well as a literary type. For what the intellectuals of the eighteenth century attributed to "nature," we can confidently assign to "culture." It is hard to believe, furthermore, that the effects of this great "sentimental revo'ution," which has so much softened or suppressed many varieties of p; n-inducing human conduct, will ever be reversed.[44] However, as has of en been noted, one of the things that happened to the man of feeling in t e romantic period is that the enjoyment of the emotion of pity, the sympathetic identification with the sufferer, became an end in itseh and the compul-

[43]*Ibid.,* I, 31–32. Bishop Edward Reynolds had noticed that the mind of a sufferer "doth receive (as it were) some lightness and comfort, when it finds itself *generative* unto others, and produces *sympathy* in them." The torment of hell will be all the greater, Reynolds commented, because grief there "shall not be any whit *transient,* to work commiseration in any *Spectator,* but altogether *immanent* and *reflexive* upon its self." *A Treatise of the Passions and Faculties of the Soul of Man* (London, 1678), in Edward Reynolds, *The Works* (London, 1679), 631.

[44]Cf. Dr. Samuel Johnson's comment on the novelist Samuel Richardson, that he had "taught the passions to move at the command of virtue." The complex of doctrines supporting the man of feeling "was something new in the world," according to Ronald Crane; "Suggestions toward a Genealogy of the 'Man of Feeling,' " *Journal of English Literary History,* I (1934), 207. "Neither in antiquity, nor in the Middle Ages, nor in the sixteenth century, nor in the England of the Puritans and Cavaliers had the 'man of feeling' ever been a popular type."

sion to relieve the suffering proportionately less urgent. This is the same as saying that compassion became more literary and less a matter of practical morals. The cultivation of humane literature, ironically, may be a refuge from and a substitute for feelingful responses to painful human situations in the real world.[45]

If the teaching of compassion sometimes resulted in people feeling more and doing less, it has also been noticed that the reverse can happen, too. Bishop Butler in his *Analogy* made one of the shrewdest observations about the practical distortions of fellow-feeling. The repeated exercise of compassionate responses, Butler noted, has the paradoxical effect of strengthening the *habit* of providing relief and succour while at the same time weakening the emotional impetus behind compassion. This is the result of the general psychological rule that repetition strengthens active habits but weakens passive impressions.[46] Repeated subjection to excitements or stimulants from outside will gradually weaken the effect these stimulants have; on the other hand, repeated action tends to form indelible habits.

Perception of distress in others is a natural excitement, passively to pity, and actively to relieve it; but let a man set himself to attend to, inquire out, and relieve distressed persons, and he cannot but grow less and less sensibly affected with the various miseries of life, with which he must become acquainted; when yet, at the time, benevolence, considered not as a passion, but as a practical principle of action will strengthen: and whilst he passively compassionates the distressed less, he will acquire a greater aptitude actively to assist and befriend them.[47]

Social reform or benevolence, in other words, always tends to become bureaucratic. Fervent reform ends up as mere form.

Even worse than the misplaced compassion of the littérateur or than the benevolence without heart of the professional social worker is the outright perversion of the doctrine of natural compassion. It has been fairly well established that the philosophical defense of cruelty and diabolism, beginning especially with the Marquis de Sade, which has followed like an ominous shadow behind humanitarianism, was an ironic by-product of the age of sensibility.[48] Philosophical sadism—as

[45]For discussion see George Steiner, *Language and Silence* (New York, 1967), 5, 61. Late in the nineteenth century William James lamented the "habit of excessive novel-reading and theater-going," which he felt would produce "monsters" of indifference to real life situations. "The weeping of a Russian lady over the fictitious personages in the play, while her coachman is freezing to death in his seat outside, is the sort of thing that everywhere happens on a less glaring scale." *Habit* (New York, 1890), 63.

[46]*Works of Joseph Butler,* ed. Gladstone, I. 111.   [47]*Ibid.,* I, 112.

[48]Nietzsche was perhaps the first to expose this relationship between Sadism and sentimental humanitarianism. De Sade is discussed in the context of eighteenth-century moral thought in Lester Crocker, *An Age of Crisis: Man and World in Eighteenth Century French Thought* (Baltimore, 1959), and as an influence on the nineteenth

opposed to simple Caligula-like corruption from unlimited power—becomes a real possibility when the "Nature" that the eighteenth-century moralists vaunted ceases to be a secular metaphor for the Creation and becomes an antigod in its own right. This fact should indicate to us the importance of Christian underpinnings in sentimental humanitarianism. The belief in the eighteenth century that natural compassion was a divinely ordained and sanctioned human expression saved the whole theory of the moral authority of the passions from unlimited distortion by the libertines.

Both politics and theology were profoundly affected by humanitarian forces in the eighteenth century, and therefore indirectly by the dogma of irresistible compassion. Philosophers in particular, more than historians, have stressed the revolutionary implications of the increase in the scope and intensity of sympathy.[49] In Hannah Arendt's *On Revolution* the connection between compassion and revolutionary politics, which first began in the eighteenth century, is stated explicitly. The "passion of compassion," Arendt believes, above all other forces has "haunted and driven" the best men in all the modern revolutions, with the exception of the American.

History tells us that it is by no means a matter of course for the spectacle of misery to move men to pity; even during the long centuries when the Christian religion of mercy determined moral standards of Western Civilization, compassion operated outside the political realm and frequently outside the established hierarchy of the Church.

But in the eighteenth century, Arendt observes, "this age-old indifference was about to disappear, and . . . in the words of Rousseau, an 'innate repugnance at seeing a fellow creature suffer' had become common in certain strata of European society and precisely among those who made the French Revolution."[50]

---

century in Mario Praz, *The Romantic Agony* (Cleveland, 1967; first publ., 1933); also Michel Foucault, *Folie et Déraison. Histoire de la folie à l'âge classique* (Paris, 1961), 437: "Le sadisme n'est pas un nom enfin donné à une pratique aussi vieille que l'Éros; c'est un fait culturel massif qui est apparu précisément à la fin du XVIIIe siècle, et qui constitue une des plus grandes conversions de l'imagination occidentale."

[49]Thus, for example, Nietzsche's *Genealogy of Morals;* Alfred North Whitehead, *Adventures of Ideas* (New York, 1933); Bertrand Russell, *Human Society in Ethics in Politics* (New York, 1955), 155–56: "Sympathy has produced the many humanitarian advances of the last hundred years. . . . Perhaps the best hope for the future of mankind is that ways will be found of increasing the scope and intensity of sympathy."

[50]*On Revolution* (New York, 1963, 1965), 66. Arendt's analysis of the social and political implications of modern pity and compassion—she carefully distinguishes the two—is superb. It follows up an insight of Bernard Mandeville's that Arendt was probably unaware of: pity resembles virtue, Mandeville noted, "but as it is an impulse of nature, that consults neither the public interest nor our own reason, it may produce evil as well as good." See Lester Crocker's discussion of Rousseau in *An Age of Crisis, op. cit.,* 362, where may be found the above quotation from Mandeville.

Theology in the eighteenth century was faced with the difficult problem of reconciling the new psychological dogma of irresistible compassion with traditional Christian teaching on reprobation, hell, and eternal punishment. What had been earlier simply a perennial theological tension between God's mercy and His justice, became, as a result of humanitarian pressure, open conflict or contradiction. If God had in fact given man involuntary compassionate responses, then God must be at least as compassionate as man. Moreover, truly divine teaching could hardly include eternal punishment, since eternal punishment was wholly incompatible with the divine lesson taught to every man by his own instinct for pity and sympathy. As William Ellery Channing said early in the nineteenth century in opposition to the old orthodox teaching on reprobation, "We ask our opponents to leave us a God . . . in whom our moral sentiments may delight."[51] That is to say, a God that humanitarian feeling may approve of.

Channing's point of view has many antecedents, of course.[52] And the basis of opposition to the doctrines of hell and reprobation is quite varied.[53] But historians have more often mentioned the so-called "rational" objections to eternal punishment than the affective.[54] The doctrine of hell offended both reason and "humanity," good sense and compassion, and perhaps it was the latter that was more effective in changing minds than the former; but the most convincing argument in the eighteenth century was a mixture of feeling and logic: God gave men

[51]*Unitarian Christianity, and other essays,* ed. I. Bartlett (Indianapolis, 1957), 25.

[52]A weakness in the excellent article by Howard R. Murphy, "The Ethical Revolt Against Christian Orthodoxy in Early Victorian England," *American Historical Review,* **60** (July 1955), 800–17, is that the author seems to date the revolt against Original Sin, Reprobation, Eternal Punishment, etc., from the nineteenth century, whereas already in Britain before the mid-eighteenth century all of the humanitarian arguments Murphy cites had been fully expressed.

[53]Murphy, "Ethical Revolt," for example, singles out "meliorism," "the idea that the world was susceptible to systematic improvement through a sustained application of human effort and intelligence," as the force that "gradually took hold in men's minds and fired (or seduced) their imaginations." The root of humanitarian repugnance to doctrines like infant damnation and eternal punishment, according to this view, was the sense of incongruity between the Christian teaching and the meliorist bias of the time.

[54]Paul C. Davies, "The Debate on Eternal Punishment in Late Seventeenth- and Eighteenth-Century English Literature," *Eighteenth-Century Studies,* 4 (Spring 1971), 257–76, refers to the "reasonable" desire, on the part of opponents to orthodoxy, to avoid "extremism, absurdity, and irrationality." When it comes to the affections and passions, Davies primarily notes the manner in which their existence in the human breast tended to sustain teaching about hell: since men are motivated principally by hope and fear, or the desire for pleasure and the fear of pain, the threat of hell is necessary for social control. Davies observes in the romantic period the "insistence upon the human values of sympathy, compassion, and forgiveness," but scarcely mentions the growth of these values in the pre-romantic eighteenth century and their vital bearing on the debate over eternal punishment.

and women compassion, and He would not contradict in His own performance His moral expectations of His creatures.

The belief that God or even a pious man would feel the least bit of pity for the suffering of sinners in hell had to overcome a tremendous weight of tradition. The predominant view, which goes back to Tertullian at least, was that God and the angels together would derive not uneasiness but an augmentation of bliss from the contemplation of the punishment of the damned. D. P. Walker in *The Decline of Hell: Seventeenth Century Discussion of Eternal Torment*[55] remarks about Peter Sterry (d. 1672) and Jeremiah White (d. 1707), both of whom preached universal salvation based on God's preeminent attribute of love, that these men are "almost unique in the theology of that age," insofar as they expressed a "compassion for the suffering of sinners" and projected it unto God. In the eighteenth century, under the influence of figures like Bishop John Tillotson (d. 1694) and others, it became commonplace to reconstruct God's image into that of the benevolent ruler.[56] George Turnbull in 1740 spoke representatively for many when he maintained:

Nothing can be more absurd than the doctrine which has sometimes been advanced; that goodness in God is not the same as goodness in men, but something of quite another kind and which we understand not. . . . The true notion . . . of the divine benevolence must be learned by considering what it is in man. And by augmenting the idea of a good man to boundless perfection, we arrive at the nearest conception that is possible for us to frame of the goodness of an all-perfect mind.[57]

Since compassion by this time had become so conspicuous a factor in human nature, extension to the godhead of this quality of mercy would inevitably lead to the abolition of eternal torment.

The encounter in the eighteenth century between irresistible compassion and orthodox theology is a more complex matter than there is space to go into here. I will conclude, however, with an example of the conflict that shows clearly the tensions within theology. In America, at Harvard College, at almost the same moment that Turnbull was writing, the Hollis Professor of Divinity Edward Wigglesworth was also

---

[55](Chicago, 1964), 111.

[56]This point has been made many times; e.g., Norman Sykes, "Theology of Divine Benevolence," *Historical Magazine of the Protestant Episcopal Church,* **16** (1947), 278–91.

[57]Turnbull, *Principles,* preface. For the same idea in a later period: Tom Paine, *Age of Reason,* Part I: "The moral duty of man consists in imitating the moral goodness and beneficence of God. . . . The goodness of God to all men . . . is an example calling upon all men to practice the same toward each other; and consequently, . . . everything of persecution and revenge between man and man, and everything of cruelty to animals, is a violation of moral duty."

addressing the problem of reconciling God's sovereignty with human compassion. Wigglesworth had turned to the subject, he said, after reading some pamphlets from England that defended "Universal Redemption" on the basis of a "dangerous Deduction" from the consideration of divine mercy.

Wigglesworth's tack was to distinguish sharply the divine attribute from its human counterpart. Not surprisingly, however, he found the psychological doctrine of irresistible compassion altogether compelling, and elaborated on it in his address, never realizing that once he admitted its validity he would be trapped. "When we speak of the Mercy of Men," Wigglesworth said, "we intend by it a compassionate painful sense of the Miseries we see others groaning under . . . , which excites us to endeavour to prevent those Miseries . . . and to deliver them from, or to relieve and comfort them under those miseries." The Scriptures, in order to give us "a more lively affecting Sense of the Greatness of the Mercy of God," represent the divine virtue in the same way, "as attended with all that inward Commotion and uneasy Sensation, which we experience in ourselves upon the Appearance of an Object of Pity." But it is a serious mistake, Wigglesworth insisted, to use this analogy as the basis for attributing the "Imperfections of human Passions to the Divine Nature." Humankind, he explained, "whose Wisdom reaches but a little way," has been given by God a "Readiness to shew Mercy to all that are in Misery," for if left "to our own Liberty in this Matter," "many Mischiefs both of a private and publick Nature" would result. In the case of the passion of compassion, in other words, man could not be trusted with freedom and was given an indiscriminate or at least controlling amount. "We . . . whose Disposition to Acts of Kindness and Mercy is many times too feeble, and whose angry Passions are not seldom too strong, are not left to our own Discretion to shew Mercy, or to refuse it, when, and where we please."

On all of these counts, however, God is quite different. He experiences no "inward Disturbance or Uneasiness at the Misery of Creatures," for it would be inconsistent with His absolute perfections, and "an Interruption of his perfect Happiness." Moreover, God is "absolutely free and unconfined in his Acts of Grace and Mercy." He is not subject to the involuntariness or the passivity of any passion.[58] With these words Wigglesworth appears to be simply reiterating the old truths rather than confronting the disturbing challenges to them. In the end, all that Wigglesworth can offer, it seems, is the weak protestation

[58]The paradox of God's passions, especially the nature of His love in comparison to human love, was widely discussed in the patristic period. A Harvard College commencement *quaestio* in 1723, answered in the negative by the M. A. candidate Thomas Smith, reads: "An dentur in Deo affectus Vere & proprie dicti?" (Are there affections in God, truly and properly speaking?)

that God "hath the Government of the World upon him," and "Mercy and Justice are both alike dear and essential to him."[59]

Wigglesworth's evasiveness, the unsatisfying incompleteness of his response, only serves to point up the revolutions in theological and moral thought that irresistible compassion was working in his day. But he can hardly be blamed for his helpless predicament. When a human feeling is elevated to a moral absolute, there can be no answer to it.

Institute of Early American History and Culture, Williamsburg, Va.

[59]Edward Wigglesworth, *The Sovereignty of God in the Exercises of his Mercy. . . . consider'd in Two Public Lectures at Harvard College in Cambridge* (Boston, 1741), 6–12.

VI

THE IDEA OF THE SAVAGE IN NORTH AMERICAN
ETHNOHISTORY

By David Bidney

Among the encouraging features of contemporary American scholarship is the renewed interest in American ethnohistory. This is an aspect of our culture history which professional anthropologists have tended for the most part to neglect, owing in large measure to their preoccupation with the gathering of ethnographic data and the description of exotic cultures. Functional relationships between the elements of culture rather than ethnohistorical studies have been characteristic of modern ethnological work. With the publication of J. H. Kennedy's *Jesuit and Savage in New France* [1] and *The Savages of America: A Study of the Indian and the Idea of Civilization* [2] by Roy H. Pearce, students of American ethnohistory have been provided with two first-rate, interdisciplinary studies which should stimulate interest in this much neglected field. It is worthy of note that Professor Kennedy is a historian and Professor Pearce is a scholar in the field of English literature.

The colonization of North America by the English and French during the seventeenth and eighteenth centuries brought them into intimate contact with the Indians. For the colonial Americans, the problem of the savage was both theoretical and practical. On the one hand, they were confronted with the Indian and had to make their peace with him. On the other hand, the manner in which they resolved their practical problem depended on their theoretical understanding and evaluation of the Indian as a type of man. The early colonists brought with them certain preconceptions as to the nature of savage man which they promptly transferred to the Indians. In the course of time, as they were made aware of the culture of the Indians they revised their original ideas and rationalized on the basis of their experience and the practical requirements of their social and environmental conditions.

The seventeenth-century colonists thought of the Indians as " natural men " living in a precivilized " state of nature." Civilization was conceived as a historical system of beliefs, customs and institutions which supervened upon man's original natural condition. It was thought to be the duty of Christian civilized man to bring the benefits of religion and civilization to the savages and to humanize them in accordance with the ideals and practices of European culture. Thus, Christian humanism and missionary zeal were allied closely with imperialism and trade interests in the colonization of the New World. The colonists assumed that the savages would be willing

---

[1] J. H. Kennedy, *Jesuit and Savage in New France* (New Haven: Yale University Press, 1950).

[2] Roy H. Pearce, *The Savages of America: A Study of the Indian and the Idea of Civilization* (Baltimore: The Johns Hopkins Press, 1953).

and able to accept the benefits of their civilization once they were made
conscious of them and that Europeans and Indians could live peacefully and
profitably together. As Christians, the colonists, and especially their clergy,
felt the obligation to bring the Indians from a state of nature to a state of
Christian civility.

Kennedy has shown clearly how the Jesuits in particular prepared careful ethnographical reports on the Indians of New France, especially the
Algonquins and Hurons, whom they were concerned to convert to Christianity. The Jesuits took a sympathetic, scholarly interest in the character and
culture of their Indian charges. Not being in competition with the Indians
either for territory or trade, the Jesuits tended to be on friendly terms with
them and to appreciate their rude virtues. According to Kennedy, it was
owing in large part to these Jesuit reports, published each year from 1632
to 1674, that contemporary Europe of the seventeenth century formed the
concept of the " noble savage." The savages of New France were looked
upon as " natural men " with all the innate goodness and disposition to
virtue with which they were endowed by their Creator, requiring but the
Christian gospel to illuminate their intelligence and humanize their conduct.
Unlike their civilized contemporaries, they had not acquired the vices of
civilization and so were saved from the accumulated corruptions of that
civilization. The Jesuits, however, underestimated the difficulties of ac-
culturation and found great difficulty in making converts, some of them
becoming martyrs for their missionary zeal.

What was especially significant in the Jesuit approach was their scholarly interest in the culture and language of the Indians; " it became standard practice for every missionary to study first the language of the tribe to
which he was assigned " (Kennedy, 61). However, in the interest of conversion, the Jesuits came to sanction conquest and colonization, although at
times they objected strenuously to the military and mercantilist concomi-
tants of such programs (*Ibid.*, 62).

In theory, the Jesuits tended to combine cultural relativism with religious absolutism. The Indians were said to live in an " environment of
innocence " and the Jesuits concluded that the effects of barbarism were
not all harmful (*Ibid.*, 100). Some thought " their nature has something
of the goodness of the terrestrial paradise before sin entered it " (100).
The Indians were said not to lack intelligence but merely education and the
knowledge of the true God (102). The Jesuits, therefore, tended to allow
great latitude in the sphere of natural conduct while insisting upon absolute
conformity in the sphere of supernatural religion (104). It was not necessary, they thought, to brand as criminal things that were done with an innocent intent. Thus they tried to establish a common ground between Indian
standards and their own dogma and morality, and to construct a religion
at the same time native and Catholic (109). For long they persisted in
regarding evil traits as temporary and contingent upon paganism, and to
the end they remained ardent advocates of the Indians.

In France the savages, as known from the Reports of the Jesuits as well as from actual observation of Indians brought from America by explorers such as Champlain, served the philosophers with material for criticizing prevailing institutions. Thus while for the Jesuits the conversion of the Indians was an end in itself, for the French intellectuals the savages were a means to an end. In time, with the advent of the spirit of Cartesian rationalism in the eighteenth century, the savage was utilized in the arguments against the Church which had done so much to foster an appreciation of him (*Ibid.*, ch. x). In Rousseau and Voltaire, French intellectuals found champions of the savage in the name of freedom and equality for Europeans.

Pearce's study serves to complement nicely the picture presented by Kennedy. From Pearce's account we learn how the idea of the savage affected the colonizing of English America during the period from 1609 to 1851. His work is in essence a critical appraisal of the literature bearing upon the ideas of savagism and civilization as expressed by Anglo-American writers and of the changing significance of these ideas as interpretations of the symbol and image of the Indian during this period.

The early colonists of British America as of New France thought it to be their duty to Christianize the natives and to civilize them. Assuming the Indians to be rational men deprived of the advantages of the Christian religion, they thought the Indians would be glad to accept the benefits of their religion once they were made aware of them. But the Puritans of New England and the Protestants of Virginia lacked the broad tolerance of the Jesuits. The massacre of 1622 in Virginia made the hope of Christianizing the Indians seem hopeless. The New England clergyman with their Calvinistic division of mankind into the saved and the damned soon began to think of the Indians as instruments of the devil destined for ultimate destruction. The settlers of New England thought of the pagan Indians as symbols of Satan opposing the Word of God; the savage symbolized the fall of men and his degraded spiritual condition. Hence the Puritans were not interested in studying the Indian, as were the Jesuits, but in converting him and saving him from himself. If the Indian resisted, he brought a well-merited retribution upon himself, just as did witches and all sinners who opposed the word of God. The Quakers in Pennsylvania also hoped to bring the Indians out of heathenism, but attempted to do so by gentler and less dogmatic methods. But Quaker freedom and love were at once too much and too little for the savages (Pearce, 37). Eventually, with the advent of the war of 1756 with the French and Indians, the settlers of Pennsylvania, too, found that the principle of survival prevailed over the principle of divinity (39).

Whatever the attitude of the clergy, British policy was governed primarily by considerations of trade and colonization. Traders and settlers conflicted over land rights with the Indians. By the middle of the eighteenth century the original idealistic and evangelical vision of civilizing the

Indians was superseded by the practical struggle for survival against Indian resistance to colonial expansion. Instead of saving savages for Christianity, the major objective was that of saving American civilization from the savages. Gradually the thought was formulated that the savage was incapable of civilization and an obstacle in the development of American civilization. After 1775 Americans came to believe that the savages in their midst could have no share in the progress of their civilization.

In the course of the nineteenth century the policy of the administration and the attitudes of philosophers, historians and men of letters converged upon a common articulated conclusion, namely, that in the conflict of American civilization and Indian culture the former as the higher and mightier was bound to prevail and that the Indian together with his culture would be destroyed. Since the Indian could not, and would not, be saved for American civilization, that civilization was bound to destroy him in the end. It was not without a feeling of guilt and remorse that American thinkers came to this tragic and pessimistic conclusion. The Indian, it was argued, though a savage, had many noble qualities and virtues; but since he could not bring himself either to accept the white man's gifts or to withstand them he was inevitably doomed to destruction. The Indian was to be pitied, but he had to make way for the realization of the American dream. This was the consensus of opinion of historians such as Francis Parkman, administrators such as Henry Rowe Schoolcraft, and literary figures of the stature and popularity of Longfellow and Cooper.

Pearce attributes this crystallization and articulation of American thought towards a negative evaluation of the Indian and his image in the nineteenth century as owing to the influence of the idea of the savagism which American thinkers derived from eighteenth-century Scottish historians and moral philosophers, such as Adam Ferguson and Lord Kames. The idea of savagism as developed by these writers was based on the thesis that the savage represented " the zero of humanity " and that savagism was bound to be superseded by civilization in the natural course of development. This implied an anti-primitivistic attitude which went counter to the glorification of the Indian as the noble savage. While it was granted that the savage had some natural virtues, it was pointed out that he lacked all progressive tendencies towards self-improvement and also had many ignoble traits which spelled his doom. Thus, Pearce argues, the idea of savagism prepared the way for a negative evaluation of the savage as symbolized by the Indian and imaged by early nineteenth-century writers.

I do not, however, find that the ethnohistorical facts serve to substantiate Pearce's thesis. The concept of the savage in eighteenth-century philosophical and historical thought involved no such pragmatic and historical consequences. The thesis that savagery constituted the lowest rung of the cultural ladder is quite compatible logically and practically with an attitude of broad tolerance and benevolence towards people of lower stages of development. Contrary to Pearce's argument, the logical inference which was made on the basis of this philosophy of culture history was that since all peoples are perfectible and tend to develop through parallel stages, it was the duty of the more advanced and civilized to assist those less advanced. Cultural inferiority as well as superiority were historical achievements and hence subject to change in time. There is no room on this assumption for the notion that a given people is incapable of civilization and outside the historical process which makes for cultural progress. I find myself, therefore, in agreement with Pearce when he observes that the concept of savagism as put forth by the eighteenth-century historians was anti-primitivistic, but I am opposed to his thesis that American belief in the idea of savagism led logically to a negative evaluation of the Indian and to his exclusion from participation in the advance of American civilization.

Pearce makes the point that the idea of savagism was not supported by ethnographical facts. According to him, " We may work with hypotheses which do not press us to see primitive cultures as at once historically anterior and morally inferior to ours. Indeed, we feel committed to avoid such historicizing and moralizing, and rigorously to separate anthropology from philosophy, description from evaluation " (105). He implies that an attitude of cultural relativism which precludes normative moral judgments is more in accord with the ethnographic facts and would have made for greater tolerance. In this respect, it seems fair to say, Pearce has not kept up with developments in contemporary ethnological theory. Contemporary anthropologists no longer insist upon a rigorous separation of anthropology from philosophy, and of description from evaluation.[3] The modern science of anthropology is very much concerned with problems of values and with the value attitudes of anthropologists. It is being realized that the anthropologist cannot avoid making value judgments even in the name of cultural relativism, and that the latter doctrine is untenable in a world of conflicting ideologies.[4]

It seems to me that Pearce has failed to reckon seriously with the historical and sociological conditions prevailing in the America of the late eighteenth and nineteenth centuries and with the circumstances which led Americans to rationalize their efforts to settle the West and develop their civilization. It was not so much an a priori theory of savagism developed in Europe and transported and diffused to America which determined the attitude of the colonists who settled the country, but the hunger for land, a growing population, and the economic development of the country. The Indians who resisted the expansion of American society were considered as

[3] David Bidney, " The Concept of Value in Modern Anthropology," in *Anthropology Today, An Encyclopedic Inventory,* prepared by A. L. Kroeber (Chicago, 1953).

[4] A. L. Kroeber and Clyde Kluckhohn, *Culture: A Critical Review of Concepts and Definitions* (Harvard University Press, Cambridge, 1952), 174–79; Bidney, *Theoretical Anthropology* (New York, 1953), ch. xiv.

obstacles to be overcome and removed from the way. The official policy of removal of the Indians was a temporary expedient which was superseded by the march of events. In the course of this inevitable expansion towards the ocean thoughtful Americans rationalized their destiny and expressed "double-mindedness" and equivocation in their statements justifying the destruction of the Indian. But once the continent was opened up for settlement, and the settlers felt relatively secure, the official American attitude softened and the right of the Indian to a share in American civilization as full citizens was gradually recognized. Even at present, however, much remains to be done to rectify historic abuses.

Thus the early attitude expressed in the maxim "civilization or extinction" was not one born of philosophical theory but of historical expediency. Neither Morgan's scientific study of the *League of the Iroquois* in 1851 nor any of the later ethnographical studies brought about any significant change in policy. The evolutionary anthropologists, such as Morgan, shared the very idea of savagism which Pearce holds responsible for the "century of dishonor." What brought about the change in attitude towards the Indian was a change in social conditions which assured American security and expansion.

It is of interest in this connection to reflect that the typical rationalization employed by nineteenth-century Americans to validate their claim to expansion on the North American continent and to exclude the Indians from participating in their civilization, was duplicated in the twentieth century by the claims of land-hungry nations of Europe, Germany and Italy, before the Second World War. In their quest for *Lebensraum* similar claims were made as to the rights of powerful civilized peoples at the expense of the so-called less civilized, weaker peoples. One has but to recall the arguments advanced to justify the conquest of Ethiopia or the destruction of ethnic minorities in Europe. But in the twentieth century it was the American and British peoples with their allies who insisted that this mode of rationalization to justify conquest was not valid and based on nothing more than myth. It is precisely because of the contemporary belief in the universal moral values of civilization and in the rights of all peoples to participate in the development of a common human civilization that the United States and the United Nations are taking steps to assist in every possible way less fortunate, underdeveloped countries. Our idealism is bolstered by our realism, by our belief that survival in the modern world depends on a democratic view of civilization which includes participation by all the peoples of the world regardless of their present stage of cultural development. It is the modern union of anthropology and philosophy which is providing the theoretical justification for this new approach to ethnic problems.

Indiana University.

VII

THE AMERICAN DEBATE ON THE NEGRO'S PLACE IN NATURE, 1780–1815

By John C. Greene

Are all human beings of one biological species? This was a momentous question in Jefferson's day. Theologically it bore upon the Christian doctrine of the spiritual unity of mankind in their common descent from Adam. Politically it colored conceptions of the white man's rights and duties with respect to the inhabitants of those regions of the earth which were being subjected to his control. Scientifically it involved the distinction, enormous in the eyes of eighteenth-century naturalists, between a species and a variety. If the various types of human beings were separate species, the task of the natural historian was to classify them according to their specific characters, accepting these as permanent and divinely ordained. But if human races were but varieties of a single species, science must account for their peculiarities by natural causes.

In the United States there were special incentives to the study of these questions. The Americans were themselves a mixture of European peoples undergoing transformation by intermarriage and by exposure to a new physical and social environment. On the frontier they came into conflict with the Indian tribes. In the settled areas, particularly in the South, were the Negroes, an alien race transplanted from Africa and held in bondage to the white man despite the resounding affirmations of the Declaration of Independence. It is not surprising, then, that the current of anthropological speculation ran strong in the United States and that it swirled around the question of the Negro's place in nature.

The most ambitious and best known American treatise on physical anthropology in the period before 1815 was the Reverend Samuel Stanhope Smith's *Essay on the Causes of the Variety of Complexion and Figure in the Human Species*,[1] first published in 1787. Smith was Professor of Moral Philosophy at the College of New Jersey and later became its President. His main concern in this work was to vindicate the Scriptural doctrine of the unity of the human race against objections drawn from the apparent diversity of mankind, in particular those set forth by the Scotch jurist Lord Kames in his *Sketches of the History of Man,* first published in 1774.[2] With respect

[1] Samuel Stanhope Smith, *An Essay on the Causes of the Variety of Complexion and Figure in the Human Species. To Which Are Added, Strictures on Lord Kames's Discourse on the Original Diversity of Mankind* (Philadelphia, 1787). A second, enlarged edition was published at New Brunswick, N. J., in 1810.

[2] Henry Home (Lord Kames), *Sketches of the History of Man* (Edinburgh, 1774). A second enlarged and revised edition was issued in four volumes in 1788.

to the Negro, therefore, he confines himself to showing that the physical peculiarities of this, as of every, human race are the product of two great kinds of natural causes: climate and the state of society. On the subject of climate he echoes the arguments of Buffon, Montesquieu, and others, maintaining the slow and imperceptible modification of the human constitution by heat and cold, the transmissibility of the characteristics thus acquired, and the general correlation of latitude and skin color. He speculates that the complexion in any climate will be changed towards black, in proportion to the degree of heat in the atmosphere, and the quantity of bile in the skin."[3] The hair, he declares, follows the law of the complexion, hence it is not surprising that Negroes born in the United States have longer, straighter, denser hair than those brought directly from Africa, or that their body odor is less powerful. The change wrought in the Negro constitution by the American environment appears most strik-

---

Smith's "Strictures" on this work were appended to both editions of the *Essay*. Kames was a common sense polygenist, theologically heterodox but decidedly conservative in his general view of nature. He had no use for fine-spun distinctions between species and varieties. To him it seemed axiomatic that every kind of creature had been perfectly adapted by the Creator to its peculiar environment and function in nature. He conceded that environment might produce random variations from the original models of nature but denied that it could ever create a new type. Applying these principles to the case of man, he concluded that the various human types found on the earth had been created separately and adapted by their Maker to the regions which they were to inhabit. No other hypothesis, he felt, could account for the racial peculiarities of the Negro and the Indian or explain the tendency of varieties to degenerate when exposed to climates different from their native ones. None other could illustrate so clearly the wisdom of the Creator. As for the Scriptural account of man's descent from a single pair, it could be saved by supposing that the confusion of tongues at the tower of Babel had plunged mankind into barbarism and scattered them far and wide, so that it became necessary for God to alter their makeup so as to adapt them to the variety of conditions in which they found themselves. "Without immediate change of bodily constitution, the builders of Babel could not possibly have subsisted in the burning region of Guinea, or in the frozen region of Lapland." Smith was equally solicitous to uphold the wisdom of the Creator, of course, but found it to consist in man's being given a constitution sufficiently plastic to adapt itself to the whole range of climates on the globe. Lord Kames' reconciliation of sacred and profane history Smith rejected as both disingenuous and unnecessary.

[3] Smith, *op. cit.*, 16. Smith did not discover until later that Blumenbach had advanced a similar theory in 1775 in his *De Generis Varietate Humani Nativa*. He cites Buffon and Montesquieu, however. P. M. Spurlin, *Montesquieu in America 1760–1810* (Louisiana State University Press, 1940), shows that Montesquieu's works were widely read in the United States at this time. In general, however, the writers discussed in the present paper drew more heavily on European naturalists, such as Buffon, Camper, Cuvier, and Charles White, than on Montesquieu.

ingly in domestic slaves, because in their case the influences of civilized society are added to those of the climate. How much more
rapidly, then, would the Negro take on the physical characteristics of
the white man if he were admitted to the society of his masters.

In Jefferson's *Notes on Virginia* a quite different view of the matter
was set forth. There the Negro is represented as inferior to the white
man in both body and mind. Negro men, Jefferson asserts, confess
the superior beauty of white women by preferring them to black as
uniformly as the orang-outang prefers the Negro woman to the female
of his own species. If superior beauty is thought worthy of preservation in breeding animals, why should it not be regarded in controlling
the intercourse of human beings? In mental endowment, he continues, Negroes lack foresight and imagination; they are equal to the
whites in memory but vastly inferior in the powers of reason, more
ardent in sexual passion but less delicate. " In general, their existence
appears to participate more of sensation than of reflection." [4] Jefferson admits that the Negro slaves' condition of life has not been favorable to the development of their faculties, but he adduces the artistic
and intellectual achievements of the Roman slaves and the art and
oratory of the Indians as proof that adverse conditions cannot completely suppress natural genius. He thinks that interbreeding with
the whites produces a marked physical and mental improvement in
the Negro and regards this supposed fact as proof that the Negro's
inferiority is grounded in nature as well as in social condition.

The question whether the Negro is a separate species of man, distinct from all others since the day of creation, or merely a variety,
" made distinct by time and circumstances," Jefferson leaves open.
He is not concerned to corroborate Scripture, nor does he feel that any
moral issue hangs on the answer to this problem in natural history.
His denunciation of slavery in another passage of the *Notes on Virginia* and his reply in 1809 to the remonstrances of the Abbé Grégoire
show that he viewed the question of the Negro's rights as one quite
distinct from that of his rank in the scale of being. The real problem
from Jefferson's point of view was: how to give the Negro the liberty
which is his due without deteriorating the dignity and beauty of
human nature by removing obstacles to the intermixture of white and
Negro blood. " Among the Romans emancipation required but one
effort. The slave, when made free, might mix with, without staining
the blood of his master. But with us a second is necessary, unknown

[4] Thomas Jefferson, *Notes on the State of Virginia* . . . , in Saul K. Padover, *The
Complete Jefferson Containing his Major Writings, Published and Unpublished,
except his Letters* (New York, 1943), 662.

to history. When freed, he is to be removed beyond the reach of mixture." [5]

The American public was exposed to a much less cautious and temperate view of the Negro's endowments and rights when, in 1788, the *Columbian Magazine* reprinted two extracts from Edward Long's *History of Jamaica*.[6] The work had been published anonymously in 1774, five years after Long's return to England from a residence in Jamaica. In the chapter on " Negroes," extracted in the *Columbian Magazine*, Long attempts to prove that the African Negroes constitute a separate species of human beings. He finds them peculiar not only in their black skin but also in their woolly hair, their features, their odor, and even in their lice. Mentally, says Long, they are void of genius, destitute of moral sense, and incapable of making progress in civilization or science. As plantation slaves they do their work " perhaps not better than an *orang-outang* might, with a little pains, be brought to do." [7]

These differences, Long claims, prove a difference of species. They cannot be explained as effects of climate and living conditions. In one hundred and fifty years of residence in North America the Negro has remained as black and woolly-headed as ever, except where he has mixed with the whites. Moreover, the whole analogy of nature leads one to expect a multiplicity of human species analogous to the variety of animal species and an arrangement of these human species in a graded series bridging the gap between the apes and the most perfect type of man. The facts known about the orang-outang indicate, says Long, that the creature may be a savage man. An animal which walks erect, lives in society, builds huts, learns easily to perform menial services, and shows a passion for Negro women cannot be summarily excluded from the human family. Indeed, there is not much to choose as between Hottentot and an orang-outang, nor would an orang-outang husband dishonor a Hottentot female. Too little is known of the orang-outang to render it certain that he is incapable of speech and education. No one has tried seriously to train one from infancy.

[5] *Ibid.*, 665. In his letter to the Abbé Henri Grégoire, dated Washington, 25 February, 1809, Jefferson says: " . . . whatever be their degree of talent it is no measure of their rights. Because Sir Isaac Newton was superior to others in understanding, he was not therefore lord of the person or property of others." See A. A. Lipscomb, ed., *The Writings of Thomas Jefferson* (Washington, 1903–1904), XII, 255.

[6] [Edward Long], *The History of Jamaica, or, General Survey of the Antient and Modern State of That Island: with Reflections on Its Situation, Settlements, Inhabitants, Climate, Products, Commerce, Laws, and Government* (London, 1774).

[7] [Edward Long], " Observations on the Gradation in the Scale of Being between the Human and the Brute Creation. Including Some Curious Particulars respecting Negroes," *The Columbian Magazine or Monthly Miscellany*, 2 (1788), 15.

" For my own part," concludes Long, " I conceive that probability favors the opinion, that human organs were not given him for nothing: that this race have some language by which their meaning is communicated; whether it resembles the gabbling of turkies like that of the Hottentots, or the hissing of serpents, is of very little consequence, so long as it is intelligible among themselves: nor, for what hitherto appears, do they seem at all inferior in the intellectual faculties to many of the Negroe race; with some of whom, it is credible that they have the most intimate connexion and consanguinity." [8]

But even supposing with Buffon that intellect proceeds from a principle superior to matter and that the orang-outang's brain, for all its similarity to man's is but a parody of the human, the probability is still strong that there is a natural diversity of intellectual endowment among the various types of human beings. Since the Negro resembles the orang-outang in general form and structure, is it not probable that his brain too, though similar in appearance to the white man's, does not give rise to the same effects?

The Negroe race (consisting of varieties) will then appear rising progressively in the scale of intellect, the further they mount above the orang-outang and brute creation. The system of man will seem more consistent, and the measure of it more compleat, and analagous [sic] to the harmony and order that are visible in every other line of the world's stupendous fabric . . . . The series and progression from a lump of dirt to a perfect human being is amazingly extensive; nor less so, perhaps, the interval between the latter and the most perfect angelic being, and between this being and the Deity himself. Let us shake off those clouds with which prejudice endeavours to invelope the understanding; and, exerting that freedom of thought which the Best of Beings has granted to us, let us take a noon-tide view of the human genus; and shall we say, that it is totally different from, and less perfect than, every other system of animal beings? [9]

The extracts from Long's *History of Jamaica* were followed in the next issue of the *Columbian Magazine* by a reprint of Jefferson's views on the intellectual faculties of the Negro. In May, 1788, appeared " An Answer to a Circumstance on Which Some Writers, in Defense of the Slave-Trade Have Founded Much of Its Legality." The circumstance indicated was the supposition that many of the Negroes transported from Africa as slaves were the offspring of intercourse between orang-outangs and Negroes. From this it had been argued that the institution of slavery in the West Indies had contributed indirectly toward humanizing these hybrid creatures by promoting their intercourse with the white colonists, " ' to the honour of the

[8] *Ibid.*, 74.
[9] *Ibid.*, 74–75.

human species, and to the glory of the Divine Being.' " [10] The author
of the article, who signs himself " R," is not disposed to deny that
intercourse between orang-outangs and Negroes may sometimes occur,
but he objects vehemently to the idea that these unions could produce
fertile offspring. If fertile crosses between species were possible, the
distinctions in nature would soon become effaced and the whole animal economy would be thrown into confusion. Fortunately, says
" R," the Creator has guarded against this eventuality by rendering
crosses between species sterile. Conversely, the fact that all human
beings can interbreed freely proves that they belong to a single species.
If further proof is required, it can be found in the anatomical differences between man and the apes observed by Tyson, Buffon, Camper,
and others. The absence of calf muscles and the inability of the
orang-outang to speak mark him off from man as a separate species,
a species which connects the rational to the brute creation.

In July, 1792, Benjamin Rush, a leading figure in American medical circles, entered the lists on the side of the unity of mankind by
communicating to the American Philosophical Society his " Observations Intended to Favor a Supposition That the Black Color (as it is
called) of the Negroes Is Derived from the LEPROSY." The phenomenon of albinism shows, says Rush, that skin color is often affected by
disease. If albinos are white because of a diseased condition, may not
the black skin of the Negro be produced by a similar cause? In Africa
the climate and the diet and mode of life of the Negroes make them
very susceptible to leprosy. There is a striking correspondence, moreover, between the typical Negro features and the characteristic effects
of leprosy on the human being: black skin, insensibility in the nerves,
strong venereal desires, big lips, flat noses, and woolly heads. Since
leprosy is hereditary, its effects continue from generation to generation. Perhaps, then, congenital leprosy which has lost its virulent and
infectious quality is the cause of the Negro's physical peculiarities.

If this be true, Rush goes on, " all the claims of superiority of the
whites over the blacks, on account of their color, are founded in ignorance and inhumanity." [11] There is, indeed, a sound medical reason
for discouraging interbreeding between whites and Negroes until such
time as the disease will have been cured. But there is no basis for
denying the specific unity or the natural equality of all human beings.

[10] " R.," " An Answer to a Circumstance on Which Some Writers, in Defence of
the Slave-Trade, Have Founded Much of Its Legality," *Columbian Magazine*, 2
(1788), 266.
[11] Benjamin Rush, " Observations Intended to Favor a Supposition That the
Black Color (As It Is Called) of the Negroes is Derived from the LEPROSY," *Trans.
Amer. Philos. Soc.*, 4 (1799), 295.

The racial issue becomes a medical problem of discovering a cure for leprosy. Thus, the leprosy hypothesis not only confirms revealed anthropology but also removes a barrier to the exercise of Christian benevolence.

Rush's " Observations " were published in the *Transactions* of the American Philosophical Society in 1799. In the same year appeared an English work which soon played an important part in the American controversy concerning the Negro, providing an arsenal of arguments for those who would assign him an inferior rank in the scale of being. This was Charles White's *Account of the Regular Gradation in Man, and in Different Animals and Vegetables.* In it the author, a Manchester physician, disclaims any purpose to justify Negro slavery. His only interest, he declares, is to investigate nature and discover her laws. " Nature exhibits to our view an immense chain of beings, endued with various degrees of intelligence and active powers suited to their stations in the general system." [12] The gradation of natural forms is not simply an observed fact; it is a law of nature. Hence, says White, Lord Monboddo's notion that some human beings have tails is patently absurd, for such a condition would break nature's law of gradation.

The idea that the principle of gradation applies to human as well as to animal types came to White upon hearing the British anatomist John Hunter discuss the gradation of skulls in some lectures on midwifery. Hunter illustrated his remarks with the skulls of a European, an Asiatic, an American, an African, a monkey, and a dog. It occurred to White that " nature would not employ gradation in one instance only, but would adopt it as a general principle." He undertook, therefore, to compare several characters of Europeans and Negroes to see whether in every case the Negro character was intermediate between that of an ape and that of a European. Upon comparing a Negro skeleton with several European skeletons, he discovered that the Negro skeleton had longer arm bones and a flatter arch in the foot. Extending his comparisons to living persons, he became convinced of the existence of constant constitutional differences between the Negro and the European in cartilages, muscles, tendons, skin, hair, sweat, odor, size of brain, reason, speech, and language, as well as in the skeleton. Even the body lice proved different. He concluded that in mankind, as in all nature, there is a steady gradation of forms, leading in the case of man from the ape-like Negro to the European.

Ascending the line of gradation, we come at last to the white European;

[12] Charles White, *An Account of the Regular Gradation in Man, and in Different Animals and Vegetables; and from the Former to the Latter* (London, 1799), 1.

who being most removed from the brute creation, may, on that account, be considered as the most beautiful of the human race. No one will doubt his superiority in intellectual powers; and I believe it will be found that his capacity is naturally superior also to that of every other man. Where shall we find, unless in the European, that nobly arched head, containing such a quantity of brain, and supported by a hollow conical pillar, entering its centre? Where the perpendicular face, the prominent nose, and round projecting chin? Where that variety of features, and fulness of expression; those long, flowing, graceful ringlets; that majestic beard, those rosy cheeks and coral lips? In what other quarter of the globe shall we find the blush that overspreads the soft features of the beautiful women of Europe, that emblem of modesty, of delicate feelings, and of sense. Where that nice expression of amiable and softer passions in the countenance; and that general elegance of features and complexion? Where, except on the bosom of the European woman, two such plump and snowy white hemispheres, tipt with vermillion? [13]

Having described the characteristic differences between Negro and European, White turns to the problem of accounting for them. He is certain that they cannot be explained by climate and mode of life, since skeletal formations are largely removed from these influences. Even color is not permanently affected by climate. One hundred and fifty years of residence in North America have not blanched the Negro's skin. If, says White, the Reverend Samuel Stanhope Smith, " one of the latest and ablest writers who attribute the color of the human race to climate," would look into the cases he reports of modification of Negro characters in America, he would discover that they result from miscegenation. If he would then consider the distribution of quadrupeds and human beings between the Old and the New Worlds, he would realize that the types of men and animals found in America must have been placed there in the beginning by the hand of the Creator.

In November, 1808, the medical students of the College of Physicians and Surgeons in New York were introduced to the controversy concerning the unity of mankind and the Negro's place in nature by their professor of anatomy, John Augustine Smith, a young man recently returned from his studies in London. Smith's lecture appeared in the *New York Medical and Philosophical Journal and Review* in the following year.[14] The lecturer begins by disclaiming any intention to settle the question whether the observable differences

13 *Ibid.*, 134–135.

14 John Augustine Smith, " A Lecture Introductory to the Second Course of Anatomical Instruction in the College of Physicians and Surgeons for the State of New York," *The New York Medical and Philosophical Journal and Review,* 1 (1809), 32–48.

among men are native and original or produced by climate and mode of life. He proposes instead to show that the European is superior in anatomical structure to the Asiatic, the American Indian, and the African in the sense of being farther removed from the brute creation. To this end, he undertakes to prove that the European and the Negro constitute the two extreme types in the scale of human anatomy.

As if to create a presumption in favor of his thesis, Smith turns for a moment to the subject of man's place in nature. He adopts Buffon's idea of a gradation of forms descending from man to the polyp and illustrates it with reference to Camper's facial angle and Cuvier's statistics on the relative proportions of face and cranium in man, orang-outang, and monkey. He states that he has tested a collection of human skulls in his own possession by these criteria and found them to form a series rising from the Negro to the European. He laments with Jefferson the black man's inability to blush and recapitulates White's table of anatomical differences between European and Negro.

He then turns to the problem of accounting for these differences. Scripture, he declares, states incontrovertibly that all mankind are offshoots of one stock, but those writers who have attempted to corroborate revelation by attributing the differences among men to the agency of climate and the state of society have injured both science and religion. Their works are distinguished more for piety than for sound philosophy. The Reverend Samuel Stanhope Smith displays a vast ignorance of anatomy in his discussion of pigmentation and grossly exaggerates the correlation between complexion and climate. Moreover, even supposing that climate can permanently alter complexion, how can it affect the structure of the bones? The reverend doctor's supposition that cold enlarges the heads of the Laplanders by contracting their faces and limbs is ludicrous. The causes of most variations in the human form being unknown, it is better to confess one's ignorance than to invent preposterous explanations. On this note of humility Smith closes the lecture, leaving his audience to form their own conclusions. "Different minds are satisfied with different degrees of evidence; and far be it from me to fix the bounds of your faith."

In 1810 Samuel Stanhope Smith returned to the fray with a second, considerably enlarged edition of his *Essay,* to which he appended some remarks on the arguments advanced by White, J. A. Smith, and Jefferson concerning the Negro. In these addenda he concedes that White's description of the African Negro is fairly accurate. He argues, however, that climate and mode of life have made the Negro what he is and hence are capable of making him a quite different creature. In proof of this contention he offers his own observations and measurements on the Negroes of Princeton, many of whom he finds as well-formed as the laboring classes of Europe. The anatomical differences *within* the white and the black races are more striking than those *between* them, says Smith. As for the Negro's black color, it must be expected to change very slowly. In one case, however, a Maryland Negro named Henry Moss turned from black to white in the course of a lifetime.

> The change commenced about the abdomen, and gradually extended over different parts of the body, till, at the end of seven years, the period at which I saw him, the white had already overspread the greater portion of his skin. It had nothing of the appearance of a sickly or albino hue, as if it had been the effect of a disease. He was a vigorous and active man; and had never suffered any disease either at the commencement or during the progress of the change.[15]

This case, argues Smith, disposes of the notion that the Negro is a species immutably different from the European.

He then turns his attention to his countryman of the same name, Dr. J. A. Smith. He repays the young doctor's insults in kind, quoting at length from Blumenbach's treatise to show that his critic cannot be so well acquainted with that work as he pretends to be. " Can it be because Blumenbach's work is written in Latin! " Why, if the young professor of anatomy has really read Blumenbach, does he not inform his students that Blumenbach is highly skeptical concerning Camper's theory of gradation in the facial angle, instead of leaving them to infer that this hypothesis is generally accepted in the scientific world. The Negroes of Princeton, Smith declares, exhibit a range of variation from seventy to seventy-eight degrees in their facial angles. Many of them have high and prominent foreheads. Who, then, is the smatterer in philosophy, the Princeton Smith or the New York Smith? The young doctor's ignorance can be forgiven but not so the disingenuous manner in which he appeals to the authority of Scripture to settle the question of the unity or diversity of mankind. It is a favorite trick of infidels to assert the infallibility of Scripture at the same time that they labor to show that the facts cannot be reconciled with it. " These puny and half-learned scientists, who affect to treat with sarcastic leer the oracles of God, would do well

[15] Samuel Stanhope Smith, *An Essay on the Causes of the Variety of Complexion and Figure in the Human Species. To Which Are Added, Animadversions on Certain Remarks Made on the First Edition of This Essay, by Mr. Charles White . . . Also, Strictures on Lord Kaims' Discourse on the Original Diversity of Mankind. And an Appendix* (2nd ed., New Brunswick, 1810), 92–93.

to remember, if they are susceptible to advice, or of shame, with what modesty and humility of heart those sublime and genuine sons of nature, from Newton, down to Sir William Jones have thought it their glory to submit their superior minds to that wisdom which came down from heaven." [16]

Toward Jefferson, Smith is more lenient. He observes that the arguments by which Jefferson defends the Indian and the Anglo-American from the charge of mental and physical debility apply with equal force to the Negro. Indeed, they apply with greater force, since the Negro has the added disadvantage of being a slave. No wonder he has not produced noble flights of oratory. The Indians themselves degenerate into lazy, wretched, demoralized creatures when subjected to the influences of civilization. " They afford a proof of the deterioration of the mental faculties which may be produced by certain states of society, which ought to make a philosopher cautious of proscribing any race of men from the class of human beings, merely because their unfortunate condition has presented to them no incentives to awaken genius, or afforded no opportunities to display its powers." [17]

Not long after Smith's second edition appeared, it was reviewed in the *Medical Repository,* published in New York City by Dr. Samuel Latham Mitchill and colleagues. The review, though ostensibly laudatory, has an undertone of antagonism. It begins with a long summary of the Biblical account of man's origin and goes on to state that Smith is a firm believer in the veracity of Scripture, bent on corroborating Genesis by showing that all mankind can be derived from a single stock. The reviewers agree that this hypothesis is more defensible philosophically than the gratuitous assumption of several species of mankind, but they object to limiting the causes of human diversity to the agency of climate and mode of life. The most important single source of variety in successive generations is the mechanism of heredity, say the reviewers. " Enough for our present purposes is the statement of the fact, established on broad induction, ' that a man and woman may beget a child of a different complexion from either of the parents, and the complexion of the offspring may be perpetuated in his or her descendants.' " [18] Secondly, there may

---

[16] *Ibid.,* 305.

[17] *Ibid.,* 270.

[18] *Medical Repository,* 15 (1812), 159. See also *ib.,* 9 (1806), 64–70, in which the editors of the *Repository* review with approval Felix d'Azara's *Essays on the Natural History of the Quadrupeds of the Province of Paraguay,* M. Moreau-Saint-Méry, tr. 2 vols. (Paris, 1801). Say the reviewers: " . . . he traces the variegated forms of the hair, skin, and exterior parts of man and other animals, to a generative agency, or operation coeval with the production of the creature."

have been differences in " the primitive family " which were propagated to their posterity. Thirdly, the power of imitation operates powerfully to recreate in each generation family, national, and other group resemblances. The agency of climate is thus but one, and by no means the most important, source of variation in man.

This argument suggests that there were those in the United States who questioned the careless environmentalism of the day, who doubted the transmissibility of acquired characters and sought the secret of race formation in the unpredictable functioning of the mechanism of heredity. The problem from this point of view was to find some selective agency by which random heredity variation could eventuate in the production of stable types. When the Englishman Prichard attempted a solution of this problem in 1813, he found Samuel Stanhope Smith's notion of the selective influence of cultural standards a considerable help. By assuming the operation of a " natural standard of human beauty " in the choice of marriage partners Prichard thought to account for " the transmutation of the characters of the Negro into those of the European, or the evolution of white varieties in black races of men." [19] He thus opened the way to conceiving the process of race formation as a progress from rude and savage beginnings rather than as a decline from a perfect model of the species, to regarding Negroid traits as the traits of the human species at an early stage in its development. It was an Anglo-American, William Wells, however, who hit upon the idea of struggle for existence and survival of the fittest as the means whereby stable varieties might result from the sporting of the generative mechanism. His investigations into a case of a white woman with patches of black skin confirmed him in the opinion that difference of skin color was no sure proof of a difference of species and that the dark hue of the Negro was not produced by long exposure to the tropical sun. He was impressed with the susceptibility of both Negroes and whites to disease when they were transplanted to unaccustomed climates. Perhaps, he suggested, the prevalence of dark-skinned people in Africa could be explained by assuming an unknown cause correlating darkness of skin color with resistance to African diseases. If such were the case, those tribes with an hereditary tendency to dark skin would eventually drive out those tending toward a fair complexion. Thus, different human types might come to predominate in different regions of the earth by a process of natural selection. As to Prichard's

[19] James Cowles Prichard, *Researches into the Physical History of Man* (London, 1813), 233. Prichard makes specific acknowledgment of Smith's suggestions along this line (p. 41, note a).

idea that men become light-skinned in proportion as they become civilized, Wells was in doubt. He agreed that the features and woolly hair of Negroes were "somehow connected with their low state of civilization." But whether they were connected as *effects* of that low state or rather, in some obscure way, as *causes* of its continuance he was not prepared to say.[20]

Several conclusions may be drawn from the foregoing review of opinions concerning the Negro's place in nature. In the first place, the tendency to look to anthropology for a "scientific" defense of the institution of slavery, though clearly present in the years before 1815, had not yet become a major theme in American anthropology. Instead, the chief extra-scientific source of interest in the question of the Negro's origin and characteristics was its bearing on the credibility of revealed religion. The issue forced the defenders of Scripture to argue the mutability of the human constitution, while their theologically heterodox opponents were appealing to the old notion of the great chain of being—a highly conservative notion, scientifically speaking. Actually, the monogenists were as convinced of the stability and wise design of nature as their polygenist opponents, but the necessity which they felt to discover mechanisms whereby the variety of human types might have evolved in a few thousand years was bound, in the long run, to influence speculations concerning the nature and stability of species. Long before the origin of species had become a scientific problem in biology the related problem of race formation was challenging the best efforts of monogenist anthropologists. These efforts produced, among other ideas, the related concepts of random variation and natural selection with which Darwin was later to revive the languishing "development hypothesis."[21]

University of Wisconsin.

[20] William Wells, "An Account of a Female of the White Race of Mankind, Part of Whose Skin Resembles That of a Negro; with Some Observations on the Causes of the Differences in Color and Form between the White and Negro Races of Men," appended to *Two Essays: One upon Single Vision with Two Eyes; the Other on Dew* . . . (London, 1818), 425–439. Wells' "Account" was submitted to the Royal Society in 1813 but not published until 1818.

[21] This is not to say that Wells was the first to advance ideas of this kind. On the history of speculation along this line, see Conway Zirkle, "Natural Selection before the 'Origin of Species,'" *Proceedings Amer. Philos. Soc.*, 84 (1941), 71–123. Also Arthur O. Lovejoy, "Some Eighteenth Century Evolutionists," *Popular Science Monthly*, 65 (1904), 238–251, 323–340. The present article is not the place for an extended discussion of the relation of theories of race formation to the development of the idea of organic evolution. The author intends, however, to develop the subject more fully in a work now in progress, to be entitled *The Genesis of the Evolutionary Idea*.

VIII

DR. BENJAMIN RUSH AND THE NEGRO

By Donald J. D'Elia

"I love even the name of Africa," declared Benjamin Rush in 1788: these words of the co-founder, secretary, and later president (1803–13) of America's first abolitionist society (in Pennsylvania) were more than rhetorical.[1] For Rush realized that his revolutionary program of social, political, and religious reform, a program dramatized by his signing the Declaration of Independence, required the abolition of slavery.[2] Anything less than freedom for all men, black and white, would, he knew, give the lie to the republican idealism of '76. This Rush believed with great certainty. And so from that day in 1766 when, bound for studies at Edinburgh, he, a "free-born son of liberty," was outraged by the sight of a hundred slave ships in Liverpool harbor, to his death in 1813, Rush dedicated himself to Negro freedom and prosperity in a free America.[3]

If there was any one person who inspired Rush's crusade against slavery it was Anthony Benezet. The gentle Quaker reformer and philanthropist was to young Dr. Rush, back in his native Philadelphia in 1769 after study abroad, one of the most disinterested men of all time. Friend Anthony Benezet urged Rush to publish his thoughts on slavery, and the young physician's *An Address to the Inhabitants of the British Settlements in America, upon Slave-Keeping* appeared in Philadelphia, Boston, and New York in 1773. The *Address* was the first of many attacks by Rush on the social evils of his day, and perhaps his best.[4] And to his lifelong campaign against slavery and his great work in promoting the welfare of the Negro, the *Address* was to be an inspiring monument.

Negroes, Dr. Rush argued scientifically, were not by nature intellectually and morally inferior. Any apparent evidence to the contrary was only the perverted expression of slavery, which "is so foreign to the human mind, that the moral faculties, as well as those of the understanding are debased, and rendered torpid by it." He continued in the *Address*:

All the vices which are charged upon the Negroes in the southern colonies and the West-Indies, such as Idleness, Treachery, Theft, and the like, are the

[1]Rush to Jeremy Belknap, August 19, 1788, Lyman H. Butterfield, ed., *Letters of Benjamin Rush* (2 vols., Princeton, 1951), I, 482. Rush (1746–1813) and James Pemberton (1723–1809), the Quaker philanthropist, were the chief organizers of the Pennsylvania Society for Promoting the Abolition of Slavery, and the Relief of Free Negroes Unlawfully Held in Bondage (1774).

[2]The standard biography is Nathan G. Goodman, *Benjamin Rush, Physician and Citizen, 1746–1813* (Philadelphia, 1934). L. H. Butterfield's editorial commentary on Rush's letters and his "Benjamin Rush as a Promoter of Useful Knowledge," Proc. American Philosophical Soc., XCII (March 8, 1948), 26–36, are indispensable to what follows.

[3]Rush, "Journal Commencing Aug. 31, 1766," Indiana University MS, (Oct. 28, 1766), 13.

[4]Rush to Barbeu Dubourg, April 29, 1773, and to Granville Sharp, May 1, 1773, *Rush Letters*, I, 76, 80–81; George S. Brookes, *Friend Anthony Benezet* (Philadelphia, 1937), 93.

genuine offspring of slavery, and serve as an argument to prove that they were not intended by Providence for it.[5]

Science, then, made clear that human bondage was monstrous and that it not only vitiated the body but the faculties as well.[6] Restore the mind and the body to their natural state of freedom, the young medical philosopher asserted, and the vices of slavery would inevitably disappear and a new, more virtuous humanity emerge.

Rush was not content with mere professions of equality, however noble. Facts were what he needed, and in his early pamphlet on slavery and in later writings he marshalled all that he could find to prove the Negro's fitness for civilized society. Even as he wrote in 1773, the Negro poet Phillis Wheatley was charming Boston audiences with her literary gifts. The girl, it was true, was free and talented—no average Negro in America—but Rush believed that she shared with the most primitive African in the slave trade and with all human beings the inborn principles of taste and morality, which slavery corrupted and perverted, yet could not destroy. For God Himself had given men and women of every color a native appreciation of the sublime and the beautiful.[7]

Certainly, Rush argued, the only hope for the Negro (and for the moral reformation of the white society that had enslaved him) was emancipation and education. Separately emancipation and education were powerless to effect real and lasting changes in the Negro's status. What they could accomplish together was strikingly evident in the case of Rush's friend and brother physician, James Durham, about whom Rush wrote in the *American Museum*:

I have conversed with him upon most of the acute and epidemic diseases of the country where he lives, and was pleased to find him perfectly acquainted with the modern simple mode of practice in those diseases. I expected to have suggested some new medicines to him, but he suggested many more to me. He is very modest and engaging in his manners. He speaks French fluently and has some knowledge of the Spanish language.[8]

As a slave boy in Philadelphia, Dr. Durham had been educated in reading, writing, and the Christian religion; then he had served as a kind of apprentice under three physicians, the last finally allowing him to purchase his freedom.[9] Of course Rush, as secretary of the Pennsylvania Abolition Society and

---

[5]*An Address to the Inhabitants of the British Settlements in America, upon Slave-Keeping* (Philadelphia, 1773), 2–3.

[6]Rush to Granville Sharp, July 9, 1774, John A. Woods, ed., "The Correspondence of Benjamin Rush and Granville Sharp 1773–1809," *Journal of American Studies*, I (April 1967), 6–7, hereafter "The Correspondence."

[7]*An Address to the Inhabitants of the British Settlements in America, upon Slave-Keeping*, 2; Rush to Granville Sharp, July 9, 1774, Woods, ed., "The Correspondence," 6–7. Phillis Wheatley's *Poems on Various Subjects, Religious and Moral* appeared in 1773 (*DAB*).

[8]Rush to the Pennsylvania Abolition Society, Nov. 14, 1788, *Rush Letters*, I, 497; this letter was printed in *The American Museum*, V (Jan. 1789), 61–62. Another letter by Rush, submitted at the same time to the Society, concerned the Negro slave prodigy, Thomas Fuller, the illiterate "African Calculator." See Prof. Butterfield's note, *Rush Letters*, I, 497–498.   [9]*Ibid.*, 497.

a leading doctor and medical teacher, relished this opportunity to inform the public of a former slave's competence in the practice of medicine. Later, in the terrible yellow fever epidemic of 1793, when Rush was in dire need of help in treating the sick, and Durham was absent, other black men assisted him in battling death. Male nurses like the faithful Marcus demonstrated to him anew that the Negro was inferior in neither skill nor courage.

Marcus, Rush's friend and household servant, was no Dr. Durham. But his value to Rush and the ailing humanity of Philadelphia in the great plague of 1793 is evident in letter after letter from Rush to his wife, who was safely in New Jersey. Weak himself with the fever, Rush wrote on September 21 of the comforting presence of his devoted Negro assistant:

Marcus has not, like Briarius, a hundred hands, but he can turn his two hands to a hundred different things. He puts up powders, spreads blisters, and gives clysters equal to any apothecary in town.[10]

And a month later, now seriously ill but improving under Marcus' tender care, the grateful Doctor confided to Mrs. Rush that "with a little instruction" Marcus "would exceed many of our bark and wine doctors in the treatment of the present fever."[11] Rush owed his life to Marcus, just as Marcus and Peter, a little mulatto servant boy who assisted Rush in treating fever victims, owed their lives to him.[12] To Rush this was dramatic evidence of the moral equality of all men!

Outside his household but dear to him as friends and humanitarians were Absalom Jones, Richard Allen, and William Gray, leaders of the Negro community in Philadelphia. It was they who nobly joined the battle against yellow fever at Rush's request by providing Negro nurses and workers for the stricken city.[13] After the deadly and seemingly interminable epidemic was over, Rush once again took up his pen to defend the Negro—this time because of the charge that the black nurses had exploited the helpless and dying whites they had attended during the crisis. In a letter to Mathew Carey, who was preparing an account of the fever, Rush tried to set the record straight:

In procuring nurses for the sick, Wm. Grey and Absalom Jones were indefatigable, often sacrificing for that purpose whole nights of sleep without the least compensation. Richard Allen was extremely useful in performing the mournful duties which were connected with burying the dead. Many of the black nurses it is true were ignorant, and some of them were negligent, but many of them did their duty to the sick with a degree of patience and tenderness that did them great credit.[14]

[10]Rush to Mrs. Rush, *ibid.*, II, 673. The best account of the yellow fever epidemic is John H. Powell, *Bring Out Your Dead; The Great Plague of Yellow Fever in Philadelphia in 1793* (Philadelphia, 1949).

[11]Rush to Mrs. Rush, Oct. 14, 1793, *Rush Letters,* II, 716.

[12]*Ibid.,* Sept. 22, 1793, Oct. 17, 1793, 674–675, 717; Powell, 117.

[13]Rush to Mathew Carey, Oct. 29, 1793, *Rush Letters,* II, 731–32; George W. Corner, ed., *The Autobiography of Benjamin Rush: His "Travels through Life" Together with His Commonplace Book for 1789–1813* (Princeton, 1948), 221 and Dr. Corner's note; Powell, 94–101.

[14]Rush to Mathew Carey, Oct. 29, 1793, *Rush Letters,* II, 731–732; also, Rush's classic *An Account of the Bilious Remitting Yellow Fever, As It Appeared in the City of Philadelphia, in the year 1793* (Philadelphia, 1794) for his praise of the Negroes.

What made their conduct even more exemplary, Rush noted dramatically, was the discovery that Negroes did not possess the immunity to yellow fever that Rush himself and the public had attributed to them during the epidemic.[15]

Working together in great humanitarian causes was not new to Rush, Jones, Allen, and Gray. At the very time the fever raged these men and John Nicholson, another white philanthropist, were seeing their dream of an African church in Philadelphia come true. The African Episcopal Church of St. Thomas, dedicated on August 22, 1793, was America's first Negro church; and for Rush, who had done so much to bring it about, the event marked a turning point in the history of the Negro's quest for freedom.[16] He and others had pioneered the antislavery movement which had won a triumph in 1780 with the passage (in Pennsylvania) of the nation's first abolition law.[17] To add to her honor, Rush's state now had a church for the advancement of her freedmen in religion and morals.

The revolutionary significance which Rush attached to the Negroes' having their own church is nowhere better expressed than in his commonplace book:

I conceive it will collect many hundred Blacks together on Sundays who now spend that day in idleness. It may be followed by churches upon a similar plan in other States, and who knows but it may be the means of sending the gospel to Africa, as the American Revolution sent liberty to Europe? Then perhaps the Africans in America may say to those who brought them here as slaves, what Joseph said to his brethren when they condemned themselves for selling him into Egypt.[18]

Indeed, there was no doubt in Rush's mind that what he called the "Spirit of the Gospel" was regenerating the world in his time: that just as the political evil of monarchy had been destroyed by the divinely commissioned American Revolution, in which Rush himself had so actively participated, so the moral and social evil of slavery was being destroyed, too, by a merciful God acting through the agency of Rush and other reformers. The historic ignorance and misery of the Negroes, accordingly, were predestined to give way before the civilizing forces of religion and education, which God in His infinite wisdom had released in the epoch of the American Revolution. Rush believed that the United States was the center from which God was reforming the world through perfected reason and progressive revelation.[19]

[15]Rush to Mathew Carey, Oct. 29, 1793, *Rush Letters*, II, 731–732; Powell, 95.

[16]Rush to John Nicholson, Nov. 28, 1792, to Mrs. Rush, July 16, 1791, August 22, 1793, and to John Nicholson, August 12, 1793, Rush *Letters*, I, 624, 599–600, II, 639–640, 636–637; Corner, 202–203.

[17]Ira V. Brown, *Pennsylvania Reformers: from Penn to Pinchot* (University Park, 1966), 7.

[18]"Now therefore be not grieved, nor angry with yourselves, that ye sold me hither: for God did send me before you to preserve life." Genesis XLV, 5; Corner, 202–203; Rush to Granville Sharp, August 1791, *Rush Letters*, I, 608–609.

[19]Rush to Jeremy Belknap, June 21, 1792, to Rev. Elhanan Winchester, Nov. 12, 1791, and to Thomas Jefferson, August 22, 1800; *ibid.*, I, 620–621, 611–612; II, 820–821; Rush to Granville Sharp, Oct. 29, 1773, "The Correspondence," 3; Corner, 161–162. Rush, "Lectures on Pathology. Influence of Government upon Health," Library Company of Philadelphia, Rush MSS (Yi2/7396/F22), 312–314.

That America was chosen by God as the place for man's ultimate deliverance from slavery was evidenced, Rush believed, in the New World's providing a religious and political sanctuary for Europeans from earliest times. Closer to his own day, Quaker antislavery reformers and educators of the Negro like John Woolman and Anthony Benezet manifested in their work the special divine presence. Rush himself had written his *Address* under the spell of Benezet and, again because of the Quaker's influence, had opened a lifelong correspondence with Granville Sharp, the English abolitionist.[20] To Sharp, in fact, he wrote excitedly of the Continental Congress's pledge of October 1774 *"never* to import any more slaves into America." "This resolution does our Congress the more honor," he observed with transparent pride, "as it was proposed and defended entirely upon *moral* and not political principles."[21] Congress's motives in the Continental Association were, of course, not so simple and noble, but Rush viewed the resolution idealistically as a sign of his country's moral regeneration:

Thus have we stopped the avenue of a vice which we have good reason to fear brought down the vengeance of Heaven upon our country—a vice so infinite in its mischief upon the liberty, morals and happiness of a people that no wisdom, or power could have established an empire which it would not have destroyed. We have now *turned from our wickedness.* Our next step we hope will be to do that *which is lawful and right.* The emancipation of slaves in America will now be attended with but few difficulties except such as arise from instructions given to our Governors, not to favour laws made for that purpose.[22]

There was hope, Rush went on, even the probability that, should Americans persevere in this antislavery feeling, Negro bondage would disappear from the continent in forty years.[23] Then Britain's shame as the creator of the African Company would be complete.[24] The very climate and rich soil of the slave colonies seemed to cooperate with the new moral purpose in that forced labor was unnecessary in the divine economy. "The natural fertility of the earth in all warm countries," Rush argued teleologically, "shows that heaven never intended hard labor to be the portion of man in such countries."[25]

Rush believed, too, that the hand of God could be seen in the Declaration of Independence, which he signed as a delegate from Pennsylvania. And for him there was absolutely no doubt that the Negro possessed (and had been denied) the natural rights which the Declaration celebrated. So certain was Rush of divine wrath at the Anglo-American enslavement of the Negro that he fearfully suggested that a bloody civil war might be necessary "to expiate their guilt."[26]

The triumph of American arms in 1783 was also unmistakable evidence to

[20]Rush to Granville Sharp, May 1, 1773, "The Correspondence," 2; Rush to Thomas Jefferson, Oct. 6, 1800 and to Mrs. Rush, June 1, 1776, *Rush Letters,* II, 825–826, I, 102; Rush, *An Address to the Inhabitants,* 28.

[21]Rush to Granville Sharp, Nov. 1, 1774, "The Correspondence," 13.   [22]*Ibid.*   [23]*Ibid.*

[24]Cf. Rush, *An Address to the Inhabitants,* 21; Rush to Nathanael Greene, Sept. 16, 1782, *Rush Letters,* I, 286.   [25]*Ibid.;* Rush, *An Address to the Inhabitants,* 8.

[26]Corner, 119; Rush, *An Address to the Inhabitants,* 7, 30; Rush to Nathanael Greene, Sept. 16, 1782, *Rush Letters,* I, 286; Rush to Granville Sharp, July 9, 1774, "The Correspondence," 8; Rush, *An Address to the Inhabitants,* 30.

Rush of God's being on the side of freedom—for black and white. "I remember the time (about 15 years ago)," he wrote to Granville Sharp in November, "when the advocates for the poor Africans were treated as fanatics, and considered as the disturbers of the peace of society. At present they are considered as the benefactors of mankind and the man who dares say a word in favor of reducing our black brethren to slavery is listned (sic) to with horror, and his company avoided by every body."[27] This was not true, he hastened to admit, in South Carolina. But there and in the other southern states reason and Christianity were prevented from operating successfully by a collective mental disease which Rush, in his investigations as a medical philosopher, called "negromania."[28]

A form of madness, which in Dr. Rush's broad definition meant "a want of perception, or an undue perception of truth, duty, or interest," negromania had before the Revolution affected people in all parts of the country. Now, in 1783, the disorder was prevalent only in the South. Negromaniacs in their collective illness and misery failed to perceive that Negro slavery violated the laws of nature and God and that the interest, health, and happiness of white Southerners lay in their own free honest labor.[29] Any healthy-minded person could see that God had not created the Africans for hard work. It was obvious to any man of sound perceptions that the Divine Governor of the universe had placed Africans in easy tropical surroundings and fitted them only for light employments. In seven years, though, the revolutionary Doctor was confident, the negromania could be cured, at least in South Carolina.[30]

Rush's faith in the Revolution as the harbinger of an age of freedom and equality among black and white seemed to be gloriously confirmed when in September 1787 the proposed Federal Constitution appeared to prohibit the importation of slaves, beginning in 1808. Later as a member of the Pennsylvania state convention to consider ratification of the Constitution, he would have much to do with its acceptance in his home state. But even before ratification Rush proudly wrote to his English abolitionist friend, John Coakley Lettsom, of his native province's role in ending the slave trade:

To the influence of Pennsylvania chiefly is to be ascribed the prevalence of sentiments favorable to African liberty in every part of the United States. You will see a proof of their operation in the new Constitution of the United States. In the year one thousand seven hundred and eight (sic) there will be an end of the African trade in America.[31]

[27]Rush to Granville Sharp, April 7, 1783, and his November 28th letter from which the quotation is taken, "The Correspondence," 17, 20; Corner, 161–162.

[28]Rush to Granville Sharp, Nov. 28, 1783, "The Correspondence," 20; Rush, "On the Different Species of Mania," D. D. Runes, ed., *The Selected Writings of Benjamin Rush* (New York, 1947), 212–13. This edition of Rush's writings should be used only when absolutely necessary—as in this instance—and with extreme caution; see L. H. Butterfield, "The Reputation of Benjamin Rush," *Pennsylvania History*, XVII (1950), 19.

[29]Rush, "On the Different Species of Mania," 212–13; Rush to Granville Sharp, Nov. 28, 1783, "The Correspondence," 20; Rush, *An Address to the Inhabitants*, 7–8.

[30]Rush to Granville Sharp, Nov. 28, 1783, "The Correspondence," 20.

[31]Goodman, *Benjamin Rush*, 78; Rush to John Coakley Lettsom, Sept. 28, 1787, and to James Madison, Feb. 27, 1790, *Rush Letters*, I, 442, 541.

So pervasive was the spirit of liberality and humanity among all the framers of the Constitution, Rush triumphantly declared, that nowhere did the words "slaves" or "Negroes" appear in the great document. The use of those ugly words, it was agreed, would serve only to "contaminate the glorious fabric of American liberty and government."[32]

By December 25, 1787 Rush had seen his early optimism for the Constitution's adoption redeemed. Delaware, Pennsylvania, and New Jersey had by now ratified and hopes were high for general adoption by the states. Rush was ecstatic at the thought that the slave trade was doomed in America. "O! Virtue, Virtue, who would not follow thee blindfold? The prospect of this glorious event more than repays me for all the persecution and slander to which my principles and publications exposed me about 16 or 17 years ago."[33] With the abolition of the slave trade assured and the revolutionary spirit of liberty becoming everywhere more powerful and obvious, Rush directed his energies to destroying slavery itself, and to ameliorating the Negro's miserable condition and preparing him for real social and political equality.

Rush, a physician and medical teacher as well as a humanitarian, was convinced that slavery was physically and morally injurious to the Negro. This was so despite proslavery arguments that the Negro was merry, as could be seen in his singing and dancing, and therefore perfectly happy. The Negro slave was merry, true, but his mirth had nothing to do with happiness. The Africans' merry singing and dancing were, in fact, "physical symptoms of melancholy or madness, and therefore are certain proofs of their misery." This was science—not a slave-master's fancy. The life and health of man, Rush's science and revealed religion confirmed, depended upon the natural stimulus of liberty. Slavery deprived man of liberty which, like the other natural stimuli of food, clothing, and fuel, was essential to life and health. Without liberty there was only fear, which was destructive of life. No wonder, then, that slaves suffered from peculiar disorders of mind and body like melancholy, lockjaw, the many dietary diseases, and dangerous child-bearing complications. Christianity and natural reason should be outraged by such unnecessary human misery![34]

A practicable and God-given way of helping to end slavery, Rush believed, was to be found in the manufacture and use of American maple sugar rather than West Indian slave-produced cane sugar. "Whoever considers that the gift of the sugar maple trees is from a benevolent Providence," he wrote

[32]Rush to John Coakley Lettsom, Sept. 28, 1787, *ibid.*, 442.

[33]Rush to Elizabeth Graeme Ferguson, Dec. 25, 1787, *ibid.*, 446–447; Wayland F. Dunaway, *A History of Pennsylvania* (2d ed.; Englewood Cliffs, 1961), 190; Sylvester K. Stevens, *Pennsylvania: Birthplace of a Nation* (New York, 1964), 121.

[34]Rush to Jeremy Belknap, May 6, 1788, and to John Coakley Lettsom, April 21, 1788, *Rush Letters,* I, 460, 457–458. For the quotation on singing and dancing as symptomatic of melancholy, see *ibid.,* 458–459. In his famous *Medical Inquiries and Observations upon the Diseases of the Mind* (Philadelphia, 1812), 41, Dr. Rush again noted a connection between Negro insanity and "the toils of perpetual slavery." In the same work, 39, he observed that "fear often produces madness," but his most elaborate discussion of this idea and the natural stimulus of liberty is to be found in "An Inquiry into the Cause of Animal Life in Three Lectures," Rush, *Medical Inquiries and Observations* (5th ed.; 2 vols., Philadelphia, 1818), I, 39, 13, *et passim.*

Thomas Jefferson, who was much interested in the project,

that we have many millions of acres in our country covered with them, that the tree is improved by repeated tappings, and that the sugar is obtained by the frugal labor of a farmer's family, and at the same time considers the labor of cultivating the sugar cane, the capitals sunk in sugar works, the first cost of slaves and cattle, the expenses of provisions of both of them, and in some instances the additional expense of conveying the sugar to market in all the West-India Islands, will not hesitate in believing that the maple sugar may be manufactured much cheaper and sold at a *less price* than that which is made in the West-Indies.[35]

What this meant in Rush's teleological view was that God had planned free maple sugar to replace slave cane sugar at this revolutionary time in the history of the world. "In contemplating the present opening prospects in human affairs," he concluded his letter,

I am led to expect that a material part of the general happiness which Heaven seems to have prepared for mankind will be derived from the manufactory and general use of maple sugar, for the benefits which I flatter myself are to result from it will not be confined to our own country. They will I hope extend themselves to the interests of humanity in the West-Indies. With this view of the subject of this letter, I cannot help contemplating a sugar maple tree with a species of affection and even veneration, for I have persuaded myself to behold in it the happy means of rendering the commerce and slavery of our African brethren in the sugar islands as unnecessary as it has always been inhuman and unjust.[36]

Here certainly was a workable program of undermining the economic foundations of slavery.

Negroes, though rescued from slavery and unnatural fear, needed special care, Rush held. He observed of the almost 3,000 freedmen in Philadelphia in 1791 that they were "still in a state of depression, arising chiefly from their being deprived of the means of regular education and religious instruction."[37] The fine educational work of Anthony Benezet and the other Quakers notwithstanding, it was imperative that bold, new projects be undertaken for the Negro's relief.

One of these projects, as we have seen, was the founding of Negro churches like that of St. Thomas. Rush was so excited about this cause that he took the matter to the President of the United States himself, who pledged a contribution. And to Granville Sharp, Rush wrote, "The favor I now solicit for them is more substantial than even freedom itself. It will place them in a condition to make their freedom a blessing to them here and prepare them for happiness beyond the grave."[38] Sharp responded generously with his own and other English contributions. As late as 1810 when, by Rush's information, there were in excess of 12,000 Negroes in Philadelphia, their indefatigable partisan

[35]Rush "To Thomas Jefferson: An Account of the Sugar Maple Tree," July 10, 1791, *Rush Letters,* I, 592–593; Goodman, *Benjamin Rush,* 286–287. For Jefferson's interest, see the "Account," 587.

[36]*Ibid.,* 596–97; Corner, 177; Butterfield, "Benjamin Rush as a Promoter of Useful Knowledge," 28–32.

[37]Rush to Granville Sharp, August 1791, *Rush Letters,* I, 608.

[38]Rush to Mrs. Rush, Aug. 12, 1791; to Granville Sharp, Aug. 1791, *ibid.,* 602, 609.

was still trying to collect money for new African churches.[39]

Another of Rush's enterprises to help the "poor blacks" of the nation was his projected Negro farm settlement. Named "Benezet" in honor of the dead Quaker reformer, who had so influenced Rush in his career as a benefactor of the Negro, the model farm colony was planned for Bedford County, Pennsylvania, where Rush in February 1794 had purchased 20,000 acres. Near the end of the year he saw a perfect opportunity to advance his project. Determined to act on his belief that yeoman farming was the best way of life for the Negro, Rush presented 5,200 acres of his Bedford holdings to the Pennsylvania Abolition Society. Along with his offer, Rush characteristically suggested a plan by which the land might be distributed in fee simple to worthy Negro farmers. Should the enterprise fail, a possibility he realistically conceded, the Negro could still benefit, as the lands could then be sold and the proceeds "applied for the emancipation and melioration of the condition of the blacks."[40] Invincibly optimistic, the good Doctor made even possible failure serve his humane purposes. A decade later, though, he was still confident enough in the project of Negro farm colonies to make another donation of land to the Society, this time in Cambria County, Pennsylvania.[41]

We have seen that all of Rush's programs to help the Negro were carefully reasoned and planned. And, again typically for the Age of the Enlightenment in which he lived, Rush employed science—as he understood it—to destroy fear and superstition and to advance the civilization of man. Science demonstrated, for example, that slavery was contrary to nature, that it corrupted the faculties of slaves and masters and, by the natural laws of association, of all men.[42] Rush argued, too, in a scientific paper read before the American Philosophical Society, that even the Negro's black skin color was explicable in natural terms—as symptomatic of a leprous disease. "The inferences" of this for the Negro, he noted to Thomas Jefferson, "will be in favor of treating them with humanity and justice and of keeping up the existing prejudices against matrimonial connections with them."[43] Another and truly radical

[39]Rush to Mrs. Rush, Oct. 17, 1793, and to Samuel Bayard, Oct. 23, 1810, *ibid.,* II, 717, 1071; Rush to Granville Sharp, June 20, 1809, "The Correspondence," 37.

[40]The deep respect that Rush had for Anthony Benezet can be seen throughout his writings but most notably in his "Biographical Anecdotes of Anthony Benezet" and his "Paradise of Negro-Slaves—A Dream," Rush, *Essays, Literary, Moral, and Philosophical* (2d ed.; Philadelphia, 1806), 302–304, 305–310. On Rush's planned Negro farm colony, see his letter to the President of the Pennsylvania Abolition Society, [1794?], *Rush Letters,* II, 754–55, and Prof. Butterfield's note on 755–56; Goodman, *Benjamin Rush,* 303.

[41]Rush to the President of the Pennsylvania Abolition Society, [1794?], *Rush Letters,* Prof. Butterfield's note on II, 755–56.

[42]Rush, *An Address to the Inhabitants,* 2–3, 6, 21–22; Rush, "On the Utility of A Knowledge of the Faculties and Operations of the Human Mind to A Physician," *Sixteen Introductory Lectures to Courses of Lectures upon the Institutes and Practice of Medicine. . . .To Which are Added Two Lectures upon the Pleasures of the Senses and of the Mind; with an Inquiry into Their Proximate Cause* (Philadelphia, 1811), 270; Rush to American Farmers About to Settle in New Parts of the United States, March 1789, I, 504; Corner, 219–20, 176.

[43]Rush to Thomas Jefferson, Feb. 4, 1797, *Rush Letters,* II, 786. His paper, "Observations Intended to Favour a Supposition That the Black Color (as It Is Called) of the Negroes Is Derived from the Leprosy," was read in July 1797 and published in the

implication, more helpful to the Negro, was that a cure would someday be found in the perfection of medicine for his leprous skin disease.

But Rush's science, for all its integrity and ingenuity, was really the hand-maid of his theology, as was his humanitarian concern for the Negro itself. Ultimately, the Negro was important and his freedom and prosperity necessary because of the perfect divine creation in which Rush implicitly believed and whose benevolent purposes he sought to discover and explain. God's benevolent purpose in allowing Negro slavery was a question that deeply troubled Rush. But it was a question that he seems to have answered to his satisfaction. "And when shall the mystery of providence be explained which has permitted so much misery to be inflicted upon these unfortunate people?" he wrote his Boston friend, Rev. Jeremy Belknap. "Is slavery *here* to be substituted among them for misery *hereafter?* They partake in their vices of the fall of man. They must therefore share in the benefits of the Atonement. Let us continue to love and serve them, for they are our brethren not only by creation but by redemption."[44]

Slavery, it appeared, was a special means of salvation granted to Negroes by God. It was a condition of relatively short worldly misery greatly preferable to the long, almost infinite, punishments which other men must undergo after death in order to achieve the same reconciliation with God. When Rush's reason and science failed, it was this teleological explanation of the Negro slave's place in the divine government that sustained Rush. Most of his projects for the Negro's freedom and welfare came to nought: the Negro farm colony of "Benezet" never materialized; the American sugar maple tree was never to be as widely cultivated as he hoped. And in the end, as Rush had gloomily foreshadowed, a civil war between English-speaking people was necessary to end slavery.

But Negro slavery *was* abolished officially—first in Great Britain and then in the United States. Negro churches and colleges *have* flourished, and the African-American has increasingly taken his place as a major force in American life. For the Negro, however, the potential meaning of the American Revolution, with respect to freedom and prosperity, is only beginning to be realized: "THE REVOLUTION IS NOT OVER!"[45]

State University, New Paltz, N.Y.

Transactions of the American Philosophical Society, old ser., IV (1799), 289–97. For an interesting and thoughtful discussion of Rush's "supposition," see Daniel J. Boorstin, *The Lost World of Thomas Jefferson* (Boston, 1960), 89 ff. Prof. Boorstin's comparison of Jefferson's and Rush's ideas on the Negro, as well as on other subjects, is always insightful. A more general study is Winthrop D. Jordan, *White Over Black: the Development of American Attitudes Toward the Negro, 1550–1812* (Chapel Hill, 1968), which examines the subject of the Negro in a different context. The revolutionary (and political) character of Rush's medical ideas is treated in Donald J. D'Elia, "Dr. Benjamin Rush and the American Medical Revolution," *Proceedings of the American Philosophical Society*, CX (Aug. 23, 1966), 227–34.

[44]Aug. 19, 1788, *Rush Letters*, I, 482–483; Rush, "Paradise of Negro-Slaves.—A Dream," *Essays, Literary, Moral, and Philosophical*, 306; Donald J. D'Elia, "The Republican Theology of Benjamin Rush," *Pennsylvania History*, XXXIII (April 1966), 187–203, esp. 197.

[45]Rush, "An Address to the People of the United States....On the Defects of the Confederation," *American Museum*, I (Jan. 1787), 8–11. The quotation comes from H. Niles' reprint of the "Address" in his *Principles and Acts of the Revolution in America* (Baltimore, 1822), 236.

IX

LOCKEAN IDEAS IN THOMAS JEFFERSON'S *BILL*
FOR ESTABLISHING RELIGIOUS FREEDOM

By S. Gerald Sandler

While the influence of John Locke on religious thinkers in America during the eighteenth and nineteenth centuries was considerable, there is probably no single document in American religious history which exemplifies this influence more clearly than Thomas Jefferson's *A Bill for Establishing Religious Freedom*. This bill, presented to the House of Delegates of Virginia in 1779, contains not only a Jeffersonian interpretation of Locke's theory of religious toleration, but also a discernible paraphrasing of several passages from Locke's *A Letter Concerning Toleration*. Scholars may question the extent to which Jefferson is indebted to Locke for his political theory and for the Declaration of Independence, but there can be little doubt of his indebtedness to Locke for his ideas on religious toleration.

That Jefferson read *A Letter Concerning Toleration* we may be certain, for among his papers is found a series of four folio pages containing extensive reading notes and some brief commentaries on Locke's *Letter*.[1] Editors of the Jefferson Papers have given these notes on Locke varying significance, although I believe that their rôle as the intermediary step in Jefferson's interpretation of Locke's *A Letter Concerning Toleration* has not yet been realized. The notes were first published in *The Writings of Thomas Jefferson* (1893), edited by Paul Leicester Ford, who suggested that they were employed by Jefferson as materials for his speeches in the House of Delegates on petitions concerning the disestablishment of the Episcopal Church.[2] In the most recent publication of the papers, *The Papers of Thomas Jefferson*, edited by Julian P. Boyd, the notes on Locke are included in the section " Notes and Procedings on the Discontinuance of the Church of England " in which Boyd relates these notes to Jefferson's *Outline of Argument in Support of his Resolutions*.[3] The truth is that the notes on Locke are only indirectly related to Jefferson's *Outline*. They do form, however, the essence of Jefferson's outline for his famous *Bill for Establishing Religious Freedom* and, thus, they constitute the link which connects Jefferson's bill with the work which inspired it, John Locke's *A Letter Concerning Toleration*.

To demonstrate the three-way relationship between Locke's *A Letter Concerning Toleration*, Jefferson's reading notes on Locke, and Jefferson's *A Bill for Establishing Religious Freedom*, I have selected five ideas from Jefferson's bill which I shall examine and trace back through Jefferson's

[1] *The Papers of Thomas Jefferson*, ed. Julian P. Boyd (Princeton, 1950), I, 544–548.

[2] *The Writings of Thomas Jefferson*, ed. P. L. Ford (New York, 1893), II, 92.

[3] Boyd, *The Papers of Thomas Jefferson*, I, 528–9. Bernhard Fabian has also compared these notes with Jefferson's *Outline of Argument* in " Jefferson's *Notes on Virginia:* The Genesis of Query xvii, The different religions received into that state? " *William and Mary Quarterly*, 3rd Series, XII (1955), 131–2, 138. Fabian, admittedly, shows some similarity of *thought* between the two documents. However, as I shall show, a more obvious textual similarity will be found by comparing the notes on Locke with Jefferson's *A Bill for Establishing Religious Freedom*.

notes on Locke to their ultimate origin in Locke's *A Letter Concerning Toleration*. To further illustrate that Jefferson's indebtedness is not merely one of ideas, but often one of phraseology, I have quoted freely from both authors, especially where I feel that the textual parallels are significant. Occasionally, selections from the *Letter* and the *Bill* may seem entirely unrelated until the juxtaposition of Jefferson's notes on Locke furnishes the necessary link for tracing the ideas to their apparent origin. While I do not claim that the following five points of comparison exhaust the similarities, I do feel that they are representative and that they furnish sufficient evidence for establishing Locke's *A Letter Concerning Toleration* as the primary source of inspiration for Jefferson's *A Bill for Establishing Religious Freedom*.

The five ideas concerning religious toleration which I have selected for comparison are as follows:

I. *True belief is inspired by reason, not force*

This, Jefferson's first argument for religious freedom, should be considered as two separate ideas: first, that true belief cannot be inspired by force, and second, that it *is* inspired by the rational persuasion of the mind. Jefferson states that because religious belief cannot be willed consciously, either by the person himself or by others coercing him, all attempts to force a person to worship against the dictates of his own conscience must eventually be futile. This statement closely parallels Locke's assertion that unless a man truly believes, i.e., unless he is " fully satisfied " in his own mind, any outward profession of faith is meaningless. The following quotations from each author illustrate the similarity of their ideas in this first part of the argument. Notice particularly that both Locke and Jefferson regard persuasion by force to be the breeder of " hypocrisy."

Locke: *A Letter Concerning Toleration*	Jefferson: Notes on Locke	Jefferson: *A Bill for Establishing Religious Freedom*
All the life and power of true religion consists in the inward and full persuasion of the mind; and faith is not faith without believing. Whatever profession we make, to whatever outward worship we conform, if we are not fully satisfied in our own mind . . . we add unto the number of our other sins, those also of hypocrisy, and contempt of his Divine Majesty.[4]	the life and essence of religion consists in the inward persuasion or belief in the mind. external forms of worship, when against our belief, are hypocrisy and impiety.[5]	Well aware that the opinions and belief of men depart not on their own will, but follow involuntarily the evidence proposed to their minds . . . that all attempts to influence it by temporal punishments, or burthens, or by civil incapacitations, tend only to beget habits of hypocrisy and meanness. . . .[6]

The second part of Jefferson's argument, that true religion is inspired by " influence on reason alone," can be traced more directly to Locke's philosophic writings than it can to a specific reference in his *A Letter Concerning*

---

[4] John Locke, *Works*, II (1714), 234–5.
[5] Boyd, *The Papers of Thomas Jefferson*, I, 545.   [6] *Ibid.*, II, 545.

Toleration.[7] However, in describing the manner by which God chose to
"propagate" his will, Jefferson is restating an idea which does have a definite counterpart in Locke's *A Letter Concerning Toleration*. In this latter
work God is depicted as the "Prince of peace" whose soldiers set the perfect example by subduing nations by the persuasion of the Gospel, rather
than by instruments of force. In examining the following passages, the
reader should be particularly aware of the textual similarities which link
both the *Bill* and the *Letter* to Jefferson's notes.

Locke: *A Letter Con-cerning Toleration*	Jefferson: Notes on Locke	Jefferson: *A Bill for Establishing Religious Freedom*
If, like the Captain of our salvation, they sincerely desire the good of souls, they would tread in the steps, and follow the perfect example of that Prince of peace, who sent out his soldiers to the subduing of nations, and gathering them into his church, not armed with the sword, or other instruments of force, but prepared with the Gospel of peace, and with the exemplary holiness of their conversation. This was his method.[8]	. . . our Savior chose not to propagate his religion by temporal pnmts or civil incapacita-tion, if he had it was in his almighty power . . . but he chose to [enforce] extend it by its in-fluence on reason, thereby shewing to others how [they] should proceed.[9]	. . . attempts to influence it by temporal punish-ments . . . are a depar-ture from the plan of the holy author of our religion, who being lord both of body and of mind, yet chose not to propagate it by coer-cions on either, as was in his Almighty power to do, but to extend it by its influence on rea-son alone. . . .[10]

II. *That civil magistrates may be fallible in religious matters is justified
in history*

In tracing the development of this idea from Locke to Jefferson, it will
be helpful once more to distinguish its two components: first, that civil
magistrates "being themselves but fallible and uninspired men" know no
more of "true" religion than do other citizens, and second, that this assertion has been proven in many instances throughout the history of the world.
The origin of the first part of the argument lies in Locke's definition of the
limits of human capability which he claims applies equally to civil magistrates as well as to all other persons. Locke further states that while the
path to heaven is narrow and that there is only "one way," the magistrate
has no more knowledge of this way than do "private persons." The second
part of Jefferson's argument, the historical justification for the above judgments, does not utilize Locke's extensive examples, but merely accepts his
conclusion. It would seem that Locke's background in systematic philosophy accounts for his treatment of the history of the Jews, the English kings,
and the English queens as separate proofs, whereas Jefferson in his desire to

[7] See, for example, John Locke, *An Essay Concerning Human Understanding*
(1690), IV, x.

[8] Locke, *Works*, II, 233–4.

[9] Boyd, *The Papers of Thomas Jefferson*, I, 544.   [10] *Ibid.*, II, 545.

be concise summarized Locke's examples in a general, but inclusive, statement proposing his conclusion to be true for " the greatest part of the world and throughout all time."

Locke: *A Letter Concerning Toleration*	Jefferson: Notes on Locke	Jefferson: *A Bill for Establishing Religious Freedom*
Perhaps some will say that they do not suppose this infallible judgment, that all men are bound to follow in the affairs of religion, to be in the civil magistrate, but in the church. . . . Who sees not how frequently the name of the church, which was venerable in people's eyes, in the following ages? . . . Amongst so many of the kings of the Jews, how many of them were there whom any Israelite, thus blindly following, had not fallen into idolatry. . . . Or if those things be too remote, our modern English history affords us fresh examples in the reigns of Henry VIII, Edward VI, Mary, and Elizabeth.[11]	I cannot give up my guidance to the magistrate; because he knows no more of the way to heaven than do I & is less concerned to direct me right than I am to go right, if the jews had followed their kings, amongst so many, what number would have led them to idolatry? consider the vicissitudes among the emperors, Arians, Athans. or among our princes, H.8. E.6. Mary, Elizabeth.[12]	. . . that the impious presumption of legislators and rulers, civil as well as ecclesiastical, who being themselves but fallible and uninspired men, have assumed dominion over the faith of others, setting up their own opinions and modes of thinking as the only true and infallible, and as such trying to impose them on others, hath established and maintained false religions over the greatest part of the world and throughout all time.[13]

III. *Because the domains of church and state are separate, a citizen's (religious) opinions should have no effect upon his civil capacities*

At the heart of Jefferson's *Bill* is the doctrine of the separation of the church and state, and although the fact that Jefferson employs the doctrine is not in itself evidence of an indebtedness to Locke, the similarity of his supporting arguments to their counterparts in Locke's *Letter* is striking. For example, in defining the limits of civil jurisdiction, Jefferson implies that because governments are established for the protection of civil interests, it is beyond the powers granted to the magistrate for him to exert influence in religious affairs. Jefferson states clearly that while men have conceded certain civil liberties to the jurisdiction of the magistrate, their opinions are private and free from external censure. I have selected the following passages for illustrating the parallels in Locke and Jefferson on this subject of civil jurisdiction. In comparing the passages, one should notice particularly that Jefferson, unlike Locke, does not qualify the phrase " opinions of men." While in *A Letter Concerning Toleration*, Locke considers " opinions " specifically as religious opinions, Jefferson makes no such distinction and, thus, he may be regarded as one of the early advocates of complete intellectual freedom.

[11] Locke, *Works*, II, 241–2.
[12] Boyd, *The Papers of Thomas Jefferson*, I, 547.   [13] *Ibid.*, II, 545–6.

Locke: *A Letter Concerning Toleration*	Jefferson: Notes on Locke	Jefferson: *A Bill for Establishing Religious Freedom*
Now that the whole jurisdiction of the magistrate reaches only to these civil concernments . . . these following considerations seem unto me abundantly to demonstrate. . . .[14]	the magistrate's jurisdn. extends only to civil rights and from these considns. . . .[15]	. . . that the opinions of men are not the object of civil government, nor under its jurisdiction; that to suffer the civil magistrate to intrude his powers into the field of opinion and to restrain the profession or propagation of principles on the supposition of their ill tendency is a dangerous fallacy. . . .[16]

Another of Jefferson's arguments related to the doctrine of the separation of church and state is that no man's civil capacities shall be affected, favorably or otherwise, because he maintains a particular religious belief. The domains of church and state are separate and, therefore, a person's profession of faith should have no effect upon his eligibility for public office. Locke, too, makes a similar assertion, claiming that no citizen should be prejudiced in his civil " enjoyments " because he belongs to " another church." Thus, this may be considered to be the common goal of both writers: a society in which men may freely follow the dictates of their own reason and where religious belief has no effect upon civil capacity. The following are passages which I feel are significant in determining the source of Jefferson's ideas on this subject. Notice, once again, how the notes serve as an intermediate step in the Jeffersonian interpretation.

Locke: *A Letter Concerning Toleration*	Jefferson: Notes on Locke	Jefferson: *A Bill for Establishing Religious Freedom*
Secondly, no private person has any right, in any manner, to prejudice another person in his civil enjoiments, because he is of another church or religion.[17]	we have no right to prejudice another in his civil enjoiments because he is of another church.[18]	. . . that our civil rights have no dependence on our religious opinions . . . that therefore the proscribing any citizen as unworthy the public confidence by laying upon him an incapacity of being called to offices of trust and emolument, unless he profess or renounce this or that religious opinion, is depriving him injuriously of those privileges and advantages to which, in common with his fellow citizens, he has a natural right. . . .[19]

IV. *Civil governments must interfere, however, when principles break out into overt acts against peace and good order*

Aware that faction and private meetings represent a potential danger to

---

[14] Locke, *Works*, II, 234.
[15] Boyd, *The Papers of Thomas Jefferson*, I, 545.   [16] *Ibid.*, II, 546.
[17] Locke, *Works*, II, 237.
[18] Boyd, *The Papers of Thomas Jefferson*, I, 546.   [19] *Ibid.*, II, 546.

civil interests, both Locke and Jefferson concede that unlimited religious freedom is not practical from the standpoint of protecting civil liberties. Thus, in Locke's *Letter*, as well as in Jefferson's *Bill*, one finds the provision for civil intervention wherever sedition or other acts threatening the general peace and good order of society are perceptible.

Locke: *A Letter Concerning Toleration*	Jefferson: Notes on Locke	Jefferson: *A Bill for Establishing Religious Freedom*
If anything pass in a religious meeting seditiously and contrary to the public peace, it is to be punished in the same manner, and no otherwise, than as if it had happened in a fair or market. These meetings are not to be sanctuaries for factious and flagitious fellows.[20]	[If] anything pass in a religious meeting seditiously & contrary to the public peace, let it be punished in the same way & no otherwise than as if it had happened in a fair or market. these meetings ought not to be sanctuaries for faction and flagitiousness.[21]	... it is time enough for the rightful purposes of civil government for its officers to interfere when principles break out into overt acts against peace and good order. ...[22]

V. *Truth, unaided, has sufficient power to prevail over error*

While the previous comparisons have relied primarily upon a similarity of ideas rather than of specific phraseology, the evidence seems to be conclusive that Jefferson's commentary on the power of truth has at least one sentence paraphrased directly from Locke's *A Letter Concerning Toleration*. With a strikingly similar vocabulary Jefferson restates Locke's argument, asserting that truth is the sufficient combatant for error and that "she" will prevail if not corrupted or hindered by human intervention. Of further significance is the fact that by repeating *identically* his own commentary in his Notes on Locke (truth is "the proper and sufficient antagonist to error"), Jefferson has furnished us with evidence for believing that these Notes, rather than a later reading of the *Letter*, provided the material for the *Bill*.

Locke: *A Letter Concerning Toleration*	Jefferson: Notes on Locke	Jefferson: *A Bill for Establishing Religious Freedom*
For the truth certainly will do well enough, if she were once left to shift for herself. She seldom has received, and I fear never will receive much assistance from the power of great men, to whom she is but rarely known, and more rarely welcome. She is not taught by laws, nor	[Tr]uth will do well enough if left to shift for herself. she seldom has received much aid from the power of great men to whom she is rarely known & seldom welcom. she has no need of force to procure entrance into the	... that truth is great and will prevail if left to herself; that she is the proper and sufficient antagonist to error, and has nothing to fear from the conflict unless by human interposition disarmed of her natural weapons. ...[25]

[20] Locke, *Works*, II, 253.
[21] Boyd, *The Papers of Thomas Jefferson*, I, 545.
[22] *Ibid.*, II, 546.

has she any need of force	minds of men. error
to procure her entrance	indeed has often pre-
into the minds of men.	vailed by assistance
Errors indeed prevail by	of power or force.
the assistance of foreign	truth is the proper
and borrowed succours.[23]	and sufficient antago-
	nist to error.[24]

Among the Jefferson Papers in the same sequence of documents that contains the Notes on Locke, a smaller sheet of paper with miscellaneous notes on heresy and religion is also found.[26] Ford has combined these notes on heresy with the other notes of the same sequence in a single category, " Notes on Religion." [27] Boyd distinguishes the former notes in his edition as " Notes on Heresy," and he identifies many of the authors whose works are quoted or referred to by Jefferson.[28] Significantly, Boyd cites no source for the first three notes on heresy which, as I shall show, are actually not the beginning of a separate sequence as they are presented, but rather, the concluding portion of the aforementioned Notes on Locke.

Appended to all early editions of Locke's *A Letter Concerning Toleration* is a postscript in which the author considers the nature of heresy and schism. It is this portion of Locke's *Letter* that inspired Jefferson's introductory comments on heresy, and a comparison of these notes on heresy with Locke's postscript should not only demonstrate the origin of Jefferson's notes, but also furnish sufficient evidence to justify the combining of the two sequences and the restoring of their original order in future editions of the Jefferson Papers. Jefferson's entry on Locke's postscript is as follows:

A heretic is an impunger of fundamentals. what are fundamentals? the protestants will say those doctrines which are clearly & precisely delivered in the holy scriptures.[29]

Although Jefferson's notes are actually comments on Locke's postscript rather than transcriptions of specific passages, the following quotation selected from Locke's postscript should adequately identify the source of Jefferson's notes:

Both these are heretics, because they err in fundamentals, and they err obstinately against knowledge, for when they have determined the Holy Scriptures to be the only foundation of faith, they nevertheless lay down certain propositions as fundamental, which are not in the Scriptures. . . .[30]

These notes on heresy conclude Jefferson's record of his reading in Locke's *Works;* the remaining notes on the page and in the sequence are unrelated and refer to miscellaneous historical and theological tracts.

N.Y.U.–Bellevue Medical Center.

[23] Locke, *Works*, II, 248.
[24] Boyd, *The Papers of Thomas Jefferson*, I, 547–8.   [25] *Ibid.*, II, 546.
[26] Manuscripts of the Jefferson Papers, Library of Congress, II, 226–7.
[27] Ford, *The Writings of Thomas Jefferson*, II, 95.
[28] Boyd, *The Papers of Thomas Jefferson*, I, 555.
[29] *Ibid.*, I, 553.   [30] Locke, *Works*, II, 255.

X

JAMES MADISON AND THE NATURE OF MAN

By Ralph L. Ketcham

In the first book of his *Politics* Aristotle stated that "what each thing is when fully developed, we call its nature," and then added his famous dictum that "man is by nature a political animal."[1] Once Aristotle has asserted that man can realize the full potentiality of his humanness only when participating in the social (political) life of a civilized state (city), it is not difficult to imagine some of the broad principles of his political philosophy. The place of man in the community will receive more attention than the delineation of individual rights. Concepts of moderation and lawfulness essential to civilized social intercourse will be emphasized. The obligations of the good citizen will be pre-eminent over the duties and privileges of the good man. Indeed, once a philosopher has divulged what sort of creature he takes man to be, both in fact and in potentiality, his arguments in other fields of inquiry are often readily anticipated. The view which James Madison had of human nature offers such insight into the theories and policies which he developed and followed throughout his long career, and is important in understanding his overall philosophy.

The task, however, is not an easy one. There is no recorded evidence that Madison ever spelled out in systematic detail his thoughts on the nature of man. Yet, his writings are full of reflections and comments on the subject. A further complication is introduced by the indiscriminate mixing of statements of fact and observations about human motivation and action with injunctions about the way men could or should act. Finally, throughout Madison's writings about human character there is an ambivalence which at first glance appears contradictory.

The picture, as it emerges from letters, speeches, and notes covering the sixty-five years of Madison's adult life, is a fascinating one, and contains every shade of opinion from optimism to despair concerning the nature of man. That mankind ought to be free, and indeed *had* to be free if life was to be human rather than brutish, was an unquestionable axiom to Madison, student of Locke and friend of Jefferson. On this point Madison accepted the faith of the Age of Reason to which he was heir. On another great ideal of the day he stood four-square: "The perfect equality of mankind . . . is an absolute truth."[2] Late in life he wrote that the distinction between

---

[1] Jowett translation (Modern Library ed., N.Y., 1943), Bk. I, ch. 2: 1252b and 1253a, 54.

[2] Gaillard Hunt, ed., *The Writings of James Madison*, 9 vols. (New York, 1904), V, 381.

the Republican and Federalist Parties "had its origin in the confidence of the former in the capacity of mankind for self-government, and in the distrust of it by the other . . . and is the key to many of the phenomena presented by our political history." [3]   In a eulogy of his associates at the Federal Convention of 1787, he wrote that "there never was an assembly of men . . . who were more pure in their motives, or more exclusively or anxiously devoted to the object committed to them [of] devising and proposing a constitutional system . . . to best secure the permanent liberty and happiness of their country." [4]   Clearly, Madison believed that men of right ought to be free and equal, and that both individually and collectively they possessed faculties which enabled them to lead lives of independence and justice.

His application of this faith to the fundamentals of government was explicit. Madison stated many times that the vital republican principles were those of " numerical equality " and " the will of the majority," and asked " if the will of the majority cannot be trusted," what can? [5]   These principles he carried into practice in favoring the election of the president by the people at large, arguing that such an election " would be as likely as any that could be devised to produce an Executive Magistrate of distinguished character." [6]   In 1800 at the height of the uproar over the Alien and Sedition Acts, Madison wrote Jefferson that he was confident " a demonstration of the rectitude and efficacy of popular sentiment would rescue the republican principle from the imputation brought on it by the degeneracy of the public Councils." During the embargo crisis in 1808–1809, he praised the " spirit of ardent and determined patriotism " in the nation, and trusted " the well-tried intelligence and virtue of my fellow citizens." [7]

Throughout, Madison's faith in the virtue and intelligence of man and his consequent ability to govern his own affairs, is sober but unwavering. From his earliest public act in writing a more liberal and trusting law regulating road repair in Orange County (1772), until his days of proud, confident reflection on the record of nearly fifty

[3] Letter to William Eustis, May 22, 1823, *ibid.*, IX, 136.

[4] Manuscript dated 1835 on the " Origin of the Constitutional Convention " printed with the posthumous publication of his Convention Journal. *Ibid.*, II, 411–412.

[5] See, for example, a letter to George Hay, August 23, 1823, and an essay on " Majority Governments," 1833, *ibid.*, IX, 151, 528.

[6] Speeches in the Federal Convention, Thurs., July 19, 1787, *ibid.*, IV, 8, 62.

[7] Letter to Jefferson, March 15, 1800; letter to James Armstrong and James Bowdoin, July 15, 1807; and First Inaugural Address, March 4, 1809; *ibid.*, VI, 408; VII, 462; VIII, 50.

years of free government under the Constitution, the sage of Montpelier was steadfast in his adherence to *the* republican principle that men could be entrusted with carefully constructed mechanisms of self-government. Although the ecstasy of a Paine or Condorcet is notably absent, his calm, practical confidence in human nature is unmistakable, and a fact of the utmost significance in understanding the mind of James Madison.

On the other hand, there is an equally constant strain of skepticism and even pessimism about human nature that runs like a stream of grandfatherly advice through his writings. In a famous passage from the fifty-first *Federalist Paper*, Madison stated most bluntly his skepticism:

What is government itself, but the greatest of all reflections on human nature? If men were angels, no government would be necessary. If angels were to govern men, neither external nor internal controls on government would be necessary. In framing a government which is to be administered by men over men, the great difficulty lies in this: you must first enable the government to control the governed; and in the next place oblige it to control itself.[8]

In a speech to the Virginia Constitutional Convention of 1829, as he approached his eightieth birthday, Madison applied this pessimism more directly to human motives:

In republics, the great danger is, that the majority may not sufficiently respect the rights of the minority. Some gentlemen, consulting the purity and generosity of their own minds, without averting to the lessons of experience, would find a security against that danger in our social feelings; in a respect for character; in the dictates of the monitor within. . . . But man is known to be a selfish, as well as a social being. Respect for character, though often a salutary restraint, is but too often overruled by other motives. . . . We all know that conscience itself may be deluded; may be misled . . . into acts which an enlightened conscience would forbid. . . . These favorable attributes of the human character are all valuable, as auxiliaries; but they will not serve as a substitute for the coercive provisions belonging to Government and Law.[9]

It is significant that in support of this sober view Madison joined with ex-President James Monroe and Chief Justice John Marshall in backing property qualifications for suffrage at the 1829 Convention.

Almost random comments from Madison's letters and speeches reflect a realism about the frailties of mankind. He wrote James Maury that however valid his ideas on tobacco culture were, nothing would

[8] Henry Cabot Lodge, ed., *The Federalist Papers* (New York, 1900), No. 51, 323.
[9] Hunt, *Writings*, IX, 361.

come of them " because good advice is apt to be disregarded." [10]   During the ratifying debates of 1788 he remarked that " there can be no
doubt that there are subjects to which the capacities of the bulk of
mankind are unequal." [11]   Madison ridiculed Rousseau's plan for
universal peace arguing that such a plan was one which "in the catalogue of events, will never exist but in the imagination of visionary
philosophers, or in the breasts of benevolent enthusiasts." [12]   During
the War of 1812 he asked for higher pay for volunteers since " patriotism alone " would not produce a sufficient number of soldiers.[13]   Two
years later he complained that the " leaders and priests " of New
England had brought the people " under a delusion scarcely exceeded
by that recorded in the period of witchcraft." [14]

In an almost Hobbesian comment deploring the evils of war during the crisis of 1793, Madison wrote that " the strongest passions
and most dangerous weaknesses of the human breast; ambition, avarice, vanity, the honorable or venial love of fame, are all in conspiracy
against the desire and duty of peace." [15]   In 1820, he noted that "nothing has been found more difficult in practice than to guard charitable
institutions against mismanagement fatal to their original objects,"
and three years later just before a presidential election he reported
without displeasure or alarm that, " what most nearly concerns the
mass of the people is the state of the crops and the prospect of
prices." [16]   Finally while being pestered by James Callender for political spoils following Jefferson's election in 1800, Madison impa-
tiently wrote Monroe that " besides his [Callender's] other passions,
he is under the tyranny of that of *love*." [17]

Two items illustrate more systematically Madison's skepticism
about human nature, and indicate an important positive aspect of his
concept of man.   First was his attitude toward utopian schemes for
improving the lot of mankind.   In commenting on Robert Owen's
New Harmony Community, Madison observed that

Mr. Owen's remedy for [all] vicissitudes implies that labour will be relished
without the ordinary impulses to it; that the love of equality will supersede

[10] *The Letters and other Writings of James Madison*, 4 vols., published by order
of Congress (New York, 1865), IV, 1–2.

[11] Letter to Edmund Randolph, January 10, 1788, Hunt, *Writings*, V, 81.

[12] Essay on " Perpetual Peace," Feb. 2, 1792, *ibid.*, VI, 88.

[13] Fourth Annual Message, Nov. 4, 1812, *ibid.*, VIII, 227.

[14] Letter to Wilson Cary Nicholas, Nov. 26, 1814, *ibid.*, VIII, 319.

[15] " Letters of Helvidius," No. 4, Sept. 14, 1793, *ibid.*, VI, 174.

[16] Letters to Joel K. Meade, Oct. 16, 1820, and to Richard Rush, July 22, 1823,
Congress Ed., *Works*, III, 183, 331.

[17] Letter to James Monroe, June 1, 1801, Hunt, *Writings*, VI, 421.

the desire of distinction, and that increasing leisure . . . will promote intellectual cultivation, moral enjoyment and innocent amusements, without any of the vicious resorts, for the ennui of idleness. Custom is properly called second nature; Mr. Owen makes it nature itself.

After comparing Owen's scheme to " Helvetius' attempt to show that all men come from the hand of nature perfectly equal," Madison asserted that evil and diseases are " too deeply rooted in human society to admit of more than great palliatives." [18] At another point he stated that " a Utopia exhibiting a perfect homogeneousness of interests, opinions and feelings [is] nowhere yet found in civilized communities." [19] Clearly, Madison felt that evil in human nature and in world affairs was indelible, and that the hardships of life spring from " basic nature," not from custom or " second nature." Furthermore, he saw the hopes of those who would " plan " the end of human suffering foundering on the fact of the heterogeneity of mankind.

This crucial diversity of human beings was the essential factor beneath the brilliant logic of the tenth *Federalist Paper* which T. V. Smith has called " a studied and profound view of human nature itself." [20]

As long as the reason of man continues fallible, and he is at liberty to exercise it, different opinions will be formed. . . . The diversity in the faculties of men, from which the rights of property originate, is not less an insuperable obstacle to a uniformity of interests. . . .

The latent causes of faction are thus sown in the nature of man; and we can see them everywhere brought into different degrees of activity. . . . A zeal for different opinions concerning religion, concerning government, and many other points; an attachment to different leaders ambitiously contending for pre-eminence and power . . . have, in turn, divided mankind into parties, inflamed them with mutual animosity, and rendered them much more disposed to vex and oppress each other than to cooperate for their common good.[21]

In a letter to Jefferson written at the same time he was turning out the *Federalist Papers,* Madison was more explicit:

Those who contend for a simple Democracy, or a pure republic, actuated by the sense of the majority . . . assume or suppose a case which is altogether fictitious. They found their reasoning on the idea, that the people composing the society, enjoy not only an equality of political rights; but that they have all precisely the same interests, and the same feelings in every respect.

[18] Letter to Nicholas P. Trist, April 1827, Congress Ed., *Works,* III, 576–7.

[19] " Majority Governments," 1833, Hunt, *Writings,* IX, 526.

[20] T. V. Smith, " Saints, Secular and Sacerdotal—James Madison and Mahatma Gandhi," *Ethics,* LIX (Oct. 1948), 59.

[21] Lodge, ed., *The Federalist,* No. 10, 53–54.

... We know however that no society ever did or can consist of so homogeneous a mass of citizens. . . . In all civilized societies, distinctions are various and unavoidable. A distinction of property results from that very protection which a free government gives to unequal faculties of acquiring it. There will be rich and poor; creditors and debtors; a landed interest, a monied interest, a merchantile interest, a manufacturing interest. . . . In addition to these natural distinctions, artificial ones will be founded, on accidental differences in political, religious, or other opinions. . . . However erroneous or ridiculous these grounds of dissention and faction may appear to the enlightened statesman or the benevolent philosopher, the bulk of mankind, who are neither statesmen nor philosophers, will continue to view them in a different light.[22]

This emphasis on the diversity of human talents and the multiplicity of human desires and interests is the key to the resolution of Madison's ambivalence on the strength or frailty of human character. Obviously, Madison felt that some men were good and others were bad, and indeed, individuals had within themselves varying amounts of honor and perversity. Without a doubt he counted Alexander Hamilton among the " pure and devoted " men assembled at Philadelphia during the summer of 1787, while this same gentleman was the monster who led the " stockjobbers " in reaping the profits of debt assumption in 1790–91, and who clamored for war with Republican France during the decade of Federalist power.

In short, Madison was on the whole less inspired by the past performance of mankind than he was about his hopes for the future, especially the future of a land blessed with the free Constitution of the United States of America. Concerning questions, what had men been like, and how had he generally observed them to be, Madison was almost Hobbesian. Life was usually guided by avarice, vanity, cruelty, and depravity, but there was a reasonable hope that free institutions would brighten the future in some cases. In fact, his views were close to what one would expect from a philosopher of the Enlightenment. Yet, Madison refused to take the next step and envision the end of human suffering and strife once the chains of the past had been undone. What he conceded, and patiently hoped for, was that the lot of mankind could be improved, especially in the presence of the greatest possible amount of freedom for individuals, and that there was enough virtue, honor, and intelligence distributed in the human race to make republican government at least a viable alternative to the twin evils of tyranny and anarchy. To concede or hope for more, according to the Father of the Constitution, would have been to build on the sands of human weakness and in blindness to the lessons of human history.

[22] Letter to Jefferson, Oct. 24, 1787, Hunt, *Writings*, V, 28–29.

On the whole, Madison was inclined to center his attention on the observable facts of human nature, and leave the moralizing and speculating to less sober and less realistic minds. His commentary on the potentiality of human nature would have been confined, in the Aristotelian fashion, to a statement that "man is by nature a *free* animal." To say more would run the risk of ignoring or prejudging the diversities which so impressed Madison as he observed and read about his fellow creatures. Over and over again, it is possible to see Madison's probing mind start from the conditional propositions "if men are heterogeneous in their talents and virtue" and "if men must be free to be human," then such-and-such will or should follow in politics or economics or religion or any other field of endeavor.

If to assert that men are both good and bad and that they are both frail and free involved taking notice of contradictions and complicating the understanding and regulation of human society, one would simply have to learn to live with contradictions and face with humility the fact that the problems of men might not admit of complete or final solution or even resolution. This was, in fact, the point of view from which James Madison dealt with private and public affairs during the eighty-five years of his life.

At this point, one would almost be justified in raising doubts as to the adequacy or rigorousness of Madison's education on the question of human nature. Whence came this apparently paradoxical view which equivocated on the goodness or badness of mankind? Although it is not possible to assemble anything resembling proof on the origins of Madison's ideas on this subject,[23] it is possible, and highly instructive, to examine some of the obvious sources available to him and see what thoughts are there that correspond with ideas expressed by Madison.

Madison's relationship to Enlightenment learning has already been suggested. That he owed a huge intellectual debt to such figures as Locke, Hume, Montesquieu, Addison, Pope, and Voltaire is unquestionable. What has been often overlooked is that in the eighteenth century, before young scholars read the great contemporaries, they read the classics: Plato, Aristotle, Thucydides, Tacitus, Homer, Virgil, and Cicero. Since explicit reference to these authors

---

[23] Curiously enough, there is less evidence on the source of Madison's ideas on an important subject such as his view of human nature than on some lesser topics like finance and international law. He never wrote a footnoted treatise on the subject, and treated it as something tacitly assumed, not painstakingly explained. Furthermore, since there are no explicit references in his writings to the origins of these ideas, the influence of such factors as friends, family, and community are in the final analysis imponderable. What follows, then, suggests what might have been in the line of intellectual origins, and does not pretend to "prove" that Madison got his ideas from the suggested sources.

was exceedingly rare, even though all educated men of the day had studied them, their precise impact is difficult to evaluate. In Madison's case, however, it must at least be attempted since it suggests an answer to the riddle of Madison's ambivalence regarding the nature of man. Many of the ancients, especially the historical philosopher Aristotle and the philosophic historian Thucydides, were not heirs to the concepts of rationalism, progress, and perfectibility which permeated the Age of Reason. Their writings study the past and seek lessons in the observable actions of men in society, rather than start in a more abstract way and then follow reason wherever it led in establishing the truths of human nature. If the wisdom of Aristotle and Thucydides is added to the later philosophy and history of Locke and Hume, an interesting and almost strikingly obvious pattern of thought, closely akin to that of Madison's, emerges.[24]

One of the most stirring and graphic episodes in Thucydides' *History of the Peloponnesian War* is the description of the Corcyrean Revolution in the fifth year of the war. In the wake of some local victories by the Corinthians, allies of the Spartans, a group of intriguers attempted to detach Corcyra from her Athenian alliance. After the Corcyreans had voted to continue the Athenian connection, the conspirators assassinated the leaders of those who favored the alliance. The enraged " commons," as Thucydides called the populace of Corcyra, rose, rioted in the city, and

engaged in butchering those of their fellow citizens whom they regarded as their enemies: and although the crime imputed was that of attempting to put down the democracy, some were slain also for private hatred, others by their debtors because of monies owed them. Death thus raged in every shape; and as usually happens at such times, there was no length to which violence did not go; sons were killed by their fathers, and suppliants dragged from the altar or slain upon it; while some were even walled up in the temple of Dionysus and died there.[25]

In commenting on the results of this bloody revolution, Thucydides made eminently clear what he thought of human nature:

[24] The specific relevance of ancient writers was suggested to me by Douglass Adair's unpublished doctoral dissertation " The Intellectual Origins of Jeffersonian Democracy," Yale, 1944. Adair points out the existence of physiocratic ideas in Aristotle and balance-of-power concepts in Polybius, for example. My own studies have confirmed Adair's emphasis on the importance of classical traditions, especially on such a basic concept as that of the nature of man. Cf. G. Chinard, " Polybius and the American Constitution," this *Journal*, I (1940), 38–58; also Charles F. Mullett, " Classical Influences on the American Revolution," *Classical Journal*, XXXV (Nov. 1939), 92–104.

[25] Thucydides, *History of the Peloponnesian War*, translated by Crawley (Modern Library ed., N.Y., 1934), Bk. III, Ch. 10, 184–9.

The sufferings which revolution entailed upon the cities were many and terrible, such as have occurred and always will occur, as long as the nature of mankind remains the same. . . . Places where [the revolution] arrived last . . . carried to still greater excess . . . the cunning of their enterprises and the atrocity of their reprisals. . . . Prudent hesitation came to be considered specious cowardice; moderation was held to be a cloak for unmanliness. . . . Frantic violence became the attribute of manliness; cautious plotting, a justifiable means of self-defense. . . .

Thus every form of iniquity took root in the Hellenic countries by reason of the troubles. The ancient simplicity into which honor so largely entered was laughed down and disappeared; and society became divided into camps in which no man trusted his fellow. . . .

In the confusion into which life was now thrown in the cities, human nature, always rebelling against the law and now its master, gladly showed itself ungoverned in passion, above respect for justice, and the enemy of all superiority. . . .[26]

These accounts of the excesses and evils of revolution, and the depravities of human nature attending it, were essentially reflected in the discussions of revolution in the eighth book of Plato's *Republic* and the fifth book of the *Politics* of Aristotle. It is not difficult to picture the images which might have come to the minds of men like James Madison, students of the classical writers, as they heard of the uprising of Daniel Shays in the winter of 1786–87.

In the second book of the *Politics,* in the course of his criticism of the ideal and communal aspect of Plato's *Republic,* Aristotle made some sober comments on the nature of man:

The error of Socrates [Plato] must be attributed to the false notion of unity [about human nature] from which he starts.

It is said that the evils now existing in states, suits about contracts, convictions for perjury, flatteries of rich men and the like . . . arise out of the possession of private property. These evils, however, are due to a very different cause—the wickedness of human nature.

The avarice of mankind is insatiable. . . . It is not the possessions but the desires of mankind which require to be equalized, and this is impossible, unless a sufficient education is provided by the laws.

. . . want is not the sole incentive to crime; men also wish to enjoy themselves and not be in a state of desire. . . . The greatest of crimes are caused by excess and not by necessity. Men do not become tyrants in order that they may not suffer cold. . . .

Let us remember that we should not disregard the experience of ages. . . . The habit of lightly changing laws is an evil, and, when the advantage is small, some error both of lawgivers and rulers had better be left; the citizen will not gain so much by making the change as he will lose by the habit of disobedience.[27]

[26] *Ibid.,* 189–191.

[27] Aristotle, *Politics* (ed. cit. f.n. 1), 88, 89, 90, 99, 100, 101, 106, Bk. II, chs. 5, 7, 9.

The lessons and impressions Madison might have gained from this kind of commentary are obvious. In addition, the familiar assumptions and tenets of Greek political philosophy, found in such standard works as Thucydides' account of Pericles' funeral oration, Plato's *Republic,* and Aristotle's *Politics,* of the social obligations of citizens, the importance of rule by the wise and able, and the necessity for stable continuity, equilibrium, and moderation in government, should be taken into account in assessing the impact of classical traditions on one who was trained rigorously in the ancient learning. Although there is but one direct reference to Aristotle and Thucydides in all of Madison's extant writings,[28] it is very likely that he was well acquainted with the ancient authors. His tutors, notably Donald Robertson and John Witherspoon, were learned classical scholars, and made innumerable references to that learning in the conduct of their instruction.[29] Although there is no direct proof of Madison's debt to the ancient authors, the ideas they expressed fill out an otherwise poorly explained facet of Madison's recorded attitude on the nature of man.

The debt which nearly all the Founding Fathers owed to the political philosophy of John Locke has long been acknowledged. That Madison shared this heritage is clear, both from the principles he espoused and his reference to Locke as an author " admirably calculated to impress on young minds the right of Nations to establish their own governments, and to inspire a love of free ones." [30] The familiar assumptions regarding human rationality and the need for and right of individual freedom in the *Second Treatise,* impressed Madison just as they did Jefferson, Franklin, the Adamses and all the others. For a more detailed account of Locke's view of the nature of man, however, it is necessary to turn to his great philosophic work, *An Essay Concerning Human Understanding.* [31]

[28] In his essay on " Government," January 2, 1792, Hunt, *Writings,* VI, 81.

[29] See Irving Brant, *The Life of James Madison,* 4 vols., (Indianapolis, 1941–1954), I, 58–60, 76–78 for detailed accounts of Madison's schooling under Robertson (1763-1767) and Witherspoon (1769–1772). The notes taken by Witherspoon's students at Princeton are full of citations of the classical authors, and Witherspoon's own treatment of political theory is taken straight from the *Politics.* See John E. Calhoun's copy of Witherspoon's " Lecture on Moral Philosophy " (1774), William Bradford's copy of " Lectures on Eloquence " (1772), and Andrew S. Hunter's copy of " Lectures on Oratory " (1772), for examples of Witherspoon's devotion to the classics. All notes deposited in the Rare Books and Manuscripts Division of the Firestone Library, Princeton University.

[30] Letter to Jefferson, Feb. 8, 1825, Hunt, *Writings,* IX, 218–219.

[31] There is no explicit reference to the *Essay* in Madison's extant writings. In a private letter, however, Irving Brant wrote that " it would be incredible if Madison did not have every work of Locke that was extant." There is evidence that the *Essay* was used at Donald Robertson's school, and the controversy over its psy-

In Chapter 21, Book II of the *Essay,* entitled " On Power," Locke entered the great debate on the freedom of the will, in the course of which he explained how men came to have the thoughts and wills they had. He took the firm ground to begin with that liberty meant the choice open to a man to do or not to do something, depending on what his preference was. The rest of the complex debate over whether man was free to prefer what he wanted, was related to the fundamental motivation of human life which Locke defined vaguely as " happiness." The path toward this " happiness " was guided by a variety of anxieties and desires that motivated men in many different ways. In answering the question how these various desires and motivations could be explained and evaluated, Locke made some profound observations on man's nature:

the various and contrary choices that men make in the world do not argue that they do not all pursue good: but that the same thing is not good to every man alike. This variety of pursuits shows that everyone does not place his happiness in the same thing, or choose the same way to it. . . .

Hence it was, I think, that the philosophers of old did in vain inquire, whether *summum bonum* consisted in riches, or bodily delights, or virtue, or contemplation: and they might have as reasonably disputed whether the best relish were to be found in apples, plums, or nuts, and have divided themselves into sects upon it. . . . It is not strange nor unreasonable that men should seek their happiness by avoiding all things that disease them, and by pursuing all that delight them; wherein it will be no wonder to find variety and difference. . . . Though all men's desires tend to happiness, yet they are not moved by the same object. Men may choose different things, and yet all choose right. . . .[32]

Locke concluded the chapter " On Power " by asserting that within each man there were conflicting desires that competed with one another, and that the essence of human rationality was the ability of conscience and judgment to sort these desires and move the will to act in pursuit of some conscious objective.

Although Madison would probably have been less confident about the amount of rational judgment exercised by human beings, and would have been less willing to find the source of human conduct in sensory impressions than Locke was, the similarity on the subject of human diversity is striking. In fact, Locke's analysis of the origin

chology was at the core of the debates at Edinburgh among the Scottish " Common Sense " philosophers with whom Witherspoon studied in the years immediately before his coming to Princeton in 1768. See Brant, *Madison,* I, 61 and 73–74. That Madison had studied and discussed the *Essay* is therefore fairly certain.

[32] John Locke, *An Essay Concerning Human Understanding* (Philadelphia, James Kay, Jr. and Co., no date), Bk. II, Ch. 21, Sect. 54, 168–169.

and resolution of individual motivation is a neat microcosm of Madison's famous doctrine of controling factions by extending the republic. The humility and toleration required for a man to believe that "men may choose different things, and yet all choose right," was typical of Madison, and perhaps indicated a more fundamental debt owed John Locke than the one readily conceded in the matter of basic political propositions. Once the pluralism of the passage quoted above is accepted, it would be difficult to justify political axioms much different from those found in the *Second Treatise on Civil Government* or in the tenth and thirty-ninth *Federalist Papers,* for that matter.

Of all the philosophers of the eighteenth century, the one who was in many respects closest to the edge of Madison's mind was the sophisticated and skeptical David Hume. That is to say, whereas the impressions of Aristotle and Locke were so deep and basic as to call forth no particular acknowledgment, Hume was contemporary enough to be the subject of controversy and hence more likely to elicit specific reference. There are half-a-dozen references to Hume's *Essays* and *History of England* in Madison's correspondence and speeches. Furthermore, and perhaps of more significance, Hume's writings and ideas were much on the mind of the Rev. John Witherspoon as he began his presidency of Princeton in 1768. He had known and studied with Hume in Edinburgh, where the famous skeptical philosopher was one of the intellectual giants of the day. Witherspoon used Hume as a whipping boy in moral philosophy, exorcising him for his utilitarian ethics, applying such epithets to him as " skeptical " and "infidel." [33] On the other hand, in his lectures on eloquence, Witherspoon referred to Hume as being " of great reach and accuracy of judgment in matters of criticism," and changed his adjective to " sagacious " in describing the infidel! [34] In many respects, some of Witherspoon's classes must have been a kind of running debate between the orthodox Presbyterian's views and the noxious and nettlesome ideas of the skeptical philosopher.

Because of the freshness of Hume's thought, and its probing, questioning, yet urbane quality, one can imagine its peculiar attractiveness to a person of Madison's analytical turn of mind. Hume's willingness to balance probabilities and distinguish empirical factors, regardless of systems or dogma, also would have appealed to Madison. The affinity between the two men is neatly illustrated in Hume's short essay on " The Dignity or Meanness of Human Nature."

In this essay, Hume undertook to examine just exactly what was meant when men made comments about human nature, since it was

---

[33] Calhoun's notes, " Lectures on Moral Philosophy," 36, 56.
[34] Bradford's notes, " Lectures on Eloquence," 208.

" a point that seems to have divided philosophers and poets, as well as divines, from the beginning of the world to this day." Contrary to the attitude of his optimistic contemporaries, Hume admitted that he was " sensible that a delicate sense of morals, especially when attended with a splenetic temper, is apt to give a man a disgust of the world." Having conceded this regrettable but nevertheless true observation about mankind, he proceeded to find considerable grounds for avoiding despair. In the first place, Hume observed that the goodness or badness of human nature depended upon the standard of comparison. If compared to animals, men appeared wise and virtuous, but if compared to angels, men certainly seemed mean and lowly. Secondly, " it is usual to compare one man with another; and finding very few whom we can call wise or virtuous, we are apt to entertain a contemptible notion of our species in general." Hume softened this judgment by pointing out that the terms " wise " and " virtuous " were comparative, since, " were the lowest of our species as wise as Tully or Lord Bacon, we should still have reason to say that there are few wise men."

Hume's final observation on human nature was a direct attack on the Hobbesian contention that all human motivation was basically selfish.

In my opinion, there are two things which have led astray those philosophers, that have insisted so much on the selfishness of men.

I. They found, that every act of virtue or friendship was attended with a secret pleasure; whence they concluded that, friendship and virtue could not be disinterested. But the fallacy of this is obvious. The virtuous sentiment or passion produces the pleasure, and does not arise from it. . . .

II. It has always been found, that the virtuous are far from being indifferent to praise; and therefore they have been represented as a set of vainglorious men, who have nothing in view but the applause of others. But this is also a fallacy. . . . Vanity is so closely allied with virtue, and to love the fame of laudable actions approaches so near the love of laudable actions for their own sake . . . it is almost impossible to have the latter without some degree of the former. . . . Nero had the same vanity in driving a chariot that Trajan had in governing the empire with justice and ability.[35]

The contribution which this kind of writing, and it is typical of Hume's polite but incisive essays, might have made to Madison's thinking was more one of mood and temper than one of bold, new ideas. Hume took a sensible, sophisticated middle ground on human nature. Of course, there was a great deal in the observable behavior of mankind that would give rise to a " disgust of the world." On the other hand, it was important to keep in mind that man was supposed

[35] David Hume, " Of the Dignity or Meanness of Human Nature," *Essays, Literary, Moral. and Political* (London, 1870), 45–49.

to be "a little lower than the angels." Finally, Hume's sharp mind bared the sophistry of those who would utterly blacken the character of man. The pattern is a significant and interesting one: logical errors exposed, regrettable realities admitted, but modest hope maintained in spite of the recognition of human imperfectibility. The Master of Montpelier dealt with many perplexities in precisely this fashion.

What, then, might Thucydides, Aristotle, Locke, and Hume have finally meant for James Madison? [36] Most important, the emphasis on Aristotle and Thucydides, who perhaps were representatives of much more of the classical tradition, denoted a major break with the dominant mood of the Age of Reason—realistic, sagacious moderation, instead of simple, naïve optimism. This is not to say that there is no compatibility between Classical and Enlightenment thought, or that Madison's contemporaries were not exposed to the same ancient authors. It simply suggests that Madison was more impressed, and enough more impressed by the idea of moderation in the classical tradition of freedom to make a crucial difference in his thought and philosophy. Comparison with both Jefferson and Hamilton is instructive. Hamilton was perhaps too much impressed with the élitism and power-consciousness of such classical figures as Plato and Caesar, and saw too little of the hope for human dignity and freedom which Christian and humane learning might have revealed to him. Jefferson, on the other hand, saw too much of the vision of the "heavenly city of the eighteenth-century philosophers," and was too neglectful of the sobering wisdom he might have gleaned while he was learning Greek and Latin.

In short, Madison's view of human nature, whether borrowed from the authorities suggested or merely a coincidental combination similar to them, can be summarized in a somewhat systematic fashion: the great truth, which critics of Plato from Aristotle to Karl Popper have pointed out so forcefully, that the talents and motivations of mankind are many, not one, was placed at the keystone of Madison's thought. Furthermore, the diversity ran not just in shades of black or shades of white, but covered the whole gamut of possibilities from very black to very white, from men who stoned dissenting preachers to George Washington. Also, since the passions and desires of individuals were sometimes modulated by rational judgment and sometimes not, it was not easy to predict what men would do, or indeed depend

---

[36] No comprehensive analysis of the thought of the four men has been attempted, of course. Two things, perhaps, will excuse this. First, the passages quoted are not secondary or extreme views of the authors; they are relatively important and representative selections. Second, passages have been chosen which bear most directly on the question of human nature.

finally on the wisdom or virtue of any particular person. Viewed as a whole, this unpredictability left society in a somewhat precarious position. At worst, the picture of the Corcyrean noblemen slain on the altar of Dionysus came to mind. At best, if a mixed system of government such as was formed under the Constitution of 1787 was devised, there was reasonable hope that men would be able to pursue their various kinds of happiness. Finally, the indispensable moral absolute, and the only unchanging star in Madison's philosophic firmament, was that men of right ought to be, and in practice had to be free if civilized society was to survive and life was to be " human " in the fullest sense of the word.

It is scarcely possible to over-emphasize the importance of this view of human nature to Madison's thought and philosophy. Not only does it indicate the substantive positions he took on any number of political, economic, social, diplomatic, and religious questions, but it offers keen insight into the frame of mind with which Madison faced the world. He was realistic, tolerant, tentative, and cautiously hopeful. In short, he saw the sensibleness of finding in store for the world what he could see in the nature of the men who gave it life and being.

University of Chicago.

XI

JOHN ADAMS ON
"THE BEST OF ALL POSSIBLE WORLDS"

By Constance B. Schulz*

The popular picture of John Adams is that of a conservative in spite of himself, a man obsessed with human shortcomings, hiding his own behind a prickly pride, determined to preserve the liberty of free men by hindering their actions. There is a widespread assumption among historians that John Adams was, as Trevor Colbourne has put it, "essentially pessimistic," finding in history "a record of human errors" so convincing that "since he did not anticipate any great change in human nature" he spent his entire career devising and then defending political institutions designed to defend human society against human foibles.[1] To anyone who has read widely in his political and personal writings, such a portrait of Adams is persuasive but incomplete. To dwell on its darker shadows is to ignore the importance of an equally important strain of optimism and liberality within Adams' thought. Adams' optimism and its philosophical roots are most conspicuously and luminously displayed in a little-known series of notes, inspired by his readings (during his retirement) of the philosophies of the Greek writers Ocellus and Timaeus Locrus, translated into French and annotated with extensive commentary by Jean Baptiste de Boyer, the Marquis d'Argens. The purpose of my paper is to evaluate the contribution of Adams' notes to our understanding of his thought and its classical Greek roots by first summarizing the contents and the purposes of the books themselves, and then analyzing his reactions to them.

His notes on Timaeus Locrus and Ocellus tell us several important facts about John Adams. First, they bear witness to the remarkable acuity of his skills and the range and depth of his knowledge. His facility in three languages is impressive: he quarrels occasionally with d'Argens' translation of the Greek into French; he fluently translates Greek, French, and Latin into a pungent and idiomatic English. His command of an

---

* A version of this paper was first read at the December 1980 meeting of the American Historical Association in Washington, D.C.

[1] H. Trevor Colbourne. *The Lamp of Experience: Whig History and the Intellectual Origins of the American Revolution* (Chapel Hill, N.C., 1965), 87. Other historians who have attributed Adams' conservatism to a pessimistic outlook upon human history are Randall B. Ripley, "Adams, Burke, and Eighteenth Century Conservatism," *Political Science Quarterly*, **80** (1965), 230-31; Clinton Rossiter, *Conservatism in America* (New York, 1962); Russell Kirk, *The Conservative Mind from Burke to Santayana* (Chicago, 1953); Peter Viereck, *Conservatism from John Adams to Churchill* (Princeton, 1956). In *The Changing Political Thought of John Adams* (Princeton, 1966), John R. Howe has argued that Adams shifted from an early optimism and liberalism into a mid-life conservatism and then back into a post-1812 optimism, but he concludes (249) that Adams never fully shook off "his earlier disenchantment about American society or his forbodings about its fate," and that while he was inclined in his last years to be hopeful, there was nevertheless "a tension between hope and pessimism."

extensive literature on philosophy, religion, mythology, and history is equal to that of d'Argens.[2] Though he complained to Jefferson about the deterioration of his physical condition, the notes, written when Adams was nearly eighty, are in a firm and readable hand, although there are traces of the arthritic quiver that would soon become so noticeable.

More important than the firmness of his hand, however, is the strength and vitality of his mind. His continued commitment of liberty of conscience, and his faith in the ability of the human intellect to operate within the sphere of the secular universe bear witness to Adams' continued involvement in the intellectual debate of a republican ideological revolution. The particular nature of Adams' optimism is important. His is no abstract philosophical conviction of universal benevolence; it is rooted, as is so much of his writing, in a sensual, physical, joyful affirmation of the dignity of being human. Adams was a creature of the eighteenth century, and of an orderly world view that was becoming outmoded even as he asserted it; but he was also a man who served as a bridge into a new epoch. In his notes on Timaeus Locrus and Ocellus, Adams repeatedly reaffirms the essential happiness of human experience; in this conviction lay the fertile soil for a nineteenth-century view of progress based on individual pursuit of happiness and accomplishment. All Adams' reading convinced him that there is no man totally depraved. "The most abandoned Scoundrel that ever existed, never Yet wholly extinguished his Conscience, and while Conscience remains there is some Religion." For that reason, declared Adams to Thomas Jefferson in a luminous burst of wisdom shortly after he had completed reading Ocellus and Timaeus:

the vast prospect of Mankind, which these Books have passed in Review before me, from the most ancient records, histories, traditions and Fables that remain to us, to the present day, has sickened my very Soul; and almost reconciled me to Swift's Travels among the Yahoo's [sic]. Yet I can never be a Misanthrope.

---

[2] John Adams' linguistic and scholarly accomplishments are analyzed in Alfred Iacuzzi, *John Adams, Scholar* (New York, 1952). Adams' classical skills are surveyed in Dorothy M. Robathan, "John Adams and the Classics," *New England Quarterly*, **19** (1946), 91-98, and less usefully in Susan Wiltshire Ford, "Thomas Jefferson and John Adams on the Classics," *Arion*, **6** (Spring 1967), 116-32. More useful both for understanding Adams and comparing his abilities and appreciation for the classics with those of his contemporaries are two articles by Meyer Reinhold, "Opponents of Classical Learning in America during the Revolutionary Period," American Philosophical Society, *Proceedings*, **112** (1968), 221-34, and "The Quest for Useful Knowledge in Eighteenth Century America," *ibid.*, **119** (1975). Richard M. Gummere, "The Classical Politics of John Adams," *Boston Public Library Quarterly*, **9** (1957), 167-82, Edwin A. Miles "The Young American Nation and the Classical World," *Journal of the History of Ideas*, **35** (1974), 259-74, and Linda Kerber, "Salvaging the Classical Tradition" in *Federalists in Dissent: Imagery and Ideology in Jeffersonian America* (Ithaca, 1970) also deal with classical studies and Adams' interest in them. Frank E. Manuel, "John Adams and the Gods" in *The Eighteenth Century Confronts the Gods* (New York, 1967), 271-82, describes Adams' interest in mythology.

Homo Sum. I must hate myself before I can hate my Fellow Men: and that I cannot and will not do. No! I will not hate any of them, base, brutal and devilish as some of them have been to me.[3]

The dismal catalogues of the depth of human folly that he had read were unable to change Adams' moral and religious creed, which "has for 50 or 60 Years been contained in four short Words, 'Be just and good.' In this result they all agree with me. . . . My conclusion from all of them is Universal Tolleration [sic]."[4]

The Platonic ideas of Ocellus and Timaeus Locrus that had in part inspired this conclusion formed an important part of the extensive program of reading that filled Adams' days at Quincy during his retirement. They are first mentioned by Adams in 1813. In August, Jefferson had described to Adams the Abbé Batteux translations of Ocellus and Timaeus Locrus stating only that it was they who "first committed the doctrines of Pythagoras to writing."[5] In a subsequent letter to Adams on the existence of a natural aristocracy, Jefferson cited Ocellus' pronouncements "concerning the interprocreation of men," and translated a long passage into English for his friend.[6] Adams' response on Christmas day made it clear that he was already quite familiar with both works. Scolding Joseph Priestley for failing to deal with the Pythagoreans in his compendium of the doctrines of heathen philosophy, Adams charged "He barely mentions Ocellus, who lived long before Plato. His Treatise of Kings and Monarchy has been destroyed. . . . His Treatise of 'The Universe' has been preserved. He labours to prove the Eternity of the World." Nor did Priestley include Timaeus, Adams continued, although

it does appear that he had read him. . . . He was before Plato and gave him the Idea of his Timaeus, and much more of his Phylosophy. After his Master he maintained the existence of Matter: that Matter was capable of receiving all sorts of forms: that a moving Power agitated all the Parts of it: and that an Intelligence produced a regular and harmonious World. This Intelligence had seen a Plan, an Idea (Logos) in conformity to which, it wrought, and without which it would not have known what it was about, nor what it wanted to do. This Plan was the *Idea*, Image or Model, which had represented, to the Supream [sic] Intelligence, the World before it existed, which had directed it, in its Action upon the moving Power, and which it contemplated in forming the Elements the Bodies and the World. This Model was distinguished from The Intelligence which produced the World as the Architect is from his plans. He divided The productive Cause of the World into a Spirit, which directed the moving Force, and into an Image, which determined it in the choice of the directions which it gave to the moving Force, and the forms which it gave to matter.

[3] April 19, 1817, in Lester J. Cappon, ed., *The Adams-Jefferson Letters, The Complete Correspondence Between Thomas Jefferson and Abigail and John Adams* (Chapel Hill, 1959) II, 509.

[4] Adams to Jefferson, Dec. 12, 1816; Cappon, II, 499.

[5] Cappon, *Adams-Jefferson Letters*, II, 368.

[6] Jefferson to Adams, Oct. 28, 1813, Cappon, *ibid.*, II, 387.

I wonder that Priestley has overlooked this because it is the same Phylosophy with Plato's and would have shewn that the Pythagorean as well as the Platonic Phylosophers probably concurred in the fabrication of the Christian Trinity.[7]

Such a detailed account of the content of the Timaeus Locrus suggests that Adams had either seen the work or discussed it at length with someone who had read it. The edition of the Timaeus Locrus—and of Ocellus—that Adams wished to read was not the more popular one prepared by the Abbé Batteux in 1768, but an earlier translation by the Marquis d'Argens. "D'Argens not only explains the text," Adams wrote to Jefferson, "but sheds more light upon the ancient systems. His remarks are so many treatises, which develope the concatenation of ancient opinions. The most essential ideas of the theology, of the physics and of the morality of the ancients are clearly explained, and their different doctrines compared with one another and with the modern discoveries."[8]

Adams did not have a chance to read these two volumes—and a third by d'Argens on the Emperor Julian—until the spring and summer of 1815.[9] The three small volumes are intact in the collection of Adams' books in the Rare Book Room of the Boston Public Library. Adams' usual habit of making notes in the margins was foiled by the lack of sufficient margin in which to write, and the books themselves are almost devoid of his marks. The comments appear instead in a sheaf of papers folded to make a small booklet; there are twenty-six manuscript pages of notes on Ocellus, forty-nine on the Timaeus Locrus, and an additional sixteen on the work by the Emperor Julian.[10] In each case, Adams' notes

[7] Cappon, *Adams-Jefferson Letters*, II, 409-13.

[8] Adams to Jefferson, Dec. 25, 1813, Cappon, *ibid.*, II, 411. Jefferson later responded that his own translation by Batteux was but "a meagre thing", although D'Argens' principal biographer points out that the Batteux edition is by far the better translation of the Greek into French. Jefferson to Adams, Jan. 1814, Cappon, II, 424; Elsie Johnston, *Le Marquis d'Argens, Sa vie et ses oeuvres, Essai biographique et critique* (Paris 1928), 109. Jefferson's copy of *Timée de Locres, de l'âme du monde avec la traduction françoise & des remarques*, par M. l'abbé Batteux (Paris 1768) is in the Jefferson Collection in the Rare Book Room of the Library of Congress.

[9] On June 20, 1815, Adams wrote to Jefferson: "I have at last procured the Marquis D'Argens' Ocellus Timaeus and Julian. Three such Volumes I never read," (Cappon, *op. cit.*, II, 546). Although he implied to Jefferson that he had already read all three, he was still plowing through the Timaeus Locrus on August 16, when he interrupted his comments upon d'Argens' lengthy discussion of the fall of Adam (and whether or not God was thus the author of sin) to note: "Went to Church, and Mr. Whiting opened the Service by Setting us to sing the 158th Himn intitled Divine Goodness," p. 20 of Adams' notes on Timaeus Locrus, Reel 188 of the Microfilm Edition of the Adams Papers, hereafter cited as APM.

[10] *Ocellus Lucanus, en grec et en françois* has John Adams' signature and the date "1815" written both on the title page and on the dedication page, where, at the end of a lengthy panegyric to "Votre Altesse Royale" Adams has commented: "Un Philosophe Adulateur." On page 321 of *Timée de Locres*, the phrase "la marche de l'esprit humain" is underlined in pencil, and in the margin in a shaky hand is written "Webster, 1824."

begin much like those of a diligent student, as jottings summarizing the content of the text. These parallel the one-word memory devices that litter the margins of his other books. But the pages of his homemade notebook provided Adams with more space, and perhaps the dissertations of d'Argens stimulated his argumentative personality to more effort. Soon the summaries are replaced with essays and dissertations by Adams. Those essays reflect Adams' own skills in translation, and his wide ranging literary and philosophical interests. They also illustrate Bernard Bailyn's perceptive observation that John Adams had "to an extraordinary degree . . . a sensuous apprehension of experience. For all his mental efforts and intellectual accomplishments, his knowledge and ideas, he responded first and fundamentally to the physical—the tangible, audible, visual—qualities of life." [11]

Although a modern (and sympathetic) student of the philosophical speculations of d'Argens has apologized that he was "one of the host of writers of every age whose opinions remain significant historically but who are condemned to oblivion by their intrinsic lack of talent," his works were widely known and read during his own time in intellectual circles in England and on the continent. [12] The Marquis d'Argens, Jean-Baptiste de Boyer (1703-1771), was one of the intimates of Frederick the Great. He served Frederick as chamberlain, friend, confident, butt of practical jokes, correspondent, and philosopher until his retirement in 1768. Though French, d'Argens gave Frederick his absolute loyalty, and near the end of the Seven Year's War he translated and embellished with copious notes the Greek philosophies of Ocellus and Timaeus Locrus as an anodyne for the abuse he received from the French clergy and conservative intellectual circles.

D'Argens was an amateur at translation, having mastered the Greek language during the eighteen-month period in which he completed both works, although Adams assured Francis Vanderkemp that d'Argens' translations were "not superficial," and that "his Greek and Latin are remarkably correct." [13] For his part, d'Argens had bragged to Frederick, "I left your Majesty stammering Greek and I will return knowing it like the Dacians and the Saumais." [14] The volumes are ostensibly translations,

[11] Bernard Bailyn, "Butterfield's Adams: Notes for a Sketch," *William and Mary Quarterly*, 3rd series, **19** (1962), 246.

[12] Newell Richard Bush, "The Marquis D'Argens and his Philosophical Correspondence: A Critical Study of d'Argens' *Lettres juives, Lettres cabalistiques*, and *Lettres chinoises*," (Unpublished Ph.D. Dissertation, Columbia University, 1953, printed by University Microfilms, Ann Arbor), 221. In addition to the biography by Elsie Johnston, reprinted in Geneva in 1971 (Slatkine reprints), and Bush's dissertation, Louis Thomas edited the *Mémoires du Marquis D'Argens* (Paris, 1941) with an introduction and critical discussion of its contents.

[13] Adams to Vanderkemp, July 13, 1815, in Charles Francis Adams, ed., *The Works of John Adams* (Boston, 1850-1856), X, 168.

[14] Johnston, *Le Marquis d'Argens*, 109.

with parallel Greek and French texts (in both cases the first such translation of these works into French), but d'Argens' real purpose found fruition in the lengthy notes or "dissertations" in French with learned digressions and quotations from Latin and Greek authorities.

D'Argens' interest in the translation of Ocellus resulted from its subject matter, the eternality of the world. He used this as a springboard to show that the ethical standards of the true Epicurean philosophers— foremost among whom were the circle of *philosophes* in Berlin—were superior to the standards proposed by the theologians. In so doing, he stopped just short of attacking revelation, for fear, he said, of raising anew the cries of "les fanatiques et les imbéciles." [15] The translation of Timaeus Locrus which followed that of Ocellus also had a polemical purpose for d'Argens; "I have composed the dissertations on Timaeus Locrus to pour out on the world, the most detestable of possible worlds, a small part of the bile that our enemies have poured on me. . . . That was the sole consolation that I have had in this unhappy time. I confided my chagrin to paper." [16]

Modern classicists have questioned the antiquity of both of these Greek texts, but Adams and d'Argens considered them genuine, that is, followers of Pythagoras and precursors of Plato. [17] Regarded as minor philosophers even before they were dismissed by the nineteenth century as frauds, both authors would seem to have but a minimal claim on our interest, perhaps worthy of notice in a footnote but not a fit subject for an article-length discussion in a serious journal of ideas. On the contrary, the combination of the Greek texts, d'Argens' *dissertations*, and Adams' voluminous notes form a three way dialogue that reveals some of the complexities of the transmission of ideas from two classical Greek texts, via a French commentator, to America, with consequent shifts in meaning and occasional distortion.

---

[15] Johnston, *Le Marquis d'Argens*, 110; Bush, "D'Argens' Philosophical Correspondence," 41.   [16] D'Argens to Frederick, Oct. 1762, Bush, 43.

[17] "Ocellus" is the name currently attributed to an anonymous forger around 150 B.C., see esp. Richard Harder, *Ocellus Lucanus, text und kommentar* (Berlin, 1926); this was given as Harder's 1924 inaugural lecture at Berlin. See also the entry on Ocellus in the *Oxford Classical Dictionary*, 1970 ed. In an interesting note, Anton-Herman Chroust, "Pseudo-Ocellus, De universe natura, A Fragment of Aristotle's *On Philosophy*?" *Classical Philology*, **69** (1974), 209-10, points out that there are close parallels between fragments of the Ocellus forgery and Aristotle's advance of the theory of the uncreatedness and indestructibility of the universe. Attribution of the Timaeus Locrus text is more complex. Alfred Edward Taylor, *A Commentary on Plato's Timaeus* (Oxford, 1928), 37, 655-64, argues that it is a first century A.D. Neo-Pythagorean forgery; Richard Harder, in *Pauly Wissowa* (1936), also labels it a forgery but believes it to be an abstract of a still earlier and unknown précis of Plato's *Timaeus*. Gilbert Ryle, "The Timaeus Locrus," *Phronesis*, **10** (1965), 74-90, argues that it might be a very early précis of Plato's *Timaeus* prepared while the latter was known only in an oral version within the Academy. Ryle suggested that it was ghost-written by a young Aristotle as a gift for Dionysius, when Aristotle was part of a delegation to Syracuse in the summer of 361 B.C., thus explaining the

The principal concerns of both Greek texts were the problems of the eternality or 'createdness' of the universe, the nature and origin of beings in it, and their relationship to each other and to the whole of which they were a part. In Ocellus' treatise, *On the Universe*, he argued that the universe, "has been eternal and will be eternal, uncreated, unproduced, imperishable," that it "gives no indication of Change," that its "Parts change, the whole never."[18] How then, it might be asked, can we account for those parts of the universe that are not eternal but have only a temporal existence? Are they less intrinsically a part of the universe than that which is eternal? What in the universe is eternal, what temporal, and how are they related to each other? What forces generate temporal beings? Is the essence of man his temporal physical existence, or some eternal spiritual nature? Ocellus answered these questions in four brief chapters that mixed material philosophy with a curious and labored scientific analysis of the nature of matter. The transitory nature of much existence in a material and eternal universe he explained by drawing a distinction between permanent matter and the perpetually changing, generated forms it takes "beneath the moon." Since the world is eternal and the existence of things of impermanent nature in it must be perpetual, they therefore must be generated in their own respective regions, the "Gods in the heavens, men on earth, and in the region on high demons."[19]

D'Argens, although he assured Frederick that he had stopped short of attacking revelation, made it clear in his comments on Ocellus that he rested his own ideas of a first cause not in revelation, but in the world of reason and of nature. His method, however, was that of Bayle, of quoting extensively from the sacred authorities to show the absurdity of those authorities. Ever ready to display the pomposity and foolishness of the Church Fathers, he annotated Ocellus' brief comment on demons at great length with the speculations of ancient, learned, and holy authorities upon the carnal origins of demons, their relationships with

---

"amateurish Doric" in which it is written. The definitive text of the Timaeus Locrus, prepared by Walter Marg, appeared in H. Theslaff's *The Pythaogrean Texts of the Hellenistic Period* (Abo, 1965); in 1972 Marg's student, Matthias Baltes, published an extensive commentary on that text, Timaios Lokrus, *Über die Natur des Kosmos und der Seele* (Leiden, 1972), #XXI in the Philosophia Antiqua series; that same year Marg added a discussion of the manuscript tradition of the text he had already edited for Theslaff; see Walter Marg, ed., Timaeus Locrus, *De Natura Mundi et Animae. Überlieferung, Testimonia, Text und Übersetzung* (Leiden, 1972), # XXIV, Philosophia Antiqua. Reviewers G.J.P. O'Daly, "Timaeus Locrus," *The Classical Review*, **25** (1975), 197-99; and R.E. Witt, *Journal of Hellenic Studies*, **94** (1974), 189-90, find no basis for Baltes's conclusion that the text is "a serious forgery" that may have been synthesized from an epitome of the Platonic *Timaeus* by Eudorus of Alexandria, and student lecture notes on Plato's *Timaeus*, and note that there is "no overwhelmingly convincing reason why" Ryle's more provocative thesis is wrong.

[18] Adams' translation, APM, reel 188, notes on Ocellus, p. 1.

[19] Translation by Taylor, p. 20.

women, and their physical attributes.[20] Demons, according to this mythology and to medieval Christian doctrine, were punished by God or the Gods for their carnal knowledge of women—for straying outside of their proper sphere. Indeed, D'Argens, who had a particular antipathy to the teachings of the Church on sin, struck a receptive chord in John Adams with a series of pointed questions:

How can one conceive that God condemns millions of creatures to eternal unhappiness, when he can deliver these same creatures after their faults have been purged and erased. . . . If God can end the sufferings of the damned, and make them useful and profitable, why would he wish to endlessly and fruitlessly reject them. . . ? The light of nature shows us that the idea we have of clemency and goodness, is against the belief in the supreme wisdom inflicting eternal pain when that wisdom could make them short and useful.

Remarked Adams, "This is very curious and very affecting."[21]

Although Ocellus insisted on the eternality of the universe, he could not deny that "violent corruptions and mutations take place in the parts of the earth," both in nature and in history. D'Argens, in expanding upon this theme, attributed men's ignorance of the extent of these changes to the accidental or deliberate destruction of the books that record them. Adams, for whom the disappearance of the ancient libraries was a favorite theme, responded "I can scarcely read this Page without Tears. . . . Shall I tell my suspicion? It is that Sacerdotal, Monarchical, Aristocratical and democratical Knavery, have all in their turns conspired to deprive us of these Sources of Information."[22]

Having discussed generation of demons, Ocellus turned in the final chapter of his treatise to the question of the generation of men, and here too d'Argens found inspiration for copious notes attacking the teachings of the church, most notably those on the miraculous story of the virgin birth. Ocellus's premise was simple: if individual men are finite and mortal, mankind as part of an infinite and eternal world must have some means of perpetuating itself. "The powers, instruments and appetites" imparted to men were not given for pleasure, "but for the sake of the perpetual duration of the human race."[23] Translated Adams: "We ought not to approach Women for pleasure: but for the procreation of Men!"

---

[20] Adams, dutifully taking notes, stopped long enough to inject learnedly that d'Argens "does not appear to have known any thing of the Hindoos or that Pythagoras had travelled in India, where the History of Demons was known in perfection before Moses was born." He raised the question "whether Hebrews, Greeks, Romans, and Christians have not derived their knowledge of Demons from Indostan?" and cited his own knowledge of this influence through "the splendid but uncertain Speculations of Sir William Jones" and the "futile effusions of Dr. Priestley," APM reel 188, notes on Ocellus, pp. 11-12.

[21] Jean-Baptiste de Boyer, Marquis d'Argens, *Ocellus Lucanus* (Utrecht, 1762), 114-15, translation my own; APM reel 188, notes on Ocellus, p. 14.

[22] APM reel 188, notes on Ocellus, p. 17.   [23] Taylor translation, p. 22.

adding his own anecdote: "John Torrey of Weymouth was as sage as Ocellus. He said Children ought never to be gotten, but religiously. And I think so too!" Ocellus did not, "like several fathers of the Church" insist that "the pleasures of Love are criminal in themselves,"[24] but d'Argens concluded his commentary on Ocellus with a forty-page note on the learned theologians' pious and detailed discourses on sex, written under the pretext of instruction against sin.

At first glance, the subject of Timaeus Locrus, "On the Soul of the World," seems much like that of Ocellus, but both the Greek author's treatment of it and d'Argens' notes give the treatise a distinctly different thrust, and inspired Adams to explore a new direction for his thinking. It is in the notes on the Timaeus Locrus that Adams' most profound insistence on a philosophical optimism are found. Notwithstanding his concern with human sexual relations, and the moral responsibility of men to use their generational powers wisely, Ocellus portrayed a material universe that was morally neutral. Timaeus Locrus addressed a more complex series of teleological and ontological questions by seeking moral values within the very design of the universe. Like Plato, he taught that the physical world known to men is produced from the tension between matter/force/necessity and spirit/mind/reason. Idea, or form, is unproduced, and fixed; matter, though eternal, is moveable. From the combination of the male/father/idea and the female/mother/matter, come those engendered produced things that men (who are themselves produced and engendered) discover through sensation and experience. Because the Idea is good, says Timaeus, the world "is the most excellent of Things that could be produced."[25]

In his dissertations illuminating Timaeus Locrus' statement of the Platonic principals, d'Argens moved considerably beyond the position in favor of a philosophical materialism that he had taken in his commentaries on Ocellus. In an immense note of one hundred and sixty three pages, ranging in subject matter from more discourses on the sexual behavior of the gods to a chronicle of the horrors of the religious wars of Europe, d'Argens attempted to show that this was far from being the best of worlds, that it might indeed be the worst. Page after page listed the terrors of persecution, savagery, debauchery, all in the name of the noble cause of religion, and formed the basis for a sneering attack on human pretensions to understand the nature and purpose of the universe. D'Argens chronicled all these things, he claimed, to show how destructive conflicting convictions in matters of faith had been to humanity. He suggested disingenuously that a possible alternative to brute strength was the creation of a sovereign judge—i.e., a Pope—to proclaim an infallible

[24] APM reel 188, notes on Ocellus, p. 18.

[25] This summary of the philosophy of the Timaeus Locrus is based on Adams' notes on the Greek text and d'Argens' French translation of it, in the APM, reel 188, page 3 of Adams' notes on the Timaeus Locrus, hereafter cited as TL.

truth, known through revelation. Though he cited long excerpts from church authorities on the need for such a spiritual sovereign, d'Argens then proceeded to fill an equal number of pages with examples of the absurdity of the pretensions of past Popes to any such authority or wisdom. D'Argens' French contemporaries understood that this exercise, veiled though it was in a mockingly pious and learned deference for ancient authorities, was a virulent attack on the central tenets of the Roman Catholic Church. D'Argens' works, though disguised as translations, were in reality an unequal debate between an angry *philosophe* and his defenseless Greek texts. Or, as D'Argens succinctly expressed it when his patron Frederick questioned his motives in publishing these works: "If your Majesty will be so kind as to read my dissertations, he will see that I have not made the sauce for the fish, but that I have cooked the fish in order to have a pretext to make the sauce."[26]

John Adams' response to the conflicting ideologies bound together through d'Argens' fiction of expanding upon the translation with "notes" and reflections, adds yet another dimension to the debate. Just as d'Argens used the Greek texts as a pretext for his own defense of a philosophical position of skeptical materialism against the attacks of the French clergy, Adams too used the Greek and d'Argens' learned discourses as a springboard for his own concerns. In part he became immersed in his readings on ancient religions[27] because they addressed the central question of the origin and purpose of evil in the universe. Cosmological speculation was not an idle hobby; solution to this problem was necessary for vindication of Adams' political ideas, because it was to control the bad or evil effects of human nature that he believed in the necessity of a political balance. Governments can devise political methods for controlling these evil effects only if the men who create them understand the source and nature of those evil tendencies that make such control necessary.

Adams' observations in response to Ocellus and Timaeus Locrus need to be divided into two general categories, which coexist, jumbled together throughout the manuscript notes. First are a series of reactions that form a kind of high-spirited argumentative debate on the specific textual content of d'Argens' work. Adams argued with a translation, was shocked by examples used by d'Argens to prove a point, was reminded by d'Argens' text of yet other more appropriate examples. These notes of Adams are informed by a philosophical position of cautious optimism that is at the same time almost Kantian in its denial of the efficacy of metaphysical speculation; nevertheless they are primarily surface reactions to the immediate stimulus of the text. There is, however, a second and more

---

[26] D'Argens to Frederick, 4 November 1761, Johnston, *Le Marquis d'Argens*, 111.

[27] After Adams had completed d'Argens' three works, he turned to the work of Dupuis to satisfy his curiosity about solutions to these problems in mythology; see F. Manuel, "John Adams and the Gods," 271-80.

important aspect to Adams' notes contained in a litany of luminous statements of testimony from the heart of his optimism: this is the best of all possible worlds, and human experience in it is fundamentally happy.

A series of recurring themes comprise the first category of his notes, showing that Adams had little use for the scientific thinking of the Greeks which he dismissed as "a mass of Ignorance of natural Philosophy and Chemistry," and "a parcell of Ignorance and nonsense."[28] He was fascinated and outraged by d'Argens' lengthy dissertations on human sexuality and reproduction, and suspected d'Argens of prurient motives in reprinting such extensive theological writing on the topic. "St. Justin again discusses the question concerning Adam + Eve, very anatomically + casuistically," John Adams recorded in his notes, remarking as he followed d'Argens' dissertations, "Outrageous," "D'Argens must have inserted all this dispicable [sic] and indecent stuff, merely to make the theologians ridiculous." Finally, after a long and learned discourse from St. Augustine on the thesis that copulation was not known to Adam and Eve until after their expulsion from Eden, Adams could stand it no longer. "Had Eve Bubbies?" he exploded. "Could Adam see them, or feel them, without Concupiscence? Were they not made to Suckle Infants? For what was the Uterus made?" Ocellus, he concluded, was "more reasonable" than the learned Church Fathers. As d'Argens assembled more examples of the teachings of the Church on the celibacy of priests, of its doctrinal insistence on the necessity of immaculate conception, and of its rejection of "carnal commerce," Adams perceptively queried, "Is not all this Hindoo and Pythagorean Contempt of Matter and flesh?" and, for once, he had nothing but approval for d'Argens' dissertations. "Sound Reflection" expressed Adams' praise: "Well said, D'Argens" while he dismissed the learned Church Fathers—Ambrose, Jerome, and Tertullian—as "Mad! Stark Mad!" on the subject.[29] When Ocellus counselled that laws should be instituted to prevent "incest and marriages of consanguinity," Adams found it "Excellent advice," and added, "And I could give good Advice to the Masters of Negroes, English French Spanish Dutch Portugese, and Swedish, with fear and trembling I must add the Planters in my beloved Country to forbid familiarities between their Boys and their Negro Girls."[30]

Adams, whether because of difficulties with the French language or ignorance of d'Argens' philosophic career, sometimes failed to grasp the mocking purpose of d'Argens' dissertations, particularly his tongue-in-cheek insistence on the need for a Pope as a spiritual sovereign. Adams' confusion in this case, however, prompted him to pen an impassioned

---

[28] APM reel 188, notes on Ocellus, pp. 8-9.
[29] APM reel 188, notes on Ocellus, pp. 18-19.
[30] APM reel 188, notes on Ocellus, pp. 24-25.

plea for liberty of conscience. D'Argens devoted the last half of the notes on the first chapter of Timaeus Locrus to an extensive exercise in Biblical criticism, aimed at the central theological problems of the nature of revelation and of Christian teaching about the origin of good and evil. "Mystery!" exclaimed Adams, is "The Mortal Poison to all freedom of speech Writing and Printing. There can be no Mystery in Religion or Morality. The Head and the heart must be united; The Understanding the Will and the Affections must concur in every Act of Religion or Morality."[31] But he could not accept d'Argens' tongue-in-cheek insistence that a judge of the faith was required to eliminate mystery. "Truth says if Liberty of Conscience had been established, those Wars would have been more effectually avoided," he insisted; "I infer the necessity of Liberty of Conscience, which would secure the Peace of Society much better than Popes and general Counsells. . . . Liberty of Conscience and freedom of Investigation ought to be unlimited."[32]

Adams first became deeply engaged with the central philosophical questions of both the Greek and French texts over the question of whether the universe was essentially matter or spirit. Although Adams denied allegiance to the materialism of Ocellus and d'Argens, his perception of the dilemma of both materialists and spiritualists was unabashedly based on his appreciation for the richness of physical experience. After one of d'Argens' long notes, Adams commented:

Come let me be a little saucy, with Gassendi, Descartes, and Lock[e]. What Extension divisibility, height, depth, length, or Breadth, has the simple Sensation, the Smell of the Rose. the Feeling of Velvet? The Sight of the Sun? The hearing of Musick? The Taste of a Grape? A Strawbury [sic]? or a Pine Apple? How long or how short, how high or how deep, is a simple apprehension or Perception? of Memory and Imagination? of Judgment? of Reason? of Method, Order, Arrangement?

Adams' own conclusion was that of the rationalist realist who wished to affirm not only the utility of reason but also his perception of his own limitations as a reasoner. "Vain man! fall into thyself and be a Fool. Acknowledge thy Ignorance of the Nature of God Matter and Spirit. Their Effects only are known to thee and that very Superficially and imperfectly; but enough for thy nature and thy State and as much as they can bear."[33] He did not argue with either Ocellus or d'Argens against the eternality of the universe. Indeed, Adams believed that "All Christians will agree in this. The universe comprehends the Deity, all Intelligible Beings, all Matter. The first cause is self existent. Whatever changes he may make in Minds, Bodies, or Motions, the Universe will still exist."

[31] APM reel 188, notes on the TL, p. 35.
[32] APM reel 188, notes on the TL, pp. 42-43.
[33] APM reel 188, notes on Ocellus, comments upon d'Argens' note to S 14.

It seemed to Adams, however, that d'Argens claimed too much for human intelligence in going beyond a simple observation of the eternality of the universe to argue for its material origins:

Presumptuous mortal! Drop into thyself and be a Fool. An animalcule in pepper Water! A Mite in a Cheese! an Atom floating in the Sun Beams, is proud enough to aspire to the comprehension of the TO ΠΑV! Is there more than one omni[s]cient Being? Was there ever more than one? Will there ever be more than one! Man! Thy duty and thine interest, and thine happiness, are confined to a narrow Gird; they are written on thine heart; and are confirmed by Jesus. Yet I fear I am as proud as vain and as conceited as any of you.[34]

In this comment, though it is tinged with orthodox piety, Adams reflects the cautious optimism of most eighteenth-century deists and of Lockean practicality. An understanding of the world that included a hierarchy of all possible created beings placed man's intelligence considerably below that of the Creator and of other higher sorts of existence. Men therefore best fulfilled their place in nature's rational order if they bent their reason and their energy to those things they could understand. It is human pride that leads man astray; Adams' refrain finds echo in Pope's lament:

> In pride, in reas'ning pride, our error lies'
> All quit their sphere and rush into the skies.[35]

For Adams, Pope, and d'Argens, of course, the outcry is primarily against theologians and metaphysicians, for progress in human society is possible only when people deal with what they can understand in order to behave morally and rationally towards one another, and foreswear acting on the basis of superstition and mystery. Among those superstitions and mysteries, Adams insisted, was the quarrel among theologians and philosophers over matter and spirit. "Why quarrel for matter," he challenged Ocellus and d'Argens,

when you know not what it is? Why quarrell Against or for spirit when you know not what it is. Here is a depth in which We are all drowned. It should admonish us, to dogmatize no longer upon Subjects too deep and too vast for our Faculties. Instead of appealing to a Pope; appeal to God. Do your duty which is plain before you. Do no Wrong! Do all the good you can! lament your faults and correct them. Submit to eternal Wisdom! and essential Goodness.[36]

The Platonic metaphysical dualism that divided the universe into phenomena and "form" or into matter and spirit, underlies an equally fundamental moral dualism. It formed the basis in medieval and Christian thought for attributing what is good in the universe to that which is

---

[34] APM reel 188, Adams' notes on Ocellus, p. 4.

[35] Arthur O. Lovejoy, *The Great Chain of Being* (Cambridge, Mass., 1936), Chap. 6, esp. 192-93.

[36] APM reel 188, Adams notes on Ocellus, pp 5-6.

spiritual, and evil to that which is material. Adams could not accept the Manicheean heresy of the two principles. "Plutarch! Thou liest! Thine assertion is a Libel on the Universe and its Author, Father, Creator, Principle!" he exploded at one of d'Argens' learned authorities. "The World composed equally of good and Evil is a lie!" On the contrary, wrote Adams in a bold hand, "There is a thousand times more good than Evil in the Universe! Philosophers have taken their own fretfull peevish humours for Evils. Does the Universe exist for them? to gratify their Vanity and justify their presumption? So thinks a pampered Goose."[37] When d'Argens brought Plato forth as an expert witness on the dualist principles, Adams added an exponential power to his ratio: "Many Persons still pretend that God is the Author of all Evil, even of sins and crimes," he noted, but "Plato libells [sic] God and his Universe, When he says there is much more Evil than good in the Universe. On the contrary there is ten thousand times more good than Evil in the Universe!"[38]

In this Adams engaged himself in a debate that deeply troubled enlightened philosophers of the eighteenth century. Arthur O. Lovejoy has brilliantly outlined the history of the idea of plenitude and its relationship to the Platonic ideal of an essentially benevolent universe.[39] Neither Adams nor d'Argens made particularly innovative contributions to this optimistic ideal as it was developed in the eighteenth century. Indeed, d'Argens addressed the central problem of that philosophy, "If God and the universe are good, why do men suffer?" by quoting at length the attempts of Leibniz to answer it:

It results from the supreme Perfections of God that in producing the Universe, he chose the best plan that was possible. The best of all possible Worlds. The greatest possible Varieties with the best possible order. Space Time Bodies and Spirits, the best managed to the best advantage. . . . The most knowledg, [sic] Happiness and Goodness that the Universe could bear. . . . The result of all these productions must be the present World as it is; and the most perfect that is possible.[40]

Leibniz's answer was not one that d'Argens could accept, and he set out to prove instead "not only that this World does not deserve to be considered, the best among possible Worlds; but, on the contrary that it is the worst, for Evil, Physical or moral infinitely exceeds all the Good in it."[41] He proposed to do this by reciting "The History of France, from Francis 1st to the death of Louis 14," to show "as proof, for 200 years,

---

[37] APM reel 188, notes on the TL, p. 6.

[38] APM reel 188, notes on the TL, p. 7.

[39] In *The Great Chain of Being, op. cit.*, passim.

[40] The translation of Leibniz is that made by Adams, and found in the APM reel 188, p. 13, notes on page 40 of the TL.

[41] APM reel 188, notes on the TL, p. 14.

that Evil was tryumphant over good." Adams took extensive notes: "Henry 2nd Who can read this Reign without tears, indignation and horror?" when "circumstances of Cruelty too horrible to relate, were the amusement of King and Courtiers after their Debauches." No less affecting were "the horrors of St. Bartholomews day and Week." He even thought that d'Argens could have added to the catalogue of misery: "You might have remembered Guy Fauks's Powder Plott, the Irish Massacre, and all the Wars of Religion for 1500 Years."[42]

But Adams could not agree that these events proved what d'Argens claimed. His emphatic response foreshadows the utilitarianism of Jeremy Bentham, and reflects a peculiarly American tendency toward individualism.[43] Leibniz, and the philosophers of the enlightenment who wished to celebrate the benevolence of the universe, had done so by stressing its diversity, and the positive role that evil in it might play. Theirs was a philosophical and intellectual argument, based it is true, on the physical evidence of the plenitude of existence. For Adams, the proof of benevolence was not in an optimistic and abstract intellectual philosophy, but in a utilitarian psychology that stressed individual rather than corporate experience. "This short Sketch of the Calamities of Europe is not Exaggerated," he admitted.

It might have been aggravated consistently with Truth. But does it follow from all this that there was more Vice than Virtue in Europe for those 200 Years? There was probably an immense overballance of Virtue. Was there more pain than pleasure in Europe during those two Centuries. Probably there were thousands of times more Pleasure than Paine. Probably there was not one Individual in Europe during that whole Period who did not experience ten times more Pleasure than pain during his whole Life. This is the only fair Way of stating the question. To me there appears an immense Preponderance of Virtue and happiness even in this World wicked and miserable as it is represented.[44]

What is revealing here is not Adams' use of the principles of pleasure and pain, of measuring virtue by assessing happiness, but his application of it to a philosophical optimism. Equally revealing is the common sense observational basis for his conclusion that history's sufferers experienced more pain than pleasure: "Upon your Principles," he tells d'Argens, "it would be wise and philosophical in every Individual of the human race to commit Suicide, to get out of the worst of possible Worlds, and extricate himself from infinitely more Evil than good, as soon as possible. There are bodkins, Swords Pistols, Halters, Ponds Lakes Rivers, Opium Arsenick enough at hand to deliver you at once, from the Worst World and the greatest Evil."[45]

[42] APM reel 188, notes on the TL, pp. 15-16.

[43] I am indebted for the suggestion of this influence to the work of J.R. Pole, *American Individualism and the Promise of Progress*, an Inaugural Lecture delivered before the University of Oxford on 14 February 1980 (Oxford, 1980).

[44] APM reel 188, notes on the TL, p. 18. [45] APM reel 188, notes on the TL, p. 21.

But Adams observed that very few people, even given the assurances from religion of a future life of happiness, chose escape from the world as it is. "Vain presumptuous Mortal! Has there been one second of thine Existence that you would not have preferred to Non Entity?" he asked d'Argens.[46]

Yet even as he made this luminously optimistic, and in some ways naive, statement about human physical experience, Adams nevertheless realized that he had not solved the problem of the origin and purpose of evil. "The Reasoning of D'Argens . . . I acknowledge I cannot Answer. I cannot reconcile the Existence of Evil, with infinite Wisdom, Goodness and Power. On the other hand I cannot reconcile a World, mechanically necessarily chimically happy, with the Existence of Liberty or Morality in the Universe."[47] From Richard Price (1723-91) he borrowed a halfway answer: that the triumph of justice and the assurance of the goodness of the created universe was possible if one accepted the idea of future rewards and punishments. "The Doctrine of a future State is or ought to be a consolation to the just under all the pains of Life but even this does not account for the Existence of Evil physical or moral even for one moment in any part of the universe, tho it ought to reconcile our Minds to its Existence."[48] Even as he puzzled, Adams dropped back from the precipice to take refuge in his knowledge of his own ignorance and human limits:

If Liberty and Morality are necessary in the best of possible or conceivable Worlds, this may be the best. But where are you and I wandering D'Argens? We are but Glow Worms, vainly conjecturing the Essence of the Sun and the Theory of Light. We are Ants reasoning on the Influence of the Dog Starr[;] to employ your own Style We are Still infiniment Petits, reasoning on Subjects infiniment grand. With Horace and Pope, "Trust the Ruler with his Skies." "Fall into thyself."[49]

Even as he counselled resignation, however, Adams could not escape recognition that he had plunged himself into another dilemma; "Liberty and morality" demanded the existence of a choice, for there could be no virtue in doing that good which had been determined by another, nor liberty in doing what had been preordained or foreknown. To "Trust the ruler with his skies," to acknowledge divine foreknowledge and the ultimate adjustment of good over evil in the balance of the world, in some future state, seemed to deny free will. "That Morality, and Liberty which

[46] APM reel 188, notes on the TL, p. 8.

[47] APM reel 188, notes on the TL, p. 20.

[48] APM reel 188, notes on the TL, p. 23. Richard Price's most cogent statement of the necessity of belief in a future state of rewards and punishments if one believed in the virtue of the universe is found in Price's *A Review of the Principal Questions in Morals* (London, 1787), published shortly before Adams left London. See esp. Chap X and Price's conclusions, 443 ff.

[49] APM reel 188, notes on the TL, p. 20.

is essential to it have an eternal foundation in the Universe I have no doubt. That they are consistent with the Wisdom Power and Goodness of God I have no doubt. But how they are reconcileable, and how they are reconciled, I know not, Is this a Wonder? No. Vain Mortal! were you summoned to the eternal Counsells of this immense Universe. As well might an Ant or a Bee, pretend to such distinctions."[50]

Nor could Adams accept comfort from answers to this puzzle that were proffered by revelation. Adams himself claimed to believe in revelation, but his idea of revelation was quite different from that of the theologians. For him, it was human understanding that was the principle "revelation from its maker which can never be disputed or doubted. We can never be so certain of any Prophecy, or the fulfillment of any Prophecy; or of any miracle, or the design of any miracle as we are, from the revelation of nature; i.e. of nature's God that two and two are equal to four."[51] Yet even here, he believed, caution demanded that the observer separate the revelations of nature from speculation on causes: "Causes are all hidden: effects only are seen felt, heard, smelled, tasted. Intellectual Causes are equally unknown: Moral causes are felt. Conscience and common Sense feels and perceives are the only guide to duty and Interest."[52]

Adams' lifelong study of human nature convinced him that "conscience and common Sense" demanded a simple moral and religious creed: "Be just and good;" while "duty and Interest" led him to the conclusion of "Universall Tolleration."[53] These are the conclusions that lay behind Adams' notes on Ocellus and the Timaeus Locrus. Like d'Argens he used the text that he read as a springboard for the expression of his own convictions. Historians have rightfully shown the importance of Adams' reservations about human nature as the basis of his particular political solutions for the experiment in republican government which he helped to launch; but it is not amiss to point out that his reservations were those of a realist, not of a pessimist. Adams, more perhaps than any of his contemporaries ever realized, knew all too well his own faults, sins, ignorance, limitations. He saw clearly that his countrymen and his friends shared those human qualities in varying degrees; but he never lost sight of, nor ceased to celebrate, the possibilities as well as the limitations of human existence.

College of Wooster, Ohio.

---

[50] APM reel 188, notes on the TL, p. 22.
[51] Adams to Jefferson, 14 September, 1813, Cappon, *Adams-Jefferson Letters*, II, 373.
[52] APM reel 188, notes on Ocellus, pp. 8-9.
[53] See discussion (n. 4 above), Adams to Jefferson, Dec. 12, 1816.

XII

JOEL BARLOW, ENLIGHTENED RELIGIONIST

By Joseph L. Blau

When Joel Barlow was graduated from Yale, in 1778, he needed a job and found it as a chaplain in the Revolutionary Army. At this time he was a conservative thinker about religion as about other subjects. He was one of the group who, under the name of "the Hartford wits," scathingly denounced any extremist point of view. He was not insincere in becoming a chaplain. One of his earliest literary labors was a rewriting of Isaac Watts' hymn book in smoother verse. His first major work was an epic, "The Vision of Columbus," which was marked throughout by genuine piety and a constant reference to an anti-Catholic, conservative religious position.[1]

Some years later, however, while Barlow was in Europe as the agent for one of our earliest fraudulent land-promotion schemes, as a free-lance commercial speculator, and as the official representative of the American government in occasional matters, he came under the influence of Tom Paine, Godwin, and other advanced thinkers of their circle.[2] These revolutionaries may not have produced a revolution in his economic ideas, but they certainly affected his religious views.

These later religious ideas, as expressed in Barlow's prose and poetry, reveal very clearly the tendency of the enlightened among the men of the enlightenment to place organized religion on the periphery of human affairs. Any authoritarianism, any dogmatism makes religious belief central to life; it is to the interest of the churches and their clergy to maintain or to regain this central position. Enlightened religionists were, therefore, anticlerical and opposed to church establishments. They favored freedom of wor-

[1] Cf. Joel Barlow *The Vision of Columbus; a Poem in Nine Books* (Hartford, 1787), 28, 53, 205–7, 216–17, 230, 235. Some passages, however, reveal that special brand of eighteenth century piety which was called Natural Religion, and which was a half-way house on the road to Deism, Unitarianism, or open infidelity.

[2] Details may be found in Charles Burr Todd, *Life and Letters of Joel Barlow, LL.D. Poet, Statesman, Philosopher,* (New York, 1886); an interpretation of this phase of Barlow's life was recently presented by Joseph Dorfman, "Joel Barlow: Trafficker in Trade and Letters," *Political Science Quarterly,* LIX (1944), 83–100; cf. also J. Dorfman, *The Economic Mind in American Civilization* (New York, 1946), I, 459–71.

ship because it precluded the growth of any single strong church. They approved of freedom of thought and were free in their own thinking without necessarily being freethinkers.

What makes them especially significant is their dominance in the early period of our history. The first six presidents of the United States, from Washington to John Quincy Adams, whatever their nominal church affiliation, were in all essentials enlightened religionists. The first forty years of our existence under the Constitution, the years during which the attitude of our government towards religion was crystallized, were marked by an indifference to formal religion on the part of our chief executives.

In the writings of Barlow, then, we will look to find both the negative, destructive elements characteristic of his enlightened group, and the positive formulation of beliefs which, because they held spiritual meaning for him and for many of his fellows, we may call his religion and theirs. His work is a convenient source because he was literate in ideas, profuse in their expression, and typical of a large group in his day. It is interesting to note that the matters with which we deal fell, in Barlow's mind, into the class of self-evident truths which "are as perceptible when first presented to the mind, as an age or a world of experience could make them."[3]

Barlow's contention in the *Advice to the Privileged Orders* is that "The establishment of general liberty will be less injurious to those who now live by abuses, than is commonly imagined."[4] In marshalling his evidence to prove this statement, he suggests that no law and no government can last for any length of time without benefiting a sufficiently large section of the aristocracy. "The tyrannies of the world . . . are all aristocratic tyrannies . . . which go to enrich the whole combination of conspirators, whose business it is to dupe and to govern the nation."[5] No one group within the aristocracy being sufficiently numerous to impose its interests, combinations of privilege arise for mutual benefit. Out of the conflict of what we today would call pressure groups

[3] Joel Barlow, *Political Writings, containing Advice to the Privileged Orders. Letter to the National Convention. Letter to the People of Piedmont. The Conspiracy of Kings.* (New York, 1796), iv. From the Introduction to "Advice to the Privileged Orders."

[4] *Ibid.*, vii.

[5] *Ibid.*, ix–x.

"has arisen the necessity of that strange complication in the governing power, which has made of politics an inexplicable science; hence, the reason for arming one class of our fellow creatures with the weapons of bodily destruction, and another with the mysterious artillery of the vengeance of heaven."[6] Not only the army and the church, but also the courts of justice join with the wealthy feudal nobility to perpetuate privilege and to prevent commerce and industry from improving the condition of men.

It is in the context of privilege, then, that Barlow considers the church. "Mankind are by nature religious," and the church subverts this natural characteristic to the purpose of sustaining the feudal system. The authoritarianism of the church helps to keep the greater part of the people ignorant of their strength, which is necessary because "men . . . are as naturally disposed to calculation, as they are to religion" and can, if not distracted, realize their united power to overthrow their oppressors. "Recourse must therefore be had to mysteries and invisibilities; an engine must be forged out of the *religion* of human nature, and erected on its credulity, to play upon and extinguish the light of reason, which was placed in the mind as a caution to the one, and a kind companion to the other." The church under various names has been the means used to keep men in proper subordination to authority. Which church has been most harmful is hard to decide, but "Were it not for the danger of being misled by the want of information, we should readily determine, that under the assumption of christianity it has committed greater ravages than under any other of its dreadful denominations."[7]

He is very careful to point out that he is not talking about religion as such, but only about the church, which he sees as a system of abuse, "darkening the consciences of men, in order to oppress them."[8] In discriminating between religion and the church, Barlow uses the United States of America as an example of a country in which there is no national establishment, but in which the people are very religious. Where religion is a personal rather than a corporate matter, heresy, schism, apostasy, and priesthood have no place. Men may profess, maintain, or change their beliefs without running counter to organized dogmatism. This leads

[6] *Ibid.*, x.
[7] *Ibid.*, 34–35.
[8] *Ibid.*, 35, *n.*

to the conclusion that *"The existence of any kind of liberty is incompatible with the existence of any kind of church. By liberty,* I mean the enjoyment of equal rights, and by *church,* I mean any mode of worship declared to be national, or declared to have any preference in the eye of the law."[9] In fact, the absence of a church establishment is the security for the continuance of both religion and liberty in the United States.[10]

Again, in his "Letter to the National Convention of France," dated September 16, 1792, Barlow argues against the necessity of maintaining a "national church." Such an establishment he declares to be "an imposition upon the judgment of mankind, . . . one of those monarchial ideas, which pay us the wretched compliment of supposing that we are not capable of being governed by our own reason." He denies the assertion that public support of the Catholic priesthood was "founded on the idea of the property supposed to have been possessed by that church" and expropriated by the nation, for "the church . . . signifies nothing but a *mode of worship;* and to prove that a mode can be the proprietor of lands, requires a subtilty of logic that I shall not attempt to refute."[11]

Finally, Barlow maintains that the abolition of an established church would not cause the destruction of religion itself, for religion is a "natural propensity of the mind, as respiration is of the lungs." He advocates, therefore, unrestricted exercise of freedom of worship without governmental subvention of any sort, and maintains that this will further the cause of true religion.

I can see no more reason for making laws to regulate the impression of Deity upon the soul, than there would be, to regulate the action of light upon the eye, or of air upon the lungs. I should presume therefore, that, on stripping this subject of all the false covering which unequal governments have thrown upon it, you will make no national provision for the support of any class of men, under the mock pretence of maintaining the worship of God. But you will leave every part of the community to nominate and pay their own ministers in their own way. The mode of worship which they will thus maintain, will be the most conducive to good order, because it will be that in which the people will believe.[12]

[9] *Ibid.*, 40.
[10] *Ibid.*, 49.
[11] *Ibid.*, 172–73.
[12] *Ibid.*, 173–74.

Just as Barlow distinguished church and religion, he differentiated priest and minister. To the extent that he saw the clergy as an organized force working for the perpetuation of privilege, he called clergymen ''priests'' and maintained a strongly anti-clerical point of view. To contrast with this priesthood, this ''hierarchy,'' he presented a view of congregationalism, under which there existed a ministry dependent upon the choice of the people, and living in a society protected against their encroachments.

As long as public teachers are chosen by the people, are salaried and removeable by the people, are born and married among the people, have families to be educated and protected from oppression and from vice,—as long as they have all the common sympathies of society, to bind them to the public interest, there is very little danger of their becoming tyrants by force and the liberty of the press will prevent their being so by craft.[13]

For the most part, however, he concerns himself with criticism of ''the hierarchy'' which ''is every where the same engine of state; and whether it be guided by a Lama or a Mufti, or by a Pontifex or a Pope, by a Bramin, a Bishop or a Druid, it is entitled to an equal share of respect.''[14]

Every order of privilege must be able to demonstrate in some way its unique possession. The rich own land or buildings; the lawyers can plead in the jargon of the courts. The stock-in-trade of the priesthood is a peculiar relationship with divinity. ''The first great object of the priest is to establish a belief in the minds of the people, that he *himself is possessed of supernatural powers.* ... This article once established, its continuation is not a difficult task. For, as the church acquires wealth, it furnishes itself with the necessary apparatus, and the trade is carried on to advantage.''[15] This peculiar relationship redounds to the disadvantage of the people in various ways. It makes democracy impossible; ''as long as governors have an established mode of consulting the auspices, there is no necessity . . . of consulting the people.''[16] It raises the priest, as man, above other men and thereby causes him to lose sight of common motives and common decencies.

[13] *Ibid.,* 49.
[14] *Ibid.,* 41.
[15] *Ibid.,* 41.
[16] *Ibid.,* 42.

The moment you give one member of society a familiar intercourse with God, you launch him into the region of infinities and invisibilities; you unfit him, and his brethren, to live together, on any terms but those of stupid reverence and of insolent abuse. . . . When a person believes that he is doing the immediate work of God, he divests himself of the feelings of a man. And an ambitious general, who wishes to extirpate or to plunder a neighbouring nation, has only to order the priest to do his duty, and set the people at work by an oracle; they then know no other bounds to their frenzy than the will of their leader pronounced by the priest; whose voice to them is the voice of God. In this case the least attention to mercy or justice would be abhorred as a disobedience to the divine command. This circumstance alone, is sufficient to account for two-thirds of the cruelty of all wars—perhaps in a great measure for their existence—and has given rise to an opinion, that nations are cruel in proportion as they are religious. But the observation ought to stand thus, *That nations are cruel in proportion as they are guided by priests;* than which there is no axiom more undeniably without exception.[17]

Thus Barlow saw the need for the downfall of hierarchy as one step in the upbuilding of humanity. He approved, therefore, of the suppression of the monasteries by the constitution of the French Republic. In his letter of December 27, 1792 to the citizens of Piedmont, he returns to one of his favorite themes, the improvement of religion by the destruction of hierarchy. The authors of the French constitution, he declares, have worked for the advantage of religion by suppressing "those haunts of idleness, hypocrisy, and vice, known by the name of monasteries and convents . . . for religion teaches men to do good, and to labour for their living; but these institutions teach them to do nothing, and live upon the labours of others."[18]

Barlow's anticlerical views and his opposition to a church establishment persisted beyond the immediate revolutionary period in France which led him to the expressions which have been presented. In the course of his epic poem, the *Columbiad*, published in 1807, he frequently associates kings, priests and ministers of state as agents of human bondage.[19]

There is less of the church in the *Columbiad;* there is, however, a repeated reëmphasis on the author's antagonism to the priests. Montezuma, for example, is pictured as "A sovereign

[17] *Ibid.*, 42–43.

[18] *Ibid.*, 212.

[19] E.g., *Columbiad*, Book VII, lines 659–74.

supplicant with lifted hands'' attempting to placate with treasures
and cession of sovereignty the conquering Spaniards, who stand
unmoved

> While blind religion's prostituted name
> And monkish fury guide the sacred flame.[20]

In general, anticlericalism appears here as a phase of Barlow's
belief in freedom of thought; for the most part, it is ''the bondage of the mind'' which the priesthood promotes to which Barlow
is opposed. He asserted that the discovery of America would
spread benefits

> Wide thro the world while genius unconfined
> Tempts loftier flights and opens all the mind.[21]

He declared that Erasmus had torn

> . . . the deep veil that bigot zeal has thrown
> On pagan books and science long unknown,[22]

while Luther had walked forth ''From slavery's chains to free
the captive mind.''[23]

Again, one function of Truth, ''on these regenerate shores'' of
America, is to bid

> . . . Bright instruction spread her ample page
> To drive dark dogmas from the inquiring age.[24]

Indeed, he was certain that even the clergy in the new world was
tolerant, undogmatic, unified in moral purpose.

> Tho different creeds their priestly robes denote,
> Their orders various and their rites remote,
> Yet one their voice, their labors all combined,
> Lights of the world and friends of humankind.[25]

Out of the background which has thus far been presented, Barlow incorporated into the ninth book of the Columbiad a history of
the growth of religion. This is preceded by a developmental account, first of the earth and then of man. Barlow was assuredly
not taking the biblical account of creation literally when he wrote
of the earth:

20 *Ibid.*, Book II, lines 334; 341–342.
21 *Ibid.*, Book IV, lines 59–60.
22 *Ibid.*, Book IV, lines 139–40.
23 *Ibid.*, Book IV, line 150.
24 *Ibid.*, Book IV, lines 483–84.
25 *Ibid.*, Book VIII, lines 535–38.

> . . . What an age her shell-rock ribs attest!
> Her starry spines, her coal-incumber'd breast!
> Millions of generations toil'd and died
> To crust with coral and to salt her tide,
> And millions more, ere yet her soil began,
> Ere yet she form'd or could have nursed her man.[26]

Nor was he orthodox in his account of the coming of man.[27] No more is his tale of the origin of religion grounded in revelation.

In those dark days, those innumerable ages, when the primitive ancestor of man wandered a prey to every beast, before he had developed "the pinions of his lofty mind," superstitious error was born.

> And when, as oft, he dared expand his view
> And work with nature on the line she drew,
> Some monster, gender'd in his fears, unmann'd
> His opening soul and marr'd the works he plann'd.[28]

The forces of nature, still beyond the control of man, were animistically considered as personal powers. Out of these personalized natural forces arose the god idea, of which monarchy is an earthly expression.

> Hence rose his gods, that mystic monstrous lore
> Of blood-stain'd altars and of priestly power.
> Hence blind credulity on all dark things
> False morals hence and hence the yoke of kings.[29]

After some account of the worship of heavenly bodies,[30] Barlow restates in more detail his view that the habit of faith in supernatural beings led to the development of monarchy, and describes the union of priest and king to continue the slavery of mankind.

> His pliant faith extends with easy ken
> From heavenly hosts to heaven-anointed men;
> The sword, the tripod join their mutual aids
> To film his eyes with more impervious shades,
> Create a sceptred idol and enshrine
> The robber chief in attributes divine,
> Arm the new phantom with the nation's rod

[26] *Ibid.*, Book IX, lines 95–100.
[27] Cf. *Ibid.*, Book IX, lines 101–14.
[28] *Ibid.*, Book IX, lines 141–44.
[29] *Ibid.*, Book IX, lines 157–60.
[30] Cf. *Ibid.*, Book IX, lines 161–74.

> And hail the dreadful delegate of God.
> Two settled slaveries thus the race control,
> Engross their labors and debase their soul;
> Till creeds and crimes and feuds and fears compose
> The seeds of war and all its kindred woes.[31]

Now Barlow directs his attention to priestcraft in Egypt, Greece, Tibet, and India, in the Apollonian mystery cults, in Islam and "the Magian faith;" everywhere we see that the "fraudful drama" first enacted by "sainted hierophants"

> Forms local creeds, with multifarious lore
> Creates the god and bids the world adore.[32]

Paralleling these realms of priest-led darkness, Barlow shows the few scant signs of the ripening of reason, in Tyre, in Carthage, and in Syracuse, until finally the true dawn of reason came in Greece. Dashed down in Greece, human reason established itself in Egypt. "From Egypt chased again," reason found a home in "sage, considerate Rome," until, in the monk-ruled middle ages, man forgot "the gorgeous glare he made,"

> Wars with his arts, obliterates his lore
> And burns the books that rear'd his race before.[33]

Finally, the development of scientific knowledge of the universe, of the compass, and of the printing press led to an era of progress for man in which there will be no setbacks. In fact, he declares, had these been discovered sooner, there would have been no dark ages.

> Rome, Athens, Memphis, Tyre! had you but known
> This glorious triad, now familiar grown,
> The Press, the Magnet faithful to its pole,
> And earth's own movement round her stedfast goal;
> Ne'er had your science from that splendid height
> Sunk in her strength nor seen succeeding night.[34]

Despite his scattered references to the role of the monks in keeping the minds of men fettered, Barlow's comments on religion in the *Columbiad* are for the most part, non-specific. It would be quite possible for a member of any Christian denomination to

[31] *Ibid.*, Book IX, lines 177–88.
[32] *Ibid.*, Book IX, lines 247–48.
[33] *Ibid.*, Book IX, lines 437–38.
[34] *Ibid.*, Book IX, lines 657–62.

read most of the passages which have been quoted and agree that
other religious groups had at various times been guilty of the
offenses listed by the poet. This is not true, however, of the last
passage in which Barlow mentions religion, for here the cross
is associated with the symbols of other religions as ''destructive
things'' and ''agents of the woes of man.''

> Beneath the footstool all destructive things,
> The mask of priesthood and the mace of kings,
> Lie trampled in the dust; for here at last
> Fraud, folly, error all their emblems cast.
> Each envoy here unloads his wearied hand
> Of some old idol from his native land;
> One flings a pagod on the mingled heap,
> One lays a crescent, one a cross to sleep;
> Swords, sceptres, mitres, crowns and globes and stars,
> Codes of false fame and stimulants to wars
> Sink in the settling mass; since guile began,
> These are the agents of the woes of man.[35]

It was to this passage in particular that the Abbé Henri Gregoire, former Bishop of Blois, adverted in his celebrated *Critical
Observations on the Poem of Mr. Joel Barlow, the Columbiad.*[36]
An engraving, in the first edition of the poem, illustrated these
lines; this illustration was titled ''Final destruction of prejudices.'' Of these lines and illustration, Gregoire observed that
no one desired the destruction of prejudices more than he did but
that Barlow was at fault in classing with the dangerous emblems
of prejudice ''the attributes of the catholic ministry, and, above
all, the standard of christianity, the cross of Jesus Christ!''
Even without the evidence of eighteen centuries of Christian history, ''it would be easy to shew that this picture is an attack
against all christian societies, that it is an act of intolerance, of
persecution, which offends God and man.''[37]

After an assertion of the benefits of Christianity and a description of the attacks directed against that religion during the excesses of the French revolution, Gregoire continues with the charge
that Barlow is condemnable before the tribunal of public opinion
because his publication offended both propriety and justice.

[35] *Ibid.,* Book X, lines 599–610.
[36] Washington City: Printed by Roger Chew Weightman. 1809.
[37] Gregoire, *Critical Observations,* 3–4.

"Your presbyterian countrymen will perhaps ask, if you have abjured the principles that you professed when you were the chaplain of a regiment in the war of independence."[38] Again, Gregoire concluded: "The true foundation of political liberty is in the gospel, for it perpetually reminds men, that, having all proceeded from the same stock, they compose only one family; that there exists among them, not a species of relationship, as has been said in a well known work, but a real consanguinity, whose bond is indistructible."[39] Thus Gregoire attempted, as did so many others thinkers of his day, to make belief in democracy dependent upon belief in the Christian religion, to insist that the brotherhood of man is meaningful only as a corollary of the Fatherhood of God.

Gregoire's letter was given wide publicity in conservative ecclesiastical and political periodicals. Barlow's reply,[40] therefore, displayed prominently the request that editors who had published Gregoire's letter should also publish Barlow's answer to it. "It is an act of justice due to him, and to the character of their Journals, as well as to the Author."[41]

Barlow opened his reply with expressions of personal esteem for Gregoire, and a disclaimer of responsibility for the engraved illustration against which Gregoire had directed his attack. He then remarked on the relation of religious beliefs to one's birthplace, and explained his lack of concern for the cross as a result of his having been born and educated in the iconoclastic sect of puritans. He insisted that he still adhered to the religious beliefs of his youth because of "a conviction that they are right."

Next, he emphasized his distinction between a symbol and the reality it signifies, and reassured his correspondent that his opposition was only to the symbol.

I mention these things, my worthy friend, not with the least idea of levity or evasion; but to prove to you how totally you have mistaken my meaning and my motive; to show by what chain of circumstances . . . our habits of opinion, our cast of character are formed; to show how natural it is that a man of my origin and education, my course of study and the views I must

[38] *Ibid.*, 10.

[39] *Ibid.*, 14.

[40] Joel Barlow, *Letter to Henry Gregoire, Bishop, Senator, Compte of the Empire and Member of the Institute of France, in Reply to his Letter on the Columbiad.* Washington City: Printed by Roger Chew Weightman. 1809.

[41] *Ibid.*, 2.

have taken of the morals of nations, their causes and tendencies, should attribute much of the active errors that afflict the human race to the use of emblems, and to the fatal facility with which they are mistaken for realities by the great vulgar of mankind; how the best of christians of one sect may consider the christian emblems of another sect as *prejudices* of a dangerous tendency, and honestly wish to see them destroyed; and all this without the least hostility to their fundamental doctrines, or suspicion of giving offence.[42]

He accused Gregoire himself of having identified symbol and substance by treating the cross and the gospel as the same thing. To Gregoire's assertion that Barlow would be offended were the symbols of liberty to be trampled underfoot,[43] Barlow's consistent reply was "Leave to me and my country the great realities of liberty, and I freely give you up its emblems."[44]

In defense of the *Columbiad*, Barlow defied any critic "to point out a passage, if taken in its natural unavoidable meaning, which militates against the genuine principles, practice, faith and hope of the christian system."[45] On the contrary, he asserted it to be "more consonant to ... the spirit of the gospels than all the writings of all that list of christian authors of the last three ages, whom you have cited as the glory of christendom."[46] He repeated the claim made in the preface of the *Columbiad*, that the poem is a highly moral work.

Gregoire had mentioned the setting up of the image of a Goddess and a temple of Reason by the French revolutionists.[47] Barlow explained that the minds and hearts of the people of France had become so habituated to concrete representations of divinity by the practice of the Catholic church, that even liberty, reason, and the rights of man had to be made visible and tangible before they could be understood. Personification became deification, which, in its turn, became reification in the hands of the populace. "*August* liberty, *holy* reason, and the divine rights of man" had to be bodied forth in marble and plaster of Paris before the people could understand; "they must create before they could adore."[48]

[42] *Ibid.*, 5–6.
[43] Gregoire, *Critical Observations*, 10.
[44] Barlow, *Letter to Henry Gregoire*, 7.
[45] *Ibid.*, 8.
[46] *Ibid.*, 8.
[47] Gregoire, *Critical Observations*, 6.
[48] Barlow, *Letter to Henry Gregoire*, 11.

In this way, Barlow shifted the guilt for the failure and the excesses of the French revolution to the Catholic Church.

It has been shown that Barlow considered himself a Christian, but that he objected to both church organization and clerical dominance. For him as for Thomas Jefferson, Christianity meant the moral code of the gospels rather than the theological dogmas of the churches. Both church and clergy seemed to Barlow agents of oppression, maintaining over the minds and the spirit of men a despotism similar to and associated with that which kings and nobles maintained over men's bodies. He saw the forms of worship as a substitution of the shadow of spirituality for its substance, and advocated an iconoclastic, anticlerical, congregational religion.

By the elimination of the church and its hierarchy and symbols, Barlow thought men would be brought nearer to the essence of Christian belief which he found in the ideas of freedom and of progress. The free mind served as an illustration of the divine in man; the free life made possible the free use of reason. Freedom of the press, freedom of speech, freedom of trade, freedom from oppressive taxation and governmental interference, and freedom of worship were to him the preconditions of the unfettered divine mind in man. Progress was the external and visible sign of this inner and spiritual grace. It is, therefore, in Barlow's apostrophes to freedom and progress that the positive content of his enlightened religion is revealed.

The *Columbiad* begins with an invocation to freedom "to teach all men where their interest lies."[49] Again, Columbus is urged by the guardian spirit of the western world, Hesper, not to despair of good arising from his discovery of America, despite the immediate evils of the Spanish conquest.

> Now borne on bolder plumes, with happier flight,
> The world's broad bounds unfolding to the sight,
> The mind shall soar; the coming age expand
> Their arts and lore to every barbarous land;
> And buried gold, drawn copious from the mine,
> Give wings to commerce and the world refine.[50]

Columbus himself, after visions of the future greatness of America

[49] *Columbiad*, Book I, line 27.
[50] *Ibid.*, Book II, lines 389–94.

have been revealed to him, exults in the coming glories of the race
of men.

> Predestined here to methodize and mold
> New codes of empire to reform the old.
> A work so vast a second world required,
> By oceans bourn'd, from elder states retired;
> Where, uncontaminated, unconfined,
> Free contemplation might expand the mind,
> To form, fix, prove the well adjusted plan
> And base and build the commonwealth of man.[51]

The faith of the enlightenment in the regenerative power of
reason finds clear expression in the Columbiad. A this-wordly
conception of salvation through the creation of a new social order
founded upon a reasonable morality of liberty and industry
marches through Barlow's verse.[52] Man's salvation will come in
the United States because

> FREEDOM, his new Prometheus, here shall rise,
> Light her new torch in my refulgent skies,
> Touch with a stronger life his opening soul,
> Of moral systems fix the central goal,
> Her own resplendent essence.[53]

Freedom is apostrophized as the "Sun of the moral world." She
is to point out to men how inequality is the source of all conflict;
she is to "unfold at last the genuine social plan," when men shall
reach their full dignity and nations dare "to be just and wise."[54]
   The gospel of progress is associated by Barlow with the evolutionary development presented in the ninth book of the *Columbiad*.

> Know then, progressive are the paths we go
> In worlds above thee, as in thine below.
> Nature herself (whose grasp of time and place
> Deals out duration and impalms all space)
> Moves in progressive march; but where to tend,
> What course to compass, how the march must end,
> Her sons decide not; yet her works we greet
> Imperfect in their parts, but in their whole complete.[55]

[51] *Ibid.,* Book IV, lines 335–42.
[52] Cf. especially, *Ibid.,* Book IV, lines 417–42.
[53] *Ibid.,* Book IV, lines 473–77.
[54] *Ibid.,* Book IV, lines 495–98.
[55] *Ibid.,* Book IX, lines 39–46.

Although the goal of progress is not clearly revealed in its inception, Barlow shows what he thinks the end is to be, for man. It is to be complete freedom of thought, by virtue of which man may

> Lift keener eyes and drink diviner day,
> All systems scrutinize, their truths unfold,
> Prove well the recent, well revise the old,
> Reject all mystery and define with force
> The point he aims at in his laboring course.

This freedom will lead man to a deeper understanding of the world, and of the true nature of right and wrong. It will help him to define the proper limits of civil power. In this visioned end, man

> Gives to just government its right divine,
> Forms, varies, fashions, as his lights increase,
> Till earth is fill'd with happiness and peace.[56]

This ideal will be achieved first in the United States, and soon every nation will imitate her, and thus a league of enlightened nations will come about.

> Each land shall imitate, each nation join
> The well based brotherhood, the league divine,
> Extend its empire with the circling sun,
> And band the peopled globe within its federal zone.[57]

In Barlow, we have a fair representation of what the earliest political leaders of the United States thought about religion, and about freedom of religion. By no means everyone agreed with this view. Elihu Palmer, Ethan Allen, and other Deists went much further in advocating the destruction of Christianity. Conservative thinkers like the Connecticut group from which Barlow broke away agreed with Gregoire that liberty and Christianity (preferably their own brand of both) were truly one and inseparable. The dominant view, for a time, was, however, that of the liberal, enlightened religionists, and it was over this liberalism that Christianity in America had to triumph to reestablish its centrality in the life and thought of Americans.

Columbia University.

[56] *Ibid.,* Book IX, lines 672–76; 692–94.

[57] *Ibid.,* Book IX, lines 699–702; cf. also Book X, in which details of the league are presented.

PART TWO

DISCOURSES OF
POLITICS AND NATION

XIII

THE MEANING OF COLONIZATION IN AMERICAN REVOLUTIONARY THOUGHT

By Michael Kammen*

One of the most enduring and intriguing inquiries in American intellectual history concerns the nature and development of revolutionary ideas between 1763 and 1776. In the many constitutional, political, philosophical, and literary studies that have appeared, the historical assumptions of Americans in these years have been a secondary, if not marginal, consideration. Those assumptions have usually been regarded as incidental to the central thrust of an emerging ideology which tended to be ahistorical or primarily whiggish in its reading of the past.[1] My purpose here, therefore, is to consider pre-revolutionary American attitudes toward colonial origins, particularly colonization before 1652.[2] Such attitudes were inextricably intertwined with the better known political ideas of these years, but their relationship has not hitherto been fully explored.

Students of American thought in the revolutionary era have generally presupposed the importance and inevitability of intellectual change as colonials groped for secure and tenable ground in the Great Debate. In 1922 Arthur M. Schlesinger characterized such change as "a strategic retreat," and his view was accepted and adopted by many others.[3]

---

*An earlier version of this paper was read before the Southern Historical Association, Nov. 10, 1967, in Atlanta, Georgia.

[1]There are two significant exceptions. Wesley F. Craven, *The Legend of the Founding Fathers* (N.Y., 1956), ch. 2, is concerned with tradition as a force that shaped the developing contest with England, and especially with the extent to which the colonists' case depended upon an appeal to their own history. H. Trevor Colbourn, *The Lamp of Experience: Whig History and the Intellectual Origins of the American Revolution* (Chapel Hill, 1965) concentrates on books the provincials read, particularly English history. The author gives much attention to their reading of Saxon history and the Norman conquest, but then skims down to the later seventeenth century. While displaying the colonists' distaste for the Stuarts generally, Colbourn devotes little space to the Stuarts' historic role in New World colonization. See also Richard M. Gummere, *The American Colonial Mind and the Classical Tradition* (Cambridge, Mass., 1963), ch. 6.

[2]In New England the concern with colonization concentrated on the years 1620–1640. In Virginia the years 1584–1624 were only slightly more important than 1624–1652. Craven, *Legend of the Founding Fathers*, 54, 56.

[3]*New Viewpoints in American History* (N.Y., 1922), 179; also Carl L. Becker, *The Declaration of Independence: A Study in the History of Political Ideas* (N.Y., 1922), 133; Randolph G. Adams, *Political Ideas of the American Revolution* (Durham, N.C., 1922), *passim*; Charles F. Mullett, *Fundamental Law and the American Revolution, 1760–1776* (N.Y., 1933), 79, though Mullett feels there were some who took a consistent stand through the whole polemic. Max Beloff's Introduction to *The Debate on the*

MICHAEL KAMMEN

In 1948 Edmund S. Morgan rejected the notion "that the colonists were guilty of skipping from one constitutional theory to another, like so many grasshoppers." Nevertheless he saw a growth in radicalism after 1770, and admitted that "American revolutionary thought went through two stages, [if] not three."[4] In recent years historians have abandoned the attempt to reconstruct revolutionary thought as a kind of three-stage rocket. Whether they regard the changes as a liberating progression of propulsive discoveries, or as a "strategic retreat," all join in viewing the intellectual history of these years as a matter of flux. In the main they are right to do so, for the patterns of change are by now well-documented. Nonetheless their emphasis has tended to obscure the most constant consideration in the colonial mind: the historical meaning of early colonization.

What emerges from an examination of pre-revolutionary writings, private as well as public, is a cluster of preliminary observations on the importance of provincial origins in American thought. First, there was an interpretative debate of significant proportions on this issue, conducted on both sides of the Atlantic. Second, the patriots' completely Lockean position helped to sustain their faith in the justness of their cause. Third, it led them to question and challenge parliamentary sovereignty as early as 1765. Fourth, the patriot position utterly infuriated their opponents. And finally, it constituted a major line of consistency and continuity in revolutionary political thought. Until the fullest implications of the meaning of colonization became clear after 1772, and reliance upon this argument was augmented, Americans of very diverse political persuasions shared a common body of historical assumptions: John Dickinson, William Smith, *and* their opponent Benjamin Franklin in Pennsylvania; Samuel Adams, James Otis, *and* Thomas Hutchinson in Massachusetts; Richard Bland, George Wythe, *and* Arthur Lee in Virginia.

The two most striking tendencies in early American historical thought and writing seem oddly paired: an emphasis upon colonizing origins coupled with a desire to explicate "the present state" of a given colony. To some extent this juxtaposition encouraged a foreshortening of the intervening narrative, as well as an inability to develop fully both the inherent continuities and patterns of change. Not surprisingly, by the 1760's, the century since Cromwell and the Restoration

---

American Revolution, 1761-1783 (London, 1949) refers to "the shifting of the grounds of the discussion as it proceeded" (8).

[4] "Colonial Ideas of Parliamentary Power 1764-1766," *William and Mary Qtly.*, ser. 3, V (July 1948), 341. I agree with Morgan that the patriot position was more advanced in 1764-66 than most historians have recognized. In analyzing the colonists' rejection of Parliament's right to tax, however, Morgan does not treat the historical basis of their argument.

had been intellectually telescoped and blurred. Yet there were advantages in doing so, for during that century the colonies, however inadvertently, had seemed to acquiesce in parliamentary sovereignty. This might have been a much greater source of embarrassment after 1765 had not the first generations *already* been staked out by writers on the past as constitutionally determinative. Just where "the first generations" ended is not clear; but the years 1641–52 formed a twilight zone beyond which most patriotic Americans of the revolutionary period were reluctant to reach. And with good reason. After 1641 all "dominions of the Crown" had effectively become part of "the Commonwealth of England and the dominions and territories thereunto belonging," though that terminology would not become official until 1649 when Parliament passed the Act establishing the Commonwealth, an indivisible entity ruled absolutely by a Parliament of the English nation. The full exercise of Parliament's power over her colonies came in 1651 with passage of the first Navigation Act on October 9th.[5] Some provincial historians and polemicists would wind their accounts through the years after 1652; but most preferred to confine their investigations to the earlier decades.

After 1763, when the prolonged controversy with Parliament made arguments based upon the original character of English colonization politically useful, the best documented part of that polemic involved Puritan New England. Michael Wigglesworth's vision of the purpose and nature of early settlement had become widely read after 1662 in "God's Controversy With New England." The following generation added such laments as Joshua Scottow's *Narrative of the Planting of the Massachusetts Colony* (1694) and Cotton Mather's *Magnalia Christi Americana* at the turn of century. John Callender's centennial work on Rhode Island (1738) focused on that colony's origins, hoping thereby to develop provincial self-consciousness through the use of history. Thomas Prince's purpose in compiling his narrative was partially to show that Puritan colonization had been the true culmination of the Protestant Reformation.[6]

In contrast, the earliest historical treatments of colonial origins in New York were not used to praise the pious and exhort the impious, but rather to justify conflicting Dutch and later Anglo-Dutch claims. From Adriaen van der Donck's *Representation of New Netherland* (1650) until the *History* of William Smith, Jr. (1757), Yorkers examined their provincial genesis with a critical eye. Smith's title page

[5]C. H. McIlwain, *The American Revolution: A Constitutional Interpretation* (N.Y., 1923), 21, 28, 44, 108, 110, 112–13.

[6]Callender, *An Historical Discourse on the Civil and Religious Affairs of the Colony of Rhode-Island*, R.I. Hist. Soc. *Collections*, IV (1838); Prince, *Chronological History of New England in the Form of Annals* (Boston, 1736).

quoted from James Thomson's *Liberty* five lines emblematic of the meaning of colonization accepted well before the revolutionary crisis unfolded.

> Lo! Swarming o'er the new discover'd World,
> Gay Colonies extend; the calm Retreat
> Of undeserv'd Distress.....
> .... Bound by social Freedom, firm they rise;
> Of *Britain's* Empire the Support and Strength.

In Virginia William Stith's long history (1747) was essentially devoted to clarifying the historical circumstances of Chesapeake colonization—an effort to rectify Captain John Smith's misleading story. Samuel Smith's bulky *History of the Colony of . . . New Jersey,* published in 1765 but written earlier, followed the well-established doctrine: the first Americans had emigrated to seek or preserve civil and religious liberty.[7]

For more than a century then, as Carl Bridenbaugh has shown, "the colonists had been constructing the version of history employed during the debate of the 'sixties."[8] In all of these narratives, whether Robert Beverley's Virginia, Provost Smith's Pennsylvania, or Thomas Hutchinson's Bay Colony, the legal arrangements and charter provisions of colonization received great attention alongside the hardships and motivations for migrating. Meanwhile such historical discussions were paralleled by the political writings of the pre-revolutionary years. By 1760 the surviving charters had long been consulted as special documents of higher law inextricably involved in the circumstances of colonization. New England received her charters, according to Jeremiah Dummer in 1721, in order to settle colonies: "to strip the country of their charters after the service has been so successfully performed is abhorrent from all reason, equity and justice."[9]

In 1728 the elder Daniel Dulany insisted that the first settlers of Maryland were Englishmen entitled to the benefits of English statutes as well as the common law. His argument, rooted in the earliest circumstances of colonization, stressed the reciprocal nature of allegiance and protection. A decade later a dispute in South Carolina elicited from Maurice Lewis the view that "the Common Law and the Principles of our Constitution immediately take Place upon the forming of

[7]*The History of the First Discovery and Settlement of Virginia* (Williamsburg, 1747), 329; *History of . . . New Jersey . . . to the Year 1721* (Burlington, 1765), xi.

[8]*Mitre and Sceptre: Transatlantic Faiths, Ideas, Personalities, and Politics, 1689–1775* (N.Y., 1962), 172–78.

[9]Dummer, *A Defence of the New-England Charters* (Boston, 1721, 1745, *1765*), 7–8; Perry Miller, *The New England Mind from Colony to Province* (Cambridge, Mass., 1953), 389.

a new Colony of British Subjects, and . . . no Usage or Royal Instructions can take away the Force of it in America." Once again the colonists would cherish and defend "a fundamental Right . . . handed down to us from our Ancestors."[10] In New York during the 1740's, Cadwallader Colden, a learned Newtonian and conservative Scot, devoted to the Crown, depicted the earliest history of New England in terms that would be repeated again and again by patriots a quarter century later.

The first settlers of New England at First underwent great difficulties having little assistance from their Mother Country & became in a great measure independent of it. It is probable that without that enthusiastic zeal which animated the first planters they must have succumbed under the difficulties they met with in a wilderness destitute not only of all the comforts of life but even of necessaries otherwise than by hard labour and a penurious manner of liveing. By Voluntarly subjecting themselves to the strictest discipline in the performance of all religeous civil & military duties they established a numerous & flowrishing colony with little or no assistance from their mother country.[11]

Thus by the time of the Seven Years' War a consistent and well-developed view of colonial origins had been in common use for decades. Portents of trouble ahead, however, lay in the rather different understanding held by imperial administrators, such as Arthur Dobbs or Benjamin Martyn. As Secretary to the Trustees of Georgia, Martyn was deeply involved in administrative aspects of colonization in the 1730's. To his mind colonies were unquestionably dependencies, fully subject to imperial authority from the very outset. Governor Dobbs believed that the establishment of colonies was due to overpopulation and the lust for dominion. Because land had been grabbed in America by greedy settlers regardless of the rights of the natives, much trouble had ensued, not to mention great expense incurred by the Crown in protecting her colonies. Nothing could have been farther from the patriot view of colonization adumbrated with growing intensity after 1764.[12]

The patriot view during the pre-revolutionary decade essentially comprised answers to five questions: why had the first English settlers

[10]*The Right of the Inhabitants of Maryland to the Benefit of the English Laws* (Annapolis, 1728); M. Eugene Sirmans, *Colonial South Carolina: A Political History, 1663-1763* (Chapel Hill, 1966), 203–4; J. H. Easterby and R. S. Green, eds., *The Colonial Records of South Carolina: the Journals of the Commons House of Assembly* (8 vols., Columbia, S.C., 1951–61), 1736–1739, p. 720.

[11]Colden, "Account of the Government of the New England Colonies" [c. 1742], in N.Y. Hist. Soc. *Collections*, LXVIII (N.Y., 1937), 247–48.

[12]Albert B. Saye, "The Genesis of Georgia Reviewed," *Georgia Historical Quarterly*, L (June 1966), 159 and n22; Caroline Robbins, *The Eighteenth-Century Commonwealthmen* (Cambridge, Mass., 1961), 151–52.

emigrated? under what circumstances? what had become of their relationship to England after settling here? what constitutional and
social consequences of lasting importance ensued? and finally, why
were all of these matters significant a century and a half later?

The first of these queries was the most simply answered. At a
critical point in the history of England and Liberty, the colonizers
had escaped an arbitrary reign, marked by oppression and bad legislation, in order to enjoy civil and religious liberties undisturbed and
pass such cherished treasures on to their posterity.[13] More important were the circumstances of their coming, for as Samuel Adams
noted in 1765, they "emigrated at their own Expence, & not the
Nations; As it was their own & not a National Act; so they came to
& settled a Country which the Nation had no sort of Right in." They
brought with them all the privileges, immunities, and rights of Englishmen—rights assured in the future by virtue of royal charters.
"By all these charters," wrote Stephen Hopkins, "it is in the most
express and solemn manner granted, that these adventurers, and
their children after them forever, should have and enjoy all the freedom and liberty that the subjects in *England* enjoy."[14]

The first settlers brought with them the "full and absolute power
of governing all the people of this place, by men chosen from among
themselves," because when men "withdraw themselves from their
country, they recover their natural Freedom and Independence: The
Jurisdiction and Sovereignty of the State they have quitted ceases;
and if they unite, and by common Consent take possession of a new
country, and form themselves into a political Society, they become a
Sovereign State, independent of the State from which they separated."[15] This view of Richard Bland's, written in Virginia in 1766,
was reiterated in 1768 by William Hicks of Philadelphia, in 1774 by
Peter Whitney of Boston, and throughout these years by countless
others. The colonizers had brought with them the spirit of English
government, and assumed that "they should be allowed to make such
regulations as might answer the purposes of their emigration." Once
colonial governments were organized (with the concurrence of Crown

[13] James Lovell, *An Oration Delivered April 2d, 1771* (Boston, 1771), 13–14; Oliver
Noble, *Some Strictures upon the . . . Book of Esther . . .* (Newburyport, 1775), 21n.

[14] Harry A. Cushing, ed., *The Writings of Samuel Adams*, I (N.Y., 1904), 27–28;
[Stephen Hopkins], *The Rights of Colonies Examined* (Providence, 1765), 5, 8–9;
[Daniel Dulany], *Considerations on the Propriety of Imposing Taxes* ([An-
napolis], 1765), 14–15, 29–30.

[15] Cf. John Locke, *Two Treatises of Government: A Critical Edition With an Introduction and Apparatus Criticus*, by Peter Laslett (2nd ed., Cambridge, Eng., 1967),
363–64.

officials), Hicks observed, they "totally disclaim[ed] all *subordination* to, and dependence upon, the two inferior estates of their Mother country."[16]

Because only the King, and not Parliament, had entered into compacts with the first settlers, he alone retained any sort of relationship to "all the lands in America." "The great enquiry, therefore," as young Alexander Hamilton put it, "is concerning the terms on which these lands were really dispensed."[17] The responses to this enquiry were not of a piece. Most essayists agreed that the colonizers had passed through a "state of nature" in coming, that (Blackstone to the contrary notwithstanding) the colonies were not obtained by Crown conquest, and that if anyone had conquered the New World it had been the patriot's forebears.[18]

But insisting that the colonizers had been conquerors rather than conquered, like the Irish, raised embarrassing questions about the Americans' just title to the soil—in the eyes of God as well as man. Consequently the preferred and popular argument persisted that the early settlers had duly purchased their land from the Indians and then elected (quite voluntarily) to become subjects of the English King by subscribing to a compact. Additional lands had been added later through defensive wars. Therefore the Crown had never had any legal right to grant these lands, "for they were not seized of them, and consequently had no property in them." The crucial factor was that the land had previously been inhabited. The charters could not so much grant the land as merely convey a royal assurance that the colonizers would not be disturbed in their enjoyment of it once tenure had been legitimately secured.[19] By cultivating "the barren soil by their incessant labour," and by instituting provincial legislatures which were complete in themselves, the colonizers established and legitimized their total independence of Parliament. Even the Crown

[16]Bland, *An Inquiry Into the Rights of the British Colonies* (Williamsburg, 1766), 14, 20–22; [William Hicks], *The Nature and Extent of Parliamentary Power Considered* (Philadelphia, 1768), 5–8; Peter Whitney, *The Transgression of a Land* (Boston, 1774), 48.

[17]*The Farmer Refuted* (N.Y., 1775) in Harold C. Syrett, ed., *The Papers of Alexander Hamilton*, I (N.Y., 1961), 108.

[18][John Allen], *The American Alarm* (Boston, 1773), 22; [James Wilson], *Considerations on the Nature and the Extent of the British Parliament* (Philadelphia, 1774), 14, 25–26, 29; [John Dickinson], *An Essay on the Constitutional Power of Great-Britain* (Philadelphia, 1774), 97–98. Cf. Locke, *Two Treatises of Government*, 295–96, 402–03.

[19]Noble, *Some Strictures*, 21n; William Stearns, *A View of the Controversy* (Watertown, 1775), 12–15; Samuel Webster, *The Misery and Duty of an Oppress'd and Enslav'd People* (Boston, 1774), 21–22.

became more symbolic than real as an effective bond and source of original authority.[20]

The social consequences of colonization were less complicated, though scarcely less important. Americans were decidedly not descended from the scum of Europe, but rather from her substantial and better families. Consequently they deserved rights and privileges consistent with their social origins. William Livingston of New York, for whom American beginnings held a compelling fascination, felt that the several generations of colonials had been pious, and had given due attention to social institutions in an effort to maintain a flourishing culture despite great hardships. Although some writers envisioned the earliest environment as "a howling wilderness," while others depicted "an uncultivated desert," all were agreed on the strong moral fibre of the people who had surmounted the environment.[21]

Most revolutionaries had no doubts whatever about the enduring significance of colonization in the American experience. As their fathers and grandfathers had, they turned for reassurance and strength to the founders' intentions and relevant provisions of early governmental documents. For those canny enough to see through the mist of myth and historic obfuscation, it mattered little "whether the Colonists were invested with a *Right* to these liberties and privileges that ought not to be wrested from them, or whether they were not; tis the truth of fact, that they really *thought* they were." Joseph Warren could thus look back in 1775, just as Charles Chauncy had in 1766, in order to rationalize the non-rational, and clarify the obscure circumstances of American origins.[22]

As early as the Stamp Act crisis, then, the colonists' understanding of their seventeenth-century origins contributed significantly to the widening chasm of contrasting conceptions and positions that made it so difficult for Americans and Englishmen to communicate meaningfully with one another. Moreover, the Americans' reading of provincial history helped to clarify their quest for identity during the long crisis by establishing securely who they were and how they had come to be there. By defining the nature of the great migrations in essen-

---

[20]Joseph Warren, *An Oration Delivered March 5th, 1772* (Boston, 1772), 7–8; [Silas Downer], *A Discourse Delivered in Providence* (Providence, 1768), 6.

[21][Arthur Lee], *An Essay in Vindication of the Continental Colonies of America* (London, 1764); William Livingston, *A Letter to the . . .Bishop of Landaff* (N.Y., 1768), 5–6, 8.

[22]J. R. Pole, *Political Representation in England and the Origins of the American Republic* (N.Y., 1966), 269; Charles Chauncy, *A Discourse on "the Good news From a Far Country"* (Boston, 1766), 14–15 (my italics); Joseph Warren, *An Oration Delivered March Sixth, 1775* (Boston, 1775), 6–8.

tially Lockean terms, such pamphleteers as Richard Bland established their own peculiar criteria for judging the colonists' obligation to obey the laws of England. Thus Bland's view of the original settlement of Virginia, and especially of the origins and powers of the colonial assembly, helped to shape and reinforce the provincial repudiation of the English concept of virtual representation.[23]

As early as 1765 the colonists had begun to relate their particular origins to a more general conception of the history of colonization. In so doing they elevated their appeal to a higher level of abstraction and universal justice. When Stephen Hopkins examined *The Rights of Colonies*, he included a brief survey since antiquity of "what hath generally been the condition of colonies with respect to their freedom." Not surprisingly, Hopkins and his contemporaries found that "colonies in general, both ancient and modern, have always enjoyed as much freedom as the mother state from which they went out." Surely then Britain's American possessions would not be "an exception to this general rule?"[24] With the whole history of human colonization to bolster their cause, and with axioms of constitutional propriety extrapolated therewith, the colonists might well feel secure in their historical heritage and future forensic fights.

After 1772, as the related issues of taxation and representation gave way to a stark problem of sovereignty, the whole historical question took on a new urgency, causing colonists to look to their books more intensively in search of definitive answers. In 1773 George Mason of Virginia made elaborate extracts from the Virginia charters with his own commentaries appended. For Mason,

every clause relating to the people and inhabitants in general . . . under the Faith of which our Ancestors left their native land, and adventured to settle an unknown country, operated and inures to the benefit of their posterity forever, notwithstanding the dissolution of the Virginia Company, had such dissolution been ever so legal. . . . When America was discovered, the sending abroad colonies had been unknown in Europe from the times of the ancient Greeks and Romans. . . . To the people of Great Britain the scene then opening was entirely new; and altho' the people removing from thence, to settle Colonies in America, under the auspices and protection and for the benefit of Great Britain, would by the laws of Nature and Nations, have carried with them the Constitution of the Country they came from, and consequently been entitled to all its advantages, yet not caring to trust altogether to general principles applied to a new subject, and anxious to secure to themselves and

[23]Bernard Bailyn, ed., *Pamphlets of the American Revolution, 1750–1776* (Cambridge, Mass., 1965), I, 319, 321, 323; Bland, *An Inquiry Into the Rights of the Colonies*, 9–10, 13–14, 20–22.

[24][Hopkins], *Rights of Colonies Examined*, in Bailyn, ed., *Pamphlets of the American Revolution*, I, 508–10.

their posterity, by every means in their power, the rights and privileges of
their beloved laws and Constitution, they entered into a solemn compact with
the Crown for that purpose. Under the faith of these compacts, at their own
private expense and Hazard, amidst a thousand Difficulties and Dangers, our
Ancestors explored and settled a New World: their posterity have enjoyed
these rights and privileges from time Immemorial; and have thereby (even if
the Charters had been originally defective) acquired a legal Title. It ought to
wear well; for it has been dearly earned.[25]

Mason had been driven to research and analysis by critics of the
colonial position whom we shall discuss below. In Massachusetts that
same year a confrontation flared up directly. In January 1773 Governor
Hutchinson spoke to the General Court in terms that body could not
stomach. He informed them that both colonizers and Crown early in
the seventeenth century had assumed they would remain subject to the
supreme authority of Parliament. The response of the Court's committee, drafted by John Adams and reported by Samuel, analyzed the
history of American colonization, especially its constitutional and
legal aspects. What emerged was not so much new in substance as
more comprehensive in its implications and thrust. The New Englanders relied heavily on Virginia origins and even upon the late sixteenth-
century voyages and patents. The meaning of colonization in revolutionary thought had thus come to transcend the provincial bounds of
experience. Patriots borrowed freely from one colony's narrative or
another in buttressing arguments. The significance of colonization by
1773 was that it had an *American* application.[26]

Nowhere was this more true than in New York and Jamaica, which
had in fact been conquered provinces. A century earlier the second
Jamaican Assembly had declared "the laws of England in force in this
island," thereby hoping to ensure the enjoyment of constitutional liberties. In 1678–80 an attempt to apply the Poynings' system of control to Jamaica as a conquered colony failed once and for all in the face
of determined opposition by the planters.[27] In New York, however,
such ambiguities were not early put to rest, and by mid-eighteenth century haunted some Yorkers and perplexed others. Where the constitutional implications of English conquest in 1664 were not ignored altogether, authors were obliged to make concessions or modifications

[25]Kate M. Rowland, *The Life of George Mason, 1725–1792* (N.Y., 1892), I, 393–
414. The quotation appears on 398–99.

[26]*The Speeches of His Excellency Governor Hutchinson* (Boston, 1773), 4, 19, 36–37
et passim; Cushing, *The Writings of Samuel Adams*, II, 403–9, 415–23; Silas Deane to
Patrick Henry, Jan. 2, 1775, in *Collections of the New York Historical Society for the
Year 1886; Deane Papers*, I (New York, 1887), 37–41.

[27]Frederick G. Spurdle, *Early West Indian Government* (Palmerston North, N.Z.,
[n.d.]), 27, 222n4.

not required elsewhere: colonizers had been lured to New York by extraordinary concessions from the Crown; they had not been banished from Britain, however, and they brought with them both the allegiances and rights of Englishmen. Colonial disputes had been decided by the Privy Council, patriots admitted; but, they contended, that body had eventually usurped more power than it was justly entitled to.[28]

Despite such glibness, and given New York's hybrid history, Parliament's power over the province could not be so easily disregarded as in other colonies. In 1770, however, William Livingston's *America: or, a Poem on the Settlement of the British Colonies* anticipated the common direction of colonial thought after 1773.

> Forc'd from the pleasures of their native soil,
> Where Liberty had lighten'd every toil;
> Forc'd from the arms of friends and kindred dear,
> With scarce the comfort of one parting tear . . .
>
> To these far-distant climes our fathers came,
> Where blest NEW-ENGLAND boasts a parent's name.
> With Freedom's fire their gen'rous bosoms glow'd,
> Warm for the truth, and zealous for their God; . . .
>
> Penn led a peaceful train to that kind clime,
> Where Nature wantons in her liveliest prime, . . .
>
> Brave Oglethorpe in Georgia fix'd his feat,
> And deep distress there found a calm retreat.

Livingston's own ancestry was as mixed as his colony's, and he was very much a Yorker; but he drew upon the experience of New England, Pennsylvania, and Georgia, in short, upon American origins generally in composing his patriotic paean. (Four years later his brother Philip took a more cautious view of colonization than most colonial patriots, but with some cause. Contested lands along the Massachusetts border were adjacent to the Livingston estates. Steadily after 1767 the family petitioned for a favorable settlement; but their arguments were contingent upon the conquest of 1664 and the extent of Dutch claims acquired by the Duke of York. Hence the muted tones of both Livingstons on the colonization question.)[29]

---

[28]James Fenimore Cooper, *Satanstoe; or, the Littlepage Manuscripts. A Tale of the Colony* (N.Y., 1845), 218; Britannus Americanus, *Liberty, Property and No Stamps* (N.Y., 17 Dec. 1765) [Evans #10041]; *Considerations Upon the Rights of Colonists to the Privileges of British Subjects* (N.Y., 1766), 4, 9–10.

[29][William Livingston], *America: or, a Poem on the Settlement of the British Colonies* (New Haven, [1770]), 4–5; [Philip Livingston], *The Other Side of the Question: Or, A Defense of the Liberties of North America* (N.Y., 1774), 16; Irving Mark, *Agrarian Conflicts in Colonial New York, 1711–1775* (N.Y., 1940), 51–56; "William Livingston," *Dictionary of American Biography*.

In 1774 Samuel Seabury offered whiggish New Yorkers a challenge by contending that legislation was not an inherent right in colonies. He examined many colonial charters in support of this view, and then taunted his readers by pointing out that New York lacked a charter altogether. To this Alexander Hamilton, still a college student, responded in ways the Livingstons must have quietly applauded. Hamilton was obliged to concede New York's particular deficiency; but following Mason in Virginia and the General Court's committee in Massachusetts, he insisted that he could, "with justice, plead the *common* principles of colonization: for, it would be unreasonable, to seclude one colony, from the enjoyment of the most important privileges of the rest." With that established, Hamilton had an easy time examining the general history of colonial settlement and charters, finally rejecting any parliamentary dependency.[30]

By the eve of independence, then, the meaning of colonization in American revolutionary thought had been enunciated with consistency in sermons, pamphlets, private correspondence, and public documents. After 1773 the traditional refrain swelled into a crescendo that would be sustained for more than two years by a chorus of American patriots.[31] All that was needed was a director to set the refrain in measured, dignified cadences heard beyond the seas. They found two in fact: Thomas Jefferson and John Adams.

The Stamp Act had led Adams to see in the original settlement of the colonies "the opening of a grand scene and design in providence for the illumination of the ignorant and the emancipation of the slavish part of mankind all over the earth." In the subsequent decade he embellished and enlarged this view; but he did not change it. His fear of any combination of civil and ecclesiastical tyranny underlay his understanding of American history and forged links in his mind between the earliest settlements and his own time. "British liberties are not the grants of princes or parliaments," he proclaimed in 1765, "but original rights, conditions of original contracts." Because the first settlers had not been a conquered people, feudalism had no place in America. Adams's ancestors had *chosen* to hold their land from the Crown, he

[30][Seabury], *A View of the Controversy Between Great-Britain and Her Colonies: Including a Mode of Determining their Present Disputes* (N.Y., 1774), 9, 11–14; [Hamilton], *The Farmer Refuted* (N.Y., 1775) in Syrett, *Papers of Hamilton*, I, 91, 104, 108–09, 114, 121–22 (italics mine).

[31]In addition to titles already cited, see Roger Clap, *Memoirs of Capt. Roger Clap* (Boston, 1774), 15; Joseph Bean, *A Sermon Delivered at Wrentham* (Boston, 1774), 9; *A Brief Review of the Rise, Progress, Services and Sufferings of New England* (Norwich, Conn., 1774), 5, 10; [Arthur Lee], *An Appeal to the Justice and Interests of the People of Great Britain* (N.Y., 1775), 11; [Moses Mather], *America's Appeal to the Impartial World* (Hartford, 1775), 6–7, 24; Samuel Webster, *Rabshakeh's Proposals Considered* (Boston, 1775), 20–22.

declared in the *Dissertation*. Ten years later his *Novanglus* pursued the same theme: those ancestors were entitled to as much of the common law as they chose to adopt upon emigration; moreover they could have erected any form of government they wished in the wilderness. Finally, "their children would not have been born within the king's allegiance, would not have been natural subjects, and consequently not entitled to protection, or bound to the King." Adams drew upon the Chesapeake story as well as New England to support his view that the early inhabitants had been in full accord on their proper relationship to England.[32]

Jefferson, eight years Adams's junior, emerged in 1774 with the most comprehensive American statement concerning the meaning of colonization: the *Summary View*, written in July 1774 as draft instructions for Virginia's delegates to the Continental Congress. It was not, as historians have suggested, an especially radical breakthrough in colonial political thought, and certainly not in historical thought. To summarize the *Summary View*'s historical perspective would be to recapitulate the essence of this paper: our earliest ancestors were free inhabitants of Britain; they had a perfect right to emigrate, colonize, and establish good laws; their Saxon ancestors had done likewise centuries before; if America *had* been conquered it was by colonizers rather than the British State; Crown treasuries never helped the colonies until long after they were established; the emigrants *chose* to accept English law and continue in political union with Britain by submitting to a common sovereign; the colonizers were victimized by English politicians, and their hard earned lands were parcelled out to various favorites and followers of the court. Despite some new emphases (and an admirable clarity of exposition), like the Declaration of Independence, it basically summed up what had been said and was being said by patriots everywhere.[33]

Jefferson's understanding of the motives and circumstances of colonization had not gone much beyond Richard Bland's in 1766. The future president's research was more comprehensive, for he had carefully worked through Virginia's early records, and his coverage included New England. But the basic historical contentions are the same: the pact of 1651 had been accepted voluntarily; there had been no conquest; and the 1652 articles of surrender remained determinative (as they had been for Bland) because they specifically acknowledged that the surrender was "a voluntary act not forced nor constrained by a

[32]*The Works of John Adams*, ed. Charles F. Adams (Boston, 1851), III, 452, 463; IV, 108–12, 121–24, 126, 173–77.

[33]Julian P. Boyd, ed., *The Papers of Thomas Jefferson*, I (Princeton, 1950), 121–24, 133, 136n5.

conquest upon the countrey." Professors Dumas Malone and Elisha
Douglass properly credit Jefferson with an ingenious but unhistorical
composition. Like his contemporaries Jefferson was making history
the handmaiden of politics; but unlike many English counterparts he
was not re-writing history to suit the occasion. If *A Summary View* was
not a faithful rendering of the history of English colonization, it was at
least the traditional rendering, familiar to generations of Americans.[34]

Jefferson's concern with colonial origins remained a vital one.
During the summer of 1775 he recapitulated all the familiar arguments in writing the *Declaration of the Causes and Necessity for Taking Up Arms:* why the forefathers had emigrated, what they had done
upon arrival, the constitutional consequences, and subsequent assumptions of parliamentary power by Great Britain. When George III's
speech upon the convening of Parliament in October 1775 dwelled
upon England's nurturing the colonies with great tenderness, news
of such a declaration stung Jefferson into renewing his documentary
research into the history of colonization. Early in 1776 he completed
those efforts with conclusions that would form part of his early draft
of the Declaration of Independence.

This short narration of facts, extracted principally from Hakluyt's voiages, may
enable us to judge of the effect which the charter to Sr. Walter Ralegh may
have on our own constitution and also on those of the other colonies within its
limits, to which it is of equal concernment. It serves also to expose the distress of those ministerial writers, who, in order to prove that the British parliament may of right legislate for the colonies, are driven to the necessity of
advancing this palpable untruth that 'the colonies were planted and nursed at
the expence of the British nation': an untruth which even majesty itself, descending from it's dignity, has lately been induced to utter from the throne.

These lengthy investigations were never published as such, but they
colored the outlook of the founders at a critical juncture. They were
communicated to Ebenezer Hazard of Pennsylvania for his *Historical
Collections*, and in an abstract and highly idealized form they may be
found embodied in Thomas Paine's *Common Sense.*[35]

[34] Dumas Malone, *Jefferson the Virginian* (Boston, 1948), 182–86; Elisha P. Doug-
lass, *Rebels and Democrats, The Struggle for Equal Political Rights and Majority Rule
During the American Revolution* (Chapel Hill, 1955), 291–92; A. M. Lewis, "Jefferson's
Summary View as a Chart of Political Union," *William and Mary Quarterly*, ser. 3, V
(Jan. 1948), 34–51; Colbourn, *Lamp of Experience*, 161–63; Craven, *Legend of the
Founding Fathers*, 55–57.

[35] Declaration of the Causes and Necessity for Taking Up Arms, Boyd, *Papers of
Jefferson*, I, 199; Refutation of the Argument that the Colonies were Established at the
Expense of the British Nation, *ibid.*, 283–84; correspondence with Hazard and
memoranda, *ibid.*, 144–48, 164; Becker, *Declaration of Independence*, 122–23, 191;
William M. Van der Weyde, ed., *The Life and Works of Thomas Paine* (New Rochelle,
N.Y., 1921), II, 98–101.

American opponents of the dominant view we have been describing emerged rather slowly. Martin Howard, for example, was one of the few in 1765 who regarded the original charters as restrictive rather than permissive grants of authority. Nor did he directly oppose the traditional understanding of colonial origins. By 1773, however, potential Loyalists, such as Thomas Hutchinson, had changed their minds considerably on the constitutional circumstances of colonization. Not until 1774, however, did whole-hearted critiques of the patriot stand appear.[36]

Jonathan Boucher agreed that the early history of the colonists might be important, but wondered whether their ancestors' status and rights had been clearly understood or asserted: "even these legal constitutional Privileges were encumbered with a Thousand legal Customs, which they patiently submitted to." John Mein found that the patriot assertions were based on the most extravagant and impudent absurdities. An inhabitant of Middlesex might move to the Isle of Man without being outside the British dominions; why therefore would an Englishman in North America be so since that country "appertained" to the Crown? Mein cleverly twisted the knife several times, noting the blatant intolerance of provincials who had emigrated to escape oppression, and the attempt by Massachusetts to exert authority over Connecticut because settlers there had formerly resided in the Bay Colony. Isaac Hunt divided colonization into two sorts of enterprises: discovery and purchase on the one hand, and conquest on the other. In the former case the laws of England unquestionably took effect immediately upon discovery and settlement, while in the latter not until the conqueror so declared. But in both situations acts of Parliament bound the colonies where they were specifically named.[37]

In England contempt for the settlers, and especially for their devious descendants, had long been in evidence. By 1763 it was manifest to imperial bureaucrats in London that colonization was somehow a subversive process viewed altogether differently by men living on opposite sides of the Atlantic.[38] By the time of the Stamp Act crisis such men searched the annals of Greek and Roman colonization to

[36][Martin Howard], *A Letter from a Gentleman at Halifax* (Newport, 1765), 8–10, 14–15; Becker, *Declaration of Independence*, 84; Hutchinson, *The History of the Colony and Province of Massachusetts Bay*, ed. Lawrence S. Mayo (Cambridge, Mass., 1936), III, 266; McIlwain, *American Revolution*, 123–29.

[37][Boucher], *A Letter from a Virginian to the Members of the Congress* ([New York], 1774), 9–10; [Mein], *Sagittarius's Letters* (Boston, 1775), 5–6, 10, 22–24, 32; Hunt, *The Political Family* (Philadelphia, 1775), 8–9.

[38]Sydney W. Jackman, *Man of Mercury. An Appreciation of the Mind of Henry St. John, Viscount Bolingbroke* (London, 1965), 136; Thomas C. Barrow, ed., "A Project for Imperial Reform: 'Hints Respecting the Settlement for our American Provinces,' 1763," *William and Mary Quarterly*, ser. 3, XXIV (Jan. 1967), 114, 117.

support the assertion that colonies were, always had been, and always would be subordinate to the laws of the mother country. The first Anglo-Americans had gone abroad "under the authority of the state . . . to remain Subject to, and under the Power and Dominion of the Kingdom of England." One placeman spelled out such a view for George Grenville in 155 manuscript pages. Charles Townshend, meanwhile, voiced the commonplace conception of "children planted by our care," and debated the issue with Isaac Barré in the House of Commons early in 1765.[39]

In 1769 Israel Mauduit, sometime agent and general placeman, published *A Short View of the History of the Colony of Massachusetts Bay*, which in subsequent expansions became a general *History of the New England Colonies, With Respect to Their Charters and Constitutions*. The Pilgrims, he declared, had been totally subject to the authority of England, while the 1620 grant to some Dorsetshire patentees had *not* included an exemption from parliamentary jurisdiction. In Mauduit's view colonial writers

who talk so arrogantly about the original Terms of Colonization, would do well to ask themselves, whether they really think, that Mr. *Matthew Cradock* and Mr. *Thomas Goff*, and 18 other Gentlemen living in *London*, could send over by Mr. *John Endicott* to the Rev. Mr. *Conant*, and a Number of poor Creatures in *America*, who were starving, and wanting to come home again, a Right of Independence on the Parliament *of England*.

With very ill Grace must these Men now upbraid us with their original Terms of Colonization; or set up what they call their constitutional Rights against the Authority of Parliament, when their first Charter and their original Constitution in New England knew nothing of any House of Representatives at all.

Whatever Privileges therefore can now be claimed as original Charter Rights, or Motives of their first Settlement, or Covenants of Colonization, as they now call them, ought to be produced from Grants or Charters prior to this Period. For since that no new Settlements were made, and all the after Enlargements were only Continuations of the old.

American Whigs were simply deluded, he argued, and had distorted their own constitutional history.[40]

By 1775 Britons had hardened their historical outlook. The Rev. Andrew Burnaby, a reasonably sympathetic visitor to the colonies, believed "they settled in America under the charters, which expressly

---

[39][James Abercromby], *De Jure Coloniarum*, or An Inquiry into the Nature and the Rights of Colonies Ancient and Modern [c. 1765-66], MS in the John Carter Brown Library, Providence, R.I., esp. pp. 9, 84; Ian Christie, *Crisis of Empire. Great Britain and the American Colonies, 1754-1783* (London, 1966), 52-53.

[40]Editions of Mauduit's book appeared in London in 1769, 1774 twice, and the 1776 edition which I have used (pp. 8-13, 14, 16, 20-22, 30).

reserved to the British Parliament the authority . . . now asserted." Dr. Samuel Johnson, unsympathetic as ever, described the colonization process in terms that made sense to every true Englishman.

An English colony is a number of persons, to whom the king grants a charter, permitting them to settle in some distant country, and enabling them to constitute a corporation enjoying such powers as the charter grants. . . . As a corporation they make laws for themselves; but as a corporation subsisting by a grant from higher authority, to the control of that authority they continue subject. . . . If their ancestors were subjects, they acknowledged a sovereign; if they had a right to English privileges, they were accountable to English laws; and, what must grieve the lover of liberty to discover, had ceded to the king and parliament, whether the right or not, at least, the power of disposing, "without their consent, of their lives, liberties, and properties."[41]

Writing that same year, William Knox echoed Johnson's sentiments. The right to American soil had inhered in the Crown before English subjects settled there. From the very outset planters carried grants from the King, who had every right to prescribe conditions for those who received such rights. Adventurers had been assisted in many ways by fellow subjects at home, and the power of the state had been exercised in their behalf. Finally, no act passed by Parliament since the beginning of colonization had ever distinguished between a man born in England and one born in America.[42]

In 1760 David Hume admonished Benjamin Franklin for using such a peculiar word as "colonize" in his Canada pamphlet. The word was already an accepted part of American usage; owing to the forthcoming debate over the meaning of colonization it would soon gain currency even in the King's English.[43] Such an etymological discrepancy was symptomatic of a larger gap. Just when Americans were coming to glorify colonization as a great era in the history of freedom, Britons were regarding it as a period of waste, suffering, and tyranny over heathen natives. By 1775 the two conceptions of colonization were counterpoised: the noble purposes of emigration as against the ignoble processes of settlement.[44] The patriot conception

[41]Burnaby, *Travels Through the Middle Settlements in North America* (Ithaca, N.Y., 1960), x; Samuel Johnson, *Taxation No Tyranny; An Answer to the Resolutions and Address of the American Congress* (London, 1775) in *The Works of Samuel Johnson* (Troy, N.Y., 1903), xiv, 107–9, 114.

[42][Knox], *The Interest of the Merchants and Manufacturers of Great Britain in the Present Contest* [London, 1775], 3–6.

[43]Franklin to Hume, 27 Sept. 1760, Leonard W. Labaree, ed., *The Papers of Benjamin Franklin*, IX (New Haven, 1966), 95, 229.

[44]See David Brion Davis, *The Problem of Slavery in Western Culture* (Ithaca, N.Y., 1966), 423–24, 431–32.

reinforced the Americans' view of themselves as a people peculiarly descended and chosen for a special destiny. By the 1770's a sense of *American*, as opposed to provincial history, was born of the inevitable borrowing by essayists and politicians. Especially was this true in New York, where William Livingston, Alexander Hamilton and others adopted the more congenial history of other colonies as part of their own heritage.[45]

The historic sense of the significance and meaning of colonization shared by most Americans was neither sound nor even consistent. But it at least antedated the controversy that had fired it with a glaze of glowing lustre. On this account it had a greater measure of persuasiveness during the revolutionary crisis, and perhaps more integrity than the utterly contrived whig history produced during the most troubled years of Stuart England.[46] Despite the absence of substantiating evidence, despite Poyning's Law (1495), the Declaratory Act of 1719, and other evidence to the contrary, Irish nationalists would persistently foster the myth of Henry II's grant to John of an independent kingdom in Ireland. By contrast, the Puritan leaders of the Massachusetts Bay Company had *indeed* tried to eliminate the Crown by insisting that, in approving the grant of the charter in 1629, the Crown had divested itself of all right to interfere in the affairs of the new colony. The Puritans *had* shrugged off the authority of Parliament by asserting that the statute law of England did not concern them. And Roger Williams, moreover, *had* denied the right of Charles I to grant lands that he did not properly own. To be sure, there was sophistry and casuistry in these early American arguments. But they endured, so that after five or six generations of repetition they had a certain ring of integrity and familiarity.

When the colonists' sense of their past was reinforced by persuasive currents of Enlightenment thought, the resulting ideology acquired

---

[45]William Smith, Jr. of New York had a serious interest in colonial origins; but he was also shrewd and forthright enough to recognize that "the Empire, long after the Constitution was formed, acquired a *new, adventitious* State. And the question therefore is not, what the Constitution was, or is, but what, present Circumstances considered, it ought to be." Robert M. Calhoon, ed., "William Smith Jr.'s Alternative to the American Revolution," *William and Mary Quarterly*, ser. 3, XXII (Jan. 1965), 113. In 1777, while simultaneously revising his *History of the late Province of New-York* and agonizing over his allegiances, Smith noted that "our ancestors claimed every social benefit not injurious to the Mother Country, nor inconsistant with their loyalty to the Crown or their dependence upon Great Britain." MS marginalia on p. 109 of Smith's copy of his *History*, Philip H. and A. S. W. Rosenbach Foundation, Philadelphia.

[46]Quentin Skinner, "History and Ideology in the English Revolution," *Historical Journal*, VIII (1965), 151-78; J. G. A. Pocock, *The Ancient Constitution and the Feudal Law: A Study of English Historical Thought in the Seventeenth Century* (Cambridge, 1957).

both momentum and a certain self-righteousness. The very essence of Lockeanism, for example, seemed to confirm the significance of the seventeenth-century migration in the American mind, and the two became intertwined in revolutionary thought. Locke's understanding of the origins of society presented a clear picture of persons emigrating with their property and then contracting together for its preservation. Locke had said that men are naturally in a state of nature, "and remain so, till by their own Consents they make themselves Members of some Politick Society." The Great Philosopher had also observed that "many have mistaken the force of Arms, for the consent of the People; and reckon Conquest as one of the Originals of Government. But *Conquest* is as far from setting up any Government, as demolishing an House is from building a new one in the place." Here was special comfort and sustenance for colonists in New York and Jamaica.[47]

More important than Locke's chapters on "The State of Nature" and "Conquest," however, was his long section "Of the Beginning of Political Societies." Lawful government derived *only* from "the consent of any number of Freemen capable of a majority;" and when such a society had been joined, its members "might set up what form of Government they thought fit." Each man who gave his consent to such a community put "himself under an Obligation" to every other member. Therefore the colonist's greatest allegiance must have been to his immediate community, and not to such larger political abstractions as the English constitution or Empire. The Lockean axiom most relevant to the colonists' understanding of colonial origins, however, came in chapter 116 of *The Second Treatise*. There Locke rejected the notion that birth into one polity restrained the individual's ability to give consent to another. " 'Tis true, that whatever Engagements or Promises any one has made for himself, he is under the Obligation of them, but *cannot* by any *Compact* whatsoever, bind *his Children* or Posterity."[48] The seventeenth-century settlers, therefore, had simply left a corrupt country and created a new "Politick Society" in America. Their descendants cherished this simple truth and used it to underpin maxims of their natural rights philosophy during the revolutionary crisis.

It is ironic, if not surprising, that English conceptions of the state of nature were changing during the 1760's and 1770's. Just when the colonists were finding analytical uses for Locke's abstract state of

[47]Pole, *Political Representation and the American Republic*, 25; Locke, *Two Treatises of Government*, 295–96, 362, 402–403.

[48]Locke, *Two Treatises of Government*, 350–31, 355, 363–64. Cf. John Adams's view, cited above from *Novanglus*.

nature and Rousseau's state of nature as a historical condition, English writers—especially the antiradicals—were ridiculing both conceptions and thereby drifting away from the traditional Lockean domination of British political ideas. Surely this trend, occurring quite independently of the debate on the colonial-constitutional question, contributed to Anglo-American misunderstanding. The Americans' Lockean view of the seventeenth-century migration simply did not fit into most advanced English schema; and they, in turn, were irrelevant to the colonists' quest for a rational past. There was consequently no possible hope for a meeting of minds where colonial origins and political theory were concerned.[49]

In addition to the colonists' very obvious Lockeanism, their views of Stuart colonization must also have been buttressed by their deeply ingrained Protestantism. Martin Luther's *Open Letter to the Christian Nobility,* for example, had described the process whereby colonizers create viable instruments of self control in response to their primitive needs. "If a little group of pious Christian laymen," Luther wrote, "were taken captive and set down in a wilderness, and had among them no priest consecrated by a bishop, and if there in the wilderness they were to agree in choosing one of themselves, married or unmarried, and were to charge him with the office of baptising, saying mass, absolving and preaching, such a man would be as truly a priest as though all bishops and popes had consecrated him. . . . It was in the manner aforesaid that Christians in olden days chose from their number bishops and priests."[50] The sermon literature of the pre-revolutionary decade contains numerous echoes of these thoughts, and similar sentiments designed to justify the historical understanding of colonization, which I have described above.[51]

It is important to realize that patriotic Americans were not in complete agreement on every aspect and detail of the seventeenth-

[49]H. V. S. Ogden, "The State of Nature and the Decline of Lockian Political Theory in England, 1760–1800," *American Historical Review*, XLVI (1940), 21–44.

[50]*An Open Letter to the Christian Nobility of the German Nation Concerning the Reform of the Christian Estate* (Wittenberg, 1520), in C. M. Jacobs, ed., *Works of Martin Luther* (Philadelphia, 1915), II, 67–68.

[51]Amos Adams, *A Concise Historical View of the Perils . . . Which Have Attended the Planting and Progressive Improvements of New England* (Boston, 1769), 7–9, 13, 51–52, 63–64; Judah Champion, *A Brief View of the Distresses, Hardships and Dangers Our Ancestors Encounter'd in Settling New-England* (Hartford, 1770), 10–19; James Dana, *A Century Discourse* (New Haven, [1770]), 22 ff.; Gad Hitchcock, *A Sermon Preached at Plymouth December 22d, 1774* (Boston, 1775), 5–6, 17, 36; Samuel Baldwin, *A Sermon, Preached at Plymouth, December 22, 1775* (Boston, 1776), 16–17, 24; Samuel Williams, *A Discourse on the Love of Our Country* (Salem, 1775), 15; Joseph Montgomery, *A Sermon Preached at Christiana Bridge* (Philadelphia, 1775), 23–24.

century migration and its meaning. In 1774, for example, John Adams, Benjamin Franklin, and Thomas Jefferson differed over whether their forefathers had had a perfect right to leave England. (Adams believed the King's permission was required; Franklin and Jefferson felt that it was not.)[52] But they all—Calvinists and Liberals—read the same broad lessons from the history of colonization, and saw the same constitutional implications.[53] Hence the emphatic meaning behind the sixth resolution of the First Continental Congress: "That they [the colonies] are entitled to the benefit of such of the English statutes, as existed at the time of their colonization; and which they have by experience, respectively found to be applicable to their several local and other circumstances."[54]

In the years from 1764 until 1776 Americans were simultaneously obliged to understand the present and anticipate the future in terms consonant with their past. Unlike the moderate reformers in England who simply wished to wash away the corruption that had eaten into the system since 1688, and unlike the Old Whigs who looked back to a fictive Gothic constitution which had been overthrown by the Normans, colonial patriots concentrated on an intermediate period of English history: the first half of the seventeenth century. These variant historical emphases would lead to divergent interpretations of the present, thereby weakening the bonds among segments of the trans-Atlantic community.[55] New Englanders especially "paid tribute to their ancestors and themselves simultaneously by identifying their own cause—political and religious liberty—as the one that had animated the founding of New England." But to patriots generally, it became a commonplace that overseas territories had long been the natural sanctuaries for liberty and virtue, especially when they were suffering "at home" from corruption and authoritarianism.[56]

In 1776 and the years following, when intellectual energies in the new states were applied to creating new sets of constitutional arrangements, the history and meaning of colonization—less relevant for the moment—faded temporarily into the background. In England, however,

[52]Cf. *Works of John Adams*, IV, 121–22; *Papers of Thomas Jefferson*, I, 121; Verner W. Crane, *Benjamin Franklin, Englishman and American* (Baltimore, 1936), 117.

[53]Alan Heimert, *Religion and the American Mind from the Great Awakening to the Revolution* (Cambridge, Mass., 1966) 98, 245–46, 358–59, 429, 438, 450n2, 462, 470.

[54]*Journals of the American Congress: From 1774 to 1778* (Washington, 1823), I, 21.

[55]Pole, *Origins of the American Republic*, 427–28.

[56]Edmund S. Morgan, "The Historians of Early New England," in *The Reinterpretation of Early American History: Essays in Honor of John Edwin Pomfret*, Ray A. Billington, ed. (San Marino, California, 1966), 43. See also Bernard Bailyn, *The Ideological Origins of the American Revolution* (Cambridge, Mass., 1967), 140–41.

the interest in colonization that had been stimulated by the Great Debate was diverted eastward to the new imperial outposts, and after 1776 to scholarship; so that the modern scholarly study of ancient colonization dates from the late 1770's.[57]

Cornell University.

[57]Richard W. Van Alstyne, *Empire and Independence; The International History of the American Revolution* (N.Y., 1965), 45–46; [William Barron], *A History of the Colonization of the Free States of Antiquity, applied to the present contest between Great Britain and her American colonies* (London, 1777); John Symonds, *Remarks upon an essay entitled the History of the Colonization of the Free States of Antiquity* (London, 1778); A. J. Graham, *Colony and Mother City in Ancient Greece* (Manchester, Eng., 1964), xvii–xviii.

XIV

THE AMERICAN REVOLUTION AND NATURAL LAW THEORY

By Lester H. Cohen*

The authors of the Declaration of Independence were not interested in stating a *fait accompli*. They sought to justify the American separation from Britain on the ground that the separation was historically necessary. They attempted, therefore, to state unambiguously not only the reasons that justified America's separation from England, but also a set of general rules for determining whether or not any revolution is justified. Affirming the notion that a people ought not to revolt for "light and transient causes," the document stated that a revolution is justified only when the course of human events makes it "necessary"; only when conditions become "intolerable"; only "when a long train of abuses and usurpations, pursuing invariably the same object, evinces a design to reduce them under absolute despotism. . . ." Under such conditions a people has not merely the right but the obligation to revolt, and therefore, its revolution is justified.

According to the Declaration and to commonly received maxims of eighteenth-century political theory, government is in itself merely a convenience. It operates on the basis of positive law, law created by men for the administration of the state. When government is properly constituted, however, deriving its authority from popular consent, its aim is to secure the happiness of the people and the people's inalienable rights, rights which are rooted in the Laws of Nature and of Nature's God. The government that is properly constituted, then, makes positive law an organic outgrowth of Natural Law.

The Declaration's argument is elegantly constructed to demonstrate the truth of its claims. It is designed to explain and to justify not only this revolution by these revolutionaries at this time. It articulates, in addition, a set of conditions under which any people might justifiably revolt, thereby establishing the universality of its argument and, at the same time, preempting the anticipated counter-claim that it was merely an expedient way of rationalizing actions which had already been taken. Similarly, to avoid the suggestion that it was designed solely for expediency, the Declaration rests the morality of revolution on its historical necessity: because British policies subverted the British constitution, leading inexorably toward the creation of an "absolute despotism," the revolution was necessary; and because it was necessary, it was morally justifiable.

More important, the argument of the Declaration is a subtle, if ambiguous, blending of empirical historical analysis and the metaphysics of Natural Law. To prove its central contention—that the revolution was made necessary by British policies—the document enumerates twenty-seven specific events in

* This essay grows out of a paper which I delivered to the History Conference of the Indiana Academy of the Social Sciences, October 17, 1975. I am grateful to Professor Lester Schmidt, editor of the Academy's *Proceedings*, for allowing me to publish this expanded version of the paper.

recent history which reveal precisely how Britain acted to establish a despotism. These twenty-seven events, listed as grievances, constituted a strong case for the expediency of a revolution, for this people's rebelling at this time; and the reader of the document who would be satisfied with arguments of expediency alone, could accept that the enumerated grievances called for strenuous action, even action of a revolutionary nature.

But the revolutionaries meant to transcend arguments of expediency, for such arguments were always subject to the vicissitudes of opinion and opinion might lead one to conclude that a revolution was in fact unnecessary and therefore unjustifiable. To remove their claims from the arena of opinion and to ground them with certainty, the revolutionaries felt constrained to found the argument for justification on the principle of Natural Rights which was rooted in the theory of Natural Law as applied to politics and society. Thus the grievances enumerated in the Declaration, weighty in themselves for some readers, were for others concrete examples of how one nation attempted to subordinate another to an "absolute despotism." The grievances, taken together, demonstrated that British policies had violated the fundamental principles of Natural Law itself.

By thus attempting to join universal rules with specific conditions, moral truths with historical necessity, and metaphysical principles with empirical historical facts, the Declaration sought to justify as well as to account for the American separation from Britain. But "justification" meant more than the creation of a useful myth or an expedient rationale for the revolutionaries' actions. It entailed the articulation or, at the very least, the presupposition of an immutable standard of value against which the necessity and the propriety of revolution could be measured. That standard was Natural Law, a standard which assured epistemological certitude because it was transcendent, universal, and immutable, and thus beyond the ravages of historical exigency.

At the heart of the Declaration, then, was an unstated epistemological assumption about the universal truth of Natural Law and about how men could in practice know that truth. Because the Declaration was not only a statement about a practical political event, but was in itself a crucial aspect of that event, this unstated epistemological assumption could remain unstated. Precisely by juxtaposing, without resolving, the empirical and the theoretical, the immanent and the transcendent, the Declaration left to its readers or auditors the problem of making clear the relationship between specific historical events and the truths of Natural Law. Attempting to justify the revolution in retrospect, however, proved a more difficult task. For in retrospect the ambiguity that persisted through the Declaration—the ambiguous relationship between the historical and the transcendent—became glaring. To justify the revolution in retrospect on the basis of principle required a new mode of interpretation, and that new mode, practiced by the historians of the revolution, involved the transformation of Natural Law into an historical process.[1]

[1] See in general, Carl Lotus Becker, *The Declaration of Independence: A Study in the History of Political Ideas* (1922; rpt. New York, n.d.); Leo Strauss, *Natural Right and History* (1950; rpt. Chicago, 1974); Otto Gierke, *Natural Law*

America's "revolutionary historians," those contemporaries of the Revolution who wrote histories of the era, sought to accomplish what the authors of the Declaration seemed to have achieved so elegantly and easily: to justify the separation from England on the ground that historical conditions had made a revolution necessary. Like the authors of the Declaration, the historians, as Mercy Otis Warren put it, meant "to justify the *principles* of the defection and final separation from the parent state." The purpose was educational, even didactic, and the aim could not be achieved without relying on arguments of principle. John Lendrum said that he wrote history in order to provide future generations of Americans with the means "to form just ideas of the liberties and privileges to which the colonies were entitled by their charters." No argument for expediency would suffice to justify the revolution. Justification required statements of fundamental principle.[2]

Indeed, the historians, even more than the authors of the Declaration, were careful to make clear the distinction between arguments for expediency or utility and arguments for necessity which could only be founded on fundamental principle. Jedidiah Morse, for example, sharply distinguished between what he called "a mere quesion of EXPEDIENCY," and "metaphysical disquisitions about abstract rights," each of which was a valid form of argumentation as long as each was confined to its proper sphere.[3] Mercy Warren emphasized the same distinction, stating her disgust with some members of parliament who would "shamelessly . . . avow the necessity of leaping over the boundaries of equity, and [wink] out of sight the immutable laws of justice." Accusing parliament of giving in to arguments of expediency, she observed that the greatest evils lay in the idea espoused by Lord Mansfield, "that the original question of *right* ought no longer be considered; that the justice of the cause must give way to the present situation. . . ." Warren railed at this sacrifice of principle to a relativistic, situational ethic, reaffirming the idea that, when questions of truth and right were concerned, one properly appealed to "the immutable laws of justice" and to "the principles of rectitude."[4]

---

and the Theory of Society, 1500 to 1800, trans. with an intro. by Ernest Barker (Cambridge, 1950), esp. Ch. 2. For a discussion of scientific natural law and its application to society: Caroline Robbins, *The Eighteenth-Century Commonwealthman* (New York, 1968), 67-72.

[2] Mercy Otis Warren, *History of the Rise, Progress and Termination of the American Revolution* . . . (3 vols.; Boston, 1805), I, viii; John Lendrum, *A Concise and Impartial History of the American Revolution* . . . (2 vols.; Boston, 1795), I, 107. See in general, William Gordon, *The History of the Rise, Progress, and Establishment of the Independence of the United States of America* . . . (4 vols.; London, 1788), II, 295; Timothy Pitkin, *A Political and Civil History of the United States of America* . . . (2 vols.; New Haven, 1828), I, iii; David Ramsay, *The History of the Revolution of South Carolina* . . . (Trenton, 1785), I, Preface, and *The History of the American Revolution* (2 vols.; Philadelphia, 1789, rpt. London, 1793), I, Preface.

[3] Jedidiah Morse, *Annals of the American Revolution* . . . (Hartford, 1824), 109.

[4] Warren, *American Revolution,* I, 280-81; III, 414.

Justification depended upon arguments of principle, and only arguments
of principle could constitute the necessity of a movement for independence.
Timothy Pitkin found the emphasis upon necessity in the colonies' instructions to their delegates to the Continental Congress. New Jersey, for example,
instructed its delegates to support a motion for independence "in case they
judged it necessary and expedient for supporting the just rights of America.
. . ." Similarly, Pennsylvania stated that it would support independence, but
"at the same time, asserted, that this measure did not originate in ambition
or in an impatience of lawful authority, but that they were driven to it, in
obedience to the first principles of nature, by the oppressions and cruelties
of the king and parliament, as the only measure left to preserve their liberties,
and transmit them inviolate to posterity."[5] Maryland, according to Pitkin,
affirmed the same notion that independence was a proper action only if it
were deemed a necessary action, and only if it were taken as a last resort to
preserve fundamental rights and liberties.[6]

The historians' concern for demonstrating the necessity of the separation
from Britain was nowhere clearer than in David Ramsay's simple assertion
that "Necessity, not choice, forced [the Americans] on the decision" to
revolt.[7] Following the argument of the Declaration itself, he added that the
historical conditions then prevailing "made a declaration of independence
as necessary in 1776, as was the non-importation agreement in 1774, or
the assumption of arms in 1775." The logic of necessity was inexorable:
the declaration "naturally resulted" from these earlier events, just as they
had been necessitated by still earlier ones.[8]

Writing in 1788, William Gordon presented a similar case for the necessity of the revolution. By the time British and American forces engaged at
Lexington and Concord, the contest would have to "issue in independence
or slavery" for the colonies. The decision to declare independence "may be
deemed by some presumptuous," he continued. "But how could it have
been avoided?"[9] Likewise, Jedidiah Morse was convinced that in 1776 the
"immediate necessity [of independence] was proved."[10]

Morse coupled his claim for the necessity of independence with the
notion that the stakes of the contest involved nothing less than Americans'
"natural and indisputable rights," the parameters of which were "certain and
thoroughly understood."[11] Mercy Warren presented perhaps the clearest
case for the relationship between historical necessity and the Natural Right-
Natural Law thesis when she observed that the American people "considered [Britain's] measures as the breach of a solemn covenant; which at
the same time that it subjected them to the authority of the King of England,
stipulated to them all the rights and privileges of free and natural born subjects." When such a solemn covenant is broken, when the King demands
subjection at the same time refusing to acknowledge the people's rights, then
the obligation to obey is annulled and, as Warren stated it, the people must
"hazard the consequences of returning to a state of nature, rather than
quietly submit to unjust and arbitrary measures continually accumulating."

---

[5] Pitkin, *Political and Civil History,* I, 363.
[6] *Ibid.,* 364.   [7] Ramsay, *American Revolution,* I, 335.   [8] *Ibid.,* 338.
[9] Gordon, *History* II, 296-97.   [10] Morse, *Annals,* 246.   [11] *Ibid.,* 255.

Precisely when a people is returned to a state of nature Natural Law and its concomitant Natural Rights begin to operate directly and immediately.[12]

These historians sound confident that the separation from Britain was justified because historical conditions had made a revolution necessary. The Crown's policies constituted a threat not merely to positive law but to the Law of Nature itself. But the historians were writing in retrospect and they became aware of certain difficulties that arose as a consequence of retrospective analysis. The easiest argument to make, after all, was that what happened in fact, happened by necessity. The historians had no difficulty *asserting* the necessity of the revolution, but the ground upon which they argued that necessity was eroding under their feet. They discovered that necessity and justification could exist independently of one another, and that even if they could demonstrate that the revolution was necessary they still might not be able to make an absolute case for its justification.

In fact, the historians found themselves arguing the case for necessity on the ground of expediency, and yet it was exactly such arguments which they felt constrained to transcend. David Ramsay noted that "Several [people] on both sides of the Atlantic, have called the declaration of independence 'a bold, and accidentally, a lucky speculation,' but subsequent events have proved, that it was a wise measure."[13] John Marshall also resorted to a retrospective analysis based upon expediency when he observed that, despite the opposition of a "formidable minority," "It cannot, however, be questioned, that the declaration of independence was wise and well timed. . . ."[14] The problem, of course, was that it *could* be questioned. Relying on "subsequent events" seemed to prove nothing.

Similarly, when William Gordon claimed that the separation from England was "unavoidable," he attempted to demonstrate the truth of his claim by asserting: "The people were ripe for it. Prudence dictated a compliance with their expectations and wishes. A disappointment might have disgusted [them], and produced disorder." By the same token, declaring independence, according to Gordon, might result in many advantages to the Americans; it might make the French less "timid" and "animate" them to exertions on behalf of the new nation. The people, moreover, "have nothing worse to apprehend from the declaration than before. . . . Besides, the quarrel is in such a stage, that it cannot be ended with safety to the inhabitants, but by their separating from Great Britain, and becoming independent. . . ."[15]

What more utilitarian argument for expediency could Gordon have presented? He not only made no reference to the transcendent, immutable Laws of Nature, nor to "the principles of rectitude," but he depicted the declaration of independence as a cunning subterfuge, a ploy to gain material

---

[12] Warren, *American Revolution,* II, 145; John Locke, *Two Treatises of Government,* ed. with intro. by Peter Laslett (Cambridge, 1960; rpt. 1963), *Second Treatise,* Ch. 2, sects. 1-12; Ch. XVI; Strauss, *Natural Right and History,* 202-51.

[13] Ramsay, *American Revolution,* I, 347.

[14] John Marshall, *The Life of George Washington* . . . (5 vols.; Philadelphia, 1804-07), II, 413.

[15] Gordon, *History,* II, 297; Jeremy Belknap, *The History of New Hampshire* (3 vols.; Boston, 1792), II, 405.

and political advantages for the American cause. Indeed, Gordon's argument represented the same cynical sacrifice of principle to expediency for which Mercy Warren had excoriated parliament.

Even Jedidiah Morse, the historian who had so scrupulously distinguished between questions of mere expediency and metaphysical principles of Natural Law resorted in his own writings to the argument for expediency. With the events of 1775, Morse wrote, "the question of the expediency of independence [was] decided." "While the *legality* of the measure was thus argued," he continued, "its immediate necessity was proved."[16] Here the final twist of logic is turned, confusing altogether the usual terms of the debate. For Morse was willing to see the necessity of independence as a function of its expedience; and the obvious implication of his statement is that, even if debate were to conclude that independence was illegal it was, nevertheless, necessary, and because it was necessary it was justifiable.

The problem of reconciling arguments of expedience with arguments of principle which would justify the revolution was nowhere clearer than in the historians' attempts to discuss a sympathetic figure who had opposed independence. Tories were one thing; John Dickinson was another. Almost all of the historians made it a point to observe that some "worthy men," among whom they numbered John Dickinson, had given serious thought to the implications of a decisive break with Britain. When the Continental Congress was debating the issue of independence men like Dickinson had doubts that a separation was even desirable, much less necessary. David Ramsay referred to men like Dickinson as "misguided" but "honest" men, "respectable people whose principles were pure, but whose souls were not of that firm texture which revolutions require." William Gordon added that when Dickinson opposed independence he did so "openly, and upon principle."[17]

But how could one say with such certainty that John Dickinson, a man who had been in the forefront of the struggle against British policies since the 1760's, was "misguided?" And if he were an "honest" man whose principles were pure, did that imply that Dickinson was appealing to some standard or set of principles other than the Laws of Nature, or "the immutable laws of justice," or "the principles of rectitude" to have arrived at his erroneous opinions? Insight into Natural Law required intuition, according to John Locke. Whose intuition into the Laws of Nature was brighter, more immediate, more certain: Ramsay's or Dickinson's? Any answer would be as absurd as the question.[18]

Something clearly was wrong, and the problem seemed to lie in the traditional theory of Natural Law or with its retrospective application to concrete historical events. Indeed, the traditional theory seemed to be flying back in the face of the historians, for its greatest virtue—the fact that it offered epistemological certitude because it was transcendent—now seemed to be its greatest pitfall. For the gap between the transcendent and the his-

---

[16] Morse, *Annals,* 246; my emphasis.

[17] Ramsay, *American Revolution,* I, 337; Gordon, *History,* II, 289; Marshall, *Life of Washington,* II, 412-13.

[18] John Locke, *An Essay Concerning Human Understanding,* Collated and Annotated by Alexander Campbell Fraser (2 vols.; New York, 1959), II, 176-78.

torical seemed to have widened beyond man's ability to bridge it philosophically. Peter Gay has observed that by the end of the eighteenth century
European thinkers had given up the Natural Law thesis and had become
confirmed proponents of the principle of utility. Leo Strauss has also suggested that the seeds of the crisis of Natural Rights theory which were being
harvested in the late eighteenth century had been sown as early as the mid-
seventeenth century, when Thomas Hobbes had written *De Cive* and *Levia-
than*.[19] America's revolutionary historians, however, tried to face the difficulties which others had either avoided or overcome to their own satisfaction.
But in the face of such troubling logic, Mercy Warren, for one, resigned herself to the idea that, try as man might to understand and to live by transcendent imperatives, he "yet discovers an incapacity to satisfy his researches,
or to announce that he has already found an unerring standard on which
he may rest."[20]

If the logic of transcendent, immutable Natural Law seemed no longer
to work in practice, why, then, did the historians persist in using the rhetoric?
It is tempting to conclude with good twentieth-century "political realism"
that Natural Law had become a fiction, providing no more than a rhetorically
strategic language which was enormously useful for disguising the real, less
than divine, reasons for separating from Britain. It is also tempting to see
the revolutionary historians' use of Natural Law theory in the light of how
nineteenth-century idealistic philosophers transformed it, or in the light of
the Utilitarians' rejection of the theory altogether. The historians, however,
did not articulate an incipient theory of dialectical idealism, nor were they
prepared to abandon the theory of Natural Law and to replace it with the
principle of utility. For they feared that to eliminate a transcendent standard of truth and value meant to plunge man into a chaos of relativism,
leaving him to sink or swim in an ethical and historical whirlpool which was
devoid of certitude or even meaning.

There was, however, already present in the histories an alternative to relativism and to transcendent absolutism, although the modern reader will
almost doubtless agree with Daniel Howe's judgment that the alternative
was at best "a brave front," which for a time "helped stave off intellectual
chaos."[21] The alternative involved the perpetuation of the theory of Natural
Law, but it was a Natural Law no longer conceived as a static body of immutable principles. Rather, Natural Law was historicized; it was seen as a
process by which fundamental principles were made concrete in the course
of history itself. Natural Law was thus conceived to require historical action
or practice for it to be "legal."

James Wilson, America's most important legal philosopher of the period,
came closest to stating this processive theory of Natural Law *as* a theory. By
doing so he pointed to the problem and to the possibility of its solution in
practice. In his essay "Of the Law of Nature," Wilson wrote unequivocally

[19] Peter Gay, *The Enlightenment: An Interpretation: The Rise of Modern
Paganism* (New York, 1967), 18; Strauss, *Natural Right and History*, Chs. 5, 6.

[20] Warren, *American Revolution*, III, 423.

[21] Daniel Walker Howe, *The Unitarian Conscience: Harvard Moral Philosophy,
1805-1861* (Cambridge, Mass., 1970), 29.

that "The law of nature is immutable," and that "The law of nature is universal." But he also observed that "It is the glorious destiny of man to be always progressive," and that man's progress was directed by immutable principles.[22] Perhaps contrary to one's expectations, Wilson did not resolve this apparent ambiguity by suggesting that man's progress was itself a law of nature. Rather, he argued that "the law of nature, though immutable in its *principles,* is progressive in its operations and effects. Indeed the same immutable principles will direct this progression."[23]

Insofar as Wilson continued to affirm the transcendence of Natural Law, his thesis failed to overcome the difficulties inherent in the traditional theory, difficulties which the historians ran into when they attempted to justify the revolution in retrospect on the ground of necessity. But Wilson had opened another dimension of Natural Law theory by seeing it is a process in which "[the natural law] will not only be fitted, to the contemporary degree, but will be calculated to produce, in future, a still higher degree of perfection."[24] Natural Law, then, while immutable in its *principles,* required history for its fulfillment.

If Wilson and, to some extent Thomas Jefferson, pointed the way to a processive theory of Natural Law, it remained for the historians of the era to realize the theory and to make it work in practice.[25] In the writings of the historians the processive theory of Natural Law was, in the first place, shorn of its transcendence. The Natural Rights of man, which are rooted in the Law of Nature, wrote Mercy Warren,

are improved in society, and strengthened by civil compacts; these have been established in the United States by a race of independent spirits, who have freed their posterity from the feudal vassalage of hereditary lords.[26]

The significance of Warren's formulation is two-fold: in it she implies that Natural Rights are abstract rights; they become actual rights only in historical situations, only when "a race of independent spirits" practices them. Secondly, to demonstrate the legality of Natural Rights and to know, therefore, when they have been violated, the historian must establish that those rights have a tradition, that they have been practiced for generations.

In his historical survey of the *Canon and Feudal Law,* John Adams exhorted:

Be it remembered, that liberty must, at all hazards, be supported! We have a right to it, derived from our maker! *But if we had not,* our fathers have

---

[22] Robert Green McCloskey, ed., *The Works of James Wilson* (2 vols.; Cambridge, Mass., 1967), I, 145-46.

[23] *Ibid.,* 147; Wilson, "Of the General Principles of Law and Obligation," *ibid.,* 97-125.   [24] *Ibid.*

[25] Jefferson's "A Summary View of the Right of British America . . . (1774)" in *The Portable Thomas Jefferson,* ed. Merrill D. Peterson (New York, 1975), 3-21, can be read as a harbinger of the processive theory of Natural Law. Like the Declaration of Independence, however, it is still more an uneasy mixture of the historical and the transcendent than a synthesis of them.

[26] Warren, *American Revolution,* III, 327; Ramsay, *The History of South Carolina . . .* (2 vols.; Charleston, 1858), II, 75.

earned it and bought it for us, at the expence of their ease, their estates, their pleasure and their blood.[27]

Liberty is an absolute right, derived from God, according to Adams; it is in *principle* eternal and immutable. But what gives Adams' point its power is his reliance on tradition, for experience has shown that principle is frequently trampled under the boot of expediency. Therefore, even if liberty were not a right derived from God, Americans still had an absolute right to it because of what the fathers had done to earn it. Liberty is, in short, a fundamental dimension of the American constitution.

As a practical form of historical analysis the processive theory of Natural Law echoed Edmund Burke's theory of tradition. Burke identified concrete historical practice with Natural Law, arguing that the natural constitution is identical to the constitution which a society had developed in the course of generations.[28] It was with this conception of Natural Law, incidentally, that Burke found the means of supporting the American Revolution but not the French. Consistent with Burke's view, Jedidiah Morse wrote that Americans' rights had not only been "stipulated and confirmed by royal charters, [and] acknowledged by the people of Great Britain"; in addition, the had been practiced by Americans, "enjoyed by the colonies for more than a century. . . ." Any violation of such rights "would be inconsistent with the British constitution and an infringement on [sic] [Americans'] natural and essential rights."[29] Morse thus blurred any distinction between Natural Rights and traditional rights, precisely as he blurred the distinction between a people's "natural charter" and their "constitutional rights" elsewhere.[30]

The historians applied the same reasoning to the great issue of taxation and representation. The English Lord Camden, quoted by practically every historian, said in 1766 that "Taxation and representation are inseparable. This position is founded on the laws of nature. It is more, it is itself an eternal law of nature."[31] The American historians, of course, agreed with Camden in principle. But they recognized that it was no longer sufficient to invoke the self-evidence of Natural Law, however satisfying self-evidence was epistemologically. One had to show that the rights at issue were rights in practice. Thus Timothy Pitkin wrote that taxation and representation were indeed inseparable; but it was because

The colonists, from their first settlement, considered themselves entitled to the rights of Englishmen as secured by magna charta and confirmed by the

[27] Quoted in Pitkin, *Political and Civil History*, I, 191; my emphasis.

[28] Edmund Burke, "Speech on Conciliation with the Colonies" (March 22, 1775), Intro. and Notes by Jeffrey Hart (Chicago, 1964), *passim;* Strauss, *Natural Right and History*, 294-323; Sheldon S. Wolin, *Politics and Vision: Continuity and Innovation in Western Political Thought* (Boston, 1960), 409-10; Leslie Stephen, *History of English Thought in the Eighteenth Century* (2 vols.; 1876; rpt. London, 1962), II, 197ff.

[29] Morse, *Annals*, 99; Ramsay, *Revolution of South Carolina*, II, 213; Warren, *American Revolution*, I, 274.   [30] Morse, *Annals*, 92.

[31] Quoted in Lendrum, *American Revolution*, I, 244.

bill of rights. . . . The most important of these rights, were those of *taxation and representation*.[32]

Similarly referring to the seventeenth century, David Ramsay noted that "Long before the declaration of independence, several of the colonies on different occasions declared, that they ought not to be taxed but by their own provincial assemblies, and that they considered subjection to acts of a British Parliament, in which they had no representation, as a grievance."[33] And Mercy Warren, believing that Natural Rights were "improved in society," thought that "old opinions, founded in reason" had become so firmly intrenched in the American mind since the settlement that they had become no less than a "part of the religious creed of a nation."[34]

The processive theory of Natural Law, involving as it did the reliance upon traditional practice, prompted the historians to treat the ancestors as incipient revolutionaries themselves. To show that the Natural Rights of which they spoke were not mere abstractions, the historians argued that the principles of the revolution "were the principles which the ancestors of the inhabitants of the United States brought with them . . . to the dark wilds of America. . . ." Indeed, even before the settlement,

These were the rights of men, the privileges of Englishmen, and the claim of Americans: these were the principles of the Saxon ancestry of the British empire, and of all the free nations of Europe previous to the corrupt systems introduced by intriguing and ambitious individuals.[35]

These long-standing, traditional principles were supported, even institutionalized by the settlers of America who "were all of one rank; and were impressed with the opinion that all men are born entitled to equal rights." Those "sober, industrious, and persevering people" established "the same spirit among their descendents, finally [leading] them to liberty, independence and peace." David Ramsay stated the point clearly and emphatically: "The English Colonists were from their first settlement in America, devoted to liberty, on English ideas, and English principles. They not only conceived themselves to inherit the privileges of Englishmen, but though in a colonial situation, actually possessed them."[36]

Such idealized portraits of the fathers are more befitting hagiography than biography. But even if they sound like mythology to the modern ear one must appreciate the historians' intent in idealizing their forebears. By "creating a usable past" the historians meant to demonstrate that Natural Law and Natural Right had been established in the constitution of American society. But by "constitution" the historians, like Edmund Burke, did not mean a compact which symbolized the transition from the state of nature

[32] Pitkin, *Political and Civil History*, I, 85. Jedidiah Morse observed that taxation and representation were one right which amounted to "a privilege of ancient date" (*Annals*, 98).

[33] Ramsay, *American Revolution*, I, 16.

[34] Warren, *American Revolution*, III, 370.   [35] *Ibid.*, 306-07.

[36] Lendrum, *American Revolution*, I, 204; John McCulloch, *A Concise History of the United States . . .* (4th ed.; Philadelphia, 1813), 32; Ramsay, *American Revolution*, I, 27.

to civil society; they meant the order of things, how principles were lived in practice—constitution meant, in short, the way in which society was "constituted."

By understanding Natural Law as an historical process rather than as a static body of transcendent principles, one can return with an altered perspective to the historians' efforts to justify the revolution on the ground of its necessity. The revolution was justified, according to this view, because the British had violated rights which traditionally had been believed and practiced by the American people. They were "Natural Rights" precisely because they had grown up *in* historical experience, modified by the demands of the environment, and organically transmitted, generation by generation, from the settlers to the revolutionaries.[37] They were "Natural Rights" because they were taken-for-granted; they were assumed in the very process of living in the colonies. British policies, then, threatened not merely abstract rights—models of what rights would be like if they were ideal; nor did British policies threaten merely positive laws which were practiced by convenience. What the British threatened were "constitutional rights," rights which had been practiced for so long that they *were* the constitution of society. They threatened, therefore, the very structure of American existence.

With this view of Natural Law the tension between necessity and expediency was overcome, for by seeing both Natural Law and specific historical events as immanent in the historical-societal order of things the historians no longer had to create a bridge between the transcendent and the mundane. Thus an appeal to traditional practice—to concrete historical usage and custom—was itself an appeal to Natural Law. It was, of course, conceivable that some revolution might not be justified because it was merely expedient, because it was not demonstrated that traditional, practical rights had been abridged. This was the ground of Edmund Burke's hostility to the French Revolution.[38] Necessity was still established by appealing to Natural Law, but an appeal to Natural Law had become an appeal to history itself.

The effect of historicizing Natural Law theory was double-edged. At the same time that the historical theory of Natural Law resolved certain problems and ambiguities it tended to generate others. While, for example, it overcame the epistemological separation between the transcendent and the immanent, it also required the historians to repudiate in practice what had amounted to a religious faith in the transcendent as an immutable standard against which historical action could be measured with certainty. Equally important, while the historical theory freed the historians to make moral judgments about events without being required to point to any standard outside the events themselves, the Tory historian could argue that historical

---

[37] Ramsay, *American Revolution*, I, 28ff.

[38] Compare Burke's "Speech on Conciliation" with his *Reflections on the Revolution in France*, ed. Thomas H. D. Mahoney (Indianapolis, 1955), esp. 39-102. Mahoney summarizes the point: "One of the main reasons why Burke opposed the French Revolution was precisely because the French were breaking violently with their past instead of using it . . . as the foundation for the future" (*ibid.*, xxii).

morality thereby became situational—not only relativistic philosophically, but suspiciously subject to the vagaries of ideology.

Similarly, the historical theory of Natural Law made problematic the idea of "historical necessity." As long as necessity was understood in the context of the divinely-ordained providential, it was taken to be an absolute imperative of the transcendent. And there is reason to think that some of the historians continued to affirm the providential historical order. Once historicized, however, necessity was seen to arise *in* history rather than from without, and as a uniquely historical principle necessity raised problems of interpretation. For in the revolutionary histories, historical necessity meant something more like the manifest tendency of events rather than the absolute determination of history. But in presenting an argument for the general tendency of events the historian, who was as much the participant in those events as he was their narrator, opened himself to the charge of bias. His claim that the American Revolution was indeed historically necessary was easily construed as the product of political blindness or, less charitably, of ideological motive.[39]

These difficulties with the historical or processive theory of Natural Law underscore the point that there was still room to debate the justifiability of the American Revolution. The "patriot historians" were not going to convince the Tories that the revolution was justified because Natural Rights— traditional American rights and practices—had been violated. Jonathan Boucher, the Tory exile, would still write with bitterness that historical writings were too often "entirely exculpatory—compiled on purpose to vindicate [the historians'] own characters and conduct."[40] But precisely by denying that the revolution had been necessary, precisely by arguing that Natural Law had not been violated because traditional American rights and practices had not been abridged, Boucher and the Tories affirmed the revolutionary historians' new mode of analysis. For by quarreling with the patriot historians' interpretation of the past, the Tories had to quarrel in a new context. They could no longer question whether abstract, transcendent principles had been violated and, in the absence of revelation or intuition, disagree as a matter of opinion. Henceforth the debate would have to be conducted in the arena of historical fact and historical experience.

Purdue University.

---

[39] The problems of "necessity" and "inevitability" in the revolutionary histories are too complex to explicate here. See the author's "The Course of Human Events: American Historical Writings in the Revolutionary Era (Unpub. Ph.D. diss., Yale Univ. 1974), Ch. 4.

[40] Jonathan Boucher, *A View of the Causes and Consequences of the American Revolution* . . . (Repro. of 1797 edit.; New York, 1967), xx.

XV

POLYBIUS AND THE AMERICAN CONSTITUTION

By Gilbert Chinard

The part played by neo-classical influences in the development of American architecture is well-known. Following in the steps of Thomas Jefferson and of French refugees such as Godefroy and Joseph Mangin, American architects for generations covered the country, and particularly college grounds, with replicas of the *Maison carrée,* Greek temples and classical colonnades. Less evident and almost ignored is the influence of the classical tradition and of classical precedents in the establishment of institutions which, more or less amended and modified, have constituted the framework of American political life for a century and a half. So far as this writer has been able to discover, the many orations delivered and papers read on the occasion of the sesquicentennial of the Constitution have failed to mention the debt of the "founding fathers" to the "opinions and reasonings of philosophers, politicians and historians . . . whose writings were in contemplation of those who framed the American constitution," to quote no less an authority than John Adams.

This omission is understandable. The philosophy of the eighteenth century is still so close to us, we live in societies so deeply transformed and so completely remolded by eighteenth-century thinkers, that our natural tendency has been to attribute to English liberals and deists, to the French *philosophes* and to the American founders, an originality which they themselves would usually not have claimed. We have learned that during the "age of enlightenment" there was so little chauvinism that ideas circulated freely between England and France, and from both countries to America. Tracing the transfer of these ideas and estimating the debts of different countries to one another has proved a fascinating sport. We may wonder, however, whether it has not been too often forgotten that, in some cases at least, ideas for which we gave credit to a particular country had not a remote but quite ascertainable origin in a common treasure house and in a common tradition.

This seems to be particularly true of America. We have so often been told that the American experiment opened a new era, American historians have been so eager to trace the system of government finally formulated in 1787 to colonial beginnings, and have done it in so plausible and convincing a way, that we have naturally come to the conclusion that the form of civilization developed on this continent, while maintaining some so-called Anglo-Saxon principles of government, was a new and original departure from the older systems. To a certain extent we have been misled by the "Fathers" themselves, and by their historians. When Senator Lodge published the works of Hamilton, he inscribed as an epigraph these words taken from the *Farmer Refuted,* written by Hamilton when he was eighteen years old:

The sacred rights of mankind are not to be rummaged for among old parchments or musty records. They are written, as with a sunbeam, in the whole volume of human nature, by the hand of the Divinity itself, and can never be erased or obscured by mortal power.

And he supplemented it with another quotation:

We are laboring hard to establish in this country principles more and more *national,* and free from all foreign ingredients, so that we may be neither "Greeks nor Trojans," but truly Americans.[1]

When, a little over fifty years ago, Charles Francis Adams, Jr., delivered his famous Phi Beta Kappa address in Sanders Theater, he maintained that the time had come "to seek fresh inspiration at the fountains of living thought; for Goethe I hold to be the equal of Sophocles, and I prefer the philosophy of Montaigne to what seem to me the platitudes of Cicero." He even went so far as to declare that none of his great ancestors, neither John, nor John Quincy Adams, had derived any profit from what their descendant called "fetich worship." The least that can be said is that such an assertion reveals either surprising depths of ignorance or a vehement partisan spirit in a man who was in a position to be better informed. Even the most rapid survey would show that the assertion was as untrue of the Adamses as of most of their contemporaries.

I

The achievements of Jefferson as a classical scholar are so well known and so generally admired that they somewhat obscure the no less remarkable achievements of his contemporaries in the same field. In New England even more than in Virginia the classical

[1] Hamilton to King, 1796.

tradition was well established, and most of the men who made a name for themselves during the revolutionary era were no mean classical scholars. That they read Locke and later Montesquieu cannot be disputed; but at all times they studied and memorized Cicero and some of the Greek historians. It was from Cicero particularly, among the ancients, that they derived their ideals of liberty and government. It would be instructive to study more closely than has hitherto been done the knowledge of the classics that men of that generation could acquire in the colleges. No doubt the system of teaching could easily have been improved upon; but the fact remains that, however tedious may have been the training to which college students were subjected, most of them when they graduated were able to read ordinary Greek without much difficulty, and to read and write Latin with facility.

After leaving college, Jefferson compiled the curious *Commonplace Book,* which I published a few years ago, in which Greek and Latin authors occupy such a prominent place. John Adams, realizing that his teachers at Harvard had neglected to make him read the masterpieces of Latin literature, undertook to complete his classical education and, at twenty-nine, organized the *Sodalitas* Club, with Messrs. Gridley, Fitch and Dudley, to read in concert the Feudal Law and Tully's *Orations;* they started with the *Pro Milone.*[2] James Otis, in 1760, published a treatise entitled *The Rudiments of Latin Prosody, with a Dissertation on Letters, and the principles of Harmony, in poetic and prosaic composition, collected from the best writers,* and he composed a similar work on Greek prosody, which he could not have printed, for, he said, "there were no Greek types in the country, or if there were, no printer knew how to set them." It is difficult to realize today the influence that these readings of the Greek and Latin authors could have upon young minds uncluttered with the perishable trash against which no double lock and no ivory tower can offer complete protection. Having few books at their disposal and only very brief newspapers, they eagerly sought in the classics allusions to contemporary events, they found in them principles of public and political morality, and they looked on them as masters and guides.

A few days after the Stamp Act was to have gone into operation, a Boston minister, Dr. Mayhew, whom the younger generation of Harvard graduates considered as their intellectual leader, preached

[2] *Works,* II, 149.

a sermon on ''The Repeal of the Stamp Act.''   Towards the end of
the discourse he dwelt on his own principles:

> Having been initiated in youth in the doctrines of civil liberty, as they
> are taught by such men as Plato, Demosthenes, Cicero, and other persons
> among the ancients; and such as Sidney and Milton, Locke and Hoadley,
> among the moderns, I liked them; they seemed rational.[3]

There is little doubt that the same admission could have been
made by most of the men who from 1776 to 1787 cooperated in the
formulation of the American system of government.

This is the period which would give the most fruitful rewards
in such an investigation as is here proposed.   During the agitation
directly preceding the Declaration of Independence, the problems
discussed were somewhat limited.   The real question then was rather
to prove, that, in coming over to America, the colonists had severed all the political bonds which, nominally and apparently, still
connected them with the mother country.   In a few instances we
find allusions to the status of the Greek colonies, but in most cases
the colonists claimed the same rights as had been enjoyed by their
''Saxon ancestors'' when they settled in a sparsely populated
territory.

From 1776 to 1787 the questions uppermost in their minds were
of an entirely different nature.   Independence could be considered
as a *fait accompli,* but at one stroke the Declaration had abolished
all the forms of government which proceeded in any degree from
the British Crown.   New governments had to be established for the
new States and some formula had to be devised to regulate the relations of the States with one another.   Such was the task before
the men who wrote the different State constitutions, and who felt
the need of a national or federal constitution when the Articles of
Confederation proved inadequate and inefficient.   To these problems, solutions taking into consideration what was unique in the
situation of America had to be found, and the members of the Continental Congress and of the Constitutional Convention were no
doubt mindful of the unprecedented character of the American experiment.   On the other hand, most of them had been trained in the
study of the common law, which had developed in them the legalistic
disposition so apparent in the behavior of all American deliberative
assemblies.   Their arguments would have been less convincing, the

[3] Tudor, *Life of James Otis,* Boston, 1823, p. 144.

speakers themselves would have felt less confident of the soundness of their positions, if they had not been able to find precedents and to quote authorities for the measures they were advocating. This explains why the name of Montesquieu reappears so often in the debates of the time. It is not that Montesquieu really exerted a decisive influence or could be considered as the real and immediate "source" of any feature of the American constitution. Both Federalists and Republicans quoted him with equal confidence for he was much more than a foreign political philosopher. His book, *The Spirit of Laws,* was in fact the most compact and the most complete handbook on the science and history of government at their disposal. In it were to be found countless facts and countless quotations which could be used as precedents and illustrations in support of practically any and all opinions. Among the many questions which retained the attention of the Constitutional Convention, two only have been selected here: the famous theory of checks and balances, and the organization of the Senate, which might well be considered as a corollary to the first. On these two points, the delegates called upon Montesquieu as an authority in support of their views; but a careful study of the *Records* and the *Federalist* would show that more frequently they went back to the ancient sources from which Montesquieu himself had derived his information, and that they had apparently a first hand acquaintance with ancient historians and ancient history.

To a certain extent, their really surprising knowledge of classical analogies and precedents may be explained by the fact that John Adams had published, early in January 1787, his *Defence of the Constitutions of Government of the United States of America.* The first part of the work, dealing exclusively with ancient governments and writers, had reached America in March, long before the opening of the Federal Convention. It was immediately reprinted in Boston, New York and Philadelphia. In many respects, it was even better adapted to the use of the American legislators than the book of Montesquieu, since the author had dealt more extensively with problems of particular importance for the country he represented abroad. Among the students of government Adams had particularly singled out Polybius to whom he had been introduced by Swift, "one who, though seldom quoted as a legislator, appears to have considered this subject, and to have furnished arguments enough forever to determine the question." Swift had observed "That the best legislators of all ages agree in this, that the absolute power, which originally is in the whole body, is a trust too great to be committed to any man or assembly; and therefore. . . it will be an eternal rule in politics among every free people, that there is a balance of power to be carefully held by every state within itself.''[4]

This theory, however, had not originated with Swift, and the Doctor himself had quoted his authority—no less than Polybius—who tells us, ''the best government is that which consists of three forms, *regis, optimatium et populi imperium.''* Cicero had expressed the same idea almost in the same words when he asserted: ''*Statuo esse optime constitutam rempublicam, quae ex tribus generibus illis, regali, optimo, et populari, modice confusa,''* and Adams as well as his contemporaries was familiar with it, but nowhere had this ''fusion'' of the three orders balancing one another been expressed so clearly and so perfectly as in the Greek historian of Rome.[5]

To the discussion of Polybius Adams gave considerable space, more than ten pages of the modern edition, freely acknowledging his debt to the ancient writer:

I wish to assemble together the opinions and reasonings of philosophers, politicians, and historians, who have taken the most extensive views of men and societies, whose characters are deservedly revered, and whose writings were in the contemplation of those who framed the American constitutions. It will not be contested that all these characters are united in Polybius, who, in a fragment of his sixth book translated by Edward Spelman, at the end of his translation of the *Roman Antiquities of Dionysius Halicarnassensis,* says,—''It is customary, with those who professedly treat this subject, to establish three sorts of government,—kingly government, aristocracy, and democracy. . . . It is manifest that the best form of government is that

[4] *A Discourse of the Contests and Dissensions between the Nobles and Commons of Athens and Rome, with the Consequences they had upon both those States,* in *The Works* of John Adams, IV, 383–389.

[5] Adams already had in his library an edition of Dionysius Halicarnassensis, published in Frankfort in 1686, with the Greek and Latin in parallel columns, which he purchased in Paris in 1784. He added to it the English translation, *The Roman Antiquities translated into English; with Notes and Dissertations,* by Edward Spelman, London, 1758; he also possessed a French translation of Polybius, *Les Histoires de Polybe, avec les fragmens ou extraits du mesme auteur,* par Du Ryer, Paris, 1669–1670, 3 vols. and an English translation, *The History of Polybius . . . principally of the Roman People, during the first and second Punick Wars,* translated by Sir Henry Sheeres. Added a character of Polybius and his writings, by Mr. Dryden. London, 1698, 3 vols.

which is *compounded of all three*. This is founded not only in reason, but in experience.[6]

Then follows a long quotation which would deserve full elaboration and discussion, for it contains already two of the principles often attributed to Montesquieu who, in fact, did nothing but generalize and modernize the lessons of ancient history:

Lycurgus concluded that every form of government that is simple, by soon degenerating into that vice that is allied to it, must be unstable. The vice of kingly government is monarchy; that of aristocracy, oligarchy; that of democracy, rage and violence; into which, in process of time, all of them must degenerate. Lycurgus, to avoid these inconveniences, formed his government not of one sort, but united in one all the advantages and properties of the best governments; to the end that no branch of it, by swelling beyond its due bounds, might degenerate into the vice which is congenial to it; and that, while each of them were mutually acted upon by *opposite powers*, no one part might incline any way, or *outweigh* the rest; but that the commonwealth being equally *poised* and *balanced*, like a *ship* "or a *wagon*," acted upon by *contrary powers*, might long remain in the same situation; while the king was restrained from excess by the fear of the people, who had a proper share in the commonwealth; and, on the other side, the people did not dare to disregard the king, from their fear of the senate, who, being all elected for their virtue, would always incline to the justest side; by which means, that branch which happened to be oppressed became always superior, and, by the accessional weight of the senate, *outbalanced* the other. This system preserved the Lacedaemonians in liberty longer than any other people we have heard of ever enjoyed it.

All three principal orders of government were found in the Roman commonwealth; everything was constituted and administered with that equality and propriety by these three, that it was not possible, even for a Roman citizen, to assert positively, whether the government, in the whole, was aristocratical, democratical, or monarchical. For, when we cast our eyes on the power of the consuls, the government appeared entirely monarchical and kingly, when on that of the senate, aristocratical; and when any one considered the power of the people, it appeared plainly democratical.[7]

[6] *Defence* . . . chapter VI, in *Works* of John Adams, IV, 435–445.

[7] Whether or not he remembered Polybius, Benjamin Franklin, according to Adams himself, had used a similar comparison "in 1776, in the convention of Pennsylvania when speaking on" a motion to add "another assembly, under the name of a senate or council," the Doctor has said that: "two assemblies appeared to him like the practice he had somewhere seen, of certain wagoners, who, when about to descend a steep hill with a heavy load, if they had four cattles, took off one pair from before, and chaining them to the hinder part of the wagon drove them down hill; while the

Polybius had concluded his long dissertation with the assertion that, "such being the power of each order to hurt and assist each other, their union is adapted to all contingencies, and *it is not possible to invent a more perfect system.*" Such an enthusiasm and such an optimism Adams felt himself unable to share. In fact, the monarchical, aristocratical and democratical powers were unequally mixed in Rome. The consuls had no negative; the people had a negative, but a very unequal one, because they had no opportunity for cool deliberation. The appointment of tribunes was a very inadequate remedy. This appears from Adams's commentary on the speech of Manlius Valerius, found in the seventh book of Dionysius Halicarnassensis, in which the old senator proposed to strengthen the tribunitian power. He found facts to support his criticism in Adam Ferguson's book entitled *History of the Progress and Termination of the Roman Republic*, 1783, 3 vols. There the student of government is able to trace the development of the Roman constitution from the earliest days to "that state of maturity, at which Polybius began to admire the felicity of its institutions, and the order of its administration." For Adams the history of republican Rome could be summed up in this picturesque fashion: *Plebeians scrambling after Patricians; or Democracy hunting down Aristocracy; or Tribunes in chase of a Senate.* The lesson to draw from all this scramble and this continuous contention between the different powers was clear:

From this example, as from all others, it appears that there can be no government of laws without a balance, and that there can be no balance without three orders: and that even three orders can never balance each other, unless each in its department is independent and absolute. For want of this the struggle was first between the king and senate; in which case the king must always give way, unless supported by the people. Before the creation of the tribunes, the people were in no sense independent, and, therefore, could not support the kings. After the abolition of kings, the senate had no balance either way, and accordingly became at once a tyrannical oligarchy. When the people demanded their right, and obtained a check, they were not satisfied; and grasped at more and more power, until they obtained all, there being no monarchical power to aid the senate. But the moment the power became collected into this one center, it was found in

pair before and the weight of the load, overbalancing the strength of those behind, drew them slowly and moderately down the hill." *Defence*, ch. IV; in *Works*, IV, 390.

reality split into three; and as Caesar had the largest of the three shares, he instantly usurped the whole.

Thus the system outlined by Polybius was not perfect, though the principles on which it rested were excellent: .or the executive was never sufficiently separated from the legislative, nor had these powers a control upon each other defined with sufficient accuracy. This precedent made very clear the task of the American legislators: it was to preserve the principle of checks and balances without which no form of government can attain any permanency. This principle, which had been reaffirmed by Montesquieu, constituted the essence of the political philosophy of ancient thinkers whose works were available to the delegates either directly or in the abridged form given by John Adams in his *Defence*. It was the duty of the American legislators to keep in mind these ancient experiments, to derive from them whatever profit they could, to remember that to a certain extent "the constitution of England, if its balance is seen to play, in practice, according to the principles of its theory, . . . is a system much more perfect." But there was no reason to believe that the American architects could not erect a much better structure on the old foundations, and Adams concluded that "The constitutions of several of the United States, it is hoped, will prove themselves improvements both upon the Roman, the Spartan, and the English commonwealths."

II

Supplemented by the book of Ferguson, Rollin's *Ancient History* and Montesquieu's *Spirit of Laws*, the *Defence of the Constitutions of Government of the United States of America* became the text book, or rather the handbook of the American legislators. There were few occasions when the ancient writers were not called upon to provide precedents and illustrations for the different speakers. A complete enumeration cannot be undertaken here, but a few examples may not be out of place.

Shortly after the opening of the Convention, Madison thought it necessary to remind his colleagues of former experiments and he,

in a very able and ingenious speech ran through the whole Scheme of the Government,—pointed out all the beauties and defects of ancient republics; compared their situation with ours wherever it appeared to bear any analogy, and proved that the only way to make a Government answer all the end of its institution was to collect the wisdom of its several parts in aid of each other whenever it was necessary.   Hence the propriety of incorporating the Judicial with the Executive in the revision of the Laws.   (*Records, I, 110*).[8]

When the question of the presidential powers was brought up for the first time, George Mason indicated his preference for an executive in three persons, for a single executive would be too much like a monarchy.   He praised the democratic spirit which makes citizens fight *pro aris et focis* and enabled "the little cluster of Grecian republics to resist, and almost constantly to defeat the Persian monarch."

Ancient precedents were mentioned again and again in the fierce discussion which raged around the sovereignty of the States of the Union.   Hamilton made an impassioned plea for a strong executive and a strong federal bond, and pointed out that the Greek confederacies were of short duration because of an inherent weakness:

> The Amphyctionic Council had, it would seem, ample powers for general purposes.   It had in particular the power of fining and using force against delinquent members.   What was the consequence?   Their decrees were mere signals of war.   The Phocian war is a striking example of it.   Philip at length taking advantage of their disunion, and insinuating himself into their Councils, made himself master of their fortunes.   (*June 18, Records, I, 285*).

The same argumentation, with the same examples, was presented by Madison on the next day: "Did not Persia and Macedon distract the councils of Greece by acts of corruption?   And is not Jersey and Holland at this day subject to the same distractions?" (*Records, I, 326*)

Charles Pinckney apparently was the only one who had the courage to protest that conditions were entirely different and precedents out of place.   He did not do so however, without some display of historical erudition:

> The people of this country are not only very different from the inhabitants of any State we are acquainted with in the modern world; but I assert that their situation is distinct from either the people of Greece or Rome, or of any State we are acquainted with among the antients.—Can the orders introduced by the institution of Solon, can they be found in the United States?   Can the military habits and manners of Sparta be resembled to our habits and manners?   Are the distinctions of Patrician and Plebeian known among us?   (*June 25th, Records, I, 401*)

[8] All the following quotations are taken from *The Records of the Federal Convention of 1787*, edited by Max Farrand, New Haven and London, 1911, 1937.

Apparently he was not followed, for three days later, arguing for the establishment of a strong federal government and trying to allay the apprehension lest the small States be crushed by the larger ones, Madison pointed out that the smaller States had nothing to fear from a government in which the federal bond would be powerful enough to protect the weaker members against the enterprises of the ambitious ones. Once again he brought in an array of historical precedents: "Among the principal members of antient and modern confederacies, we find the same effect from the same cause. The contentions, not the coalitions of Sparta, Athens and Thebes, proved fatal to the smaller members of the Amphyctionic Confederacy . . . The more lax the bond, the more liberty the larger will have to avail themselves of their superior force. Here again Experience was an instructive monitor." After mentioning "the heroic period of antient Greece, the feudal licentiousness of the middle ages of Europe, the existing condition of the American savages," he finally added:

> But there are cases still more in point. What was the condition of the weaker members of the Amphyctionic Confederacy? Plutarch (Life of Themistocles) will inform us that it happened but too often that the strongest cities corrupted and awed the weaker, and that Judgment went in favor of the more powerful party. (*June 28th, Records, I, 449*)

At this juncture Franklin rose in despair. The Convention threatened to degenerate into a classical meeting, which we may surmise was somewhat over the heads of some members. To his colleagues he addressed a piteous appeal:

> The small progress we have made after 4 or five weeks close attendance and continual reasonings with each other—our different sentiments on almost every question, several of the last producing as many noes as ays, is methinks a melancholy proof of the imperfection of the Human Understanding. We indeed seem to feel our own want of political wisdom, since we have been running about in search of it. We have gone back to ancient history for models of Government, and examined the different forms of those Republics which having been formed with the seeds of their own dissolution now no longer exist. And we have viewed the Modern States all round Europe, but find none of their Constitutions suitable to our circumstances. (*June 28th, Records, I, 451*)

His conclusion was that "we have not hitherto once thought of humbly applying to the Father of lights to illuminate our understanding," and he proposed to institute daily prayers, as in the old Congress.

Although fully trusting in the divine guidance, the scholars in the Convention were not ready to give up their most precious arguments. In Franklin's own words, "The Convention, except three or four persons, thought Prayers unnecessary," and when Martin took up the floor again on the same day, he went back to the old confederacies, advancing that

> The states forming the amphictionic council were equal, though Lacedemon, one of the greatest states, attempted the exclusion of three of the lesser states from this right. The plan reported, it is true, only intends to diminish those rights, not to annihilate them.—It was the ambition and power of the great Grecian states which at last ruined this respectable council. (*June 28th, Records, I, 454*)

Madison retorted that the great States in the Amphyctionic Confederacy never oppressed the smaller, never combined to oppress the other cities, but that they were rivals and fought each other. Martin, nevertheless, stuck to his guns contending that: "Amphictyonick Council of Greece represented by two from each town—who were notwithsg. the dispn. of the Towns equal"; that "All the *Ancient* and *Modern* Confedns. and Leagues were as *equals* notwithstanding the *vast* disproportions in size and wealth," and in support of his position, he triumphantly quoted from "Rollin's *Ancient History*, 4 vol., p. 79." (*June, 28th, Records, I, 459*)

Who could have thought, unless such positive texts were produced, that the limitation of two senators for each State might perhaps be traced to the "Amphictyonick Council of Greece?"

When Ellsworth, as a compromise, proposed an amendment, "That in the second branch each state shall have an equal vote," he admitted that the effect of this motion was to make the general government partly federal and partly national. He thought, however, that if some conspicuous faults appeared in this organization, they could be remedied in time.

This, in Madison's opinion would never do. It was a most dangerous doctrine. "The Defects of the Amphictionick League were acknowledged, but they never could be reformed" (*June 29th*). He maintained that, on another important point, Mr. Ellsworth "had also erred" in saying, in support of the equal representation of the States, that:

No instance had existed in which confederated States had not retained to themselves a perfect equality of suffrage. Passing over the German system in which the K. of Prussia has nine voices, he reminded Mr. E. of the Lycian confederacy, in which the component members had votes proportioned to their importance, and which Montesquieu recommends as the fittest model for that form of government. Had the fact been as stated by Mr. E. it would have been of little avail to him, or rather would have strengthened the arguments against him; the History & fate of the several Confederacies modern as well as Antient, demonstrating some radical vice in their structure. (*June 30th, Records, I, 485*)

This question was necessarily very closely connected with the organization of the Senate, and as the discussion was not conducted very systematically, it is practically impossible to distinguish between the two in an analysis of the debates. It does not appear that the possibility of limiting the legislative power to one house was very seriously or very long considered in the Convention, although outside the Convention the unicameral system was favored by a number of writers.

Madison insisted that the Senate should remain a small body, and here again he drew his illustrations from ancient history:

Their weight would be in an inverse ratio to their number. The example of the Roman Tribunes was applicable. They lost their influence and power in proportion as their number was augmented. The reason seemed to be obvious: They were appointed to take care of the popular interests & pretensions at Rome, because the people by reason of their number could not act in concert; were liable to fall into factions among themselves, and to become a prey to their aristocratic adversaries. The more the representatives of the people therefore were multiplied, the more they partook of the infirmities of their constituents, the more liable they became to be divided among themselves either from their own indiscretions or the artifices of the opposite factions, and of course the less capable of fulfilling their trust. (*June 7th, Records, I, 151*)

A week later, Patterson made a very interesting speech, no less erudite, on the dangers of the unicameral system:

A single legislature is very dangerous.—Despotism may present itself in various shapes. May there not be legislative despotism if in the exercise of their power they are unchecked or unrestrained by another branch? On the contrary an executive to be restrained must be an individual. The first triumvirate of Rome combined, without law, was fatal to its liberties; and the second, by the usurpation of Augustus, ended in despotism.—The two kings of Sparta and the consuls of Rome, by sharing the executive, distracted their governments. (*June 16th, Records, I, 261*)

It is clear that in the opinion of several delegates, the executive represented the monarchical power, the senate the aristocratical, and the house the popular power. This appears even more clearly in a speech of Madison on the same subject. Insisting that the term of the Senator should be nine years rather than four or six, and answering Pinckney, who had opposed a long term, Madison frankly declared that it was necessary to insure to the Senate as much permanency as possible. It was impossible to prevent the rise of an aristocracy: "There will be debtors and creditors, and an unequal possession of property, and hence arises different views and different objects in government. This, indeed is the ground-work of aristocracy; and we find it blended in every government, both ancient and modern." In conclusion, he did not hesitate to state that: "Landholders ought to have a share in the government to support these invaluable interests and to balance and check the other. They ought to be so constituted as to protect the minority of the opulent against the majority. The senate, therefore, ought to be this body; and to answer these purposes, they ought to have permanency and stability. Various have been the propositions; but my opinion is, the longer they continue in office, the better will these views be answered." (*June 26th, Records, I, 431*)

Hamilton agreed with Madison and was equally outspoken:

If we incline too much to democracy, we shall soon shoot into a monarchy. The difference of property is already great amongst us. Commerce and industry will still increase the disparity. Your government must meet this state of things, or combinations will in process of time, undermine your system.

Then he drew again from ancient history to illustrate his thesis, and once more he evidently remembered Polybius:

What was the tribunitial power of Rome? It was instituted by the plebeans as a guard against the patricians. But was this a sufficient check? No—The only distinction which remained at Rome was, at last, between the rich and poor. (*June 26th, Records, I, 432*)

These quotations and illustrations could easily be multiplied. Incomplete as they are, they may serve to support the contention that the framers of the Federal Constitution, far from being unmindful of the past, were eager to connect the American experiment with the efforts of the generations of old to establish a balance of powers. Such an analysis of the weaknesses of ancient as well as modern constitutions would, they hoped enable America to escape the sort of fatality which, according to Montesquieu, had seemed to make it impossible for any government not to decay.

This constant preoccupation with the past and this prestige of the ancient writers extended beyond the walls of the Federal Convention. The same historical considerations reappeared, although somewhat less frequently during "the debates in the several State Conventions on the adoption of the Constitution."[9]

In Massachusetts, evidently alluding to Sedgwick, Ames, Heath and perhaps John Adams, Gore protested against the speakers who held that "we ought to consult the sentiments of wise men who have written on the subject of government and thereby regulate our decision on this business," and he maintained that "certainly observations drawn from such sources can have no weight in considering things so essentially different." He was upheld by King, who reiterated that "history can afford little on this subject" and that "from the continent of Europe we could receive no instruction." (*Elliot, II, 16, 17, 19*)

On the other hand, the learned Dr. Willard "entered largely into the field of ancient history," to be contradicted by the Hon. Mr. Cabot "in a clear and elegant manner." This display of erudition would have probably occupied much more space had not Mr. Randall abruptly cut it short by saying that "the quoting of ancient history was no more to the purpose than to tell how our forefathers dug clams at Plymouth." A few days later, Bowdoin, unimpressed by this rugged profession of Americanism, discussed at length Solon and Montesquieu. (*Ib., II, 68, 126*)

In Connecticut, Ellsworth indulged in a long disquisition on the Amphictyonic Council, the Achaean league, and the Aetolian league (*Ib., II, 187*), and so did Hamilton in New York (*Ib., II, 233, 302*). In Pennsylvania Wilson attempted to check the scholarly enthusiasm of those who drew false analogies between the present situation and the Achaean league, the Lycian confederacy and the Amphictyonic council, and claimed an entire and unprecedented originality for the system on which rested the Constitution—namely "the doctrine of representation altogether unknown to the ancients." (*Ib., II, 423*)

[9] This is the title of the well known compilation of Jonathan Elliot, Philadelphia, 1861, from which the following quotations are taken.

In Virginia, Nicholas discussed the system of balances introduced in the government of Rome by the "creation of tribunes of the people" (*Ib., III, 19*); Madison enumerated "the various reasons whereby nations had lost their liberties" (*Ib., III, 91*). Monroe, in a long and scholarly discussion reviewed the history of the ancient and modern confederations and "read several passages from Polybius to elucidate and prove the excellent structure of the Achaean league and the consequent happy effects of this excellency." (*Ib., III, 209–211*)

III

No attempt has been made to study from this point of view the editorials appearing in the press during the debates. We know however that the writers of the *Federalist* found it necessary on many occasions to resort to ancient history in order to strengthen their argumentation. In fact, they displayed their erudition much more freely than during the debates and to the sources already mentioned they added among others "an intelligent writer," "l'abbé de Mably," whom they quoted extensively.[10]

Attempting to show the dangers resulting from men who abuse the confidence placed in them either by a king or a people, and consequently the desirability of establishing proper checks, Hamilton discovered a conspicuous example in the life of Pericles, who "in compliance with the resentment of a prostitute, at the expense of much of the blood and treasure of his countrymen, attacked, vanquished, and destroyed the city of the Samnians," then of the Megarensians, and "was the primitive author of that famous and fatal war, distinguished in the Grecian annals by the name of the Peloponnesian war; which, after various vicissitudes, intermissions and renewals, terminated in the ruin of the Athenian commonwealth."[11]

Protesting against the belief that a republic would necessarily enjoy peace, and that no standing army was necessary, Hamilton again recalled the examples of Sparta, Athens and Carthage, for "Sparta was little better than a well-regulated camp; and Rome was never sated of carnage and conquest."

Against those who would like to give equal representation to all the States, irrespective of their population, and to maintain a confederate rather than a national government, in order to preserve the

[10] See particularly *Federalist*, VI, XVIII, XX.
[11] *Federalist*, VI.

full independence and sovereignty of the individual States, Hamilton took the ground that the proposed plan of government made them "constituent parts of the National Sovereignty, by allowing them a direct representation in the Senate, and leaves in their possession certain exclusive and very important portions of Sovereign power." In this respect the American plan was far better than the Lycian Confederacy, which had been represented by Montesquieu as "a model of an excellent Confederate Republic," for "In the Lycian Confederacy, which consisted of twenty-three CITIES, or republics, the largest were entitled to *three* votes in the COMMON COUNCIL, those of the middle class to *two,* and the smallest to *one.*"[12]

Madison gave a whole number of the *Federalist*[13] to a discussion of the ancient confederacies, of which "the most considerable was that of the Grecian Republics, associated under the Amphictyonic council. From the best accounts transmitted of this celebrated institution, it bore a very instructive analogy to the present Confederation of the American States." He then proceeded with a detailed analysis of the Amphictyonic Council, pointing out its faults, and particularly its lack of balance, which enabled the larger cities, in spite of the equality of representation, to dominate the assembly. "Athens, as we learn from DEMOSTHENES, was the arbiter of Greece seventy-three years. The Lacedaemonians next governed it twenty-nine years; at a subsequent period, after the battle of Leuctra, the Thebans had their turn of domination." "The smaller members, though entitled by the theory of their system, to revolve in equal pride and majesty around the common centre, had become, in fact, satellites of the orbs of primary magnitude." "Had Greece, says a judicious observer on her fate, been united by a stricter Confederation, and persevered in her union, she would never have worn the chains of Macedon; and might have proved a barrier to the vast projects of Rome."

The Achaean League supplied Madison with no less "valuable instruction." In Madison's opinion, it was by far the most interesting of the ancient confederations; it was also the most united, and so well-balanced that "the popular Government, which was so tempestuous elsewhere, caused no disorders in the members of the Achaean republic, *because it was there tempered by the general authority and laws of the Confederacy.*" This was so true that

[12] *Federalist,* IX.
[13] *Ibid.,* XVIII.

when the Romans undertook the conquest of Greece they found that the easiest way to overcome the Greeks was to proclaim "universal liberty throughout Greece," which was "but another name more specious for the independence of the members on the Federal head." "By these arts, this union, the last hope of Greece, the last hope of ancient liberty, was torn into pieces; and such imbecility and distraction introduced, that the arms of Rome found little difficulty in completing the ruin which their arts had commenced." Madison deeply regretted that such imperfect monuments should remain of this curious political fabric; but enough of it, he opined, was known to provide an important lesson for the American States.

When Hamilton tried to refute the objection that coördinate authority could not exist in the matter of taxation, he quoted the Roman organization, according to which "the legislative authority, in the last resort, resided for ages in two different political bodies— not as branches of the same Legislature, but as distinct and independent Legislatures, in each of which an opposite interest prevailed; in one, the patrician; in the other, the plebeian. Many arguments might have been adduced, to prove the unfitness of two such seemingly contradictory authorities, each having power to *annul* or *repeal* the acts of the other. But a man would have been regarded as frantic, who should have attempted at Rome to disprove their existence. It will be readily understood, that I allude to the COMITIA CENTURIATA and the COMITIA TRIBUTA . . . these two Legislatures coexisted for ages, and the Roman Republic attained to the utmost height of human greatness."[14]

When, finally, the *Federalist* took up the organization of the Senate, Madison thought it necessary again to go back to ancient history to justify the establishment of a second house. In speaking of the constitution of the Senate, he said:

It adds no small weight to all these considerations, to recollect that history informs us of no long-lived republic, which had not a senate. Sparta, Rome, and Carthage are, in fact, the only states to whom that character can be applied. In each of the two first, there was a senate for life. The constitution of the Senate in the last is less known. Circumstantial evidence makes it probable, that it was not different in this particular from the two others. It is at least certain, that it had some quality or other which rendered it an anchor against popular fluctuations.[15]

[14] *Federalist*, No. XXXIV.
[15] *Ibid.*, No. LXIII.

Even in the pure democracies of Greece, it was found necessary to elect some smaller bodies: the nine archons of Athens before Solon, and, subsequent to that period, an assembly of at first four, then six hundred members annually elected by the people, and partially representing them in their legislative capacity. Madison tried to demonstrate that such an assembly did not constitute a danger for the more popular branch of the government. He presented it as a necessary check against the tyranny of popular passions and, to make his point in a more forceful way, he could do no better than quote again from Polybius:

As far as antiquity can instruct us on this subject, its examples support the reasoning which we have employed. In Sparta, the Ephori, the annual representatives of the people, were found an overmatch for the senate for life, continually gained on its authority and finally drew all power into their own hands. The Tribunes of Rome, who were the Representatives of the people, prevailed, it is well known, in almost every contest with the senate for life, and in the end gained the most complete triumph over it. The fact is the more remarkable, as unanimity was required in every act of the Tribunes, even after their number was augmented to ten. It proves the irresistible force possessed by that branch of a free government, which has the people on its side. To these examples might be added that of Carthage, whose senate, according to the testimony of POLYBIUS, instead of drawing all power into its vortex, had, at the commencement of the second Punic War, lost almost the whole of its original portion.[16]

IV

It is, of course, undeniable, that the American Constitution rests largely upon the colonial governments and upon British traditions modified in order to fit new circumstances. This having been granted, it is not superfluous to recall that the legislators of 1787 were aware, in the words of John Adams, that "the English have, in reality, blended together the feudal institutions with those of the Greeks and Romans, and that out of all have made that noble composition which avoids the inconveniences, and retains the advantages of both." Some of them had little use for the past and for Europe, either because, like Mr. Bass, a member of the North Carolina Convention, "who never went to school, and had been born blind," they flattered themselves, "with the possession of common sense and reason" (*Elliot, IV, 174*), or simply because they were distrustful

[16] *Federalist,* LXIII.

of any foreign ideas. Most of the delegates, however, were willing and eager to refer to the past and from it to derive whatever lessons had been preserved for the use of future generations. Two points particularly attracted their attention: the experiments in federal organization which had been carried out more or less successfully by the Greeks; then the imperfect but interesting system of checks and balances established by the Romans and described by Polybius. In the discussion of these fundamental problems, they often quoted Montesquieu, but Montesquieu was only one of their authorities; they utilized modern historians like Stanyan and Ferguson and they did not neglect the original texts available either in full or in the convenient compilation of John Adams.

To evaluate exactly the influence of the ancient philosophers and historians upon the formulation of the American system of government would be a long and difficult undertaking. In many cases the legislators used the ancient examples and precedents simply to illustrate and confirm conclusions which they might have reached independently. When J.-J. Mounier, a former member of the French "Constituent Assembly" attempted to estimate the responsibility of the *philosophes* in the upheaval which had overthrown the old régime, he maintained that: "the principles advanced by a few of the eighteenth century writers and chiefly the example of the Long Parliament, assumed a disastrous importance. But the Revolution was not brought about by the influence of these principles. On the contrary, the Revolution made them influential. Even if they had not been already circulated, the circumstances in which France happened to be would have caused the creation and development of such deleterious systems."[17]

In a similar way, to claim too much for "Polybius," who is taken here as a sort of symbol, would be erroneous and dangerous. One of the writers of the Federalist papers who had read on the subject as much as any man of his time and had been an actor as well as an observer during the framing of the Constitution, summed up the whole question in words which might well be remembered by historians of constitutional history and historians of ideas. After enumerating the causes which made unstable the ancient republics and pointing out that the history of Sparta, Rome and Carthage

---

[17] *De l'influence attribuée aux philosophes, aux francs-maçons et aux illuminés sur la Révolution de France.* Paris, 1822. 1st edition, Tubingue, 1801.

alone provides "very instructive proofs of the necessity of some institution that will blend stability with liberty," he concluded:

> I am not unaware of the circumstances which distinguish the American from other popular governments, as well ancient as modern; and which render extreme circumspection necessary, in reasoning from the one case to the other. But after allowing due weight to this consideration, it may still be maintained, that there are many points of similitude which render these examples not unworthy of our attention.[18]

A very moderate conclusion, but a conclusion which could be taken as a program by all those who believe that the American experiment had more than a local and circumstantial value; that it was in fact a sort of culmination, and that, to understand and appraise it, it is necessary to realize that the most modern form of government is not unconnected with the political thought and the political experience of ancient times.

Princeton University.

---

[18] *Federalist,* LXIII.   The author is either Madison or Hamilton; the display of historical erudition seems to point to Madison.

XVI

DUTCH AND AMERICAN FEDERALISM *

BY WILLIAM H. RIKER

Since the United Netherlands was by far the most successful of modern federal republics prior to 1787, one might reasonably suppose that the framers of the United States Constitution drew heavily on Dutch experience. And indeed, when the records of the Constitutional Convention and the state ratifying conventions are superficially examined, it appears that our heritage from the Netherlands is considerable. The records show that members of the conventions referred to the government of the United Provinces more frequently than to any other modern European government, except that of Great Britain. In all, Dutch institutions are mentioned thirty-seven times and ten of these references are substantial discussions of history and authorities.[1] John Marshall remarked, as he began his highly rhetorical interpretation of the Dutch constitution in the Virginia ratifying convention (Eliott, III, 255): " We may derive from Holland lessons very beneficial to ourselves ", and the tone of most of the rest of the thirty-seven references is quite similar. It might seem justifiable, therefore, to conclude that Dutch institutions of the seventeenth and eighteenth centuries have a significant historical relevance to our own.[2]

* The author wishes to thank the Rockefeller Foundation for a grant that allowed him sufficient freedom from academic duties to prepare this essay, for the contents of which the Foundation is in no way responsible.

[1] A list of the substantial discussions of the United Provinces in the Federal Convention of 1787 and the state ratifying conventions:

a. In Max Farrand, *Records of the Federal Conventions of 1787* (New Haven, 1911 and 1937, 4 vols.), hereafter cited as " Farrand ":

(1) I, 89, 90, 91; 2 June 1787; Pierce Butler (S.C.); discussion of the executive. (2) I, 102–03; 4 June 1787; Benjamin Franklin (Pa.); epitome of Dutch history. (3) I, 254, 261, 266, 272; 16 June 1787; James Wilson (Pa.); discussion of legislative unanimity. (4) I, 449, 458; 28 June 1787; James Madison (Va.); discussion of Holland.

b. In Jonathan Eliott, *Debates on the Federal Constitution* (Washington, 1856, 5 vols. revised), hereafter cited as " Eliott " : (5) II, 55–56; 21 January 1788; Rufus King (Mass.); discussion of the unanimity principle. (6) II, 188; 4 January 1788; Oliver Ellsworth (Conn.); discussion of stadtholderate. (7) II, 218–19; 20 June 1788, John Lansing (New York); discussion of the unanimity principle. (8) III, 131; 7 June 1788; James Madison (Va.); discussion of unanimity principle. (9) III, 189–90; 9 June 1788; Edmund Randolph (Va.); discussion of constitution. (10) III, 268; 11 June 1788; George Mason (Va.); discussion of prosperity.

[2] In *Federal Government* (London, 1953) K. C. Wheare, for example, does indeed remark (43) that the United Netherlands served as a lesson of weakness for subsequent federations.

But the pitfalls in the study of the history of ideas are many and some of them are in the path here. Despite the framers' fairly extensive discussions, despite their own obvious confidence in their knowledge, despite, even, their citation of authorities, close examination of their speeches reveals that they had only a cursory knowledge of Dutch history and that they knew even less about the operation of Dutch institutions. Nearly all the framers who spoke on the subject seemed certain of one statement about the Netherlands; and in this they were mistaken. Nearly all seemed to believe that the decisions of the general government required unanimity of the seven provinces—an even more stringent requirement than in the Continental Congress. But, misled by inaccurate commentaries, they did not know what this requirement meant or how it worked in practice or what significance it had in Dutch politics. And, of course, they did not know that unless they allowed for significant exceptions they were wrong. Because, however, of the superficial similarity of this supposed rule of Dutch legislatures to the provisions about legislative decision in the Articles of Confederation, they concentrated on this constitutional rule—torn out of its political and historical context—and quite erroneously interpreted it in the light of their own recent experience. As a consequence, their discussions of Dutch institutions, far from constituting an attempt to learn from Dutch history, are simply a device for praise or calumny of the Articles of Confederation, from the history of which the framers had learned much. As a member approved or disapproved of the Articles, so he eulogized the Netherlands as " a free and happy republic " or condemned it as an example of " the characteristic imbecility of federal governments."

Tempting though it may be, therefore, to conclude from the records that our federalism owes something to the example of this earlier one, such a conclusion is nevertheless false. Constitutional experience is not readily transmitted from one culture to another; and, as suggested by the detailed examination of the supposed transmission of ideas from the Netherlands to America, an examination to which the rest of this essay is devoted, statements about the influence of one constitution on another are difficult to substantiate.

I

One of the reasons Dutch experience could exert little influence on the United States is the paucity of information about the Netherlands available to members of the Philadelphia convention. John Adams, then the only American ambassador to The Hague ever actually in residence and hence one of the few Americans qualified to speak on Dutch politics, was in Europe in 1787. Only one of the delegates at Philadelphia, Pierce Butler of South Carolina, purported to discuss Dutch affairs on the basis of a traveller's knowledge. Yet his one contribution was so clearly without foundation in the customary interpretation of Dutch politics that the following day Dr. Franklin, in one of the few speeches he personally delivered, reviewed Dutch history in some detail in order to point out Butler's errors (items 1 and 2, note 1). Butler had asserted that the direction of Dutch military affairs was so divided that the States-General had recently been forced to employ a French commander. Franklin demonstrated on the contrary that the employment of a French officer was merely an incident in the perpetual conflict between republicans and the House of Nassau and that the danger to the republic was not the division of military command but rather the concentration of it in the hands of a stadtholder. Franklin's 300 word epitome of Dutch history from 1570 to 1787 is, with one exception, reasonably accurate in fact, consistent in interpretation, and obviously based on knowledge obtained at the French court in the previous decade. His prestige and the content of his speech were sufficient to crush Butler's pretentions to authority. So far as the record shows and quite understandably, Butler did not mention his travels again.

Since the members of the convention lacked personal knowledge of Dutch politics, they were forced to rely on published accounts. Here language was a barrier. So far as I can discover from an extensive reading of biographies and papers, all of the framers were ignorant of Dutch and thus lacked access to any comprehensive account of Dutch history or to the several collections of state papers. Consequently they could know only what was written about the Dutch constitution in English and, for the best educated, in French, though it is not certain that they used any French sources. Numerous Latin works on the Netherlands were available of course; but by the latter part of the 18th century Latin had ceased to be the language of history writing and diplomacy. Few of the framers read Latin with facility and even one as well educated as Madison would ask Jefferson to get titles in French rather than Latin. It may be safely assumed, I believe, that none of the framers ploughed through any of the detailed Latin chronicles of affairs in the Netherlands.

Materials on the subject in English or French were, however, difficult to come by. At least one of the framers, James Madison, who is not undeservedly called " the father of the Constitution," had for some years sought to study Dutch government. In March, 1784, he wrote to Jefferson, who was then at Annapolis, asking him to buy books: " You know tolerably well," he added, " the objects of my curiosity. I will only particularize my wish of whatever may throw light on the general Constitution and droit public of the several confederacies which have existed. I observe in Boinaud's [sic] catalogue several pieces on the Duch [sic], the German, and the Helvetic. The operation of our own must render all such lights of consequence." [3] Jefferson delayed the purchases until he went to the better and cheaper bookstores of France, where, during the winter of 1784–85, he selected a library of 192 volumes. He shipped it 1 September 1785 and Madison received it 24 February 1786, nearly two years after the original request.[4] But not one volume in the 192 dealt more than cursorily with the Netherlands. Clearly, it was not easy for an isolated Virginia planter to study the " droit public of the several confederacies." Madison did subsequently acquire a copy of De Witt (?), *Political Maxims*—he read from it at the Virginia convention—and this acquisition ought to be regarded, I think, as part of the everyday heroism of the scholarly politician.

Madison's difficulty in getting books was partly occasioned by the fact that there were few titles to get. The catalogue of Jefferson's

[3] *The Papers of Thomas Jefferson*, ed. Julian F. Boyd (Princeton, 1951 ff.), VI, 37; Madison to Jefferson, 16 March 1784. It would be fortunate for our understanding of the transmission of ideas if we knew or could easily guess what titles caught Madison's eye. Unfortunately, no copy of this catalogue has come down to us, according to assurances given me by Mr. Clifford Shipton, Librarian of the American Antiquarian Society, Worcester, Massachusetts. Although the catalogue is described in several bibliographies, the descriptions all stem, so Mr. Shipton tells me, from a Boinod and Gaillard advertisement in the *Pennsylvania Journal* of 17 January 1784. We do know, however, at least two of the titles that must have interested Madison. Washington ordered some books from the catalogue (see: *The Writings of George Washington*, ed. by John C. Fitzpatrick [Washington, 1931 ff.], XXVII, 338–39, 18 February 1784). Among the items he ordered was William Lothian, *History of the United Provinces of the Netherlands* (Dublin, 1780). Quite possibly Washington also thought that light from the Dutch confederacy was of consequence to ours. If he expected light from this work, however, he was probably disappointed, for it is a year-by-year chronicle, based on about fifty French and Latin chronicles, of war, diplomacy, and exploration in the Netherlands and the East Indies from 1598 to 1609. Although it is adequate as a chronicle, it has only incidental material on Dutch political forms and only by laborious inference could one obtain from it a picture of the operation of Dutch institutions. Even the scholarly Madison would, I am certain, have found little light in Lothian. John Williams, *On the Rise, Progress and Present State of the Northern Governments: Viz: The United Provinces, Denmark, Sweden, Russia, and Poland; or Observations . . .* , etc. (London, 1777, 2 vols.) another item Washington ordered, has 150 pages on Dutch commerce, history and government and might, thus, be expected to throw more light. Although it purports to contain a traveller's first-hand observations, it is, in the section on the Netherlands, both inaccurate and derivative, since it is mostly an inept reworking of Temple's *Observations*. Williams failed even to note that voting power in the admiralty boards differed from that in the States General; yet he asserted that he had acquired special knowledge about marine affairs in the Netherlands.

[4] *The Papers of Thomas Jefferson*, VIII, 460–64.

library, as he sold it to Congress in 1815, lists only two works in English published prior to 1787 on Dutch history and public law, and these are in fact about the only ones that were readily available.[5] Indeed, every scrap of specialized or detailed knowledge about the Netherlands used in the several conventions can be readily traced to one of the following short list of sources:

1. Sir William Temple, *Observations upon the United Provinces of the Netherlands* (London, 1672. The third edition of 1676, which has minor additions, seems to be the one customarily found in the United States. It was reprinted in 1932, from the third edition, by the Cambridge University Press with an introduction by G. N. Clark. I shall quote from this reprint.) Sir William, who was subsequently Swift's patron, served as ambassador to the United Provinces in 1668. On the occasion of the Anglo-Dutch war of 1672, he used the leisure of his political retirement to write this delightful and discursive little essay on Dutch geography, history, trade, manners, religion, and government. On this last subject he is fairly well informed and well-organized. His work displays sympathy with republican forms and, considering that his country and his subject were at war, a surprisingly friendly attitude toward the Netherlands. The *Observations* was probably readily available to the framers, since it is listed in several almost contemporary library catalogues, especially the catalogue of the Library Company of Philadelphia.[6]

2. John De Witt, *Political Maxims of the State of Holland: Comprehending a General View of the Civil Government of that Republic, and the Principles on which it is Founded: the Nature, Rise, and Progress of the Commerce of its Subjects, and of their True Interests with Respect of all their Neighbors,* translated by John Campbell with a memoir of Cornelius and John De Witt (London, 1743. There

---

[5] The works were Aitzema, *Notable Revolutions* (see Appendix) and De Witt (?) *Political Maxims* (see above: 2). As a further illustration of the difficulties over books, note that Jefferson tried to purchase a French, Italian, or English translation of Grotius, *Annales*. An English translation had been published in the previous century; but Jefferson never found a copy. See E. Millicent Sowerby, *Catalogue of the Library of Thomas Jefferson* (Washington, 1952 ff., 4 vols.), I, 125.

[6] According to an estimate made for me by Mr. Edwin Wolf, 2nd, Librarian of the Library Company of Philadelphia, on the basis of the 1789 catalogue and extrapolation of accession numbers, the *Observations* was in the Library Company in 1787. According to the *Catalogue of the Books in the Library of American Academy of Arts and Sciences* (Boston, 1802), it was in the Boston library of that organization in 1802. Since the library consisted almost entirely of the books of Governor Bowdoin, books collected prior to 1786, it was doubtless available in Boston in 1787. According to Henry Adams, *A Catalogue of the Books of John Quincy Adams* (Boston, 1938), John Adams gave a copy of it to his son in 1780, but this volume was probably not physically in the United States until after 1787.

was a second edition in 1746; but since most copies in the United States seem to have been the first edition, I have used it for citations.) This work is a translation of *Aanwysing der Heilsame Politike Gronden en Maximen Van de Repulike Van Holland* (1669), which is in turn a revision and enlargement of Pieter De La Court, *Interest Van Holland* (1662). John De Witt was Grand Pensioner of Holland, 1652–72, and the chief politician of the United Netherlands of this era. Intensely republican, he and his brother Cornelius were in 1672 lynched by a mob instigated by the party of William III. The De Witt volume is an analysis, still impressive today, of the commercial and political policy appropriate for Holland, as distinct from the United Netherlands. Its main dogmas are: (1) that Holland ought to beware of monarchy, that is, of a stadtholder of the House of Nassau, (2) that Holland ought to avoid foreign alliances except in time of war, even, apparently, too close alliances with the other provinces, and (3) that Holland ought to follow a policy of free trade, free seas, free religion, and peace. Unlike Sir William Temple, De Witt (?) did not describe the government of either Holland or the United Provinces, since he assumed that knowledge on the part of his readers. As a tract on public policy, this book is less informative than the more carefully organized and more introductory treatment in the traveller's essay. It was, however, readily available. The Library Company of Philadelphia almost certainly had a copy in 1787. The Boston library of the American Academy of Arts and Sciences had a copy in 1802 and, very probably, in 1787. Both Jefferson and John Qunicy Adams had copies, although the dates they acquired them are unknown.

3. Philip Dormer Stanhope, Fourth Earl of Chesterfield, " Some Account of the Government of the Republic of the Seven United Provinces." This is item 433 of *Letters Written by the Right Honorable Philip Dormer Stanhope, Earl of Chesterfield, to his Son*, ed. by Mrs. Eugenia Stanhope (London, 1774, and often reprinted thereafter). The most recent critical edition, from which I shall quote, is one edited by Bonamy Dobrée (London, 1932, 6 vols.), in which the " Account " appears in II, 605–12. Mr. Dobrée dates the essay from Chesterfield's second embassy to the Hague (1745), although he believes that Chesterfield added the notes in 1761. In any event, this characteristically lucid and succinct essay was intended to instruct his son and hence is a useful text for others who want instruction. Roughly two-thirds of the "Account" consists of a condemnation of the supposed requirement of unanimity of legislative decision in the States General. This essay is without question the most influential source of information the framers had, possibly

because it was the most readily available. According to Evans, *American Bibliography*, the *Letters* were printed in full in New York in 1775, in Boston in 1779, in Providence in 1779, in Philadelphia in 1786, and, in abbreviated form, in several other places.

4. Benjamin Franklin, " Speech to the Philadelphia Convention " (item 2, note 1, above). So far as I can discover, this epitome of Dutch history does not depend on any written source but is simply a distillation of what Franklin knew about the Netherlands, which, though little, was considerably more than what any one else at the convention knew. Since his speech was not printed, it probably had little influence beyond the convention; but we do have the assurance of Madison's notes that the speech was actually delivered.

5. An oral tradition, the existence of which can be clearly discerned, consisting chiefly of the belief that legislative decision in the States General was by unanimity of provinces. In the debates in the Continental Congress in the summer of 1776 on the provisions of the Articles of Confederation, Dutch institutions were several times mentioned in connection with the draft article: " In determining questions each colony shall have one vote." According to John Adams' notes, Roger Sherman of Connecticut cited the practice of " the States of Holland " in support of the draft.[7] So also did Stephen Hopkins of Rhode Island (p. 1105). According to Jefferson's notes of the same debate, James Wilson of Pennsylvania argued against the draft thus: " the greatest imperfection in the constitution of the Belgic confederacy is their voting by provinces. The interest of the whole is constantly sacrificed to that of the small states " (p. 1106).

Dr. Benjamin Rush of Philadelphia discussed the Dutch forms in more detail than anyone else, saying that the " decay of the liberties of the Dutch republic proceeded from . . . : 1. the perfect unanimity requisite on all occasions. 2. their obligation to consult their constituents. 3. their voting by provinces. This last destroyed the equality of representation: . . ." (p. 1105). According to John Adams' notes, Dr. Rush cited the Abbé Raynal as his authority, doubtless referring to his *Histoire du Stadhoudérat Depuis Son Origine Jusqu'à Présent* (Paris, 1747, although I quote from the fourth edition, The Hague, 1748). At the time Raynal wrote, the English had just succeeded in installing William IV, son-in-law of George II of England, as stadtholder, much to the discomfiture of the French, who supported the republic. Raynal, as a civil servant of the French monarchy, attacked monarchy (in its low country form) and defended

---

[7] *Journals of the Continental Congress, 1774–1789*, edited by Worthington Chauncey Ford (Washington, 1906), VI, 1081.

republican institutions (for the Dutch). While one would not thus expect severe criticism of the republic from him, he did say that " si les deux tiers pouvoient conclurre [sic] pour tout le corps, le Gouvernement en seroit plus sur at plus fort " (83). We can be certain that several members of the convention of 1787 received this tradition about the weakness of legislative decision in the Netherlands. Roger Sherman and James Wilson, both of whom discussed Dutch government in these terms in 1776 and both of whom doubtless heard Dr. Rush's speech, were present at the Constitutional Convention of 1787, where Wilson again discussed Dutch government in detail. Benjamin Franklin and Elbridge Gerry were present in Philadelphia in both 1776 and 1787. Since Franklin participated actively in the debate with Sherman, Hopkins, Wilson, and Rush, one can be certain that he carried this tradition in his person. Furthermore, Jefferson gave his notes on this debate in 1776 to Madison, and they remain in Madison's papers to this day. Hence it can be assumed that Madison read at least once the abstract of Dr. Rush's severe condemnation of Dutch voting procedure.

In addition to these five sources, perhaps fifty or so other works had been published in English or French, and might therefore have influenced the framers. The most important of these works are listed and described in the Appendix. Some of them doubtless contributed to the tradition that assigned the requirement of unanimity to Dutch legislatures; but since, so far as I can discover, none of the detailed references in the conventions derive from them, I have consigned them to a concluding note.

In addition to knowledge gained from books, the framers of course possessed the common and often inaccurate information of educated men of their time and place, i.e., such statements as: that the United Provinces were a republic, that they had successfully revolted against Spain some two hundred years previously, that they had prospered in trade and fisheries, that their present circumstances in the war with England were exceedingly perilous, and that, as Montesquieu blandly told them in a sentence (*The Spirit of the Laws,* Book IX, Chap. 3), all the provinces had an equal voice in the States General.

II

The thirty-seven discussions of the Netherlands in the several conventions may be divided into two categories, those that depend simply on the stock of common statements of the sort mentioned in the previous paragraph and those that depend on some specialized knowledge. All but one of the thirteen discussions in the second category depend on the five sources listed above; and the one that does not, Pierce Butler's already mentioned speech, depends on a traveller's observation rather than a written source. In most of the instances, the source is apparent, not merely by reason of similarity of content, but by reason of verbal parallels and direct quotations.

Turning to a demonstration of the framers' dependence on these few sources, James Wilson's speech of 16 June 1787 (item 3, note 1, above) is one of the earliest discussion of the Netherlands in the convention and, I believe, one of the most influential. It is reported in the notes of Madison, Robert Yates, Rufus King, and William Paterson. All four of these auditors agree that he emphasized that the affiirmative vote of all provinces was necessary to legislative decision. Paterson's notes on the Netherlands passage of the speech consists of only nine words and Madison's notes are somewhat confused, but Yates and King make it clear that Wilson told or read the following story from Lord Chesterfield:

> . . . When I was soliciting the accession of the Republic to the treaty of Vienna, in 1731, which the Pensionary, Count Sinzendorf, and I, had made secretly at the Hague, all the towns in Holland came readily into it, except the little town of Briel [i.e., Brill]; whose deputies frankly declared, that they would not give their consent, till *Major-Such-a-one*, a very honest gentleman of their town, was promoted to the rank of Lieutenant-Colonel, and that, as soon as that was done, they would agree, for they approved of the treaty. This was accordingly done in two or three days, and then they agreed. This is a strong instance of the absurdity of the unanimity required, and of the use that is often made of it (II, 605–07, ed. Dobrée).

This story was used again by John Lansing in the New York convention (item 7, note 1); but he gave it both a new source and a new application. Lansing says " an important measure was delayed by the dissent of a single town until one of its citizens was accommodated with a commission." Obviously this is Chesterfield's story, but Lansing attributed it to Sir William Temple, who nowhere mentioned such an event. (Indeed, Temple, in reciting the details of his embassy, remarked on pp. 71–72 that such bribes were unnecessary.) While Wilson used the story to condemn the Articles insofar as they required unanimity in decision, Lansing, an Anti-federalist, used it to show that the Articles were superior to the constitutions of other confederacies, such as the Dutch, whose experience was therefore, so he argued, irrelevant to a judgement of the Articles.

In a speech on June 28, Madison commented (item 4, note 1): " Holland contains about ½ the people, supplies about ½ the money, and by her influence, silently and indirectly governs the whole Republic." The simple statistical fact, which is several times repeated in the conventions, could well have come from Temple, De Witt, Chesterfield, or indeed from several of the writers cited in the Appendix, all of whom mention that Holland paid 58 guilders out of every 100 assessed by the States-General. The inference about Holland's influence doubtless came, however, from Chesterfield. Temple did not notice and of course De Witt would not admit the overweening influence of the province of Holland; but Chesterfield observed: " It is very natural to suppose, and it is very true in fact, that Holland . . . should have great weight and influence in the other six provinces " (II, 607). In connection with his story of the major from Brill, Chesterfield explicitly asserts that Holland had a controlling influence in the other provinces.

Gouverneur Morris, echoed by Butler (Farrand, II, 31, 202) asserted that in Holland " their Senates have engrossed all power." This too is clearly reminiscent of Chesterfield, who wrote in the second paragraph of his essay. " It is very true, that the sovereign power is lodged in the States-General; but who are those States General? Not those who are commonly called so; but the Senate, Council, or *Vrootschaps* [i.e., vroedschaps] call it what you will, of every town, in every province that sends deputies to the Provincial States of the said Province." This comment about the town councils occurs in connection with assertions that the people have lost all right to vote and that the councils perpetuate themselves by co-option. Hence the phrase, " engrossed all power," is a fair summary of Chesterfield's observation.

Chesterfield is also the source, I believe, for a paragraph in Oliver Ellsworth's speech to the Connecticut convention (item 6, note 1). Ellsworth emphasized the rôle of the stadtholder who was, he said, necessary " in order to set their unwieldy machine of government in motion." " Without such an influence," he concluded, " their machine of government would no more move, than a ship without wind, or a clock without weights." Considering that Chesterfield assigned the same rôle to the stadtholder—even to the point of using the metaphor of clock machinery: ". . . a Stadtholder was originally the chief spring upon which their government turned " (II, 609)—considering that he alone of the five sources discussed the stadtholder's duties in detail, considering that he ascribed to William the Silent a Machiavellian intent to render a stadtholder necessary to break deadlocks that resulted from the unanimity requirement, and considering finally that both he and Ellsworth emphasized Holland's hostility to the office (though, of course, De Witt does that also), it seems likely that Ellsworth relied on Chesterfield, at least indirectly. It should be noted, however, that the Abbé Raynal hints at something like this when he says (84–85): " On crut devoir terminer tous ces arrangemens [i.e., of the Union of Utrecht] per intéresser personellement le Prince d'Orange à la conservation de l'edifice, qu'il avoit lui-même construit; il fut élu Stadhouder." But since this remark is brief and buried, it seems unlikely that it could have inspired Ellsworth, even if he had had access to the *Histoire du Stathoudérat.*

De Witt's (?) *Political Maxims* is the source of two major analyses of Dutch government in the ratifying conventions, one by Rufus King (item 5, note 1) and one by James Madison (item 8, note 1). Citing John De Witt, "a celebrated political writer, formerly pensioner of Holland," King noted (1) that provinces of the United Netherlands were free to comply or not as they chose with requisitions of money by the States-General, (2) that Holland paid 58 parts in 100 of the war with Spain, (3) that two provinces paid not a single guilder, (4) that Holland collected requisitions from other provinces by force, (5) that the Prince of Orange doubled the requisitions, collecting only from Holland, so that Holland paid all the expenses of the war. Items two through five in this list appear in exactly this order on page 257 of *Political Maxims.* It seems likely that King had the volume before him as he prepared his speech. Although Madison's speech is not quoted verbatim, but merely summarized, it is apparent that he quoted from the same passage. The reporter cited items two through four on the foregoing list in that order, even naming, as in *Political Maxims,* the recalcitrant provinces, Gelderland and Overissel.

The same material, much abbreviated serves Chancellor Livingston in the New York convention (Eliott, II, 214) for a one sentence condemnation of the Dutch confederation which, he said, "permitted the burden of the war to be borne, in great measure, by the province of Holland; which was, at one time, compelled to attempt to force a neighboring province, by arms, to compliance with their federal engagements." The *Political Maxims,* or a verbal tradition based on it, must have been the source for Livingston's comment because any of the more extensive sources of the story (e.g., Lothian, pp. 80–82) would have made it clear that not Holland, but the States General, sent a force to compel payment.

Later on in the Virginia convention, William Grayson undertook to explain party politics in the Netherlands (Eliott, III, 290) or rather to state the names and chief principles of the two opposing parties. Since these names and principles are similarly set forth (on page xxxiv) in the "Memoir of Cornelius and John De Witt" which serves as an introduction to *Political Maxims,* it can, I think, be safely assumed that this volume is also the source of Grayson's information.

Sir William Temple, although mistakenly cited by Lansing in the New York convention, is clearly enough the source of two discussions of the Netherlands in the Virginia convention. Governor

Randolph (item 9, note 1) observed: " Consult all writers—from Sir William Temple to those of modern times—they will inform you that the government of Holland is an aristocracy." And so Temple does (p. 58), though he used the stronger and perhaps more accurate word, " oligarchy." One of the " writers of modern times "—possibly the only one—is certainly Chesterfield, who makes the same observation in a footnote to the first sentence of his essay. When Edmund Pendleton and Madison echoed Randolph (Eliott, III, 310, 617), they emphasized that the people had no right to vote. Since Chesterfield in the second sentence of his essay observed that the unfranchised people " have nothing to do but to pay and grumble," it seems likely also that Chesterfield is also the source that impressed these latter two.

Randolph, as a proponent of the Constitution, wished to condemn the government of the Netherlands, which he identified with the government of the Articles. George Mason, on the other hand, as an adherent of the Articles, used Temple's *Observations* to demonstrate the felicity of the Dutch people (item 10, note 1). The reporter simply summarizes and does not cite the source of Mason's quotations: but it seems to me fairly certain that Mason quoted selected paragraphs from the fourth chapter of Temple's work.

So it appears that, for all the members besides Franklin (and perhaps Butler) every bit of detailed information about the Dutch in the several conventions probably came from Chesterfield, De Witt, or Temple, or perhaps indirectly from Raynal). It is possible that some of the brief references could have derived from some of the works listed in the Appendix. But since all the extensive references derive clearly from these three books, which were also the three most readily available, it is reasonable to suppose that these and the oral tradition were the framers' only sources.

III

The foregoing analysis has demonstrated the paucity of information about the Netherlands available to the framers of the Constitution. Lacking, except in the case of the aged Franklin, a deep personal experience with European politics, they were forced to rely on the written word. Lacking a knowledge of Dutch, they were forced to rely on books in English or French. This meant a library of at most fifty or so volumes, of which only three or four were easily available and regarded as authoritative. Of these, one was the observation of an ambassador who had spent only a short time in the Netherlands; the second was a tract that grew out of party politics in Holland (the implications and innuendoes of which must certainly

have been obscure to the framers); the third was an inaccurate
pamphlet written as a political duty by a French civil servant who
had never been in the Netherlands; and the fourth was a seven-page
essay which, although written for a schoolboy aged twelve, is the
most judicious and informative of the four. The first pair of these
works was based on experience as of 1668; the second pair as of the
mid–1740's. A library of three and a fraction volumes, the two most
recent of which were forty years out of date, the others 120 years,
could hardly be expected to provide sympathetic or detailed understanding of Dutch government from 1579 to 1787.

In short, the framers had little to learn from. Further, they
learned little from what they had. Considering how remote Dutch
affairs were from their own, a complete mastery of those works is
about all that one might reasonably expect from an American politician of the 1780's. But it is abundantly clear that the framers had
not mastered even these sparse materials.

Even the best of them were quite vague about Dutch affairs.
Pierce Butler's misinterpretation of his observation has already been
mentioned. Butler, though a man of judgment, had no scholarly pretensions. Madison, however, did pretend to a knowledge of Dutch
history. Yet when he took notes on Franklin's speech, he both
improved and confused the detail. Franklin's written speech reads
in part:

On his [i.e., William the Silent's] Death, They [i.e., the provinces] resum'd
and divided those Powers [i.e., of the Stadtholder] among the States and
Cities . . . . In the last century the then Prince of Orange found means to
inflame the Populace against their Magistrates, excite a general Insurrection in which an excellent Minister, *Dewit*, was murdered, all the old
Magistrates displac'd, and the Stadtholder re-invested with all the former
Powers.

Madison's notes on the last sentence are:

Still, however there was a party for the Prince of Orange, which descended
to his son who excited insurrection, spilt a great deal of blood, murdered
the de Witts, and got the powers revested in the Stadtholder.

Of course, Franklin may not have delivered his speech as written;
but since he felt his infirmities of age sufficiently to write out all his
speeches, it is very likely that he read this speech word for word.
Assuming that his spoken words tally with his written ones, Madison's deviations are of considerable interest. Franklin referred presumably to the murder of only John De Witt. Madison uses the
plural, thereby including Cornelius—an action that indicates some
special knowledge. On the other hand, Madison mixed up the

genealogy of the House of Nassau. Franklin referred to the "then Prince of Orange," thereby carefully dodging the genealogical problem. It was a wise choice of words, for the descent of the House of Nassau was somewhat involved: from William the Silent (d. 1584) to his son Maurice (d. 1625), from Maurice to his brother Frederick Henry (d. 1647), from Frederick Henry to his son William II (d. 1650), and from William II to his posthumous son William III, who was chosen stadtholder in 1672 and King of England in 1689. Madison, apparently unaware of these genealogical facts, transformed William III, the "instigator" of the murder of the De Witts, into a son of William the Silent, whereas he was in fact the great-grandson. A slip of the pen, perhaps, but not a slip likely to be made by one conversant with the course of Dutch history.

Franklin clearly knew enough about Dutch chronology and the descent of the House of Nassau to avoid Madison's error. But Franklin too seems hazy on detail. For example, he asserted that on the death of William the Silent the stadtholder's powers were divided among the "states and cities" and from that event he jumped to the accession of William III. It is certainly true that Prince Maurice did not immediately attain his father's position; but Franklin overlooked entirely the rôles of both Maurice and Frederick Henry, both of whom were, like their father, stadtholders of five provinces. Franklin intended, of course, only a brief history, but one has the impression that he ignored William's sons because he was unaware of them.

One would not expect American politicians of the 1780's to know much Dutch history of the previous two centuries, any more than one would expect American politicians today to know much about the history of, for example, Austria from the 1750's to the 1830's. But while this lack of knowledge of Dutch politics is quite pardonable and not at all surprising, it does substantially preclude the use of Dutch experience in the several conventions. Further, the lack of knowledge suggests the possibility that the framers' quotations from authorities may be misleading. Such is indeed the fact, for not one of the substantial quotations was judiciously abstracted from its source.

Madison and Rufus King in their respective conventions quoted extensively from De Witt. Both of them used the quotations to prove that the Dutch confederacy, like the government under their own Articles, was ineffective and unfair. It could not compel the payment of taxes, so they said. Yet the very passage they quoted relates that Holland [sic] sent troops to collect (presumably with success) from the recalcitrant state of Groningen. The Union of Utrecht was, they also said, unfair in that Holland had to pay more than its share of the cost of the Spanish war. (Parenthetically it should be noted that Madison and King were doubtless impressed by the parallel with their own states: Virginia and Massachusetts paid requisitions when the smaller states did not and thus bore more than their share of the cost of the central government.) They blamed this unfair taxation of Holland, just as they blamed their own unfair taxation, on the requirement of unanimity in legislative decision. Quite probably this unanimity (or rather extraordinary majority) was one of the chief factors in the excessive taxation of Massachusetts and Virginia; but, according to the very sources they quoted from, it was not so important a factor in the Netherlands. The author of *Political Maxims,* much as he complained of the injustice, did not blame the requirement of unanimity. Instead he blamed Prince Frederick Henry who, he asserted, packed the States General with his own men. And further: he complained not that Holland was balked in action by its failure to persuade the States to unanimity, but rather that Holland was out-voted by the Prince's men, " even in such matters wherein plurality of votes should have no place " (p. 259). Clearly, this Hollander did not think that the constitutional provision was a problem. He was angered, not by its existence, but by its desuetude.

James Wilson and John Lansing both refer to Chesterfield's story of the major from Brill; but both also misapply it. Although the one wished to identify, the other to distinguish, the Continental Congress and the States-General, still both accepted Chesterfield's story as a sample of the normal course of public business in the Dutch Republic. Wilson concluded therefrom that, as a general rule, the requirement of unanimity leads to corruption. Lansing, who was certain no such corruption occurred in Congress, concluded that the operation of the two legislatures was quite different. The conclusions of both men were invalid, however, because the promotion of the major was not a normal procedure, as Chesterfield himself specifically pointed out:

The unanimity, which is constitutionally requisite for every act of each town, and each province, separately, and then for every act of the seven collectively, is something so absurd, and so impracticable in government, that one is astonished that even the form of it has been tolerated so long; for the substance is not strictly observed. And five provinces will often conclude, though two dissent, provided that Holland and Zealand are two of the five; as fourteen or fifteen of the principal towns of Holland will conclude an affair, notwithstanding the opposition of four or five of the lesser (II, 607).

Furthermore, Chesterfield called the story of the major from Brill " a strong instance," that is, an exceptional instance, and then added:

However, should one, or even two of the lesser provinces, who contribute little, and often pay less, to the public charge, obstinately and frivolously, or perhaps corruptly, persist in opposing a measure which Holland and the other more considerable provinces thought necessary, and had agreed to, they would send a deputation to those opposing provinces, to reason with, and persuade them to concur; but, if this would not do, they would as they have done in many instances, conclude without them. The same thing is done in the provincial States of the respective provinces; where if one or two of the least considerable towns pertinaciously oppose a necessary measure, they conclude without them. But as this is absolutely unconstitutional, it is avoided as much as possible, and a complete unanimity procured, if it can be, by such little concessions as that which I have mentioned to the Briel Major (II, 607, note).

There can be no doubt that in the matter of unanimity the framers misapplied their sources. They also ignored the direct statement of Sir William Temple on this point, when he described the duties of the President of the States-General:

[He] Makes the Greffier [i.e., the Secretary] read all Papers; Puts the Question; Calls the Voices of the Provinces; and forms the Conclusion. Or, if he refuses *to conclude according to the plurality*, he is obliged to resign his Place to the President of the ensuing week, who concludes for him.

This is the course in all Affairs before them, except in cases of Peace and War, of Foreign Alliances, of Raising, or Coining, of Monies, or the Priviledges of each Province or Member of the Union. In all which, All the Provinces must concur, Plurality being not at all weighed or observed .... And in other important matters, *though decided by Plurality*, they frequently consult with the Council of State (p. 70, emphasis added.)

On the whole, Sir William thought the system worked well. Speaking of the fact that, by persuasion, a committee of the States-General had obtained the agreement of all provinces to the treaty he had negotiated, he said:

Nor have they ever used, at any other time, any greater means to agree and unite the several Members of their Union, in the Resolutions necessary, upon the most pressing occasions, than for the agreeing-Provinces to name some of their ablest persons to go and confer with the dissenting, and represent those Reasons and Interests by which they have been induced to their Opinions (72).

Clearly, the framers' major sources indicate that the Dutch were not nearly so disturbed by the requirement of unanimity as the framers supposed them to be. And two of them clearly state also that the rule was not as general as the framers supposed, for as Temple pointed out, the circumstances in which unanimity was required were few. Temple was quoting fairly accurately the provision of voting in the ninth article of the Union of Utrecht of 1579 and is, therefore, accurate in his statement of constitutional provisions. He too failed to understand, however, that the requirement of unanimity in the

States General and the Provincial States was much mitigated by other institutions. In the States General, it is true, matters of war, peace, treaties, and taxes could not be concluded without unanimity and even then could not be concluded finally until approved by the provincial states in which each town had a veto power. And it is also true that in all other matters in the States General, the province of Holland, which had over half the people and wealth and which contributed over half of the taxes, army and navy, still had only one-seventh of the vote. But there were other national institutions besides the States General. The Council of State, which in the absence of a stadtholder was the executive head with authority to direct the army, negotiate treaties, prepare the agenda of the States, appoint judges, and govern the dependencies in Flanders and overseas, concluded by a plurality of members. Furthermore, one-fourth instead of one-seventh of its members were chosen by Holland. Even more significant a deviation from unanimity and provincial equality is found in the five boards of admiralty. These boards, located in Rotterdam, Amsterdam, and Hoorn in Holland, in Middleburg in Zealand, and in Harlingen in Friesland, were without doubt the most important administrative bodies in the Netherlands. Since the Navy was the most important part of the national defense system, since more of the funds of the generality went for it than for any other purpose, and since colonial expansion and foreign trade and hence the prosperity of the Netherlands depended on the protection of the navy, the admiralty was in the seventeenth and eighteenth centuries the very heart of the government. And here the notion of unanimity and provincial equality was ignored. Holland dominated three of the boards, especially the one in Amsterdam, which received one-third of the national naval funds while the others received only one-sixth each; and in all five taken together, Holland had forty-two per cent of the voting power.[8] In the East India company, a state within a

---

[8] The figure of forty-two per cent is calculated as follows: Assuming on the basis of the division of funds from the generality that the board at Amsterdam controlled one-third of naval affairs and that the other boards controlled one-sixth each, and multiplying the fraction of naval authority on each board by the fraction of voting power each province had on the board, then Holland had forty-two per cent of the voting power; Zealand, seventeen per cent; Friesland, fourteen per cent; Utrecht, nine per cent; Gelderland, seven per cent; Overissel six per cent; and Groningen, five per cent—a distribution roughly in proportion to the charges paid to the generality. See: "Instructie, vande Heeren Generale Staten der Vereenighde Nederlanden, voor de Collegien vander Admiraliteyte inde respective Provincien ende Quartieren Opgerecht . . . 13 August 1 1597 " in *Groot Placaet Boeck, Vervattende de Placaten Ordonnantien Ende Dicten Vande Doorluchtige Hoogh-Mog: Heeren Staten Generael Der Vereenighde Nederlanden* . . . etc. (The Hague, 1664), vol. II, folios 1529-31. See also: F. M. Janicon, *État Present Des Provinces-Unies et des Pais Qui en Dépendent* (Hague, 1729), 195ff.

state and in effect the Dutch colonial office, Holland was even more
dominant, for Hollanders held eighty per cent of the capital and had
seventy-six per cent of the voting power in the board of directors.
Indeed, the merchants of Amsterdam, who probably held half the
capital, held nearly half the directorships and were clearly in a position to dominate the affairs of the society. In short, in commercial
and naval affairs, in a high degree, and in administrative affairs to a
somewhat lesser degree, the principle of provincial equality was
ignored and wealth and population served as the basis of representation. In an age when legislation was popularly regarded as less important than it is now, and when administration was the essential
political activity, the disregard of the principle of unanimity in administration explains why Dutchmen at least were less upset than
foreigners by the requirement of provincial unanimity in some of the
business of the States General. Certainly, taking the Dutch government as a whole, the unanimity rule was not as serious a disability as
foreign publicists suggested. It was indeed a far less stringent re-
striction on governmental activity than the provisions of the Articles
of Confederation.

Leaving aside the failure of the framers to quote justly from their
sources—a failure doubtless occasioned by their pardonable ignorance
of Dutch affairs—the framers displayed radical misunderstanding of
the Netherlands generally. They did not comprehend the depth of
civic loyalty, which was far deeper than their own state patriotism
and which was the social justification of the constitutional requirement of unanimity in some decisions. They did not comprehend the
rôle of the House of Nassau, which often had had more of the loyalty
of the common people than the patriciate of the town councils. They
did not comprehend that unanimity on some legislative decisions by
seven provinces that would fit into the state of New York four times
was quite different from the unanimity of thirteen large states
sprawled out over a thousand miles of coast. They did not even
comprehend current events in the Netherlands. Contemporary history was neither much studied nor well reported in 1787 and hence
they knew almost nothing about eighteenth century Dutch politics.
If they knew about the strengthening of the stadtholderate in 1747–
48, an event that minimized the problem of unanimity, or about the
revolutionary movement of the 1780's, they gave no hint of their
knowledge in their speeches.

Instead they read Dutch problems (what they knew of them)
in the light of their own. Since they were worried about the provision of the Articles that required unanimity for amendment and an
extraordinary majority for ordinary business, they assumed that
Dutch politicians were worried about similar problems. But the

Dutch had more pressing things to worry about than this (perhaps unwise) constitutional provision which they had long since learned how to manipulate and evade.

IV

The analysis has so far demonstrated that the framers of the Constitution had only inaccurate and inadequate information about the Netherlands. It follows that the actual Dutch political forms had little influence on our own.

But, if that is so, what then is the significance of the thirty-seven references to Dutch institutions that crop up throughout the several convention reports? With the exception of Franklin's epitome of Dutch history and Mason's quotations from (presumably) Temple's *Observations,* all the extended and detailed references to the Dutch constitution, as well as many of the briefer ones, deal with its provision for unanimity in some legislative decisions. As I have already pointed out, the provision they deal with is an idealized one, torn out of its political context and only by illegitimate descent related to the one the Dutch people knew. But that idealized provision is still of no little importance. It provided an Awful Example.

Supporters of the Constitution and of a strong central government used the mythical provision of the Dutch constitution as an indication of the future of our confederacy. The Articles of Confederation contained superficially similar provisions: They required unanimous consent of the states for amendment (Art. XIII); they required nine-thirteenths of the states to declare war, ratify treaties, coin money, tax, borrow, construct navies, recruit soldiers and sailors, and appoint army and navy commanders (Art. IX); they required an absolute majority of seven-thirteenths, regardless of how many states were represented in Congress at the time of voting, on all other matters (Art. IX). The supporters of a strong central government in effect asserted that the miseries of the Dutch were the result of a corresponding provision. By analogy between Dutch institutions and ours, they prophecied similar miseries for the American confederacy, with its similar provisions, if a strong central government were not adopted. "Happy that country," said John Marshall (Eliott, III, 225), "which can avail itself of the misfortunes of others." By observing what Madison called "the characteristic imbecility of federal governments" as displayed in this mythical constitution of a mythical Netherlands, we might, he urged, avoid the unhappy state of that besieged republic.

Regardless of its validity— which was dubious—this was an influential argument. At least it was sufficiently impressive to inspire opponents of the Constitution to answer it. In the New York convention, John Lansing (item 7, note 1) sought to distinguish the United Provinces from the United States:

The United Dutch provinces have been instanced as possessing a government parallel to the existing confederation; but I believe it will be discovered that they were never so organized, as a general government, on principles so well calculated to promote the attainment of national objects as that of the United States.

In the Virginia convention, where the Dutch example was referred to more frequently and where the opponents of the Constitution were more articulate than elsewhere, there are several examples of a similar attempt to refute the argument drawn from the mythical Dutch constitution. Patrick Henry, the leading opponent of ratification in Virginia, remarked sarcastically of Madison's use of the Dutch example (Eliott, III, 160–61):

Notwithstanding two of their provinces have paid nothing, yet I hope the example of Holland will tell us that we can live happily without changing our present despised government.

And James Monroe, the most learned of the Virginia opponents of the Constitution, argued at length that, because of the many differences of situation between the United States on the one hand and the Swiss and Dutch on the other, the experience of the latter two was irrelevant to the former (Eliott, III, 211).

It does not seem likely that the Awful Example persuaded many people to support ratification. It was only one of the many subsidiary propositions in the argument for a strong central government. Yet, as in all such great controversies, each subsidiary proposition, however subordinate, contributed to the whole. The very fact that the opponents of the Constitution so vigorously disputed the relevance of the Dutch example indicates that it was a telling argument.

This Awful Example was not entirely of the framers' own construction, although it doubtless had more meaning to them than to those who had constructed it originally. As has already been indicated, the framers obtained it from several Anglo-French histories and commentaries on public law. And further, it was a part of a still wider European juristic tradition, a tradition that was based almost entirely on a two-century-old misreading of the ninth article of the Union of Utrecht. This article provided that no treaty of peace, no declaration of war and no tax might be enacted or levied without the unanimous consent of the provinces, that all other matters would be decided by a plurality of votes of the provinces, and that, in the event of a disagreement on subjects requiring unanimity, the issue should be put to the stadtholders, who might in turn select an arbitrator. Hasty readers, mistakenly believing that war, treaties, and taxes are the only important subjects of legislation, had long before 1787 construed this to mean "unanimity of the provinces on all subjects." Those who so construed knew little more than this one detail about the Dutch republic. They did not know the structure of the council of state nor the boards of admiralty nor the customs by which Dutch politicians operated under the ninth article. Since most of the European knowledge of Dutch procedures came from ambassadors and since ambassadors are chiefly concerned with two subjects requiring unanimity (i.e., war and treaties), it is not surprising that this one detail was magnified out of all proportion in non-Dutch commentaries on Dutch government. Sir Ralph Winwood, one of the earliest English ambassadors to the Netherlands, complained bitterly that the reluctance of Zealand, occasioned largely by irrelevant commercial rivalry, delayed for long a treaty between the States and James I.[9] Chesterfield, Janicon, and other ambassadors all assert that the unanimity principle delayed business; but whether the delay inconvenienced mostly the ambassadors or mostly the Dutch is a question far too complex to enter into here. Suffice it to say that ambassadors emphasized the unanimity requirements and repeatedly asserted that it caused bad government. The non-Dutch writers on public law and history picked up this point and emphasized it further—often, as with Montesquieu and Raynal, it was the only specific thing they could say about the Dutch government. Other authors who depended primarily upon ambassadors' writings (e.g., Lothian, Williams) emphasized it at the expense of all other features of Dutch government. Not unreasonably, therefore, this half-truth became the one widely known detail about the Dutch constitution, a half-truth remembered because it was a curiosity, just as today the only widely known detail about the Australian government is the equally misinterpreted system of compulsory voting.

This half-truth reached the framers from numerous sources; but it took on special significance when it reached them through the pages of Lord Chesterfield. His essay is the only one of their major sources that deals extensively with the requirement of unanimity. It contains a detailed report of a conversation on the subject between Chesterfield and the Pensionary Slingelandt, in which the Pensionary is reported as agreeing with Chesterfield that in operation the requirement of unanimity almost necessitated a quasi-monarchical

[9] Edmund Sawyer, *Memorials of Affairs Of State In The Reigns Of Queen Elizabeth and King James I, Collected Chiefly From The Original Papers Of The Right Honorable Sir Ralph Winwood, KT., Sometime One Of The Principal Secretaries Of State.* . . . (London, 1725, 3 vols.), III, 42, 79, 100.

stadtholder. (Compare the quotation from the Abbé Raynal above). It does not take a great stretch of the imagination to visualize the horror that this conclusion must have aroused in all good republican Whigs in the United States. Certainly this conclusion aroused deeper emotions in Americans, who lived with similar provisions in the Articles, than in Europeans like Chesterfield, who were only mildly vexed by Dutch delay. In any event, it seems likely that Chesterfield's essay, which had certainly been read by Wilson, Madison, Gouverneur Morris, and Ellsworth and which, because of its brevity and availability, had probably been read by many others, confirmed and strengthened their convictions on the folly of this requirement. It is thus possible that Chesterfield's essay, written for the wholly private instruction of his son, quite accidentally offered an Awful Example to American constitution-makers. To one who, like the present writer, has always respected the warm humanity and urbane maturity of that great Whig lord, it is pleasing to observe that he had, in this quite unconscious and unanticipated way, some slight influence for the good on our institutions.

V

To say that the framers of the Constitution failed to learn from Dutch history and public law is not to say that they failed to learn from history and politics at all. They were representative men of the eighteenth century and as such they thoroughly believed in the possibility of rational comprehension of human experience and in the possibility of reconstructing institutions on the basis of their comprehension. The experience they comprehended, however, was in this instance only slightly Dutch and mostly American. The discussions of Dutch institutions are to be regarded as an elaborate figure of speech, an extended but not wholly conscious metaphor. The literal reference of the words to the Dutch constitution and the States General are to be understood, I believe, as an intended reference to the Articles of Confederation and the Continental Congress. So understood, the ignorance of the framers about Dutch affairs is irrelevant to the validity of their arguments. And so understood, their disputes have some relevance to experience and are not wholly and irrationally concerned with a myth.

This figure of speech is not to be regarded, however, as merely an ornament of belles-lettres. The framers seized upon this current European half-truth with great eagerness and referred frequently to it in their discussions. What was merely a minor curiosity to Montesquieu and merely a vexation to Chesterfield had deep significance for Madison, Wilson, Ellsworth, and others. This difference in the emotional reaction to the half-truth on the two sides of the Atlantic is clear evidence that the Awful Example was indeed a metaphor for American experience. The metaphor helped to bolster the framers' confidence in the universal validity of their assertions about the Articles of Confederation. In the eighteenth century, when political propositions attained intellectual respectability only under the guise of universals, the service of the metaphor was of some emotional value. Although it really generalized chiefly about experience in the United States and only secondarily and vaguely about experience in the Netherlands, still it assured (doubtless irrationally) the proponents of a strong central government that the requirement of extraordinary legislative majorities hampered the operation of government, not only in the United States, but everywhere.

And so to this conclusion: The framers of the Constitution were influenced neither by the constitution that existed in the Netherlands nor by the history that occurred there. Rather they were influenced—and that only slightly—by the inaccurate descriptions of the Dutch constitution and by the poorly written histories of Dutch events. And on still closer examination it turns out that the framers used this inaccurate description and poorly written history not as foreign experience from which they could learn, but as a metaphor for domestic experience from which they had *already* learned very much. Thus, Dutch federalism is twice and distantly removed from American.

And this conclusion leads to two observations, one of interest to students of the American Constitution, the other of interest to students of the history of ideas. First, in this instance, it has been found naïve to accept at face value the framers' discussions of Dutch public law. If, in this connection, the Constitution owes something to European sources, the debt is not to the Dutch but to the Anglo-French commentaries. And at most the debt is literary, not a debt for an actual transfer of ideas. In this instance, then, the American Constitution has been found to be more indigenous than is usually asserted. (I suspect, without on this occasion undertaking to prove, that the extended references in the conventions to ancient confederations and even to the then contemporary English institutions may be of equally figurative character; [10] if they are, then the Constitution is still more indigenous than the traditional interpretation admits.)

Second, this conclusion suggests that the transmission of consti-

---

[10] If analyzed by the method here used, I suspect that, for example, the much talked of influence of Polybius on the American Constitution would prove to be equally metaphorical. See, however, Gilbert Chinard, " Polybius and the American Constitution " this *Journal*, I, 38–58, and Kurt von Fritz, *The Theory of the Mixed Constitution in Antiquity* (New York, 1954), v ff.

tutional ideas is less direct than might be supposed, were the framers' comments to be taken literally. It has been demonstrated (a) that the existent Dutch federalism had no influence on ours and (b) that the non-Dutch commentaries served merely to provide a metaphor; but the demonstration has been possible only because, by a happy accident, we can identify all the framers' sources and can trace in precise detail the actual transmission and use of information. For more difficult studies of the transmission of ideas, for studies, that is, where the material is less abundant, the present conclusion suggests a cautionary observation. It suggests that students of the history of ideas ought to be extremely wary—in the absence of clear and irrefutable evidence—about attributing to the institutions and commentaries of one time and place an influence on the institutions of another. Even when those who are purportedly influenced assert, as in this instance they asserted most sharply, that they have been influenced by the example of others, it does not follow that they have actually been so influenced. It may well be that they have been influenced only by poor descriptions of the examples of others. Or it may even be that—as in this instance—the supposed influence is conjured up by those who purport to feel it for wholly rhetorical purposes of their own.

Lawrence College, Appleton, Wisconsin.

APPENDIX

In addition to the sources discussed in the text, the following works, listed roughtly in the order in which it is most likely that they might have influenced the framers, were also available in English or French. I have omitted from the list translations of Dutch public documents, of which, for example, eighteen are listed in A. F. Pollard and G. R. Redgrave, *A Short Title Catalogue* . . . 1475–1640 (London, 1948) and twenty-three are listed in Donald Wing, *Short Title Catalogue* . . . 1641–1700 (New York, 1945, 3 vols.). I have also omitted guide books, of which there are a considerable number, often reprinted. These occasionally contain constitutional detail, especially the half-truthful misreading of article nine of the Union of Utrecht; but, since it is unlikely that the framers would have regarded these as authoritative sources, I have not attempted to list them in detail. For similar reasons I have omitted yearbooks, which appear under such titles as *The Present State Of Holland,* and which contain little constitutional detail. Finally, I have also omitted ephemeral pamphlets on public affairs, except for those printed in the 1780's. On the other hand, I have tried to include all major works known to have been in the United States in 1787 or within a generation thereafter.

1. Abbé [Guillaume Thomas François] Raynal, *Histoire Du Stathoudérat* (see above). The only evidence I can find that this volume was in the United States is

the fact that Benjamin Rush cited it in 1776. Of course he may have seen it when he studied medicine at Edinburgh.

2. John Williams, *On The Rise, Progress And Present State Of The Northern Governments* (see note 3). If Washington actually obtained this work from Boinod and Gaillard, then it was probably in his library. At least we know that it was for sale in the United States in 1784. It almost certainly was in the Library Company of Philadelphia in 1787.

3. William Lothian, *History Of The United Provinces Of The Netherlands* (see note 3). This too was for sale in Philadelphia in 1784 and probably was in the Library Company of Philadelphia in 1787. It is also listed in the 1809 catalogue of the Library Company of Baltimore.

4. *A History Of Holland From Its First Foundation To The Death Of King William* (London, 1705, 2 vols.). I have not been able to examine this work. In 1787 it probably was in the Library Company of Philadelphia.

5. Walter Harris, *A New History Of The Life And Reign Of William Henry, Prince Of Orange And Nassau; King Of England, Etc. . . . To Which Is Prefixed A Dissertation . . . On The Government Of Holland* (Dublin, 1747, 4 vols.). The " dissertation " (in vol. 1) is a brief reworking of the chapter on government in Temple's *Observations*. It lacks Temple's qualifying detail; but it does contain these sentences (page X):

All Questions are here [i.e., in the States General] determined by the Majority of Voices, except in cases of Peace or War, raising or coining Money, Foreign Alliances, and particularly the Sovereignty and Privileges of each Province or Member of the Union; in all which, the Provinces must give universal Concurrance. Nor can they chuse Ambassadors, or answer Foreign Ministers . . . without consulting the *States* of each Province by their Deputies; . . . and this is the Reason, that the Consultations and Resolutions of the *States-General* are so exceeding slow.

Following Sir William Temple, Harris also noted that voting in the Council of State was by plurality of voices, not provinces, and that on both the Council of State and the Admirality Boards representation of provinces was unequal. The four volumes of this work were probably in the Library Company of Philadelphia in 1787.

6. Onslow Burrish, *Batavia Illustrata: or a View of the Policy and Commerce of the United Provinces: Particularly of Holland with an Enquiry into the Alliances of the States General with the Emperor, France, Spain and Great Britain* (London, 1728, 2 vols.). Volume I, on the government, contains a description of each province, the admiralty, and the stadtholderate. Burrish emphasizes that each province is sovereign; but his detail on legislative procedure is meager. In many places, it seems to be a translation of Charles Basnage, *Annales Des Provinces Unies Depuis Les Négotiations Pour La Paix de Munster Avec La Description Historique De Leur Gouvernement* (La Haye, 1719). This work has good detail on legislative procedure in the provincial estates and on the structure of the Admiralty; it is unfortunate that Burrish did not translate more carefully. The Burrish work probably was in the Library Company of Philadelphia in 1788; but I can find no evidence that the Basnage volumes were in this country in 1787.

7. Baron [Louis Aubery] du Maurier, *The Lives Of All The Princes Of Orange From William The Great, Founder Of The Commonwealth Of The United Provinces*, translated by Thomas Brown (London, 1693). This work, translated from the French original of 1682, is by the son of the French ambassador to The Hague in 1613 and after. Baron Louis knew Princes Maurice, Frederick Henry, William II and William III and hence his work has a certain personal authority; but by reason of its form it contains no constitutional detail and is of little use for the study

of public law. It undoubtedly served Raynal as his chief source, next to Grotius, *Annales*. The *Lives* probably was in the Library Company of Philadelphia in 1787 and it was in the New York Society Library in 1813. Baron du Maurier also wrote *Mémoires Pour Servir L'Histoire De La République Des Provinces-Unies* (1680), a work that I have not been able to examine.

8. Lion Aitzema, *Notable Revolutions; Being A True Relation Of What Happened In The United Provinces Of The Netherlands In The Years MDCL and MDCLI, Somewhat Before And After The Death Of The Late Prince Of Orange* (London, 1653). This is a translation from the Dutch original of Lieuwe van Aitzema, published in 1652. As a chronicle, it is difficult to use in the study of public law, although next to De Witt, *Political Maxims*, it is the most authoritative work available to the framers. It probably was in the Library Company of Philadelphia in 1787 and Jefferson had it in 1815.

9. Hugo Grotius, *De Rebus Belgicis; Or The Annals And History Of The Low Country Wars*, translated by T. Manley (London, 1665). As a translation of Grotius' chronicle, this is an important work; but it is of limited use for the study of public law, even though it contains a summary of the Union of Utrecht and does emphasize that in the Council voting was by persons rather than provinces. An English translation, probably this one, was almost certainly in the Library Company of Philadelphia in 1787, although, as indicated in note 5, it was not easy to come by. Harvard College had in 1790 a Latin version of the *Annales*. Grotius wrote also a little work, *De Antiquitate Respublicae Batavicae*, which was translated by T. Woods under the title, *The Antiquity Of Commonwealths* (London, 1652). This is clear, but too brief to be of much help; and I can find no evidence to suggest that a copy was in the United States in 1787.

10. Bernard Romans, *Annals Of The Troubles In The Netherlands. From The Accession of Charles V. Emperor Of Germany. In Four Parts. A Proper And Seasonable Mirror For The Present Americans* (Hartford, 1779 and 1782, 2 vols). The author of this work, the only one on the Netherlands published in the United States prior to 1787, is notable for having discerned the resemblance of the American Revolution to the Dutch. (In his preface he remarks " May the dreary examples through which I lead you be a comfort to you (respected Americans) who are so highly favored by Providence, as in all appearance to obtain the glorious blessings contended for, with infinite less trouble and hardships, than fell to the lot of those heroes, whose sufferings are exhibited in this work.") Unfortunately, as a translation of chronicles (chiefly, of Grotius' *Annales*), it is not particularly informative on public law and the section on the Union of Utrecht contains no detail on its provisions.

11. L. G. F. Kerroux, *Abrégé De L'Histoire De La Hollande Et Des Provinces-Unies Depuis Le Tems Le Plus Anciens Jusqu'à Nos Jours* (Leyden, 1778, 4 vols.). This is a well-organized chronicle, based very largely on the elaborate history, Jan Wagenaar, *De Vaderlandsche Historie Vervattende De Geschiedenissen Der Vereenigde Nederlanden* (Amsterdam, 1749–60, 21 vols.). Kerroux's work, the most recent full-scale history available in 1787, contains only incidental and buried comments on public law. It was in the Harvard College Library in 1787.

12. Adrien Baillet [pseudonym; M. de la Neuville] *Histoire De Hollande Depuis Le Trêve De 1601 Où Finit Grotius Jusqu'à Notre Tems* (Paris, 1702, 4 vols.). This was in Jefferson's library in 1815, but I have not been able to examine it.

13. Edward Grimstone, *A Generall Historie Of The Netherlands . . . Continued Unto 1608 . . .* (London, 1609). This is a very detailed chronicle based on Latin

works. While it contains mention of the Union of Utrecht, it does not give adequate detail on its provisions. This work was in the New York Society Library in 1813. Grimstone also translated from the French of Jean Francois Petit a volume entitled, *The Low Country Commonwealth, Containing An Exact Description Of The Eight United Provinces Now Made Free* (London, 1609). I have not seen either this volume or its source.

14. Adrien Richer, *Vie De Michel De Ruiter, Lieutenant Admiral General De Hollande Et De West Frieze* (Paris, 1783). Jefferson had this in 1815, but I have not been able to examine a copy.

15. Isaac Lamigue, *Histoire Du Prince D'Orange Et De Nassau* (Leyden, 1715). Jefferson also had this in 1815, but again I have not been able to examine a copy.

16. M. Le Clerc, *Histoire Complette Des Provinces-Unies, Depuis La Naissance De La République Jusqu'à La Paix D' Utrecht* (Hague, 1728, 4 vols.). This is a careful and detailed chronicle, with, however, almost no detail no political forms.

17. *An Address To The People Of The Netherlands On The Present Alarming And Most Dangerous Situation Of The Republick Of Holland Showing The True Motives Of The Most Unpardonable Delays Of The Executive Power In Putting The Republick Into A Proper State Of Defense, And The Advantages Of An Alliance With Holland, France And America* (London, 1782). Following a suggestion of the referee, I find that this is a translation of Joan Van der Capellen tot de Pol, *Aan het Volk van Nederland* (1781). Van der Capellen blames the Stadtholder and the oligarchy for the "dangerous situation." It is hardly conceivable that any of the framers could have read this pamphlet with its angry detail, for, had they read it, they would have been in no doubt as to whether or not Dutch government was oligarchic.

18. F. M. Janicon, *État Present Des Provinces-Unies Et Des Pais Qui En Dépendent* (The Hague, 1729). This is, without question, the most impressive work on Dutch government available in French or English in 1787. Had any of the framers read it, they could hardly have misinterpreted Dutch government so greatly.

19. *Résolution De L. N. P. Les Etats De Zélande Justifiée* (Holland, 1780). This pamphlet on the unwisdom of war with England contains little material of interest on public law.

20. Jean de Witt, *Lettres Et Négotiations Entre Mr. Jean De Witt, Conseiller Pensionnaire Et Garde Des Sceaux Des Provinces De Hollande Et De West Frise. Et Messieurs Les Plénipotentiaires Des Provinces-Unies Des Pais Bas Aus Cours De France, D'Angleterre, De Suéde, De Danemare, De Polonge, Etc., Depuis L'Année 1652 Jusqu'à L'An 1699* (Amsterdam, 1725). Jefferson bought this work in 1803.

XVII

JAMES MADISON AND THE SCOTTISH ENLIGHTENMENT

By Roy Branson

When the definitive book on the ideological origins of the American Constitution is written it should not ignore the remarkable similarities between the political and social theory of Madison and that of the Scottish Enlightenment thinkers. While they may have been independently responding to social and political realities common to Scotland and America, it is striking that at points where they differed from contemporaries Madison and the Scotsmen agreed with each other.[1] Comparison of their thinking underscores both the richness and complexity of Madison's political theory and the surprisingly neglected relevance of the social and political ideas of the Scottish Enlightenment to American Constitutional thought.[2]

Unfortunately, Madison seldom discussed or even referred to previous thinkers, but it is clear that Madison had ample opportunity to read the Scottish writers. When Madison attended Princeton, its President John

[1] Some who underline the importance of ideas during the Revolutionary years de-emphasize their significance in the Constitutional period. Bernard Bailyn is perhaps more responsible than any other single historian for establishing the importance of the ideological origins of the American Revolution. By contrast, Bailyn declares that "Constitutional thought . . . tended to draw away from the effort to refine further the ancient traditional systems," and moved "toward a fresh, direct comprehension of political reality," which led to organizing the national government, and "achieved its classic expression in *The Federalist.*" *The Ideological Origins of the American Revolution* (Cambridge, Mass., 1967), 301. Gordon Wood, acknowledging an incalculable debt to Bailyn, analyzes American history from 1776 to 1778. He agrees with Bailyn that intellectual traditions were not as important as "a simple response to the pressures of democratic politics." *The Creation of the American Republic* (Williamsburg, Va. and Chapel Hill, N.C., 1969), 615. Wood is certain that the result was pivotal in the history of political thought. The Constitution was "the finale to the American Enlightenment," indeed "an end of the classical conception of politics and the beginning of what might be called a romantic view of politics." *Ibid.,* 605-06. Having the assumptions that they do, it is perhaps not surprising that they do not relate the ideas found in the Scottish Enlightenment to the Constitutional thinkers. One can agree that the Constitutional thinkers, including Madison, were powerfully impressed by the empirical realities they observed in America and still believe that certain patterns of ideas helped them interpret the facts they observed. If the Constitution was actually as momentous a shift in the history of political thought as Wood claims, it seems strange not to explore the intellectual traditions (even if they are admittedly only part of the story) lying behind such an important change.

[2] On the validity of characterizing the eighteenth-century Scottish thinkers as a group, despite the differences among them, see Gladys Bryson, *Man and Society: The Scottish Inquiry of the Eighteenth Century,* (New York, 1968), 1-3. Sidney Ahlstrom, in a very helpful and much cited article, draws attention to eighteenth-century Scottish thinkers, but he concentrates on the importance of Scottish common

Witherspoon had recently come from Scotland where he had been immersed in its intellectual and public life. A prominent conservative, evangelical cleric opposing the domination of the Church of Scotland by liberal Moderates with whom the leading intellectual figures of Scotland were associated, Witherspoon was hardly an apologist for David Hume, Adam Smith, John Millar, or Adam Ferguson. But Witherspoon had never followed the even more conservative Secessionists out of the Church of Scotland. Among the hundreds of volumes that he brought with him when he came to America were the works of all the leading Scottish authors, Moderate or agnostic. He put the works of Hume, Smith, and Ferguson on his reading lists, and in his lectures could recommend the works of William Robertson, the leader of the Moderates. He even announced that David Hume, though an infidel, was "of great reach and accuracy of judgment in matters of criticism."[3]

When the Federal Congress wanted "a list of books to be imported for the use of the United States in Congress assembled," it put Madison in charge of the committee to draw it up. He submitted the requested list in January 1783. It included Scottish authors throughout. The section on "Politics" specifically included "Hume's political essay," "Smith on the wealth of Nations," "Ferguson's History of Civil Society," and "Millar on distinction of Ranks in Society."[4] Other works of Hume and Ferguson appeared elsewhere on the list. Madison had purchased Ferguson's

---

sense or "natural realism" philosophy (particularly Thomas Reid and Dugald Stewart) for American theologians debating epistemology. He does not explore the impact on American thought of the political and social theories of thinkers such as Hume, Smith, Millar, and Ferguson. "The Scottish Philosophy and American Theology," *Church History,* 14 (Sept. 1955), 257-72. Douglass Adair was interested in the political and social theories lying behind Madison's thinking. However, he narrowed his focus primarily to David Hume's relation to Madison, most notably their common defense of a large republic, and similarities in their analyses of the source of faction. "That Politics May be Reduced to a Science: David Hume, James Madison and the Tenth *Federalist," Huntington Library Quarterly,* 20, 1956-57, 343-60. Cf. "James Madison," in *Fame and the Founding Fathers: Essays by Douglass Adair,* ed. Trevor Colbourn (New York, 1974), 124-41.

[3] Quoted in Douglas Sloan, *The Scottish Enlightenment and the American College Ideal,* (New York, 1971), 133; cf. James H. Smylie, "Madison and Witherspoon: Theological Roots of American Political Thought," *The Princeton University Library Chronicle,* 12, no. 3 (Spring, 1961), 118-32; and Ralph Ketcham, *James Madison: A Biography,* (New York & London, 1971), Ch. III, esp. 41-46.

[4] *The Papers of James Madison,* VI, eds. William T. Hutchinson and William M. E. Rachal (Chicago and London, 1969), 62-115, esp. 84-90 on "Politics." On purchase of Ferguson, see *Papers,* 1, 131; 133, no. 1; 143; 148-49. On Madison's inscription of his name in a copy of Millar's *Origin of the Distinction of Ranks,* see copy in Rare Book Division of the Library of Congress.

History for himself in 1775, and inscribed his name on his copy of the third edition of John Millar's *The Origin of the Distinction of Ranks.*[5]

Much more important, of course, than these external relationships between Scottish Enlightenment writers and James Madison are the internal similarities in their thought. Obviously, the Scottish Enlightenment was not the only eighteenth-century intellectual tradition to which Madison was exposed. He never gave up his adherence to popular sovereignty, natural rights, or the contractual interpretation of politics, all hallmarks of British radical and opposition thought. But Madison was able to maintain those principles while appreciating that continuing changes taking place in society were more significant than revolution of the government. Like the Scotsmen, Madison emphasized the importance of the emerging professions and competing factions for the vitality and order of a nation.[6]

It is important to note that in confronting the Scotsmen, Madison was not merely finding an intriguing source for defending extended republics here or a new characterization of parties there. David Hume, Adam Smith, Adam Ferguson, and the other eighteenth-century Scotsmen were launched on nothing less than the demanding venture of analyzing modern, Western society. As J. G. A. Pocock has said, "The great achievement of the Scottish School of sociological historians was the recognition that a commercial organization of society had rendered obsolete much that had been believed about society before it."[7] Auguste

[5] William C. Lehmann, *John Millar of Glasgow,* 1735-1801 (Cambridge, 1969), 154. This volume includes an edition of the entire *Origin of the Distinction of Ranks.*

[6] Clearly, I am distinguishing the Scottish writings from "the writings of the English radical and opposition leaders," which provided a "harmonizing force for the other discordant elements in the political and social thought of the revolutionary generation" (Bailyn, 52, 53). Bailyn himself has been careful not to claim for English radical thought the same dominant influence in the Constitutional period. Caroline Robbins, however, does. She refers to a "revolutionary tradition" of ideas in eighteenth-century Britain whose representatives she calls Commonwealthmen or Real Whigs: "In Ireland and Scotland may be found the most radical thinkers," and their most important influence was on America of the Constitutional period. "The American Constitution employs many of the devices which the Real Whigs vainly besought Englishmen to adopt and in it must be found their most abiding memorial." *The Eighteenth-century Commonwealthman,* (Cambridge, 1950), 95, 96. If my essay is correct, the radical thinkers that Bailyn argues were the dominant shaping force during the revolutionary period, and the overlapping group of Real Whigs or Commonwealthmen that Caroline Robbins credits for the Constitution, were not as important an influence on Madison, at least, as was a more moderate strain of thinkers in Scotland. This is true, even if Caroline Robbins bewilderingly includes such anti-revolutionary, non-radical Scots as Smith, Ferguson, and Millar within her overly-broad and diffuse category of Commonwealthmen. Ralph Ketcham continues the confusion in his large biography, attaching Madison's name to those in the canon of the "English dissenting tradition." Ketcham, 38.

[7] J. G. A. Pocock, "Machiavelli, Harrington, and English Political Ideologies in the Eighteenth Century," *William and Mary Quarterly,* 3rd series, 22 (1965), 549-83.

Comte, Karl Marx, and Werner Sombart all saluted Scottish Enlightenment figures as pioneer sociologists and economists of modern society.[8]

This essay cannot provide a full exposition of the social and political thinking of the Scottish Enlightenment and James Madison. Nor will the essay attempt to demonstrate a causal relationship between their thinking and his. Instead, it will explore selected ideas in Madison's thinking and note parallels in the writing of David Hume, Adam Smith, John Millar, and Adam Ferguson to suggest that they were a significant influence on his thought. The work of these particular Scotsmen receives special attention because their prominence is widely acknowledged and because points of similarity between their ideas and Madison's are especially noteworthy.

I. Madison's similarities with the Scotsmen are dramatized by the way the positions they held in common differed from those of Madison's lifelong friend from the Revolutionary era, Thomas Jefferson. Jefferson adhered to the common assumption that society was founded on a contract among individuals. Indeed, he told Madison that "what is true of every member of the society individually, is true of them all collectively, since the rights of the whole can be not more than the sum of the rights of the individuals."[9] When the majority decided a change in government was needed, it was legitimate for those having the preponderance of rights to prevail. If resistance to change forced revolution, so be it. "I hold it," Jefferson wrote Madison, "that a little rebellion now and then is a good thing, and as necessary to the political world as storms in the physical. . . . It is a medicine necessary for the sound health of government."[10]

Jefferson's famous letter to Madison arguing that "the earth belongs in usufruct to the living," was an attempt to make revolution automatic. Each generation should have the opportunity to return to a state of nature and as individuals renegotiate the contract forming society. Every nineteen years, at the expiration of each generation, not only were debts forgiven, but "every constitution then, and every law, naturally expires at the end of nineteen years. If it be enforced longer, it is an act of force and not of right."[11] Madison replied with several criticisms showing that he placed greater value on sustaining the ongoing human relationships of society than on returning to a primitive state of nature.

If the earth be the gift of nature to the living, their title can extend to the earth in its *natural* state only. The *improvements* made by the dead form a

[8] Bryson, 254, n. 1; see also David Kettler, *The Social and Political Thought of Adam Ferguson* (Columbus, Ohio, 1965), 10, n. 3.

[9] Jefferson to Madison, Sept. 6, 1789, *The Papers of Thomas Jefferson*, XV, ed. Julian Boyd (Princeton, 1958), 393.

[10] Jefferson to Madison, Jan. 30, 1787, *Papers*, XI, 93.

[11] Jefferson to Madison, Sept. 6, 1789, *Papers*, XV, 396.

debt against the living, who take the benefit of them. This debt cannot be otherwise discharged than by a proportionate obedience to the will of the Authors of the improvements.

There seems then, to be some foundation in the nature of things; in the relation which one generation bears to another, for the *descent* of obligations from one to another.

Madison's appreciation of the achievement of society and the contributions of succeeding generations to one another made him apprehensive of thoroughgoing revolutions. "Would not a Government so often revised become too mutable & novel to retain that share of prejudice in its favor which is a salutary aid to the most rational government?"[12]

In 1790 when Jefferson became desperate about the dominance of the Federalists and wrote to Madison his willingness to "sever ourselves from that union we so much value," Madison quickly made a trip to see Jefferson. Two weeks later, when Jefferson sent a list of suggested legislative resolutions to Kentucky in the form of a letter to Wilson Cary Nicholas, he omitted the phrase. Jefferson said Madison had talked to him and he had altered the language of his recommendation partly, he admitted, "in deference to his [Madison's] judgment."[13]

Madison did not stress the need for periodic overthrows of the government and violent changes in society, at least partly because he believed that all nations were involved in a constant process of development.[14] The thinkers of the Scottish Enlightenment suggested an alternative to the idea that change meant revolution of government and a return to nature. The Scots even challenged the Lockean concept of individuals in a state of nature consenting to an original contract creating society. The Scotsmen agreed with Hume that "almost all the governments which exist at present, or of which there remains any record in story, have been founded originally either on usurpation or conquest or both, without any pretense of a fair consent."[15] Hume's terms were standard for Scotland: he observed there had been a development from "rude, unpolished nations" up to "polished nations" with increasing commercial activity. In rude nations the agricultural class was doomed to "slavery and subjection," but in polished nations,

where luxury nourishes commerce and industry, the peasants, by a proper cultivation of the land, become rich and independent; while the tradesmen and

---

[12] Madison to Jefferson, Feb. 4, 1790, *The Writings of James Madison*, V, ed. Gaillard Hunt (New York, 1904), 438, 439.

[13] Jefferson to Wilson Cary Nicholas, Sept. 5, 1799, *The Writings of Thomas Jefferson*, X, ed. Andrew A. Lipscomb (Washington, D.C., 1903), 131; see Adrienne Koch, *Jefferson and Madison: The Great Collaboration* (New York, 1950), 196-201.

[14] July 26, 1787, *Debates on the Adoption of the Federal Constitution*, ed. Jonathan Elliot (Philadelphia, 1861), 371.

[15] David Hume, *David Hume's Political Essays*, ed. Charles W. Hendel (New York, 1953), 47.

merchants acquire a share of the property and draw authority and consideration to that middling rank of men who are the best and firmest basis of public
liberty.[16]

With society improving economically and politically, revolution was unreasonable. Political change must come gradually, part of the ongoing
process of society's development. "Some innovations must necessarily
have place in every human institution. . . . But violent innovations no
individual is entitled to make."[17] Hume, contrary to the accepted theory
of his day, argued that the republican form of government better suited
a large than a small territory because distance can moderate sudden
changes attempted by any group within the commonwealth.[18]

Adam Smith and, even more, his student John Millar were more
specific than their mutual friend David Hume about the development
of society from rude to polished. Improvement had come in four stages.
In his University of Glasgow lectures on private law, Adam Smith said
that they "vary according to the periods of human society. The four
stages of society are hunting, pasturage, farming and commerce."[19]

Several years later, John Millar, having also become a professor at the
University of Glasgow, organized his *Origins of the Distinction of the
Ranks in Society* around the same stages. He was convinced that "the
several stages" were "accompanied with peculiar laws and customs."[20] In
the "rude period of society," a savage "earns his food by *hunting and
fishing,* or by gathering the spontaneous fruits of the earth."[21] Next,
there is the invention of taming and pasturing cattle, which may be regarded as the first remarkable improvement in the savage life."[22]

The improvement of *agriculture,* which in most parts of the world has been
posterior to the art of taming and rearing cattle . . . gives rise to property in
land, the most valuable and permanent species of wealth; by the unequal distribution of which a greater disproportion is made in the fortune and rank of
individuals.[23]
When agriculture has created abundance of provisions, people . . . endeavour
to be clothed and lodged, as well as maintained, in a more comfortable manner . . . commodities of different kinds are produced. These are exchanged
for one another, according to the demand of different individuals; and thus
manufacturers, together with *commerce,* are at length introduced into a country.[24] (Italics mine)

Millar believed that man's abilities, talents and desires were driving society from one stage of improvement to another.[25] What should be of

---

[16] *Ibid.,* 128.   [17] *Ibid.,* 52.   [18] *Ibid.,* 158.

[19] Adam Smith, *Lectures on Justice, Police, Revenue and Arms* (Oxford, 1896),
107.

[20] John Millar, "The Origin of the Distinction of Ranks," in Lehmann, *op cit.,*
176.

[21] *Ibid.,* 183.   [22] *Ibid.,* 204.   [23] *Ibid.,* 208.   [24] *Ibid.,* 218.   [25] *Ibid.*

concern is "when a great and polished nation begins to relapse into its primitive rudeness and barbarism."[26]

Adam Ferguson, like his Scottish colleagues, regarded the development of society as one of "improvement" and "progress." Although he did not use Smith's and Millar's four stages, he did set aside parts of his *Essay on the History of Civil Society* to discuss rude nations emerging from "savage" and "barbarous" conditions advancing to polished, commercial nations. But more than the other Scotsmen, Ferguson saw the deficiencies and possible decline of commercial society. While Millar acknowledged the possibility, Ferguson devoted an entire section of his book to the issue. He believed that "man is not made for repose. In him, every amiable and respectable quality is an active power."[27] A polished nation should reflect that energy. The principal sign of its decaying was relaxation and languor among the citizenry.

Madison described social change in similarly evolutionary terms. While others may have also come to recognize the validity of this framework for understanding society, Madison employed both the concepts and terminology of the Scottish thinkers. In a statement that deserves greater attention—his extended presidential address before the Agricultural Society of Albemarle, Virginia—Madison repeated his unflattering view of the natural, uncivilized state and applauded the march of man from his most natural to increasingly complicated forms of living. "The hunter becoming the herdsman; the latter a follower of the plough; and the last reparing to the manufactory or workshop." This basic outline for his remarks relied on the same four stages Adam Smith and John Millar identified in the evolution of society. Madison went on to articulate Ferguson's concern at society's devolution, even incorporating his term "savage" into the discussion.

Madison worried about "the possibility of a transition from a better state of human society to a savage state."[28] That this was a real, not an imagined concern, is illustrated by the fact "that our own people, nursed and reared in these habits and tastes, easily slide into those of the savage, and are rarely reclaimed to civilized society with their own consent." He specified the steps of regression, reversing the four stages of society's evolution.

The manufacturer readily exchanges the loom for the plough, in opposition often to his own interest, as well as that of his country. The cultivator, in situations presenting an option, to the labors of the field, the more easy employment of rearing a herd. And as the game of the forest is approached, the hunting life displays the force of its attractions.[29]

[26] *Ibid.*, 282.

[27] Adam Ferguson, *An Essay on the History of Civil Society, 1767*, ed. Duncan Forbes (Edinburgh, 1966), 210.

[28] "Address to the Agricultural Society of Albermarle, Virginia," May 12, 1818, *Letters and Other Writings of James Madison*, III (Philadelphia, 1865, imprint of R. Worthington, N.Y., 1884), 66.   [29] *Ibid.*

Madison did not attribute either progression or regression to the physical environment. Rather, it was man who was praised for his ability to manipulate nature.

He possesses a reason and a will, by which he can act on matter organized and unorganized. He can, by the exercise of these peculiar powers, increase his subsistence, by which his numbers may be increased beyond the spontaneous supplies of nature; and it would be a reasonable conclusion, that making, as he does in his capacity of an intelligent and voluntary agent, an integral part of the terrestial system, the other parts of the system are so framed as not to be altogether unsusceptible of his agency, and unliable to its effects.[30]

Deterioration was not due to some intrinsic quality of nature, reclaiming its own, but man's "fascination of that personal independence which belongs to the uncivilized state," his "disrelish and contempt of the monotonous labor of tillage, compared with the exciting occupations of the chase," and (in terms reminiscent of Ferguson) man's penchant for "the indolence enjoyed by those who subsist chiefly on the mere bounties of nature, or on their migratory flocks."[31]

That civilization generally was the result of man's ability to change his environment and advance beyond the primitive level of subsistence was seen in the particular case of the United States. Consistent with the outlook of the Scotsmen, but in contrast to some of his contemporaries, Madison refused to celebrate America as the embodiment of an ideal state of nature.

The enviable condition of the people of the United States is often too much ascribed to the physical advantages of their soil and climate, and to their uncrowded situation. Much is certainly due to these causes; but a just estimate of the happiness of our country will never overlook what belongs to the fertile activity of a free people and the benign influence of a responsible Government.[32]

Reflecting on the accomplishments Americans had already achieved in changing their environment allowed Madison to reassert his usual optimism about the future. There was continuing need for agricultural reform, but there were groups to accomplish the task. The institution he cited as the instrument for change led Madison to touch on another aspect of his political theory where he and at least some of the Scots held parallel views. In ancient times charismatic individuals might have improved conditions. In contemporary America,

Patriotic societies, the best agents for effecting it, are pursuing the object with the animation and intelligence which characterize the efforts of a self-governed people, whatever be the objects to which they may be directed.[33]

[30] *Ibid.*   [31] *Ibid.*   [32] *Ibid.*, 76.   [33] *Ibid.*, 77.

Madison primarily meant by reform agricultural progress, no doubt, but only as part of a general pattern of ongoing, gradual reform. And the voluntary associations, like the Albemarle society, were "the best agents for effecting it."

II. Throughout his career Madison made the nature and function of groups in society central to his thinking. Remaining remarkably consistent in his remarks, Madison's position coincided with that of the Scottish thinkers at many points where both he and they differed from most contemporaries. Most importantly, seeing Madison's remarks on faction within the framework of the Scottish Enlightenment's general theories of politics and society highlights the complex view Madison had of America benefitting from a stable, carefully crafted government, while expressing itself as an actively changing, improving society.

Madison's intellectual peers noticed the diverse groups flourishing in America, but overlooked their importance as innovators of moderate social change because in their analyses they persisted in forcing all groups within the traditional European categories of aristocracy and democracy. John Adams doggedly imposed the two-part European scheme on the varied scene he observed in America.

Whether there are not distinctions arising from corporations and societies of all kinds, even those of religion, science, and literature, and whether the professions of law, physic and divinity are not distinctions? Whether all of these are not material for forming an aristocracy? Whether they do not in fact constitute an aristocracy that governs the country?

On the other side, the common people, by which appellation I designate the farmers, tradesmen, and laborers, many of the smaller merchants and necessitous who are obliged to fly into the wilderness for a subsistence.[34]

He could be rather dispassionate in his description because Adams was satisfied to maintain a permanent balance between aristocracy and democracy.

Jefferson sounded a more openly partisan note.

Men by their constitutions are naturally divided into two parties: 1. Those who fear and distrust the people, and wish to draw all powers from them into the hands of the higher classes. 2. Those who identify themselves with the people, have confidence in them, cherish and consider them as the most honest and safe, although not the most wise depository of the public interests. In every country those two parties exist, and in every one where they are free to think, speak and write, they will declare themselves. Call them therefore, Liberals and Serviles, Jacobins and Ultras, Whigs and Tories, Republicans and Federalists, Aristocrats and Democrats, or by whatever name you please, they are the same

[34] John Adams, *The Works of John Adams*, VI, ed. Charles Francis Adams (Boston, 1851), 531.

parties still, and pursue the same object. The last appellation of Aristocrat and Democrat is the true one expressing the essence of all.[35]

Jefferson was clearly and consistently on the democratic side, but like Adams he saw the conflict in traditional terms. It was one of the reasons that Jefferson's prescription for change in a society remained revolution of the many against the few controlling government.

Madison declared the use of the European orders of aristocracy and democracy irrelevant to understanding groups in America.

We had not among us those hereditary distinctions of rank which were a great source of the contests in the ancient governments, as well as the modern states, of Europe; nor those extremes of wealth or poverty which characterize the latter.[36]

This assumption freed Madison to call the myriad groups he found in America by a variety of terms: parties, factions, interests, classes, institutions.

Madison began his major statement on faction with a discussion of non-economic groups. He mentioned those "made up of followers of different leaders ambitiously contending for pre-eminence and power."[37] Madison also found factions forming around "persons of other description whose fortunes have been interesting to the human passions.[38] There were also religious groups, inevitable called sects, and factions brought into existence by zeal for points "of speculation."[39]

David Hume had described parties or faction in very similar terms. He did refer to "two orders of men, such as the nobles and people," but orders now also included soldiers and merchants.[40] And all of these were only one kind of party or faction—factions of interest. In addition there were personal factions and factions of affection, based on "personal friendship or animosity," or "founded on the different attachments of men toward particular families and persons whom they desire to rule over them."[41] Finally, there were parties of principles, "especially abstract speculative principle," of which religious groups were an example.[42]

Madison's analysis of economic groups in Federalist #10 has received considerable notice. He acknowledged that these groups formed according to whether people did or did not enjoy wealth: creditors and debtors, rich and poor, propertied and non-propertied. What is much more significant is that Madison also recognized occupational groups,

---

[35] Jefferson to Henry Lee, August 10, 1824, *Works* XII, ed. Paul Leceister Ford, 375.

[36] Federalist #10, in *The Federalist*, Alexander Hamilton, James Madison, and John Jay, ed. Benjamin Fletcher Wright (Cambridge, Mass., 1961), 13.

[37] "Vices," *Writings*, II, 367; also *Federalist* #10, 131.

[38] *Federalist* #10, 131; cf. Madison to Jefferson, Oct. 24, 1787, Writings, V, 29.

[39] *Federalist* #10, 131.

[40] Hume, "Of Parties in General," *David Hume's Political Essays*, 81.

[41] "Of Parties in General," 78, 84.   [42] *Ibid.*, 81.

cutting across distinctions of wealth. He mentioned landed, manufacturing, mercantile, and moneyed classes.[43] Elsewhere he referred to the "regular branches of manufacturing and mechanical industry," as well as sailors, and "several professions of more elevated pretensions, the merchant, the lawyer, the physician, the philosopher and the divine."[44]

Madison has been praised for his originality in recognizing the importance of a multiplicity of professions intersecting the two-part distinction between aristocratic and democratic orders or wealthy and poor classes.[45] It surely is no denigraton of his acuity to point out that one of the Scotsmen in Madison's library had made the importance of professions a principal focus of his writings. Adam Ferguson believed that "mankind, when in their rude state, have a great uniformity of manners; but when civilized, they are engaged in a variety of pursuits."[46] He was convinced that "a people can make no great progress in cultivating the arts of life, until they have separated, and committed to different persons, the several tasks, which require a peculiar skill and attention."[47] Rather than the modern word differentiation, Ferguson used the word complication.

> The establishments and men . . . arose from successive improvements that were made, without any sense of their general effect; and they bring human affairs to a state of complication. . . . Who could anticipate or even enumerate, the separate occupations and professions by which the members of any commercial state are distinguished?[48]

He identified the highest form of society with the appearance of these groups. "The term polished, if we may judge from its etymology, originally referred to the state of nations in respect to their laws and government. In its later applications, it refers no less to their proficiency in the liberal and mechanical arts, in literature, and in commerce."[49] In the polished, commercial society Ferguson saw at least as many professional groups as Madison. Those he called mechanical included "the labourer, who toils that he may eat; the mechanic, whose art requires no exertion of genius."[50] Enjoying more respect are the liberal professions resembling those Madison called "professions of more elevated pretensions." Ferguson included merchants, literary scholars, artists, "men of science," and statesmen. He conjectured that "thinking itself in this age of separations, may become a craft."[51] The analytic importance of the established

---

[43] *Federalist* #10, 131.

[44] "Republican Distribution of Citizens," *The National Gazette,* (March 5, 1792). *Writings,* VI, 99.

[45] Douglass Adair, "The Tenth Federalist Revisited," *William and Mary Quarterly,* 3rd Series, VIII (Jan., 1951), 48-67; Benjamin F. Wright, "The Federalist on the Nature of Political Man," *Ethics,* LIX (Jan., 1949), 1-31; Benjamin Wright, "Introduction," to his edition of *The Federalist,* 36.

[46] Adam Ferguson, 188.   [47] *Ibid.,* 180.   [48] *Ibid.,* 182.
[49] *Ibid.,* 205.   [50] *Ibid.,* 184.   [51] *Ibid.,* 183.

orders began to erode in Hume's work. It disappeared in Ferguson's fascination with the emergence of new groups in a polished, commercial society.

One reason that Madison's comments on groups have not been linked with the theories of social development in the Scottish Enlightenment may be a misconception that Madison fundamentally condemned factions. The fact is, Madison, like the Scots, provided not only a negative, but a positive description of factions.

It is certainly true that in the Federalist #10 Madison did give a negative definition of faction.

By a faction, I understand a number of citizens, whether amounting to majority or a minority of the whole, who are united and actuated by some impulse of passion, of interest, adverse to the rights of other citizens, or to the permanent and aggregate interests of the community.[52]

Factions, according to this passage, are by definition evil, and minorities or majorities, if they are opposed to the rights and interests of the community, can be called a faction. Indeed, Madison talked about minorities and majorities that are factions.

If a faction consists of less than a majority, relief is supplied by the republican principle, which enables the majority to defeat its sinister views by regular vote. . . . When a majority is included in a faction, the form of popular government, on the other hand, enables it to sacrifice it to its ruling passion or interest both the public good and rights of other citizens.[53]

If one concentrated solely on these passages, Madison would be in the awkward position of saying that factions are by definition evil and that a majority, which he stoutly defends as the final political authority in a state, can be such an evil group.[54] With only this definition, Madison could not be understood as giving the majority final authority in republican society while he simultaneously regarded factions as voluntary associations acting through a variety of interests to disperse and divide the potentially tyrannical purpose of the majority.

But in addition to this negative definition, Madison provided a positive description of faction, a description that understood factions as voluntary associations of interest and purpose groups intersecting the quite different entities called majorities and minorities. Four paragraphs after his negative definition of factions, Madison gave his reason for rejecting the abolition of factions: they arise from liberty being granted to the diverse aspects of man's nature. In addition to deplorable self-love, factions reflect man's reason arriving at opinions. Man tries to make his views more pervasive and potent by creating groups to inculcate and propagate them. Man's nature includes certain "faculties" or talents which

---

[52] *Federalist* #10, 132.   [53] *Ibid.*
[54] Robert A. Dahl, *A Preface to Democratic Theory* (Chicago, 1956), 25.

lead him to possess certain interests. Again, man creates groups to achieve these interests. Madison never applauded self-love, but expression of opinion and exercise of talents were considered by him to be legitimate aspects of man's activity. The right to hold and communicate opinions is a basic right, and in this same essay, Federalist #10, Madison indicated how important he considered the right to exercise one's talents when he said that "the protection of these faculties is the first object of government.[55]

Factions, according to Madison's first definition, are unacceptable either as majorities or minorities any time they arise. If Madison had limited himself to this definition he would have had an understanding of faction quite different from that of the Scots, who were at worst equivocal and often enthusiastic about factions. However, according to the second characterization Madison employs, factions are inevitable combinations not only of man's passion of self-love, but the opinions of his reason and the interests of his faculties. Factions seen in this way appear to be necessary extensions of man's rightful freedom to express his nature.

Indeed, in other writings Madison did say that factions were not only needed to allow man the full expression of his nature, but necessary to the functioning of a nation. "An extinction of parties necessarily implies either a universal alarm for the public safety, or an absolute extinction of liberty."[56] Madison could even assert that the United States Constitution encouraged faction.

Besides the occasional and transient subjects on which parties are formed they seem to have a permanent foundation in the varience of political opinions in free states, and of occupations and interests in all civilized States. The Constitution itself, whether written or prescriptive, influenced as its exposition and administration will be by these causes, must be an unfailing source of party distinctions. And the very peculiarity which gives pre-eminent value to that of the United States, the partition of power between different departments of government, opens a new door for controversies and parties.[57]

According to this view, factions are a legitimate part of American society.

Madison's characterization of faction would have seemed familiar to the Scotsmen. Hume had anticipated Madison in seeing factions arising from the basic nature of man, and having both good and evil effects.

When men act in a faction they are apt, without shame or remorse, to neglect all the ties of honor and morality in order to serve their party; and yet, when a faction is formed upon a point of right or principle, there is no occasion where men discover a greater obstinancy and a more determined sense of justice and equity. The same social disposition of mankind is the cause of these contradictory appearances.[58]

[55] *Federalist*, #10, 131.   [56] *Federalist*, #51, 354.
[57] Madison to H. Lee, June 25, 1824, *Letters*, III, 441-42.
[58] "Of the First Principles of Government," *Hume's Political Essays*, 25.

In his essay "Parties in General," Hume had related the social disposition of mankind to his interests and passions and concluded that factions were unavoidable and deplorable.[59] But in his essay "Of the Parties of Great Britain" Hume said of Britain what Madison said of America; that there were "parties of *principle* involved in the very nature of our constitutions."[60] From this viewpoint parties were unavoidable and natural. In fact, "to abolish all distinction of party may not be practicable, perhaps not desirable in a free government."[61]

Like Hume, Smith thought that parties could both wreak havoc and accomplish good. If a group hit upon an "ideal plan of government" and insisted "upon establishing all at once and in spite of all opposition, everything which that idea may seem to require," the effect would be cruel and temporary. "The violence of the party, refusing all palliatives, all temperaments, all reasonable accommodations, by requiring too much frequently obtains nothing."[62] On the other hand, if parties can be motivated by more than narrowly partisan interests, they become admirable agents for moderate social change.

The leader of the successful party, however, if he has authority enough to prevail upon his own friends to act with proper temper and moderation (which he frequently has not), may sometimes render to his country a service much more essential and important than the greatest victories and the most extensive conquests. He may re-establish and improve the constitution, and from the very doubtful and ambiguous character of the leader of a party he may assume the greatest and noblest of all characters, that of the reformer and legislator of a great state, and by the wisdom of his institution secure the internal tranquility and happiness of his fellow citizens for many succeeding generations.[63]

Smith thought that parties were more than inevitable; they could be instruments for needed innovation and reform.

However, on the nature, role, and interaction of factions, Ferguson must have seemed to Madison the most compatible of the Scotsmen. He thought man possessed a variety of talents and emotions which he expressed in corporate activity. "Man is by nature the member of a community," and "mankind are to be taken in groups, as they have always subsisted."[64] He was as clear-eyed as any of the Scots that man-in-groups acted from self-interest, but he arrived at the same surprising conclusion which was to bring Madison lavish praise for originality. "Faction is ever ready to seize all occasional advantages; and mankind, when in hazard from any part, seldom finds a better protection than that of its rival."[65] Precisely his inability to be idealistic about man's capacity for selflessness committed Ferguson to the necessity of factions opposing one another.

[59] "Of Parties in General," *ibid.*, 77.
[60] "Of the Parties of Great Britain," *ibid.*, 85.
[61] "Of the Coalition of Parties," *ibid.*, 93.
[62] Smith, 245.   [63] *Ibid.*, 245.   [64] Ferguson, 57, 4.   [65] *Ibid.*, 134.

Amidst the contentions of party, the interests of the public, even the maxims of justice and candour, are sometimes forgotten; and yet . . . the public interest is often secure, not because individuals are disposed to regard it as the end of their conduct, but because each, in his own place, is determined to preserve his own. Liberty is maintained by the continued differences and oppositions of numbers, not by their concurring zeal in behalf of equitable government.[66]

It was because polished societies were filled with so many diverse groups that they were the most free. There, "law is literally a treaty, to which the parties concerned have agreed."[67] He was reassured by the fact that in complex, polished societies agreement came by way of factional disputes. The great danger to polished nations was that conflict would cease and laws would become dead letters. "Political rights, when neglected, are always invaded; and alarms from this quarter must frequently come to renew the attention of parties."[68] A constitution merely records the extent to which parties intend to protect their rights and interests; it cannot in itself guarantee rights.[69]

Both Ferguson and Madison realized that beneficial conflict must take place among groups that share some things in common. Ferguson talked about the need for "similar dispositions" and "mutual dependence," and stressed the value of a "national spirit."[70] Madison praised "mutual confidence and affection," leading people to "concur amicably, or to differ with moderation."[71]

III. Seeing within faction and party the full panorama of groups described by Scottish thinkers, and approving them to the point of encouraging their proliferation, was crucially important for Madison's theory. He recognized that voluntary groups could both bring needed improvements in society and that conflict among those groups could prevent the changes from being tyrannous. Madison could endorse the principle of popular sovereignty in spite of his fears.

Madison was committed to the majority acting for the whole society. Indeed, he talked of the will of "the majority—that is, of the society."[72] Both in the forming of society and in its continued actions, the majority assumes the dominant role. "Whatever be the hypothesis of the origin of the *lex majoris partis,* it is evident that it operates as a plenary substitute of the will of the majority of the society for the will of the whole society."[73] Because government in a republic was controlled by society the majority ultimately controlled the coercive power of government. But as early as his 1787 essay on the "Vices of the U.S. Constitution," Madison expressed concern over the power of the majority. His speech to the 1829

---

[66] *Ibid.,* 128. [67] *Ibid.,* 165.

[68] Ferguson, *Principles of Moral and Political Science,* II (Edinburgh, 1792), 352.

[69] Ferguson, *Essay on the History of Civil Society,* 166.

[70] Ferguson, *Principles of Moral and Political Science,* 311, 315.

[71] "Consolidation," *The National Gazette* (Dec. 5, 1791); *Writings,* VI, 68-69.

[72] *Federalist* #51, 358.   [73] "Majority Governments," 1833, *Writings,* IX, 528.

Virginia Constitutional Convention showed that this fear of the unchecked power of the majority was prominent in Madison's thinking
through his public life.[74]

Madison would not allow himself to be reassured into thinking that a
neutral, truly fair government could be created to control the majority.
Dividing the government into competing federal and state levels, and into
legislative, executive, and judicial departments was necessary to make
government as disinterested as possible, but one had to remember that
government was ultimately dependent on the will of the majority in society. It was one principal reason Madison could never share Jefferson's
urgency about the government declaring a Bill of Rights.[75] Dispersal of
the power of the majority in society was the essential protection of corporate and individual rights.

That is why, of course, the insight that factions were not peripheral
but central to the development of society was so important for Madison's
thinking. He could assure the readers of Federalist #51 that while in the
"federal republic of the United States," "all authority in it will be derived
from and dependent on the society, the society itself will be broken into
so many parts, interests and classes of citizens, that the rights of individuals, or of the minority, will be in little danger from interested combinations of the majority."[76]

Madison's Lockean views of popular sovereignty, could have allowed
him to believe that the path of authority could travel directly from an
individual to a majority in society and on to a determination of governmental policy. Madison actually argued that the desires, passions, and
opinions of individuals create groups and that coalitions of them constitute a majority setting the terms for governmental policy. Just as in government there is "the intermediate existence of the State governments,"
between the citizen and the national level of government, so in society
there are voluntary groups between the individual and the majority.[77]

Madison's particular achievement was that as he refined forms of
the United States government he recognized the importance of the non-
governmental parts of the nation. Madison was able to synthesize the
Lockean rationalistic understanding of contractual majorities dominating
governmental action with the Scottish historical-developmental view of
society full of active occupational, political, and commercial groups
achieving moderate reforms.

Kennedy Institute of Ethics, Georgetown University.

[74] "Vices of the Political System of the United States," *Writings*, II, 367;
"Speech in the Virginia Constitutional Convention," Dec. 2, 1829, *Writings*, XI,
361.

[75] Madison to Jefferson, Oct. 17, 1788, *Writings*, V, 272; cf. Speech in Congress,
June 8, 1789, *Writings*, V, 382.   [76] *Federalist* #51, 358.

[77] "Virginia Resolutions of 1798," *Writings*, VI, 405.

XVIII

JEFFERSON ON LIBERTY

By J. W. Cooke

"The beginning and end of all philosophy," wrote Friedrich Schelling, "is—Freedom." Similarly, it can be argued that the beginning and the end of all attempts to understand the American past center around the effort to comprehend what Americans have meant when they used the words *liberty* and *freedom*. Yet such an understanding is extraordinarily difficult, if only because some two hundred definitions of these ambiguous and connotative terms have been noted in the western intellectual tradition. Despite an evident lack of agreement concerning meaning, the uses to which Americans have put these key words can indicate much about the character of their aspirations, the sort of prejudices they were likely to display, the blind spots in their culture, and the kind of values they were willing to defend with words and bullets. And, as Alfred North Whitehead has pointed out, much can be learned about the character of an era by studying the constantly shifting boundary between what he calls "Individual Absoluteness" and "Individual Relativity"; i.e., by analyzing how the articulate members of a given group or generation define their individual freedom, their obligations to the community, and the relationship which exists between these two concepts.[1]

It is impossible to read for very long in the voluminous correspondence, state papers, and miscellaneous writings of Thomas Jefferson without becoming aware that a concept of liberty, remarkably consistent but with a shifting emphasis for different audiences, was a controlling assumption in his religious, social, and political thought. Without understanding what Jefferson meant when he used the word "liberty" or its synonym "freedom," it becomes quite difficult, or impossible, to understand what was meant when he used such other key words or phrases as "moral sense," "virtue," "natural rights," "reason," "government," "education," and "property."

There were three basic ideas of freedom available to the generation of Thomas Jefferson. First, freedom was sometimes described as a result of certain favorable circumstances which enabled men to behave as they wished in pursuing their chosen interests. Men were free in this

---

[1]Quoted in Jacques Barzun, *Darwin, Marx, Wagner: Critique of a Heritage* (rev. 2nd ed., Garden City, N. Y., 1958), 354; Sir Isaiah Berlin, *Two Concepts of Liberty: An Inaugural Lecture Delivered Before the University of Oxford on 31 October 1958* (Oxford, 1958), 6, hereafter cited as Berlin, *Two Concepts;* Alfred North Whitehead, *Adventures of Ideas* (New York, 1935), 50–51, 54–55.

sense when they were exempt from the coercive power of other men or of institutions. External conditions were supremely important in this idea of freedom because they could assist or hinder bodily movements, enlarge or diminish alternative ways of acting, and encourage or discourage emotions or ideas which, in turn, encouraged or discouraged action. Liberty under law, that form of liberty which is a result of a government of laws impartially administered, is a special variant of this idea of freedom. Second, liberty could also be acquired through a rigorous, self-induced change in the individual's mind, character, or personality. As a result of this new character, personality, or ability the individual was able to live according to an ideal or "moral law" of his own choosing. No external circumstance, whether threats of hell, the pressures of public opinion, or the seductiveness of power and beauty could deprive a man of this kind of freedom. This idea of liberty was quite compatible with being a slave or a prisoner; indeed, under some circumstances, it might be the jailer or the slaveowner who was really enslaved. And last, freedom was sometimes construed as a gift from God, a natural right which all men possessed, although they might temporarily be hindered or prevented from exercising it because of adverse conditions, or because they had not yet acquired the necessary knowledge or virtue. Nevertheless, freedom was theirs because they were God's creatures, and not because of unusually propitious circumstances or because they had achieved a significant and lasting alteration in their character.[2]

As a deist Jefferson accepted the creation and ordering of the world by what he called "an intelligent and powerful Agent," a divine, essentially benevolent first cause, and the source of all absolute values. The Creator had not left man an entirely unformed, plastic entity. In the first place, almost all individuals (Jefferson did not explain the exceptions) were endowed with a "moral sense," an innate faculty which developed within the individual as his understanding grew. "The moral sense," Jefferson commented to John Adams in 1816, "is as much a part of our constitution as that of feeling, seeing, or hearing; as a wise creator must have seen to be necessary in an animal destined to live in society. . . ." This sense, peculiar to man, was most often displayed in benevolent actions aimed at promoting the well-being of his fellow creatures. The individual with a fully developed "moral sense" would find pleasure in the happiness of his friends and neighbors, and in practicing the classic virtues of prudence, temperance, fortitude, and justice. Or, to put it another way, "nature has constituted *utility* to man, the stan-

[2]Mortimer J. Adler, *The Idea of Freedom: A Dialectical Examination of the Conceptions of Freedom* (Garden City, N. Y., 1958), 112, 125, 230, 586, 83, 134–36, 143, 147, 154–56.

dard and test of virtue." Everything is useful, Jefferson wrote to Robert Skipwith, which helps us to make virtuous acts habitual. Regrettably, not all men possessed a "moral sense," but society could secure conformity to its standards from the recalcitrant individual through education, "appeals to reason and calculation, by presenting to the being so unhappily conformed, other motives to do good and to eschew evil, such as the love, or the hatred, or rejection of those among whom he lives; and whose society is necessary to his happiness and even existence; demonstrations by sound calculation that honesty promotes interest in the long run; the rewards and penalties established by the laws; and ultimately the prospects of a future state of retribution for the evil as well as the good done while here. . . . " [3]

Men were also born with natural rights (rights necessary for moral and intellectual achievement), the most important of which were "individual liberty and social freedom." More specifically, Jefferson had in mind three essential liberties: freedom of thought, freedom from tyrannical political authority, and freedom in choosing and plying one's livelihood. Such liberties were never to be abridged or denied by any man-

[3] Jefferson to John Adams, April 11, 1823, in Lester J. Cappon, ed., *The Adams-Jefferson Letters: The Complete Correspondence Between Thomas Jefferson and Abigail and John Adams* (2 vols., Chapel Hill, 1959), published for The Institute of Early American History and Culture at Williamsburg, Virginia, II, 592: Jefferson to John Adams, April 8, 1816, *ibid.*, 467; Jefferson to John Adams, Aug. 1, 1816, *ibid.*, 484; Jefferson to Abigail Adams, Jan. 11, 1817, *ibid.*, 504, hereafter cited as Cappon, ed., *Adams-Jefferson Letters;* Jefferson to Mr. Miles King, Sept. 26, 1814, in Andrew A. Lipscomb and Albert Ellery Bergh, eds., *The Writings of Thomas Jefferson* (20 vols., Monticello edition, Washington, D. C. 1904), XIV, 197–98; Jefferson to David Barrow, May 1, 1815, *ibid.*, 297, hereafter cited as Lipscomb and Bergh, eds., *Writings;* Jefferson to John Adams, Oct. 14, 1816, in Cappon, ed., *Adams-Jefferson Letters,* II, 492; Jefferson to William Short, Oct. 31, 1819, in Lipscomb and Bergh, eds., *Writings,* XV, 224; Jefferson to Thomas Law, Esq., June 13, 1814, *ibid.,* XIV, 141–43; Jefferson to Robert Skipwith, Aug. 3, 1771, in Julian P. Boyd, ed., *The Papers of Thomas Jefferson* (17 vols. to date; Princeton, 1950–65), I, 76–77, hereafter cited as Boyd, ed., *Papers;* Jefferson to Francis Gilmer, June 7, 1816, in Richard Beale Davis, ed., *Correspondence of Thomas Jefferson and Francis Walker Gilmer, 1814–1826* (Columbia, 1946), 41, hereafter cited as Davis, ed., *Correspondence;* also, *Opinion on the question whether the United States have a right to renounce their treaties with France, or to hold them suspended till the government of that country shall be established,* April 28, 1793, in Lipscomb and Bergh, eds., *Writings,* III, 229; Jefferson to Peter Carr, Aug. 10, 1787, *ibid.,* VI, 257; Jefferson to James Fishback, Sept. 27, 1809, *ibid.,* XII, 315; Jefferson to Mr. Miles King, Sept. 26, 1814, *ibid.,* XIV, 197–98; Jefferson to Charles Thompson, Jan. 9, 1816, *ibid.,* 386; Jefferson to Dupont De Nemours, April 24, 1816, *ibid.,* 490; Jefferson to Judge William Johnson, June 12, 1823, *ibid.,* XV, 441; Jefferson to John Adams, May 5, 1817, in Cappon, ed., *Adams-Jefferson Letters,* II, 512; Jefferson to Martha Jefferson, Dec. 11, 1783, in Boyd, ed., *Papers,* VI, 380; Jefferson to Peter Carr, Aug. 19, 1785, *ibid.,* VIII, 406; Jefferson to Maria Cosway, Oct. 12, 1786, *ibid.,* X, 450; Jefferson to Peter Carr, Aug. 10, 1787, *ibid.,* XII, 15. Italics in the original.

made institution. They were the gift of God to all men and were, further, the only sound basis upon which a society or a government could be founded. Men did not give up a single one of these natural rights when they entered society; it was the duty of the legislator, Jefferson wrote Francis W. Gilmer, "to declare and enforce only our natural rights and duties, and to take none of them away from us." The great Virginian's acknowledgment of "duties" indicates that he was aware of the need to resolve the tensions that would inevitably arise between what different men might define as their inalienable rights. Jefferson resolved this problem, at least to his own satisfaction, by explaining that "the law of the *majority* is the natural law of every society of men," although this natural right, like most others, might be abridged by mutual consent or through laws which were freely assented to. In the last analysis, Jefferson affirmed to a committee of the Danbury Baptist Association in 1802, that no man has any natural right in opposition to his "social duties." Here Jefferson's "moral sense" played a significant conciliatory role by predisposing men to behave honestly and benevolently toward their fellows, and thus negating some of the otherwise irreconcilable tensions which might be prompted by man's self-love. As Jefferson rather too neatly summarized the matter: "Man was created for social intercourse; but social intercourse cannot be maintained without a sense of justice; then man must have been created with a sense of justice."[4]

The idea of natural rights served both a normative and a descriptive function in Jefferson's thought. It was, first, a moral absolute useful in measuring the amount of "morality, compassion, [and] generosity" present in purely personal relations, in relations between states, and in

[4]Adrienne Koch, *The Philosophy of Thomas Jefferson* (Gloucester, 1957), 137, 142–43, hereafter cited as Koch, *Philosophy of Jefferson;* Carl Becker, "What Is Still Living in the Political Philosophy of Thomas Jefferson," *The American Historical Review,* **48,** 4 (July 1943), 695; Jefferson to Francis W. Gilmer, June 7, 1816, in Lipscomb and Bergh, eds., *Writings,* XV, 24; *Jefferson's Opinion on the Constitutionality of the Residence Bill* in Boyd, ed., *Papers,* XVII, 195; Jefferson to Messrs. Nehemiah Dodge, Ephraim Robbins, and Stephen S. Nelson, A Committee of the Danbury Baptist Association, in the State of Connecticut, Jan. 1, 1802, in Lipscomb and Bergh, eds., *Writings,* XVI, 282; Jefferson to Francis W. Gilmer, June 7, 1816, *ibid.,* XV, 25; also, Jefferson to John W. Eppes, Sept. 11, 1813, *ibid.,* XIII, 357; Jefferson to Dupont De Nemours, April 24, 1816, *ibid.,* XIV, 490; Jefferson to Judge William Johnson, June 12, 1823, *ibid.,* XV, 441; Thomas Jefferson, *Notes on the State of Virginia,* ed. Thomas Perkins Abernethy (New York, 1964), 83, 152, 156, hereafter cited as Abernethy, ed., *Notes; The Declaration of Independence as Adopted by Congress in Congress,* July 4, 1776, in Boyd, ed., *Papers,* I, 429; Jefferson to David Humphreys, Mar. 18, 1789, *ibid.,* XIV, 678; *The Response, ibid.,* XVI, 179; *Jefferson's Opinion on the Constitutionality of the Residence Bill, ibid.,* XVII, 195; Jefferson to Francis W. Gilmer, June 7, 1816, in Davis, ed., *Correspondence,* 40; Jefferson to Francis W. Gilmer, Dec. 26, 1820, *ibid.,* 75. Italics in the original.

relations between persons and institutions. Natural rights also served as a sound utilitarian (and therefore moral) basis upon which to construct a viable society; i.e., men were certainly more likely to give a strong and uncoerced loyalty to those institutions (and especially government) that acknowledged and respected the existence of certain privileges and immunities which were, under no circumstances, to be abridged or denied. And such a concept might protect a creative minority (Jefferson's "natural aristocracy" composed of individuals who possessed an abundance of "virtue and talents") from an oppressive majority, those whom Jefferson once referred to as "the unreasonable . . . the largest part of mankind. . . ." Jefferson's thoughts on this vitally important subject sometimes seem vague and inconsistent. In an opinion written in 1790 concerning the constitutionality of the Residence Bill he argued that all natural rights *might* be abridged by the consent of the majority, or its representatives, provided they were honestly and freely chosen. Yet he also affirmed in separate communications to David Humphreys and Francis Gilmer over a 27 year interval that there were rights which should never be submitted to government. Perhaps a reconciliation between these two seemingly contradictory statements was effected in a comment made in the *Notes on the State of Virginia.* Here Jefferson distinguished between natural rights which could be legitimately modified through the moral actions of majorities and the "rights of conscience" which were absolute. These "rights of conscience" were never clearly defined, but perhaps Jefferson's comments to David Humphreys in 1789 give the clearest outline of what he regarded as the truly inalienable liberties. "There are rights," he wrote, "which it is useless to surrender to the government. . . . These are the rights of thinking, and publishing our thoughts by speaking or writing: the right of free commerce: the right of personal freedom."[5]

Men also possessed the faculty of reason. This, like other human faculties, was God-given, but its development depended to some extent upon human effort. Jefferson seems to have used the word in three distinct ways. First, reason was an instrument employed to comprehend,

[5]Jefferson to Dupont De Nemours, April 24, 1816, in Lipscomb and Bergh, eds., *Writings,* XIV, 490; Jefferson to John Adams, Oct. 28, 1813, in Cappon, ed., *Adams-Jefferson Letters,* II, 388; Jefferson to Hugh Williamson, Feb. 6, 1785, in Boyd, ed., *Papers,* VII, 642; *Jefferson's Opinion on the Constitutionality of the Residence Bill, ibid.,* XVII, 195; Jefferson to David Humphreys, Mar. 18, 1789, *ibid.,* XIV, 678; Jefferson to Francis W. Gilmer, June 7, 1816, in Lipscomb and Bergh, eds., *Writings,* XV, 24; Abernethy, ed., *Notes,* 152; also, Jefferson to Major John Cartwright, June 5, 1824, in Lipscomb and Bergh, eds., *Writings,* XVI, 44, 48; Jefferson, *To the Republicans of Georgetown,* Mar. 8, 1809, *ibid.,* 349.

analyze, and discriminate between sense impressions. "Fix reason firmly in her seat," he advised Peter Carr, "and call to her tribunal every fact, every opinion." Second, Jefferson occasionally equated the reasonable with the rightful; i.e., what was according to reason was right, or moral, or virtuous. As he admonished his fellow republicans and federalists on the occasion of his First Inaugural, ". . . though the will of the majority is in all cases to prevail, that will to be rightful must be reasonable. . . ." And last, Jefferson identified reason with nature, thus making the reasonable equivalent to the natural, and both equivalent to the moral.[6]

Reason, of course, had many significant functions but there are five which seem particularly prominent in Jefferson's thought. First, it was to render whatever assistance was necessary to guide the conscience (or "moral instinct"). Not much strength of reason would be required here however; common sense was almost always sufficient. "Morals," Jefferson wrote, "were too essential to the happiness of man to be risked on the uncertain combinations of the head. She [Nature] laid their foundation therefore in sentiment, not in science." Reason was also called upon to assess the dogmatic assertions of organized religion, and to discriminate between the conflicting claims of various churches and sects. Ultimately, Jefferson thought, by using the criterion of reasonableness the true could be differentiated from the false, in religion as in secular affairs. Reason was valuable in more mundane affairs, as well. It was supremely important in understanding and manipulating the New World environment for the glory of God and the happiness and well-being of men; this helps to explain Jefferson's lifelong interest in agronomy and its allied disciplines. Reason was also to be used in discovering and defining both man's natural rights (hidden from him for ages by "kings, priests and nobles") and the civil liberties of Americans, and in fixing them firmly in civil legislation. "The standard of reason [is] at last erected," wrote Jefferson exultantly after the Virginia Statute for Religious Freedom became law. And last, reason was to be employed in judging the histories of great men and of past societies in an effort to gain guidance for future actions.

Liberty and reason were conceptually interdependent ideas because without liberty, there was little opportunity for reason to develop.

[6] Jefferson to Peter Carr, Aug. 10, 1787, in Lipscomb and Bergh, eds., *Writings,* VI, 258; James D. Richardson, ed., *A Compilation of the Messages and Papers of the Presidents, 1789-1897* (2 vols., Washington, 1896), I, 322, hereafter cited as Richardson, ed., *Messages and Papers;* Sidney Hook, *The Paradoxes of Freedom* (Berkeley and Los Angeles, 1962), 6-7; this three part definition of reason was first suggested by Roland Bainton and later used by Gerald Stourzh in "Reason and Power in Benjamin Franklin's Political Thought," *American Political Science Review,* 47 (Dec. 1953), 1097.

When Jefferson campaigned tirelessly for public education, when he defended freedom of the press and freedom of conscience he was, in effect, acknowledging this close relationship. Unless men could freely search history for lessons and principles to guide their actions in the present and future, unless they were at liberty to study nature and comprehend its laws, unless they were free to observe, experiment, and deduce in government and in their private affairs there was little chance for circumstantial liberty to develop. The use of reason also led to the discovery that God created the mind free. If such an awareness was lacking, Jefferson warned, the cause of liberty might well be lost. "The sufficiency of human reason for the care of human affairs" and a respect for the will of the majority, he once wrote, were the only reliable guardians of the "rights of man."[7]

Jefferson did not, however, place unlimited faith in the powers of rationality. As he noted in a letter to John Randolph, "I see too many proofs of the imperfection of human reason, to entertain wonder or intolerance at any difference of opinion on any subject. . . ." His doubts concerning the all-sufficiency of reason were based on four reservations. First, all judgments concerning the nature of reality were dependent upon "sensation . . . matter and motion. . . ." Upon this fragile base, Jefferson asserted, "we may erect the fabric of all the certainties we can have or need." Rejecting what he called "*immaterialism*" and "all organs of information . . . but my sense," Jefferson warned that

[7]Jefferson to Maria Cosway, Oct. 12, 1786, in Boyd, ed., *Papers*, X, 450; Jefferson to Peter Carr with Enclosure, Aug. 10, 1787, *ibid.*, XII, 14–16; Jefferson to James Fishback, Sept. 27, 1809, in Lipscomb and Bergh, eds., *Writings*, XII, 315; Jefferson to Monsieur N. G. Dufief, April 19, 1814, *ibid.*, XIV, 127; Jefferson to Mr. Miles King, Sept. 26, 1814, *ibid.*, 197–98; Jefferson to Monsieur D'Ivernois, Feb. 6, 1795, *ibid.*, IX, 297–98; *Autobiography, ibid.*, I, 74; Jefferson to Thomas Cooper, July 10, 1812, *ibid.*, XIII, 176–77; Jefferson to Dr. Thomas Cooper, Oct. 7, 1814, *ibid.*, XIV, 201; *Plan for Elementary Schools*, Sept. 9, 1817, *ibid.*, XVII, 436–37; Jefferson to Peter Carr, Sept. 7, 1914, *ibid.*, XIX, 211–21; Jefferson to John Adams, Oct. 28, 1813, in Cappon, ed., *Adams-Jefferson Letters*, II, 390; Jefferson to John Adams, Oct. 14, 1816, *ibid.*, 491; Jefferson to James Madison, Dec. 16, 1786, in Boyd, ed., *Papers*, X, 604; *A Bill for the More General Diffusion of Knowledge, ibid.*, II, 526–27; Abernethy, ed., *Notes*, 142; *The Response*, Boyd, ed., *Papers*, XVI, 179; also, Jefferson to Robert Skipwith, Aug. 3, 1771, *ibid.*, I, 77; Jefferson to Edward Carrington, Jan. 16, 1787, *ibid.*, XI, 49; Jefferson to William Stephens Smith, Nov. 13, 1787, *ibid.*, XII, 356; Jefferson to John Norvell, June 11, 1807, in Lipscomb and Bergh, eds., *Writings*, XI, 223; Jefferson to Horatio G. Spafford, Mar. 17, 1814, *ibid.*, XIV, 120; Jefferson to John Adams, Aug. 1, 1816, in Cappon, ed., *Adams-Jefferson Letters*, II, 485; Jefferson to John Adams, Nov. 25, 1816, *ibid.*, 498–99; H. Trevor Colbourn, *The Lamp of Experience: Whig History and the Intellectual Origins of the American Revolution* (Chapel Hill, 1965), published for the Institute of Early American History and Culture at Williamsburg, Virginia, 158–84; Clinton Rossiter, *Seedtime of the Republic: The Origin of the American Tradition of Political Liberty* (New York, 1953), 142.

"once we quit the basis of sensation, all is in the wind." Nevertheless, the combined testimony of the senses, together with the "faculty of reasoning," gave men all the knowledge they needed to direct their affairs successfully. Second, Jefferson believed that both moral and physical qualities were to some undefined extent transmissible from parents to offspring. And, if this was the case, to what extent could they be effectively controlled and guided by reason, an essentially acquired faculty? The great Virginian was fond of asserting that men were born either Whigs or Tories, either "healthy, strong and bold" or "sickly, weakly, timid." In fact, Jefferson asserted, just as every human face was to some extent unique, so was each human mind and probably each human creed. Third, reason was often inadequate to restrain the seductions of self-love. Egotism, Jefferson wrote to Thomas Law, was "the sole antagonist of virtue. . . ." Reluctantly he conceded that "the human character requires in general constant and immediate control. . . ." And last, "accident, chance, and circumstances" were factors in man's life that reason, no matter how efficacious, was insufficient to fully explain or control. For these reasons, Jefferson did not expect absolute rationality or truth from men. Rather, "integrity of views more than their soundness, is the basis of esteem." It was not so much what an individual believed, but the sincerity with which he held his views that seemed important to Jefferson.[8]

Republican government (or representative democracy), "the only form of government which is not eternally at open or secret war with the rights of mankind," was that political contrivance best designed to secure men's happiness and well-being by offering them equal access to freedom, property, education, and justice. The essential features of such a government, Jefferson believed, were "freedom of religion, freedom of the press, trial by jury, *habeas corpus*, and a representative legislature." At other times Jefferson warned that standing armies, monopolies, banks, and a concentration of power in the hands of the

---

[8] Jefferson to John Randolph, Dec. 1, 1803, in Lipscomb and Bergh, eds., *Writings*, X, 436; Jefferson to John Adams, Aug. 15, 1820, *ibid.*, XV, 274–76; Jefferson to John Adams, Oct. 28, 1813, in Cappon, ed., *Adams-Jefferson Letters*, II, 387–88; Jefferson to Joel Barlow, May 3, 1802, in Lipscomb and Bergh, eds., *Writings*, X, 320–21; Jefferson to Thomas Law, Esq., June 13, 1814, *ibid.*, XIV, 140; Jefferson to Monsieur Dupont De Nemours, April 24, 1816, *ibid.*, 489; Koch, *Philosophy of Jefferson*, 124; Jefferson to Elbridge Gerry, Jan. 26, 1799, in Lipscomb and Bergh, eds., *Writings*, X, 85; also, Jefferson to Peter Carr, Aug. 10, 1787, *ibid.*, VI, 261; Jefferson to Benjamin Waring, Esq. and Others, Mar. 23, 1801, *ibid.*, X, 235; Jefferson to James Fishback, Sept. 27, 1809, *ibid.*, XII, 315; Jefferson to Dr. Benjamin Rush, Dec. 5, 1811, *ibid.*, XIII, 116; Jefferson to Dr. John Manners, Feb. 22, 1814, *ibid.*, XIV, 98; Jefferson to Timothy Pickering, Esq., Feb. 27, 1821, *ibid.*, XV, 324; Jefferson to Marquis De La Fayette, Nov. 4, 1823, *ibid.*, 492–93; Jefferson to Henry Lee, Aug. 10, 1824, *ibid.*, XVI, 73–74. Italics in the original.

federal government were dangers to political freedom. It should not be too energetic or paternalistic. "God send," he wrote to Francis Hopkinson, "that our country may never have a government, which it can feel. This is the perfection of human society." The best government, said Jefferson in his First Inaugural, was one "which shall restrain men from injuring one another, [which] shall leave them otherwise free to regulate their own pursuits of industry and improvement, and shall not take from the mouth of labor the bread it has earned." Yet every form of government contained some defect, some seed of tyranny and corruption, that had to be constantly guarded against. "The natural progress of things," Jefferson warned Edward Carrington, "is for liberty to yeild [sic], and government to gain ground." But the government of the republic, by giving its citizens a "free right to the unbounded exercise of reason and freedom of opinion," had hopefully minimized the dangers of tyranny and maximized their chances of remaining free.

Jefferson further sought to create an atmosphere congenial to liberty by stressing the need to consider all relevant circumstances— population density, geography, the level of literacy, experience in self-government, virtue, and the like—in determining the type of government best suited for Americans. Here in the New World, he believed, conditions were uniquely favorable to the creation of an "Empire for liberty." In a republic with abundant, easily procured land, a small population, a system of public education open to all, a government dedicated to the "equal rights of man, and the happiness of every individual," and a minimum of tyrannous customs and institutions inherited from the past, there would be room for liberty, virtue, and happiness.[9]

[9]*Response to the Address of Welcome,* Mar. 11, 1790, in Boyd, ed., *Papers,* XVI, 225; Jefferson to Monsieur Dupont De Nemours, Feb. 28, 1815, in Lipscomb and Bergh, eds., *Writings,* XIV, 255; Jefferson to James Madison, Dec. 20, 1787, in Boyd, ed., *Papers,* XII, 440; Jefferson to Uriah Forrest, with Enclosure, Dec. 31, 1787, *ibid.,* 476; Jefferson to William Stephens Smith, with Enclosure, Feb. 2, 1788, *ibid.,* 558; Jefferson to Alexander Donald, Feb. 7, 1788, *ibid.,* 571; Jefferson to C. W. F. Dumas, Feb. 12, 1788, *ibid.,* 583; Jefferson to Francis Hopkinson, Mar. 31, 1789, *ibid.,* XIV, 650; Jefferson to Colonel Humphreys, Mar. 18, 1789, in Lipscomb and Bergh, eds., *Writings,* VII, 323; Jefferson to Elbridge Gerry, Jan. 26, 1799, *ibid.,* X, 77; Jefferson to Gideon Granger, Aug. 31, 1800, *ibid.,* 167–69; Jefferson to Monsieur Destutt De Tracy, Jan. 26, 1811, *ibid.,* XIII, 19; Jefferson to John Taylor, May 28, 1816, *ibid.,* XV, 23; Jefferson to Francis Hopkinson, May 8, 1788, in Boyd, ed., *Papers,* XIII, 145; Richardson, ed., *Messages and Papers,* I, 323; Jefferson to Edward Carrington, May 27, 1788, in Boyd, ed., *Papers,* XIII, 208–09; Jefferson to Roger C. Weightman, June 24, 1826, in Lipscomb and Bergh, eds., *Writings,* XVI, 182; Jefferson to Monsieur A. Coray, Oct. 31, 1823, *ibid.,* XV, 482; also, Answers to Demeunier's First Queries, Jan. 24, 1786, in Boyd, ed., *Papers,* X, 19–20; Jefferson to James Madison, Dec. 20, 1787, *ibid.,* XII, 442; Jefferson to Martha

Popular education was another necessity if liberty was to be safe. "No other sure foundation [than education], can be devised for the preservation of freedom and happiness," Jefferson wrote George Wythe. A common school system was "the key-stone of the arch of our government." In 1779 Jefferson proposed a system of public education to the legislators of the state of Virginia. Without going into great detail, the plan called for three years of instruction in reading, writing, simple arithmetic (and, indirectly, history since the pupils were to be taught to read using books of Greek, Roman, English, and American history) for all "free" boys and girls. Counties were to be divided, for educational purposes, into "hundreds" and a schoolhouse was to be built in each of these districts to serve the surrounding area. Beyond this point the school system was to be much more selective: only the most intellectually promising students (supported at public expense if their parents were too poor to pay) and the children of well-to-do parents were to be taught the Latin and Greek languages, English grammar, geography, and "the higher part of numerical arithmetick . . ." at district grammar schools so located that they could offer an education to pupils coming from several counties. In each of the first two years at this second level there was to be a further winnowing of genius and talents among the young scholars. Eventually, after four more years, the remaining students would emerge prepared for the rigors of a college education. The plan was rejected by his fellow Virginians.

Many years later Jefferson again became absorbed in designing a suitable educational curriculum, this time for the "natural aristoi" who would attend the University of Virginia. The list of proposed courses is notable for its comprehensiveness. In addition to further study in the disciplines of history, geography, mathematics, and languages the students were to have instruction in "natural philosophy," agriculture, chemistry, medicine, anatomy, zoology, botany, mineralogy, geology, law, government, rhetoric, "belles lettres, and the fine arts generally,"

Jefferson, Mar. 28, 1787, *ibid.,* XI, 251; Jefferson to Mr. Wythe, Aug. 13, 1786, in Lipscomb and Bergh, eds., *Writings,* V, 396; Jefferson to Jean Baptiste Say, Feb. 1, 1804, *ibid.,* XI, 2; Jefferson to Baron Alexander Von Humboldt, Dec. 6, 1813, *ibid.,* XIV, 22; Jefferson to Benjamin Waring, Esq., Jan. 9, 1816, *ibid.,* 392; Jefferson to Amos J. Cook, Preceptor of Fryeburg Academy in the District of Maine, Jan. 21, 1816, *ibid.,* 405; Jefferson to C. F. C. De Volney, Feb. 8, 1805, *ibid.,* XI, 64; Jefferson to John Adams, June 27, 1813, in Cappon, ed., *Adams-Jefferson Letters,* II, 337; Jefferson to John Adams, Oct. 28, 1813, *ibid.,* 391; Jefferson to John Adams, May 17, 1818, *ibid.,* 524; Abernethy, ed., *Notes,* 142. Italics in the original.

ideology (in the sense of the *Idéologues*), ethics, and "military and naval science." Given such intensive and extensive training, the intellectual elite of the country would be well equipped to discover, define, and defend their natural right to liberty and their civil liberties (as well as those of their fellow citizens), and they would be equally competent to exploit the country's natural resources to enhance and expand their circumstantial liberty.[10]

Property and freedom were related in two ways in Jefferson's thought. In one sense, liberty was every man's "property"; it was an inalienable and intrinsic part of his being. No one could deprive him of it, but its exercise might be rather effectually hindered by a lack of virtue (laziness, for instance) or crippling circumstances. Property was also described by Jefferson as one of man's "natural wants." In this sense it was something tangible and alienable—land for instance—and a guarantee that circumstantial liberty might exist. If a man could not support his dependents and himself, how could it be argued that he was a free man? Would he not, inevitably, be coerced by those who could give him work, money, food, or shelter? "Dependence," warned Jefferson, "begets subservience and venality, suffocates the germ of virtue, and prepares fit tools for the designs of ambition." A man's liberty was his property, and his property (in land at least) guaranteed a minimum of liberty.

Jefferson also found a relationship between certain forms of property and virtue. Men were more free, happier, and more virtuous when farming than when working at any other occupation. In part this was because most farmers, while making an adequate living, could never expect to accumulate any great amount of wealth; thus they would be spared the dangerous allurements of luxury, dissipation, and vice. A certain austere style of life was absolutely necessary if men

---

[10] Jefferson to George Wythe, Aug. 13, 1786, in Boyd, ed., *Papers,* X, 244; Jefferson to John Adams, Oct. 28, 1813, in Cappon, ed., *Adams-Jefferson Letters,* II, 390; *A Bill for the More General Diffusion of Knowledge,* in Boyd, ed., *Papers,* II, 526-33; *Plan for Elementary Schools,* Sept. 9, 1817, in Lipscomb and Bergh, eds., *Writings,* XVII, 436–37; ideology is defined clearly in Koch, *Philosophy of Jefferson,* 65–82; also, Jefferson to John Adams, Dec. 10, 1819, in Cappon, ed., *Adams-Jefferson Letters,* II, 549–50; *Autobiography,* in Lipscomb and Bergh, eds., *Writings,* I, 74; Jefferson to Thomas Cooper, July 1, 1812, *ibid.,* XIII, 177; Jefferson to Thomas Law, Esq., June 13, 1814, *ibid.,* XIV, 141; Jefferson to Dr. Thomas Cooper, Oct. 7, 1814, *ibid.,* 201; Jefferson to the Marquis De Lafayette, Feb. 14, 1815, *ibid.,* 245; Jefferson to Dupont De Nemours, April 24, 1816, *ibid.,* 491-92; Jefferson to Cornelius Camden Blatchly, Oct. 21, 1822, *ibid.,* XV, 399–400; Jefferson to Monsieur A. Coray, Oct. 31, 1823, *ibid.,* 483; Jefferson to Judge Augustus B. Woodward, Mar. 24, 1824, *ibid.,* XVI, 19; Jefferson to Peter Carr, Sept. 7, 1814, *ibid.,* XIX, 211–21.

were to remain free and virtuous. What a pity, Jefferson reflected while touring pre-revolutionary southern France, that a rich country could not long remain a free one. "We must," he warned Samuel Kercheval, "make our election between *economy and liberty, or profusion and servitude.*" Yet in the United States men could be free because their labors earned them adequate compensation and enough extra to provide for their old age. This fortunate concatenation—liberty and property—would help immeasurably to insure the success of the American experiment in self-government. "Here," he wrote John Adams, "every one may have land to labor for himself if he chuses [sic]; or, preferring the exercise of any other industry, may exact for it such compensation as not only to afford a comfortable subsistence, but wherewith to provide for a cessation from labor in old age. Every one, by his property, or by his satisfactory situation, is interested in the support of law and order. And such men may safely and advantageously reserve to themselves a wholesome controul [sic] over their public affairs, and a degree of freedom, which in the hands of the Canaille of the cities of Europe, would be instantly perverted to the demolition and destruction of everything public and private." Jefferson's often repeated affirmation that the earth belonged to the living may also be understood as, in large part, a result of his love of liberty. "The earth," he wrote to James Madison, "is given as a common stock for men to labour and live on." But if the ownership of land could be concentrated in the hands of a few men, then liberty for most men would be impossible. Without liberty, the acquisition of property was impossible; and, without property men would be hard put to remain virtuous. Property, then, was a necessity for virtue.[11]

[11]Jefferson to Dupont De Nemours, April 24, 1816, in Lipscomb and Bergh, eds., *Writings,* XIV, 490; Abernethy, ed., *Notes,* 157; Notes on a Tour into the Southern Parts of France, and etc., in Boyd, ed., *Papers,* XI, 420; Jefferson to Samuel Kercheval, July 12, 1816, in Lipscomb and Bergh, eds., *Writings,* XV, 39; Jefferson to John Adams, Oct. 28, 1813, in Cappon, ed., *Adams-Jefferson Letters,* II, 391; Jefferson to James Madison, Oct. 28, 1785, in Boyd, ed., *Papers,* VIII, 682; also, Jefferson to John Jay, Aug. 23, 1785, *ibid.,* 426; Jefferson to Geismar, Sept. 6, 1785, *ibid.,* 500; Jefferson to Archibald Stuart, Jan. 25, 1786, *ibid.,* IX, 218; Jefferson to John Page, May 4, 1786, *ibid.,* 445–46; Jefferson to Thomas Pleasants, May 8, 1786, *ibid.,* 472–73; Jefferson to Brissot De Warville, Aug. 16, 1786, *ibid.,* X, 262; Jefferson to George Washington, Aug. 14, 1787, *ibid.,* XII, 38; Jefferson to James Madison, Dec. 20, 1787, *ibid.,* 442; Jefferson to Edward Rutledge, July 18, 1788, *ibid.,* XIII, 378; Abernethy, ed., *Notes,* 157; Jefferson to John Taylor, May 28, 1816, in Lipscomb and Bergh, eds., *Writings,* XV, 18; Jefferson to Major John Cartwright, June 5, 1824, *ibid.,* XVI, 48; Jefferson to John Adams, April 25, 1794, in Cappon, ed., *Adams-Jefferson Letters,* I, 254; Jefferson to John Adams, Feb. 28, 1796, *ibid.,* 260. Italics in the original.

Only once, late in his life, did Jefferson attempt a formal definition of his idea of freedom. Liberty, he wrote to Isaac H. Tiffany in 1819, "is unobstructed action according to our will, but rightful liberty is unobstructed action according to our will within limits drawn around us by the equal rights of others." This is very close to being the least edifying comment Jefferson ever made on the subject. It is abstract and colorless, little more than an outline, and possessing none of the eloquence which seemingly came so easy to the great Virginian. The conventional distinction was made between the freedom men possessed in a state of nature and that liberty under law ("rightful liberty") which they acquired as a result of their coming together with other men to create a civil society. Yet Jefferson chose to ignore another significant distinction, often made in previous comments, between the normative (i.e., natural rights) and the descriptive (circumstantial) aspects of his idea of liberty. There was, in fact, nothing in his definition which gave the least hint that he was aware of the spaciousness and the richness of the American continent and its enormous potential for liberty, although, in fact, such awareness conditioned all his thinking. Nor did he acknowledge in writing to Tiffany that only when there is reasonable agreement among men concerning the goals of their society, only when compromise is accepted as a normal part of the political and social process, did his idea of liberty have a reasonable chance of success. And, despite his admiration for both Epictetus and Epicurus, Jefferson ignored the point of their comments concerning freedom: that men can become truly free only as a result of a deliberate, self-induced effort to change the nature of their desires and aspirations. Jefferson's idea of liberty was, in fact, very much in the tradition of what the English philosopher, Sir Isaiah Berlin, has called "negative" freedom. In this formulation the individual is free when he is completely exempt from the coercion of other men or of institutions in at least some significant areas of endeavor. The philosophers of "negative" liberty also assert that men possess a measure of freedom if they have rights and immunities which may not be taken away from them without due cause, and when there are opportunities to choose and acceptable choices available. Jefferson appears to have accepted this conventional definition throughout most of his adult life. From the *Summary View* of 1774 and the *Declaration* of 1776 until his death fifty years later there is no evidence of a significant modification in his basic idea of freedom. His thinking about liberty, original only in detail and emphasis, became identifiably American when he wrote with eloquence, as in the *Declaration of Independence,* of man's inalienable right to liberty, and when he spoke and wrote with the passion of a lover and the vision of a prophet about his country's future as an "Empire for liberty."[12]

University of Tennessee at Nashville.

[12] Jefferson to Isaac H. Tiffany, April 4, 1819, in Edward Dumbauld, ed., *The Political Writings of Thomas Jefferson: Representative Selections* (Indianapolis, 1955), The American Heritage Series, 55; Berlin, *Two Concepts,* 7-16; Isaiah Berlin, *Four Essays on Liberty* (New York, 1969), pp. XXVIII-XL, XLVIII, 122-24, 126, 158; for further evidence of Jefferson's bias toward a circumstantial definition of freedom see Lieutenant Francis Hall, *Travels in Canada, and the United States, in 1816 and 1817* (2nd ed., London, 1819), 292.

XIX

JEFFERSONIAN REVISIONS OF LOCKE: EDUCATION, PROPERTY-RIGHTS, AND LIBERTY

By David M. Post

This essay considers the history of a particular interpretation of individual liberty during the period it was reconstructed and introduced in the United States by the Jeffersonian Republicans. The interpretation of freedom here considered—a positive or, following C. B. Macpherson, a "developmental" one—showed two faces in the early U.S. republic.[1] Theories of education and of property-right, when taken together, indicate the reworking of prevalent Lockean beliefs about political liberty. The parallel republican deviations from Lockean theory should be examined not only by those wishing to focus a clearer image of the Jeffersonian movement; consideration of these deviations also enriches current debate over what our own conceptions of liberty need to include. Locke's formulation of the natural right to property and knowledge by fully rational members of society remained influential ideas in the early U.S. Departures from Locke by the Jeffersonians, however, indicate a transformation.

Historiographic Perspectives. Sixty years have softened the too-sharp image which Carl Becker presented of Jeffersonian political theory. Today historians have a far broader, though less focused view. "The lineage is direct," Becker had asserted. "Jefferson copied Locke and Locke quoted Hooker."[2] Historians, in reacting to this view of Jefferson as Locke's direct heir, have widened our understanding of Jeffersonian thought. Just as surely, earlier understandings have been eroded, and little agreement now remains as to exactly what any definition of the Jeffersonian Republicans should include. Who were they? One of the most useful characterizations was provided by Louis Brandeis: "Those who won our independence believed that the final end of the state was to make men free to develop their faculties. . . . They valued liberty as both an end and as a means."[3] In order to consider this evaluation, interpretations of the republican movement need to deal with the associated Jeffersonian transformations of educational theory and property theory. And the literature of the period suggests that a key to understanding these transformations is the emergence of a developmental concept of liberty.

The original point of contention following Becker's study concerned Jefferson's deviation from Locke on the inclusion of property among the trilogy of natural rights. Jefferson substituted "pursuit of happiness" within the famous Lockean "life, liberty, and property." Locke's own phrase was preserved in the

---

[1] For an exposition of a "developmental" concept of freedom, aimed at revising the firm division set by Isaiah Berlin between negative and positive liberty, see C. B. Macpherson, *Democratic Theory* (New York, 1973). Such a concept inheres in the premise that "man is not a bundle of appetites seeking satisfaction but a bundle of conscious energies seeking to be exerted" (5). For a defense of positive liberty see Lawrence Crocker, *Positive Liberty* (Boston, 1980).

[2] Carl Becker, *The Declaration of Independence* (New York, 1922), 79.

[3] *Whitney vs. California*, 274 U.S. 357, 375.

standard common law *Commentaries* of William Blackstone,[4] and in such other
eighteenth-century American documents as the 1777 *Declaration on the Violation
of Rights.* While the historians Adrienne Koch and Stuart Brown continued to
affirm Jefferson's basic adherence to Lockean property theory, others began to
question this view. In the 1930s and 1940s Gilbert Chinard, T. V. Smith, Eugene
Perry Link, and Herbert Schneider, among others, all departed from Becker's
thesis. Gary Wills and Morton White have further reinterpreted Jeffersonian
thought.[5]

Recently one reviewer has suggested that republican "revisionism" may have
over-extended itself with regard to sweeping away Locke's influence. "This new
broom has also swept away much that is the truth," notes Isaac Kramnick, and
he finds the reports of Locke's intellectual death to be (*pace* Mark Twain)
"greatly exaggerated."[6] Nevertheless, in the past half century historians generally
have come to accept the deviation of the republicans from parts of Lockean
theory. Interpretations now must deal with the character of those republican
deviations in order to form a clearer image of early intellectual life in the U.S.A.
We should therefore narrow the discussion of republicanism to a question which
is central to the understanding of republican style: was the movement, as Brandeis

---

[4] "The third absolute right, inherent in every Englishman, is that of property." William
Blackstone, *Commentaries* (Oxford, 1768), I, 138.

[5] Adrienne Koch, *The Philosophy of Thomas Jefferson* (New York, 1943). She reported
(175) that "there is ample proof, therefore, for Jefferson's recognition of property as a
basic 'natural right.' "

Stuart Brown, *The First Republicans* (Syracuse, 1954). Brown asserted (10) that "the
language of the *Declaration* intended no departure from the familiar concepts."

Gilbert Chinard, *Thomas Jefferson, the Apostle of Americanism* (Boston, 1929).
Chinard discovered (84) that "when Lafayette submitted to Jefferson his 'Declaration
des droits de l'homme,' Jefferson put in brackets the words 'droit a la propriete,' thus
suggesting their elimination from the list of natural rights."

T. V. Smith, "Thomas Jefferson and the Perfectibility of Mankind," *Ethics* (July,
1943). Smith suggested that Jefferson might have viewed property as a social right.

Eugene Perry Link, *Democratic-Republican Societies, 1790-1800* (New York, 1942).
Link wrote that Jefferson and Paine probably diverged from Lockean principles.

Herbert W. Schneider, *A History of American Philosophy* (New York, 1946). Schneider
found (246) that "the Scottish enlightenment was probably the most potent single tradition
in the American enlightenment."

Gary Wills, *Inventing America* (Garden City, 1978). Wills further corroborates
Schneider on the influence of the Scottish enlightenment.

Morton White, *The Philosophy of the American Revolution* (New York, 1978). White
terms property an "adventitious" right in the Jeffersonian view, and he traces the origin
of this idea primarily to Jean Jaques Burlamaqui (1694-1748), the Swiss jurist who based
all political rights on principles of natural law.

[6] Isaac Kramnick, "Republican Revisionism Revisited," *The American Historical
Quarterly* (June 1982). As Jefferson did consider Locke one of Europe's three greatest
thinkers, and hung his portrait at Monticello, it is impossible to dispute this point. More
debatable is Professor Kramnick's assertion that "Chapter 5 of the Second Treatise, 'On
Property,' became the received wisdom in advanced radical circles in the late eighteenth-
century," at least unless American radicals are excepted by Kramnick. On the contrary,
it is the very pervasiveness of Locke's influence which makes so significant the departure
from his theories of education and property right.

suggested, indeed a move toward what might today be described as a developmental concept of individual liberty? Answers to this question must begin with the parallel concerns of the republican movement, namely, public education and property as a social right, best understood as divergences from the type of individualism which republicans associated with English thought. In departing from a concept of negative liberty championed by Locke, did not the republicans consciously approach a developmental concept of freedom?[7]

If Kramnick is correct in suspecting Locke's influence to be alive and well in the late eighteenth-century, then it is necessary to review the points of Lockean theory from which Americans diverged. Only against the backdrop of Locke's pervasive influence can Jeffersonian republican features be historically appreciated.

Locke on Property and Education. "It is necessary for me to be as I am," wrote Locke, "God and nature have made me so; but there is nothing I have is essential to me. An accident or disease may very much alter my color or shape; a fever or fall may take away my reason or memory, or both; and an apoplexy leave neither sense, nor understanding, no nor life." In Locke's view the relationship of an individual to his behavior, character, or *properties* is similar to an individual's relationship to his knowledge. In both cases all humans equally must acquire their character or knowledge in the world. "So if it be asked," Locke concluded, "whether it be essential to me or any other particular corporeal being to have reason, I say no, no more than it is essential to this white thing to have words on it."[8]

Despite the egalitarian premise, Locke's theory of property attempted to explain and justify as rightful the divisions of social class. He wanted to show "how men might have come to have property in several parts of that which God gave to Mankind in common, and that without any express compact of all the commoners."[9] Justification for the institution of property was obtained first by granting man control and propriety over his own person. "Though the Earth, and all inferior creatures be common to all men, yet every man has a property in his own *person.* This no body has any Right to but himself. The labor of his body, and the work of his hands, we must say, are properly his." Because Locke regarded individuals the proprietors of their own person, they are able to acquire property freely. "Whatsoever he removes out of the State that Nature hath provided, and left in it, he hath mixed his Labor with and joyned to it something that is his own, and thereby makes it his Property" (*ibid,* 328-29). In the remaining step of explaining the institution of a class society, Locke argued that those who *have* used their labor to appropriate property are also those who most have obeyed God's will—they then must be regarded as the most rational

[7] For a differing interpretation see J. W. Cooke, "Jefferson On Liberty," *Journal of the History of Ideas,* 34 (1973, 563-76). Cooke presents Jefferson as an exponent of negative liberty. However, he does not fully deal with Jeffersonian educational programs or the property theory of republicanism as a movement, nor does he examine Lockean views comparatively.

[8] John Locke, *An Essay Concerning Human Understanding,* Alexander Campbell Fraser, ed., (New York, 1959), II, 58.

[9] John Locke, *Two Treatises of Government,* Peter Laslett, ed., (New York, 1965), 327.

in addition to being the most industrious, for God gave the world "to the use of the Industrious and Rational (and Labour was to be his title to it); not to the Fancy or Covetousness of the Quarrelsome and Contentious" (*ibid*, 333). Thus, Locke was able to justify the ownership of property by the contemporary landowners and gentry, since appropriation had marked that class as the most rational. Macpherson terms the differential rationality in Locke's notion a "bourgeois concept," different from prior, Aristotelian views of masters and slaves. "With Locke the difference in rationality was not inherent in men, not implanted in them by God or Nature; on the contrary, it was socially acquired by virtue of different economic positions."[10]

Having explained the establishment and division of social class, Locke's definition of "property" at once excluded the landless laborer from society while also binding him to it. For the purpose of limiting full membership in the state to the upper class, Locke regarded *land* as representative of *all* property, since civil government was formed by landowners who were its primary participants: "The great and *chief end,* therefore, of men's uniting into Commonwealths, and putting themselves under government, is the *Preservation of their Property.*" States owed their existence to the collective action of the fully rational, property-holding class. One aim of government was the protection of rights to property acquisition; "property" in this sense meant physical capital. However, for purposes of including the landless laborer under the laws of the state, "property" was sometimes broadened to have a meaning nearer to that of "properties" in an environmental sense. Although the right to liberty and property was natural, liberties and human properties were acquired by labor from use of the environment, just as surely as all knowledge was a comprehension of the external world. For the purposes of including the laborer under the law, Locke defined the term "property" broadly to mean "lives, liberties, and estates," including what economists of education today term "human capital."[11] Finally, this ambiguity in Locke's egalitarianism, could result by regarding a proletariat as *in* but not *of* society.

Individuals are born without inherent difference. However, they develop and distinguish themselves in the world just as social classes were developed. Both individuals and classes acquire from the world their properties (in the two senses of the word). But what can be acquired can also be alienated. Thus, because *liberty* and *property* are phrased together in Locke's trilogy of natural rights and have equal status by origin, the terms also have equal economic status. Liberty as well as property may freely be transferred by one class to another in a contract, since Locke gave individuals propriety over their own person. Furthermore, for Locke, appropriation rather than production most fulfilled divine mandate; liberties and labor of the lower classes were acquired in justice.

Lockean educational theory is consistent with his thinking on human development and personality. His *Thoughts Concerning Education* was first written as a letter to Edward Clarke for the benefit of instructing Clarke's son at home. Earlier Locke had written: "Where the hand is used to the plough and the spade, the head is seldom elevated in mysterious reasoning. 'Tis well if men of

[10] C. B. Macpherson, *The Political Theory of Possessive Individualism* (New York, 1962), 246.

[11] Laslett, 21.

that rank (to say nothing of the other sex) can comprehend plain propositions." [12] In his *Thoughts* Locke wrote that "virtue is harder to be got than knowledge from the world." [13] Accordingly, moral education was of paramount importance to him. Locke did not think moral intuition was innate, and he stated clearly that "children cannot well understand what injustice is until they understand property" (*ibid.*, 84). Because Locke conceived education as of primarily moral importance, it was understandable that he would advise gentlemen to give their sons a *private* education (i.e., taking place in the private households of the gentry): "A father that breeds his son at home has the opportunity to have him more in his own company, and there give him what encouragement he thinks fit; and can keep him better from the taint of servants and the meaner sort of people than is possible to be done abroad" (*ibid*, 54). In a Lockean perspective, education never was designed to equalize the differential rationality and property-right assumed by his political theory. Locke was clear as to just who should take the time to study: "Those, methinks, who by the industry and parts of their ancestors have been set free from a constant drudgery to their backs and bellies, should bestow some of their spare time on their heads and open their minds by some trials and essays in all sorts of reasoning." [14]

A view of education for the consumption of rational property-owners, education beyond the access of "the meaner sort of people," set the stage for eighteenth-century English debates over grammar and charity schools. Taken to the extreme, Locke's egalitarian epistemological premises eventually led Bernard de Mandeville to criticize educational reform. Mandeville's essay on charity schools, in his 1723 edition of *The Fable of the Bees,* was a frank defense of inequality. "Thinking and reasoning justly, as Mr. Locke has rightly observed, require time and practice. Those that have not used themselves to thinking but just on their present necessities, make poor work of it when they try beyond that." [15] Mandeville was genuinely concerned with the effect on society of educating the poor. Who would perform menial work, if not the poor? Not even the Christian evangelism of the charity-school movement could persuade Mandeville that such education would not have dangerous consequences. "The knowledge of the working poor should be confin'd within the verge of their occupations," he warned, "and never extended beyond what relates to their calling. The more a shepherd, a plowman or any other peasant knows of the world, and things that are foreign to his labour or employment, the less fit he'll be to go through the fatigues and hardships of it with chearfulness and content" (*ibid*, 288).

The Jeffersonian Republicans. When turning to consider the republican divergence from Locke, it is useful to recall the original wording of the *Declaration of Independence:* "inherent and inalienable rights." Because Locke considered

---

[12] John Locke, *The Reasonableness of Christianity,* George Ewing, ed. (Chicago, 1965), 193. Contrast this comment with Jefferson's letter to Peter Carr: "State a moral case to a ploughman and a professor. The former will decide it as well and often better than the latter. . . ." Lee, 146.

[13] Peter Gay, ed., *John Locke on Education* (New York, 1964), 49.

[14] John Locke, *Of the Conduct of the Understanding,* Francis Garforth, ed. (New York, 1966), 53.

[15] Mandeville, *The Fable of the Bees* (Oxford, 1924), II, 190.

virtue and character to be acquired, any notion of moral "development" in the "state of nature" in his theory was out of place. Jeffersonians thought rights inalienable precisely because they had roots inherent in the human being. That property right was not similarly viewed by Jefferson to have such inherent roots is also clear from his substitution of "pursuit of happiness" for Locke's "property."

"Revisionist" historians, to use Kramnick's term, have detected the influence of Scottish moral sense philosophy in Jeffersonian thought. To cite but one example, Henry Home (Lord Kames) reported a universal moral sense, present even in uncivilized man. Moral sense "proceeds from a direct feeling we have upon presenting the object, without the intervention of any sort of reflection. . . ." Home claimed that "the Author of our nature has not left our action to be directed by so weak a principle as reason."[16] Compare Jefferson's statement to Peter Carr: "He who made us would have been a pitiful bungler if he had made the rules of our moral conduct a matter of science." Jefferson then goes on to explain that "the moral sense, or conscience, is as much a part of man as his leg or arm. It is given to all human beings in a stronger or weaker degree, as force of members is given them in greater or weaker degree. It may be strengthened by exercise, as may any particular limb of the body."[17] Jefferson wrote to DuPont de Nemours explicitly: "I believe . . . that morality, compassion, generosity are innate elements in the human constitution."[18]

The Jeffersonian belief in an essentially inherent moral capacity inspired republican views of property and of education quite different from those of John Locke. Since for Jefferson natural rights had roots in human nature, he thought the right to liberty to be in a separate class from the right to property. Locke had treated all rights as though they were properties; indeed, they were represented and symbolized by property and could, like property, be acquired or alienated. Individuals were considered to be without inherent character, but distinctions of both class and individuals were produced by the environment. For Jeffersonians human nature indicated a basic set of rights, but property was incidental and adventitious, a right produced only after formation of a social contract, a social rather than natural right. Thomas Paine gave the most detailed explanation:

Of the first kind there are rights of thinking, speaking, forming and giving opinions, and perhaps all those which can be exercised by the individual without the aid of exterior assistance—or in other words, rights of personal competency. Of the second kind are those of personal protection, of acquiring and possessing property, in which the individual power is less than the natural. . . . These are civil rights or rights of compact, and are distinguishable from natural rights."[19]

Joel Barlow, in 1793, asserted that "it is the person, not the property, that

---

[16] Henry Home, *Essays* (Edinburgh, 1751), 63, 98-99. See also Arthur McGuinness, *Henry Home, Lord Kames* (New York, 1970), 43.

[17] Adrienne Koch and William Peden, eds., *The Life and Selected Writings of Thomas Jefferson* (New York, 1944), 430-31.

[18] Gilbert Chinard, ed., *The Correspondence of Jefferson and Du Pont de Nemours* (Baltimore, 1931), 257.

[19] Cited in Chinard, *Correspondence,* LXXII.

exercises the will, and is capable of enjoying happiness. It is therefore the person for whom government is instituted."[20] It was with this understanding of property right that Jefferson could make his well-known statement to James Madison: "The earth belongs to the living," he charged. "The Portion occupied by any individual ceases to be his when himself ceases to be, and reverts to society. If the society has formed no rules for the appropriation of its lands in severalty, it will be taken by the first occupants.... But the child, the legatee, or the creditor takes it not by any natural right, but by the law of society of which they are members, and to which they are subject."[21] Comments such as these do support a revision of Becker's thesis, and a conclusion that Jeffersonians deviated from Locke's including property among the natural rights.

Two policies in particular reflect the demotion of property from a natural to a social right. The first was Jefferson's own campaign to abolish primogeniture. His concern was to govern the rules of inheritance by passing a law to divide the Virginia estates of the "pseudo-aristocracy." In his autobiography he reflected that "if the eldest son could eat twice as much, or do double work, it might be a natural evidence of his right to a double portion. But being on par with his brothers and sisters, he should be on par also in the partition of the patrimony" (*ibid*, 45). Yet more revealing than this issue was the linkage Jefferson placed between suffrage and a fifty-acre state gift of land. Like Locke, Jefferson did view landowners as the most responsible guardians of social welfare. They had a physical stake in the preservation of society and were "tied to their country by ... the most lasting bonds" (*ibid*, 377). However, at the same time that Jefferson limited suffrage to landowners, he also included in the Virginia constitution a provision giving to all white males over twenty-one the necessary property—no great contribution, perhaps, from the viewpoint of those excluded from the plan. And yet, in its direction, does not Jefferson's move verge on the conception, as in Macpherson, of man as a "doer, an exerter, a developer and enjoyer of his human capacities?"[22]

The answer is clearly yes, if one considers the associated views of liberty found in Jeffersonian theories of education. One finds everywhere a linkage between property reform and general enlightenment, for the "pseudo-aristocracy" of wealth was thought challenged by education. Educators were assigned a new responsibility in the republic, and they felt a special mission. Enlightened, literate citizens were seen to benefit society as well as themselves, and their participation was thought at least as important as that of property owners. Therefore education was conceived to be a public task. Jefferson's 1779 *Bill For the More General Diffusion of Knowledge* expressed the provision of education as a positive duty on the state: "... Whence it becomes expedient for promoting public happiness that those persons, whom nature hath endowed with genius and virtue, should be rendered by liberal education" capable of government.[23] Years later, in a note to John Adams on Virginia's abolition of primogeniture, Jefferson would recall that "these laws, drawn up by myself, laid the ax to the foot of pseudo-aristocracy. And had another which I prepared been adopted by

[20] Joel Barlow, *Letter to the National Convention of France* (New York, 1793), 32.
[21] Koch & Peden, 488.
[22] Macpherson, *Democratic Theory*, 51.
[23] *The Papers of Thomas Jefferson* (Princeton, 1950), Julian P. Boyd, ed., II, 526-33.

the legislature, our work would have been complete. It was a bill for the more general diffusion of knowledge."[24]

Robert Coram, a leader in the Newcastle, Delaware, Patriotic Society, directly attacked the Lockean theory of property in 1791. In a diatribe against Sir William Blackstone, Coram wrote that the English jurist should well have known that "the unequal distribution of property was the parent of almost all disorders of government." Rather than to suggest redistribution of property, Coram saw in this "plain truth a foundation whereon to erect a system, which like the sun in the universe, will transmit light, life, and harmony to all under its influence, I mean—A System Of Equal Education."[25] Coram saw a misuse of schooling in aristocratic societies, which he opposed to an idealized vision of the American Indians. "Among those people all the gifts of providence are in common. We do not see, as in civilized nations, part of the citizens sent to colleges to learn to cheat the rest of their liberties, who are condemned to be hewers of wood and drawers of water."[26] This concern led the Newcastle Patriotic Society to pass a motion recommending establishment of schools "whereby the unfortunate children of indigence and neglect may be educated and enlightened among the children of opulence and vigilance, which is an essential means of preserving that equality so necessary to preservation of a pure republican government."[27]

Samuel Harrison Smith was a co-winner of the American Philosophical Society prize for essays on the type of education proper in a republic. He wrote that "if any circumstance be more connected with the virtue and happiness of the United States than another it is the substitution of works defining correctly political, moral, and religious duty" in accordance with "the radical ideas we have already established and which are in great measure peculiar to us."[28] Although a stalwart federalist on many issues, even Noah Webster could write that "two regulations are essential to the continuance of republican governments: 1) such a distribution of lands and such principles of descent and alienation as shall give every citizen a power of acquiring what his industry merits; 2) such a system of education as gives every citizen an opportunity of acquiring knowledge and fitting himself for places of trust" (ibid, 65).

Republican writers on education exhibited a bias against Lockean individualism. "The republican student," wrote Benjamin Rush (1745-1813), "must be taught to amass wealth, but it must be only to increase his power of contributing to the wants and needs of the state" (ibid, 14). What educational view could be more compatible with Jefferson's comment that "stable ownership is the gift of social law?"[29] Even more than property owners, educated citizens were considered to be the guard against tyranny. Through the individual's pursuit of hap-

---

[24] Gordon C. Lee, ed., *Crusade Against Ignorance, Thomas Jefferson On Education* (New York, 1961), 164.

[25] Frederick Rudolph, ed., *Essays On Education in the Early Republic* (Cambridge, Mass., 1965), 111.

[26] Rudolph, 130.

[27] Philip S. Foner, ed., *The Democratic Republican Societies, 1790-1800: A Documentary Source Book* (Westport, Conn., 1976), 32.

[28] Rudolph, 216.

[29] Koch & Peden, 630.

piness and development of potential, the general good of republican society was also thought to be increased. "If a nation expects to be ignorant and free, in a state of civilization, it expects what never was and never will be," wrote Jefferson.[30] A nation's freedom was correlated with knowledge, and so was individual liberty. Jefferson told Edward Carrington that to have newspapers without government was preferable to government without newspapers. "But I should mean that every man should receive those papers and be capable of reading them."[31] In his American Philosophical Society essay, which shared honors with Smith's, Samuel Knox also connected knowledge with freedom: "Ignorance, more especially literary ignorance, has often been the parent and stupid nurse of civil slavery." Smith simply stated that "an enlightened nation is always most tenacious of its rights."[32]

The Jeffersonian Republicans consistently drew a connection between the general welfare and the development of its citizens. Perhaps for this reason, despite the pervasiveness of Lockean views, they placed more responsibility for education upon the state. Samuel Knox wrote in his A.P.S. essay that "the celebrated Locke himself not excepted, we find very few who have attempted to offer any plausible objections to a public education." Samuel Harrison Smith agreed. He acknowledged Locke as a partisan of private education because of the "sacrifice, alleged to be produced, of morality and honesty." Smith nonetheless favored public education, outside the control of private households. Associating private education with the aristocracy, Smith observed that "prejudices are as hereditary as titles, and you may almost universally know the sentiments of the son by those of the father" (ibid, 307, 208).

If the nation did benefit from the education of its citizens, if the state was to control the process, and if the equal opportunity to develop one's potential was an emerging ideal, then Jeffersonians were also clear that the public must pay for it. Jefferson wrote to the Virginia judge George Wythe that "the tax which will be paid is not more than the thousandth part of what will be paid to kings, priests, and nobles, who will rise up among us if we leave the people in ignorance."[33] Benjamin Rush had similar thoughts: "Shall the estates of orphans, bachelors and persons who have no children be taxed to pay for support of schools from which they can derive no benefit? I answer in the affirmative to the first part of the objection, and I deny the truth of the latter part of it. Every member of the community is interested in the propagation of virtue and knowledge in the state. . . . The bachelor will in time save his tax for this purpose by being able to sleep with fewer bolts and locks."[34]

Republicans were united in a belief that the state had some positive function in raising its citizens from ignorance and servitude to knowledge and freedom. Representative is Joel Barlow's advice to French republicans: "In order to be consistent with yourselves in removing those abuses which have laid the foundation of all offences against society, both in crimes and punishment, you ought to pay a farther attention to the necessity of public instruction. It is your duty

---

[30] Lee, 18-19.
[31] Koch & Peden, 411-12.
[32] Rudolph, 288, 307.
[33] Koch & Peden, 395.
[34] Rudolph, 6.

to establish a system of government that shall improve the morals of mankind. In raising a people from slavery to freedom, you have called them to act on a new theater, and it is a necessary part of your business to teach them how to perform their parts."[35] New York Governor DeWitt Clinton, President of the Free School Society, had this to say in an 1809 address: "the celebrated Locke . . . devoted the powers of his mighty intellect to the elucidation of education; but in the very threshold of his book we discover this radical error: his treatise is professedly intended for the children of gentlemen. . . . The consequence of this monstrous heresy has been that ignorance, the prolific parent of every crime and vice, has predominated over the great body of people."[36]

The popular appeal of this counter-Lockean movement surfaced in such newspaper editorializing as the following: "it may be said by some that it is reasonable there should be no such [public school] establishment, but that every man should pay for the education of his own children. Let it not be considered, however, that the general fund of knowledge is private property merely: it is public stock on which depends the well-being of the community."[37] Such counter-Lockean sentiments culminated in the rhetoric (if not always actions) surrounding the establishment of early State school systems. In Kentucky, for example, a report of the first Commission on Education (1823) concluded that "the cultivated minds of the people constitute the chief treasure of the state. There is an infinite expansibility in the mind of man; and it is among the first and most important duties of the government to improve the elasticity and cultivate the intellectual energy of the whole community. . . . Knowledge is power, and the only way to preserve an equality of the latter is to promote a general diffusion of the former."[38] Far from the Lockean model which had allowed rational property owners freely to choose an education for their children, Jeffersonians consciously expressed a different ideal. Samuel Harrison Smith, in the A.P.S. essay written just ninety years after John Locke's death, could nonetheless depart radically from Locke's views. Locke had written, "nobody is under an obligation to know everything. Knowledge and science in general is the business only of those who are at ease and leisure."[39] Smith proposed, however, that "it be made punishable by law for a parent to neglect offering his child to the preceptor for instruction."[40]

Care always must be taken to avoid reading nineteenth-century conflicts into prior periods. The Jeffersonian Republicans, after all, were not nascent socialists. Nor can their concerns easily be applied to educational problems of the twentieth-century, or to our ongoing attempt to conceptualize liberty. But the continuing discussion of these issues is deepened by consideration of the Jeffersonians. Locke had emphasized property as a right antecedent to government, and took unequal distribution as proof that property owners were the fully rational members of a society and, thus, its fullest participants. For the Jeffersonians property-right

[35] Barlow, 58.
[36] Carl F. Kaestle, ed., *Joseph Lancaster and the Monitorial School Movement* (New York, 1973), 154.
[37] (Louisville) *Public Adviser,* Nov. 17, 1818.
[38] George Robertson, Broadside, copy in Filson Club, Louisville.
[39] Garforth, 55.
[40] Rudolph, 210.

derived from social life, and reason was equally sufficient in all individuals. They believed that moral education, explicitly as such, was not necessary since there was thought to exist an innate, universal moral capacity. Locke thought virtue to be acquired environmentally and, at his most extreme, had seen education to expand the powers of those having property and leisure. Both in regard to property and to knowledge, Jeffersonians shifted responsibility for the development of human powers away from the exclusive domain of propertied individuals. The divergence of early U.S. thinkers from Lockean educational and property theories marked the start of a divergent view of individual liberty as well. If they valued freedom as an end as well as a means, then they also began to view the opportunity for human development as a proper concern of republican government.

University of Chicago.

XX

BENJAMIN FRANKLIN AND THE PENAL LAWS

By Marcello Maestro

Benjamin Franklin's biographers point out in their studies that he was a man of many talents: printer, engraver, bookseller, journalist, educator, scientist, inventor, statesman, diplomat, humanitarian, essayist, philosopher. It is strange that one subject to which Franklin devoted much time and thought has to date drawn little attention: the criminal law.

Franklin was slow to show interest in penal legislation. His first writing dealing with penal justice was a semi-facetious piece entitled *The Speech of Polly Baker,* published anonymously in 1747 and often described as one of Franklin's hoaxes because many readers were led to believe that it was the account of a real event. Smyth included this "Speech" in his edition of Franklin's works despite the fact that he had no absolute proof of its authorship.[1] A thorough study by Max Hall has since proved conclusively the authenticity of Franklin's authorship, and Hall's conclusion has been endorsed by the editors of *The Papers of Benjamin Franklin,* now being published under the auspices of the American Philosophical Society and Yale University.[2]

On the surface, *The Speech of Polly Baker* was a light-hearted piece, intended to entertain its readers. It presented a fictional trial in which an unmarried and obviously attractive Polly Baker, accused of having had a fifth natural child, not only was acquitted, but by her plea so moved one of the judges that he decided to marry her and become the father of all her future children. It was an amusing story, but also a protest against existing legislation, in particular against the law which prohibited sexual intercourse outside wedlock and condemned the mother of an illegitimate child to the payment of a fine and to a public whipping. This law, a product of puritanical attitudes, was also unfair because the father of the child usually went entirely free. Franklin not only protested against this particular law, but by having Polly ask several rhetorical questions of the court, showed that the whole penal code needed reexamination. Several passages in the "Speech" imply a criticism of the existing system of justice. In one of these passages Polly Baker affirms that laws are sometimes too severe and unjust, and that unjust laws should be repealed. At another point Polly makes an eloquent plea for the elimination of religious influence on the administration of secular justice. Referring to the accusation that her transgressions violated the precepts of religion, Polly says: "If mine is a religious offence, leave it to religious punishments. You have already excluded me from the comforts of your church communion. Is not that sufficient? You believe I have offended Heaven, and must suffer eternal fire:

[1] *The Writings of Benjamin Franklin,* ed. A. H. Smyth (New York and London, 1905–07), II, 463–64n.

[2] Max Hall, *Benjamin Franklin and Polly Baker: The History of a Literary Deception* (Chapel Hill, 1960); *The Papers of Benjamin Franklin* (New Haven, 1960–), III, 120–23 (complete text of *The Speech of Polly Baker,* 123–25).

will not that be sufficient? What need is there, then, of your additional fines and whipping?"

The thesis that violations of religious rules should be of no concern to secular justice was later upheld by Montesquieu and Beccaria, who, speaking in terms very similar to Franklin's, stated that those guilty of religious offenses should be punished here on earth, simply by their exclusion from religious services. The absurdities and contradictions of certain laws are described by Polly Baker: "What must poor young women do, whom customs and nature forbid to solicit men, and who cannot force themselves upon husbands, when the laws take no care to provide them any; and yet severely punish them if they do their duty without them; the duty of the first and great command of nature and nature's God, *increase and multiply?*"

The Speech of Polly Baker was the first criticism made by Franklin of the existing penal system. Its influence is proved by the attention it received everywhere and by the popularity it quickly acquired. First printed in *The General Advertiser* (London, April 15, 1747), it was reprinted within a month by a number of newspapers in London and other English cities. On July 20 it was printed in America by *The Boston Weekly Post-Boy* and soon after reprinted by *The New York Gazette* and *The New York Weekly Journal*. The "Speech" soon became known also in France where several writers—among them Voltaire, Diderot, and Morellet—found its contents helpful and made use of it in their fight for a more enlightened society.[3]

Despite its success, *The Speech of Polly Baker* remained for a long time an isolated item. Franklin was then occupied with many other activities. In 1748 he was elected a member of the city council of Philadelphia and in 1750 he became a member of the Assembly of Pennsylvania, an office to which he would be reelected several times. During those years he traveled to Europe and also worked on his scientific studies, as shown by the publication of several papers on electricity. All this did not prevent him from following with constant attention new books and pamphlets which dealt with penal problems. These were the years in which Montesquieu published *The Spirit of Laws,* Frederick II enacted the first reforms in the penal system of Prussia, Louis de Jaucourt wrote his thoughtful article on crime for the French Encyclopedia, and Voltaire began his fight against the miscarriages of French justice.

In 1762 Jean Calas was executed in Toulouse after being found guilty of killing his own son. Voltaire studied the case and was able to demonstrate that the judges had condemned the man unjustly, that Jean Calas was the victim of a judicial error, and that his son had not been killed but had, instead, committed suicide. In his pamphlet, *Treatise on Tolerance,* Voltaire gave a detailed account of the case, showing how faulty the legal system was, and how much the criminal law in France was in need of reform, as indeed, it was in all countries. Franklin read Voltaire's booklet, which had been published anonymously, and commented on it:

I have lately received a number of new pamphlets from England and France, among which is a piece of Voltaire's on the subject of religious toleration. . . .

[3]For the success of the "Speech" and the reactions of French writers: Max Hall, *op. cit.,* 58–75, 87–88, 126ff.; Carl Van Doren, *Benjamin Franklin* (New York, 1952), 721–22.

There is in it abundance of good sense and sound reasoning, mixed with some of those pleasantries that mark the author as strongly as if he had affixed his name. Take one of them as a sample: "The Toulouse tribunal and several others have a peculiar jurisprudence; they admit a third, or a fourth, or a sixth of a proof, and with six hearsays on one side, three on the other, and four fourths of presumptions, they form three complete proofs. This splendid evidence entitles them to place a man on the wheel and put him to death.[4]

While this happened in France, an event occurred in Pennsylvania which stirred Franklin's feelings and led him to proclaim that complete respect for the laws was necessary in order to preserve a civilized society. The event was the massacre in December 1763, in Lancaster County, of Indian families by white men from the town of Paxton. These men—"the Paxton boys"—then threatened to come to Philadelphia and kill the Indians sheltered there. It became clear to many that they would find many sympathizers in the city who would do nothing to stop them and who might even join them in the onslaught. In an effort to influence public opinion against the tragedy that had already occurred and the threatened violence, Franklin speedily wrote and published, in January 1764, *A Narrative of the Late Massacres in Lancaster County*. This tract is a most eloquent plea for justice and morality, as well as a warm evocation of humanitarian sentiments. Referring to the murderers of the innocent Indians, Franklin expressed his indignation at their pretense that their action was justified by God's will: "These people think they have as their justification nothing less than the *Word of God*. With the Scriptures in their hands and mouths, they can set at nought that express command, *Thou shalt do no murder;* and justify their wickedness by the command given Joshua to destroy the heathen. Horrid perversion of Scripture and of religion! to father the worst of crimes on the God of peace and love!" Franklin then appealed to all citizens of good will for a determined stand against barbarism and lawlessness: "Let us rouse ourselves for shame and redeem the honour of our province from the contempt of its neighbours; let all good men join heartily and unanimously in support of the laws and in strengthening the hands of Government; that justice may be done, the wicked punished, and the innocent protected; otherwise we can, as a people, expect no blessing from Heaven; there will be no security for our persons or properties; anarchy and confusion will prevail over all, and violence without judgment dispose of every thing."

With great difficulty Governor John Penn and other notables succeeded in deterring the Paxton boys from carrying out their threats against the Indians of Philadelphia. Franklin's intervention undoubtedly contributed to averting new criminal acts, but the government was too weak to prosecute the guilty for the crimes already committed. For Franklin this failure was the cause of great disappointment and apprehension.[5]

---

[4]Franklin's letter to Henry Bouquet, Sept. 30, 1764, in *The Papers of Benjamin Franklin*, XI, 366–68.

[5]For the text of Franklin's *Narrative of the Late Massacres in Lancaster County* and the history of the episode: *The Papers of Benjamin Franklin*, XI, 42ff.; also R. E. Amacher, *Benjamin Franklin* (New York, 1962), 98–99, and Van Doren, *op. cit.,* 308–10.

In that same year, 1764, soon after Franklin's plea for justice and respect for the laws, Cesare Beccaria published in Italy his *Dei delitti e delle pene* which called for an attitude toward criminal legislation based on reason and opposed to all unnecessary cruelty. This little volume was to be recognized as the most important book of the century on penal law and was most influential on the reforms which would be enacted in the following decades. Since Franklin had a good reading knowledge of Italian, it may well be that he was able to acquaint himself with Beccaria's views from the original edition of the book. At any rate, the first English translation, *Essay on Crimes and Punishments,* appeared in 1767, only a few years after the Italian edition. In 1770 John Adams quoted Beccaria when he defended the British soldiers implicated in the so-called "Boston Massacre," and a few years later Jefferson transcribed in his *Commonplace Book* the most important passages of Beccaria's *Essay.* Franklin, a friend of both Adams and Jefferson, did not, however, discuss Beccaria in his writings or letters; nor did he ever correspond personally with the Milanese jurist. He did correspond, instead, with Gaetano Filangieri, a young Neapolitan writer of an old and distinguished family, whose ideas on legislation were strongly influenced by Beccaria.

It was Filangieri who helped sharpen Franklin's interest in criminal law and encouraged him to express his own views on the subject. The great difference in age between the two men—Franklin born in 1706, Filangieri in 1753[6]—did not prevent them from having the most friendly feelings and the greatest admiration for each other. Filangieri was undoubtedly flattered by the attention with which the American sage followed his publications. Franklin, on the other hand, was pleased to see in the work of Filangieri many ideas that he recognized as his own. Not only was Filangieri's Catholicism modified by a philosophical approach and desire to reform it, but, like Franklin, he had entered the universal fraternity of the Freemasons. This fact and the views expressed in his writings made the condemnation of his books by the Church of Rome unavoidable.

The first two volumes of Filangieri's opus, *The Science of Legislation,* appeared in 1780. In them the author dealt with general principles and the role of laws in the political and economic fields. He advocated political liberty, public education, religious tolerance, a more equitable distribution of property, and the curtailment of the clergy's excessive wealth. Franklin was then in Paris as American minister to France. He obtained a copy of Filangieri's volumes from Luigi Pio, the chargé d'affaires of the Kingdom of Naples in Paris, and was impressed by Filangieri's enlightened ideas, recognizing in him a courageous and skillful fighter for human progress.

Luigi Pio was a good friend of Filangieri, and on September 11, 1781 wrote him a letter:

Mr. Franklin, to whom I am bound by feelings of friendship, expressed the desire of reading your work, of which I had talked to him. I am glad I was able to satisfy him. To show his gratitude the American philosopher gave me a

---

[6]Several historians had accepted 1752 as the year of Filangieri's birth, but a careful study of original documents has shown that he was born on August 22, 1753: *Riformatori napoletani,* ed. Franco Venturi (Milan-Naples, 1962), 779–80.

large quarto edition of his essays on scientific experiments and I have been reading them with great enjoyment. Mr. Franklin reads Italian rather slowly, but he understands it perfectly well. He told me that he derives much pleasure from your theories which—these are his words—are presented with the utmost clarity and precision. He asked me to tell you that he is anxiously waiting for the volumes dealing with criminal legislation because they will be of special interest to his nation, still needing to be enlightened on this subject.[7]

A few days later Pio wrote to Filangieri that Franklin had handed him some of his political publications and had asked him to send them to Filangieri as a personal gift. This shipment reached Naples after a long delay and Filangieri acknowledged its arrival in his letter to Franklin of August 24, 1782. To show his gratitude for the "precious gift," Filangieri wrote that he was sending to Mr. Pio, at the Neapolitan Embassy in Paris, several copies of his *Science of Legislation,* which would be at Franklin's disposal if he wanted to pass them on to some of his friends. Filangieri also informed Franklin that he had almost finished the part of his work dealing with criminal law: it will consist, he added, of two volumes, one concerning the system of procedure, the other dealing with the penal code.[8]

On December 2, 1782, Filangieri wrote Franklin that the two volumes on criminal law were in the press and that he was anxious to have Franklin's opinion of them. In his letter, Filangieri, who was eager to marry the royal governess Carolina (or Charlotte) Frendel, also asked about the possibility of settling with her in America, where he might contribute with his legal knowledge to the preparation of laws for the new republic.[9]

Franklin received this letter on January 10, 1783, and promptly answered it the next day. His failure to answer the previous letter, he explained, was due to

[7]Translated from the Italian, letter preserved in the Municipal Museum "Gaetano Filangieri" of Naples; original text in *Riformatori napoletani,* 772–73n. As regards Franklin's knowledge of Italian, he wrote in his autobiography that in 1733 he began to study languages, first French and then Italian and Spanish (*The Works of Benjamin Franklin,* ed. J. Sparks [Boston, 1840], I, 126–27). He made good progress in Italian and acquired a perfect reading knowledge of the language, as confirmed by the above letter of Luigi Pio and by his own statement to the scientist Giambattista Beccaria (no relation to Cesare Beccaria), to whom he wrote on May 29, 1766: "I am pleased to hear that you read English, although you do not write it. I am in the same case with Italian. Hence we can correspond, if this pleases you, more easily if each of us writes his own language" (*The Papers of Benjamin Franklin,* XIII, 288). As a matter of fact, Franklin managed also to write in Italian, as shown by his letters to some Italian correspondents who presumably did not read English. His written Italian was far from perfect, but he was able to express his thoughts with sufficient clarity. Examples of Franklin's Italian are in A. Pace, *Benjamin Franklin and Italy* (Philadelphia, 1958), 9–10 and 367.

[8]Letter preserved in the Library of the Historical Society of Pennsylvania; original text in Pace, *op. cit.,* 398–99, or in *Riformatori napoletani,* 772–74. Filangieri's letters to Franklin were all written in Italian, while Franklin wrote to Filangieri in English. I wish to thank the Editorial Office of *The Papers of Benjamin Franklin* at Yale University, now directed by William B. Willcox, for letting me check the photostats of Franklin's correspondence. Special thanks go to Miss Mary L. Hart for her help in my research.

[9]Letter preserved in the Library of the Historical Society of Pennsylvania. For the original text in Italian: Pace, *op. cit.,* 399–401; *Riformatori napoletani,* 775–77.

a fairly long illness and to "the multiplicity of business that followed." After stating that the first two volumes of Filangieri's work had been read with great pleasure by him and some "very judicious persons" to whom he had lent them, Franklin added that he was now anxiously waiting for the next volumes on penal legislation. The criminal laws, said Franklin, were everywhere in so great disorder, and so much injustice was committed in the execution of them, that he had been sometimes inclined to think that it would be better to leave the punishment of injuries to private resentment. Concerning the possibility of Filangieri's settling in America, Franklin advised him to try to make a trip to America on some diplomatic mission for the Court of Naples. Such a trip, said Franklin, would enable Filangieri to see for himself if life in America would be satisfactory for him and his future wife.[10]

Filangieri's two volumes on criminal law were published in the summer and fall of 1783. On July 14, 1783, Filangieri informed Franklin that he was sending him the third volume of his work and that in a few days he would send him the fourth. In his letter Filangieri also informed Franklin that he was about to settle in the countryside, where he would have more peace than in the big city, and that in a few days he would marry Miss Frendel. Finally, he thanked Franklin for his advice about going to America, saying that in any case he would not do anything until the Court of Naples decided to send a minister to the new republic.[11]

On October 27, 1783 Filangieri thanked Franklin for a copy of the American state constitutions which he had received since his letter of July 14.[12] Franklin was slow in acknowledging receipt of the two volumes on criminal legislation, and Filangieri wrote him again on April 21, 1784: he wanted to know if everything had arrived and was eager to have Franklin's opinion of his new volumes.[13] Franklin's reply has not been preserved: one may surmise that he gave a favorable judgment on Filangieri's new work.

[10]Letter preserved in the Municipal Museum "Gaetano Filangieri" of Naples. For the text of this letter: *The Writings of Benjamin Franklin*, ed. A. H. Smyth, IX, 1–3.

[11]Letter preserved in the Library of the Historical Society of Pennsylvania; original text in Pace, *op. cit.*, 402. This letter is dated July 14, 1784; it is so classified by the Historical Society of Pennsylvania, and the date has not been questioned by Pace who reproduced the letter in his book. There is no doubt, however, that the letter is misdated and that Filangieri wrote by mistake 1784 instead of 1783. The date of July 14, 1783, is the correct one for the following reasons. The letter confirms that the third volume of *The Science of Legislation* is being shipped, while the fourth volume will follow shortly; the two volumes were, in fact, published and shipped in 1783, at the dates indicated. Filangieri informs Franklin that he will soon move to the country, away from Naples, and in fact a week or two later he moved to Cava. He also says that he is going to marry Miss Frendel in a few days, and the marriage did take place soon after July 14, 1783. Finally, in a letter of August 10, 1783 (preserved in the Library of the American Philosophical Society) Luigi Pio wrote Franklin that he was sending him the third volume of *The Science of Legislation* together with a letter just received from Filangieri: it clearly was the letter of July 14, 1783, wrongly dated July 14, 1784.

[12]Letter preserved in the Library of the Historical Society of Pennsylvania; full text in Pace, *op. cit.*, 401.

[13]Letter preserved in the Library of the Historical Society of Pennsylvania; text in Pace, *op. cit.*, 401–02.

In his volumes on criminal law Filangieri developed skillfully and systematically the principles which had been outlined by Beccaria in his *Essay on Crimes and Punishments*. As the Piedmontese jurist Francesco Dalmazzo Vasco put it: "Beccaria went directly and brilliantly to the point and sowed the seeds of the useful truths which aroused the interest of the enlightened men of Europe in the establishment of a just and peaceful society, while Filangieri was the first man who had enough courage, patience and intelligence to write out a complete plan of criminal legislation."[14]

Using his vast knowledge of the history of events and ideas, Filangieri drew up a juridical system based on reason and on the ideals of liberty and tolerance embodied in the philosophy of the Enlightenment. He called for a code of clear and precise laws, a just proportion between crimes and punishments, the extension to all countries of the jury system already adopted in England and North America, the complete abolition of torture, and the rejection of the inquisitorial procedure which had evolved in many countries under the influence of the Roman Church. These were all principles which had been advocated by Beccaria. But Filangieri did not follow the Milanese jurist in his call for the complete abolition of the death penalty. Beccaria believed that no man had the right to take away the life of another human being. In his *Essay* he had written:

If human passions or the necessities of war have taught men to shed one another's blood, the laws, which are intended to moderate human conduct, ought not to extend the savage example, which in the case of a legal execution is all the more baneful in that it is carried out with studied formalities. It seems an absurdity that the laws, which are the expression of the public will, and which abhor and punish murder, should themselves commit one; and that, to deter citizens from private assassination, they should themselves order a public one.[15]

Beccaria was convinced that a system of moderate laws and the elimination of cruel punishments would contribute to molding the character of the people accordingly, making them kinder and gentler, less prone to commit crimes. But not everyone agreed with Beccaria's reasoning; and the historian Franco Venturi may be right when he says that Filangieri, as well as Pagano and other Neapolitan intellectuals, did not have the courage to reject the death penalty because they were surrounded by a harder and more violent society than that of Milan and the Lombard region.[16] Although Filangieri did not subscribe to Beccaria's outright stand against capital punishment, he nevertheless made it clear that he wanted the application of the death penalty reduced to a minimum; and in accordance with the principle of a right proportion between crimes and punishments he asked that it be reserved only for those guilty of treason or deliberate murder.

Franklin was seventy-seven when he received from Filangieri the two volumes on criminal legislation. Having found himself in agreement with most of Filangieri's views, he soon presented his own ideas in what may be

[14] *Riformatori napoletani,* 633.

[15] J. A. Farrer, *Crimes and Punishments, Including a New Translation of Beccaria's "Dei Delitti e delle Pene"* (London, 1880); chapter on the death penalty, 169–80.

[16] Beccaria, *Dei delitti e delle pene,* ed. F. Venturi (Turin, 1965), xvi–xvii.

considered Franklin's most important writing on the subject of penal legislation: his "Letter to Benjamin Vaughan on the criminal laws and the practice of privateering." In it Franklin aimed especially at the penal legislation of England and at some of its most cruel and absurd provisions. While in the former English colonies of North America a serious reform movement was already making good progress, the situation in England was still far from encouraging. It is true that some jurists—Bentham and Romilly among them—were dissatisfied with the existing situation and were sponsoring a number of penal reforms, but they were frustrated in their endeavors by several stubborn men whose aim was to delay, as much as possible, the enactment of more humane legislation. In 1784 one of these men, Martin Madan, wrote a book, *Thoughts on Executive Justice,* in which he defended the whole existing system with all its cruelties and absurd punishments. Romilly decided not to let Madan's statements go unchallenged and under the title *Observations* he wrote a refutation of Madan's theories, upholding the view that the English system of justice was in need of urgent reforms. At the end of his own text Romilly printed Franklin's letter to Benjamin Vaughan, calling it *A Letter from a Gentleman abroad to his Friend in England.* The name of the author was withheld, and Romilly said in an explanatory note that, having received a copy of the letter from a friend of his to whom it was addressed, he thought he should render a service to the public by printing it. Then he added: "The writer of the foregoing *Observations* cannot but feel it incumbent on him to make some apology for publishing it in the form of an *Appendix* to a work, which it very far surpasses in every kind of merit. The truth is, he was not at liberty to print it in any other manner. The simplicity of style and liberality of thought, which distinguish it, cannot fail of discovering its venerable author to such as are already acquainted with his valuable writings. To those, who have not that good fortune, the editor is not permitted to say more, than that it is the production of one of the best and most eminent men of the present age."[17]

Franklin himself later confirmed that he was the author of this writing.[18] Although Romilly's book was published in 1786, Franklin's letter to Benjamin Vaughan was written much earlier, a few months before his resignation as minister to France and his return to Philadelphia. In this letter, dated March 14, 1785, Franklin discussed the aspects of the English law which seemed to him most reprehensible: the lack of proportion between crimes and penalties, and the cruelty of a legislation which in many cases did not hesitate to put to death people guilty of what Franklin considered minor offenses. At the very outset of his letter Franklin takes Madan to task for defending the right to inflict the death penalty on all thieves, no matter how small the value of the stolen articles:

If we really believe, as we profess to believe, that the law of Moses was the law of God, the dictate of divine wisdom, infinitely superior to human; on what principle do we ordain death as the punishment of an offence which, according to that law, was only to be punished by a restitution of fourfold? To put a man to death for an offence which does not deserve death, is it not murder? .... Is

---

[17] *The Writings of Benjamin Franklin,* ed. A. H. Smyth, IX, 291–92n.
[18] Letter to Louis Le Veillard, April 15, 1787; *ibid.,* IX, 561.

not all punishment inflicted beyond the merit of the offence, so much punishment of innocence?[19]

Franklin then takes up the question of the purpose of punishments. Both Beccaria and Filangieri had agreed that the purpose of penalties was to prevent the offender from doing more harm and to deter others from committing similar offenses. But at the same time both Beccaria and Filangieri advocated a just proportion between crimes and punishments, and opposed excessive penalties whose only justification was the deterring effect they might have on other evildoers. Franklin agrees with the two Italian jurists and attacks Madan for holding the opposite view and for stating that such penalties were justified. Franklin finds Madan's defense of the death penalty for thieves particularly objectionable. Madan had justified it on the ground that "every man's property, as well as his life, should be held sacred and inviolate." For Franklin this is most unreasonable: "Is there no difference in value between property and life? If I think it right that the crime of murder should be punished with death, not only as an equal punishment of the crime, but to prevent other murders, does it follow that I must approve of inflicting the same punishment for a little invasion of my property by theft?"

While it is clear from this statement that Franklin favored punishments proportionate to the offenses, it is also clear that on the question of capital punishment he did not follow Beccaria, but sided, instead, with Filangieri in the view that the crime of murder deserved the death penalty. For some unexplained reason Franklin has sometimes been described as an opponent of capital punishment. Pasquale Mancini, speaking on February 24, 1865, before the Italian Chamber of Deputies in defense of his bill for the abolition of the death penalty, mentioned Franklin as one of the men who had, after Beccaria, opposed the taking of human life in the name of justice.[20] This simply is not true: Franklin, like Filangieri, wanted the death penalty reserved only for the worst crimes, but he did not completely reject it as a matter of principle, as Beccaria had.

In his volumes on criminal law Filangieri had dealt also with the crime of piracy and had criticized those governments which punished this crime in peacetime and encouraged it in times of war. It was Filangieri's hope that new laws would soon be enacted which would prevent belligerent nations from using "this infamous method of harming their enemies." In the second part of his letter to Vaughan Franklin shows that he agrees with Filangieri's strong condemnation of piracy, and he develops the theory that crime thrives in an atmosphere of violence and in a nation where immoral acts are committed or tolerated by the government. Why, Franklin asks, are there more thefts and other crimes committed in England than in the rest of Europe? May not one of the causes be "the deficiency of justice and morality in the English Government?" Here Franklin cites several examples of such deficiency, and high on the list is the last war upon Holland: a war, says Franklin, which was seen by impartial Europe as a war of rapine and pillage. Is it strange, he asks, that the people employed in robbing the Dutch, being put out of that employment by the peace, should continue robbing and rob one another?

[19] *Ibid.*, IX, 292–94 (complete "Letter to Benjamin Vaughan": 291–99).
[20] *Atti del Parlamento Italiano, Sessione del 1863–64–65* (Rome, 1891), XI, 8475.

If the government's policy is reprehensible, says Franklin, so is the behavior of the merchants who voluntarily engage a gang of ruffians to attack the merchants of another nation in order to plunder them of their property: "Yet these things are done by Christian merchants, whether a war be just or unjust; and it can hardly be just on both sides; they are done by English and American merchants, who nevertheless complain of private thefts and hang by dozens the thieves they have taught by their own example."

In his conclusion Franklin invites all nations to stop the practice of privateering and points out that the government of the United States of America has taken a first step to this end by offering to all other powers treaties in which such a practice would be outlawed. It is of interest to note that an article to this effect was incorporated in the treaty of amity and commerce which was concluded between the United States and Prussia in the summer of 1785. The wording of this article was largely the work of Franklin who had taken part, with Jefferson and Adams, in the negotiations for the treaty.[21]

The letter to Vaughan is important because it reflects with clarity Franklin's views on some aspects of criminal justice, as well as his attitude toward war and the conduct of nations. It also shows that, like other men of his time, Franklin earnestly hoped that before long a more civilized behavior would prevail in the relations among nations; he himself certainly did his best to bring about the improvement to which he aspired. In his edition of Franklin's work, Jared Sparks recalls the praise bestowed on Franklin by Romilly and had this comment in his own presentation of Franklin's piece: "This testimony is valuable from such a man as Sir Samuel Romilly. And indeed the letter may be classed among the best of the author's writings, whether regarded as to the vigor and clearness of the style, the benign spirit it breathes, or its bold defence of the rights of humanity and justice."[22]

Soon after the signing of the treaty with Prussia Franklin left Europe and in September 1785 arrived once more in America. Having been elected president of the State of Pennsylvania, he was able to accelerate the adoption by the Assembly of several measures which had been debated during his long absence. In the field of criminal legislation the Assembly had been directed already in 1776 "to proceed as soon as might be to the reformation of the penal laws and to invent punishments less sanguinary and better proportioned to the various degrees of criminality."[23] The task was an arduous one. After Penn's unsuccessful effort to enact a more humane legislation in the seventeenth century, the laws of Pennsylvania had remained unchanged. Death by hanging was still the prescribed punishment for the following offenses: murder, treason, robbery, burglary, rape, arson, sodomy, malicious maiming, manslaughter, and counterfeiting. Bodily mutilations, as well as the pillory and whipping were current penalties for most minor offenses. Because of the disruption caused by the war the desired reforms were long delayed, but finally in September 1786, during Franklin's administration, an act was passed which limited the punishment of death to four crimes: murder, treason, rape, and

[21]Van Doren, *op. cit.*, 712. For the article in the treaty with Prussia see *The Writings of Benjamin Franklin*, ed. A. H. Smyth, IX, 299–300n.

[22]*The Works of Benjamin Franklin*, ed. J. Sparks, II, 478.

[23]R. J. Turnbull, *A Visit to the Philadelphia Prison* (London, 1797), 6.

arson. All other major crimes were made punishable by imprisonment at hard labor. Branding with a hot iron, ear cropping, whipping, and use of the pillory were abolished.[24]

It is difficult to assess the part Franklin had in the enactment of this new law. It is probably safe to say that he did not do much more than endorse the result of the long debates which had preceded the final adoption of the new act.

After the passage of this law the advocates of reform worked for further changes in the penal laws. Several new editions of Beccaria's *Essay* had meanwhile been published in the United States, and his appeal for the complete abolition of the death penalty found a sympathetic response in the writings of several distinguished citizens, among them the historian Robert J. Turnbull and the well-known professor of medicine Benjamin Rush, an old friend of Franklin and a signer of the Declaration of Independence.[25] These men were not entirely successful, but, as a result of their pressure, some years later only murder of the first degree was left as a capital crime in Pennsylvania.[26]

The exchange of correspondence between Franklin and Filangieri continued in the meantime, and not long after his return to America Franklin received a letter announcing the shipment of three more volumes of Filangieri's work: volumes which had as their subject the laws concerning education, morals, and public instruction.[27] We do not have Franklin's comments on the new books: he probably wrote about them to Filangieri in some letter which has disappeared.

In May 1787 the Constitutional Convention was assembled in Philadelphia to draw up the document which would guide the conduct of the government of the United States for years to come. Among the famous men attending the sessions sat Benjamin Franklin, the eighty-one year old delegate from Pennsylvania. In September of that year the great work was accomplished and on October 14 Franklin sent a copy of the new constitution to his friend Filangieri. In his letter Franklin ordered additional copies of Filangieri's volumes, including the ones dealing with criminal law, as well as copies of any volume that might be published in the future.[28]

This letter took an unusually long time even for those days to reach its destination. It arrived at the beginning of July 1788, almost nine months after being sent: too late for Filangieri to read it and to rejoice at the drafting of the

[24]R. Vaux, *Notices of the Original and Successive Efforts to Improve the Discipline of the Prison of Philadelphia and to reform the Criminal Code of Pennsylvania* (Philadelphia, 1826), 10, and Van Doren, *op. cit.*, 739. Van Doren says that the new act made only murder and treason capital offenses; to be exact, the law also made rape and arson still punishable by death.

[25]Turnbull, *op. cit.*, 49ff. and B. Rush, *Considerations of the Injustice and Impolicy of Punishing Murder by Death* (Philadelphia, 1792).

[26]Turnbull, *op. cit.*, 10.

[27]Filangieri's letter to Franklin, Dec. 24, 1785, preserved in the Library of the American Philosophical Society; original text in Pace, *op. cit.*, 403; Eng. translation (under erroneous date of Oct. 24, 1785) in *The Works of Benjamin Franklin*, ed. J. Sparks, X, 233–35.

[28]Letter preserved in the Municipal Museum "Gaetano Filangieri" of Naples, press copy in the Library of Congress, Washington; cf. *The Writings of Benjamin Franklin*, ed. A. H. Smyth, IX, 618–19.

constitution for the country which had aroused in him great hope and admiration. Some time in the first months of 1789 Franklin received a letter from Filangieri's wife, dated September 27, 1788:

Sir, attribute this long delay to my grief and sympathize with me in my affliction. The Chevalier Gaetano Filangieri, my husband and my friend, is no more. He died on the 21st of July, in the flower of his age, the victim of a cruel disease, and with him my happiness has gone. He has left three children, with no other patrimony than the memory of his virtues and his reputation. If the letter which you wrote to him on the 14th of October, 1787, had reached him before the 1st of July, the day on which the disease attacked him, he would not have failed to answer it, and to send you the copies of his work on legislation which you had requested. I shall myself perform what would have been his wish, and you will receive all that you desire.[29]

Filangieri died at the age of thirty-five. Franklin himself was then approaching the end of his much longer life. His body was weakening, but his mind was as alert as ever, and his will to fight for good causes never faltered. A few months before his death, in November 1789, as president of the Pennsylvania Society for Promoting the Abolition of Slavery, he wrote an address in which he said with perceptive vision: "Slavery is such an atrocious debasement of human nature, that its very extirpation, if not performed with solicitous care, may sometimes open a source of serious evils."[30] Nothing could be done, however, because the times were not ripe for the enactment of laws prohibiting slavery, and the serious evils so clearly foreseen were not to be avoided.

In conclusion, it is apparent from all that has been said in this study that Franklin, besides his many other titles, should be recognized also as a penal reformer. He certainly contributed to the reform movement with his writings, his activity, his prestige, his encouragement of other men fighting for better laws; and we may well say with Romilly that in this field, as in so many others, he was one of the best and most eminent men of his time.

New Rochelle.

[29]Letter preserved in the Library of the American Philosophical Society (original French text in Pace, *op. cit.,* 403–04; Eng. translation in *The Works of Benjamin Franklin,* ed. J. Sparks, X, 359). One more volume of Filangieri's *Science of Legislation,* on laws concerning religion, was published posthumously in 1791.

[30]*The Writings of Benjamin Franklin,* ed. A. H. Smyth, X, 66–68.

XXI

FROM LIBERALISM TO RADICALISM:
TOM PAINE'S *RIGHTS OF MAN*

By Gary Kates

In a fundamental sense, we are today all Paine's children. It
was not the British defeat at Yorktown, but Paine and the
new American conception of political society he did so much
to popularize in Europe that turned the world upside down.
— Jack P. Greene*

Thomas Paine's pamphlet, *Rights of Man,* stands as one of the fundamental texts of modern democracy. Written during the stormy days of the French Revolution, the pamphlet became an instant success throughout the European world, selling some 200,000 copies in two years, making Paine the era's best-known revolutionary writer. "I know not," John Adams wrote in 1805, "whether any man in the world has had more influence on its inhabitants or affairs for the last thirty years than Tom Paine."[1]

One of Paine's most cherished purposes was to convince readers that the various political changes affecting late eighteenth-century Europe and America were all part of a coherent and rational development towards a better world. "It has been my fate to have borne a share in the commencement and complete establishment of one revolution (I mean the Revolution of America)," he wrote to his French constituents in 1792. "The principles on which that Revolution began, have extended themselves to Europe." Despite obvious differences, Paine's vision unified Philadelphia merchants, British artisans, French peasants, Dutch reformers, and radical intellectuals from Boston to Berlin into one great movement: "it is the great cause of all; it is the establishment of a new era, that shall blot despotism from the earth and fix, on the lasting principles of peace and citizenship, the great Republic of Man."[2]

In his person as well, Paine seemed to embody the unity of an era

* Jack P. Greene, "Paine, America, and the 'Modernization' of Political Consciousness," *Political Science Quarterly*, 93 (1978), 92. I wish to thank John Martin, Char Miller, Linda Salvucci, Dena Goodman, Lynn Hunt, Tom Cragin, Gayle Pendleton, and Lloyd Kramer for their helpful suggestions. An early version of this paper was presented to the Consortium on Revolutionary Europe, Atlanta, 1986. Funds for research were generously provided by the Faculty Development Committee of Trinity University.

[1] John Adams to Benjamin Waterhouse, 29 October 1805, quoted in David Freeman Hawke, *Paine* (New York, 1974), 7.

[2] "Address to the People of France," *The Complete Writings of Thomas Paine*, Ed. Philip S. Foner (2 vols.; New York, 1945), II, 538-39 (here cited as *Complete Writings*).

of universal revolution. Born in England, where he lived the first half of his life and later sought radical change, Paine was, with Lafayette, one of the very few activists to have played significant roles in both the American and French Revolutions. On the laurels of his writings, Paine was the only Anglo-American elected to the National Convention. More important, Paine himself later insisted that his entire life was devoted to the same democratic principles. If we believe Paine, he brought his ideas for representative democracy with him from England in 1774 and his ideas changed little during his tumultuous political career. "It was to bring forward and establish the representative system of Government," he wrote a year before his death, "That was the leading principle with me in writing that work [*Common Sense*], and all my other works during the progress of the revolution. And I followed the same principle in writing the *Rights of Man*...."[3]

Paine's biographers have accepted his claim at face value. R. R. Fennessey, for example, asserts that Paine's "political ideas were completely *a priori*, and he was incapable of modifying them to suit the facts."[4] Obviously this is what Paine wanted readers to believe. But it is far from an accurate picture of Paine's ideological development. A more critical review of Paine's French Revolutionary writings, particularly *Rights of Man*, reveals fundamental change in his ideas. Tom Paine's radicalism was not prefabricated, but grew out of his own participation in France during the early years of the Revolution. As a result, his ideology was not simply modified, it was transformed.

Any analysis of *Rights of Man* must begin with the observation that it was written and published in two separate sections. Part One was completed in early 1791 and was in London bookshops by February of that year. Its purpose was to refute Edmund Burke's *Reflections on the Revolution in France*, published four months earlier. Part Two was written during the second half of 1791 and published in February, 1792. Even before Part Two appeared Paine's public expected it to be a sequel to Part One. "Its title is to be a repetition of the former 'Rights of Man,'" announced one London newspaper, "of which the words, 'Part the Second' will show that it is a continuation."[5] Indeed, Paine himself emphasized this connection between the two parts in his preface to Part

---

[3] *Complete Writings*, II, 1491.

[4] R. R. Fennessey, *Burke, Paine, and the Rights of Man* (The Hague, 1963), 31. Paine himself made virtually the same claim in 1802: "The principles of that work [*Rights of Man*] were the same as those in 'Common Sense'" (*Complete Writings*, II, 910). See also Eric Foner, *Tom Paine and Revolutionary America* (New York, 1976), 216; Harry Hayden Clark, ed., *Thomas Paine: Representative Selections* (New York, 1961), xxxiii–lviii; and, for a helpful introduction to Paine scholarship, A. O. Aldridge, "Thomas Paine: A Survey of Research and Criticism Since 1945," *British Studies Monitor*, 5 (1975), 3-27.

[5] *The Gazetteer*, 25 January 1792, quoted in Monroe D. Conway, *Thomas Paine* (2 vols.; New York, [1892] 1980), I, 335.

Two: "When I began the chapter entitled the 'Conclusion' in the former part of the Rights of Man, published last year, it was my intention to have extended it to a greater length. . . ." Later in the same preface Paine offered "another reason for deferring the remainder of the work . . . that Mr. Burke promised in his first publication to renew the subject at another opportunity. . . . I therefore held myself in reserve for him."[6]

Biographers have taken Paine's remarks at face value and assume that the two parts deliver essentially the same message. Paine's Part Two, they agree, "went on with the belabouring of Burke and was equally successful."[7] At best, the more sensitive of Paine scholars believe that while Paine's rhetoric in Part Two may have become more militant, exhibiting "a 'jovial ferocity' toward sacred institutions," his ideas did not really change. "The shibboleths are the same," notes David Freeman Hawke, "but the tone of the attack has changed."[8]

But a careful examination of Rights of Man reveals that much more changed than simply rhetorical tone. In fact Part Two is not a sequel to Part One. The two parts have little in common, each espousing contradictory ideologies. The first fits squarely with what later came to be known as (nineteenth-century European) Liberalism, which argued for a constitutional monarchy based upon political freedom but an unequal electoral system. The other ideology found in Rights of Man is properly known as (nineteenth-century European) Radicalism: democratic republicanism based upon universal manhood suffrage and a commitment to the amelioration of the lower classes through significant social and economic legislation. Today the distinction between Liberalism and Radicalism may have become somewhat blurred. But from 1789 to at least 1848 these two ideological systems stood in as much opposition to each other as Socialism and Communism would after 1917. Some of the last century's most famous political struggles, such as English Chartism or the French Bloody June Days of 1848, suggest the potency of the conflict between Liberals and Radicals. During the French Revolution and the first part of the nineteenth century, therefore, Radicalism was not simply a more progressive variant of Liberalism (just as Communism was not simply a more progressive variant of Socialism), but rather Radicalism constituted a profound critique of Liberalism's anti-democratic features.[9] Paine's Rights of Man is a work at odds with itself.

---

[6] Thomas Paine, Rights of Man, ed. Eric Foner (Harmondsworth, 1984), 153. All citations will be from this Penguin Books edition, referred to as RoM.

[7] J. Hampden Jackson, "Paine" in David Thomson, Political Ideas (New York, 1966), 108. Foner describes Part Two as "a companion volume" to Part One in Tom Paine, 216.

[8] Hawke, Paine, 241-42. See also Conway, Thomas Paine, I, 332; and Alfred Owen Aldridge, Man of Reason: The Life of Thomas Paine (Philadelphia, 1959), 157.

[9] On these ideologies see Guido de Ruggiero, The History of European Liberalism, tr. R. G. Collingwood (Boston, 1959), 66-77, 99-108, 370-80, and, for the nineteenth

There is one curious fact about Part One that has eluded Paine scholars. In an essay that defends the principles and events of the early Revolution, it is remarkable that Paine chose to discuss only one revolutionary leader: the Marquis de Lafayette. Incredibly, neither Sieyès nor Mirabeau, neither the Lameths nor Barnave, neither Robespierre nor any other politician or revolutionary writer was ever discussed in Part One. Still, Paine returned to Lafayette at five different points in the essay. For Tom Paine—at least for the Paine of 1790—the French Revolution belonged to Lafayette.[10]

The portrayal of Lafayette in Part One is highly significant, and it illustrates Paine's own political position within French Revolutionary politics. Lafayette was certainly among the most powerful and influential revolutionary politicians in France. Indeed, the early years of the Revolution (1789-91) are often called "The Years of Lafayette."[11] As a member of the Constituent Assembly, founder of political clubs in Paris, and head of the capital's newly-established local militia, the Paris National Guard, Lafayette wielded enormous power.

Under Lafayette and his followers, usually called the Fayettists or Patriot Party, the National Assembly accomplished a great deal during the period between the passage of the Declaration of the Rights of Man and Citizen in August 1789 and the publication of *Rights of Man* Part One in March 1791. They nationalized church lands, abolished various "feudal" laws and taxes, established a suspensive royal veto, reorganized the country into eighty-three departments, and approved plans for a unicameral legislature. But that was as far as Lafayette wanted the Revolution to go.

The Fayettists believed in a liberal constitutional monarchy in which the power of king, church, and corporate bodies was severely limited; but like their Whig counterparts in Britain, they also tried to exclude the populace from participating directly in political affairs. In October 1789 the Fayettists easily maneuvered the Constituent Assembly to pass a decree restricting those eligible to vote in elections to taxpayers who paid direct taxes worth three days' labor; and at the same time they got the Assembly to pass a law that restricted those voters eligible for national political office to men who paid annual direct taxes equivalent to a *marc*

---

century, Benedetto Croce, *History of Europe in the Nineteenth Century*, tr. Henry Furst (New York, 1963).

[10] *RoM*, 45, 53, 62, 95, 115, and 121. Only two French Revolutionary leaders are even mentioned in passing in the text: Bailly (63) and Sieyès (105).

[11] For example, Owen Connelly, *French Revolution/Napoleonic Era* (New York, 1979), chapter 3. On Lafayette's career, Louis Gottschalk and Margaret Maddox, *Lafayette in the French Revolution* (2 vols.; Chicago, 1969-73), and more generally, C. McClelland, "The Lameths and Lafayette: The Politics of Moderation in the French Revolution" (Ph.D. dissertation, University of California, Berkeley, 1942), and G. Michon, *Essai sur le parti Feuillant, Adrien Duport* (Paris, 1924).

d'argent (silver mark), worth about fifty-four days' labor. These new electoral laws effectively split the nation into active and passive citizens, the latter having full civil rights but limited political rights.

This repudiation of French democracy did not go unchallenged. Robespierre strongly objected to the new laws from the floor of the Constituent Assembly. But his views were soundly defeated by the Fayettist majority. The real struggle for democracy did not occur there but in the new Paris municipal institutions, the communal and district assemblies, where Paine's future "Girondin" allies, including politicians such as Condorcet and Brissot, were trying to establish a democratic municipality. Brissot, for example, was thrilled when Condorcet became the president of the Paris Communal Assembly because it meant that "the democratic party will always dominate it."[12]

Thus beginning in the fall of 1789 a democratic movement composed of well-known politicians and writers rose to challenge the Fayettist hegemony of the Revolution. Among the democrats were men who would soon become Paine's closest French allies. For two years they would wage a cold war against the Fayettists for control of national politics, a struggle that became violent after the king's infamous flight to Varennes in June 1791, when any hope for a liberal constitutional monarchy was put in serious jeopardy. My point is not simply that until 1791 Paine had been a Fayettist supporter; even more significantly, his support for Lafayette had much to do with *Rights of Man*. No one has ever doubted that Part One was an attack upon Burke's conservative ideas; but what has been less clear is that it also signified a repudiation of Parisian radicalism.

Far from exporting democratic republicanism from America to France in 1789, Paine ignored the democratic aspirations of Paris radicals. As early as September 1789 he had privately endorsed Thomas Jefferson's belief that "a tranquility is well established in Paris and tolerably well throughout the countryside," which would allow the Constituent Assembly to establish "a good constitution which will in its principles and merits be about a middle term between that of England and America."[13]

---

[12] For Robespierre's activities see P. J. B. Buchez and P. L. Roux, *Histoire parlementaire de la Révolution française....* (40 vols.; Paris, 1834), III, 213; Jacques-Pierre Brissot, *Correspondance et papiers*, ed. Claude Perroud (Paris, 1911), 241. On the rise of a Paris democratic movement see R. B. Rose, *The Making of the Sans-Culottes: Democratic Ideas and Institutions in Paris, 1789-1792* (Manchester, 1983); Jack Richard Censer, *Prelude to Power: The Parisian Radical Press, 1789-1791* (Baltimore, 1976); M. Genty, "Mandataires ou représentants: une problème de la démocratie municipale, Paris 1789-90," *Annales historiques de la Révolution française*, No. 207 (1972), 1-27; Gary Kates, *The Cercle Social, the Girondins, and the French Revolution* (Princeton, 1985), 17-71.

[13] Paine to Thomas Walker, September 19, 1789, reprinted in W. H. G. Armytage, "Thomas Paine and the Walkers: An Early Episode in Anglo-American Cooperation," *Pennsylvania History*, 18 (1951), 23; *The Correspondence of Edmund Burke, Vol. VI,*

It is hard to justify calling Paine a democrat given his acceptance of this "middle term," when radicals were pressing for significant political changes.

In January 1790 tension mounted between Fayettists and radicals. When the Constituent Assembly reiterated its support for the *marc d'argent*, Condorcet attacked the Assembly, charging that this legislation was "dangerous for liberty." Condorcet predicted that its inclusion into the constitution would "establish a legal inequality against those you have declared equal in rights."[14]

More dangerously, on 22 January Lafayette took 3000 troops into the Cordeliers district, the headquarters of democratic radicalism, to arrest the notorious journalist Jean-Paul Marat. The President of the district, soon-to-be famous Georges-Jacques Danton, refused to surrender Marat to the authorities. While street violence was avoided, the confrontation was not forgotten. Never against would the radicals trust the political leadership of the Fayettists.[15]

Curiously, it was at this very moment that we catch the first glimpse of *Rights of Man*. (Paine had come to Paris in November 1789 and would return to London in March 1790.) On 12 January (some nine months before Burke's *Reflections* appeared) Lafayette wrote to George Washington that Paine was "writing for you a brochure in which you will see a portion of my adventures."[16] Since Part One was dedicated to Washington, scholars agree that Lafayette was here referring to an early draft of *Rights of Man*. This means that *Rights of Man* was begun in January 1790 as an apology for Lafayette at the very instant when that statesman was under attack for his anti-democratic policies. It is even more interesting that on 17 January 1790 Paine had written a friendly letter from Paris to none other than Edmund Burke. "If we distinguish the Revolution from the Constitution," Paine commented, "we may say that the first is compleat, and the second is in a fair prospect of being so."[17] The constitution Paine refers to here would have prevented most of the adult

---

July 1789-December 1791, eds. Alfred Cobban and Robert A. Smith (Chicago, 1967), 68 (letter of 17 January 1790).

[14] The manuscript for Condorcet's speech is in the Archives de la Seine, VD12, 48-57. It was first published in Bonneville's *Cercle Social* [February 1790], letter 8, 57-75. See also Marecel Dorigny, "Les Girondins et le droit de propriété," *Bulletin de la Commission d'histoire économique et sociale de la Révolution française* (1980-81), 15-31.

[15] *Actes de la Commune de Paris pendant la Révolution. Première série, 25 juillet 1789 à 8 octobre 1790*, ed. Sigismond Lacroix (7 vols.; Paris, 1894-98), III, 520-60. For the reactions of democratic activists later associated with the Girondins, see also Marcel Dorigny, "La Presse Girondine et les movements populaires: necessité et limites d'une alliance," *Movements populaires et conscience sociale* (Paris, 1985), 519-27.

[16] Quoted in Aldridge, *Man of Reason*, 126-33.

[17] *Correspondence of Edmund Burke*, 68. On the relationship between Paine and Burke see Thomas W. Copeland, *Our Eminent Friend Edmund Burke. Six Essays* (New Haven, 1949), 146-82.

male population from holding seats in the national assembly. The "we" in Paine's remark may have been an indirect reference to Lafayette, but it never could have included Condorcet and the rest of the Paris radicals.

By January 1790, then, Paine envisioned *Rights of Man* to be a vindication of the Revolution won by Lafayette. No wonder he ignored all other leaders, including the radicals, and focused exclusively upon his hero. Only when he caught wind in April that Burke was about to publish a complete renunciation of the Revolution did Paine shrewdly decide to change rhetorical strategies and turn the pamphlet into a response to Burke. The point, however, is that this change marked no similar transformation in Paine's ideas; if anything, his loyalty to Lafayette was intensified.

Thus *Rights of Man* Part One does not belong to the burgeoning democratic movement that surfaced between 1789-91 in opposition to the leaders of the Constituent Assembly. Instead, it belongs to that vast outpouring of literature which defended the Fayettist interpretation of the French Revolution. What that literature suggests is that the essential difference between a Fayettist Patriot and a democrat before 1792 was the latter's faith in the ability of the ordinary citizen to participate fully in political affairs.

In *Rights of Man* Part One Paine's Fayettism is nakedly revealed in at least three places: first, his defense of the *marc d'argent*; second, his criticism of the popular executions of Bertier and Foulon; and finally, his discussion of the march to Versailles during the October Days.

Given the sharp criticism of the *marc d'argent* by 1791, it is significant that Paine did not attack it in *Rights of Man*, but replied to Burke's ironic attack upon the electoral laws by endorsing them, albeit in a twisted and opaque language: "The Constitution of France says, That every man who pays a tax of sixty sous per annum . . . is an elector. What article will Mr. Burke place against this? Can anything be more limited, and at the same time more capricious, than the qualifications of electors in England?"[18] Courting primarily an Anglo-American readership, Paine pointed out that at least the French laws were still more progressive than the English. But this weak defense of Lafayette's policies ignored the large and noisy groups of Paris radicals who argued that the electoral laws of both countries were anti-democratic. Thus his arguments should not simply be interpreted as a defense against Burke; they also reveal Paine's own anti-democratic attitudes.

Perhaps it is unfair to judge a foreigner according to the same standards we might judge Paris politicians. After all, what more could be expected from a British reformer in 1791? That question, however, is easily answered by glancing at another British pamphlet that appeared within a month of Paine's. In James Mackintosh's *Vindiciae Gallicae*,

[18] *RoM*, 73.

the laws restricting suffrage were passionately attacked and the leaders of the Constituent Assembly were sharply criticized:

Here I must cordially agree with Mr. Burke in reprobating the impotent and preposterous qualification by which the Assembly have *disenfranchised* every citizen who does not pay a direct contribution equivalent to the price of three days' labour. Nothing can be more evident than its inefficacy for any purpose but the display of inconsistency, and the violation of justice. . . . [It] stained the infant constitution with this absurd usurpation.[19]

Here in Mackintosh one finds a democratic ideology that is simply absent in Paine.

Louis-Benigne Bertier de Savigny, the last royal intendent of Paris, was arrested within days of the Bastille's fall. Under intense pressure from the Paris crowd, municipal authorities agreed to an immediate trial. But when Lafayette tried to delay the trial and have Bertier imprisoned, the crowd intervened. Bertier was dragged into the streets and hung on a lamppost.

Coincidentally, Bertier's father-in-law, the financier and former Controller-General Joseph-François Foulon, had been arrested at the same time on an unrelated charge. When the crowd learned that he was in the vicinity of the Bertier execution, someone shot him. Lafayette, who as Commander of the Paris National Guard was in charge of maintaining law and order in the capital, resigned over the episodes. But neither the mayor nor the Paris Communal Assembly accepted his resignation.[20]

The immediate response of the popular press helps to put Paine's later reaction into proper perspective. Within a week of the murders one of the capital's most popular papers, the *Révolutions de Paris*, edited by the staunch democrat, Elisée Loustalot, offered a lengthy description and analysis of the executions in the radical language of popular sovereignty. For Loustalot, both Bertier and Foulon had got what was coming to them. While Bertier had been a "slave to the great" and a "vicious courtisan," Foulon "was hated and even despised" for the "obnoxious monopolies hid from an angry public." Describing the murders in terms that were shockingly graphic even for that age, Loustalot nonetheless believed that the actions demonstrated "the terrible vengeance of a people justly upset." In these murders Loustalot saw the essence of the Revolution: a just people overthrowing a despotic regime in their own popular way. "Your hatred is revolting, it is terrifying," Loustalot admitted to his readers, "but remember how shameful it is to live in slavery!"[21]

---

[19] James Mackintosh, *Vindiciae Gallicae* (London, 1791), 224. For a somewhat opposing interpretation see William Christian, "James Mackintosh, Burke, and the Cause of Reform," *Eighteenth-Century Studies*, 7 (1973-74), 193-212.

[20] Gottschalk and Maddox, *Lafayette*, I, 145-54.

[21] *Révolutions de Paris*, no. 2, 18-25 July 1789, 55-62. We know that Paine had read this paper from his footnote on p. 64 of *RoM*: "An account of the expedition to Versailles

Edmund Burke had a very different reaction to these murders. The
"old Parisian ferocity has broken out in a shocking manner," he wrote
to a friend on 9 August 1789.

It is true, that this may be no more than a sudden explosion: If so no indication
can be taken from it. But if it should be character rather than accident, then
that people are not fit for Liberty, and must have a Strong hand like that of
their former masters to coerce them. . . . To form a constitution requires wisdom
as well as spirit.[22]

This view is sharply opposed to Loustalot's. For a radical democrat like
Loustalot, politics must embody the will of the people; for a Whig like
Burke, politics must embody wisdom and deference. Thus even if Burke
approved of the Revolution in general—he was still making up his mind
in August 1789—he could never justify the actions of a popular lynch
mob. By the time Burke published the *Reflections*, he used these types
of crowd actions to demonstrate the complete chaos and lawlessness
inherent in the Revolution.

When Tom Paine sat down fifteen months later to write *Rights of
Man* Part One, he thus had at least two ideologies available to him when
he came to the section analyzing the Foulon and Bertier murders. Significantly, Paine rejected the language of the Paris democrats and chose
a discourse that was remarkably close to Burke's. "There is in all European countries," he wrote, "a large class of people of that description
which in England is called the 'mob,' " who,

incensed at the appearance of Foulon and Bertier, tore them from their con-
ductors before they were carried to the Hotel de Ville, and executed them on
the spot. Why then does Mr. Burke charge outrages of this kind on a whole
people? . . . These outrages were not the effect of the principles of the Revolution,
but of the degraded mind that existed before the Revolution, and which the
Revolution is calculated to reform.[23]

Compared to Loustalot, Paine displayed a self-conscious disagreement
with Burke that seems superficial. Paine might have defended the crowd's
actions on the grounds of revolutionary justice; certainly, neither Lafayette nor the Paris government had any doubts regarding the guilt of the
two men. After all, the incidents occurred during the first days of a
revolution; what better symbol of the old order was there than the capital's
intendent and a financier who had taken advantage of the nation's fiscal

---

may be seen in No. 13 of the *Révolution de Paris*, containing the events from the 3rd to
the 10th of October 1789." On Loustalot and his newspaper see Censer, *Prelude to Power*.
    [22] Burke, *Correspondence*, 10.
    [23] *RoM*, 58-59. For a more general discussion of these ideas see George Rudé, *The
Crowd in the French Revolution* (New York, 1959).

problems? Paine might at least have excused crowd actions as zealotry, thereby demonstrating the public's intense approval for the new regime.

But he did not. Instead, Paine largely sided with Burke in seeing the crowd as an irrational "mob," which had no sense of justice or patriotism. Burke argued that the crowd typified the revolution because it embodied anarchy; Paine agreed with Burke's views on mobs and this position forced him into the slippery argument that the activities of the Paris crowd did not belong to the Revolution. Apparently, therefore, the mark of a great revolutionary, such as Lafayette, lay in his ability to manage the populace. "In the commencement of a Revolution," Paine wrote of the street activists, "those men are rather the followers of the camp than the standard of liberty, and have yet to be instructed how to reverence it." [24]

That Paine shared Lafayette's obsession for the restoration of order is again demonstrated when the Marquis was once more pitted against "the mob" during the October Days. Describing the popular women's march to Versailles as essentially "mischief," Paine praised Lafayette for saving the king from "the mob" and thus preserving the Revolution from anarchy: "As soon therefore as a sufficient force could be collected, M. de Lafayette, by orders from the civil authority of Paris, set off after them at the head of twenty thousand of the Paris militia. The revolution could derive no benefit from confusion, and its opposers might." [25] Here is the essence of the Fayettist ideology: Lafayette embodied the Revolution in its difficult task of constructing a new order. The people are not really villainous but submissive actors, no doubt misguided partly by their own ignorance and partly by the machinations of counter-revolutionaries. In Paine's rhetoric the people who brought the king and queen back to Paris were certainly not heroes.

Again, we need to emphasize, if only because the myth of Paine's democratic ideas remains so pervasive among Paine scholars, that there were other reformers writing at the same time, such as Mackintosh, who rejected this Fayettist rhetoric. In the *Vindiciae Gallicae*, for example, the patriotic common sense of "the people" has replaced Paine's violent "mob": "A degree of influence exerted by the people . . . must be expected in the crisis of a Revolution which the *people* have made . . . that, therefore, the conduct of the populace of Paris should not have been the most circumspect . . . was, in the nature of things, inevitable." In contrast to Paine, Mackintosh expected the crowd to enact their own style of popular politics in the streets.

Likewise, Mackintosh was not offended by the October Days but saw

---

[24] *RoM*, 59. Incidentally, years after the Revolution Lafayette admitted that Foulon had been a corrupt statesmen who had earned the "people's hatred." See the *Mémoires, correspondance et manuscrits du Général Lafayette* (6 vols.; Paris, 1837-38), II, 274.

[25] *RoM*, 62.

in them the expression of popular justice. "The march to Versailles," Mackintosh wrote, "seems to have been the spontaneous movement of an alarmed populace" who had good reasons to demand "the king to change his residence to Paris." What made Mackintosh's rhetoric democratic was that in his interpretation, the people do not follow the politicians, but were rather the driving force of the Revolution; they and not their leaders controlled political affairs.[26]

Rights of Man Part One, of course, was written in English for an Anglo-American audience. Its purpose was to stimulate a peaceful Fayettist revolution in Britain. Thus while Paine disagrees sharply with Burke over political principles, there is no real debate over the extent to which "the people" ought to participate in political affairs. Paine's focus is rather on the nature of monarchy in France, and here too Paine is more moderate than republicans might expect. Against Burke's prediction that the French Revolution would destroy monarchy, Paine came dangerously close to defending Louis XVI:

It was not against Louis the XVIth, but against the despotic principles of the government, that the nation revolted. . . . The monarch and the Monarchy were distinct and separate things; and it was against the established despotism of the latter, and not against the person or principles of the former, that the revolt commenced. . . .[27]

Against the background of traditional Enlightenment views of despotism, such as the one found in Montesquieu's *Spirit of Laws*, Paine's argument sounds strange. How could there be despotism without a despot? How could despotism be attacked without the despot himself receiving the first blow? Nonetheless, Paine insisted that pre-revolutionary France was, in fact, a despotism without a despot. Displaying an attitude toward monarchy that was very different from the one found in *Common Sense*, Paine portrayed Louis XVI as a passive and neutral king, even "known to be a friend of the nation."[28] The despotism begun during the reign of Louis XIV had simply expanded beyond the control of the despot. Louis XVI could not have reformed the system even if he had wanted to.

For the Paine of Part One the French Revolution was above all against despotism but not monarchy itself. Since the key attribute of despotism was that it lacked a constitution, the prime objective of the French Revolution was not to overthrow the monarchy, but rather to make the monarchy constitutional. "Mr. Burke said in a speech last winter in parliament," Paine remarked,

---

[26] Mackintosh, *Vindiciae Gallicae*, 181, 193-94.

[27] *RoM*, 47.

[28] *Ibid*. Compare with *Common Sense*: "There is something exceedingly ridiculous in the composition of monarchy . . ." (*Complete Writings*, I, 8).

that when the National Assembly first met in three Orders . . . France had then a good constitution. This shows, among numerous other instances, that Mr. Burke does not understand what a constitution is. The persons so met were not a *constitution*, but a *convention*, to make a constitution.[29]

Thus the central distinction found in *Rights of Man* Part One is not between aristocracy and democracy or between monarchy and republic but between absolute monarchy (which Paine called "hereditary despotism of the monarchy"[30]) and constitutional monarchy.

It must be emphasized that in this first part of *Rights of Man*, Paine went no further than this relatively moderate position. There was no call to make France a republic; nor was there any insistence that the French Revolution become democratic.

As soon as *Rights of Man* Part One was published in February 1791, Paine returned to France. When he arrived in Paris, he found that the political climate in the capital was more polarized and embittered than at any time since the taking of the Bastille. Although a democratic movement had been developing since the fall of 1789, it was only now receiving support from large segments of the Paris public. A series of small but significant events had made Parisians realize that the Constituent Assembly had no real commitment to making France democratic. The activists with whom Paine made friends, and would be associated with for the rest of his political career in France—politicians such as Condorcet, Brissot, Bonneville, and the Rolands—had become thoroughly frustrated with the Fayettists and no longer had faith in their ability to lead the Revolution forward. For example, Paine's French translator, François Lanthenas, reported that his good friend Madame Roland "has been to the National Assembly" and "is now convinced that liberty and the constitution will not belong to and do not belong to, the men who have given the most to the Revolution." And a few days later Madame Roland herself scolded the Fayettists for holding views that were "false" and "dangerous."[31]

Louis XVI's infamous flight to Varennes was the final step that converted Paine and his friends to the view that only a democratic republic could save the French Revolution. Behind the king's betrayal the Brissotins saw Lafayette's Machiavellian designs. "It is virtually impossible that Lafayette is not involved," wrote Madame Roland after learning of the flight. Immediately Brissot, Condorcet, and Paine became "the rec-

[29] *Ibid.*, 72.

[30] *Ibid.*, 47.

[31] *Lettres de Madame Roland*, ed. Claude Perroud (2 vols.; Paris, 1900-1902), II, 206, 240. The best survey of this period is Marcel Reinhard, *La Chute de la royauté, 10 août 1792* (Paris, 1969). On the deterioration of Lafayette's reputation among Paris democrats see also Kates, *Cercle Social*, 138-51; Censer, *Prelude to Power*, 100-107, 144.

ognized chiefs of a republican party." They put out a journal, *Le Républicain ou Le Défenseur du gouvernement représentatif*, whose influence
among Paris clubs was important. Yet despite their efforts Madame
Roland did not believe that Lafayette's grip on the government could be
broken: "Lafayette is more powerful than ever. His game is more developed and better received than we had supposed ... he has the force
of the army; he has a reserve of blind partisans; he has allied himself
closely with the group of opportunists in the Assembly."[32]

Paine is often given credit for educating his friends in the new radical
ideology.[33] But considering Paine's previous lack of commitment to the
radical movement, there is much evidence that it was French radicals
who helped convert Paine to democracy and republicanism in June 1791.
For example, in *Rights of Man* Part Two there is an important section
in which Paine defined a republic as a "res-publica, the public affairs,
or the public good, or literally translated, the public thing." This section
was lifted practically verbatim from his friend Bonneville's daily newspaper, *Bouche de fer*. "En definissant le mot *ré-publique*," wrote Bonneville four days after the king's flight, "et le traduissant litteralement dans
notre langue, car c'est un mot latin *res-publica*, toute obscurité va dis-
paroitre ... La ré-publique, n'est autre chose litteralement que la chose
commune, la chose publique, la grande communauté nationale, LE GOU-
VERNEMENT NATIONAL."[34] Likewise, there is no evidence that
Paine had progressed very far in writing Part Two until after his return
to England. For commentators like Fennessey to suggest that Paine had
always been a pronounced democrat and had never learned anything
"from his extensive experience of American and French politics" is
grossly mistaken[35]: however much he would later deny it, Paine's democratic republicanism developed and matured because of what he and
his friends witnessed in the streets of Paris during the tumultuous period
surrounding the king's flight to Varennes.

Any further movement towards a democratic republic was soon repressed by Lafayette and his supporters in the Constituent Assembly.
They refused to abolish the monarchy, forgave the king for all misdeeds
as long as he professed support for the constitution, and prepared plans
for liquidating the democratic movement. The climax of this anti-democratic campaign was the Massacre at the Champ de Mars, where on 17
July 1791 Lafayette's troops fired on a crowd of Parisians holding a
peaceful republican rally. The suppression of the democrats was successful
from Lafayette's viewpoint, insofar as order was restored in the city and

[32] *Lettres de Madame Roland*, II, 302, 312-13.
[33] For example, Foner, *Tom Paine*, 211-34; and A. O. Aldridge, "Condorcet et Paine.
Leur rapports intellectuels," *Revue de litterature comparée*, 32 (1958), 47-65.
[34] *RoM*, 178; *Bouche de fer*, 25 June 1791, 1-4.
[35] Fennessey, *Burke, Paine*, 63.

Louis XVI and the Assembly were able to ratify the new constitution. "Yes, the National Guards are the instruments of oppression, the satellites of an abominable man," cried Madame Roland on the day of the Massacre. "We can say that the counter-revolution is being made at Paris by the majority of the National Assembly and the armed forces with Lafayette at the head."[36]

Nevertheless, Lafayette's victory was ephemeral. Unable to run for office in the new Legislative Assembly (months earlier all members of the Constituent Assembly had disqualified themselves), he and his allies quickly lost their power base. Into the political void stepped Brissot, Condorcet, and their supporters. These Girondins were frustrated by a monarchical constitution that was too conservative for their tastes. They looked to a new war to help minimize the influence of the king and maximize possibilities for French democracy. By January, 1792, the Girondins controlled both the Jacobin Club and the Legislative Assembly. In February they forced the king to replace his Fayettist ministers (who opposed any war) with Roland and Etienne Clavière, Brissot's close allies. A few weeks later, France declared war upon Austria. In the midst of these developments appeared *Rights of Man* Part Two.[37]

The schism between Paine and the Fayettists is dramatically displayed in the bizarre and awkward dedication "To M. Lafayette," that makes up the first pages of Part Two.[38] Paine acknowledged his break with Lafayette. But he claimed that the essential differences between them had to do not with "principles" but with "time." In brief but pungent prose, Paine argued that Lafayette was a misguided patriot, but he refused to call him a counter-revolutionary. Paine's attitude towards Lafayette was condescending but not hostile. Paine viewed Liberalism as only a temporary phase, with Radicalism's victory inevitable. "I wish you to hasten your principles, and overtake me," he urged Lafayette. Paine desperately needed to explain the relationship between Liberalism and Radicalism as developmental rather than oppositional, if the fiction of a "sequel" was to make any sense. Otherwise, he would leave the door open to charges that he and his hero had been opposed to progress and perhaps were even traitors to the cause of democracy.

The first pages of Part Two, therefore, announced that Paine and his hero had gone their separate ways. Nonetheless, the next few pages go over territory covered in Part One, repeating "the belabouring of Burke," until suddenly Paine comes clean with his readers, letting them know that unlike Part One, Part Two was not a response to Burke's *Reflections*: "Mr. Burke has talked of old and new whigs. If he can amuse himself with childish names and distinctions, I shall not interrupt his pleasure.

[36] *Lettres de Madame Roland*, II, 336.
[37] M. J. Sydenham, *The Girondins* (London, 1961).
[38] *RoM*, 151-52.

It is not to him, but to the Abbé Sieyès, that I address this chapter."[39]
If we take this statement together with Paine's dedication to Lafayette,
it becomes clear that *Rights of Man* Part Two was never intended as an
attack upon Burke, but rather a serious challenge to the leadership of
Lafayette and Sieyès. This point—often ignored by Paine scholars still
obsessed with the Burke/Paine debate—is the key to understanding the
real purpose and ideology of Part Two.[40]

Why Sieyès? Between 1789 and 1791 Sieyès was an ally (though
sometimes a strained one) of Lafayette. But while Lafayette was primarily
a soldier and a statesman, Sieyès's most important contribution was as
a thinker. His *What is the Third Estate?* (January 1789) became the most
important French pamphlet of the period, inspiring the Declaration of
the Rights of Man and Citizen. And as a member of the Constituent
Assembly's Constitution Committee, Sieyès had considerable opportunity
to translate his ideas into legislation. Under the direct influence of Adam
Smith's *Wealth of Nations*, Sieyès argued that only those citizens who
contributed to the national economy ought to participate in political life.
Those citizens not able to become productive workers would be protected
by the laws, but would have no right to make the laws. This idea, outlined
in *What is the Third Estate?*, became the germ for the anti-democratic
laws establishing the *marc d'argent*, which were, not surprisingly, written
by Sieyès.[41]

Rights of Man Part Two was not the first battle in print between
Paine and Sieyès. Immediately following the king's flight to Varennes in
June-July 1791, Sieyès published an article in the *Moniteur*, the most
important French daily, challenging anyone to defend republicanism over
monarchy. Paine accepted the challenge, and he published a short response in *Le Républicain*. Thus *Rights of Man* Part Two should be viewed
within the context of an ongoing debate with Sieyès over republican
principles. In that sense *Rights of Man* is something of a paradox: where
Part One defended the Fayettist Revolution, Part Two repudiated Fayettist ideology.[42]

If Paine was a spokesman for Lafayette in *Rights of Man* Part One,
Rights of Man Part Two echoed the Girondins. The new element in Part

[39] *RoM*, 171.

[40] Only Conway comes close to recognizing Sieyès's role. See his *Thomas Paine*, I,
328-29.

[41] Paul Bastid, *Sieyès et sa pensée* (Paris, [1939] 1970), 89, 369-70; and Murray
Forsyth, *Reason and Revolution: The Political Thought of the Abbé Sieyès* (New York,
1987).

[42] On this exchange between Sieyès and Paine, see Aldridge, "Condorcet et Paine,"
51-57. Aldridge makes a persuasive case that the debate was staged, suggesting that after
the king's flight Sieyès himself had at least secretly become a republican. But more
recently, Murray Forsyth (*Reason and Revolution*, 176-79) has reconfirmed Sieyès's
commitment to monarchy.

Two was Paine's emphasis on "the representative system." Although Paine had mentioned representative government in passing in Part One, he now developed the concept of representative democracy into a mature theoretical framework. Paine acknowledged the debt modern democracies owed to ancient Greece. But he, like many thinkers during the Enlightenment, also recognized that it was impossible for large nation-states to imitate the Athenian model. Paine wanted a system in which representation would become the keystone for democratic political institutions. "By ingrafting representation upon democracy," Paine said, "we arrive at a system of government capable of embracing and confederating all the various interests and every extent of territory and population."[43]

This new kind of political system had no place for monarchy. "Every government that does not act on the principle of a Republic," he wrote, "is not a good government." Although a democratic monarchy was a theoretical possibility (one toyed with by several Revolutionary leaders, including Mirabeau and Robespierre), the Paine of Part Two viewed it as "eccentric government" and realized that only a representative democratic republic could provide the kind of freedom he desired. Consequently, Paine's model of an admirable state changed from Part One to Part Two: because France in February 1792 was not yet a democratic republic, Paine advised his readers to look towards the United States: "It is on this system that the American government is founded. It is representation ingrafted upon democracy." In Part One, in spite of his focus upon Lafayette, Paine had rarely mentioned the United States. Since he was defending a constitutional monarchy the example of 1776 was somewhat irrelevant. Ironically, America only became central to Paine's arguments when he dropped Lafayette in Part Two.[44]

Paine's understanding of the nature of revolutionary change also changed from Part One to Part Two. In the first pamphlet Paine had hoped that other nations would choose to imitate the French in a short, peaceful, and above all rational transfer of sovereignty. But when Paine called for revolution to become "the order of the day" in Part Two, he meant something else. In Part One Paine expressed the belief that some kings, such as Louis XVI, were decent enough to hold national office. But Part Two returns to the view he espoused in *Common Sense* in which all kings were criminals, since all monarchies were "originally a tyranny, founded on an invasion and conquest of the country." That is why, Paine asserted, monarchies were inherently expansionist and militaristic. "War is their trade, plunder and revenue their objects." This kind of govern-

---

[43] *RoM*, 180.
[44] *RoM*, 178-80. See also 125, where America is praised largely for its inexpensive government.

ment, so different from the possibility of the kind of pacifist constitutional monarchy suggested in Part One, was unable to reform itself.[45]

In Part One, Paine hoped that the French Revolution would lead the world by example. But in Part Two that leadership took a more direct and more violent form: the French were expected to wage war on the rest of Europe, liberating the peoples of Europe from their old regimes. The first step was "the extinction of German despotism." But Germany was not enough. Only "when France shall be surrounded with revolutions" will she "be in peace and safety." And only through war could that goal be achieved quickly and efficiently. In Part One, the revolutionary process was described as pacifist and piecemeal. But now, reflecting Girondin foreign policy, Paine envisioned a war that would create a string of democratic republics from England to the Russian border, a war that led him to predict the death of monarchy: "I do not believe," Paine declared, "that monarchy and aristocracy will continue seven years longer in any of the enlightened countries in Europe."[46]

In contrast to Part One, then, Part Two was indeed radical; clearly without Part Two, *Rights of Man* would not have become the bible among nineteenth-century working-class Radicals.[47] Part Two, for example, advocates the abolition of all monarchy and the establishment of democratic republics based upon universal manhood suffrage. More importantly, its fifth chapter includes a social component, in which Paine argued for a graduated income tax, as well as health and old-age insurance, foreshadowing the idea of the welfare state. Obviously nothing in Part One had even hinted at these new and daring proposals.

The Girondins themselves were aware of the inconsistency between the two parts. Brissot's close friend, François Lanthenas, did not translate the work until after Part Two was complete. His edition appeared in April or May 1792 and was published by the most significant Girondin publishing house, the Imprimerie du Cercle Social. Nonetheless, Lanthenas edited the work in a curious fashion. First, he eliminated the preface to Part Two because, as he put it,

Owing to the prejudices that still govern *that nation*, the author has been obliged to condescend to answer Mr. Burke. He has done so more especially in an extended preface which is nothing but a piece of very tedious controversy, in which he shows himself very sensitive to criticisms that do not really affect him. To translate it seemed an insult to the *free French people.* . . .[48]

Clearly Paine's French friends did not see *Rights of Man* as primarily a

[45] *RoM*, 161, 192-93.

[46] *RoM*, 151-52, 156.

[47] E. P. Thompson, *The Making of the English Working Class* (New York, 1963), 104-11.

[48] Thomas Paine, *Théorie et pratique des droits de l'homme*, tr. François Lanthenas (Paris, 1792). Lanthenas's preface is translated in *Complete Writings*, I, 346-47.

response to Burke. The French version also eliminated the dedication to Lafayette. Not only did Lanthenas admonish Paine for addressing himself before Burke, but he refused to allow Paine to humble himself before Lafayette. "Paine, that uncorrupted friend of freedom," wrote Lanthenas, "believed too in the sincerity of Lafayette," a naiveté which Lanthenas believed proved that Paine had much to learn from the French. "Bred at a distance from courts, that austere American does not seem any more on his guard against the artful ways and speech courtiers than some Frenchmen who resemble him." By deleting the preface against Burke and the dedication to Lafayette, which had linked the two parts rhetorically, if not substantively, Lanthenas not only firmly established Part Two as an anti-Fayettist text, but he also drew attention to the problematic relationship between the two parts. This may explain why French reviews of *Rights of Man* were relatively cool and even critical, a fact that has perplexed Paine's biographers.[49]

Lanthenas' editorial efforts make clear that Paine united two works whose ideologies were contradictory. Why did Paine not renounce Lafayette more sharply in 1792, as Brissot and his colleagues were willing to do, and simply publish Part Two as a kind of Girondin manifesto? Insofar as Paine refused to attack Lafayette, he allowed his own political theory to decline into a cult of personality. His relationship with Lafayette also explains why Paine retreated from the staunch republicanism of *Common Sense* and endorsed the constitutional monarchy of Louis XVI.

During the 1770s Lafayette had become the best known European supporter of the American Revolution. And Americans were deeply proud that this young liberal nobleman admired their new state. When Lafayette took a leading role in the French Revolution, Anglo-American supporters naively supposed that he was offering France the lessons that he had learned in America. "He took a practical existing model, in operation here," commented John Quincy Adams speaking for American public opinion, "and never attempted or wished more than to apply it faithfully to his own country."[50] Perhaps we can forgive the American president for this naive interpretation, but certainly Paine ought to have

---

[49] A. O. Aldridge, "*The Rights of Man* de Thomas Paine: symbole du siècle des lumières et leur influence en France," Pierre Francastel, ed., *Utopie et institutions au xviiiᵉ siècle: le pragmatisme des lumières* (Paris, 1963), 285.

[50] Quoted in Lloyd S. Kramer, "Lafayette and the Historians: Changing Symbol, Changing Needs, 1834-1934," *Historical Reflections / Réflections historiques*, 11 (1984), 373-401. See also his "America's Lafayette and Lafayette's America: A European and the American Revolution," *William and Mary Quarterly*, 3rd Series, 38 (1981), 233-41; and Anne Loveland, *Emblem of Liberty: The Image of Lafayette in the American Mind* (Baton Rouge, 1971), 16-34. Paine praises Lafayette for his American heroism in *RoM*, 46.

known better. Nonetheless, Paine was keenly aware that representing
Lafayette as this kind of a symbol could enhance his own star as well.

Paine wanted readers to see the entire era characterized by the universal progress of human rights, a process whose unity was best embodied
by Lafayette and himself. By 1792 only Lafayette and Paine had played
a major role in *both* the American and French Revolutions; both of them
could be used to represent a linkage among the American and French
Revolutions that would make British parliamentary reform appear urgent
and inevitable.

For us *Rights of Man* reveals an ideologue's desperate search to
maintain some shred of intellectual consistency during a period of intense
revolutionary change. So long as the Revolution constituted a united
Third Estate against an entrenched and privileged aristocracy, Paine's
ideas could be endorsed by all reformers. But the moment that the Third
Estate began to argue among itself—a process that began as early as the
fall of 1789, Paine's ideology could no longer represent the entire Revolution but only the dominant faction. As the gap between Fayettists and
radicals widened between 1789 and 1791 over fundamental issues regarding democracy and republicanism, Paine's ideological frame became
even more problematic. By the time *Rights of Man* Part One was published
in March 1791 its ideology had already moved far to the right on the
spectrum of French Revolutionary politics. Within four months he
dropped his Fayettist endorsements and wrote Part Two as if it were a
sequel. But what the Girondins chose to minimize, their Montagnard
rivals later sought to exploit: Paine spent the year of the Terror in prison,
and while he would go on to write works of major importance, his political
career was over.

Trinity University.

XXII

THE YOUNG AMERICAN NATION AND THE
CLASSICAL WORLD

By Edwin A. Miles

Many historians have noted the remarkable interest of the American Revolutionary leaders in the history of ancient Greece and Rome. Perhaps Lewis Mumford overstated the case when he wrote that the educated gentlemen of that era had "one foot in their own age, and the other in the grave of Rome," but undoubtedly the classical world, as Louis B. Wright observed, "provided these men with a cultural anchor, ... a philosophical and intellectual mooring."[1] In their struggle for independence and in their quest for "a more perfect union," the Founding Fathers turned often to the renowned republics of Greece and Rome for inspiration and guidance. Samuel Adams, for example, began "by the Greeks and Romans, to get at the Whigs and Tories," as the Marquis de Chastellux expressed it.[2] Charles F. Mullett has suggested that "not less than the Washingtons and the Lees, these ancient heroes helped to found the independent American commonwealth."[3]

Yet by the middle of the nineteenth century most Americans no longer regarded the republican eras of Greece and Rome as constituting a Golden Age in man's history. Instead some tended to consider the study of the Greco-Roman civilization as valuable only for exhibiting examples to be avoided rather than imitated, while others looked upon the record of the earlier republics merely "as a matter of *curiosity,* rather than of *instruction.*"[4] Their different attitudes toward the relevance of the classical world well demonstrates the political and intellectual chasm that existed between the Revolutionary generation and their descendants who lived during the quarter century prior to the American Civil War.

Because of the prevailing influence of classical education, the

---

[1]Lewis Mumford, *Sticks and Stones: A Study of American Architecture and Civilization* (New York, 1924), 56; Louis B. Wright, "The Classical Tradition in Colonial Virginia," *The Papers of the Bibliographical Society of America,* 33 (1939), 37.

[2]Quoted in Samuel Eliot Morison, *Three Centuries of Harvard, 1636-1936* (Cambridge, Mass., 1936), 136; Richard M. Gummere, "Thomas Hutchinson and Samuel Adams, A Controversy in the Classical Tradition," *Boston Public Library Quarterly,* 10 (July 1958), 119-29 and (Oct. 1958), 203-12.

[3]"Classical Influences on the American Revolution," *Classical Journal,* 35 (Nov. 1939), 104.

[4]Thomas S. Grimké, *Address on the Expediency and Duty of Adopting the Bible as a Class Book* (Charleston, 1830), 90.

ancient world seemed close at hand to most American leaders of the Revolutionary era.[5] Before the Declaration of Independence the colonists generally cited the English tradition of self-government in their quarrel with the mother country; when they severed their ties with Great Britain, however, they tended to place less emphasis upon their Anglo-Saxon heritage, associated as it was with the lowly regarded Middle Ages.[6] Instead, they turned to the earlier examples of the republics of Greece and Rome to sustain their faith in the success of their political experiment. It was altogether natural that they should do so. Since the Renaissance the literature and history of the classical world had fascinated the educated men of the western world, and this appeal had been singularly irresistible to advocates of republicanism.

To be sure, Americans of the Revolutionary era did not view ancient history in the same light as the English classical republicans of the seventeenth century.[7] Framers of the American Constitution, like the earlier republicans, often referred to Polybius' theory of mixed government, but just as the employment of that concept by James Harrington and Algernon Sidney had been influenced by Niccolò Machiavelli, so the Founding Fathers' views on Greek and Roman government had been shaped in part by Baron de Montesquieu.[8] Revolutionary Americans, endorsing the social compact theory associated with the doctrine of natural rights, repudiated the concept of the Solon- or Lycurgus-type lawgiver so admired by Polybius, Machiavelli, and the English classical republicans. Influenced by Montesquieu, they questioned the suitability of a republican form of government for a large and expanding nation, a proposition that had not been entertained by their earlier English counterparts. Furthermore, few educated Americans of the late eighteenth century espoused the once-popular notion that the world was degenerating and hence modern man could merely strive to imitate without any hope of

[5]Richard M. Gummere, *The American Colonial Mind and the Classical Tradition: Essays in Comparative Culture* (Cambridge, 1963); John C. Miller, *Origins of the American Revolution* (Boston, 1969), 169.

[6]Talbot Hamlin, *Greek Revival Architecture in America* ... (London, 1944), 3-4; H. Wayne Morgan, "The Founding Fathers and the Middle Ages," *Mid-America,* **42** (Jan. 1960), 30-43.

[7]For the views of the seventeenth-century English republicans: Zera S. Fink, *The Classical Republicans; An Essay in the Recovery of a Pattern of Thought in Seventeenth Century England* (Evanston, 1945). There were also significant differences in the attitude of the American and the later French revolutionaries toward the ancient republics.

[8]R. A. Ames and Henry C. Montgomery, "The Influence of Rome on the American Constitution," *Classical Journal,* **30** (Oct. 1934), 19-27; Gilbert Chinard, "Polybius and the American Constitution," *JHI,* **1** (Jan. 1940), 35-58; Gummere, *The American Colonial Mind and the Classical Tradition,* Ch. 10; Lawrence Meyer Levin, *The Political Doctrine of Montesquieu's Esprit des Lois: Its Classical Background* (New York, 1936); Paul Merrill Spurlin, *Montesquieu in America, 1760-1801* (Baton Rouge, 1940).

equaling the ancients. Most of them instead accepted the cyclical theory of history as popularized by such writers as Lord Bolingbroke, while the idea of progress, which Americans later wholeheartedly embraced, was not without its New World advocates during the Revolutionary era.[9] Thus while the founders of the American republic often quoted the famous authors of antiquity and referred frequently to examples from Greek and Roman history, they were significantly influenced by the views of modern European writers in what use they made of antiquity.

Perhaps, as Samuel Eliot Morison contends, the early classical training of many American Revolutionary leaders provided them with "the wisdom to deal with other men and with the great events in the 1770's and 80's."[10] Certainly the intensive study of Greek and Latin contributed to the mastery of rhetoric by such men as John Dickinson, Thomas Jefferson, and John Adams.[11] The emulation of the heroic virtues of classical antiquity may have aided the American cause during the war, for the conflict stimulated respect not only for those ancient writers and orators who had extolled personal freedom and self-government but also for those Greek and Roman heroes who had displayed bravery, patriotism, fortitude, and perseverance.[12] More influential than all other writers in popularizing these and other classical virtues was Plutarch, the ancient Greek biographer whose *Parallel Lives* successfully combined entertaining narratives with inoffensive moralizing. The high esteem for the Plutarchian hero entertained by the American leaders of the Revolutionary and Federalist eras clearly reveals their misgivings regarding democratic rule. Such men as Camillus, Phocion, and Cicero had been virtuous men who accepted

[9]Stow Persons, "The Cyclical Theory of History in Eighteenth-Century America," *American Quarterly,* 6 (Summer 1954), 147–63; Rutherford E. Delmage, "The American Idea of Progress, 1750-1800," *Proceedings of the American Philosophical Society,* 91 (1947), 307–14.

[10]*The Ancient Classics in a Modern Democracy; Commencement Address Delivered at the College of Wooster, 12 June 1939* (New York, 1939), 23.

[11]Richard M. Gummere, "John Dickinson, the Classical Penman of the Revolulution," *Classical Journal,* 53 (Nov. 1956), 81–87; Gilbert Chinard, "Thomas Jefferson as a Classical Scholar," *American Scholar,* 1 (April 1932), 133–43; Louis B. Wright, "Thomas Jefferson and the Classics," *Proc. of the Amer. Phil. Soc.,* 87 (1944), 223–33; Karl Lehmann, *Thomas Jefferson, American Humanist* (New York, 1947); Dorothy M. Robatham, "John Adams and the Classics," *New England Quarterly,* 19 (Mar. 1946), 91–98; Gummere, "John Adams, *Togatus,*" *Philological Quarterly,* 13 (April 1934), 203–10.

[12]At any rate, the respect for the virtues of classical antiquity served as a frequent argument in favor of a thorough study of the ancient languages. "Curious Dissertation on the Valuable Advantages of a Liberal Education," *New-Jersey Magazine and Monthly Advertiser,* 1 (Jan. 1787), 53–54; Henry Stuber, "Observations on the Utility of the Latin and Greek Languages, in a Series of Letters," *New-York Magazine,* 1 (July 1790), 468; "On History," *ibid.,* 5 (Oct. 1794), 568–69; Marcus Cunliffe, *George Washington: Man and Monument* (New York, 1958), 161–65.

public office from a deep sense of public responsibility. If their exertions failed to receive popular approval, if they were reviled, ostracized, or even killed, the masses invariably suffered as a consequence of the repudiation of such noble leaders.[13] George Washington's favorite character from the *Parallel Lives* was Cato the Younger, as interpreted by Joseph Addison in his celebrated eighteenth-century play (which was performed, incidentally, at Valley Forge). Washington's admiration for Cato's stoicism was reflected in the general's "wisdom, poise, and serenity," acquired through the "severest self-discipline."[14]

Whatever the influence of antiquity upon the American Revolution, the war did much to stimulate the classical tradition in America.[15] Piqued by European conservatives who regarded their new commonwealth with skepticism, disfavor, or hostility, Americans sought reassurance in the record of the ancient republics that their experiment would succeed. In several ways they sought to identify themselves with the ancients: they chose classical names for their villages and hamlets; they adopted such pen names as "Brutus," "Cassius," or "Aristides" for their pseudonymous political writings; their statues depicted American statesmen and soldiers dressed in antique costumes; and during the early nineteenth-century classical revival architecture dictated the appearance of their public buildings.[16] But above all the classical tradition survived in the belief firmly cherished by many Americans that the United States was the modern heir of the ancient republics, an idea that found widespread expression in published orations, debates, and political pamphlets.[17] One must not be

[13]"Instances of Ingratitude in Greece and Rome," *American Museum,* 8 (Sept. 1790), 129–33; "On Party Divisions," *ibid.,* 8 (Oct. 1790), 176–77; "The Free Republican," *Boston Magazine,* 1 (Mar. 1784), 192–95; Douglass Adair, "A Note on Certain of Hamilton's Pseudonyms," *William and Mary Quarterly,* 12 (April 1955), 282–97.

[14]Samuel Eliot Morison, *By Land and By Sea* (New York, 1953), 161–80. During the Revolution Samuel Sewall wrote a new epilogue to Addison's *Cato* in which he compared George III to Caesar and Washington to Cato. "Dramatic Reminiscences," *New-England Magazine,* 2 (June 1832), 485; Henry C. Montgomery, "Washington the Stoic," *Classical Journal,* 31 (Mar. 1936), 371–73, and *idem,* "Addison's *Cato* and George Washington," *ibid.,* 55 (Feb. 1960), 210–12; Edmund G. Berry, "Latifundia in America," *ibid.,* 39 (Dec. 1943), 156–158.   [15]Mumford, *Sticks and Stones,* 57.

[16]"Letter to the Poets, Philosophers, Orators, Statesmen and Heroes of Antiquity," *United States Magazine,* 1 (Jan. 1779), 11–14; "On the Architecture of America," *American Museum,* 8 (Oct. 1790), 174–76; Geoffrey Crayon [Washington Irving], "National Nomenclature," *Knickerbocker,* 14 (Aug. 1839), 159; William Cabell Bruce, *John Randolph of Roanoke,* 2 vols. (New York, 1922), I, 353–54; Hamlin, *Greek Revival Architecture,* 17; Fiske Kimball, *American Architecture* (Indianapolis, 1928), 71, 95; Henry C. Montgomery, "The Architect of the American Republic," *Classical Weekly,* 39 (Dec. 17, 1945), 74–78; Lewis Mumford, *The South in Architecture* (New York, 1941), 35–36, 49–50, 52, 54–55.

[17]"They conjure us not to quench the light which is rising on the world. Greece cries to us by the convulsed lips of her poisoned, dying Demosthenes; and Rome

misled by the constant claims of American superiority over the Greeks and Romans; the fact that such comparisons were deemed necessary is of weightier significance.[18]

If Americans referred more often to Rome than to Greece, it was not only because the Latin classics were more familiar to them, but also because they considered the example of Rome more rewarding for their contemplation. John Adams read with "horror" of the "factions and confusions" that led to the destruction of Grecian liberty; and such accounts likewise filled Alexander Hamilton with "pain and disgust."[19] But Rome, the ancient Italian republic which sprang from humble beginnings to become mistress of the world, was a more glorious model. Consequently Americans called their nation "this embryo Rome," "the new Rome," or "our Rome of the West."[20] They designated their congressional edifice the "Capitol," its upper house the "Senate," and they adopted the Roman eagle as their national emblem. Though they did not aspire to emulate the conquests of the "Niobe of Nations," they at least hoped that their own republic might some day command the respect that Rome once elicited from the people of the world.

But in less than a half-century after the Founding Fathers had drafted the federal constitution, the examples of Greece and Rome no longer seemed so consequential to most Americans. In part the waning interest in the record of the ancient republics resulted from the declining influence of classical education, which led to less frequent allusions to antiquity. At the same time the depreciation of those

---

pleads with us in the mute persuasion of her mangled Tully." Edward Everett, *Orations and Speeches on Various Occasions*, 4 vols. (Boston, 1865-72[7]), I, 40; "Our Own Country. Number Two. The Times," *Knickerbocker*, 5 (May 1835), 417.

[18]See, e.g., James Wilson's Fourth of July 1788 oration, in which he boasted of America's superiority over the Romans while lauding the virtues of republican Rome: *Columbian Magazine*, 2 (July 1788), 394-400.

[19]*The Works of John Adams*, ed. Charles Francis Adams, 10 vols. (Boston, 1856), IV, 285; *The Works of Alexander Hamilton*, ed. Henry Cabot Lodge, 12 vols. (New York, 1904), I, 246.

[20]"Fourth of July Thoughts," *Knickerbocker*, 14 (July 1839), 62, 67; *Register of Debates*, 23 Cong., 1 Sess., 2676-77 (Feb. 6, 1834); Ralph Henry Gabriel, *The Course of American Democratic Thought* (New York, 1956[2]), 95. Thomas E. Tallmadge suggests that Thomas Jefferson's preference for Roman revival in architecture was due to his belief that "the real analogy with the infant Republic lay in Rome, not Athens": *The Story of Architecture in America* (New York, 1936), 92-93. The christening of a small stream in the District of Columbia after the famed river that flowed through the Eternal City struck Thomas Moore, the celebrated Irish poet, as ridiculously incongruous. He jocularly recalled his visit: "... o'er this 'second Rome!' Where tribunes rule, where dusky Davi bow, And what was Goose-Creek once is Tiber now...." *The Poetical Works of Thomas Moore, Collected by Himself*, 10 vols. (London, 1842), 296. He would have been even more amused had he foreseen that the American Tiber was destined to become one day a part of the capital sewage system.

commonwealths as valuable models served as an argument against the study of the learned languages.

Even during the early days of the Republic, some prominent Americans like Benjamin Franklin and Benjamin Rush had opposed the heavy emphasis upon the classics in the education of the nation's youth, and dolefully complained that theirs were voices crying in the wilderness against the entrenched studies.[21] During the Jacksonian era, however, the tide began slowly to turn in favor of the opponents of the traditional curriculum.[22] Now it was the advocates of the old-fashioned course of study who spoke out in strident tones against the encroachments of their antagonists. In 1843 Andrew P. Peabody declared that "he, who should, twenty years ago, have occupied the time of a literary society ... with a defense of classical literature, would have been regarded as performing a work of useless and Quixotic knight-errantry—as running tilt against the windmills of his own wayward fancy." But now, he warned, "the controversy has become a real and an earnest one. War to the death has been declared and waged against classical culture."[23]

In the first place, the traditional classical education was ill-adapted to the equalitarian-minded (if not equalitarian) Jacksonian era. Since the ability to read and quote Latin and Greek formerly served as a means of distinguishing the gentleman from the common man, such studies better suited a society that recognized rigid class distinctions. With their whole-hearted endorsement of democracy many Americans frowned upon a system of education that tended to set men apart according to their presumed station in life.[24] The common school, not

[21]Richard M. Gummere, "Socrates at the Printing Press: Benjamin Franklin and the Classics," *Classical Weekly,* **26** (Dec. 5, 1932), 58; "Observations upon the Study of the Latin and Greek Languages, as a Branch of Liberal Education, with Hints of a Plan of Liberal Instruction, without Them, Accommodated to the Present State of Society, Manners and Government in the United States," in Benjamin Rush, *Essays, Literary, Moral and Philosophical* (Philadelphia, 1806), 21–56. For references to Rush's and Franklin's attacks upon the classics: John C. Kunze, "Letter on the Learned Languages," *New-York Magazine,* **1** (April 1790), 213; "Improved Mode of Education," *Universal Asylum and Columbian Magazine,* **5** (Sept. 1790), 145–46.

[22]R. Freeman Butts and Lawrence A. Cremin, *A History of Education in American Culture* (New York, 1952), 76; George P. Schmidt, "Intellectual Crosscurrents in American Colleges, 1825–1855," *American Historical Review,* **42** (Oct. 1936), 46–67.

[23]*The Uses of Classical Literature: An Address Delivered before the United Literary Societies of Dartmouth College, July 26, 1843* (Boston, 1843), 5.

[24]William Hardy Alexander, "The Amiable Tyranny of Peisistratus: or the Future of Classical Studies," *Classical Weekly,* **30** (Jan. 25, 1937), 127–35; William P. Atkinson, *The Liberal Education of the Nineteenth Century* (New York, 1873), 3; Jacob Bigelow, *Modern Inquiries: Classical, Professional, and Miscellaneous* (Boston, 1870), 81; "Thoughts on the Study of the Greek and Latin Languages," *New-England Magazine,* **5** (Aug. 1833), 117n. When Robert Dale Owen proposed a vocational curriculum for the sons of workingmen, some parents objected; they wanted their children to have the advantages they believed a classical education would give them on the road to

the college or university, was the theme of panegyrics by democratic orators and writers, who stressed the diffusion of knowledge among all men and opposed the idea of an educated elite class such as existed in most European countries.[25] The strain of anti-intellectualism characteristic of the age lowered classical education in the public esteem.[26] In lauding Andrew Jackson's qualities of leadership, for example, Andrew Stevenson of Virginia suggested that the Old Hero had benefited from his lack of a classical education. "Regular and classical education has been thought, by some distinguished men," he said, "to be unfavourable to great vigour and originality of the understanding; and that, like civilization, whilst it made society more interesting and agreeable, yet, at the same time, it levelled the distinctions of nature."[27]

Paradoxically American colleges and universities, long the citadels of classical education, were attacked as undemocratic at the very time that they were proliferating as a result of a widespread popular de-

---

success. Butts and Cremin, *A History of Education in American Culture*, 269; H. R. Cleveland, *Remarks on the Classical Education of Boys* (Boston, 1834), 64; *Journal of the Proceedings of a Convention of Literary and Scientific Gentlemen, Held in the Common Council Chamber of the City of New York, October, 1830* (New York, 1831), 177. Yet the acceptance of public responsibility for the support of schools nevertheless contributed to the decline of classical education, for most taxpayers were reluctant to support the study of subjects whose utility they questioned: *ibid.*, 179.

[25] *Congressional Globe*, 29 Cong., 1 sess., Appendix, 470–71 (April 22, 1846); "Education," *Knickerbocker*, **8** (Sept. 1836), 310–11; "Nurseries of American Freeman," *ibid.*, **10** (Mar. 1837), 369–76; "Common Schools," *New-England Magazine*, **3** (Sept. 1832), 200–01, 206–07; C. C. Felton, *An Address Delivered at the Dedication of Bristol Academy in Taunton, August 25, 1852* (Cambridge, Mass., 1852), 11; Francis J. Grund, *The Americans in Their Moral, Social and Political Relations*, 2 vols. (London, 1837), I, 24–27, 31, 51; Harriet Martineau, *Retrospect of Western Travel*, 3 vols. (London, 1838), I, 48–50; "Grund's Americans," *Boston Quarterly Review*, **1** (April 1838), 163; Orestes Brownson, "American Literature," *ibid.*, **2** (Jan. 1839), 10. Opponents of the learned languages argued that the classical scholar often did not conceal his feeling of superiority over those who did not possess the same keys to the ancient tongues that he enjoyed; that he tended to hold in contempt "those who are only furnished with the knowledge indispensable for the conduct of ordinary life": *Common School Journal*, **2** (June 1, 1840), 188. Indeed some college professors indoctrinated their students with such a view. In 1846 Dr. Robert Saunders told the graduates of William and Mary upon their completion of a classical education: "You have arrayed yourselves among the votaries of knowledge. You have separated yourselves from the throng who grope in the night of ignorance, scarcely conscious of the possession of intellect." The young scholars were thus "entitled to that homage which the awakened intellect universally commands." "Baccalaureate Address," *Southern Literary Messenger*, **12** (Sept. 1846), 541.

[26] "Necessity of a Liberal Education," *Brownson's Quarterly Review*, **1** (April 1844), 199; "Who Would Be a Scholar?" *Knickerbocker*, **10** (July 1837), 39.

[27] *Monument to the Memory of General Andrew Jackson*, comp. Benjamin M. Dusenbery (Philadelphia, 1846), 253; Francis J. Grund, *Aristocracy in America*, 2 vols. (London, 1839), II, 243.

mand.[28] The institutions of higher learning were also not immune to the democratic tendencies of the times. No longer were college matriculates confined almost exclusively to those who intended to prepare for one of the learned professions.[29] According to Francis Bowen, the rivalry for students among the new colleges and universities that blossomed forth during the early nineteenth century led "in some instances to a great diminution of the severer studies, and a substitution for them of those which are more light, practicable, and agreeable."[30] Some old as well as new colleges introduced limited voluntary programs of study, though the ultimate in educational popular sovereignty, the elective system, did not flourish until the post-Civil War period.

Not only were fewer Americans being exposed to classical culture, but the liberally educated gentleman was also playing a less important role in politics and society.[31] The traditional curriculum had been strongest in the Atlantic seaboard states. With the shifting popular trend, the eastern gentleman was losing political power to the western pioneer, preoccupied with the task of taming a continent, while a rising tide of immigrants swelled the ranks of the "plain republicans" in the coastal states.[32] In the early days of the Whig party, many of its leaders, boasting that their ranks embodied "all the decency, refinement, wealth, and cultivation of practically all the States," addressed their appeals primarily to the well-educated gentry, but when the

[28]*The Works of Philip Lindsley ...*, ed. Le Roy J. Halsey, 3 vols. (Philadelphia, 1866), I, 213-15; "Observations and Hints on Education," *Boston Quarterly Review.* 3 (April 1840), 162; "Introduction," *United States Magazine and Democratic Review,* 1 (Oct. 1837), 10; "European Views of American Democracy," *ibid.,* 2 (July 1838), 348.

[29]George E. Dabney, "On the Study of the Ancient Languages in the United States," *Southern Literary Messenger,* 17 (June 1851), 331.

[30]Francis Bowen, "College Education," *North American Review,* 55 (Oct. 1842), 332-33.

[31]Francis J. Grund, *Aristocracy in America,* II, 5-6; Alexis de Tocqueville, *Democracy in America,* 2 vols. (New York, 1945), I, 202; Richard Hofstadter, *Anti-intellectualism in American Life* (New York, 1963), Ch. 6.

[32]Two speeches in the House of Representatives in 1854 reflected typical immigrant and western attitudes toward the value of a classical education. "If I am deficient in classical lore, I am pretty well booked up in the rascality of the age in which we live," said Representative Mike Walsh of New York, a native of Ireland. "I would not barter away all the practical knowledge I have received in lumber and ship-yards for all the Latin that was ever spoken in ancient Rome. I had rather speak sense in one plain and expressive language, than speak nonsense in fifty. [Laughter.]." *Congressional Globe.* 33 Cong., 1 sess., 1231 (May 19, 1854). Representative L. D. Campbell of Ohio said that it was erroneous to assume that "all the great men came from the finished fashionable institutions of New England." "I acquired my little learning," he said, "in a sort of log-cabin school-house in the West, and am quite satisfied that I never received the cold polish of what is called a fashionable education": *ibid.,* Appendix, 405 (Mar. 7, 1854). For a somewhat different view: Walter R. Agard, "Classics on the Midwest Frontier," *Classical Journal,* 51 (Dec. 1955), 103-10.

party unequivocally embraced the new democratic techniques of the era during the campaign of 1840, its leaders solicited the support of the masses, who, according to Alexis de Tocqueville, "care[d] but little for what occurred at Rome and Athens."[33] Certainly they did not esteem the Plutarchian hero who disregarded the will of the people. The politician who quoted extensively in Latin or whose references to ancient history possessed the quality of ostentation was often subject to ridicule.[34] No one enjoyed entertaining literary audiences with Latin quotations more than Daniel Webster, yet he realized that such examples of erudition repelled the common man; therefore in his appeals to juries he included "no Latin phrases, no *fieri facias*."[35] For the same reason he persuaded President William Henry Harrison, who loved to display his knowledge of ancient civilization, to delete from his inaugural address several obscure classical references. It was no easy task, but the godlike Daniel managed to kill "seventeen Roman pro-consuls as dead as smelts"—according to his own reckoning.[36]

While the learned gentleman was declining in political importance in the "Age of the Common Man," he was also being deprived of his former social prestige by the rise of the businessman. Wealth rather than family background or education was becoming the principal status determinant.[37] America's expanding economy afforded unprecedented opportunities for the acquisition of monetary fortunes, but college graduates discovered that the traditional classical education had little market value.[38] In their desire to enter "with railroad speed" into the pursuit of wealth, American youth did not relish spending long hours poring over languages that had long since been dead. They were quite willing to exchange the elegant prose of Cicero for the "dry commercial phrase of the desk and the counting house." More and more of them advocated a utilitarian education.[39] Colleges

[33]"Mr. Forrest's Oration," *United States Magazine and Democratic Review,* 3 (Sept. 1838), 51–57; Tocqueville, *Democracy in America,* II, 80.

[34]John G. Palfrey, "Congressional Eloquence," *North American Review,* 52 (Jan. 1841), 135; *Register of Debates,* 22 Cong., 2 sess., 1303, 1334 (Jan. 24, 1833), 1493 (Jan. 30, 1833); *Congressional Globe,* 29 Cong., 1 sess., Appendix, 286 (Feb. 9, 1846), 33 Cong., 2 sess., 426 (Jan. 27, 1855). "Whenever I hear a judge in court give an opinion in Latin," said Senator John P. Hale of New Hampshire, "I generally conclude that he is about to announce some infernal doctrine that he is ashamed to speak in English": *ibid.,* 35 Cong., 2 sess., Appendix, 161 (Feb. 15, 1859).

[35]*The Writings and Speeches of Daniel Webster,* 18 vols. (Boston, 1903), XIII, 582.

[36]Peter Harvey, *Reminiscences and Anecdotes of Daniel Webster* (Boston, 1877), 163.

[37]Grund, *Aristocracy in America,* II, 15, 34–38.

[38]James C. Bruce, *An Address Delivered before the Alumni and Graduating Class of the University of North Carolina, at Chapel Hill, on the Afternoon of June Third, 1841* (Raleigh, 1841), 5. Ernest Riess, "Some Remarks on 'the Future of the Classics'," *Classical Weekly,* 30 (Mar. 15, 1937), 188.

[39]For references to the utilitarian arguments against the classics: George E. Dabney,

as well as individuals were affected by this materialistic spirit. When Harvard College announced the inauguration of a limited voluntary program in 1841, its corporation defended the move as designed to attract to the support of the institution many wealthy members of the community who regarded the study of ancient languages as a waste of time.[40]

The popularity of science also contributed to the waning influence of classical education.[41] In the era of the railroad, the steamboat, the telegraph, and the mechanical reaper, science and technology, unlike the classics, appeared to meet the tests of democracy and materialism. Not only did the new inventions ameliorate the lot of the common man, but the exploitation of them by the businessman made possible the acquisition of wealth; therefore many youths were attracted to the scientific studies partly by the belief that "a knowledge of them may be made directly profitable in the pursuit of riches." Francis Bowen, an advocate of the traditional curriculum, heartily disapproved of the Lowell Scientific School, established during the 1840's at Harvard College. Regretting that the old-fashioned studies were being "pushed into a corner," he contended that the objective of most college students appeared to be "the cultivation of physical science, and even of the mechanic arts and trades."[42]

With each passing year science and invention were widening the chasm between the ancient and the modern world, thus contributing to the enthusiastic acceptance by nineteenth-century Americans of the idea of progress.[43] Why then should the ancients be aroused from

---

Lecture on the Study of the Classics, Delivered in Washington College, Lexington, Virginia, September 10, 1838 (Richmond, 1838); William Howard Gardiner, *An Address, Delivered before the Phi Beta Kappa Society of Harvard University, 28 August, 1834, on Classical Learning and Eloquence* (Cambridge, Mass., 1834); "Classical Learning," *American Quarterly Review,* 17 (Mar. 1835), 3–6; Andrew P. Peabody, "The Intellectual Aspect of the Age," *North American Review,* 64 (April 1847), 279; "The Classics," *Southern Literary Messenger,* 2 (Mar. 1836), 221–33; Mathew Carey, "The Learned Languages," *ibid.,* 2 (Aug. 1836), 558; "Instructions in Schools and Colleges," *Southern Quarterly Review,* n. s. 6 (Oct. 1852), 464; Hugh S. Legaré, "Classical Learning," *Southern Review,* 1 (Feb. 1828), 18–19.

[40]Francis Bowen, "Classical Studies at Cambridge," *North American Review,* 54 (Jan. 1842), 41–43.

[41]Matthew F. Maury, *Address Delivered before the Philodemic Society, at the Commencement of Georgetown College, August 28, 1846* (Washington, 1846), 912; William C. Richards, *The Claims of Science: An Address Delivered before the Euphemian and Philomathean Societies of Erskine College, S. C.* (Charleston, 1851), 11–12; Ogden N. Rood, *The Practical Value of Physical Science ...* (Troy, 1859), 15–16; Timothy Flint, "The Past-The Present-and the Future," *Knickerbocker,* 4 (Sept. 1834), 167.

[42]Francis Bowen, "Eliot's Sketch of Harvard College," *North American Review,* 68 (Jan. 1849), 119.

[43]E.g., Edward Everett, *Orations and Speeches,* III, 228; J. T. Headley, *The Progressive Principle* (New York, 1846), 4; Samuel M. Shute, *The Progress of the Race ...* (Baltimore, 1856), *passim.*

the sleep of two millenniums to instruct Americans about a world of which they had no conception? Particularly did American reformers stress the advances that the modern world had accomplished over ancient civilization in order to justify their faith in the future improvement of society.[44] Significantly, below the Mason and Dixon line the idea of progress was substantially modified. Southerners were willing to argue the superiority of modern slavery over ancient slavery, but they refused to acknowledge that the world-wide movement for emancipation was proof that "civilization has moved, is moving, and will move in a desirable direction."[45] Consequently the Old South displayed a determined resistance against the attacks upon the traditional educational curriculum partly because her spokesmen insisted that the successes and failures of ancient civilization bore significant meaning for modern society.[46]

To most Americans, however, there was no more striking example of progress than the record of their own republic. As their pride in the past accomplishments of their own nation waxed, their interest in Greek and Roman history waned. About the same time that Germany's Barthold Niebuhr was dismissing many "pretty stories" of Roman history as mere "idle fables," Americans were becoming increasingly conscious of their own heroic age—the American Revolution—an era that actually occurred and not one of legend and myth.[47] Furthermore they were deeply impressed by what they regarded as the impact of their struggle for independence upon world civilization.[48] "If we may judge of the ultimate consequences from those which have already followed our Revolution," said Charles Carter Lee in 1842, "it appears certain, that a deeper interest must hereafter attach to its history, than now belongs to that of ... the Commonwealth of Rome."[49] In the estimation of Americans their own virtuous heroes supplanted the great men of antiquity. Especially could they boast of George Washington (the subject, incidentally, of two Latin-language biographies published in the United States during the eighteen-

[44]E.g., A. W. Ely, "Education of the Deaf and Dumb in Europe and America," *De Bow's Review*, 17 (Nov. 1854), 435.

[45]Guy A. Cardwell, "The Idea of Progress: North and South: 1860," *Georgia Review*, 11 (Fall 1957), 271-78; George Fitzhugh, *Sociology for the South, or the Failure of Free Society* (Richmond, 1854), 158-59; Arthur Alphonse Ekirch, Jr., *The Idea of Progress in America, 1815-1860* (New York, 1944), Ch. 8.

[46]Edwin A. Miles, "The Old South and the Classical World," *North Carolina Historical Review*, 48 (July 1971), 258-75.

[47]"Editorial Miscellany," *De Bow's Review*, 14 (May 1853), 520; Henry A. Washington, "The Virginia Constitution of 1776," *Southern Literary Messenger*, 18 (Nov. 1852), 663-64; "Literary and Intellectual Statistics," *New-England Magazine*, 1 (Dec. 1831), 477-78.

[48]Grund, *The Americans*, I, 231; Robert B. Patton, *A Lecture on Classical and National Education* (Princeton, 1826), 7-8.

[49]"The American Revolution," *Southern Literary Messenger*, 8 (April 1842), 257.

thirties).[50] "History gives to Cincinnatus high civic virtues, to Aristides the quality of justice, and to Fabius Maximus consummate prudence and courage in war," said Senator Bedford Brown of North Carolina in 1839, "but the honor and glory of their being united in the person of a single individual, was reserved for exemplification in the character of George Washington."[51] Actually, growing national confidence rendered flattering comparisons of Americans to the ancients less necessary and hence less frequent; when they discovered their own history, Americans simply talked less of Thermopylae and Marathon, more of Lexington and Concord; less of Cato and Cicero, more of Washington and Jefferson.

Cultural manifestations of America's growing national consciousness also tended to weaken the prestige of the learned languages and the classical heritage. Exhibiting new found pride in American contributions to the English language, many echoed Noah Webster's oft-expressed view that hitherto the people of the United States had paid a "too general attention to the dead languages, with a neglect of our own."[52] The desire to create a genuine American culture, to forego slavish imitation of European literary standards, led some to display less respect for the authors of antiquity, for classical studies had always been more diligently pursued in the Old World than in the new.[53] Of course, European literary developments continued to influence American writers, but many of the notions of romanticism that were most enthusiastically received in the United States—the emphasis upon nature rather than books as the source of wisdom, the stress upon inspiration rather than the acceptance of authority, for ex-

[50]Francis Glass, *A Life of George Washington in Latin Prose* (New York, 1835); William Lance, *Georgii Washingtonis Vita* . . . (Charleston, 1836).

[51]Bedford Brown, *An Address Delivered before the Two Literary Societies of the University of North Carolina in Gerard Hall* (Raleigh, 1839), 34; for similar expressions boasting of Washington's superiority over the ancients: David S. Kaufman, *Address Delivered before the American Whig and Cliosophic Societies of the College of New Jersey* (Princeton, 1850), 30; William Wirt, *An Address Delivered July 20, 1830, before the Peithessophian and Philoclean Societies of Rutgers University* (New Brunswick, 1852), 44; Willis Gaylord Clarke, "Ollapodiana," *Knickerbocker,* 9 (April 1837), 407; *Annals of Congress,* 16 Cong., 1 sess., 1793 (April 6, 1820).

[52]Noah Webster, "Education," *American Magazine,* 1 (Dec. 1787), 23; Charles Caldwell, *Thoughts on Popular and Liberal Education, with Some Defence of the English and Saxon Languages, in the Form of an Address to the Philomathean Society of Indiana College* (Lexington, 1836), 32; Thomas A. Merrill, *An Essay on the Study of the Latin Language in Our Schools and Colleges, at the Expense of Writing and Speaking in English* (New York, 1860); "Editor's Table," *Knickerbocker,* 9 (Mar. 1837), 319; "Thoughts on the Study of the Greek and Latin Languages," *New-England Magazine,* 5 (Aug. 1833), 112.

[53]Thomas R. Hofland, "The Fine Arts in the United States, with a Sketch of Their Present and Past History in Europe," *Knickerbocker,* 14 (July 1839), 48–49; "Thoughts on the Study of the Greek and Latin Languages. Postscript," *New-England Magazine,* 5 (Oct. 1833), 285.

ample—likewise furnished grist for the mills of those who would decry the worth of a classical education and the value of a thorough knowledge of ancient civilization.[54]

As the Revolution and the War of 1812 faded into history, more and more Americans, influenced by certain strains of English and German romanticism, began to look with new appreciation upon their Anglo-Saxon and Teutonic origins.[55] The vogue of Gothic revival architecture and the popularity of the knightly novels reflected this trend.[56] George P. Marsh's admiration for the Gothic heritage led that "Versatile Vermonter" to a thorough disparagement of the Roman influence upon the modern world. Regarding England as "Gothic by birth, Roman by adoption," he declared that "whatever she has of true moral grandeur, of higher intellectual power, she owes to the Gothic mother; while her grasping ambition, her material energies, her spirit of exclusive selfishness, are due to the Roman nurse." According to Marsh, the Roman element had been predominant in England when the Pilgrims and Puritans left for the New World to escape its pernicious influence. "It was the spirit of the Goth," he said, "that guided the May-Flower across the trackless ocean; the blood of the Goth, that flowed at Bunker's Hill." In a remarkable address, *The Goths in New England,* he attributed the greatness of the New England character to its Gothic spirit, while he fixed responsibility upon the continuing Roman influence in Great Britain for such defects in the English moral constitution as the love of form, respect for a hereditary aristocracy, deference to titles, and family pride. In lauding the Gothic tradition Marsh thus succeeded in appealing to Novanglian provincialism and to the Anglophobia of his day; moreover, he also accommodated his thesis to anti-Catholicism. To him New England Protestantism, regarding Christianity "as a living and life-giving spirit, a mode of intercommunion between man and his maker," represented "a super-induction of the temper and spirituality of Christianity upon the soul of the Goth," while Catholicism, "holding the essence and efficacy of Christianity to consist in its ceremonies and its symbols," constituted "a middle term, a *punctum indifferens* between Judaism and [Roman] idolatry."[57]

[54]"Thoughts on the Study of the Greek and Latin Languages," *New-England Magazine,* 5 (July 1833), 53. For an attack upon the influence of Goethe and Carlyle by a classicist: Basil L. Gildersleeve, "Necessity of the Classics," *Southern Quarterly Review,* n. s. 10 (July 1854), 147.

[55]George Boas, *Romanticism in America. Papers Contributed to a Symposium Held at the Baltimore Museum of Art, May 13, 14, 15, 1940* (Baltimore, 1940), vi–viii.

[56]Agnes Addison, *Romanticism and the Gothic Revival* (New York, 1938); Hamlin, *Greek Revival Architecture,* 332, 335. Hamlin also credits the "emergence of the millionaire ... as fatal to the artistic ideals of the Greek Revival.... For if he was to enjoy his success, he must make his money obvious to all—and ostentation became a new ideal in design" *ibid.,* 334.

[57]*The Goths in New England: A Discourse Delivered at the Anniversary of the Philo-*

Usually the religious attacks upon the classical heritage merely took the form of invidious comparisons of ancient paganism to modern Christianity. Thus while Thomas S. Grimké, the leading anticlassicist of the Jacksonian era, made use of scientific arguments against the study of Greek and Latin, he also opposed the traditional studies because of their anti-Christian flavor. (In the pre-Darwinian days the battle lines between science and religion had not yet been distinctly drawn.) Believing that "the virtues of Jesus Christ are the very reverse of what are called the heroic virtues of classical antiquity," he considered it a blessing that classical studies were so imperfectly taught in the United States that not one in a thousand students "imbibe[d] the spirit of ancient literature."[58] Charles Sumner likewise regarded the classics in contention with the Sermon on the Mount. During his pacifistic days, he deprecated the notion of "exaggerated prejudice of country" obtained from the Romans.[59] Furthermore some early Victorians, objecting to the "naked sculptures" and the "lascivious" poetry of antiquity, maintained that the Pierian spring of classical culture was in reality a polluted stream.[60] Such arguments against the old-fashioned studies were hardly new, but they received a more widespread acceptance when evangelical Protestantism rather than Deism influenced the nation's religious atmosphere.

With growing national self-confidence, Americans were becoming convinced of their superiority over the citizens of the ancient republics.[61] After all, the United States was a Christian, not a pagan nation;

---

mathesian Society of Middlebury College, August 15, 1843 (Middlebury, 1843), passim; David Lowenthal, George Perkins Marsh, Versatile Vermonter (New York, 1958), 58–67; Samuel Kliger, "Emerson and the Usable Anglo-Saxon Past," JHI, 16 (Oct. 1955), 476–93.

[58] Address on the Truth, Dignity, Power and Beauty of the Principles of Peace ... (Hartford, 1832), 17, 23, 24n. On the other hand, John Quincy Adams "invariably found that a light estimate of the study of Greek and Latin and an irreverent estimate of the Bible are inseparable companions." Memoirs of John Quincy Adams, ed. Charles Francis Adams, 12 vols. (Philadelphia, 1874–77), X, 261. For similar points of view: Inaugural Oration Pronounced March 18, 1818 by Joshua Bates, A. M., President of Middlebury College (Middlebury, 1818), 19–20; Inaugural Address Delivered by the Rev. Stephen Olin, President of Randolph-Macon College, on the Occasion of His Induction into Office (Richmond, 1834), 11.

[59] The Works of Charles Sumner, 15 vols. (Boston, 1870–83), I, 67.

[60] Thomas Cooper, "The South Carolina College," Southern Literary Journal, n. s. 1 (Aug. 1837), 542, 546; Merrill, An Essay on the Study of the Latin Language, 41; William Cowper Scott, "Poetry and Religion," Southern Literary Messenger, 17 (Dec. 1851), 746–47.

[61] E.g., William H. Seward's oration on "The Destiny of America," The Works of William H. Seward, ed. George E. Baker, 5 vols. (Boston, 1887), IV, 133–36, and two speeches by Representative George McDuffie in Annals of Congress, 18 Cong., 1 sess., 857–59 (Dec. 22, 1823); Register of Debates, 19 Cong., 1 sess., 1378–85 (Feb. 16, 1826).

its citizens, who were enlightened civilians rather than barbarous warriors, were protected by constitutional rights; its government was a limited one; and the sovereign power was not vested in a single city. Furthermore they took pride in their representative system, which, in their opinion, far exceeded any ancient contributions to the science of government. Even in the early days of the republic there had been many who spoke out against the example of Rome, but usually they did so in reply to suggestions that the United States adopt policies, measures, or institutions allegedly borrowed from the ancient Latin commonwealth. Later it was more often the foes of existing trends— opponents of territorial expansion, political democracy, the growth of executive authority, and the extension of federal power, for example—who introduced the subject of Roman history to admonish lest the United States pursue the same path that led Rome through the successive stages of republic, empire, and collapse.[62] Significantly, however, while most Americans were rejecting the relevance of the experience of Rome, many Southerners were becoming increasingly drawn to a cult of Greece. Searching for assurance that a great civilization could coexist with the institution of slavery, they were attracted to ancient Hellas with its system of small independent states and its concept of Athenian democracy so different from the "progressive democracy" of the United States.[63]

If contemplation of the American past and confidence in its present strength caused a weakening of the classical tradition, reflection upon the promise of the American future contributed even more to

[62]Andrew P. Peabody, *The Uses of Classical Literature,* 22; Sidney G. Fisher, "The Science of Government," *American Monthly Magazine,* 12 (Sept. 1838), 205–06; "Our Political Errors," *American Quarterly Review,* 22 (Sept. 1837), 59–60, 75–76; "Downfall of Nations," *Knickerbocker,* 6 (July 1835), 44–53; "The Perilous Condition of the Republic," *New England Magazine,* 1 (Oct. 1831), 284–85, 288; "Democracy in America," *Southern Literary Journal,* n. s. 4 (Oct. 1838), 278; James Warley Miles, "The Danger and Safety of the Republic," *Southern Quarterly Review,* 14 (July 1848), 152, 155, 167. Edward McNall Burns, in discussing the "Lessons of Greece and Rome" in his *The American Idea of Mission: Concepts of National Purpose and Destiny* (New Brunswick, 1957) errs when he states: "no man in a position of eminence in America referred to imperialism as a major cause of Rome's downfall" (295). This argument was used repeatedly in the congressional debates involving America's territorial expansion; e.g., *Congressional Globe,* 28 Cong., 2 sess., Appendix, 342 (Jan. 14, 1845), 354 (Feb. 22, 1845); 29 Cong., 1 sess., Appendix, 129 (Jan. 16, 1846); 29 Cong., 2 sess., Appendix, 132 (Jan. 2, 1847); 30 Cong., 1 sess., Appendix, 51 (Jan. 4, 1848); 275–76 (Feb. 7, 1848); 32 Cong., 2 sess., Appendix, 289 (Mar. 21, 1853).

[63]M. R. H. Garnett, *An Address Delivered before the Society of the Alumni of the University of Virginia* . . . (Charlottesville, 1850), 14–20, 36; Thomas R. Dew, *A Digest of the Laws, Customs, Manners, and Institutions of the Ancient and Modern Nations* (New York, 1853), 210–11; Dew, "An Address, on the influence of the Federative Republican System of Government upon Literature and the Development of Character," *Southern Literary Messenger,* 2 (Mar. 1836), 273–74; Miles, "The Old South and the Classical World," 269–75; Harvey Wish, "Aristotle, Plato, and the Mason-Dixon Line," *JHI,* 10 (April 1949), 254–66.

the same tendency. As Americans came to conceive of the United States as a Providence-blessed nation whose beneficial republican institutions were designed to light the way for all mankind, they felt less dependent upon the inferior models of Greece and Rome. "Americans *love* their country, not, indeed, *as it is*," said Francis Grund, "but *as it will be*. They do not love the land of their fathers; but they are sincerely attached to that which their children are destined to inherit."[64] In 1839 the *United States Magazine and Democratic Review* editorialized: "We have no interest in the scenes of antiquity, only as lessons of avoidance of nearly all their examples. The expansive future is our arena.... We are entering on its untrodden space, with the truth of God in our minds, beneficent objects in our hearts, and with a clear conscience unsullied by the past. We are the nation of human progress; and who will, what can set limits to our onward march?"[65]

Thus Americans of the mid-nineteenth century viewed their heritage from the ancient republics of Greece and Rome in a different light from their fathers and grandfathers. The forces of democracy, materialism, anti-intellectualism, the popularity of science, and the idea of progress weakened the role of the classics in the educational curriculum. Certain elements of romanticism tended to lower in public esteem the value of classical authority and the classical example. Evangelical Protestantism created an atmosphere less congenial to the ancient world than existed when the influence of Deism led to a more sympathetic attitude toward the pagans of antiquity. Whereas in the young republic many Americans revered the wisdom of the ancients, later generations were more likely to be appalled by their ignorance.[66] Americans once boasted of the similarities between the United States and the republics of Greece and Rome; they were later struck more forcibly by the differences that made their nation far superior. Fortified by the vision of America's Manifest Destiny, they looked to the future with a confidence unshaken by the knowledge of the unfortunate record of less favorably endowed nations.

University of Houston.

[64]Grund, *The Americans*, I, 267–68. "Democratic nations," said Tocqueville, "care but little for what has been, but they are haunted by visions of what will be": *Democracy in America*, II, 73.

[65]"The Great Nation of Futurity," *United States Magazine and Democratic Review*, 6 (Nov. 1839), 427.

[66]Albert Barnes, *An Oration on the Progress and Tendency of Science* (Philadelphia, 1840), 13; "Our Own Country. Number Two. The Times," *Knickerbocker*, 5 (May 1835), 416–17; Andrew P. Peabody, "The Intellectual Aspect of the Age," *North American Review*, 64 (April 1847), 276.

XXIII

NOAH WEBSTER'S LINGUISTIC THOUGHT AND THE IDEA OF AN AMERICAN NATIONAL CULTURE

By V. P. Bynack

The decline and fall of republics was a commonplace of American political thought in the late eighteenth and early nineteenth centuries. As one orator put it, "All history has chronicled the same story—those who would be free, baffled by their own success, and buried by their own triumphs—independence leading to wealth, wealth to luxury, luxury to impatience of control, and this, by rapid stages, to effeminacy, corruption, vassalage, and destruction."[1] Before the Revolution, Americans found this *topos* useful for justifying efforts to defend colonial freedom against the policies of a decadent England. After the Revolution, however, as the new nation embarked on its future, the implications of republican history became unsettling. Fred Somkin has shown that nineteenth-century Americans themselves often were baffled by their own success, and fearful that their own triumphs would bury them. They were concerned that history would repeat this story in their own immediate future as the nation realized its own imperial promise.[2]

The development of the idea of a national culture in the United States during that period was a response to such anxieties about the future of the American republic, and to widely-held assumptions about the instability of republican politics. The intellectual and political problems with which Noah Webster struggled during his lifetime (1758-1843), together with the solutions he found, illustrate this response.[3] The lexicographer was one of the first proponents of the idea of a unified national culture

---

[1] William Adams, *New England Society Orations*, ed. Cephus and E.W. Brainerd, 2 vols. (New York, 1901), II, 189.

[2] Fred Somkin, *Unquiet Eagle: Memory and Desire in the Idea of American Freedom, 1815-1860* (Ithaca, 1967), 53.

[3] For a complete list of Webster's writings, see Edwin A. Carpenter, ed., *A Bibliography of the Writings of Noah Webster* (New York, 1958). The most recent biographical work on Webster is Richard M. Rollins, *The Long Journey of Noah Webster* (Philadelphia, 1980). See also his "Words as Social Control: Noah Webster and the Creation of the American Dictionary," *American Quarterly*, 28 (1976). Prior to Rollins' work the standard biography was Harry R. Warfel's *Noah Webster: Schoolmaster to America* (New York, 1936). The starting point for most biographical treatments of Webster is material compiled by Webster's granddaughter—Emily Elizabeth Fowler Ford, *Notes on the Life of Noah Webster*, ed. E.F. Fowler Skeel, 2 vols (privately printed, 1912). What follows here is based on my own investigation of Webster's linguistic theories, "Language and the Order of the World: Noah Webster and the Idea of a National Culture," Diss. Yale 1978.

after the Revolution, and in that idea he saw the potential basis of a stable republic, immune to the causes of decline.

History seemed to show that in republics the weaknesses of human nature eventually overwhelm the political, social, and religious institutions established to restrain or improve them. The fragility of such institutions in a republic led many to ponder the determinative role individual character would have to play in the new nation. "Our liberties may be secured in charters and constitutions," as William Adams pointed out, "but who or what shall guarantee us against the excesses of liberty but self-control in the individual man?" Many who considered the problem looked to the individual character of the nation's citizens for viable principles of self-control, seeking there what Somkin called an "internal gyroscope for self-regulating order."[4] Such principles were conspicuously absent in the citizens of other nations in the past. To discover a credible source for them in the character of American citizens would be to discover the source of the nation's claim to be the unique exemption from the history of previous republics.

The conventional means of elevating individual character by divine grace or by human ability thus furnished possible arguments for national uniqueness. From religious revivals like the Second Great Awakening with its stress (in the East) on social decorum and stability, to the public school movement with its stress on the education of the virtuous citizen, Americans sought refuge from their anxieties in the comforting ideas of spiritual election and national self-culture. They placed special value on the religious, political, and social institutions that furnished the means of individual improvement, but they also kept remembering that institutions, religious or secular, were not by themselves enough to preserve the stability of a republic against the excesses of liberty. "Our great error as a people is, that we put an idolatrous trust in our free institutions," William Ellery Channing said in 1830, "as if these, by some magic power, might secure our rights, however we enslave ourselves to evil passions." The problem was that institutions could do their work of improving the character of the citizen only when themselves "secured by . . . spiritual freedom" and by "moral power and elevation" in the American character.[5]

Few Americans were more zealous about promoting religion and education as a means of achieving this "moral power and elevation" than Noah Webster, whose numerous school texts taught piety and patriotism as well as reading and writing. Few were more zealous, however, in their concern for the existence beyond religious and secular institutions of an ultimate basis for the individual character of Americans—for the existence of some principle of order accessible to all, which would guarantee the stability and continued existence of those institutions.

[4] Adams, *New England Society Orations*, II, 191; Somkin, *Unquiet Eagle*, 53.
[5] William Ellery Channing, "Spiritual Freedom," *Works* (Boston, 1903), 483, 484.

Webster's interest in the creation of a national culture in America grew out of his sense of the problems of republican government after the American Revolution. Like many, Webster came late to the political ideas that informed Enlightenment thought. He developed his thinking along the lines of the more broadly based ideas that shaped and guided the colonial revolt, including the eclectic political philosophy of the English Real Whigs. Directed against enemies abroad who appeared to threaten America's political institutions, this way of thinking was perfectly consistent with the conservative, Connecticut "steady habit" way of life in which Webster had been reared on his father's West Hartford farm. Not until after the American Revolution did he begin to perceive it as threatening social stability. As early as 1774, his freshman year at Yale, Webster was an ardent democrat.

By reading philosophers like Rousseau during the last years of the Revolution and the first years of the peace, Webster added to this zeal for democracy a belief in the innate goodness of human nature. In 1785 he published a pamphlet called *Sketches of American Policy . . .* which contained one of the first arguments in favor of a federalized national government, and in it he expressed optimism about Americans' ability to govern themselves, an optimism he soon decided was unfounded. "On reviewing the work," he told Chancellor James Kent in 1804, "I find in the first parts" (which dealt with democratic theory and political history) "many chimerical notions respecting a popular government which I had imbibed from the writings of Dr. [Richard] Price and [Jean-Jacques] Rousseau." He had argued in the *Sketches* that the "sovereign power" in any state was "the whole body of the people generally," a power that could err, but that never knowingly could become tyrannical. This power, he maintained, was nothing but the sum of all individual interests, and "what is called *patriotism* or *public* spirit is nothing but self-interest, acting in conjunction with other interests, for its own sake." Allowing the greatest number of people freedom to pursue their self-interest therefore seemed the best way to promote social stability.[6]

Five years later, however, Webster had become a staunch Federalist. Reflecting on Thomas Jefferson's successful Presidential campaign, he told Benjamin Rush:

As to mankind, I believe the mass of them to be "copax rationis." They are ignorant or what is worse, governed by prejudices and authority—& the authority of men who flatter them instead of boldly telling them the truth. . . . We have grown so wise of late years as to reject the maxims of Moses, Lycurgus and the patriarchs—we have by our constitutions of Govt. & the preposterous use of doctrines of equality stripped old men of the [sic] dignity & *wise* men of their

---

[6] Webster to James Kent, Oct. 20, 1804, in Harry R. Warfel, ed., *Letters of Noah Webster* (New York, 1953), 148; Noah Webster, *Sketches of American Policy . . .* (Hartford, 1785), 3, 4, 11, 24n.

influence, & long, long are we to feel the mischievous effects of our modern policy.[7]

By 1802, far from declaring his support for the free expression of individual self-interest, Webster was grumbling that "the very principle of admitting every body to the right of free suffrage, prostrates the wealth of individuals to the rapaciousness of a merciless gang who have nothing to lose, and will delight in plundering their neighbors."[8]

For Webster, as for many Americans who shared his growing fear of democracy, the most important cause of his doubts about Americans' ability to govern themselves was the spectacle of the French Revolution. The events in France, as he dryly put it in 1796, together with what seemed to be a tendency toward popular tyranny in the United States, "somewhat abated my enthusiasm" for democracy.[9] As early as 1787, however, even before the Constitution was written and ratified, and only two years after his optimistic statements in the *Sketches*, Webster had begun to see something wrong with democratic politics. Things were not turning out the way he had expected they would in post-Revolutionary America. There was a gap between democratic ideals and democratic realities, and he struggled to explain why.

The reason, he decided in 1787, was that republican political institutions were not in themselves sufficient to prevent the evils that attended democracy. There had to be something prior to political, social, and economic institutions, something that would cause Americans to live together in harmony and virtue. What America needed, he decided, was something that later came to be called a national culture.

"It was expected," he wrote in 1787, that "on the ratification of peace by belligerent powers, America would enjoy perfect political tranquility." Instead, the nation was plagued by a host of evils, most of them chargeable to the consequences of democratic rule. "This," he wrote, "is the dark side of our public affairs."

Instead of general tranquility, *one* state has been involved in a civil war [Shays' Rebellion in Massachusetts] and most of them are torn with factions, which weaken or destroy the energy of government. . . . Instead of legal security of rights under governments of our own choice, and under our control, we find property at least unsafe, even in our best toned government. Our charters may be wrested from us without fault, our contracts may be changed or set aside without our consent, by the breath of a popular Legislature. Instead of a diminution of taxes, our public charges are multiplied; and to the weight of accumulating debts, we are perpetually making accessions by expensiv [sic] follies. . . .[10]

[7] Webster to Benjamin Rush, Dec. 15, 1800, in Ford, *Notes*, I, 479.

[8] Quoted in Warfel, *Noah Webster*, 280-81. Webster's growing dislike for the realities of American democratic politics reached a peak in 1814, when he was active in calling what became the Hartford Convention.

[9] Webster to C.F. Volney, July 10, 1796, in Warfel, ed., *Letters*, 137.

[10] Noah Webster, "Remarks on the Manners, Government, and Debt of the United States," in *A Collection of Essays and Fugitiv [sic] Writings on Moral, Historical, Political, and Literary Subjects* (Boston, 1790), 81-82, 83-84.

Webster wrote of democracy's problems in the language of revolutionary politics: "security of rights under governments of our own choice, and under our own control." He was not abandoning all hope for the realization of democratic ideals. At the moment, he reflected, democracy might be tending toward majority tyranny, but he still could hope that eventually, perhaps some time "beyond the lives of the present generation," America could enjoy harmony and tranquility, and at the same time self-government.

The reason republican government had not yet produced the benefits expected of it in America, he decided, was that the struggles of the Revolution were not yet over. In the wake of the political revolution, Americans still had to achieve a cultural revolution. "A fundamental mistake of the Americans has been, that they have considered the revolution as completed, when it was but just begun." Americans had fought to preserve against corruption a unique form of government; now, he argued, despite the success of the political revolution, they must realize that form of government still was doomed to corruption and failure unless, by a further revolution in their "manners," the behavior of every individual could be made to support it.[11]

The history of "manners," the history of national behavior, Webster argued in 1787, repeated the familiar story of rise and decline. "Every person tolerably well versed in history," he said, "knows that nations are often compared to individuals and to vegetables, in their progress from their origin to maturity and decay, and from virtue to vice and corruption." In terms of this analogy, America was in its very first stages of development. This made it particularly vulnerable to the corruptions characteristic of the older, declining cultures of Europe. Currently, he warned, "Men . . . are disposed to rush with heedless emulation, into an imitation of manners, for which they are not prepared."[12] The only way to ensure that Americans would behave virtuously and not fall prey to the depravity of Europe, he claimed, was to develop America's own uniquely correct habits of thought and action.

The Revolution itself had destroyed the old habits, establishing both a vacuum and the opportunity to fill it. As Webster put it, "The restraints imposed by respect and habits of obedience were broken thro [sic], and the licentious passions of men set afloat." The only viable course to take, he concluded, was to continue the process of separation from Europe begun in the political revolution, to build up new restraints, new habits of obedience, independent of the corruption that European manners threatened. What the nation now needed, he decided, was the development of a culture appropriate to the requirements of stability under a republican form of government. America's political institutions were just the framework of the new nation. A national culture would supply, in Webster's mixed metaphor, both the "superstructure" and the foundation.

Having raised the pillars of the building [Americans had] ceased to exert themselves, and seemed to forget that the whole superstructure was then to be erected.
This country is independent in government; but totally dependent in manners,
which are the basis of government. . . .

This conclusion, that "manners . . . are the basis of government," was
the kernel from which all Webster's subsequent work grew.[13]

By calling for the creation of national habits of thought and action
as the "basis" of the nation's politics, however, Webster transformed the
problem of erecting a stable American political order into a larger and
more comprehensive problem, the problem of establishing that culture
itself on a stable and enduring foundation. If Americans' unique national
"manners" were to correct their political behavior, overcoming the individual depravity that seemed to characterize political action, the way
Americans lived had to be linked in some way to constraints on that
depravity, constraints that transcended the elements of the culture itself.
People scorned law and custom, the political and social constraints society
imposed, and they scorned their duty to a seemingly distant God as well.
American behavior had to be regulated by something stronger than human art, and by something nearer than eternal rewards. It had to be
regulated by objective constraints on human action such as the essential
structure of the world in which people acted.

In the course of the eighteenth century, philosophers had become
skeptical about the ability of the human mind to know anything essential
about the world. Webster's transformation of the problem of erecting a
stable democratic government into the problem of erecting a national
culture based on the true order of things immediately raised issues of
epistemology that, if left unresolved, would render the whole transformation futile. Prior to the problem of culture, the case of Noah Webster
shows, was the problem of acquiring knowledge of that order.

Webster's interest in the creation of an American national culture
had begun with his efforts to establish a national linguistic standard. As
early as his first *Speller*, completed in 1783 as the first part of *A Grammatical Institute of the English Language*, which included a *Grammar*
(1784) and a reader (*An American Selection*, 1785), those concerns focused
on the education of Americans *as* Americans. The importance of the
problem of a national culture emerged as Webster pursued this linguistic
work. The crucial early influence on that work was the echo in America
of a debate about the character of language carried on under the aegis
of a prize essay competition conducted by the Berlin Academy in Prussia.
Beginning with the work of the Academy's President, Louis Moreau de
Maupertuis, especially with his *Réflexions philosophiques sur l'origine des
langues, et la signification des mots* (1748), and proceeding through

---

[13] *Ibid.*, 103, 84.

Johann David Michaelis' *Dissertation on the Influence of Opinions on Language and of Language on Opinions* (1760, first English edition 1769), to Johann Gottfried Herder's *On the Origin of Language* (1770), the efforts of this group established a line of thought characteristic of the proto-Romantic nature of Germany's Enlightenment. In contrast with most eighteenth-century efforts to achieve a general theory of language, this group produced linguistic theories that emphasized the national rather than the universal character of linguistic phenomena.[14] Their work reflected Germany's continuing struggle during the eighteenth and nineteenth centuries to achieve political unity and cultural self-consciousness as a unified nation. As such, it spoke directly to Webster's interest in the creation of an American national culture.

The work that directly influenced Webster was Michaelis's *Dissertation on the Influence of Opinions on Language and of Language on Opinions*. Webster was so taken by Michaelis' essay, with which Michaelis won the Berlin Academy prize essay competition in 1759, that in 1788, the year after he had decided that the solution to the problems of American democracy was a further revolution in American "manners," Webster cribbed many of Michaelis' examples, together with his entire argument, and published his own version of it, with the note that "the title and many of the following ideas are borrowed from a treatise of Mr. Michaelis, director of the Royal Society of Göttingen."[15]

Michaelis' nationalistic emphasis had attracted Webster's interest. "Languages," Michaelis wrote, "are an accumulation of the wisdom and genius of nations, and to which every one has contributed something." Not the cloistered scholar but "the bare man of wit is perhaps the larger contributor, and the illiterate has often a greater share in it, his thoughts being, as I may say, more nearly allied to nature."[16]

A national language cut across social, political, and economic lines. As the united voice of a people, "to which every one has contributed something," it united the people, transcending social, political, and economic antagonisms. Moreover, as the second part of his title implied, Michaelis suggested that a nation's language could influence the thought, and by implication, the behavior of its citizens. If this were so, Webster's

---

[14] See Hans Aarsleff, *The Study of Language in England, 1780-1860* (Princeton, 1967), 70-77, 144-54; also his essay, "The Tradition of Condillac: The Problem of Origin of Language in the Eighteenth Century and the Debate in the Berlin Academy before Herder," in Dell Hymes, ed., *Studies in the History of Linguistics: Traditions and Paradigms* (Bloomington, Indiana, 1974), 93-156. The essay is also in H. Aarsleff, *From Locke to Saussure: Essays on the Study of Language and Intellectual Activity* (Minneapolis, 1982), 146-209.

[15] Noah Webster, "A Dissertation on the Influence of Opinions on Language and of Language on Opinions," in *Essays and Fugitiv Writings*, 222.

[16] Johann David Michaelis, *A Dissertation on the Influence of Opinions on Language and of Language on Opinions* (London, 1769), 12.

philological researches were central to the national welfare. They could reveal the presence of a self-regulating principle of order in Americans' character. As he defensively put it in 1788:

I am sensible that in the eye of prejudice and ignorance, grammatical researches are the business of school boys; and hence we may deduce the reason why philosophers have generally been so inattentive to this subject. But if it can be proved that the *mere use of* words has led nations into error, and still continues the delusion, we cannot hesitate a moment to conclude, that grammatical researches are worthy of the labor of *men.*[17]

The importance of research into a nation's popular language would be particularly great if such a language not only could determine how people thought and acted but could be shown to be "more nearly allied to nature" than the sophisticated language of the learned and the elegant. Not an emphasis just on the popular and the colloquial but an emphasis on the colloquial as a means of access to the true structure of the world was central to Webster's idea of a popular national culture as it emerged during the late eighteenth century. On both sides of the Atlantic at the end of the eighteenth century, intellectuals had begun to hope that in the untutored thought and expression of a nation's ordinary people might lie a way out of a solipsistic "self-created," "arbitrary and capricious" universe, as Wordsworth put it in the 1800 "Preface" to *Lyrical Ballads,* the universe of post-Lockean epistemology.[18] They began to hope that in popular language there might be a reliable source of truth.

Unfortunately, as Michaelis showed, the influence of "the *mere use of* words" on thought and action led more often away from the truth than toward it. This was the case because of fundamental epistemological problems inherent in the relationship that seemed to exist between languages, considered as facts of human consciousness, and their putative referent, the world. These epistemological problems proved difficult to overcome. Webster's enthusiasm for Michaelis' colloquial linguistic standard and for his nationalistic conception of language did not provide Webster with a solution to the epistemological problems of post-Lockean thought. Instead, it brought him face to face with those problems.

Previous eighteenth-century linguistic philosophers had generated a great deal of enthusiasm for etymological studies, for attempts to uncover the origin of language, and for efforts to develop a general theory of linguistic universals. They did so by extending the hypothesis that human nature is everywhere the same to cover the proposition that human

---

[17] Webster, "Dissertation," in *Essays and Fugitiv[e] Writings,* 222.

[18] William Wordsworth, "Preface" (1800), *Lyrical Ballads,* ed. W.J.B. Owen, 2nd edition (London, 1969), 156-57. See also Raymond Williams, *The Country and the City* (New York, 1937), 73, 127.

perception therefore also must everywhere be the same. If perception were everywhere the same, they believed, then even arbitrary or conventional linguistic signs, as well as the ideas to which they immediately referred, possessed a uniform and intelligible relationship to the objects perceived, a relationship that cut across all the apparent differences among languages. Etymology—the study of words' original root meanings—and universal grammar together could abstract from the arbitrary differences among languages the objective, universal significance they all were supposed to share. Thus, language could be a reliable repository of knowledge about the world.

Michaelis, together with Herder and Maupertuis, questioned whether perception is everywhere the same. Arguing for national uniqueness in terms of epistemological relativism, Michaelis pointed out that different people in a different nations perceive the world in different ways. Different people saw different aspects of the same species of object, he claimed, and then they associated their different ideas of that sort of object, first, with different signs which they used to represent the object, and then with the object itself. Not only words but ideas to which they referred were different national languages, and there was no way to judge which ideas were true perceptions of their objects or which words referred to true ideas. There was no universal grammar, different languages had different origins, and etymology was just a parlor game. Language was not a means of access to truth about the world. As Michaelis put it,

What I perceive in every etymology is, that in such and such a nation, some body has thought thus or thus; but to know whether his thoughts be right or wrong requires a particular inquiry, which has nothing to do with etymology.[19]

Webster had been looking to national, colloquial language for a means of access to absolute, universal truth. He was mounting his search, however, from a position established by doubting that anyone could have access to truth of that kind. The resulting conflict was particularly evident in his early lexicographical endeavors, which he discussed in the "Preface" to his short *Compendious Dictionary of the English Language* in 1806. He had no way to resolve the conflict, and he simply papered it over. On the crucial topic of etymology, where he had to confront the issue of the original relation of words to the world, he maintained that there was a direct and intelligible relationship that cut across linguistic differences and that embodied universal constants of perception. In elucidating the primitive relationship between words and things, he said, etymology demonstrated both the universal character of human knowledge and its progressive development. As he put it, "Etymology, judiciously traced

---

[19] Michaelis, *Dissertation*, 13-14.

and displayed, exhibits not merely the origin of words, but the history of the progress of ideas and of the human intellect."[20]

But Webster had to admit that he could find no etymologies that accomplished these goals. He conceded that "imperfect etymologies or those which throw no light on the history of language and of ideas, are of little use," and he was forced to complain that existing etymologies threw no such light. Far from demonstrating the universality of the truths embodied in language, these etymologies were "defective" and "riddled with palpable errors."[21] On the one hand, all national languages were supposed to contain universal truths about the world; on the other hand, they didn't. Webster's *Compendious Dictionary* was the product of more than twenty years' thought about language, the product of more than fifteen years' interest in the relationship between a national language and a national culture, and it was a dead end.

Webster made no further progress in his study of language until he actually experienced what he took to be the absolute truth about the world. That experience made possible in his linguistic and cultural studies the use of what became, as others also discovered them, major commonplaces of the nineteenth century's argument for an American national culture. The first of these, the essentially spiritual character of reality, helped form the nineteenth-century basis of American political liberalism. The second, the privileged access to that essence enjoyed by Americans because of their racial heritage, helped form the basis of the most illiberal aspects of American politics in the modern era.

In the spring of 1808, during the Second Great Awakening, Webster struggled against his own will through the recognized stages of a conversion experience. It was while he was actually at work on his linguistic studies, he told his brother-in-law later that year, that

My mind was suddenly arrested, without any previous circumstance of the time to draw it to this subject and . . . fastened to the awakening and upon my own conduct. I closed my books, yielded to the influence, which could not be resisted or mistaken, and was led by a spontaneous impulse to repentance, prayer, and entire submission and surrender of myself to my maker and redeemer.[22]

What Webster believed he experienced at that moment was the God of Jonathan Edwards—the omnipresent Reality underlying and sustaining all phenomena. Webster had heard Edwardsean theology preached as a youth from the Rev. Nathaniel Perkins, his pastor in West Hartford during the two years prior to Webster's departure for Yale, and the tutor who prepared him for college. Perkins was one of a group of young clergymen who owed theological allegiance to the new Light of the First

[20] Noah Webster, "Preface," *A Compendious Dictionary of the English Language* (Hartford, 1806), xix.

[21] *Ibid.*, xvii, xviii, xix.

[22] Webster to Thomas Dawes, Jr., Dec. 20, 1808, in Ford, *Notes*, II, 43-46.

Great Awakening and who helped lay the evangelical foundations of the Second.[23] At Yale, however, Webster had abandoned this teaching and had embraced a vague form of religious rationalism, a doctrine he maintained for over thirty years.[24] When the revival began to stir New Haven in 1808 he was on the verge of turning Episcopalian, as many Federalists interested in reason and decorum had done, and he declared that he feared even the Second Awakening's studiously calm approach in Connecticut "would by affecting the passions too strongly, introduce an enthusiasm or fanaticism which might be considered as real religion. I expressed these fears to some friends and particularly to my family inculcating on them the importance of a *rational religion*, and the danger of being misled by the passions."[25]

Webster's thoroughly conventional belief in human ability eventually to know the truth about nature and God entailed the epistemological problems that confounded his work on language and culture. His conversion experience overthrew that belief, and at the same time it solved those problems. Counseled throughout his conversion by his family's pastor in New Haven, the young Moses Stuart, then just starting his career after studying divinity with Timothy Dwight, Jonathan Edwards' grandson, Webster learned to interpret what was happening to him in the ameliorated Edwardsean terms of Dwight's modified New Light theology, terms that more than echoed the doctrines he had been taught as a youth.[26] Edwards, Dwight, Stuart, and finally Webster in an *apologia* for his new faith that reached print in 1809, all stressed the ultimate, noumenal existence of a sovereign Creator, continuously supporting the appearances of the phenomenal world.

God's active presence appeared not just in the regeneration of the spirit, Webster declared in his *Peculiar Doctrines of the Gospel, Explained and Defended*, but in the animation of the entire physical world. What, he asked, "are the *laws of nature*" but "effects, and not causes" of that animation? "The operations of nature are evidently the effects of that power constantly exerted, which first called all things into existence. Hence their uniformity, for nothing can be uniform, but God and his operations." No one can "raise an arm or draw a breath without the agency of their Creator."[27]

[23] See Charles R. Keller, *The Second Great Awakening in Connecticut* (New Haven, 1942), 32-35, 51, 72.

[24] See, e.g., Webster Diary, 1784, 1785, in Ford, *Notes*, I, 72, 128.

[25] Webster to Thomas Dawes, Jr., Dec. 20, 1808, in Ford, *Notes*, II, 44.

[26] On general theological developments during the era, see Keller, *The Second Great Awakening in Connecticut*; and Sidney Mead, *Nathaniel William Taylor, 1786-1858: A Connecticut Liberal* (Chicago, 1942); on Stuart, see John Herbert Giltner, "Moses Stuart: 1780-1852," Diss. Yale 1965; and Gerry Wayne Brown, *The Rise of Biblical Criticism in America, 1800-1870: The New England Scholars* (Middletown, Conn., 1969).

[27] Noah Webster, *Peculiar Doctrines of the Gospel, Explained and Defended* (Poughkeepsie, 1809), 10, 12, 6.

Noah Webster found in the idea of active Spirit, of a sovereign God continuously creating all reality, the guarantee that behind the phenomena of the world there existed a stable, enduring spiritual foundation, a foundation on which Americans could rear an enduring culture. The regenerate, like Webster, actually could experience the reality of this foundation. For the unregenerate as well, though, did they but know it, this foundation gave structure to all experience. It enforced its constraints on believer and unbeliever alike. The "gospel doctrines really stand as well on the immutable order of things in the universe, as on the positive declarations of Christ and the apostles," and in that universe "nothing is uniform but truth; nothing unchangeable but God and his works."[28] As Edwards himself put it,

The only adequate definition of truth is the agreement of our ideas with existence. To explain what this existence is, is another thing. . . . In things that are supposed to be without us, it is the determination and fixed mode of God's exciting ideas in us. So that truth in these things is an agreement of our ideas with that series in God. It is existence, and that is all we can say. . . . God and real existence are the same.[29]

Webster's conversion experience helped him locate the epistemological relativism of the debate over language in the Berlin Academy's prize essay competition within a larger ontological framework. Webster's linguistic studies, once a dead end, soon began to reveal new vistas. A year after his conversion he wrote that "new discoveries of important facts, of which I had not the slightest suspicion when I began the investigation, add almost daily new incentives to my zeal and very much increase in my apprehension the value of researches into the origin and progress of languages."[30] Crucial to this revived sense of the possibilities of his project, and to its eventual fulfillment in the publication of Webster's *An American Dictionary of the English Language* in 1828, was his realization that words simultaneously could have relative and absolute significance, a national and a universal meaning.

He expressed this insight as a distinction between what he called the "appropriate" and the "primary" significance of words. In the "Introduction" to the 1828 *Dictionary*, Webster claimed that "the obscurity that still rests on the theory of language" had been the result of the failure of previous students of language to draw this distinction. On the "appropriate" level, the meaning of words was the effect of cultural and social differences between nations. *Hawking* in England, for example, denoted an aristocratic sport, the holdover of feudal customs. In the

---

[28] *Ibid.*, 6, 8.
[29] Jonathan Edwards, "The Mind," in *"The Mind" of Jonathan Edwards: A Reconstructed Text*, ed. Leon Howard (Berkeley, 1963), 101.
[30] Webster to Thomas Dawes, July 25, 1809, in Ford, *Notes*, II, 66-67.

United States, it denoted the extermination of agricultural pests by yeoman farmers. On the "primary" level, however, this and all other words had a universal meaning derived from reference to a "visible physical action."[31]

On the primary level, Webster argued, all words in all languages ultimately derived from verbs.

For example, all nations, as far as my researches extend, agree in expressing the sense of *justice* and *right*, by *straightness*, and *sin, iniquity, wrong*, by a deviation from a straight line or course. Equally remarkable is the simplicity of the analogies in language, and the small number of radical significations; so small indeed, that I am persuaded the primary sense of all the verbs in any language, may be expressed by thirty or forty words.[32]

He listed thirty-four verbs that he believed "express the literal sense of all the primary roots" of all languages, and from that list he drew an even more extreme conclusion: "As the verb is the principal radix of other words, and as the proper province of this part of speech is to express *action*, almost all the modifications of the primary sense of the verb may be comprehended in one word, to *move*."[33] The essence of reality was active Spirit, and language embodied that truth.

Behind the appropriate sense of words, and prior to the level of signification at which meaning appeared to be determined by cultural difference, there was a single, absolute, primary sense to which all words were reducible, a level of signification that could be seen, in its turn, as determinative of cultural difference. Thus Webster could argue that "the manly character of the language and the freedom of the British and American constitutions . . . may perhaps act and react upon each other mutually as cause and effect," the political institutions and customs determining the character of the national language on the appropriate level, but the national language determining the character of the political institutions and social customs on the primary level.[34]

The primordial character of the verb was a notion made current in the eighteenth century by James Harris, whose *Hermes* first appeared in 1751, and by James Burnet, Lord Monboddo, whose six-volume *Of the Origin and Progress of Language* appeared between 1773 and 1792.[35]

[31] Noah Webster, "Introduction," *An American Dictionary of the English Language*, 2 vols. (New York, 1828), (unpaginated: page cited is page-count number), 21.

[32] *Ibid.*, 21.　　　　　　[33] *Ibid.*, 21.　　　　　　[34] *Ibid.*, 40.

[35] Empiricists and materialists tended to favor the priority of the noun, among them Condillac in his *Essai sur l'origine des connaissance humaines* (1746) and John Horne Tooke, in his *Diversions of Purley* (1798, 1805). For an excellent overview, see Hans Aarleff, *The Study of Language in England, op. cit.* (n. 14 above). See also Edward Stankiewicz, "The Dithyramb to the Verb in Eighteenth and Nineteenth Century Linguistics," in Dell Hymes, ed., *Studies in the History of Linguistics: Traditions and Paradigms* (Bloomington, Indiana, 1794), 167; E.L. Cloyd, *James Burnet, Lord Monboddo* (Oxford, England, 1972), 67.

What makes Webster's treatment of this notion distinctive is that unlike his predecessors, who approached linguistics from the point of view of the Cambridge Platonists' philosophical idealism, and unlike their materialist rivals in eighteenth-century linguistics, Webster did not treat language as a human construct, an artificial system of conventions fabricated to express truths that are external to language and that have to be grasped by non-linguistic faculties appropriate to their ideal or material location. He insisted instead that language is a natural phenomenon that has been present since the Creation. He saw it not as a system of signs that individuals project on the world but (on its primary level) as a system of signs that God created when He created the original prelapsarian harmony, a system still embodying the harmony of individual, sign, and world. In Webster's post–conversion theocentric linguistics, language could be the vehicle of a truth that need not be learned by experience, by reflection, or by revelation. It could serve as the principle of order Americans needed as the basis for individual character.

Not just "the faculty of speech," the ability to form and use language, but an actual language "was *the immediate gift of God*" to Adam and Eve in the Garden, and to their posterity.[36] Webster thought he could prove the existence of this language on the primary level of the language Americans spoke. His "proof" put research into areas such as the principles governing phonological shifts at the service of one of the commonplaces of Anglo-American Whig thought, the notion of a radically privileged political heritage, a "*translatio imperii ad Teutonicus.*"[37] The chief obstacle to the development of a Whig history of language linking America with the Garden was the confusion of languages at Babel and the dispersion of "the original Chaldee" into the languages spoken by the tribes of Noah's sons—the "Shemitic," "Japhetic," and "Hamitic" languages that Webster assumed formed the principal language families. Webster thought he had discovered principles of linguistic change that could account for most differences among the languages of modern nations and among these three language groups. While "some differences of language were produced by the confusion," Babel was not the linguistic cataclysm it seems, and "neither that event nor any supernatural event is necessary to account for the differences of dialect or of languages now existing."[38] The "Japhetic" languages of Europe retained, on their primary level of meaning, a direct relationship with the language of the prelapsarian harmony, and of these languages one group—the Teutonic— dominated the others.

---

[36] Webster, "Introduction," 1828 *Dictionary*, 1.

[37] See Samuel Kliger, *The Goths in England: A Study in Seventeenth Century Thought* (Cambridge, Mass., 1952), 33-34.

[38] Webster, "Introduction," 1828 *Dictionary*, 2.

The Teutonic races legitimately had dominated Europe, according to the notion of a *"translatio,"* because they twice had assumed Rome's title to world dominion. The title to political dominion had passed to them with the fall of a decadent Empire to the virtuous German tribes, and a half century later they had assumed the title to religious dominion in the Protestant Reformation. This racial heritage supposedly was transmitted to England by the Anglo-Saxon conquest of the Celts, and Americans in search of arguments supporting claims to both republican virtue and eventual empire found useful support in the belief that Teutonic genius for liberty and title to dominion had found a final home in the New World. Webster used his linguistic research to extend this notion far back beyond Rome, creating a comprehensive vision of world history that linked nineteenth-century America with the six days of Creation and that legitimated American claims to a unique character based not so much on genetic heritage as on the language Americans spoke.

Linguistic evidence seemed to show Webster that all previous republics were Teutonic in origin. Their eventual decay, and their conquest by more virtuous Teutonic nations, as in the case of Rome, was not therefore a political catastrophe; it was a purification and reform of republican government by the race entrusted with its perpetuation.

The first inhabitants of Greece and Italy were probably of the Celtic race, but if they were, it is very evident that tribes of the Teutonic races, invaded those countries before they were civilized and intermingled with the original inhabitants. . . . This is an inference which I draw from the affinities of the Greek and Latin languages, with those of Teutonic origin. The Teutonic and Gothic races impressed their language upon all the continent of Europe. . . ."[39]

The colloquial language of America, Webster believed, was Anglo-Saxon at heart, and he was proud to be able to tell his fellow citizens that "the Saxon words constitute our mother tongue; being words which our ancestors brought with them out of Asia," all the way from the Garden of Eden.[40] Thus their language could serve as an automatic means of access to truths and principles they need not deliberately seek.

What enabled Webster to develop this conception of a national culture based on a national language was his acceptance of a view of the world that located the philosophical dualism of eighteenth-century thought within a larger, monistic framework. While the framework Webster found in Edwardsean theology was less fluid than the sense of the organic unity of all things that developed later in the nineteenth century, it did, in this respect resemble it.[41] Like Emerson's "Spirit," which "does not build up

---

[39] *Ibid.*, 3.   [40] *Ibid.*, 4.

[41] Perry Miller, however, overstates the similarities between Edwards and Emerson in "From Edwards to Emerson," *Errand into the Wilderness* (Cambridge, Mass., 1956), 185-203.

nature around us, but puts it forth through us," Webster's theology provided a comprehensive explanation which grounded individual character, and the everyday world, in an ultimate, absolute reality underlying both the individual and the world in which the individual must live and act. Webster's conversion experience taught him to trace all things, in their apparent diversity, to a single, pervasive principle, their "Almighty Author."[42]

University of California at Berkeley.

[42] Ralph Waldo Emerson, "*Nature*," in Stephen E. Whicher, ed., *Selections from Ralph Waldo Emerson* (Cambridge, Mass., 1957), 50; Webster, *Peculiar Doctrines*, 12.

XXIV

PARRINGTON AND THE JEFFERSONIAN TRADITION

By Richard Hofstadter

It is unlikely that the Jeffersonian tradition will be celebrated soon again with the generous sweep and literary grace of V. L. Parrington's *Main Currents in American Thought*. Recent studies by such critics as Lionel Trilling and Granville Hicks are ample evidence that attitudes towards Parrington's work have already passed from veneration to criticism, and that eager reception of his point of view has given way to delineation, often severe, of his limits and frailties. Among the latter are the inevitable lapses of a synthesis, however masterly, which is undertaken long before analysis reaches its proper depth.

It was appropriate that our long American heritage of grass-roots radicalism should have been summed up by a thinker whose own roots were firm in populist soil. Parrington was a Westerner; he was born in Illinois, raised in Kansas, and taught in Oklahoma and Washington. His editor, E. H. Eby, has emphasized his agrarian leanings, his suspicions of the metropolis. Parrington was acutely sensitive to the agrarian sources of American democracy, and his thinking took shape at a time when his friend J. Allen Smith and Charles Beard were interpreting the struggle between early American agrarianism and capitalism. Nothing was more natural than to find in the western rural democracy of Jefferson and Jackson a set of doctrines erected for the rationalization of an agrarian interest; to contrapose to them a clearly outlined tradition of classical Manchesterian capitalist thought; and thus to construct a symmetrical pattern of clashing economies and ideologies.

Without questioning the fundamentals of this analysis one may criticize the neatness of its schematism. I do not believe it a violation of Parrington's plan to take issue with his conception of the pattern of American economic thought. His history was not narrowly belletristic and it invites criticism on its own terms. Especially open to question is Parrington's emphasis upon the influence of French economic thought, particularly the doctrines of the Physiocrats, in forming the intellectual temper, social ideas and political action of the early Jeffersonian tradition. His stress upon the influence of Quesnay's school in coloring the American demo-

369

cratic heritage was more than a verbal one. It is true that he sometimes spoke of the Physiocratic influence in a generic and almost meaningless sense, as, for example, when he wrote of Joel Barlow's "warm humanitarian enthusiasms that had come down as a rich heritage from the Physiocratic school of social thinkers" or of Thomas Paine as "essentially a Physiocratic agrarian," or of the common tendency of leaders such as Franklin and Jefferson to idealize the agrarian way of life as the great single source of civic virtue. At other points, however, it seems clear that he conceived the Physiocratic influence to have been exerted in a direct and literal sense; that he found evidences of the economic and social doctrines of the *Economistes* written into the annals of American thought. The introduction to his second volume makes clear how central to his whole interpretation was this conception of the lines of ideological cleavage between agrarianism and capitalism and how heavily he weighted the French influence. What other interpretation could be put upon the statement that "the Physiocratic theory of social economics would be irresistible" to a plantation mind like Jefferson's, or that Jacksonianism "lost its realistic basis in a Physiocratic economics?" The following quotation from Parrington's chapter on Jefferson aptly summarizes his conception of the importance of these ideas:[1]

With its emphasis laid upon agriculture, its doctrine of the *produit net*, its principle of *laissez faire,* and its social concern, the Physiocratic theory accorded exactly with his familiar experience, and it must have seemed to Jefferson that it was little other than a deduction from the open facts of American life. He had read much of the works of the Physiocratic group, and was intimately acquainted with Du Pont de Nemours; and the major principles of the school sank deep into his mind and creatively determined his thinking, with the result that Jeffersonian democracy as it spread through Virginia and west along the frontier assumed a pronounced Physiocratic bias. The sharp struggle between Jefferson and Hamilton must be reckoned, in part at least, a conflict between the rival principles of Quesnay and Adam Smith, between an agrarian and a capitalistic economy. . . . It is this Physiocratic conception that explains [Jefferson's] bitter hostility to protective tariffs, national banks, funding manipulations, the machinery of credit, and all the agencies of capitalism which Hamilton was skillfully erecting in America.

That early American politics centered about a struggle between agrarian and capitalist interests is not likely to be questioned. But that the ideological terms in which this battle was fought were

---

[1] *The Colonial Mind,* pp. 346–7.

those of a uniquely agrarian or Physiocratic system of thought as opposed to capitalist liberalism is doubtful. Indeed, an excellent case can be made out to the effect that the principal tenets of the Physiocrats were quickly rejected or forgotten because they were fundamentally unadaptable to the American economic milieu; that whatever the Jeffersonians may have shared with the Physiocrats in their love for agriculture, the practical conclusion of the Physiocrats, the single tax on land revenue, ran directly counter to all the political efforts of the American agrarians; that the economics of Adam Smith and Quesnay were convergent rather than divergent streams in the development of economic thought; that the Jeffersonians were highly receptive to Smithian ideas; that the democratic tradition as embodied in the Jeffersonian and Jacksonian upsurges of 1800 and 1828 was not quite so hostile, at least in ideology, to the property relations of capitalism or its acquisitive spirit as Parrington has implied; and finally, that the systematic and "metaphysical" character of Physiocratic doctrine was repugnant to the spirit of American democracy, which has always been empirical and pragmatic.

To set a high valuation upon agricultural life is not in itself a uniquely Physiocratic idea. In America it generally antedated Physiocratic influence. Jefferson's remarks upon the surpassing virtue of the agricultural population—"Those who labor in the earth are the chosen people of God if ever he had a chosen people" —may be found in his *Notes on Virginia,* which was published in 1781, five years before his contact with the Physiocrats. Franklin's statement that "manufactures are founded in poverty" and his plea for an agricultural future for America dates from 1760, seven years before his meeting with Quesnay's group. John Taylor's references to the primacy of American agriculture were made without any discoverable Physiocratic influence.

The Physiocrats themselves wasted very little time in elaborating this romantic attachment to the rural life. They were too concerned with the establishment of their metaphysical system and the specific economic doctrines concerning value, wealth, distribution and taxation which they spun from its premises.

The real goal of the Physiocratic creed was the desire to save the *ancien régime* by reforming its tax system. This meant finding a means of shifting the burden of taxation upon the largely tax-exempt feudality. Quesnay, who was physician to Louis XV and Madame du Pompadour, saw prophetically that the realm would be ruined by fiscal insolvency if this were not done. The doctrine of the exclusive productivity of agriculture and the sterility of all other forms of economic activity (the Physiocrats acknowledged their usefulness, but denied that they were productive of new wealth) led naturally to the position that the only possible fund of new wealth available for taxation was the *produit net* of agriculture. Taxes levied upon other sources would only be passed on to agriculture anyway, and the most simple, economic, and effective form of taxation would be the *impôt unique,* the single tax upon the proprietor's revenue from the land. All these doctrines, together with *laissez faire,* which the Physiocrats as proponents of the free movement of agricultural products consistently advocated, seemed to flow quite naturally from the apparent physical uniqueness of agricultural production, and to be a simple deduction from God-ordained natural law. In this respect it was of one piece with the whole thought of the Enlightenment.

But a doctrine which was reasonably well adapted to the feudal society of eighteenth-century France was not suited to American agriculture, with its scattered small landowning farmers. And the conception of the single tax upon the proprietor's revenue was the last thing that a party representing this class could advocate. The Physiocratic theory was based on the conception that the landed class, having special bounties of nature and society, should pay taxes as a duty. The American agrarian doctrine was based upon the idea that the capitalist section of society was exploiting agriculture, chiefly through the medium of taxation. We might expect, then, that—contrary to Parrington's interpretation—the leaders of American democracy would shrink from the application of those tenets which were the very core of Physiocracy. This is exactly what happened in the case of Franklin and Jefferson, and the qualifications they made upon Physiocratic doctrine are especially important, since they were the American thinkers most closely associated with the Physiocrats. Both went to France while Quesnay's school was still in existence, both knew some of its leading members, and both were, in different degrees, under the influence of its leading ideas for a short time. It is especially significant, however, that neither ever advocated Physiocracy in any public writing in America, and that neither attempted to publish any works of the Physiocrats in an American edition.

Of Franklin it should be remembered that he never committed himself to an economic abstraction without some immediate practical design. During his long and useful career as a colonial agent in

Britain he was in search of an intellectual stick with which to beat the mercantilism of the mother-country. Almost any plausible body of doctrine which served as a suitable framework for *laissez faire* would have exerted considerable fascination over him; and he did, indeed, set a high value upon David Hume's *Of the Jealousy of Trade,* which in this respect anticipated the doctrines of Smith. In 1767, when the controversy with Britain had begun to sharpen, he journeyed across the channel to France, where he finally met several of the Physiocrats. There can be no doubt that the agrarianism of the Physiocrats added materially to the allure of their free trade principles. Franklin, when he was a British imperial patriot, had urged the adoption of a liberal policy on the part of the mother country on the ground that the presence of free land in America would place a natural check upon the growth of manufactures by draining the labor supply. England need have little fear of colonial competition, therefore; she would serve as the manufactory for a great agricultural commonwealth overseas. He had thus welcomed the idea that America's future would be agricultural, so that the Physiocratic combination of free trade with agrarianism was for the time being highly congenial to his practical aims. It is questionable that he ever came to grips with the full implications of the Physiocratic theory as its founders understood them. Once the bond of empire was broken, and the possibility of applying Physiocracy to American domestic taxation policy presented itself, Franklin balked. He refused to consider the application of the single tax in Pennsylvania under the Confederation. During his last years he was forced to write several letters to his Physiocratic friends in which he explained the expensiveness, impracticability and odium involved in an attempt to collect taxes from American frontier farmers. Finally he became involved in a dispute with Turgot over the universal applicability of the single tax.[2] The economic thought of his later years was scanty and confused. He tried unsuccessfully to combine the labor theory of value which he had long accepted with the Physiocratic theory of the exclusive productivity of agriculture.[3] This view, had they ever heard of it, would have profoundly shocked the Physiocrats, who believed that the expenditures of the landlords or their ancestors in clearing, draining, and enclosing the land were contributions to production as valuable as the actual labor involved in agriculture. Only with

[2] *Writings* (Smyth ed.), Vol. IX, pp. 578, 614–15, 638, 646; see also Turgot, *Oeuvres* (Schelle ed.), Vol. V, pp. 510–16.

[3] *Writings,* Vol. V, p. 195.

these sharp limitations was Franklin a Physiocrat. He accepted some of their abstract premises, with important qualifications in the direction of economic democracy. He repudiated their most important practical conclusion, and he never sought to propagate their ideas in America. That he continued to believe in them in any vital sense is unlikely. There was a gulf between him and his French friends which could not be bridged. It was the gulf between the French estate and the American frontier.

Jefferson toyed with Physiocratic ideas for a short time after his trip to France in 1786, and his friendship with Dupont de Nemours, one of the leaders of the school, lasted for many years. But it is a mistake to say that he regarded the Physiocratic theories as essentially at war with the doctrines of Adam Smith or that he was hostile to Smith. Like Franklin he was receptive to *laissez faire*, a doctrine which he at one time pushed so far as to oppose the use of taxation to level inequalities of wealth, and like Franklin he wanted to freeze American economic society at its existing agricultural level. But he was a younger man than Franklin, and by the time he became active in politics the Physiocratic school had shot its bolt. He soon came to admire Smith's contribution to political economy and thought its implications hostile to the Hamiltonian system of government intervention. In fact, as early as 1790, before the formation of his Republican party, Jefferson endorsed *The Wealth of Nations*, which in chapter nine contains an incisive refutation of the basic Physiocratic ideas, as the best existing work in political economy. In a letter written in 1813 Jefferson speaks of Smith as having "corrected some principles" of the Physiocrats.[4] Jefferson never departed from his acceptance of Smithian doctrines, although he later came to prefer the works of J. B. Say as a more readable and lucid presentation of Smith's ideas. In 1814, preparing a list of select readings for his grandson, George Wythe Randolph, he omitted the Physiocrats, but included works by Say and Malthus together with Destutt de Tracy's forthcoming *Treatise of Political Economy*, which Jefferson was then editing for its publication in America. That work, when it appeared in 1817 under his endorsement, accepted the labor theory of value and expressly repudiated the Physiocratic conception of the sterility of non-agricultural economic activity. In his preface, Jefferson settled his accounts with the Physiocrats. They had contributed sound and valuable principles now generally accepted; others were generally controverted; "and whatever may be the

[4] *Writings* (H. A. Washington ed.), Vol. VI, p. 99.

merits of their principles of taxation, it is not wonderful they have not prevailed, not on the questioned score of correctness, but because not acceptable to the people, whose will must be the supreme law. Taxation is, in fact, the most difficult function of government, and that against which, their citizens are apt to be most refractory. The general aim is, therefore, to adopt the mode most consonant with the circumstances and sentiments of the country.''[5]

As Professor Chinard has pointed out, this quotation aptly illustrates Jefferson's fundamental indifference to the abstract questions involved and his overwhelming concern with the practicable. It illustrates too, as in the case of Franklin, that Americans in rejecting the Physiocrats' ideas of taxation repudiated the greater part of their system. The tribute which Jefferson was willing to pay to the Physiocrats in 1817 was no stronger than that written into *The Wealth of Nations* in 1776, a tribute which was felt to be due them as the founders of political economy. On the idea of *laissez faire,* Jefferson, Smith and the Physiocrats were in entire agreement for varying practical reasons. Where Smith differed from the Physiocrats, Jefferson followed Smith.[6]

John Taylor of Caroline, the most systematic philosopher of Jeffersonian democracy, has often been described as a Physiocratic thinker. His *Arator,* first published in 1813, is the nearest thing to an exposition of native American agrarianism, but it falls far short of the Physiocratic system. Like most contemporary thinkers, Taylor at several times insisted upon the economic and moral primacy of the agricultural interest in America, and a few of his obiter dicta have a marked Physiocratic flavor—*e.g.,* that "a landed interest cannot tax without taxing itself"—but his statement (1822) that "highly valuable as manufactures undoubtedly are, yet all writers upon political economy agree that they are secondary and unite in allowing first place to agriculture," is perhaps as close to Physiocracy as he ever came. If this was Physiocracy, Hamilton might be classed as a Physiocrat on the basis of his ready concession in the *Report on Manufactures* (1791) that "the cultivation of the earth, as the primary and most certain source of national sup-

[5] Destutt de Tracy, *A Treatise on Political Economy* (Georgetown, 1817), p. iii; see also the Introduction to Gilbert Chinard, *The Correspondence of Jefferson and Du Pont de Nemours* (Baltimore, 1931).

[6] Joseph Dorfman, "The Economic Philosophy of Thomas Jefferson," *Political Science Quarterly,* Vol. 55 (March, 1940), pp. 98–121, emphasizes Jefferson's eclecticism.

ply . . . has intrinsically a strong claim to pre-eminence over every other kind of industry.''

Between Taylor and Jefferson there were no important differences in the interpretation of Hamilton's economic policy or the means of combating it, and Jefferson gave his unqualified approval to Taylor's prolix tome, *An Inquiry into the Principles and Policy of the Government of the United States,* which appeared in 1814. Taylor's aim, like Jefferson's, was the relief of American agriculture from the exploitation under which it labored, chiefly through the medium of unjust taxation, for the benefit of ''the complete panoply of fleets, armies, banks, funding systems, pensions, boundaries, corporations and exclusive privileges.'' If Taylor was familiar with the conception of the *impôt unique,* it must have offended him to the marrow. It was the gravamen of his argument that the injustice of the ''paper system'' lay in its monopoly features and its dependence upon the taxation of the whole agricultural community for the advantage of a single interest. His remedy for agriculture's troubles was simply a removal of government support of monopolistic financial institutions—in short, *laissez faire.* Although he had little use for Adam Smith, he was in essential agreement with the combination of governmental aloofness with reliance upon human self-interest which became such a staple of the Manchesterian creed. Declaring that love of property was the chief basis of civil society, he avowed his firm reliance in ''the idea that it is both wise and just, to leave the distribution of property to industry and talents.'' If such a policy were adopted, he believed, the dispersion of property would remain broadly democratic. One may agree or quarrel with this idea of the relation between the self-seeking of the economic man and the maintenance of democratic property relations. But if these conceptions were intrinsically hostile to capitalism, then the same must be said of the Manchester school.

It was Hamilton who could not incorporate *laissez faire* into his philosophy. He was familiar, it is true, with *The Wealth of Nations,* and made use of its vast data in his economic thinking. But the intricate system of governmental intervention which he was erecting required a new theoretical foundation. He bluntly rejected the premise ''that industry if left to itself will naturally find its way to the most useful and profitable employment,'' arguing on the contrary, that infant industries would be choked if unprotected, and that the American economy, to survive, must compete on equal terms with the subsidized industries of foreign countries. Thus, while the doctrines of Smith were a suitable *credo* for rising capitalism in England, they were quickly controverted elsewhere, particularly in America and Germany. Hamilton, far from falling within the Smithian lineage, was the predecessor of modern economic nationalism. Friedrich List, the theoretical father of nationalist economics, was deeply influenced by his reading of Hamilton's *Report on Manufactures* and by his association, while in the United States, with the Federalist-Whig "American System" which was Hamilton's legacy. The ideological side of the Jefferson-Hamilton struggle may therefore be approached as a part of the world-wide struggle between *laissez faire* and economic nationalism. Certainly there is little warrant for viewing it as "a conflict between the rival principles of Quesnay and Adam Smith.'"[7]

The ideas of Jeffersonian democracy survived in the Jacksonian era without much modification. Apologists of the new upsurge against the institutions of privilege and high finance could still find in a thinker like John Taylor a fruitful source of authority. The same central economic ideas, in urban garb, were now paraded by the new working-class element in the democracy. Both farmers and mechanics had legitimate grievances against the loose banking practices of the age. Workingmen were frequently paid in small bills of depreciating value and poor convertibility. Farmers were victimized by bank mortgages and often hated the banks because of their close connection with land speculators. High prices were attributed to bank control of currency. To those who suffered from poor paper currencies and the extravagant powers of banks the remedies seemed simple: abolish the special privilege of specific charters to banks and other enterprises; allow all applicants to incorporate by passing general incorporation laws; limit the function of banks to discount, deposit, and loan on real or personal security; and prohibit the issuance of paper bills in the small denominations in which workers were paid.

These demands may be traced in the writings of two of the more prominent economic advocates of the Democratic party, William Leggett, the editorial associate of Bryant on the *New York Post* and the hero of the young Whitman, and William Gouge, the widely known financial expert. Neither Leggett nor Gouge had any quarrel with the fundamental premises of a capitalist economy either from an agrarian or a socialist point of view. Their economics

[7] It should be noted that when Parrington formed this conclusion Gilbert Chinard's and Dumas Malone's editions of the Jefferson-Du Pont correspondence had not been published.

was chiefly a critique of government-aided financial mechanisms from a general *laissez-faire* standpoint. They did not propose to abolish capitalism or even to restrain it; they merely wished to give it a democratic bias. This is best exemplified by Leggett's demand for a general incorporation law on the ground that the poor would then be able to form corporations too![8] Gouge believed that the economic evils of the day could be cured by the overthrow of banking corporations, and the replacement of paper notes by specie. This would result in a society in which "the operation of the natural and just causes of wealth and poverty will no longer be inverted, but . . . each cause will operate in its natural and just order, and produce its natural and just effect—wealth becoming the reward of industry, frugality, skill, prudence, and enterprise, and poverty the punishment of few except the indolent and prodigal." Here, rather than in any supposed loss of realism in Physiocratic economics, lay the dilemma of Jacksonianism. It accepted the capitalist order, without desire or ability to propose an alternative society, and restricted itself to reforms which interfered with its smooth functioning.

A survey of the economic thought of the Jeffersonian and Jacksonian movements shows that at no time did they ever produce, even in theory, a design for American agrarianism. At best their philosophy led to a negative conclusion: abandon the national banking system, reduce expenditures, cut taxation, divorce government from finance, democratize incorporation, keep hands off. Such devices might impede the advance of capitalism, but never prevent it. The ultimate triumph of the capitalist order was inevitable, and it is not intended here to suggest that the Jeffersonians could or should have stemmed it; but an interesting by-product of its growth was the theoretical impotence of the agrarian opposition. Perhaps this helps also to explain the readiness of the Democracy to compromise even its most essential beliefs in a time of crisis like that following the War of 1812. It accepted fundamental economic premises which elsewhere served magnificently to rationalize the capitalist order. Visitors at Monticello in Jefferson's later years were surprised to find there a marble bust of Hamilton. With the perspective of the twentieth century, they would not have been surprised: within the mansions of Jeffersonian Democracy there were busts of Hamilton everywhere.

The College of the City of New York.

[8] *A Collection of the Political Writings of William Leggett* (N. Y., 1840), Vol. II, pp. 89–90, 142–143.

XXV

BETWEEN GOG AND MAGOG:
THE REPUBLICAN THESIS AND THE *IDEOLOGIA AMERICANA*

By J. G. A. Pocock

In a book published over a decade ago—*The Machiavellian Moment: Florentine Political Thought and the Atlantic Republican Tradition*[1]—I undertook to tell how a certain complex of writings about republican political forms and their place in history was formulated in early *cinquecento* Florence, restated in mid-seventeenth-century England, and restated once more in Revolutionary and Federalist English-speaking America, each time with measurable and sometimes repetitious consequences. These contentions have attracted both notice and criticism, and I have before me two books in which they are attacked from widely differing standpoints. In *Dal "Mito" di Venezia all' "Ideologia Americana"*,[2] Renzo Pecchioli of the University of Florence describes me, along with Hans Baron, William J. Bouwsma, and the late Frederic C. Lane, as conducting an offensive against Marxist historiography which must necessarily serve the interests of American ruling classes, and in which the thesis of a continuity of republican political values passing from Italy to England and the United States plays a leading part. In *The Lost Soul of American Politics: Virtue, Self-Interest, and the Foundations of Liberalism*,[3] John P. Diggins of the University of California at Irvine describes me, along with Bernard Bailyn and Gordon S. Wood, as intruding irrelevant republican values upon an American political tradition which in his view is founded upon Lockean individualism and very little else. If to Pecchioli I am an exponent of *ideologia americana*, which tends to draw European politics into the stifling embrace of American liberal imperialism, to Diggins I am a "historian of European political thought" who fails to understand, and indeed seeks to adulterate, the unique (but uniquely guilty) character of American liberalism.

It is evident that these criticisms differ widely in their premises and conclusions, and it would be easy and amusing to set them to destroy one another. I believe, however, that it will be more illuminating to use them to clarify one another, to explain Diggins to Pecchioli if not Pecchioli to Diggins, and in so doing to make it a little clearer what roles such terms as "republicanism," "liberalism," and "*ideologia americana*" are playing in the discussion and how I should prefer to represent my own identity, ideology, and intentions.

I. The debate begins as we discover the modes of interpretation to which Pecchioli proclaims that his own work should be seen as opposed, so that his

---

[1] Princeton, 1975. There is an Italian translation by Professor Alfonso Prandi, *Il Momento Machiavelliano: il pensiero politico fiorentino e la tradizione repubblicana anglosassone* (Bologna, 1980). An earlier version of this essay was written in English for translation into Italian and publication in the *Rivista Storica Italiana*, 98 (1986), 147-94.

[2] Subtitled *Itinerari e modelli della storiografia sul repubblicanesimo dell' età moderna* (Venezia, 1983).

[3] New York, 1984.

writings are part of what he calls "la lotta contro l'ideologia americana."[4] It becomes increasingly a matter of discovering what the *ideologia americana* is and in what terms the struggle against it is to be conducted.

I should of course agree that the ideological analysis of historiographical statements is a legitimate procedure. The relation between understanding of the past and experience of the present, and the role of language structures in social experience, are such that the historian's language will constantly convey information and messages regarding his and others' intentions and values in the present. The more we pursue the metatheoretical and metahistorical implications of his language, the likelier this is to be true and the greater the variety of information concerning the historian's social intentions that may be elicited from his language and the use that he makes of it. The assertion that there is no chaste historical language, free from ideological implications, may be taken as established, though this does not prevent the historian working to render his language as chaste and free as possible.

This being so, the conduct of ideological analysis—the enterprise of showing how the historian's language is involved in the experience of his times and conveys intentions and information concerning it—ought to be an experiment in the representation of concrete actuality; we ought to be able to see the historian's language shaping itself in response to actual pressures and to the end of conveying actual messages (conscious or unconscious, as the case may be). Concrete actuality is a concept very dear to Pecchioli; he repeatedly calls for it, he tends to regard the historical methods which he practices as possessing something like a monopoly of the means of establishing it, and he seems to consider failure to establish it with sufficient rigour evidence of ideological hostility towards the methods of which he approves. Let us then take him at his word. With what concrete actuality does he establish the existence of an *ideologia americana* and implicate the historians whom he studies in its practice?

In his fourth chapter, which concludes the first half of his book, Pecchioli reviews a great deal of British and American writing on European history published in recent years which has been non-Marxist in character, and he finds in this evidence of a "massiccia operazione" and an "offensiva storiografica condotta contro le interpretazioni marxiste del Seicento."[5] It is always difficult to tell from language of this kind how far the intellectual operations being described are supposed to have been intended, planned, and orchestrated, and how far to have been produced by impersonally convergent forces; it is an advantage of Marxist rhetoric that it permits one to alternate at will between the two readings. If what Pecchioli takes to be an "offensiva storiografica" consists simply of non-Marxist historiography going its own way without experiencing much need to engage Marxism in dialogue, then the need to struggle against it exists largely in his own perceptions. There are, however, occasions on which serious dialogue with Marxism is possible, and his book furnishes one of them. The question is whether he has demonstrated that an *ideologia americana* exists in the minds of the historians of republicanism and is itself significantly reinforced by their writings. The characteristics of *ideologia americana*

---

[4] Pecchioli, 16. The phrase is cited as the title of an article by Giuliano Procacci in *Rinascita-Il Contemporaneo* (28 April 1972).

[5] Pecchioli, 152; cf. 39.

as displayed in the work of Baron, Bouwsma, and myself are stated in Pecchioli's introduction to be as follows. Our treatments of republicanism are reducible to "una categoria metastorica," a "storia delle idee in senso schiettamente idealistico, dove manca ogni riferimento alla storia dei 'fatti,' " and "una determinata 'visione del mondo.' " These abstract entities amount "non a una conoscenza scientifica del passato ma ad una sostanziale legittimazione ideologica del presente." There is a "miracolo politologico," a "visione 'atlantica' e tendenzialmente planetaria della storia," which consists in representing the United States as the outcome and culmination of the republican tradition, and to which Pecchioli opposes his own criticisms as "legati a una visione più concreta e filologica del lavoro storico, assai distante dalle ambizione 'imperiali' della politologia."[6]

Not all of these criticisms are directed at me, though I appear to be the imperial politologist of the words last quoted (it is a difficulty that there is no exact English equivalent for *politologia*, which seems to denote a blend of political theory and historiosophy; we have plenty of that in English). But the thrust of the argument is clear enough. Non-Marxist historiography, whether intentionally or unintentionally, abstracts schematized entities from history and uses them to legitimate the present; only Marxism is apparently capable of overcoming this tendency. The arrogance of such claims, by the way, is enough to account for a good deal of the anti-Marxism that exists. It ought to be added at once, however, that Pecchioli does not fall into the trap of asserting that, because the works he criticizes display the characteristics of *ideologia* and *politologia*, they are not history at all; he is a courteous and reasonable opponent, aware that substantial history can be written even in works possessing these characteristics. But Pecchioli is writing history as well as criticism, and it is not enough for him to show that the works he analyses can be criticized and interpreted in the above senses; there has to be a concrete actuality in which they can be shown to have been written with the intentions, or to have exerted the unintended effects, attributed to them. The question I shall constantly ask is whether he has established the concrete actuality in which these things can be seen happening.

Because he is aware of the need to do so, Pecchioli has resort to the techniques of intellectual biography—though these are practiced in a different sense in Hans Baron's case than in mine, and to a far lesser degree in the case of Bouwsma. But in addition to this method, appropriate to the study of individuals, he has need of some means of presenting a history of the collective mentality of the non-Marxist and in particular of the American historical profession and of establishing the ideological climate in which the historiography of republicanism is supposed to have taken shape. This is attempted, for the most part, in chapter V, "Storiografia neo-liberale e 'ideologia americana.' " Here I do not find Pecchioli especially convincing, for the reason that he is sometimes plausible but never very specific. The first difficulty is that his interpretation smacks of that abstract division into ideal types of which he is so rightly critical whenever he finds it, or thinks that he has found it. There are only two kinds of historiography in his mind, Marxist and non-Marxist; and of these the second (or

---

[6] All the phrases quoted may be found on 11-13 of Pecchioli's introduction.

"neo-liberal") must be shown to have the characteristics which Marxist criticism traditionally and predictably attributes to all thought which is not Marxist. Pecchioli passes rapidly to the allegation that the latter constructs "grandi linee" and "tradizioni" by abstracting phenomena from the historical process and arranging them in sequences, and that the traditions thus constructed (they would be called "Whig histories" in English) turn out to legitimize the American present by depicting it as the inheritor, outcome, and culmination of the "grandi linee." Thus the history of American republicanism is supposed to represent the American republic as the heir of all the republics before it.

Let us now follow Pecchioli in his attempt to establish a climate of American historical opinion which specifically accounts for the growth of the history of republicanism as *ideologia americana*. Here he is hampered by the fact that he has only three or four historians to deal with, and of these only one has actually tried to establish linkages between Florentine and American republicanism. That this one is myself confronts him with some special problems. For one of the others, Frederic C. Lane, Pecchioli has recourse to a presidential address delivered to the American Historical Association in 1965.[7] Lane did indeed say that the economic interpretation of history was losing ground everywhere, that republicanism was more important than capitalism as a key to the Renaissance, that instead of concentrating on the study of non-western societies, American students of history should take stock of the great traditions which defined their place in the world, and that a study of republican tradition from Sebastian Ziani to George Washington would be an excellent way of doing this. Presidents of the American Historical Association issue such calls to the mobilization of tradition from time to time, but I fear Pecchioli exaggerates the authoritative character of these presidential addresses. Certainly, his description of them as "veri e propri bilanci e programmi di direzione culturale" will cause mirth among those members of the Association who may read it.[8]

II. The critical question which Pecchioli must answer in the case of the three historians whom he has chosen to study—Baron, Bouwsma, myself—is whether their historical practice conforms to his strictures upon *ideologia americana*: i.e., whether they abstract and formalize phenomena which they proceed to arrange in legitimatory "great traditions." The case of Hans Baron is the most interesting of the three, if only because Pecchioli is able to identify the concept of "civic humanism," which Baron did so much to develop, as the key to all that has been written about the recurrence of republican values and language in other times and other cultures—including my *Machiavellian Moment*. It is therefore of importance to Pecchioli to discredit this concept as far as he can.[9]

In adapting Baron's writings to my own purposes, I specifically declined to take part in the debate over what he himself regarded as his central and most crucial contention: that decisive changes in outlook which produced "civic humanism" could be located in identifiable literary compositions and dated to

[7] Pecchioli, 208-11. Frederic C. Lane, "At the Roots of Republicanism," *The American Historical Review*, 71 (1966), 403-20, reprinted in *Venice and History: The Collected Papers of Frederic C. Lane* (Baltimore, 1966).

[8] Pecchioli, 208.

[9] Pecchioli, 12, 161, n. 3, 173, 204, 169 (n. 1).

identifiable moments in the history of the Viscontian war of 1400-02. I said that "civic humanism" would be a useful concept, as far as I was concerned, whether it first appeared at those dates or not. The thrust of subsequent research has of course been to separate the assertion of civic values from the Viscontian war and discover it at increasingly earlier dates; Quentin Skinner has traced it back to Milanese *dictatores* in the time of Frederick Barbarossa.[10] Such revision has liberated the concept for employment by historians at a diversity of moments; in this precise sense I have no particular objection to saying that there was a "tradition" of civic humanism which underwent a "crisis" in the time of Machiavelli and Guicciardini.

I am at a loss to understand why Pecchioli says nothing of these matters. Baron with his Viscontian war was after all doing what Pecchioli says we should all do: seeking to relate the articulation of ideas to highly specific historical situations. Pecchioli's insistence that "storia delle idee" must be subjected to "storia dei fatti" suggests an unwillingness to recognize that "ideas"—or rather the *langues* and *paroles* in which messages are conveyed—are "facts": historical phenomena of varying duration, which inconveniently convey information concerning other facts that we frequently do not find it possible to accept. Some of these *langues* and *paroles* exist in forms durable enough to turn up more than once in the historical record; I suspect it is an issue between Pecchioli and me that he does not want to accept that the same thing can be said more than once, with effects of both continuity and discontinuity. When I say "tradition" I mean that I have found a sequence of events of this kind, not that I have discovered a grand lineage legitimating the present; I can discern no lack of historical concreteness in the assertion that I am making.

Pecchioli's biographical treatment of Hans Baron is long and detailed. It offers a portrait of a German historian in the grand manner, formed in the Burckhardtian school, who finds in the ideals of *Kleinstaaterei* matter for an understanding of liberty valuable to a liberal opponent of Nazism, who joins the emigration of German scholars to the United States, and who is therefore tempted to regard America as the last refuge of European culture and liberty (a belief which Pecchioli regards as conducive to an ideology of American imperialism). Pecchioli avoids any vulgarization of this last point; his study of Baron is careful and sympathetic and does justice to its subject's intellectual autonomy and power. There is no reason to object to the view that *The Crisis of the Early Italian Renaissance: Civic Humanism and Republican Liberty in an Age of Classicism and Tyranny* owes something to its author's experience of both liberty and tyranny, or that mythic components forming part of this debt may be found in its text; Baron's Florence in the crisis of the Viscontian war has always looked a little like, say, Britain after Dunkirk. I have given above my reasons for disagreeing with Pecchioli's contention that a "myth of liberty," which may have helped Baron create his account of the birth of civic humanism, turned the latter into an ideal type whose metahistoric adventures have been traced by subsequent historians; it seems to me that we have been doing something quite different with it. In any case the biographical approach raises a different series of questions.

[10] *The Foundations of Modern Political Thought, I, The Renaissance* (Cambridge, 1978), 23-48.

It is very proper that there should exist a considerable literature on how the German historical culture inherited from the nineteenth century responded to the devastating events of 1918-45, and the intellectual emigration to the United States in the thirties should certainly form part of it.[11] There already exists something of a "myth of the left" according to which English and American liberal thinking has its roots in Weimar and Vienna; the critics of liberalism are always anxious to prove that it conceals a worship of the ideal State (when they are not denouncing it for minimizing the State's importance). Pecchioli is not untouched by this myth, but it is both his strength and his weakness that he is unwilling to commit himself too deeply to its exploration. A strength, because he abstains from telling us that the *ideologia americana* is in fact a *congiura austro-tedesca*; he does not write nonsense or engage in witch-hunts. A weakness, because his biography of Baron, whatever its merits, is simply not a sufficiently broad scaffolding to carry the weight he needs to impose upon it.

The "sea change," as H. Stuart Hughes has termed the naturalization of European émigré philosophy and historiography in the United States,[12] is a large subject and the reinterpretation of Renaissance humanism in recent historiography is part of it. Pecchioli identifies this as the work of three scholars rather than one: Hans Baron, Felix Gilbert, and Paul Oskar Kristeller;[13] and when one is writing specifically about the historiography of Florentine republicanism, Machiavelli, and the *mito di Venezia*, the absence of a full-length treatment of Felix Gilbert from one's pages is a very large absence indeed. Gilbert has not only written extensively on these subjects but has added essays on Otto Hintze, Friedrich Meinecke, and other figures of his intellectual formation in Berlin.[14] The terms "intellectual emigration" and "ideologia americana" become more controversial as they become more concrete. They fragment, when viewed in their historical concreteness, into a plurality of complex and contradictory movements. The history of the Frankfurt school in America also needs to be considered, and so does the strange history of the late Leo Strauss and the powerful school he founded.[15] This does not mean that the phenomena Pecchioli desires to study disappear; but it does mean that his neo-liberal monolith, with the historians of republicanism at its center, begins to look like an abstract hypostatization itself, lacking in the concreteness for which he otherwise calls. His intellectual biography of Hans Baron does not follow Baron into his American years in detail sufficient to show his interactions, intellectual and otherwise, with his fellow immigrants, his hosts, or the conditions governing the growth of American historiography.

William J. Bouwsma, the next in the series of historians to be studied, differs from Baron and myself in that he once focused the whole of his attention upon both the *mito* and the *realtà di Venezia*, and has therefore been accused of

---

[11] Pecchioli, 173, n. 4.

[12] *The Sea Change: The Migration of Social Thought, 1930-1965* (New York, 1975).

[13] Pecchioli, 206.

[14] Felix Gilbert, *History: Choice and Commitment* (Cambridge, Mass., 1977).

[15] This is discussed briefly by Hughes; see also Martin Jay, *The Dialectical Imagination: a History of the Frankfurt School and the Institute for Social Research* (Boston, 1973). No independent study of Strauss's career yet exists.

confounding the two. In *Venice and the Defence of Republican Liberty*[16] he argued that the Venetian historians of the late sixteenth and early seventeenth centuries, Paolo Paruta and Paolo Sarpi, kept alive a certain style of historiography, secular, pluralist, and concerned with the fortunes of particular states in a world of unstable external and internal political relationships. Bouwsma believed that this style could be connected with the public spirit of a *Serenissima*, confident of its power to survive the displeasure of the papacy and the great European monarchies even in the years of the Interdict. Criticism of Bouwsma's thesis has focused mainly on the question whether the public philosophy of Venice was as republican and secular—or if it was, whether it was as unique in being so—as he suggested; these after all were the years in which doctrines of the *ragione* and the *interessi degli stati* were in formation all across monarchical as well as republican Europe and were not always incompatible with doctrines of hierarchy and order. *Prima facie* it would seem that Bouwsma's Venetians need to be studied in the context of a European Tacitism and Guicciardinism so widespread that any frontiers between *repubblicanesimo, Controriforma*, and Protestant monarchism would tend to disappear. We should in such a reading be looking toward "Machiavellism" in a Meineckean sense, tending towards theories of the independent action of the State, rather than towards Machiavelli's role in the formation of a republican ideology.

On the whole it seems to have been at a later date, subsequent to the wars of Louis XIV, that European historians and publicists elaborated the thesis of an international polity of emulative states; and by that time the state was seen as an actor in an increasingly complex international commerce, so that whether it was a republic or a monarchy was an important but secondary consideration. As the republic was once again seen as a commercial polity, it moved away from the profile of the "commonwealth for expansion," dependent upon swords rather than trade, which Machiavelli had fixed upon it; the concept of the republic, we see once again, was always a critical and controversial tool, never the legitimatory ideal described by Pecchioli.

But it would not follow from such criticisms of Bouwsma's position that his account of Venetian historiography in the age of Paruta and Sarpi constitutes a *mito*, an ideal type abstracted from actuality to take its place in a legitimatory sequence. It does appear in need of further contextualization, but the contexts in which it ought to be set are European and intellectual rather than Venetian and ideological. Bouwsma's offer to show that Venetian historiography was the product of a republican climate, and his critics' endeavors to demonstrate that the public ideology of Venice was not all that republican, may both have been a little wide of the mark, inspired by too simple an understanding of the problem of ideology. The intellectual phenomena generated by a particular society must always be related to its political and social structure, but there does not have to be a direct relation, of correspondence or reflection, between the two; the articulations of language may be dysfunctionally, critically, paradoxically, or playfully related to what is going on in society, and a "concrete" statement of the relationship between them may have to rest content with non-finality. We privilege the context overmuch if we insist that the text must either tell us the

[16] *Venice and the Defence of Republican Liberty: Renaissance Values in the Age of the Counter-Reformation* (Berkeley, 1968).

truth about it or tell us nothing. The doctrine of republicanism—this is what I think Pecchioli has never quite realized—need be no more than a winding and knotted thread in a complex and tangled texture.

Pecchioli does not offer us an intellectual biography of Bouwsma—who, unlike Baron or myself, has not immigrated into American culture from a formation outside it. He proposes instead to situate him in the context of the "neo-liberalism" allegedly characteristic of the American historical profession, and it is here that Pecchioli displays that reliance on the case of Frederic C. Lane about which I have already voiced certain doubts. In doing so he follows guides from within the profession itself: Eric Cochrane and Julius Kirshner, whose 1975 article, "Deconstructing Lane's 'Venice,' " [17] first stated in English the thesis of an *ideologia americana* seeking in history a "usable past" for a liberal and patrician present. What is interesting here is the diversity of standpoints from which Lane's critics operated. Cochrane's two major works are in many respects vindications of Tridentine Catholic culture against the old liberal-rational belief that Italian intellectual history stopped dead with the Counter-Reformation. [18] The attack on Lane was a much less massive offensive than that which Pecchioli attributes to Anglo-American historiography at large, but it was an offensive none the less, and at least a stage in this story, if it is a story.

III. The next stage was a colloquium on the "Myth of Venice," in which both Cochrane and Pecchioli participated. Because of certain remarks attributed to Pecchioli, I was moved, by finding myself described as a "studioso americano," to write a brief communication making two points: first, that I am not American by either formation or adoption; secondly, that my analysis of republican theory does not start with the *mito di Venezia*, but rather with the *mito di Roma*—with Machiavelli's distinction between the republic for preservation and the republic for expansion. [19] It seems to me greatly to Renzo Pecchioli's credit that he has taken me at my word and conducted a laborious and intensive study of my intellectual career. What emerges is not a biography, but a detailed and acute examination of nearly everything that I have written as a historian. Unlike Baron or Bouwsma, I have written a good deal about the theory of my method as well as about its practice and thus (I suggest) rendered it more difficult to dismiss my writings as one more expression of naive *ideologia americana*. It has to be asked, I think, whether Pecchioli's minute enquiries into my method and practice lead to results which can by any means be fitted into his account of that ideology.

Let me start from the circumstance that I am neither an American nor a European, but a product of the British antipodes. It is not reasonable to expect

---

[17] *Journal of Modern History*, 47 (1975), 321-34.

[18] *Florence in the Forgotten Centuries, 1527-1800: A History of Florence and the Florentines in the Age of the Grand Dukes* (Chicago, 1973), and *Historians and Historiography in the Italian Renaissance* (Chicago, 1981). Cf. his "The Transition from Renaissance to Baroque: the Case of Italian Historiography," *History and Theory*, 19 (1980), 21-38.

[19] Pecchioli's contribution to "Il Mito di Venezia tra rinascimento e controriforma," and my response, " 'Mito di Venezia' and 'Ideologia Americana': a correction," in *Il Pensiero Politico*, 11 (1978), 249-57, and 12 (1979), 443-45.

Pecchioli to know very much about the cultures designated by that term, or their modes of historical awareness; but since he desires to present Hans Baron and myself as historians "che, pur non essendo statunitensi di nascita o nazionalità, hanno di fatto trovato una collocazione significativa nell'ambito della cultura storica americana," [20] it should help his case to know how I as well as Baron entered that ambit and what I brought with me—an Antipodean kind of historical consciousness—for that culture to assimilate.

When I say "Antipodean," I have in mind New Zealand and Australia, the two anglophone nations of the South Pacific, cultures in many ways dissimilar but possessing certain common historical experiences. Their experience and awareness of history is governed by one material fact more than any other: "the tyranny of distance," [21] of planetary space which makes geography the precondition of sociology. The distances are oceanic, in the Australian case continental as well, and they give rise to a sense of human society and history as things fragile in themselves. Human habitation in Australia is very ancient, the work of nomadic food-gatherers who came thirty to fifty thousand years ago; in New Zealand it is very recent, the achievement of Polynesian voyagers in the first millennium A.D. The maritime civilizations of the "pre-Da Gaman age"— Indo-Malayan, Chinese, Arab—did not penetrate south-east of Indonesia, and the Europeans came very late in the eighteenth century. Only one empire brought "history" to the South Seas, and in consequence history is seen as having something of the fragility of empire.

Distance and dependency combine to mean that attachment to history is known to be real and unbreakable but at the same time contingent. One is linked to history by the memory of a voyage. The Polynesian voyage led from island to island, and so to isolation; the Maori people of New Zealand have a proverb which asks whether Kupe the first navigator ever came back, [22] and so expresses the question, still of concern to archaeologists, whether Polynesian voyaging, which never established a pattern of oceanic commerce, was other than a series of marvellous accidents. The British and European voyage led to dependency and a sense of remoteness; in the twentieth century we fought a series of wars, half a world away, for the maintenance of our place in an empire which in the end was dismantled by others; and there is a strong spatial dimension to the awareness, which we share with all other cultures, that our history is not altogether at our command. Consequently, the Anglophone cultures of the South Pacific display a sensibility in an important sense counter-mythical. New societies often base themselves on myths of foundation and regeneration; but where an American poet can write:

And Thames and all the rivers of the kings
Ran into Mississippi and were drowned [23]

[20] Pecchioli, 160, n. 4.

[21] Geoffrey Blainey, *The Tyranny of Distance: How Distance Shaped Australia's History* (Melbourne, 1966).

[22] *E hokikoki Kupe?* This hero found his fishing nets being plundered by creatures of the deep; he swore vengeance and gave chase; and after slaying the last monster at the entrance of a New Zealand harbor, returned to his Pacific Ocean homeland with information of his discovery, which his descendants followed up generations later.

[23] Stephen Vincent Benet, *John Brown's Body* (London, 1929), 4.

a New Zealand poet writes

> Still as the collier steered
> No continent appeared.
> It was something different, something
> Nobody counted on.[24]

In "the Unhistoric Story," the title of the last-quoted poem, rebirth is replaced by mere contingency; history has lost its foundation in myth. The antipodean sensibility rejects myth and is skeptical of novelty: "here is the world's end where wonders cease"; "the world one island, marvels out of date/ And all our travel circumnavigation."[25] The Australian counter-myth records the exploration of a continental interior where there is no Danube, Nile, or Mississippi, and when one has reached the other side one can only start back again. It is a sensibility deeply unlike the older American. *Homo europaeus* might step ashore at Jamestown, Plymouth, or Ellis Island and begin to pursue the westward course of empire; but *homo australis*, entering America through the Golden Gate, is already reascending the streams of history and knows there is no fifth monarchy in the remoter west. His historiosophy is eclectic, ironic, fragmentary.

I have emphasized these elements of a historical imagination because they enable me to suggest certain corrections to Pecchioli's account of my methods and intentions. Pecchioli declares that I express "una visione atlantica e tendenzialmente planetaria,"[26] but this phrase can, I think, be deconstructed. If I express a *visione planetaria*, it is because I view history across planetary distances, but it does not follow that I am trying to establish any kind of planetary synthesis. And a *visione atlantica* to me is far from being *planetaria*; the Atlantic Ocean is a great channel across which continents confront one another, but the Pacific is the true surface of the planet Aqua. If there is a historical confrontation with which I am ideologically involved, it is less that of America with Europe than that of the British Antipodes with a Britain no longer imperial. The concern with "British history" which Pecchioli has noted in my work springs from the conviction that, as Britain loses the capacity to shape history on a global scale, there is a task for the owl of Minerva to perform; cultures shaped by British history need to understand that history and their place in it and can no longer afford to have it written anglocentrically. I view American history, through the colonial and revolutionary periods but no further, as an episode in "British history": the history of one of those cultures carried to the point where it left the British orbit and began to shape a history of its own; and I enter upon the debate about American history, and the debate between Marxist and (if there is such a thing) "neo-liberal" historiography, along that route and with the predilections which it prescribes. This seems to me a further reason why Pecchioli

---

[24] Allen Curnow, *Collected Poems, 1933-73* (Wellington, 1974), 79. The "collier" is James Cook's *Endeavour*, a ship built for the coal-trade. By rounding the southern extremity of New Zealand in 1769, Cook further demolished the Ptolemaic hypothesis of a southern continent balancing Eurasia.

[25] Curnow, *Collected Poems*, 138, 119.

[26] Pecchioli, 13; cf. 239, n. 13.

is unable to fit my writings into the paradigm of *ideologia americana* as he has devised it.

I submit it follows that what Pecchioli takes to be a *politologia imperiale* is in fact a *storiografia itinerante*. For reasons entailed by my own historical formation I am interested in migrations and translations, in the movement of cultures through space and the movement of texts through time. *The Machiavellian Moment* offered an account of how certain texts, rhetorical styles, and the thought-patterns encoded in them took shape in a Florentine context and were subsequently translated into first an English and then an American context. The question in my mind is whether Pecchioli is well equipped to understand how a model of rhetoric and theory can migrate, or be translated, from one historical context to another without becoming an abstract ideal type in the process.

He quotes a passage written by Carlo Dionisotti, to the effect that rather than writing the history of an "idea" over a long period of time, it is better to study each expression of thought in the context of the specific historical situation to which it pertains.[27] This is very true; some of us have been saying so for years and have even cast doubt on whether "the history of an idea" can be traced down through the ages in any meaningful sense. But texts and established linguistic structures are another matter; the former are material objects, the latter communicable social practices, and it is an evident fact that they can be seen to undergo transference and translation—at the hands of human actors—from one local environment and from one historical moment to another. At this point we see that to study the context may be insufficient if it overprivileges the synchronous reading; to do no more than locate an utterance in a detailed context of social practice or action, move it to another which we proceed to reconstruct in the same detail, and then to another and another, would leave us in the end with a kind of Eleatic paradox in which we understood every moment of the arrow's flight or the river's flowing, but not how movement occurred or whether the arrow or the river existed at all. We need means of diachronic study of a text or language—at this point in the analysis it is probably better to avoid the term "ideas"—in order to understand the process of communication and translation; *eppur si muove.*

Translation entails reception, and communication interpretation. There is a theoretical literature which debates whether every interpretation is not a misinterpretation if we measure it by the criteria supplied by close study of the text's "meaning" at the immediately preceding moment of its trajectory; and indeed every reading, interpretation, or utterance of a text or language-pattern has a "meaning" of its own.[28] But once again we must be careful not to privilege the synchronous and return to the Eleatic paradox. There is the text, and there is the language, visible at more than one moment and in more than one culture; they are material vehicles for the bearing of encoded messages, and we cannot prejudge the question whether they transmit messages from one point or moment

---

[27] Pecchioli, 197-99.

[28] I explore this theme further in an introductory essay prefixed to *Virtue, Commerce and History: Essays on Political Thought and History, Chiefly in the Eighteenth Century* (Cambridge, 1985), a collection of essays which appeared after Pecchioli's book was published.

to another. If they do this to any extent whatever, then to that extent the text or language is an agent in determining its own translation and to structuring the situation in which it is to be interpreted. To that extent, which must vary from case to case, we may speak of continuities of communication and interpretation, in which texts or languages, with the messages encoded into them, are central and recurrent factors; and we may call these continuities "traditions" and these messages "ideas" if we cannot think of any better terms (as possibly we should try to do).

As for the complete phrase "Atlantic republican tradition," I now feel some doubts as to how far the word "tradition," taken by itself as denoting a continuum of discourse, can specify the incidence of debate, perplexity, and contradiction inherent within that discourse; but my text does not fail, I think, to emphasize at every point that the discourse concerning republicanism was inherently controversial, a quarrel with history and with itself. That is what is conveyed by calling it Machiavellian. If I had wanted to construct a "tradition" in Pecchioli's sense of a legitimatory continuum, I would scarcely have started with Machiavelli, who must be one of the least legitimatory of political writers, or emphasized that the republic, taken as an ideal, was never *serenissima* and never legitimized itself.

For all these reasons the chapter which Pecchioli has devoted to my writings seems to me to fail through its merits. Precisely because it is detailed, thoughtful, and scrupulous, it constrains him to admit that the theory and method which underlies my interpretation "non è assimilabile direttamente a quelli degli studiosi precedentemente considerati," though he continues to maintain that the interpretation itself "si inserisce ... in un'ottica storiografica e ideologica che è largemente comune ai vari indirizzi di studi sul repubblicanesimo da me analizzati." But throughout his book Pecchioli has been insisting that theory and practice, method and substance, must form a whole in the deployment of an ideology; and when in his last sentence he says that this dual reading "non riesce a mettere in ombra, secondo me, la matrice (storiografica e ideologica) fondamentalmente communi di tutte queste interpretazioni ...,"[29] I think we must admit that this forms a weak conclusion to both his chapter and his book. The fact is that he has not been able to use my writings to add substance to his claim that an *ideologia americana* exists and operates as a *verità effettuale*, any more than he was able to trace any process by which Hans Baron's thinking became "Americanized" after his settlement in the United States. He is left reiterating that *ideologia americana* does exist and that neither Baron nor I can be cleared of complicity in it; and the second part of the proposition does little to support the first. This is the more unfortunate since, as I shall show in the next part of this essay, there really is an *ideologia americana* operative in the study of history; but both its thrust and the role of the "republican synthesis" in relation to it are very different from what Pecchioli supposes.

IV. This *ideologia americana* is deeply concerned with the supposed primacy of "liberalism" in American history, but does not—Pecchioli notwithstanding—naively proclaim a *politologia imperiale* in which the United States inherits and

---

[29] Pecchioli, 268, 269, 270.

preserves all of the world's aspirations towards freedom. Rhetoric of that kind—common enough among those who seek to make popular opinion—is rare, to say the least, among the intellectuals who write and reflect upon the history of the republic. Their mood is and has long been Tocquevillean; they accept the primacy of liberalism but proceed at once to turn that thesis against itself, asking pressingly whether a society which is liberal *et praeterea nihil* can satisfy the deeper demands of the human (or the Western) spirit. The history of the reception—in many cases the rejection—of the republican reading of early national American history is the record of how a hypothesis which might have diminished the force of the thesis of inescapable liberalism has been angrily and bitterly repudiated by some of those most eloquent in denouncing liberalism's shortcomings.

Pecchioli therefore misunderstands the situation; the republican thesis is not part of a hypostasized liberalism but has been treated as an attack upon it. The present writer, denounced by Pecchioli for perpetuating a "great tradition" of liberalism, is denounced by Diggins for subverting it;[30] yet Diggins desires to subvert it far more deeply and is angry with the republican thesis because it suggests that his giant is only a windmill. The conclusion, for both Pecchioli and me, must be that Americans are odd people to find oneself among; but I wish in the latter part of this essay to explore the phenomenon of which Diggins is representative and to penetrate as far as I can into the underlying meanings of the rejection of the republican thesis.

A conventional model of American historiography would present it as obedient to two imperatives. The first is the necessity of a foundational myth, felt for obvious reasons by a nation founded in experiment and sustained by immigration; I have indicated that I come of a chain of cultures which for historical reasons do not find such myths necessary. In the United States, whose history is so largely a history of the mutations of Protestantism into civil religion, the myth of foundation further takes the form of a myth of covenant. The nation is held to have made at its beginnings a commitment, in the face of God or history or the opinion of mankind, to the maintenance of certain principles; and it is the historian's business to ascertain how the commitment was made, what the principles were, and whether the covenant has been upheld or allowed to lapse. There is a solemnity inherent in what such a historian is doing, as an exegete of the American civil religion. Having ascertained the terms of the covenant, he or she must proceed to recount the history of which the covenant was the beginning and is thereby obliged to write in a choice, or a mixture, of two styles. One is liturgical, the recital of how the covenant was kept; the other, and by far the commoner, is jeremiad,[31] the recital of how it was not kept and

---

[30] See, e.g., Diggins, 366, where I am a "historian of European intellectual history," who "has drawn upon the works of the Americanists . . . to prove that a Machiavellian interpretation should replace the present Lockean interpretation of the Revolution. . . ."

[31] The best accounts of the jeremiad as a recurrent theme in American rhetoric are to be found in Sacvan Bercovich, *The Puritan Origins of the American Self* (New Haven, 1975) and *The American Jeremiad* (Madison, 1978). Bercovich, who writes as a student of literature rather than history, drew on the two volumes of Perry Miller, *The New England Mind* (Cambridge, Mass., 1953). See also Ernest Tuveson, *The Redeemer Nation: The Idea of America's Millennial Role* (Chicago, 1968).

of what sufferings have fallen on the nation by reason of its sins and shortcomings. Diggins is a historian in the jeremiad style.

The recital of historical change, of how altering conditions of existence may have rendered the terms of the covenant obsolete or their performance impracticable, will in all probability be carried out according to the stylized rhetoric and cadences of the jeremiad mode. It should be further noted that there are few obstacles to asking whether the covenant was worth making in the first place or whether it was not radically flawed. It is perfectly permissible to criticize the covenant, as long as you do not suggest that it was not made, or that it is or ever has been possible for America to escape from it. Notoriously, American political culture is a guilt culture, whose sins and failures are necessary to the affirmation of its uniqueness as a nation chosen, whether by God or itself, to a peculiar destiny in the fulfillment of certain promises. To suggest that there was guilt in the promises themselves is permissible; to suggest that there were no promises and no covenant would be to strike at the heart.

The foregoing paragraph demonstrates that it is hard to write of a certain rhetoric without writing in it; but I have found myself accused of denying, in effect, both the unique character and the unique guilt of American history, and I need to understand the discourse in which I came to play such a role. The second conventional foundation of American historiography may be termed "the premise of inescapable liberalism," and brings us much closer to the concerns expressed by Pecchioli. Its origins may be found as far back as John Adams's *Dissertation on the Canon and Feudal Laws* (1765), and it has been developed by writers as diverse as Alexis de Tocqueville and Friedrich Engels, among others. For the present generation of historians, its decisive formulation remains that put forward thirty years ago by Louis B. Hartz in *The Liberal Tradition in America* and *The Founding of New Societies*.[32] Hartz elaborated the already existing thesis that because a feudal order had never been established in English-speaking North America, the colonial cultures had escaped the experience of revolution, defined *ex hypothesi* as the violent destruction of such an order; it could therefore be asked in what sense the American Revolution had been a revolution at all. Hartz's America had escaped the dialectic; it was liberal without the struggle to establish liberalism; and since he shared the widespread belief that John Locke was at all points and altogether the philosopher of the liberal order, he maintained that American political thought was and always had been Lockean without the possibility of an alternative—it was literally impossible for Americans to think in any other way.

The Hartzian thesis has become part of the American jeremiad. From perspectives not necessarily Marxist, though now and then touched by Marxist presuppositions, it represents America as a society isolated from mankind by the exceptionality of its liberalism and condemned to proclaim as universal sociopolitical beliefs elsewhere regarded as obsolete. The heirs of Hartz can be as critical of liberal values as he was himself; since it became the function of the intelligentsia to express alienation, the liberal intellectuals have been liberalism's most effective critics. They are, however, wholly committed to maintaining the

---

[32] Louis B. Hartz, *The Liberal Tradition in America: An Interpretation of American Political Thought since the Revolution* (New York, 1955), and (ed.), *The Founding of New Societies* (New York, 1964).

primacy of that which they would criticize—much as Marxist historians must affirm the triumph of the bourgeoisie, since without it Marxism would lose its *raison d'être*. To attack liberalism is one thing; to challenge its historical reality is unforgiveable. Writing in the conventional modes of American historiography, they have made the commitment to maintain liberalism the definition of the national identity (or "American experiment"). To doubt it is to doubt the reality of the experiment, and of the identity.

I offer this as explaining, in some cases, the vehemence with which the republican thesis has been rejected by those bent on maintaining the Lockean and liberal-capitalist interpretation of the American founding. Diggins's book places him prominently among them, but I have also in mind at least one article by Isaac F. Kramnick and (at a high level of restraint and sensitivity) a number of publications by Joyce O. Appleby.[33] These writers are bent on maintaining the view that America was founded on liberal premises, though all are concerned to criticize those premises from a variety of standpoints by no means identical with one another; Diggins is some kind of Calvinist, Kramnick some kind of Marxist, and Appleby is a neo-Jeffersonian. In order to elucidate their attack on the republican interpretation, I must proceed to state what I think this is and has been, before examining their (rather different) accounts of what they think it is.

The republican interpretation—at least in the formulation which I find myself attacked for having given—began as an attack on the paramountcy given to Locke by Hartz: that is, on the assumption that Locke was so universal, ubiquitous, and authoritative a figure that all thinking was obliged to descend from him, and that documents such as the Declaration of Independence were programmatic endeavors to put a Lockean philosophy into practice. The attack on this premise originated with the discovery that, in both Britain and America during the century 1688-1789, discourse was frequently conducted, and problems stated and contested, in terms which did not originate with Locke and in whose employment he took neither an immediate nor a posthumous part. This led to a proposal less to diminish Locke than to deconstruct him: to demolish the premise of his ubiquity and universality and to pursue lines of enquiry that led altogether away from him, until such time as the necessity of restoring him to a crucial role or roles should reassert itself. (In the writings of James Tully and others, I see signs that this is beginning to happen.)[34]

The republican (or as it may also be called, the Old Whig, Real Whig, or neo-Harringtonian) discourse of the eighteenth century was a case in point. It made no significant appeal to Lockean formulae, and neither did many of those who constructed the reply or counter-discourse which it encountered. The proposition, hitherto fairly common, that a transition from "feudal," "monarchist,"

[33] Kramnick, "Republican Revisionism Revisited," *The American Historical Review*, 87 (1982), 629-64; Appleby, "What Is Still American in the Political Philosophy of Thomas Jefferson?," *William and Mary Quarterly*, 3rd ser., 39 (1982) 287-309; *Capitalism and a New Social Order* (New York, 1985); "Republicanism and Ideology," *American Quarterly*, 37 (1985), 461-73; and "Republicanism in Old and New Contexts," *William and Mary Quarterly*, 3rd ser. 43 (1986), 20-34.

[34] *A Discourse On Property: John Locke and His Adversaries* (Cambridge, 1980) and work forthcoming.

or "traditional" values to "Whig," "capitalist," or "liberal" values could be understood by tracing the displacement of Filmer by Locke, began to crumble, as it was discovered that the republican discourse had been a means of criticizing the recovery of the monarchist-aristocratic state form in the late seventeenth century, brought about by a simultaneous intensification of court and state patronage and of capitalist methods of financing the state through public credit. Those who developed a critique of this political and economic order saw it as resting on the growth of a professional or "standing" army, and of a commerce wealthy enough to encourage the individual to pay others to defend and govern him, instead of engaging his own personality (or "virtue") directly in politics and war. Ideas about the division of labor and the alienation of personality developed, in very large measure, from this perception.

Yet it was not possible—and it was never asserted that it was possible—to find among critics of this governing order any who desired to reject the growth of trade and return to a world of agrarian or manorial self-sufficiency. The ideal type used in criticism was the citizen, not the farmer, though it was agreed that there had once been a world where the two were identical and the farmer could leave his plough to serve in the army or vote in the assembly; this had become more difficult with the growth of productive labor. The critics of Whig Britain feared the "trading interest" less than the "monied interest," the artisan or merchant less than the financial speculator in the availability of capital; when they criticized "commercial society," it was for favoring the growth of the soldier, the stockjobber, and the manipulative politician, though commercial society always found republican defenders who believed that these types could be assimilated or eliminated.

The debate among theorists was (especially in Scotland) conducted between writers who agreed that something had been lost with the decay of ancient virtue and something gained with the rise of modern commerce, but who disagreed on the moral, political, and historical conclusions to be drawn. There were those who held that unless something were done to replace or preserve ancient virtue—e.g., unless a well-regulated militia were recognized as necessary to the security of a free state—the individual would lose all identity with the public good. Some of these pessimistically doubted whether it was possible to preserve virtue under modern conditions. There were those who held on the contrary that in a society based on commercial and cultural exchange, the individual could transcend his original acquisitive egoism and achieve sympathy and community with his fellows (whether these qualities would find a political expression was not so clear). Some of these optimistically asserted that market mechanisms would ensure all the ends of virtue though individuals were not virtuous themselves, so that under modern conditions the notion of virtue itself became obsolete. There was a point at which the proposition that the self was sociable raised fundamental questions about the relation of self to society.

There is an inbuilt ambivalence in all this debate. Far from it being the case that one interest group in society employed a language of agrarian virtue, and another with incompatible interests an incommensurable language of commercial individualism, the Scottish debaters, of whom most is known, employed a shared discourse of heterogeneous origins and replete with tensions, in which alternative values might be emphasized and new concepts formulated in the confrontation with old. In *The Machiavellian Moment* I gave priority to the republican components in this discourse with the aim of showing, first, that eighteenth-century problems, realities, and historical experience could be and were analyzed in the terms it provided; second, that any new terminology framed for such purposes as the elaboration of political economy, must be hammered out in the dialogue with republicanism. In work done by various hands since 1975, the problem has been that of assigning their proper role to other languages, such as those of civil jurisprudence and moral epistemology (in both of which Locke's writings played a part); but though the map of eighteenth-century discourse has grown richer and more dynamic, this has always seemed to me a consequence not a displacement of the results achieved by deconstructing the Lockean monolith posited by Hartz and substituting a dialectic between neo-Harringtonian republicanism and Smithian political economy.[35] In the model now proposed of eighteenth-century debate, the self is shown moving from ancient to modern and never quite completing the journey; its "Machiavellian moment" is its realization of its historicity.

When in my concluding chapter I applied these concepts to the founding years of the United States, it was my intention to suggest that American thought was from its beginnings involved in what I had termed "the quarrel with history": that is, in the realization that a self involved in the movement from ancient to modern would never be fully satisfied by either, but must recognize itself as having become problematic in the transition. It was a Rousseauist reading of the eighteenth-century debate, though Rousseau's actual presence in its American formulations has never been documented to my knowledge; what is more relevant to the present essay is that I genuinely thought I had uncovered pre-Revolutionary conditions helping to bring about that underlying dissatisfaction with liberalism which characterizes the American liberal mind. The presence of agrarian and utopian components in Jeffersonian ideology; the attempt to construct a republic in order to escape Whig parliamentary corruption, only to find the specter of corruption haunting the republic as its *Doppelgänger*; the acknowledgement that the age of virtue had passed, coupled with the doubt whether the individual could be happy without it—all these seemed to furnish evidence that the language of republicanism had survived to furnish liberalism with one of its modes of self-criticism and self-doubt. Diggins's significantly titled *The Lost Soul of American Politics* seems to me to furnish quite a lot of evidence that it did; what remains to be explained is the fury with which Diggins denies that American politics ever had this particular soul to lose.

I asserted only that republican values, tending to set the self at odds with the movement of history, were present in the American mixture from the start and helped to supply it with tensions and self-doubt. What has surprised and now and then dismayed me is the vehemence with which this presence has been denied by those in whom the tensions are evident enough. I now think that I was at fault in failing to realize the extent to which my propositions were

[35] Istvan Hont and Michael Ignatieff (eds.), *Wealth and Virtue: The Shaping of Political Economy in the Scottish Enlightenment* (Cambridge, 1983); Knud Haakonssen: *The Science of a Legislator: the Natural Jurisprudence of David Hume and Adam Smith* (Cambridge, 1981); Richard F. Teichgraeber III, *Free Trade and Moral Philosophy: Rethinking the Sources of Adam Smith's Wealth of Nations* (Durham, N.C., 1986).

destructive of the American covenantal paradigm. If American thought was involved in a quarrel with history from a time before Independence, for reasons which Americans shared with British and European thinkers, then the Declaration, the Constitution, and the *Federalist Papers*—the sacred texts of the founding—could not be a covenant with history but must merely continue it, and the quarrel with its own history in which America has so manifestly been engaged could not be a simple pursuit of the terms of the covenant. The exceptionalist thesis would crumble, and in the act of offering to contribute to the explanation of American history, I would be guilty of denying the uniqueness of American guilt and exposing America to the terrors of a history it shared with other cultures. I would further be guilty of constructing an "Atlantic" interpretation of history, sure to be repudiated both by Americans refusing to continue the history of Europe and by Europeans refusing to have it continued by Americans. Their convergent wrath would seek me out even at the farthest antipodes.

That is idealist language, and I offer it ironically; but it goes some way towards explaining what has happened. I now put forward my own critique of *ideologia americana*, from a standpoint the opposite of Pecchioli's since I need to explain why exponents of that *ideologia* have treated me as an adversary. I have been perplexed, since this debate began, by the persistence with which critics of the republican interpretation (a) construct, and impute to me, a version of republican ideology which appears to me simplified to the point of caricature, and (b) insist that I said there was no available alternative to it and that the independent United States were to have been constructed on a republican blueprint. Even Gordon S. Wood—who is no crusader against the republican thesis and whose *The Creation of the American Republic* is a magisterial study of its strengths and vulnerabilities—declared in that work that it presupposed a static society of constituted orders, which is a good deal less than Machiavelli was trying to say; while more recently, in a review of Diggins's book, he has declared that it was my strategy "to eliminate Locke as the patron saint of American culture and replace him with Machiavelli."[36] Really, I had no such intention; it would be nearer the mark to say that in displacing Locke as "patron saint" I was suggesting that American politics had no patron saints, or rather no scribes of the covenant, at all, and that this has been the nature of my blasphemy. The anti-republican reaction—of which Wood has not been part—has ever since followed the two lines detectable at different points in his writings.

Their first strategy, resembling that of the eighteenth-century Scottish critics of antiquity, has been to represent the republican ideology as at all points archaic and reactionary. Following Kramnick, they have represented it as "nostalgic," serving to lament the vanished paternalism of a decaying landed gentry. They have represented it as Stoic, premised on an austere ideal of self-abnegation and service to the public good; but this fails to recognize that Machiavelli (of all people) had little faith in such virtue and was seeking means of rendering the tensions between nobility and people productive of a dynamic and expanding *virtù*. The Scottish criticism of the republic was not that it was Catonic and impractical but that it was Machiavellian and condemned to conquer the ac-

---

[36] Wood, "Hellfire Politics," *New York Review of Books*, February 28, 1985. Cf. Benjamin R. Barber, "Unscrambling the Founding Fathers," *ibid.*, January 13, 1985.

cessible world and corrupt itself thereby; how the Federalists proposed that America should escape the fate by which republics became empires is a question hinted at in *The Machiavellian Moment*. Similarly, Wood's quite proper reminder that the republic was classically composed of an aristocracy as well as a democracy does not mean that it was a stable and traditional society; the aristocracy might consist of self-made leaders in war or politics, might enjoy no more than the deference of the many, and might flourish where a hereditary or a monied aristocracy had been overthrown. The American decision to dispense even with natural aristocracies—and to confound them with hereditary in the polemic against Adams's *Defence of the Constitutions of the United States*—was a momentous one and crucial in raising the question whether virtue retained any meaning when politics was no longer a dialogue between two styles of personality. But the debate was durable, not fleeting; it was continued by Tocqueville and by the American Whigs; and the point is that even when America was no longer a classical society, it would not understand itself without saying that it was no longer a classical society and asking what were the implications of this fact. Too many of the anti-republican crusaders are looking for evidence that it had never been one, or thought that it was one, in the first place; the evidence in fact shows that the language was present and was used in discourse, and this is what I was trying to demonstrate.

The role of commerce in the eighteenth-century debate was a crucial one, and on this point I have been often misrepresented. It cannot be said too often—as I said in the first place—that the republican attitude to the growth of commerce was not one of blanket opposition but one of critical evaluation; the phenomenon was held to have brought many social and moral benefits but at the same time many actual and potential evils, and the questions which arose were (1) what remedies ought to be taken against the evils, and (2) whether they would corrupt and destroy the benefits if not checked in time. Among many typical responses, a notable and authoritative one is that of Adam Smith; he held that republican government proper was an archaic phenomenon, possible only in a slave-labor economy where the poorer citizens were at leisure for public service and doomed to disappear as they became engrossed in manufacture and commerce; but he recognized that this entailed a loss of virtue on their part, and looked to militia service and public education to remedy it.[37] Beyond any doubt, the exciting adventure of Federal America was the attempt to found a democratic republic in a commercial society; but Madison found it necessary to redefine the republic as a system of representative rather than participatory government; and attention must be paid to the warnings which he and his associates received from history concerning the possible loss of virtue under post-agrarian conditions, and the extent to which they thought it necessary to provide safeguards, just as Smith did in his theoretical writings.

It is in this context that we must examine the extent of Thomas Jefferson's agrarianism. Joyce Appleby has quite rightly stressed that he envisaged the small farmer (or yeoman, if the term be allowed) as functioning in a market economy and was often optimistic about his future there. But in the first place, I do not recall that it was ever claimed that Jefferson expected the farmer and his neigh-

[37] Adam Smith, *Lectures on Jurisprudence* (Oxford University, 1978), 18, 223-39; *An Inquiry into the Nature and Causes of the Wealth of Nations* (Oxford, 1979), 787.

bors to consume one another's produce; the yeoman carried his yield to market, the serf to be ground at his lord's mill; and in the second, what Jefferson was optimistic about was the farmer's prospect of maintaining his independence and virtue among the dangers of a commercial society, about which Jefferson knew a good deal—significantly identifying them with aristocracy—and about which he was scarcely without doubts, ambivalences, and changes in perspective. To suggest that Jefferson believed he had a solution is not to maintain that he never had a problem, and at bottom all I have been claiming is that the persistence of a republican world-view continued to render commercial society, and the role of the self in it, problematic.

I have been identifying various oversimplifications of the republican thesis and now wish to suggest that they are brought about by the desire to set it in a simple antithetical relationship to an equally simplified "Lockean" or "bourgeois" liberal capitalism. Slogans like "who's afraid of John Locke" (Diggins) or "John Locke is alive and well" (Kramnick) vociferate that any attack on the universal role attributed by Hartz to Locke is interpreted as an attack on both the American covenant and the triumph and inner contradictions of bourgeois society; America must be seen as beginning history anew, even when that history is to receive a Marxist reading. There arises a binary reading of the debate, in which the republican thesis is distorted and rigidified so that it may be set in opposition to an equally rigidified liberalism; and it is a consequence that Diggins attributes to the author of *The Machiavellian Moment* a series of positions which completely caricature the text of that book.[38] But rather than engage in a tedious rectification of Diggins, I would like to pursue the problem as it appears in the far more subtle and serious writings of Joyce Appleby.

In several published essays[39] Appleby has identified the method I practice in the history of discourse with those of Clifford Geertz and Thomas S. Kuhn and has suggested that these lead to belief in a single dominant ideology or paradigm, controlling the whole of the discourse of a given culture at a given time. I have been insisting for at least fifteen years that the political community differs from the scientific community in that it is not controlled by a single enterprise or discipline of enquiry and that therefore no single set of paradigms can be expected to control its thinking or its discourse.[40] There may in principle be as many sets of paradigms as there are contexts of debate; the same paradigm set may have its function modified or reversed as it migrates from one context to another; and there is no reason in principle why more than one set of linguistic

---

[38] For example, I do not "wish to rescue America from liberalism by demonstrating that America was founded upon a morally grounded political idea." I did not say that "the new American Republic" was "a concept derived from Renaissance humanism," that "the Constitution [was] intended to imitate or reenact English parliamentary traditions and politics," that "what is required is either the spirit of Machiavelli and virtue or the spectre of Locke and interests," that "Jacksonianism [was] the shining legacy of Machiavellian *virtù*," or that "the message of 'civic humanism' flowered in full bloom in the American West and that America may find its political bearings if historians would now look to 'the *virtù* of the frontier' " (19, 55, 57, 64, 111, 118).

[39] Above, n. 33.

[40] *Politics, Language and Time* (New York, 1971), 13-19. Cf. *Virtue, Commerce and History* (Cambridge, 1985), 8-9.

terms, rules, and presumptions may not be contending for paradigm status at the same time. Whether in these circumstances it is desirable to continue using the term "paradigm" at all may be debated, but I have long been using the term to denote an authoritative role for which several languages of discourse may be found in competition.

I therefore differ fundamentally from Appleby when she claims that my methods tend to make readers suppose that only one language can occupy paradigm status at a time, and I disclaim intention when she states that "by insisting that the only significant intellectual accommodation to change took place within a presiding paradigm, the revisionists" (a term which itself implies the preexistence of a paradigm) "have made it difficult to recognize that alongside the Machiavellian conception of citizenship, order, and liberty there grew up another paradigm."[41] I do not find this difficult to recognize in the least; all I meant by imputing "paradigm" status to "Machiavellian discourse" was that any alternative "paradigm" would find it difficult to grow up, would have to compete for paradigm status by means of an intensively contested dialogue with the pre-existing discourse, and would bear the marks of that contest in the form of some language shared with it, alongside other language antithetical to it. In *The Machiavellian Moment*, it is true, I treated the "republican" discourse to a considerable degree in isolation, establishing its paradigmatic character by showing that it possessed the capacity to offer a comprehensive account of its world; but that was a legitimate use of historiographical rhetoric, and I never concealed the fact of intimate competition between rival discourses. The political economy of Adam Smith and the commercial agrarianism of Thomas Jefferson both appear to have grown up in intimate interaction with the language of classical republicanism, and this in turn—having been framed as a critique of commercial modernity—interacted intimately with the speech of the world it criticized. In work subsequent to *The Machiavellian Moment* I have been and remain increasingly concerned with showing how the language of political economy grew out of the republican matrix, while maintaining the possibility that it was growing out of other matrices at the same time.[42] The plurality of languages interacting in a given society, not the majestic *translatio imperii* from one "paradigm" to another, has, I truly believe, been my dominant concern since I began writing.

Yet Joyce Appleby and I seem to remain deadlocked; I am not sure I shall persuade her that I write to show the limits that languages and ideologies set to one another's existence. She is neither Hartzian nor Marxian; her first book[43] was written to establish the historical specificity of the economic view of man; but in her later work she seems to have moved towards viewing economic liberalism as liberating the mind from the constraints of republican ideology. That is not how I see the history we both study; I am far more inclined to see classical republicanism and political economy as reducing one another to a common historicism, and the foundation of the United States as involved in the

---

[41] *William and Mary Quarterly*, 3rd ser. 43 (1986), 31.

[42] "Cambridge Paradigms and Scotch Philosophers," and "The mobility of property and the rise of eighteenth-century sociology," in *Virtue, Commerce and History; Barbarism and Religion: Civil History in Gibbon's Decline and Fall*, work in progress.

[43] *Economic Thought and Ideology in Seventeenth-Century England* (Princeton, 1978).

process; but there is a clear and present danger that each of us may accuse the other of reducing the history of discourse to a series of noninteracting paradigmatic monoliths.

Diggins is an interesting and powerful writer within the mythopoeic terms of the *ideologia americana*. It is important to realize that he is a historian in the jeremiad mode, concerned not to glorify or even to legitimate "liberalism" but to excoriate its moral shortcomings. His book culminates about the time of the American Civil War, taking as its central figures Herman Melville, Henry Adams—considered as a member of the Civil War generation—and above all Abraham Lincoln. These minds perceived the spiritual poverty of Lockean liberalism and set about restoring a sense of the sacred, of sin and guilt and the mysterious judgments of God, drawing upon the resources of American Protestantism and (in Diggins's view) upon a Calvinism which he thinks latent in Locke (but which recent research would probably not find there).[44] These chapters are impressively written; they give Diggins's book the character of a religious testament, a resacralization of the American civil religion by the injection of some Calvinist iron. *The Lost Soul of American Politics* is part of the literature of the covenant; it sets as the end of writing American history the discovery of the moral and religious truths appropriate to the American experience. There are of course other ways of writing history, even American history.

Diggins, then, writes in the jeremiad and not the liturgical mode; he does not celebrate the liberal hegemony over the American mind but seeks to denounce its shortcomings. What remains strange is that he cannot tolerate the "republican" suggestion that the liberal hegemony was never a complete one; in Kuhnian terms, there must be a liberal "paradigm" exercising absolute ascendancy and control in order that there may be a "revolution"—a Calvinist one—against it.[45] Diggins, Kramnick, and even Appleby are determined to eliminate the republican component from early American history—or where they cannot eliminate, at least to neutralize it—so that there shall be nothing for liberalism to quarrel with but itself, and nothing for it to do but continue that quarrel. That is as close as I know how to penetrate to the heart of *ideologia americana*, and the ineradicable root-ideas with which one is left are jeremiad and exceptionalism. But if this is merely one more case of the observer suggesting to Americans that they might be happier if they shared their history with other people, and Americans preferring the splendid misery of uniqueness, Kupe may not return to the debate.

Johns Hopkins University

---

[44] I am thinking of forthcoming work by Mark Goldie, James Tully, and John Marshall; Diggins probably has in mind John Dunn's *The Political Thought of John Locke* (Cambridge, 1969).

[45] Since this essay was written, Diggins has restated his position and argued it against both Marxist and republican readings in "Comrades and Citizens: New Mythologies in American Historiography," *The American Historical Review*, XC, 3 (1985), 614-38; there is a comment by Paul Conkin, to which Diggins replies.